Pro Spatial with
SQL Server 2012

Alastair Aitchison

Apress®

Pro Spatial with SQL Server 2012

ISBN-13 (pbk): 978-1-4302-3491-3

ISBN-13 (electronic): 978-1-4302-3492-0

Trademarked names, logos, and images may appear in this book. Rather than use a trademark symbol with every occurrence of a trademarked name, logo, or image we use the names, logos, and images only in an editorial fashion and to the benefit of the trademark owner, with no intention of infringement of the trademark.

The use in this publication of trade names, trademarks, service marks, and similar terms, even if they are not identified as such, is not to be taken as an expression of opinion as to whether or not they are subject to proprietary rights.

While the advice and information in this book are believed to be true and accurate at the date of publication, neither the authors nor the editors nor the publisher can accept any legal responsibility for any errors or omissions that may be made. The publisher makes no warranty, express or implied, with respect to the material contained herein.

President and Publisher: Paul Manning
Lead Editor: Jonathan Gennick
Technical Reviewer: Jason Horner
Editorial Board: Steve Anglin, Ewan Buckingham, Gary Cornell, Louise Corrigan, Morgan Ertel,
    Jonathan Gennick, Jonathan Hassell, Robert Hutchinson, Michelle Lowman, James Markham,
    Matthew Moodie, Jeff Olson, Jeffrey Pepper, Douglas Pundick, Ben Renow-Clarke, Dominic
    Shakeshaft, Gwenan Spearing, Matt Wade, Tom Welsh
Coordinating Editor: Anita Castro
Copy Editor: Valerie Greco
Compositor: Mary Sudul
Indexer: SPi Global
Cover Designer: Anna Ishchenko

Distributed to the book trade worldwide by Springer Science+Business Media New York, 233 Spring Street, 6th Floor, New York, NY 10013. Phone 1-800-SPRINGER, fax (201) 348-4505, e-mail orders-ny@springer-sbm.com, or visit www.springeronline.com.

For information on translations, please e-mail rights@apress.com, or visit www.apress.com.

Apress and friends of ED books may be purchased in bulk for academic, corporate, or promotional use. eBook versions and licenses are also available for most titles. For more information, reference our Special Bulk Sales–eBook Licensing web page at www.apress.com/bulk-sales.

Any source code or other supplementary materials referenced by the author in this text is available to readers at www.apress.com. For detailed information about how to locate your book's source code, go to www.apress.com/source-code.

For Douglas and Hamish

Contents at a Glance

Contents

Foreword

Spatial data has always been an important component to comprehensive information management but it has struggled to escape its "techie" origins. Spatial data management debuted in SQL Server 2008 as a comprehensive yet simple spatial implementation designed to provide solutions for both experienced and novice practitioners. Alastair's book, "Beginning Spatial with SQL Server 2008", provided an excellent introduction into the basic concepts of spatial data management and how to apply these to the spatial features in SQL Server 2008. This book remains a basic staple for those wishing to implement spatial using SQL Server regardless of version.

With the release of SQL Server 2012, Microsoft has continued to refine spatial data management, adding support for sophisticated new features such as FULLGLOBE objects, aggregates, curves on the ellipsoid and simplified spatial index creation, among many others. With the publication of "Pro Spatial with SQL Server 2012," Alastair provides the logical follow-on book by both expanding on advanced concepts while at the same time documenting the new spatial features in SQL Server 2012. It is a needed and welcome addition and will greatly assist in the effort to make spatial data management more understood and hence accessible for programmers everywhere.

Spatial Ed
(a.k.a Ed Katibah, Microsoft SQL Server Spatial Program Manager)
April 2012

About the Author

 **Alastair Aitchison** is an independent developer, consultant and trainer, specialising in spatial data reporting and analysis. His work has been used by the House of Lords, various police forces, political parties and media agencies.

Alastair is an active contributor to the development community; he is a moderator and one of the top answerers on the MSDN spatial and Bing Maps forums, he speaks at conferences, and he maintains a blog about all things to do with spatial data at http://alastaira.wordpress.com. He holds a number of certifications, and has twice been awarded the Most Valuable Professional (MVP) award from Microsoft.

He lives in Norwich, England with his wife and children.

Geographic Units of Measurement

Coordinates of latitude and longitude are both angles, and are usually measured in degrees (although they can be measured in radians or any other angular unit of measure). When measured in degrees, longitude values measured from the prime meridian range from −180° to +180°, and latitude values measured from the equator range from −90° (at the South pole) to +90° (at the North pole).

Longitudes to the east of the prime meridian are normally stated as positive values, or suffixed with the letter "E". Longitudes to the west of the prime meridian are expressed as negative values, or using the suffix "W". Likewise, latitudes north of the equator are expressed as positive values or using letter "N", whereas those south of the equator are negative or denoted with the letter "S".

NOTATION OF GEOGRAPHIC COORDINATES

There are several accepted methods of expressing coordinates of latitude and longitude.

1. The most commonly used method is the DMS (degree, minutes, seconds) system, also known as sexagesimal notation. In this system, each degree is divided into 60 minutes. Each minute is further subdivided into 60 seconds. A value of 51 degrees, 15 minutes, and 32 seconds is normally written as 51°15'32".

2. An alternative system, commonly used by GPS receivers, displays whole degrees, followed by minutes and decimal fractions of minutes. This same coordinate value would therefore be written as 51:15.53333333.

3. Decimal degree notation specifies coordinates using degrees and decimal fractions of degrees, so the same coordinate value expressed using this system would be written as 51.25888889.

When expressing geographic coordinate values of latitude and longitude for use in SQL Server 2012, you must always use decimal degree notation. The advantage of this format is that each coordinate can be expressed as a single floating-point number. To convert DMS coordinates into decimal degrees you can use the following rule.

```
Degrees + (Minutes / 60) + (Seconds / 3600) = Decimal Degrees
```

For example, the *CIA World Factbook* (https://www.cia.gov/library/publications/the-world-factbook/geos/uk.html) gives the geographic coordinates for London as follows,

```
51 30 N, 0 10 W
```

When expressed in decimal degree notation, this is

```
51.5 (Latitude), -0.166667 (Longitude)
```

Defining the Origin of a Geographic Coordinate System

Latitude coordinates are always measured relative to the equator: the line that goes around the "middle" of the earth. But from where should longitude coordinates, which are measured around the earth, be measured?

A common misconception is to believe that there is a universal prime meridian based on some inherent fundamental property of the earth, but this is not the case. The prime meridian of any spatial reference system is arbitrarily chosen simply to provide a line of zero longitude from which all other coordinates of longitude can be calculated. The most commonly used prime meridian is the meridian passing through Greenwich, England, but there are many others. For example, the RT38 spatial reference system used in Sweden is based on a prime meridian that passes through Stockholm, some 18 degrees east of the Greenwich Prime Meridian. Prime meridians from which coordinates are measured in other systems include those that pass through Paris, Jakarta, Madrid, Bogota, and Rome.

If you were to define a different prime meridian, the value of the longitude coordinate of all the points in a given spatial reference system would change.

Projected Coordinate Systems

Describing the location of positions on the earth using coordinates of latitude and longitude is all very well in certain circumstances, but it's not without some problems. To start with, you can only apply angular coordinates onto a three-dimensional, round model of the earth. If you were planning a car journey you'd be unlikely to refer to a "travel globe" though, wouldn't you? Because an ellipsoidal model, by definition, represents the entire world, you can't magnify an area of interest without enlarging the entire globe. Clearly this would get unwieldy for any applications that required focusing in detail on a small area of the earth's surface.

Fortunately, ancient geographers and mathematicians devised a solution for this problem, and the art of cartography, or map-making, was born. Using various techniques, a cartographer can project all, or part, of the surface of an ellipsoidal model onto a flat plane, creating a map. The features on that map can be scaled or adjusted as necessary to create maps suitable for different purposes.

Because a map is a flat, two-dimensional surface, we can then describe positions on the plane of that map using familiar two-dimensional Cartesian coordinates in the x- and y-axes. This is known as a *projected coordinate system*.

■ **Note** In contrast to a geographic coordinate system, which defines positions on a three-dimensional, round model of the earth, a projected coordinate system describes the position of points on the earth's surface as they lie on a flat, projected, two-dimensional plane.

Creating Map Projections

We see two-dimensional projections of geospatial data on an almost daily basis in street maps, road atlases, or on our computer screens. Given their familiarity, and the apparent simplicity of working on a flat surface rather than a curved one, you would be forgiven for thinking that defining spatial data using a projected coordinate system was somehow simpler than using a geographic coordinate system. The difficulty associated with a projected coordinate system is that, of course, the world *isn't* a flat, two-dimensional plane. In order to be able to represent it as one, we have to use a map projection.

Projection is the process of creating a two-dimensional representation of a three-dimensional model of the earth, as illustrated in Figure 1-5. Map projections can be constructed either by using purely geometric methods (such as the techniques used by ancient cartographers) or by using mathematical algorithms (as used in more modern, complex projections). However, whatever method is used, it is not possible to project any three-dimensional object onto a two-dimensional plane without distorting the resulting image in some way. Distortions introduced as a result of the projection process may affect the area, shape, distance, or direction represented by different elements of the map.

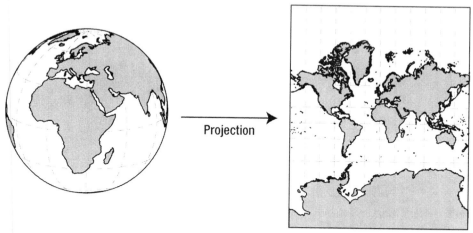

Figure 1-5. *Projecting a 3D model of the earth to create a flat map.*

By altering the projection method, cartographers can reduce the effect of these distortions for certain features, but in doing so the accuracy of other features must be compromised. Just as there is not a single "best" reference ellipsoid to model the three-dimensional shape of the earth, neither is there a single best map projection when trying to project that model onto a two-dimensional surface.

Over the course of time, many projections have been developed that alter the distortions introduced as a result of projection to create maps suitable for different purposes. For instance, when designing a map to be used by sailors navigating through the Arctic regions, a projection may be used that maximizes the accuracy of the direction and distance of objects at the poles of the earth, but sacrifices accuracy of the shape of countries along the equator.

The full details of how to construct a map projection are outside the scope of this book. However, the following sections introduce some common map projections and examine their key features.

Hammer–Aitoff Projection

The Hammer–Aitoff map projection is an equal-area map projection that displays the world on an ellipse. An equal-area map projection is one that maintains the relative area of objects; that is, if you were to measure the area of any particular region on the map, it would accurately represent the area of the corresponding real-world region. However, in order to do this, the shapes of features are distorted. The Hammer–Aitoff map projection is illustrated in Figure 1-6.

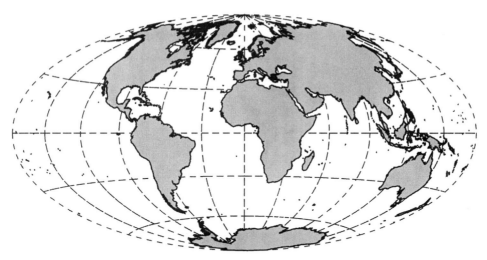

Figure 1-6. *The Hammer–Aitoff map projection.*

Mercator Projection

The Mercator map projection is an example of a conformal map projection. A conformal map projection is any projection that preserves the local shape of objects on the resulting map.

The Mercator projection was first developed in 1569 by the Flemish cartographer Gerardus Mercator, and has been widely used ever since. It is used particularly in nautical navigation because, when using any map produced using the Mercator projection, the route taken by a ship following a constant bearing will be depicted as a straight line on the map.

The Mercator projection accurately portrays all points that lie exactly on the equator. However, as you move farther away from the equator, the distortion of features, particularly the representation of their area, becomes increasingly severe. One common criticism of the Mercator projection is that, due to the geographical distribution of countries in the world, many developed countries are depicted with far greater area than equivalent-sized developing countries. For instance, examine Figure 1-7 to see how the relative sizes of North America (actual area 19 million sq km) and Africa (actual area 30 million sq km) are depicted as approximately the same size.

Despite this criticism, the Mercator projection is still used by many applications, including Bing Maps and Google Maps, and it is probably one of the most instantly recognizable of all geographical images of the world.

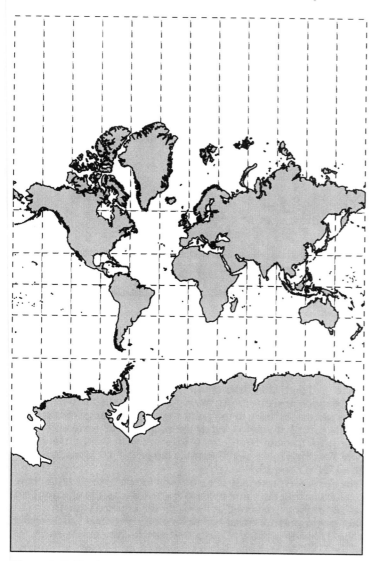

Figure 1-7. The Mercator map projection.

Equirectangular Projection

The equirectangular projection is one of the first map projections ever to be invented, being credited to Marinus of Tyre in about 100 AD. It is also one of the simplest map projections, in which the map displays equally spaced degrees of longitude on the x-axis, and equally spaced degrees of latitude on the y-axis.

This projection is of limited use in spatial data analysis because it represents neither the accurate shape nor area of features on the map, although it is still widely recognized and used for such purposes as portraying NASA satellite imagery of the world (http://visibleearth.nasa.gov/). Figure 1-8 illustrates a map of the world created using the equirectangular projection method.

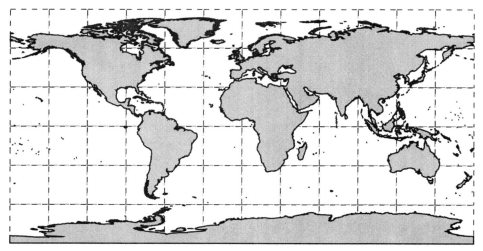

Figure 1-8. *The equirectangular map projection.*

Universal Transverse Mercator Projection

The Universal Transverse Mercator (UTM) projection is not a single projection, but rather a grid composed of many projections laid side by side. The UTM grid is created by dividing the globe into 60 slices, called "zones," with each zone being 6° wide and extending nearly the entire distance between the North Pole and South Pole (the grid does not extend fully to the polar regions, but ranges from a latitude of 80°S to 84°N). Each numbered zone is further subdivided by the equator into north and south zones. Any UTM zone may be referenced using a number from 1 to 60, together with a suffix of N or S to denote whether it is north or south of the equator. Figure 1-9 illustrates the grid of UTM zones overlaid on a map of the world, highlighting UTM Zone 15N.

Within each UTM zone, features on the earth are projected using a *transverse* Mercator projection. The transverse Mercator projection is produced using the same method as the Mercator projection, but rotated by 90°. This means that, instead of portraying features that lie along the equator with no distortion, the transverse Mercator projection represents features that lie along a central north–south meridian with no distortion. Because each UTM zone is relatively narrow, any feature on the earth lies quite close to the central meridian of the UTM zone in which it is contained, and distortion within each zone is very small.

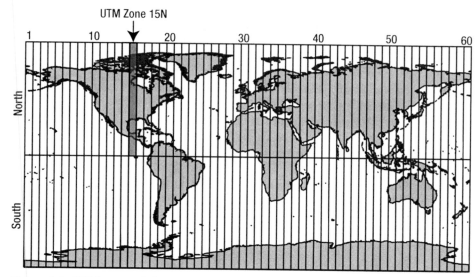

Figure 1-9. *UTM zones of the world.*

The UTM projection is *universal* insofar as it defines a system that can be applied consistently across the entire globe. However, because each zone within the UTM grid is based on its own unique projection, the UTM map projection can only be used to represent accurately those features lying within a single specified zone.

Projection Parameters

In addition to the method of projection used, there are a number of additional parameters that affect the appearance of any projected map. These parameters are listed in Table 1-2.

Table 1-2. *Map Projection Parameters*

Parameter	Description
Azimuth	The angle at which the center line of the projection lies, relative to north
Central meridian	The line of longitude used as the origin from which x coordinates are measured
False easting	A value added to x coordinates so that stated coordinate values remain positive over the extent of the map
False northing	A value added to y coordinates so that stated coordinate values remain positive over the extent of the map
Latitude of center	The latitude of the point at the center of the map projection

Parameter	Description
Latitude of origin	The latitude used as the origin from which y coordinates are measured
Latitude of point	The latitude of a specific point on which the map projection is based
Longitude of center	The longitude of the point at the center of the map projection
Longitude of point	The longitude of a specific point on which the map projection is based
Scale factor	A scaling factor used to reduce the effect of distortion in a map projection
Standard parallel	A line of latitude along which features on the map have no distortion

Projected Units of Measurement

Having done the hard work involved in creating a projection, the task of defining coordinates on that projection thankfully becomes much easier. If we consider all of the points on the earth's surface to lie on the flat surface of a map then we can define positions on that map using familiar Cartesian coordinates of x and y, which represent the distance of a point from an origin along the x-axis and y-axis, respectively. In a projected coordinate system, these coordinate values are normally referred to as eastings (the x-coordinate) and northings (the y-coordinate). This concept is illustrated in Figure 1-10.

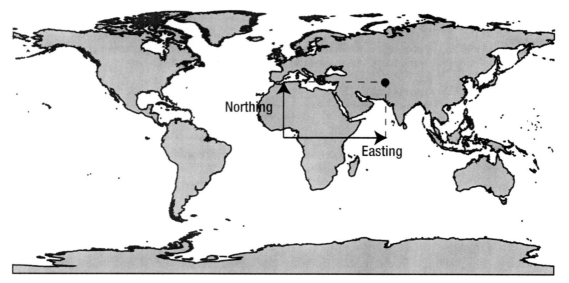

Figure 1-10. Describing position on the earth using a projected coordinate system.

Well-Known Text of a Spatial Reference System

SQL Server maintains a catalogue view, sys.spatial_reference_systems, in which it stores the details of all 392 supported geographic spatial reference systems. The information contained in this table is required to define the model of the earth on which geographic coordinate calculations take place. Note that no additional information is required to perform calculations of data defined using projected coordinates, because these take place on a simple 2D plane. Therefore SQL Server can support data defined using any projected coordinate system.

The parameters of each geographic spatial reference system in sys.spatial_reference_systems are stored in the well_known_text column using the Well-Known Text (WKT) format, which is an industry-standard format for expressing spatial information defined by the Open Geospatial Consortium (OGC).

■ **Note** SQL Server only supports geographic coordinate data defined relative to one of the spatial reference systems listed in sys.spatial_reference_systems. This table contains the additional information required to construct the model of the earth on which geographic coordinate calculations take place. However, because no additional information is required to perform calculations on a 2D plane, SQL Server supports projected coordinate data defined from any projected coordinate reference system, and the details of such systems are not listed in sys.spatial_reference_systems.

To illustrate how spatial references are represented in WKT format, let's examine the properties of the EPSG:4326 spatial reference by executing the following query.

```
SELECT
  well_known_text
FROM
  sys.spatial_reference_systems
WHERE
  authority_name = 'EPSG'
  AND
  authorized_spatial_reference_id = 4326;
```

The following is the result (with line breaks and indents added to make the result easier to read).

```
GEOGCS[
  "WGS 84",
  DATUM[
    "World Geodetic System 1984",
    ELLIPSOID[
      "WGS 84",
      6378137,
      298.257223563
    ]
  ],
  PRIMEM["Greenwich", 0],
  UNIT["Degree", 0.0174532925199433]
]
```

This result contains all the parameters required to define this spatial reference system, as follows.

Coordinate system: The first line of a WKT spatial reference is a keyword to tell us what sort of coordinate system is used. In this case, GEOGCS tells us that EPSG:4326 uses a geographic coordinate reference system. If a spatial reference system is based on projected coordinates then the WKT representation would instead begin with PROJCS. Immediately following this is the name assigned to the spatial reference system. In this case, the Well-Known Text is describing the "WGS 84" spatial reference system.

Datum: The values following the DATUM keyword provide the parameters of the datum. The first parameter gives us the name of the datum used. In this case, it is the "World Geodetic System 1984" datum. Then follow the parameters of the reference ellipsoid. This system uses the "WGS 84" ellipsoid, with a semimajor axis of 6,378,137 m and an inverse-flattening ratio of 298.257223563.

Prime meridian: The PRIMEM value tells us that this system defines Greenwich as the prime meridian, where longitude is defined to be 0.

Unit of measurement: The final parameter specifies that the unit in which coordinates are measured is the "Degree". The value of 0.0174532925199433 is a conversion factor required to convert from radians into the stated units (1 degree = $\pi/180$ radians).

Contrasting a Geographic and a Projected Spatial Reference

Let's compare the result in the preceding section to the WKT representation of a spatial reference system based on a projected coordinate system. The following example shows the WKT representation of the UTM Zone 10N reference, a projected spatial reference system used in North America. The SRID for this system is EPSG:26910.

░ **Note** Remember that, because this is a projected spatial reference system, you won't find these details in the sys.spatial_reference_systems table. Instead, you can look up the details of these systems using a site such as http://www.epsg-registry.org or http://www.spatialreference.org.

```
PROJCS[
  "NAD_1983_UTM_Zone_10N",
  GEOGCS[
    "GCS_North_American_1983",
    DATUM[
      "D_North_American_1983",
      SPHEROID[
        "GRS_1980",
        6378137,
        298.257222101
      ]
    ],
    PRIMEM["Greenwich",0],
```

```
      UNIT["Degree", 0.0174532925199433]
   ],
   PROJECTION["Transverse_Mercator"],
   PARAMETER["False_Easting", 500000.0],
   PARAMETER["False_Northing", 0.0],
   PARAMETER["Central_Meridian", -123.0],
   PARAMETER["Scale_Factor", 0.9996],
   PARAMETER["Latitude_of_Origin", 0.0],
   UNIT["Meter", 1.0]
]
```

Notice that the Well-Known Text for this projected coordinate system contains a complete set of parameters for a geographic coordinate system, embedded within brackets following the GEOGCS keyword. The reason is that a projected system must first define the three-dimensional, geodetic model of the earth, and then specify several additional parameters that are required to project that model onto a plane.

■ **Note** The Well-Known Text format in which SQL Server stores the properties of spatial reference systems in the sys.spatial_reference_systems table is exactly the same format as used in the .PRJ file used to describe the spatial reference in which the data in an ESRI shapefile are stored.

Summary

After reading this chapter, you should understand how spatial reference systems can be used to describe positions in space:

- A spatial reference system consists of a coordinate system (which describes a position using either projected or geographic coordinates), a datum (which describes a model representing the shape of the earth), the prime meridian (which defines the origin from which units are measured), and the unit of measurement. When using projected coordinates, the spatial reference system also defines the properties of the projection used.

- A geographic coordinate system defines the position of objects using angular coordinates of latitude and longitude, which are measured from the equator and the prime meridian, respectively.

- A projected coordinate system defines the position of objects using Cartesian coordinates, which measure the x and y distance of a point from an origin. These are also referred to as easting and northing coordinates.

- Whenever you state a set of coordinates representing a point on the earth, it is essential that you also give details of the associated spatial reference system. The spatial reference system defines the additional information that allows us to apply the coordinate reference to identify a point on the earth.

- For convenience, spatial reference systems may be specified by a single integer identifier, known as a spatial reference identifier (SRID).

- Details of all the geographic spatial reference systems supported by SQL Server 2012 are contained within a system catalogue view called sys.spatial_reference_systems. SQL Server also supports data defined using any projected spatial reference system.

- The Well-Known Text format is a standard format used to express the properties of a spatial reference system.

If you are interested in reading further about the topics covered in this chapter, I recommend checking out the Microsoft white paper, "Introduction to Spatial Coordinate Systems: Flat Maps for a Round Planet," which can be found in the MSDN SQL Server developer center site, at http://msdn.microsoft.com/en-us/library/cc749633(SQL.100).aspx.

CHAPTER 2

Spatial Features

In the last chapter, I stated that the purpose of geospatial data was to describe the shape and location of objects on the Earth. Although this objective may be simply stated, in practice it is not always so easy to achieve.

In many cases, although we have a rough understanding of the position and geographic extent of features on the Earth, they may be hard to define in exact terms. For example, at what point does the body of water known as the Gulf of Mexico become the Atlantic Ocean? Where exactly do we draw the line that defines the boundary of a city or forest? In some parts of the world, there is even ambiguity or contention as to where the border between two countries lies, and there are still significant areas of land and sea that are subjects of international dispute.

Even if we agree on the precise shape and location of a feature, it may be hard to describe the properties of that feature with sufficient detail; natural features, such as rivers and coastlines, have complex irregular shapes. Even man-made structures such as roads are rarely simple straight lines.

It would be very hard, if not impossible, to define the shape of these features exactly. Instead, spatial data represents these objects by storing simple geometrical shapes that approximate their actual shape and position. These shapes are called geometries.

The spatial functionality in SQL Server is based on the Open Geospatial Consortium's "Simple Features for SQL Specification", which you can view online at http://www.opensgeospatial.org/standards/sfs. This standard defines a number of different types of geometries, each with different associated properties. In this chapter, each of the different types of geometry is examined and the situations in which it is most appropriate to use each type are described.

Note In the context of spatial data, the word "geometry" can have two distinct meanings. To emphasize the difference, geometry (code formatting) is used to refer to the geometry datatype, whereas geometry (no formatting) is used to refer to simple shapes representing features on the Earth.

Geometry Hierarchy

There is a total of 14 standard types of geometries recognized by SQL Server (not counting the special cases of the FullGlobe or Empty geometries; more on those later). However, only ten of these geometry types are instantiable (that is to say, you can actually create instances of these geometries); the remaining four types are abstract classes from which other instantiable classes are derived.

Geometries can be broadly categorized into two groups, as follows.

Single geometries contain one discrete geometric element. The most basic single geometry is a Point. There are also three types of curve (LineString, CircularString, and CompoundCurve) and two types of surface (Polygon and CurvePolygon).

Geometry collections are compound elements, containing one or more of the individual geometries listed above. Geometry collections may be homogeneous or heterogeneous. A homogeneous geometry collection contains several items of the same type of single geometry only (e.g., a MultiPoint is a geometry collection containing only Points). A heterogeneous geometry collection contains one or more of several different sorts of geometry, such as a collection containing a LineString and a Polygon.

■ **Note** The Microsoft Books Online documentation refers to these two categories of geometries as "Simple types" and "Collection types" (`http://technet.microsoft.com/en-us/library/bb964711%28SQL.110%29.aspx`). The use of the word "Simple" here has been deliberately avoided because this has a separate meaning (as used by the `STIsSimple()` method) that is discussed later.

Figure 2-1 illustrates the inheritance tree of geometry types, which demonstrates how the different types of geometry are related to each other. Every item of spatial data in SQL Server is an example of one of the ten instantiable classes shown with a solid border.

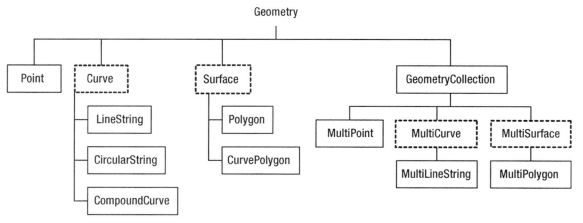

Figure 2-1. The inheritance hierarchy of geometry types. Instantiable types (those types from which an instance of data can be created in SQL Server 2012) are shown with a solid border.

SQL Server 2008 provided only a single instantiable type of Curve (the LineString), and only a single type of instantiable surface (the Polygon). Both of these geometry types are straight-edged, linear features. SQL Server 2012 added support for curved geometries, and the CircularString, CompoundCurve, and CurvePolygon curved geometries shown in Figure 2-1 are new types introduced in SQL Server 2012.

░ **Note** In the OGC Simple Features specification, geometry type names are written using Pascal case (also called Upper CamelCase) and this is the standard generally used in Microsoft documentation. For this reason, that convention is also adopted in this book by referring to geometry types as MultiPoint, LineString, and so on.

Interiors, Exteriors, and Boundaries

Once you have defined an instance of any of the types of geometry listed in the previous section, you can then classify every point in space into one of three areas relative to that geometry: every location must lie either in the geometry's interior, in its exterior, or on its boundary:

- The interior of a geometry consists of all those points that lie in the space occupied by the geometry. In other words, it represents the "inside" of the geometry.

- The exterior consists of all those points that lie in the area of space not occupied by the geometry. It can therefore be thought of as representing the "outside" of the geometry.

- The boundary of a geometry consists of those points that lie on the "edge" of the geometry in question.

Generally speaking, every geometry contains at least one point in its interior and also at least one point lies in its exterior. The only exceptions to this rule are the special cases of the empty geometry and the full globe geometry: an empty geometry has no interior, and therefore every point is considered to lie in its exterior, whereas the full globe geometry is exactly the opposite: containing every point in its interior, with no points in its exterior.

The distinction between these classifications of space becomes very important when considering the relationship between two or more geometries, because these relationships are defined by comparing where particular points lie with respect to the interior, exterior, or boundary of the two geometries in question. For example:

- Two geometries are said to *intersect* each other if there is at least one point that lies in either the interior or boundary of both geometries in question.

- Two geometries are deemed to *touch* each other if there is at least one shared point that lies on the boundary of both geometries, but no points common to the interior of both geometries. Note that this criterion is more specific than the general case of intersection decribed above, and any geometries that touch must therefore also intersect.

- If two geometries have no interior or boundary points in common then they are said to be *disjoint*.

- The distance between two geometries is measured as the shortest possible distance between any two interior points of the two geometries.

These concepts, and other related classifications, are discussed in later chapters of this book when spatial relationships are explained in more detail. For the remainder of this chapter, I instead concentrate on examining the various types of geometry in greater detail.

Points

A *Point* is the most fundamental type of geometry, and is used to represent a singular position in space.

Example Point Usage

When using geospatial data to define features on the Earth, a Point geometry is generally used to represent an exact location, which could be a street address, or the location of a bank, volcano, or city, for instance. Figure 2-2 illustrates a Point geometry used to represent the location of Berlin with respect to a map of Germany. Berlin has a fascinating and complicated history, the city itself being politically divided for much of the twentieth century between West Berlin and East Berlin, a division that famously led to the erection of the Berlin Wall. Despite the fact that West Berlin was, to all intents and purposes, a part of West Germany, it lay in a region that, for 50 years following the Second World War, was proclaimed to be the German Democratic Republic (East Germany), and was entirely isolated from the rest of West Germany.

Figure 2-2. A Point geometry marking the location of Berlin.

■ **Note** Inasmuch as a Point geometry represents an infinitely small, singular location in space, it is impossible to truly illustrate it in a diagram. Throughout this book, Point geometries are represented as small black circles, as in Figure 2-2.

Defining a Point

A Point is defined by a pair of coordinate values, either an x-coordinate value and a y-coordinate value from a planar coordinate system, or a latitude and longitude coordinate value from a geographic coordinate system.

When expressed using the Well-Known Text (WKT) format, a Point located with coordinates $x = 5$ and $y = 3$ may be written as follows,

POINT(5 3)

The WKT representation begins with the POINT keyword followed by the relevant coordinate values, contained within round brackets. The coordinate values are separated by a space (not a comma, as you might initially expect). Figure 2-3 illustrates the Point geometry represented by this definition.

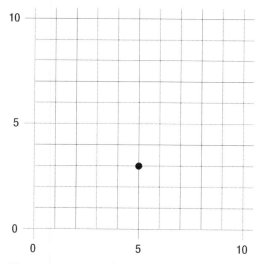

Figure 2-3. A Point located at POINT(5 3).

Defining a Point from geographic coordinates follows the same convention, but with one thing to watch out for: whereas in everyday language it is common to refer to coordinates of "latitude and longitude" (in that order), when you write geographic coordinates in WKT the longitude coordinate always comes first, then the latitude coordinate. The WKT syntax for a geography Point located at a latitude of 40° and longitude of 60° is therefore:

POINT(60 40)

The location of this Point is illustrated in Figure 2-4.

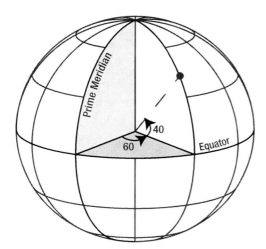

Figure 2-4. *A Point located at geographic coordinates POINT(60 40).*

To help remember the correct order for geographic coordinates, try thinking of longitude as being equivalent to the x-coordinate, because longitude increases as you travel east around the world (until you cross the 180th meridian). Likewise, latitude is equivalent to the y-coordinate, with increasing latitude extending farther north. Because you list planar coordinates in $(x\ y)$ order, the equivalent order for geographic coordinates is therefore (longitude latitude).

▓ **Caution** When defining geographic coordinates using WKT the longitude coordinate comes first, then the latitude coordinate.

Defining Points in 3- and 4-Dimensional Space

In addition to the x- and y- (or longitude and latitude) coordinates required to locate a Point on the surface of the Earth, the WKT syntax enables you to specify additional z- and m-coordinate values to position a point in four-dimensional space.

The z-coordinate is the height, or elevation, of a Point. Just as positions on the Earth's surface are measured with reference to a horizontal datum, the height of points above or below the surface are measured relative to a vertical datum. The z-coordinate may represent the height of a point above sea-level, the height above the underlying terrain, or the height above the reference ellipsoid, depending on which vertical datum is used.

The m-coordinate represents the "measure" value of a Point. The fourth dimension is most commonly thought of as time, although the m-coordinate can be used to represent any additional property of a point that can be expressed as a double-precision number. For example, if you were recording time-based data, you could use the m-coordinate to represent the time at which the location of a point was recorded. Or, if recording waypoints along a route, the *m*-coordinate could be used to express the distance of how far along the route each point lay.

The WKT syntax for a Point containing *z*- and *m*-coordinates is as follows,

$$POINT(x\ y\ z\ m)$$

Or, if using geographic coordinates:

$$POINT(longitude\ latitude\ z\ m)$$

However, you should be aware that, although SQL Server 2012 supports the creation, storage, and retrieval of *z*- and *m*-coordinate values, all of the inbuilt methods operate in 2D space only. The *z* and *m* values assigned to a Point instance will therefore not have any effect on the result of any calculations performed on that instance.

For example, when calculating the distance between the Points located at (0 0 0) and (3 4 12), SQL Server calculates the result as 5 units (the square root of the sum of the difference in the *x* and *y* dimensions only), and not 13 (the square root of the sum of the difference in the *x*, *y*, and *z* dimensions). You can, however, retrieve the *z* and *m* values associated with any instance and use them in your own calculations, as is demonstrated in a later chapter.

Characteristics of Points

All Point geometries share the following characteristics.

- A Point is zero-dimensional, which means that it has no length in any direction and there is no area contained within a Point.

- A Point has no boundary.

- The interior of a Point is the Point itself. Everything other than that Point is the exterior.

- Points are always classified as "simple" geometries.

LineStrings

Having established the ability to define individual Points, we can then create a series of two or more Points and draw the path segments that directly connect each one to the next in the series. This path defines a *LineString*.

Example LineString Usage

In geospatial data, LineStrings are commonly used to represent features such as roads, rivers, delivery routes, or contours of the Earth. Figure 2-5 illustrates a LineString that represents the route of the Orient Express railway, which traveled across Europe between Paris and Istanbul. The Orient Express was one of the world's most famous luxury railway services, and passed through many of Europe's great cities during its 1200-mile route, including Munich, Vienna, Budapest, and Belgrade.

Figure 2-5. *A LineString representing the route of the Orient Express railway.*

Defining a LineString

When expressed using the WKT format, the coordinate values of each Point are separated by a space, and a comma separates each Point from the next in the LineString, as follows.

LINESTRING(2 3, 4 6, 6 6, 10 4)

The LineString created by this WKT definition is illustrated in Figure 2-6.

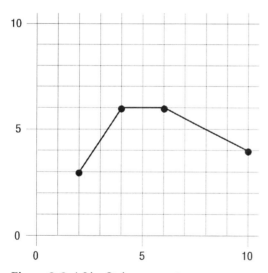

Figure 2-6. *A LineString geometry.*

▓ **Note** Some GIS systems make a distinction between a *LineString* and a *Line*. According to the Open Geospatial Consortium specification (a standard on which the spatial features of SQL Server 2012 are largely based), a Line connects exactly two Points, whereas a LineString may connect any number of Points. Because all Lines can be represented as LineStrings, of these two types SQL Server 2012 only implements the LineString geometry. If you need to define a table in which only Lines can be stored, you can do so by adding a CHECK constraint that calls the STNumPoints() method to test whether inserted LineString values contain only two points.

LineStrings created from geographic coordinates follow the same convention: the coordinates of each Point in the LineString are listed in longitude–latitude order (as they would be for an individual Point), and each Point in the LineString is separated by a comma.

Characteristics of LineStrings

All LineStrings are one-dimensional geometries: they have an associated length, but do not contain any area. This is the case even when the ends of the LineString are joined together to form a closed loop. LineStrings may be described as having the following additional characteristics.

- A *simple* LineString is one where the path drawn between the points of the LineString does not cross itself.

- A *closed* LineString is one that starts and ends at the same point.

- A LineString that is both simple and closed is known as a *ring*.

- The interior of a LineString consists of all the points that lie on the path of the line. Be aware that, even when a LineString forms a closed ring, the interior of the LineString does not contain those points in the area enclosed by the ring. The interior of a LineString consists only of those points that lie on the LineString itself.

- The boundary of a LineString consists of the two points that lie at the start and end of the line. However, a closed LineString, in which the start and end points are the same, has no boundary.

- The exterior of a LineString consists of all those points that do not lie on the line.

Different examples of LineString geometries are illustrated in Figure 2-7.

Figure 2-7. Examples of LineString geometries. (From left–right) A simple LineString, a simple closed LineString (a ring), a nonsimple LineString, a nonsimple closed LineString.

LineStrings and Self-Intersection

It is worth noting that, although the path of a nonsimple LineString may cross itself at one or more distinct points, it cannot retrace any continuous length of path already covered. Consider Figure 2-8, which illustrates the shape of a capital letter "T":

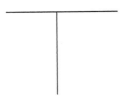

Figure 2-8. A geometry in the shape of a capital letter T.

The shape illustrated in Figure 2-8 cannot be represented by a single LineString geometry, because doing so would necessarily involve retracing at least one section of the path twice. Instead, the appropriate type of geometry to represent this shape is a MultiLineString geometry, discussed later this chapter.

CircularStrings

As described in the previous section, LineStrings are formed by defining the path segments connecting a series of Points in order. The line segments that connect consecutive points are calculated by linear interpolation: each line segment represents the shortest direct route from one Point to the next in the LineString.

However, this is clearly not the only way to connect a series of Points. An alternative method would be to define a curve that connects each Point with a smooth line and gently changing gradient, rather than abrupt angular corners between segments typical of a LineString. The CircularString geometry, which is a new geometry type introduced in SQL Server 2012, provides one such curved line by using circular, rather than linear, interpolation between points. In other words, a CircularString is defined by the paths connecting a series of points in order, where the path segments connecting each pair of points is an arc formed from part of a circle.

Example CircularString Usage

Every year, teams of rowers from Oxford University and Cambridge University compete in a boat race on the River Thames in West London. Starting from Putney Bridge, the race course follows the river upstream for slightly over four miles, ending just before Chiswick Bridge. The course is marked by three distinctive bends; the crew rowing on the north side of the river has the advantage in the first and third bends, whereas the crew rowing on the south side of the river has the advantage of being on the inside for the long second bend.

A CircularString, as illustrated in Figure 2-9, is a suitable geometry to model the course of the race, because it can represent more accurately the smooth curves of the river than is possible using linear interpolation as in a LineString.

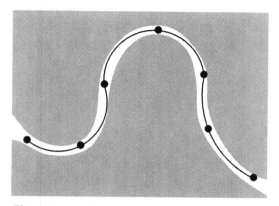

Figure 2-9. *A CircularString geometry representing the course of the Oxford–Cambridge University boat race.*

▓ **Note** Don't be misled by the name: a CircularString geometry does not have to form a complete circle (although it can); it merely means that the segments joining consecutive points are circular arcs rather than straight lines as in a LineString.

Defining a CircularString

There are an infinite number of circular arcs that connect two Points. In order to specify which of these arcs should be created, every CircularString segment actually requires three points: the start and end points to be connected, and an additional anchor point that lies somewhere on the arc between those points. The CircularString will follow the edge of the only circle that passes through all three points.

The syntax for the Well-Known Text representation of a CircularString is as follows,

CIRCULARSTRING (1 3, 4 1, 9 4)

The CircularString created from this definition is shown in the solid line illustrated in Figure 2-10. The dashed line illustrates the complete circle from which the CircularString arc has been created.

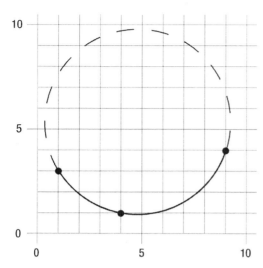

Figure 2-10. *CircularString defined by the circular interpolation of three points.*

■ **Note** The additional anchor point does not need to lie in the middle of the start and end points of a CircularString; it can be any point that lies on the circular arc between the start and end point.

Like LineStrings, CircularStrings can be created between a series of any number of consecutive points. Each segment implicitly starts at the endpoint of the previous curved segment. Each additional segment requires both an anchor point and an endpoint, therefore every valid CircularString contains an odd number of points, and must contain at least three points.

■ **Note** A valid CircularString must have an odd number of points, greater than one.

WHEN IS A CIRCULARSTRING A STRAIGHT LINE?

One interesting point to note is that it is possible to specify a CircularString in which the anchor point lies exactly on the straight line between the start and end point. The circular arc created in such cases is a straight line, effectively joining all three points with the arc taken from a circle of infinite radius. The same result can also be achieved if the anchor point is exactly equal to either the start or end point.

The set of points contained by either a LineString or a "straight" CircularString are identical, which can be confirmed using SQL Server's STEquals() method as shown in the following code listing.

```
DECLARE @LineString geometry = 'LINESTRING(0 0, 8 6)';
DECLARE @CircularString1 geometry = 'CIRCULARSTRING(0 0, 4 3, 8 6)';
```

```
DECLARE @CircularString2 geometry = 'CIRCULARSTRING(0 0, 0 0, 8 6)';

SELECT
  @LineString.STEquals(@CircularString1), -- Returns 1 (true)
  @LineString.STEquals(@CircularString2); -- Returns 1 (true)
```

Characteristics of CircularStrings

CircularStrings, like LineStrings, inherit from the abstract Curve geometry type, and share many of the same characteristics.

- CircularStrings are one-dimensional geometries; they have an associated length, but do not contain any area.

- A *simple* CircularString is one where the path drawn between the points of the CircularString does not cross itself.

- A *closed* CircularString is one that starts and ends at the same point.

- The interior of a CircularString consists of all the points that lie on the arc segments.

- The boundary of a CircularString consists of the start and end points only, except in the case of a closed CircularString, which has no boundary.

- The exterior of a CircularString consists of all those points not on the path of the CircularString.

- Every CircularString must be defined by an odd number of points greater than one.

Drawing Complete Circles

To create a CircularString that forms a complete circle, you might expect that you would need to define only three points: one point used twice as both the start and end of the CircularString, and one other anchor point that lies somewhere on the perimeter of the circle. However, the problem with this definition is that it does not specify the orientation of the created circle; that is, beginning from the start point, does the path of the CircularString travel in a clockwise or anti-clockwise direction through the anchor point and back to where it started?

   To avoid this ambiguity, in order to create a CircularString that forms a complete circle, five points are required. As with any closed LineString, the start and end points are the same. The remaining three points can be any other points that lie on the circle, listed in the desired order. The following Well-Known Text defines a clockwise circle with a radius of two units, centered about the point at (5 5):

```
CIRCULARSTRING(3 5, 5 7, 7 5, 5 3, 3 5)
```

This CircularString is illustrated in Figure 2-11.

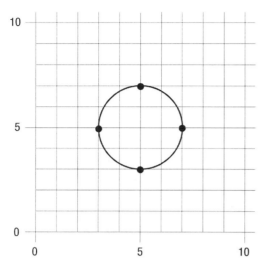

Figure 2-11. *Creating a circle using a CircularString geometry.*

■ **Note** In order to define a full circle, you must define a CircularString containing five points.

Choosing Between LineString and CircularString

Although LineString geometries can be used to approximate a curve by using a number of small segments, CircularStrings can generally do so more efficiently and with greater accuracy. However, even though the CircularString geometry may enable you to describe rounded features with greater precision, the LineString is better supported and more widely used in spatial applications. For this reason, you will probably find that many sources of spatial data still use LineStrings even in situations where CircularStrings may provide greater benefit.

You may also find that, when exporting your own data for use in third-party spatial applications, CircularStrings are not supported and you may have to convert your CircularStrings to LineStrings instead. Fortunately, SQL Server provides a method to do just this—STCurveToLine()—which is documented in Books Online at http://msdn.microsoft.com/en-us/library/ff929272%28v=sql.110%29.aspx.

CompoundCurves

A CompoundCurve is a single continuous path between a set of Points, in which the segments joining each pair of Points may either be linear (as in a LineString) or curved (as in a CircularString), or a mixture of both. The CompoundCurve geometry is a new geometry type introduced in SQL Server 2012.

Example CompundCurve Usage

The Daytona International Speedway race track in Daytona Beach, Florida, is recognizable by its distinctive *tri-oval* shape, consisting of three straights and three smooth corners. This revolutionary circuit design, conceived by Bill France, founder of NASCAR, was created to maximize the angle of vision in which spectators could see cars both approaching and driving away from them.

Figure 2-12 illustrates a CompoundCurve representing the shape of the Daytona racing circuit, consisting of three CircularString segments and three LineString segments.

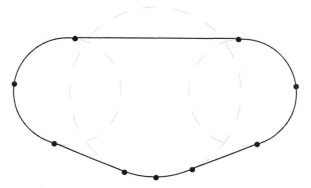

Figure 2-12. A CompundCurve representing the Daytona International Speedway racing circuit.

Defining a CompoundCurve

The Well-Known Text for a CompoundCurve geometry begins with the COMPOUNDCURVE keyword followed by a set of round brackets. Contained within the brackets are the individual LineString or CircularString segments that are joined together to form the compound curve.

Each CircularString or LineString segment in the CompoundCurve must begin at the point where the previous segment ended, so that the CompoundCurve defines a single continuous path. The coordinates of CircularString segments are preceded by the CIRCULARSTRING keyword, whereas LineString segments are not preceded by any keyword; they are simply a list of coordinates contained in round brackets.

The following code listing demonstrates the Well-Known Text representation of a CompoundCurve geometry containing two LineString segments and two CircularString segments:

```
COMPOUNDCURVE(
   (2 3, 2 8),
   CIRCULARSTRING(2 8, 4 10, 6 8),
   (6 8, 6 3),
   CIRCULARSTRING(6 3, 4 1, 2 3)
)
```

This CompoundCurve geometry is illustrated in Figure 2-13.

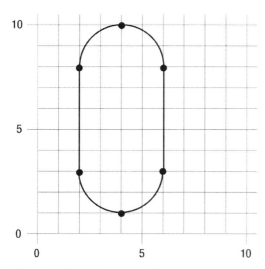

Figure 2-13. A CompoundCurve geometry.

Characteristics of CompoundCurves

CompoundCurves are constructed from one-dimensional LineStrings and CircularStrings, therefore CompoundCurves are themselves one-dimensional, and contain no area.

- A simple CompoundCurve is one that does not intersect itself.
- A closed CompoundCurve is one that starts and ends at the same point.

Polygons

A Polygon is a type of surface; that is, a Polygon is a two-dimensional geometry that contains an area of space. The outer extent of the area of space contained within a Polygon is defined by a closed LineString, called the exterior ring. In contrast to a simple closed LineString geometry, which only defines those points lying on the ring itself, the Polygon defined by a ring contains all of the points that lie either on the line itself, or contained in the area within the exterior ring.

Example Polygon Usage

Polygons are frequently used in spatial data to represent geographic areas such as islands or lakes, political jurisdictions, or large structures. Figure 2-14 illustrates a Polygon that represents the state of Texas, United States. The large state (261,797 square miles) has a very distinctive, recognizable shape, which features straight sides along the northwest border with New Mexico, the meandering path of the Red River dividing Texas from Oklahoma to the north, and the smooth border of the Gulf Coast to the southeast.

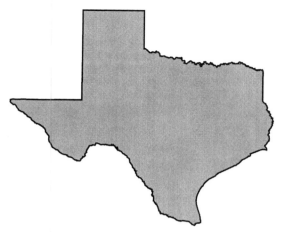

Figure 2-14. A Polygon geometry representing the U.S. state of Texas.

Exterior and Interior Rings

Every Polygon must have exactly one external ring that defines the overall perimeter of the geometry. It may also contain one or more internal rings. Internal rings define areas of space contained within the external ring, but excluded from the Polygon. They can therefore be thought of as "holes" that have been cut out of the main geometry.

Figure 2-15 illustrates a Polygon geometry containing a hole. The Polygon in this case represents the country of South Africa, and the hole represents the fully enclosed country of Lesotho.

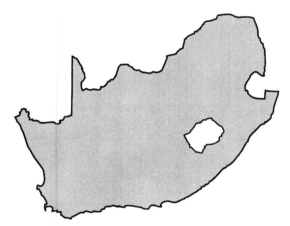

Figure 2-15. A Polygon containing an interior ring, representing South Africa. The interior ring represents the border with Lesotho.

Defining a Polygon

The Well-Known Text for a Polygon begins with the POLYGON keyword, followed by a set of round brackets. Within these brackets, each ring of the Polygon is contained within its own set of brackets. The exterior ring, which defines the perimeter of the Polygon, is always the first ring to be listed. Following this, any interior rings are listed one after another, with each ring separated by a comma.

The following code listing demonstrates the WKT syntax for a rectangular Polygon, two units wide and six units high.

```
POLYGON((1 1, 3 1, 3 7, 1 7, 1 1))
```

And the following code listing demonstrates the WKT syntax for a triangular Polygon containing an interior ring.

```
POLYGON((10 1, 10 9, 4 9, 10 1), (9 4, 9 8, 6 8, 9 4))
```

These two Polygons are both illustrated in Figure 2-16.

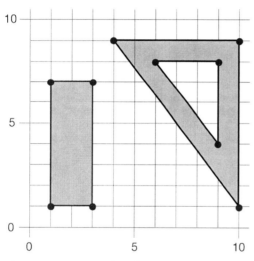

Figure 2-16. *Examples of Polygon geometries. (From left–right) A Polygon; a Polygon with an interior ring.*

▓ **Note** Because Polygons are constructed from rings, which are simple closed LineStrings, the coordinates of the start and end points of each Polygon ring must be the same.

Characteristics of Polygons

All Polygons share the following characteristics.

- Because Polygons are constructed from a series of one or more rings, which are simple closed LineStrings, all Polygons are themselves deemed to be simple closed geometries.

- Polygons are two-dimensional geometries; they have both an associated length and area.
    - The length of a Polygon is measured as the sum of the lengths of all the rings of that Polygon (exterior and interior).
    - The area of a Polygon is calculated as the area of space within the exterior ring, less the area contained within any interior rings.

CurvePolygons

The CurvePolygon, like the Polygon, is defined by one exterior ring and, optionally, one or more interior rings. Unlike the Polygon, however, in which each ring must be a simple closed LineString, each ring in a CurvePolygon can be any type of simple closed curve. Those curves can be LineStrings, CircularStrings, or CompoundCurves, so the rings that define the boundary of a CurvePolygon can have a mixture of straight and curved edges.

Example CurvePolygon Usage

Yankee Stadium, built in 1923 in New York City, hosted over 6581 home games of the New York Yankees baseball team in its 85-year history, prior to its closure in 2008 (the team now plays in a new stadium, also named "Yankee Stadium," constructed a short distance away from the site of the original Yankee Stadium). It was the first three-tiered sports facility to be built in the United States, and one of the first to be officially named a *stadium* (as opposed to a traditional baseball *park*, or *field*).

The large stadium was designed to be a multipurpose facility that could accommodate baseball, football, and track and field events, and the smooth-cornered, irregularly sided shape of the stadium can be be modeled as a CurvePolygon whose exterior ring contains four CircularString segments and four LineString segments, as illustrated in Figure 2-17.

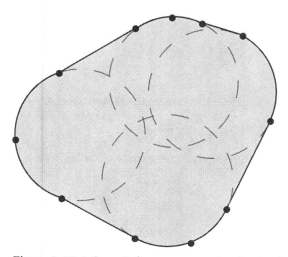

Figure 2-17. A CurvePolygon representing Yankee Stadium in New York.

Defining a CurvePolygon

The WKT representation of a CurvePolygon follows the same general syntax as that for a Polygon. However, because the CurvePolygon allows rings to be defined as LineStrings, CircularStrings, or CompoundCurves, you must specify which kind of curve is used for each ring.

The LineString is considered to be the "default" curve type, and linear rings do not need to be explicitly preceded by the LINESTRING keyword. In the following code listing, a CurvePolygon is defined by a linear ring between five points:

```
CURVEPOLYGON((4 2, 8 2, 8 6, 4 6, 4 2))
```

The result, shown in Figure 2-18, is a square of width and height 2 units, exactly the same as would have been created using the following Polygon geometry.

```
POLYGON((4 2, 8 2, 8 6, 4 6, 4 2))
```

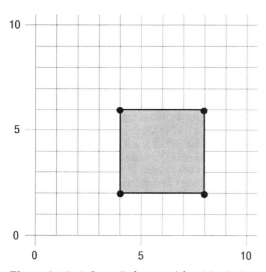

Figure 2-18. *A CurvePolygon with a LineString exterior ring.*

In the following code listing, the exterior ring of the CurvePolygon is instead defined using a CircularString geometry between the same set of points.

```
CURVEPOLYGON(CIRCULARSTRING(4 2, 8 2, 8 6, 4 6, 4 2))
```

In this case, rather than creating a square, the resulting CurvePolygon is a circle of radius 2.828 (√8), centered on the point (6 4), as shown in Figure 2-19.

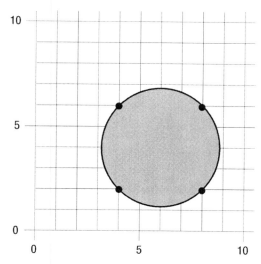

Figure 2-19. A CurvePolygon with a CircularString exterior ring.

Characteristics of CurvePolygons

With the exception of the method of interpolation between points, CurvePolygons share exactly the same general characteristics as Polygons:

- CurvePolygons are two-dimensional, simple, closed geometries.
- They have a length equal to the perimeter of all defined rings.
- The area contained by a CurvePolygon is equal to the area of space enclosed within the exterior ring less any area contained within any interior rings.

MultiPoints

A MultiPoint is a homogeneous collection of Point geometries. Unlike the LineString or CircularString, which are formed from a series of connected Points, there are no connecting lines between the individual Points in a MultiPoint: they are distinct and separate.

Example MultiPoint Usage

The Ardrossan windfarm in Ayrshire, Scotland, contains 14 wind turbines providing green electricity to around 20,000 homes. If each turbine is modeled as a distinct Point geometry, then the collection of turbines forming the entire windfarm can be modeled as a MultiPoint geometry, as in Figure 2-20.

Figure 2-20. *A MultiPoint instance representing the location of each wind turbine at the site of the Ardrossan wind farm.*

Defining A MultiPoint

To represent a MultiPoint geometry in Well-Known Text, you first declare the MULTIPOINT element name, followed by a comma-separated list of the coordinate tuples of each point contained in the instance, contained within round brackets. The coordinates of each point are listed in exactly the same manner as they would be if used to define an individual Point instance; that is, coordinates are listed in *x*, *y*, *z*, *m* order, or longitude, latitude, *z*, *m* order, with values separated by spaces.

The following code listing is an example of a MultiPoint containing three Points,

```
MULTIPOINT(0 0, 2 4, 10 8)
```

The geometry created by this WKT is shown in Figure 2-21.

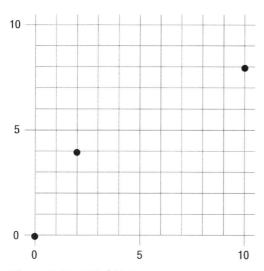

Figure 2-21. *A MultiPoint geometry.*

Be careful with the placement of the comma(s) in the Well-Known Text representation of a MultiPoint geometry; because each Point may contain between two and four coordinate values (depending on whether the optional *z*- and *m*-coordinates are defined), you must place the comma carefully to separate each coordinate tuple. Compare the following two WKT representations, which use the same coordinate values, but vary in their comma placement.

```
MULTIPOINT(0 0, 2 4, 10 8)
MULTIPOINT(0 0 2 , 4 10 8)
```

The first geometry represents a MultiPoint geometry containing three Points, each one specified with only *x*- and *y*-coordinates. The second example creates a MultiPoint containing only two Point geometries, with each one specifying *x*-, *y*-, and *z*-coordinates.

Characteristics of MultiPoints

MultiPoint geometries all share the following characteristics.

- MultiPoints, in common with the individual Point geometries from which they are formed, are always simple closed geometries.
- MultiPoints are one-dimensional, and have no length nor do they contain any area.

Many Single Points, or One Multipoint?

There are many occasions in which you will find yourself working with a set of data in which each individual item can be defined as a Point. However, this does not necessarily mean that it makes sense to combine all of the elements together into a MultiPoint. A MultiPoint should not generally be used simply as a means to group a set of Points; instead, it should be used to define a single logical feature whose geographic location and shape are best described by a set of disparate singular entities.

Consider a university campus consisting of a number of different buildings. In this case, it might be reasonable to define the entire campus as a MultiPoint geometry, with each Point representing one of the buildings on the campus.

However, what if you had a table of customers in which each customer's address was represented as a Point; would it then make sense to create a MultiPoint combining all of your customers' locations in a single geometry? Probably not. Generally speaking, the only situations in which you should do this is if it makes sense to treat that collection as a logical single unit, or if there is some operation that needs to be applied to the collection of Points as a whole. In other cases, you should just leave the data as a set of otherwise unrelated Points.

MultiLineStrings

A MultiLineString is a homogeneous collection of LineString geometries.

Example MultiLineString Usage

The River Nile Delta, formed where the River Nile joins the Mediterranean Sea, is one of the largest river deltas in the world. It extends approximately 240 km along the coastline of Northern Egypt, and begins some 160 km farther south, near Cairo. Approximately half of Egypt's population of 83 million live within the region of the Nile Delta.

The network of distributary channels formed as the River Nile bifurcates can be modeled as a MultiLineString, as illustrated in Figure 2-22.

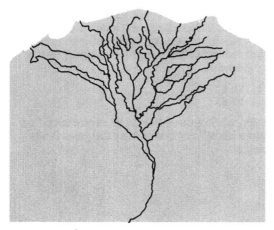

Figure 2-22. *A MultiLineString geometry representing the Nile River delta.*

Defining a MultiLineString

The WKT representation of a MultiLineString geometry is formed by a comma-separated list of individual LineString geometries, contained within a set of round brackets following the `MULTILINESTRING` keyword. Because it is known that the elements within a MultiLineString must all be LineStrings, it is not necessary to include the individual `LINESTRING` keyword in front of each element; each LineString is merely represented by a comma-separated series of coordinate values within round brackets.

The following code listing demonstrates the Well-Known Text representation of a MultiLineString containing three LineStrings: the first and second containing only two points each, and the third containing three points.

```
MULTILINESTRING((0 0, 2 2), (3 2, 6 9), (3 3, 5 3, 8 8))
```

The MultiLineString geometry represented by this WKT is shown in Figure 2-23.

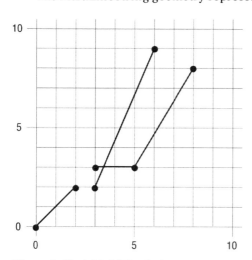

Figure 2-23. *A MultiLineString geometry.*

Characteristics of MultiLineStrings

Unlike MultiPoints and MultiPolygons, which generally contain elements that are disjoint from each other, MutiLineStrings are frequently comprised of a number of intersecting LineString elements. For example, any road or river that splits into two or more forks cannot be represented by a single LineString geometry, and must instead be represented as a MultiLineString, with each fork being represented by a separate LineString within the MultiLineString. Additional properties of MultiLineStrings are as follows.

- As are LineStrings, MultiLineStrings are one-dimensional.

- A MultiLineString is simple if all of the LineString elements contained within it are completely disjoint from each other. If any two LineStrings intersect (even if they only touch each other) the MultiLineString is not considered to be simple.

- A MultiLineString is closed if all of the LineString instances contained within it are themselves closed (i.e., every LineString forms a closed loop, ending at the same point from which it started).

MultiPolygons

A MultiPolygon is a geometry collection containing several Polygon geometries.

Example MultiPolygon Usage

MultiPolygons are frequently used to represent countries, because many countries are not defined by a single continuous border. Take New Zealand, for example, as illustrated in Figure 2-24.

Figure 2-24. A MultiPolygon representing the country of New Zealand.

It is easy to think of other countries that consist of two or more separate geographic islands or regions, including Japan, the United States of America (Alaska and Hawaii), Australia (Tasmania), France (Corsica), and many others. In all these cases, the geographic area represented by a particular political entity is best represented as a MultiPolygon.

Defining a MultiPolygon

The Well-Known Text representation of a MultiPolygon uses the MULTIPOLYGON keyword, followed by the definition of each Polygon contained in the collection, contained within round brackets.

The following code listing illustrates the WKT syntax required to define a MultiPolygon containing two Polygons, each one containing only a single exterior ring.

```
MULTIPOLYGON(((10 20, 30 10, 44 50, 10 20)), ((35 36, 37 37, 38 34, 35 36)))
```

Take care to place the brackets carefully, because brackets are used both to separate individual rings within a Polygon and also to separate Polygons within a MultiPolygon. Compare the preceding code listing to the following, which instead creates a MultiPolygon geometry containing only one Polygon that contains an interior ring.

```
MULTIPOLYGON(((10 20, 30 10, 44 50, 10 20), (35 36, 37 37, 38 34, 35 36)))
```

Characteristics of MultiPolygons

Characteristics of MultiPolygons are as follows.

- MultiPolygons are two-dimensional, simple, closed geometries.
- The length of a MultiPolygon is defined as the sum of the lengths of all the rings in all the Polygons it contains.
- The area of a MultiPolygon is the sum of the areas of all its Polygons.

GeometryCollections

The MultiPoint, MultiLineString, and MultiPolygon geometries considered previously are examples of geometry collections containing only a single type of geometry. It is also possible to define a generic, heterogeneous GeometryCollection, which may contain any number of any type of geometry (with the exception of the FullGlobe geometry, discussed later). The GeometryCollection is also the only type of collection that can contain multiple curved objects.

Example GeometryCollection Usage

GeometryCollections are commonly returned as the result of an aggregate query that returns a single record representing a varied set of features. For example, if you were to run an aggregate query to return, "All those features that lie within one mile of Trafalgar Square, London," you might expect to see geometries in the results representing Nelson's Column and the Cenotaph (Points), Downing Street and the Strand (LineStrings), and St. James' Park (Polygon). If these results were aggregated into a single record, the only geometry type capable of representing them all would be a GeometryCollection.

Defining a GeometryCollection

The Well-Known Text syntax for a GeometryCollection begins with the keyword GEOMETRYCOLLECTION, followed by the fully formed WKT representation of each element in the collection, contained within a set of round brackets. The following code listing illustrates the WKT syntax for a GeometryCollection containing a Polygon and a Point.

```
GEOMETRYCOLLECTION(POLYGON((5 5, 10 5, 10 10, 5 5)), POINT(10 12))
```

Characteristics of Geometry Collections

The characteristics of a GeometryCollection depend on the elements it contains.

- If all the elements contained in the GeometryCollection are simple then the GeometryCollection is itself simple. If any of the elements are not simple then the collection is not simple.

- Likewise, if all the elements contained within the GeometryCollection are closed then the collection itself is closed. If any element is not closed then the GeometryCollection is not closed.

- The number of dimensions occupied by a GeometryCollection is the same as the element with the highest number of dimensions that it contains. In other words, any GeometryCollection that contains only Points and MultiPoints will occupy zero dimensions; a collection containing LineStrings, CircularStrings, or CompoundCurves will occupy one dimension; and a collection that contains at least one Polygon or MultiPolygon will occupy two dimensions.

■ **Note** Although there are specific MultiLineString and MultiPolygon collections, there is no specific collection that can contain multiple instances of their equivalent curved forms; there are no MultiCircularString, MultiCurve, or MultiCurvePolygons, for example. To create a collection that contains more than one of these elements you must use the generic GeometryCollection type.

FullGlobe

The FullGlobe is a special type of geometry that encompasses the whole surface of the Earth.

Defining a FullGlobe

A FullGlobe geometry covers the entire surface of the Earth, thus there is no need to state any particular coordinate points in its construction. The Well-Known Text representation of a FullGlobe geometry is therefore very simply:

```
FULLGLOBE
```

Characteristics of the FullGlobe geometry are as follows.

- A FullGlobe does not have a boundary nor any exterior, because every point on the Earth is considered to lie in the interior of a FullGlobe.

- A FullGlobe geometry is closed.

- A FullGlobe geometry cannot be a member of a GeometryCollection.

Empty Geometries

One final type of geometry to consider is an *empty* geometry. An empty geometry is one that does not contain any points. Even though it contains no points, an empty geometry is still nominally assigned a particular type, so you may have an empty Point or empty LineString geometry, for example.

Figure 2-25. *An empty Point geometry, an empty LineString geometry, and an empty Polygon geometry. (JOKE!)*

You may be wondering why you would ever create an empty geometry: how can you represent the location or position of a feature on the Earth using a shape with no points? One way of thinking about this is as follows. If geometries represent the position (and therefore, by implication, the presence) of features on the Earth's surface, then empty geometries denote the *absence* of any such features.

You don't generally create empty geometries directly, but you do get empty geometries returned in the results of a spatial query in which no points match the specified criteria. For example, empty geometries can be used as a response to a question, "Where is *x*?" when the answer is, "Nowhere on Earth."

▓ **Note** An empty geometry is not the same as NULL. A NULL value suggests a result that has not been evaluated or is undefined. An empty geometry value suggests that a result has been evaluated, but that it does not represent a location on the Earth.

Defining an Empty Geometry

Empty geometries of any type can be defined using the Well-Known Text syntax by declaring the name of the type of geometry followed by the word EMPTY.

Some examples of different types of empty geometries are as follows.

```
POINT EMPTY
LINESTRING EMPTY
GEOMETRYCOLLECTION EMPTY
```

Characteristics of Empty Geometries

Characteristics of empty geometries are as follows.

- Empty geometries are simple geometries.

- Empty geometries are not closed.

- Empty geometries have no interior and no boundary. Everything is exterior to an empty geometry.

Choosing the Correct Geometry

There is no "correct" type of geometry to use to represent any given feature on the Earth. The choice of which geometry to use will depend on how you plan to use the data. If you are going to analyze the geographic spread of your customer base, you could define Polygon geometries that represented the shape of each of your customers' houses, but it would be a lot easier to consider each customer's address as a single Point. In contrast, when conducting a detailed analysis of a small-scale area for land-planning purposes, you may want to represent all roads, buildings, and even walls of buildings as Polygons having both length and area, to ensure that the spatial data represent their actual shape as closely as possible.

Summary

In this chapter, you learned about the different types of geometries that can be used to store spatial data in SQL Server 2012.

- Points are the most basic type of geometry, representing a singular location in space. They are used as a building block to construct the more complex types of geometry.

- LineStrings, CircularStrings, and CompoundCurves are all one-dimensional geometries that are typically used to represent paths, routes, borders, and similar features.

- Polygons and CurvePolygons are two-dimensional geometries. They have a boundary that contains an interior area, and may also have one or more interior holes.

- Elements may be combined together into collections. Homogeneous collections are MultiPoints, MultiLineStrings, and MultiPolygons, respectively. SQL Server also supports a heterogeneous GeometryCollection that may contain any number of any type of geometry (other than a FullGlobe).

- There are two special types of geometry: the FullGlobe geometry, which covers the entire surface of the Earth, and the Empty geometry, which contains no area at all.

CHAPTER 3

Spatial Datatypes

Every variable, parameter, and column in a SQL Server table is defined as being of a particular datatype. The datatype determines the range of values that can be stored and the ways in which that data can be used. You are probably already familiar with many SQL Server datatypes, such as those listed in Table 3-1.

Table 3-1. Common SQL Server Datatypes

Datatype	Usage
char	Fixed-length character string
datetime	Date and time value, accurate to 3.33 ms
float	Floating-point numeric data
int	Integer value between -2^{31} ($-2,147,483,648$) and $2^{31} - 1$ ($2,147,483,647$)
money	Monetary or currency data
nvarchar	Variable-length unicode character string

In addition to these common datatypes designed to hold numeric, character, or date and time data, SQL Server 2012 has two datatypes specifically designed to hold spatial data: geometry and geography. These are listed in Table 3-2.

Table 3-2. SQL Server Spatial Datatypes

Datatype	Usage
geography	Geodetic vector spatial data
geometry	Planar vector spatial data

There are several similarities between the geometry and geography datatypes:

- They both employ a vector model of spatial data, in which features may be represented using a range of geometries including Points, LineStrings, Polygons, and collections of these types.

- Internally, SQL Server stores values of both datatypes as a serialized stream of binary data in the same format.

- When working with items of data from either type, you use object-oriented methods based on the .NET framework.

- They both provide much of the same standard spatial functionality, such as calculating the length or area of a feature, the distance between features, or testing whether two features intersect.

However, there are also a number of important differences between the two types. When you store spatial data in SQL Server 2012, you must choose whether to store that information using the geometry datatype or the geography datatype according to the nature of the data in question, and how you plan to use that data. In this chapter, we explore the features of the two types, and show how to decide which datatype to use in a given situation.

SQLCLR Foundations

Before looking at the specific differences between the geometry and geography datatypes, it's worth spending a bit of time examining the way in which both datatypes are implemented in SQL Server.

The geometry and geography datatypes are both system-defined CLR datatypes. The abbreviation CLR in this context refers to the Common Language Runtime, the environment used to execute managed .NET code. Whereas most SQL Server queries use the T-SQL query engine, when working with CLR datatypes SQL Server additionally leverages the .NET runtime process hosted by SQL Server known as SQLCLR. The managed code environment in which SQLCLR operates allows SQL Server to deal with certain types of complex data objects, such as spatial data, more efficiently than relying on T-SQL alone.

■ **Note** SQL Server uses SQLCLR to perform operations on system-defined CLR datatypes—geometry, geography, and hierarchyid—as well as for user-defined CLR datatypes (UDTs). When querying such data, SQLCLR works alongside the T-SQL engine; it does not replace it.

In all versions of SQL Server since SQL Server 2005, it has been possible to use the SQLCLR to execute user-defined .NET code. In order to do so, however, the server must first be configured to allow such behavior, which can be done by calling the sp_configure system stored procedure and setting the clr_enabled option to 1. In contrast, system-defined CLR datatypes such as geometry and geography require no additional configuration; they are automatically available for use in all SQL Server 2012 databases. As such, you can start using spatial datatypes straight away in your database just as you would any other type of data.

Even though they require no configuration, there are still some special considerations of working with the geometry and geography datatypes (and with CLR datatypes in general) that you should be aware of, as follows.

- Each CLR data item is defined as an object, a serialized representation of a compound set of values. If you do a simple SELECT query of a column of data defined using a CLR datatype, your query will return a set of binary values.

- As with classes in object-oriented languages, a CLR datatype defines a number of methods and properties. Each individual item of geography or geometry data is an instance of the respective datatype, and inherits the methods of the datatype from which it is derived. So, methods defined by the geometry datatype can only be used on items of geometry data, and methods defined by the geography datatype can only be used on items of geography data.

- The syntax required for writing queries involving CLR data is a little bit different from regular T-SQL query syntax, and may look unfamiliar to you.

- Unlike regular T-SQL functions, such as SUM, CAST, or SUBSTRING, the methods and properties defined by CLR datatypes, such as ToString(), STArea(), or STIntersects(), are case-sensitive.

- CLR datatypes can be used within a .NET application layer as well as within SQLCLR, therefore with clever coding and application design you can develop encapsulated spatial routines that can be re-used in both the database layer and the application layer with only a minimum amount of recoding.

- Errors encountered in SQLCLR code need to be handled in a different way from T-SQL errors.

- Because spatial data are not comparable, you can't use geometry or geography data with any T-SQL operators that make a direct comparison between two values. For example, you cannot ORDER BY or SELECT DISTINCT values from a column of spatial data, nor can you UNION two result sets containing a column of the geography or geometry datatype (although you can UNION ALL two datasets). You also can't join two tables together using conventional join syntax such as TableA.GeometryColumn = TableB.GeometryColumn. Instead, you must use the appropriate comparison operator defined by the datatype itself, for example, TableA.GeometryColumn.STEquals(TableB.GeometryColumn) = 1

Many of these issues are explored in more detail in the topics covered throughout this book.

Methods and Properties

The range of methods available for a given item of spatial data (i.e., what you can actually do with that data) is dependent on the datatype in which it is defined. Although in most cases there are methods to provide equivalent functionality in both the geometry and geography datatypes, there are some methods that can only be applied to one or the other. For example, the STRelate() method, which allows you to define and test for a specific pattern of intersection between two geometries, is only available for the geometry datatype.

In some cases, there are methods that provide roughly equivalent functionality between the two types, but under a different name: for example, Lat and Long, which return the (geographic) coordinate values of a geography instance, provide equivalent functionality to STY and STX, which return the (Cartesian) coordinate values of a geometry instance.

In general, the methods available using either type can be classified into one of two categories:

- *OGC methods*: Methods that adhere to the Open Geospatial Consortium specifications are prefixed by the letters ST (an abbreviation for *spatiotemporal*). These methods provide commonly used, basic functionality for working with spatial instances such as STIntersects(), used to determine whether one instance intersects another; STDistance(), used to calculate the shortest distance between two instances; and STArea(), used to calculate the area contained within a Polygon instance.

- SQL Server also provides a number of *extended methods*, which provide additional functionality on top of the OGC standard. These include Reduce(), which simplifies a geometry; BufferWithTolerance(), which applies a buffer within a given tolerance limit; and Filter(), which performs an approximate test of intersection based on a spatial index.

Static Methods

To create an item of geography or geometry data, you must use a *static* method belonging to the appropriate datatype. The syntax for using a static method is to state the name of the datatype followed by a pair of colons, and then the name of the method. For example, the Parse() method is a static method that can be used to create an instance from a supplied Well-Known Text string. To use the Parse() method of the geometry datatype to create a Point geometry at coordinates (30,40), you would call it as shown in the following code listing,

```
SELECT geometry::Parse('POINT(30 40)');
```

■ **Note** The geometry Parse method treats all supplied coordinate values as defined using SRID 0; that is, they are abstract coordinates with no relation to a specific model of the Earth.

To provide another example, the following code listing creates a table containing a single column of the geography datatype, and then inserts three Points into that table created using the geography Point() static method. The Point() method requires three parameters representing latitude, longitude, and SRID. The return value of the method is a Point geometry at the specified location.

```
CREATE TABLE geographypoints (
  Location geography
);

INSERT INTO geographypoints VALUES
(geography::Point(51, 1, 4326)),
(geography::Point(52, -2, 4326)),
(geography::Point(50.7, -1.1, 4326));
```

After executing this code listing, the geographypoints table now contains three rows each representing a location in the south of England, defined using the EPSG:4326 spatial reference system.

Instance Methods

The process of creating an item of data using a static method is known as *instantiation*, and the geometry created is referred to as an *instance* of the geometry or geography dataype (depending on the static method from which it was created). Operations performed on individual values of spatial data are therefore called *instance methods*. Items of both the geography and geometry datatypes provide a range of instance methods for performing common calculations, including intersections, measuring distances, and addition and subtraction of geometries.

The syntax for using an instance method is to state the name of the item (or column) of data on which the method should be performed followed by a single dot (.) and then the name of the method to be called followed by a set of closed brackets (). If the method requires any parameters, these should be supplied within the brackets.

For example, the ToString() method is an instance method that retrieves the Well-Known Text representation of any item of geography or geometry data. It requires no parameters. To retrieve the WKT of each Point in the Location column of the geographypoints table created in the preceding code listing, you can execute the following.

```
SELECT
  Location.ToString()
FROM
  geographypoints;
```

As another example, the STBuffer() method is an instance method that creates a buffer zone around a geometry. It requires a single parameter stating the amount by which the geometry should be buffered. Positive values create an enlarged area around a geometry, whereas negative values create a reduced area. The following code listing declares a geometry Point variable located at (12 7) using the geometry Point() static method, and then selects a buffer of 5 units about that geometry by calling the STBuffer() method on that instance.

```
DECLARE @point geometry = geometry::Point(12, 7, 0);
SELECT @point.STBuffer(5);
```

Note that instance methods can be chained together, where the result of one method is passed directly to the next method. For example, the following code listing creates a buffered Point geometry using STBuffer() and then returns the area of that buffered geometry by calling by calling the STArea() method on the buffered instance.

```
DECLARE @point geometry = geometry::Point(3, 5, 0);
SELECT @point.STBuffer(5).STArea();
```

▓ **Note** In the preceding code listings, the coordinates from which the geometry Points were created were abstract x- and y-coordinates; they weren't intended to represent any particular feature on the Earth's surface. To indicate this, a value of 0 has been supplied as the third parameter to the Point() method, which means that these coordinates do not relate to any particular spatial reference system.

Properties

Certain properties of a geography or geometry instance can be accessed directly using property notation, which, like the syntax for instance methods, uses the column name followed by a single dot and then the name of the property to retrieve. However, because you do not need to provide parameters to retrieve the property of an instance, property names are not followed by a set of brackets.

For example, the Lat and Long properties represent the latitude and longitude coordinates of a geography Point instance, respectively. The following code listing illustrates how to retrieve the latitude and longitude coordinates of each Point in the geographypoints table.

```
SELECT
  Location.Lat,
  Location.Long
FROM
  geographypoints;
```

Some properties, such as Lat and Long are read-only. That is to say, you cannot update the latitude coordinate of a Point by running the following query,

```
UPDATE geographypoints SET Location.Lat = 20;
```

Attempting to do so will result in the following error.

```
Msg 6595, Level 16, State 1, Line 1
Could not assign to property 'Lat' for type 'Microsoft.SqlServer.Types.SqlGeography' in
assembly 'Microsoft.SqlServer.Types' because it is read only.
```

Changing the coordinate values associated with a geometry or geography instance requires you to create an entirely new geometry from a static method. However, certain properties of existing geometries can be both retrieved and set. For example, the STSrid property allows you either to return or update the spatial reference identifier associated with an instance. To change the spatial reference identifier of the Points in the geographypoints table to use the North American Datum 1983 (SRID 4269), you can execute the following code listing.

```
UPDATE geographypoints
SET Location.STSrid = 4269;
```

■ **Note** Updating the STSrid property of an instance does not reproject the coordinate values into the specified spatial reference system; it merely changes the metadata describing the system in which those coordinates are defined.

Spatial Libraries

All of the functionality of the geography and geometry datatypes is contained in two libraries: Microsoft.SqlServer.Types.dll and SqlServerSpatial.dll. These assemblies are created when you install SQL Server 2012, but they can also be installed separately as part of the Microsoft SQL Server Feature Pack, available for download from http://www.microsoft.com/downloads.

> Microsoft.SqlServer.Types.dll contains the managed (.NET) code necessary to define the spatial datatypes, and is installed by default in the \Program Files\Microsoft SQL Server\110\SDK\Assemblies directory.

> SqlServerSpatial.dll contains additional functionality required to perform spatial operations, written using native (C++) code. This assembly is installed by default in the \Windows\System32 directory.

Because these two libraries are redistributable and independent of SQL Server, you can reference them in your own applications and use exactly the same spatial methods as provided by the database in any other layer of your architecture: in a client-side app, or in a webservice, for example. The machine on which these applications are executed doesn't even need to have SQL Server installed, so long as it has the two libraries listed above (and the prerequisites to execute the code they contain, namely the .NET Framework and the Microsoft C++ runtime libraries).

■ **Note** You can import SQL Server's spatial libraries and use them from within other applications, such as a WPF application, an ASP.NET webpage, or a console application. However, because the SqlServerSpatial.dll library uses unmanaged code, these applications must be run on a Windows-based platform, and you cannot use the spatial datatypes in a Silverlight application, for example.

Whereas the SQL Server spatial datatypes are called geography and geometry, when you call directly into the SqlServer.Types.dll library from .NET, the corresponding spatial datatypes are called SqlGeography and SqlGeometry. Throughout this book, I concentrate on examples that use the geography and geometry types as they are implemented in SQL Server. However, it is worth remembering that almost all of the same functions can be applied to the equivalent SqlGeography and SqlGeometry types in a .NET application (one significant exception to this rule is that it is only possible to create and utilize a spatial index on data held in the database itself).

The geography Datatype

The most important feature of the geography datatype (and its .NET equivalent, SqlGeography) is that it stores *geodetic* spatial data, which take account of the curved shape of the Earth.

In order to define positions on a geodetic model, geography data is always stated using angular coordinates of latitude and longitude from a geographic coordinate system. Not only is geography data defined and stored on a geodetic model, but when you write spatial queries involving geography data, SQL Server uses angular computations to work out the result. These computations are calculated based on the properties of the ellipsoid model in which that data was defined.

For example, if you were to define a LineString connecting two Points on the Earth's surface in the geography datatype, the line would curve to follow the surface of the reference ellipsoid between the Points. Every "line" drawn between two Points in the geography datatype is actually a *great elliptic arc*: that is, the line on the surface of the ellipsoid formed by the plane intersecting the start and end Points of the line and the center of the reference ellipsoid. This concept is illustrated in Figure 3-1.

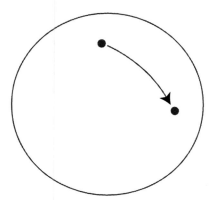

Figure 3-1. Calculations on the geography datatype account for curvature of the Earth.

Spatial Reference Systems for the geography Datatype

The geography datatype performs calculations with respect to the reference ellipsoid, therefore geography data can only be defined using one of the geographic spatial reference systems supported by SQL Server, as listed in the sys.spatial_reference_systems table. This table contains the metadata required by SQL Server to perform the appropriate ellipsoidal calculations, and its structure is shown in Table 3-3.

Table 3-3. Structure of the sys.spatial_reference_systems Table

Column Name	Description
spatial_reference_id	The integer identifier used within SQL Server 2012 to refer to this system.
authority_name	The name of the standards body that administers this reference.
authorized_spatial_reference_id	The identifier allocated by the issuing authority to refer to this system.
well_known_text	The parameters of the spatial reference system, expressed in Well-Known Text format.
unit_of_measure	A text description of the unit used to express linear measurements in this system, such as, "metre" or "foot".
unit_conversion_factor	A scale factor for converting from meters into the appropriate linear unit of measure

■ **Note** Currently all but one of the spatial reference systems supported by SQL Server are based on the EPSG registry, and the value of the internal spatial_reference_id for any system listed in sys.spatial_reference_systems is the same as the authorized_spatial_reference_id allocated by the EPSG. The only exception is SRID 104001, a system defined by Microsoft that defines coordinates on a perfect unit sphere.

The parameters that describe a geographic coordinate system (the ellipsoid, prime meridian, angular unit of measure, and the like) are defined in WKT format in the well_known_text column of the sys.spatial_reference_systems table. However, you might also have noticed that one of the other columns of data defined in the sys.spatial_reference_systems table is unit_of_measure. Why does SQL Server need to know a separate unit of measure, you might ask, when there is already a unit of measure embedded in the well_known_text definition of the system (which, for latitude and longitude coordinates as used by a geographic coordinate system, is generally *degrees*)?

The answer is that, although angular units of latitude and longitude are all very well for describing the location of Points, they are not that helpful for expressing the distance between Points, nor the area enclosed within a set of Points. For example, using the spatial reference system EPSG:4326, we can state the location of Paris, France as a point at 48.87°N, 2.33°E. Using the same system, the location of Berlin,

Germany could be described as 52.52°N, 13.4°E. However, if you wanted to know the distance between Paris and Berlin, it would not be very helpful to state that they were 11.65° apart, with the answer measured in degrees. You would probably find it much more useful to know that the distance between them was 880 km, or 546 miles, say.

To account for this, SQL Server defines an additional linear unit of measurement for every geodetic spatial reference system. When you use the geography datatype, although coordinates must be supplied in angular latitude and longitude coordinates, the results of any calculations are returned in the linear unit of measure specified in the unit_of_measure column of the sys.spatial_reference_systems table for the relevant spatial reference system.

To check the units of measurement corresponding to a particular spatial reference system, you can run a query as follows (substituting the SRID of the appropriate spatial reference system).

```
SELECT
  unit_of_measure
FROM
  sys.spatial_reference_systems
WHERE
  authority_name = 'EPSG'
  AND
  authorized_spatial_reference_id = 4326;
```

This query gives the following result, which tells us that linear measurements of any geography data defined using the EPSG:4326 spatial reference system are stated in meters.

```
metre
```

With this knowledge, we can use the geography datatype to determine the distance between Paris and Berlin based on the latitude and longitude coordinates as stated previously, but returning the answer in meters. This is shown in the following code listing.

```
DECLARE @Paris geography = geography::Point(48.87, 2.33, 4326);
DECLARE @Berlin geography = geography::Point(52.52, 13.4, 4326);
SELECT @Paris.STDistance(@Berlin);
```

The result, a distance of just under 880 km, is as follows.

```
879989.866996421
```

▓ **Note** Every time you store an item of data using the geography type, you must supply the SRID of the spatial reference system from which the coordinates were obtained. SQL Server 2012 uses the information contained in the spatial reference system to apply the relevant model of curvature of the Earth in its calculations, and also to express the results of any linear methods in the appropriate units of measurement. The supplied SRID must therefore correspond to one of the supported spatial references in the sys.spatial_reference_systems table.

Correct Ring Orientation for geography Polygons

Recall that a ring is a closed LineString, and a Polygon geometry is made up of one or more rings that define the boundary of the area contained within the Polygon. *Ring orientation* refers to the "direction," or order, in which the Points that make up the ring of a Polygon are listed.

The geography datatype defines features on a geodetic model of the Earth, which is a continuous round surface. Unlike the image created from a map projection, this geodetic model has no edges; you can continue going in one direction all the way around the world and get back to where you started. This becomes significant when defining a Polygon ring because when using a three-dimensional round model it is ambiguous as to what area is contained inside the ring, and what is outside. Consider Figure 3-2, which illustrates a Polygon defined using the geography datatype whose exterior ring is a series of points drawn around the equator; does the interior of this Polygon include the Northern Hemisphere, or the Southern Hemisphere?

Figure 3-2. *The importance of Polygon ring orientation using the geography datatype. Does the Polygon created from the ring shown here contain the Northern Hemisphere, or the Southern Hemisphere?*

To resolve this ambiguity, SQL Server applies a rule known as the "left-hand rule" (or, sometimes, the "left-foot rule"); if you imagine yourself walking along the ring of a geography Polygon, following the points in the order in which they are listed, SQL Server 2012 treats the area on the "left" of the line drawn between the Points of the ring as the interior of the Polygon, and the area on the "right" as the exterior. Another way of thinking about this is to imagine looking down at a point on the surface of the Earth from space; if that point is enclosed by a Polygon ring in a counterclockwise direction then that point is contained inside the Polygon, otherwise it is outside.

Applying this rule, we can determine that the Polygon illustrated in Figure 3-2 therefore represents the Northern Hemisphere. If the order of the points in the Polygon ring were to be reversed, then this Polygon would instead contain the Southern Hemisphere.

■ **Caution** It is a common mistake to list the points of a Polygon ring with incorrect ring orientation, in which case the resulting Polygon is "inside-out": the area that was intended to be contained within the Polygon is outside, and the interior of the Polygon actually contains the entire rest of the Earth's surface. When defining a Polygon ring in the geography datatype, ensure that the interior is on the "left" of the line connecting the points.

Remember that Polygons can also contain one or more interior rings, which mark out areas of space not included in the interior of the Polygon. To define an area of space not included in a Polygon you should therefore enclose it in a ring of Points listed in clockwise order, so that the area to be excluded lies to the right of the line. The illustration shown in Figure 3-3 demonstrates the correct ring orientation required to define a geography Polygon containing a hole.

Figure 3-3. A geography Polygon containing an interior ring.

As before, if the Points of each ring were listed in reverse order then the Polygon would become inverted: the interior of the Polygon would contain the entire surface of the globe except for the area shaded in gray in Figure 3-3.

■ **Tip** The geography datatype defines a `ReorientObject()` method, which flips the interior and exterior of a geography Polygon instance, and has the same effect as reversing the coordinate order of each ring.

The geometry Datatype

In contrast to the geography datatype, the geometry datatype operates on a two-dimensional flat plane. As such, calculations such as the distance between Points are worked out using simple geometrical methods on a flat surface. This is illustrated in Figure 3-4.

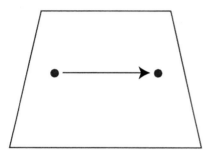

Figure 3-4. Calculations on the planar geometry type operate on a flat plane.

The geometry datatype stores planar spatial data defined using Cartesian (x, y) coordinates, which makes it ideally suited to storing coordinate data from a projected spatial reference system. In this case, the act of projection has already mapped the geographic position of features on the Earth's surface onto a flat plane. It can also be used to store "unprojected" geographic coordinates of latitude and longitude, where the longitude coordinate value is mapped directly to the x value, and the latitude value is used as the y value (in doing so, you are implicitly projecting the data using an equirectangular projection).

In fact, the geometry datatype can be used to store *any* coordinates that can be expressed using x and y values. Examples of such coordinates might be data collected from a local survey, or topological plans of a geographically small area where curvature of the Earth can be safely ignored, or geometrical data obtained from computer-aided design (CAD) packages. For example, Figure 3-5 shows the floorplan of the European SQLBits conference held at the Grand Hotel in Brighton, England in April 2012, defined entirely using the geometry datatype and displayed using the SQL Server Management Studio Spatial Results tab. This data was created from an original plan supplied in PDF format.

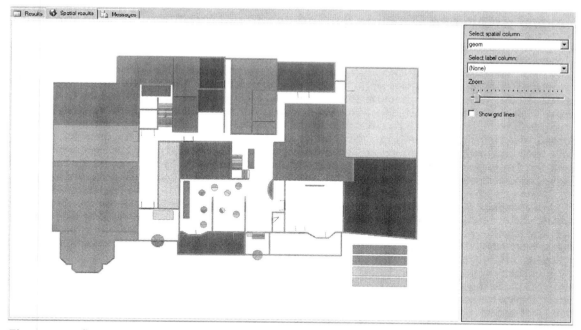

Figure 3-5. A floorplan modeled using the geometry datatype.

Because the geometry datatype uses simple planar calculations, the results of any computations will be expressed in the same units of measurement as the underlying coordinate values. The most common unit of measurement in which the coordinates of projected spatial reference systems are stated is the meter; this is the case for the Universal Transverse Mercator system and many National Grid reference systems, for example. If you use the geometry datatype to store data based on one of these systems, lengths and distances calculated using the STLength() and STDistance() methods will be measured in meters. And, if you were to use STArea() to calculate the area of a geometry, the result would be measured in square meters. In contrast, the coordinates used to create the floorplan shown in Figure 3-5 were measured in pixels, so using the STArea() method to calculate the area of each room would lead to a result measured in pixels squared.

▨ **Caution** Earlier, it was stated that the geometry datatype could be used to store "unprojected" geographic coordinates of latitude and longitude, directly mapped to the y- and x-coordinates. However, remember that these are angular coordinates, usually measured in degrees. If you use the geometry datatype to store information in this way then the distances between points would also be measured in degrees, and the area enclosed within a Polygon would be measured in degrees squared. This is almost certainly not what you want, so exercise caution when using the geometry datatype in this way. To return a geometry calculation measured in meters, say, the input coordinates must also be measured in meters.

Spatial Reference Systems for the geometry Datatype

The geometry datatype does not take account of any curvature of the Earth, nor does it rely on knowledge of the unit of measurement in which coordinates are defined, therefore stating a different SRID does not alter the numeric value of any calculations performed on geometry data. This can be a tricky concept to grasp; the first chapter of this book states that any pair of coordinates—projected or geographic—must be stated together with their associated spatial reference in order to refer to a position on the Earth. So why doesn't it make a difference what spatial reference identifier is supplied to the geometry datatype?

The answer is that choosing a difference spatial reference system *does* make a difference when initially determining the coordinates that identify a position on the Earth. However, once those values have been obtained, all further operations on those data can be performed using basic geometrical methods. Any decisions concerning how to deal with the curvature of the Earth have already been made in the process of defining the coordinates that describe where any point lies on the projected image.

When using the geometry datatype, the distance between a Point at (0 0) and a Point located at (30 40) will always be 50 units, whatever spatial reference system was used to obtain those coordinates, and in whatever units they are expressed. The actual features on the Earth represented by the Points at (0 0) and (30 40) will be different depending on the system in question, but this does not affect the way that geometry data is used in calculations. The result will always be accurate relative to the spatial reference in which the Points themselves were defined.

Consider the following code listing, which defines the Well-Known Text representation of a straight LineString geometry. The LineString in question represents the Royal Mile, which is the straight route connecting Edinburgh Castle with the Palace of Holyrood House, running along some of the oldest streets in Edinburgh. The coordinates in the Well-Known Text string are defined using SRID:27700, which is a projected coordinate system in which coordinates are measured in meters, so the result of the STLength() method gives the length of the Royal Mile in meters:

```
-- Define the WKT of the LineString
DECLARE @WKT nvarchar(max) = 'LINESTRING (325156 673448, 326897 673929)';

-- Construct a geometry LineString from the coordinates using SRID 27700
DECLARE @RoyalMile geometry = geometry::STGeomFromText(@WKT, 27700);

-- Calculate the length of the LineString
SELECT @RoyalMile.STLength();
```

The result is 1806.22313128805. Now suppose that we were to use exactly the same Well-Known Text string but, this time, change the SRID supplied to the STGeomFromText() method:

```
-- Define the WKT of the LineString
DECLARE @WKT nvarchar(max) = 'LINESTRING (325156 673448, 326897 673929)';

-- Construct a geometry LineString from the coordinates using SRID 32039
DECLARE @RoyalMile geometry = geometry::STGeomFromText(@WKT, 32039);

-- Calculate the length of the LineString
SELECT @RoyalMile.STLength();
```

The result is still 1806.22313128805, exactly as before. As demonstrated, the numeric value of any calculations performed using geometry data remains unchanged no matter in what spatial reference system the coordinates are provided. However, that doesn't mean to say that it's not still important to provide the correct SRID to identify the spatial reference system from which coordinates were derived. The spatial reference system defines the important additional information that makes those coordinates relate to a particular position on the Earth, and enable you to interpret the results appropriately:

The first code listing uses the correct SRID for the coordinates, EPSG:27700, which defines the Royal Mile as a straight line between two points in Edinburgh, 1806 meters in length.

The second code listing uses the same coordinate values but suggests that they are defined relative to the Texas Central coordinate system (EPSG:32039). Although the numerical value of the result is the same, the interpretation of this result would imply that the Royal Mile is a straight line of length 1806.22313128805 *feet*, drawn between two points in the Quitman Mountains of Texas, United States. This is clearly incorrect!

Supplying an incorrect SRID will lead to many problems farther downstream in your spatial applications. Once the metadata associated with a set of coordinates has been lost it cannot be redetermined, because looking at a set of coordinate values in isolation gives very little indication of the system from which they have been derived. By explicitly stating the SRID with every set of coordinates, not only will you retain this important metadata, but it will also ensure that you do not accidentally try to perform a calculation on items of spatial data defined using different spatial reference systems, which would lead to an invalid result.

So please, I implore you, always, *always* use the correct SRID with any spatial data in SQL Server, even when using the geometry datatype!

■ **Note** The sys.spatial_references table only contains details of geodetic spatial references, because these are required to perform calculations using the geography datatype. In order to find the appropriate SRID for a projected coordinate system, you can look it up on the EPSG website at http://www.epsg-registry.org/.

Storing Nongeodetic Data

The geometry datatype stores planar coordinates and uses standard Euclidean methods to perform calculations for which no SRID is necessary, therefore it can also be used to store any data that can be described using pairs of *x* and *y* floating point coordinates (or, if using the optional *z*- and *m*-coordinates, up to four coordinate values per item). Such items of data do not necessarily have to relate to any particular model of the shape of the Earth; for example, you could store the location of items in a warehouse using *x*- and *y*-coordinates relative to a local origin, or describe the location of components on a printed circuitboard.

When using the geometry type to record data such as these, you should use SRID 0. This SRID denotes that the coordinates are not derived from any particular spatial reference system, and coordinate values should be treated as *x* and *y* values with no specific units of measurement.

The Insignificance of Ring Orientation in a geometry Polygon

The geometry datatype operates on an infinite flat plane, thus the area contained by a closed line drawn between any set of points is unambiguous. Therefore, unlike when using the geography datatype, ring orientation (the direction in which the points of a ring are specified) is unimportant for geometry Polygons.

In the geometry datatype, a Polygon whose exterior ring is defined by the coordinates

(50,30), (52,30), (52,31), (50,31), (50,30)

contains exactly the same area as if it were specified by the following coordinates,

(50,30), (50,31), (52,31), (52,30), (50,30)

This applies to both interior and exterior rings of the geometry datatype, so the area contained by a geometry Polygon remains exactly the same even if the points are supplied in reverse order. This is illustrated in Figure 3-6, where the highlighted Polygon will always represent the Northern Hemisphere irrespective of ring orientation.

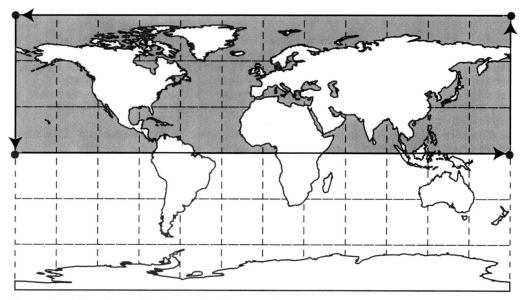

Figure 3-6. Ring orientation is not significant in the geometry datatype.

Comparing geography and geometry Datatypes

On the face of it, the decision as to which spatial datatype you should use in a given situation is pretty straightforward: if you've got projected coordinate data, measured in *x*- and *y*-coordinates, then use the geometry datatype; if, on the other hand, you've got geographic coordinate data expressed in latitude and longitude coordinates, then use the geography datatype. However, although the difference in accepted coordinate systems is certainly the single most important difference between the types, there are other factors that you should bear in mind when deciding which datatype to use for a given application.

Consistency

In order to perform operations using different items of spatial data in SQL Server 2012, all of the data must be defined using the same spatial reference system, and stored using the same datatype. It is not possible to combine geometry and geography data in the same query, nor perform operations on items of the same datatype defined using different SRIDs. If you attempt to do so, SQL Server will return a NULL result.

If you already have existing spatial data that you would like to integrate into your system, you should therefore use a datatype suitable for the format in which that data has been collected. For instance, if you have projected data collected from the National Grid of Great Britain, you should store the data in a geometry field, using the SRID of 27700. If you are using latitude and longitude coordinate data collected from a GPS system, then you should choose a geography type, with SRID of 4326. If you would like to combine multiple sets of data defined in different spatial reference systems, then you must first transform one or more of the sets of coordinate data in order to make them consistent. For more information on reprojection and transformation, refer to Chapter 8.

▓ **Note** Remember that the spatial reference identifier provides descriptive information about the system in which coordinate values have been defined; it does not dictate the system itself. You therefore cannot simply update the SRID value relating to a set of coordinates to express them in a different spatial reference system. Instead, to convert coordinates from one spatial reference system into another you must transform or reproject the data.

Accuracy

Calculations using the geometry datatype are performed on a flat plane. Any geospatial features drawn on a flat plane must have been projected and, as explained in Chapter 1, the process of projecting any three-dimensional object onto a surface will always lead to some distortion in the way those features are represented. This distortion may affect the area, shape, distance, or direction of the data. Therefore, the results of certain operations using the geometry datatype will inevitably also be distorted, with the effect of distortion varying depending on the projection used and the particular part of the Earth's surface on which the calculation is based.

Generally speaking, the greater the surface area being projected, the more distortion occurs. Although over small areas the effects of these distortions are fairly minimal, in large-scale or global applications there can be a significant impact on the accuracy of any results obtained using the geometry datatype when compared to the geography datatype (which is not distorted by projection).

In many applications that cover only a small spatial area, such as those contained within a particular state of the United States, the results of calculations performed using the geometry type on the relevant state plane projection will be sufficiently accurate. However, over larger distances, the computations based on a planar projection will become more and more inaccurate, and the geography datatype become a more suitable choice.

The End(s) of the World

One particularly extreme example of the distortion occurring as a result of projection is that, unlike the Earth itself, a projected map has edges. When storing projected spatial data using the geometry datatype, special consideration therefore needs to be taken in situations where you need to define data that cross these edges. This typically occurs in the following situations.

- Any geometries or calculations that cross the 180th meridian
- Any Polygon geometries that enclose the North or South Pole

To demonstrate how these distortions affect calculations using the geometry datatype, consider how you might calculate the shortest straight line route taken from Vancouver to Tokyo. Using the flat geometry datatype, the result (based on a map projection centered on the Greenwich meridian) might look like that shown in Figure 3-7.

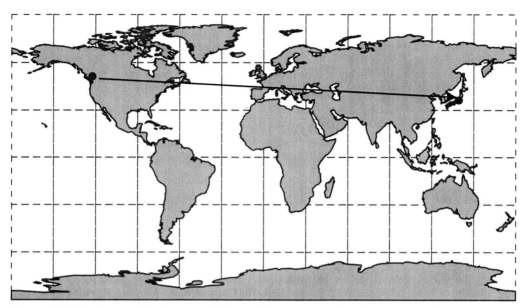

Figure 3-7. *The shortest line between Tokyo and Vancouver using the geometry datatype.*

In contrast, the geography datatype uses a continuous round model of the Earth, which is unaffected by the edges introduced as a result of projection. The answer obtained for the shortest route between Tokyo and Vancouver using the geography datatype would instead look like that shown in Figure 3-8.

Figure 3-8. *The shortest route between Tokyo and Vancouver using the geography datatype.*

It is obvious that, in cases such as these, the results obtained using the geography datatype give a more accurate answer based on the real round Earth.

A further demonstration of these issues is the problem of trying to define geometry instances that extend across the edges of the map in a given projection. Figure 3-9 highlights a Polygon geometry representing Russia.

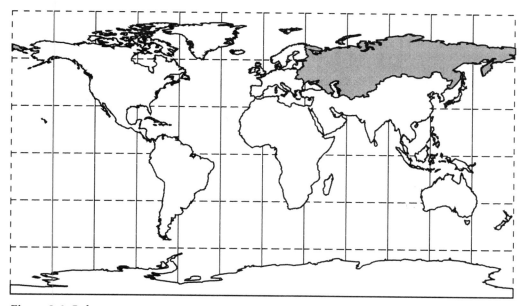

Figure 3-9. Polygon geometry representing Russia crossing edges of a projection in the geometry datatype.

Notice that although most of the Polygon is contained in the eastern hemisphere, the most northeasterly part of Russia (the region of Chukotka) actually crosses the edge of the map, to appear in the western hemisphere. Using the geometry datatype based on this projection, it would not be possible to represent Russia using a single Polygon geometry; instead you would need to use a MultiPolygon geometry containing two elements to represent the two distinct Polygons created where the edge of the map had caused the original feature to be divided in two.

Both of the problems demonstrated in this section could be mitigated to some extent by choosing an appropriate projected spatial reference system in which the geometry in question does not cross the edges of the map. However, although this would avoid the issue for a particular case, it does not solve it; even if a different projection is chosen there will always be some features that will occur on the new edges instead.

If you expect to have to deal with geometries that risk extending over the edges of a map projection, then the geography datatype would be a better choice in which to store your data.

Presentation

Because the geography datatype operates on a three-dimensional model of the Earth, if you want to present the results of any geography data in a display, they will need to be projected (unless you've got one of those fancy 3D displays). As we have already discussed, this introduces distortion. In the example above, although the geography datatype accurately works out the shortest straight line connecting two points, if we were to display this result on a projected map, this "straight" line would appear distorted and curved. The exact effect of this distortion will differ depending on the particular properties of the map projection used.

Conversely, because as the geometry datatype is based on data that has already been projected onto a plane, no further calculations or distortion need be introduced to express the results on a map: "straight" lines in the geometry datatype remain straight when drawn on a map (providing the map is projected using the same projection as the spatial reference system from which the points were obtained).

If you are storing spatial data in SQL Server specifically for the purpose of display on a particular map (say, for creating a tile overlay on Bing Maps or Google Maps), then it might be beneficial to store that data using the geometry datatype in the same projected spatial reference system as the map on which it is intended to be displayed. This reduces additional calculations required when the data is retrieved and projected onto the map, and reduces the need to introduce further distortion in the data at display time.

Performance

Performing ellipsoidal computations uses more computing resources than Cartesian computations. As a result, spatial calculations using the geography datatype may take longer to compute than the equivalent operations using the geometry datatype. This only affects methods where the geography datatype has to calculate metrics based on the geodetic model of the Earth (such as distances, lengths, or areas). When using methods that return properties of objects which do not take account of the model of the Earth, such as returning the number of points in an object, there is no difference in performance between geography and geometry types.

OGC Standards Compliance

According to their website, the Open Geospatial Consortium (OGC) is:

"a non-profit, international, voluntary consensus standards organization that is leading the development of standards for geospatial and location based services."

—http://www.opengeospatial.org/

The OGC administer a number of industrywide standards for dealing with spatial data. By conforming to these standards, different systems can ensure core levels of common functionality, which ensures that spatial information can be more easily shared among different vendors and systems.

In October 2007, Microsoft joined the Open Geospatial Consortium (OGC) as a principal member, and the spatial datatypes implemented in SQL Server 2012 are largely based on the standards defined by the OGC:

- The geometry datatype conforms to the OGC Simple Features for SQL specifications v1.1.0 (http://www.opengeospatial.org/standards/sfs) and implements all the required methods to meet that standard.

- The geography datatype implements most of the same methods as the geometry datatype, although it does not completely conform to the required OGC standards.

As such, if it is important to you to use spatial methods in SQL Server 2012 that adhere to accepted OGC standards (such as if you are replacing the functionality of a legacy system based on those standards), you should use the geometry datatype.

General Rules

If you are still unsure which type to use, consider the following general rules.

- If you have latitude and longitude coordinate data (collected from a GPS, from Google Earth, or most sources listed on the Web) use the geography datatype, normally using the default 4326 SRID.

- If you have x- and y-coordinate data (e.g., collected from a flat map), use the geometry datatype with an SRID to represent the map projection and datum used.

- If you have x- and y-coordinate data that are not defined in relation to any particular model of the Earth, use the geometry datatype with SRID = 0.

Storage Requirements

The datatypes geometry and geography are both of variable length. In contrast to a fixed-length datatype such as int or datetime, the actual amount of storage required for an item of spatial data varies depending on the complexity of the object that the data describes. Just as a varchar(max) field varies in size according to the number of characters in the string being stored, so too does a geometry or geography field vary in size according to the number of points in the corresponding geometry.

    The structure of an item of geometry or geography data begins with a header section, which defines basic information such as the type of shape being described, the spatial reference system used, and the overall number of points in the object. This header is immediately followed by the coordinate values of each x- and y- (or longitude and latitude) coordinate in the geometry, represented in 8-byte binary format. The more points that an object has in its definition, the longer this binary stream will be, and therefore the more storage space will be required.

- A Point geometry defined with only two coordinates will always occupy 22 bytes of storage space.

- A LineString between two Points, containing the minimum of four coordinates (x and y values of the start and end Point), requires 38 bytes of storage. This increases by 16 bytes for every additional line segment added to the LineString.

- A Polygon occupies a variable amount of space depending on the number of Points with which it is defined (not related to the area of space contained by the Polygon). If a Polygon contains interior rings, these also increase the storage required.

    There is no specific maximum size of an item of geometry or geography data. However, SQL Server 2012 has an overall restriction on any kind of large object, which is limited to a size of $2^{31} - 1$ bytes. This is the same limit as is applied to datatypes such as varbinary(max) and varchar(max), and equates to approximately 2 Gb for each individual item of data. You would need to store a very complex geometry object in order to exceed this limit. If necessary, remember that complex geometries can be broken down into a number of individual objects which each fit within this limit.

▓ **Tip** You can use the DATALENGTH function to find out the number of bytes used to store the value of any item of geometry or geography data (or, for that matter, any other item of data).

Internal Data Structure

Generally speaking, you do not need to know the internal format that SQL Server uses to store geography or geometry data; the dedicated methods provided by each type provide the functionality required to create and modify instances as appropriate. However, on some occasions it can be useful to modify the bytes of a geography or geometry instance directly. For example, you may be designing a spatial application using nonmanaged code (such as C or C++) that cannot use the SqlGeography and SqlGeometry types directly, and you need to programmatically construct a geography or geometry instance from its constituent elements.

To investigate the format used by SQL Server, let's first create a simple geography Point instance using the Point() static method and then SELECT the corresponding native value, as shown in the following code listing.

```
SELECT
geography::Point(40, -100, 4269);
```

The result is:

```
0xAD100000020C0000000000004440000000000000059C0
```

This value may be broken down into a number of constituent parts, as shown in Table 3-4.

Table 3-4. Elements of a Geography Instance

Element	Description
0x	Hexadecimal notation identifier
AD100000	Spatial Reference identifier (4 bytes). The integer SRID value—in this case 4269—expressed as a 4-byte binary value.
02	Version number (1 byte). SQL Server 2008/SQL Server 2008 R2 uses version 1 serialization, whereas SQL Server 2012 uses version 2 serialization.
0C	Serialization properties (1 byte). This value is set from a series of bit flags representing the following additional properties of the geometry.
	Whether the geometry is larger than a hemisphere (0×20)
	Whether the geometry is a single line segment (0×10)
	Whether the geometry is a single Point (0×08)
	Whether the geometry is valid (0×04)
	Whether the geometry contains m-coordinates (0×02)
	Whether the geometry contains z-coordinates (0×01)
	For this case, the flags for a valid (0×04), single Point (0×08) geometry have been set, leading to the value 0C

Element	Description
0000000000004440	Latitude coordinate (40) expressed as 8-byte floating point binary
0000000000059C0	Longitude coordinate (−100) expressed as 8-byte floating point binary

Suppose instead that we wanted to construct programmatically a geography Point instance defined at a latitude of 42 degrees, longitude of −90 degrees, using the SRID 4326. To do so, we could build up the geography value from the corresponding binary elements, as shown in the following code listing.

```
DECLARE @point geography =
  0xE6100000 +              -- SRID (4326)
  0x02 +                    -- Version (2)
  0x0C +                    -- Properties (Single Point [8] + Valid [4])
  0x0000000000004540 +      -- Latitude (42)
  0x00000000008056C0        -- Longitude (-90)
SELECT
  @point.STSrid,
  @point.ToString();
```

The WKT results returned by the ToString() method confirm that the geography Point has been created at the appropriate coordinates, using the 4326 SRID:

```
4326    POINT(-90 42)
```

This is admittedly a fairly contrived example, and there are few situations in which you would need to do such manual binary manipulation in T-SQL. However, it does demonstrate that it is certainly possible to do so, and you can reuse the same approach in other application layers.

▓ **Note** For more information on the serialization format used for SQL CLR datatypes, refer to the following document: http://download.microsoft.com/download/7/9/3/79326E29-1E2E-45EE-AA73-74043587B17D/%5BMS-SSCLRT%5D.pdf.

Converting Between Datatypes

Given that the two spatial datatypes are so similar, you might think that it would be an easy task to convert data between the two. However, you cannot simply CAST or CONVERT between the two types. If you try to do so, such as in the following query,

```
DECLARE @geog geography;
SET @geog = geography::STGeomFromText('POINT(23 32)', 4326);
SELECT CAST(@geog AS geometry);
```

you will receive the error,

```
Msg 529, Level 16, State 2, Line 5
Explicit conversion from datatype sys.geography to sys.geometry is not allowed.
```

Notice the wording used in this error message: conversion is not *allowed*. This is not a technical limitation of SQL Server; because geometry and geography both use the same underlying structure, converting data between the types is incredibly easy from a technical point of view. Rather, this is a deliberate restriction imposed by SQL Server to ensure that you understand the implications of working with each datatype, and that you don't casually swap data between them.

There are very few scenarios in which it makes sense to take coordinate data from one spatial datatype and convert it directly into the other. If you find a requirement to convert data between the two datatypes then it normally also involves transforming the associated coordinate data from a geographic coordinate system used in the geography datatype to a projected coordinate system for the geometry datatype, for example. Nevertheless, there are a few occasions when it is useful to be able to take geographic coordinates from a geography instance and convert them directly into the geometry datatype. This might be the case if you want to use one of the methods that is only available to the geometry datatype, such as STBoundingBox(), or STRelate().

In order to convert from geography to geometry, we can take advantage of the fact that both datatypes can be represented by, and created from, a binary stream in the Well-Known Binary format. In the following example the value of the geometry variable, @geom, is created from the STGeomFromWKB() static method. The arguments passed to this method are the Well-Known Binary representation and SRID of the geography variable @geog.

```
-- First, create a geography instance
DECLARE @geog geography;
SET @geog = geography::Point(23,32, 4326);

-- Convert to geometry via WKB
DECLARE @geom geometry;
SET @geom = geometry::STGeomFromWKB(@geog.STAsBinary(), @geog.STSrid);
```

The resulting geometry Point instance is defined using exactly the same coordinates and SRID as the original geography instance @geog.

The approach just described can be used to convert any geography instance to the geometry datatype. Inasmuch as geometry does not enforce any restrictions on the SRID used, any coordinate data stored using the geography datatype can also be stored using the geometry datatype. However, in order to perform conversion the other way, from geometry to geography, the coordinate values of the existing geometry instance must represent latitude–longitude coordinates taken from a supported geodetic spatial reference system. If you are storing Northing and Easting coordinates from a projected system, or other nongeodetic data, those data can only be stored using the geometry datatype.

Creating Spatially Enabled Tables

There are no special attributes or configurations required to enable spatial data to be stored in a SQL server database; all that is required is a table containing at least one geography or geometry column. The following code listing creates a table containing two columns: CityName, which can hold a 255-character variable length string, and CityLocation, which can be used to store the location of that city using the geography datatype:

```
CREATE TABLE dbo.cities (
  CityName varchar(255),
  CityLocation geography
);
```

New geometry or geography columns can be added to existing tables, enabling spatial information to be seamlessly integrated alongside existing items of data. Let's suppose that you have an existing table, customer, that contained the following fields of customer information.

```
CREATE TABLE dbo.customer (
  CustomerID int,
  FirstName varchar(50),
  Surname varchar (50),
  Address varchar (255),
  Postcode varchar (10),
  Country varchar(32)
);
```

Now suppose that you want to add an additional spatial field to this table to record the location of each customer's address. No problem; geography and geometry fields can be added to existing tables just like any other by using an ALTER TABLE statement as follows.

```
ALTER TABLE dbo.customer
ADD CustomerLocation geography;
```

By extending the table in this way, we have enabled the possiblity of using spatial methods in conjunction with our existing customer data, to find answers to questions such as how many customers there are within a certain area, and how far a particular customer lives from his closest store.

Enforcing a Common SRID

It is worth nothing that, although all the values stored in a single geography or geometry column must match the datatype of that column, they do not all have to share the same spatial reference system. Within a single geometry column, you may have instances defined using the UTM grid, the Alaskan State Plane coordinate system, and the National Grid of Finland, for example. However, I find that the flexibility to store instances from different spatial reference systems in the same column is rarely useful; remember that, in order to perform calculations involving two or more items of data, they must be defined using the same spatial reference system. Mixing spatial reference systems within the same column introduces an unnecessary chance of error.

Within a single column of a table, I only store instances defined using a common spatial reference system. I normally name this column according to the type of data and the spatial reference system used. For example, for a column containing geography instances defined using SRID 4326, I would choose the column name geog4326. Of course, you can name your spatial columns using any name you'd like, but I find that using this convention helps me by knowing, at a glance, important metadata about all the values in that column.

To ensure that all the instances in a column are defined using the same system, you can add a constraint on the STSrid property of that column. For example, the following code listing demonstrates how to add a constraint to ensure that only instances defined using SRID 4199 (Egypt 1930) are stored in the CustomerLocation column of the customer table.

```
ALTER TABLE dbo.customer
ADD CONSTRAINT enforce_customerlocation_srid4199
CHECK (CustomerLocation.STSrid = 4199);
```

It is now possible to perform calculations safely using any two data items from this column, knowing that they will be defined based on the same spatial reference system. You may also find it useful to enforce additional constraints on the type of spatial data stored in a particular column. For example, the following code listing creates a constraint that uses the STGeometryType() method to ensure that only Point geometries may be stored in the CustomerLocation column.

```
ALTER TABLE dbo.customer
ADD CONSTRAINT enforce_customerlocation_point
CHECK (CustomerLocation.STGeometryType() = 'POINT');
```

Summary

In this chapter you learned about the two datatypes used for storing spatial data in SQL Server 2012, geometry and geography, and examined the key differences between the two types.

- The geography datatype uses geodetic spatial data, which accounts for the curvature of the earth.

- The geometry datatype uses planar spatial data, in which all points lie on a flat plane.

- You considered the factors influencing the choice of which datatype to use, and saw some example usage scenarios for each type.

- You saw the reasons why, whichever datatype you use, it is important to state the correct spatial reference identifier associated with any coordinate data.

- You examined the structure in which SQL Server 2012 stores spatial data, represented as a stream of binary values.

- You also saw how to add a column of spatial data to a SQL Server table, and add a constraint to that column to ensure that only data of a certain SRID could be inserted.

CHAPTER 4

Creating Spatial Data

In the first three chapters of this book I introduced you to the main components necessary to define spatial data in SQL Server, namely, a set of coordinate locations, the spatial reference system in which those coordinates are defined, the type of geometry used to represent a feature, and the datatype in which that feature is stored.

In this chapter, we apply the knowledge you've gained so far in a practical context, by looking at the different methods you can use to create items of geometry or geography data. Every method requires those same key pieces of information: the spatial reference system, type of geometry, and datatype, together with the coordinates that define that instance.

The way in which you provide those elements varies depending on the method you choose; SQL Server implements methods that create data from several different standard formats: Well-Known Text (WKT), Well-Known Binary (WKB), and Geography Markup Language (GML). It also exposes an API that allows you to construct items of spatial data programmatically using the SqlGeometryBuilder and SqlGeographyBuilder classes. Each of these methods is examined in turn and the advantages and disadvantages of each discussed.

Creating Spatial Data from Well-Known Text

Well-Known Text is one of the standard formats defined by the Open Geospatial Consortium for the exchange of spatial information. It is a simple, text-based format that is easy to examine and understand. You have already seen several examples of WKT in this book; it is the format SQL Server 2012 uses to store the parameters of supported spatial reference systems in the well_known_text column of the sys.spatial_reference_systems table, and it is also used in the examples of each of the types of geometry demonstrated in Chapter 2.

Some of the advantages of the WKT format are:

- It is a simple structured format that is easy to store and share between systems.

- Because it is text-based, it is easy to examine visibly and identify the information conveyed in a WKT representation.

However, it also has the following disadvantages.

- As with any text-based representation, it is not possible to precisely state the value of certain floating point coordinate values obtained from binary methods. The inevitable rounding errors introduced when attempting to do so will lead to a loss of precision.

- SQL Server must parse the text in a WKT representation into its own internal binary format, therefore creating objects from WKT may be slower than other methods.

Because WKT is both simple to read and understand, it is the format used in most of the MSDN online documentation and code samples, as well as in other resources. It is also the format that is most widely used throughout this book.

Choosing a WKT Static Method

SQL Server 2012 implements dedicated static methods for creating each of the basic types of geometry from WKT. It also implements some generic static methods that can create any of the supported kinds of geometry. Table 4-1 lists the different methods that can be used.

Table 4-1. Methods to Instantiate Spatial Data from Well-Known Text

Geometry	Static Method
Point	STPointFromText()
LineString	STLineFromText()
Polygon	STPolyFromText()
MultiPoint	STMPointFromText()
MultiLineString	STMLineFromText()
MultiPolygon	STMPolyFromText()
GeometryCollection	STGeomCollFromText()
Any supported geometry	STGeomFromText() / Parse()

All of the methods listed in Table 4-1 are implemented by both the geometry and geography datatypes, with the datatype of any created instance matching the datatype of the method from which it was created. Note that there are no dedicated methods to create CircularString, CurvePolygon, or CompoundCurve geometries from WKT; these methods appear to have been overlooked in the OGC standard and so are not implemented by SQL Server either. To create a curved geometry from WKT you must use the generic STGeomFromText() or Parse() methods.

Passing WKT to the Method

The syntax for using any of the WKT static methods is the same: first stating the datatype to which the method belongs followed by the method name, separated by double colons. Each method itself requires two parameters: the first being the WKT of the geometry to be created, and then the SRID of the spatial reference system.

This syntax is illustrated as follows.

```
Datatype::Method( WKT, SRID )
```

Let's illustrate this with a few examples. To begin, let's take the simple example of a Point located at geographic coordinates of latitude –27.5 and a longitude of 153, measured using the WGS84 spatial reference system, SRID 4326. This is the approximate location of Brisbane, Australia.

The Well-Known Text representation of this Point is:

```
POINT(153 -27.5)
```

We can create a geography Point instance by supplying this WKT string to the dedicated STPointFromText() method, together with the associated SRID, as follows.

```
SELECT
geography::STPointFromText('POINT(153 -27.5)', 4326);
```

Notice that the WKT parameter is passed as a nvarchar(max) text string, and supplied in single quotes. If you use the SqlServer.Types.dll library in a .NET application then the WKT is passed as a SqlChars value instead, as shown in the following C# code listing.

```
SqlGeography Point = SqlGeography.STPointFromText(
  new SqlChars("POINT(153 -27.5)"),
  4326);
```

The STPointFromText() method can be used to create Point instances only. If you supply the WKT representation of a different sort of geometry to the STPointFromText() method then SQL Server will throw an exception (System.FormatException 24142). To create a LineString geometry, for example, you should use the STLineFromText() method instead, supplying the WKT of a LineString as shown in the following code listing.

```
SELECT
geometry::STLineFromText('LINESTRING(300500 600150, 310200 602500)', 27700);
```

If you know in advance that the data you will be creating will only be of a certain type of geometry, then I generally recommend that you use the method dedicated to that geometry type, STPointFromText() for Points, STPolyFromText() for Polygons, and so on. Using these methods will provide a first sanity check of your data by ensuring that it only contains geometries of the expected type; any other data will throw an exception.

However, there are also occasions when you require a method that will create spatial data from a WKT string of any sort of geometry. In these situations, you can use the STGeomFromText() method instead. The following code listing demonstrates how the STGeomFromText() method can be used to create both the Point and LineString from the previous examples.

```
SELECT
geography::STGeomFromText('POINT(153 -27.5)', 4326),
geometry::STGeomFromText('LINESTRING(300500 600150, 310200 602500)', 27700);
```

The results obtained from the STGeomFromText() method are identical to those obtained from the dedicated STPointFromText() or STLineFromText() methods used previously.

■ **Note** There is no performance benefit from using a geometry type-specific method such as STPointFromText() rather than the generic STGeomFromText() method. The sole advantage is that it restricts the types of geometry that will be accepted in the WKT input (and therefore, by implication, the type of geometry that will be returned by the method). If this is your objective, you might also want to consider adding a CHECK constraint that tests the value returned by the STGeometryType() method at the point that a geometry is inserted into a table, as demonstrated in Chapter 3.

Another alternative is to use the generic `Parse()` method. In common with the `STGeomFromText()` method, the `Parse()` method will create an item of spatial data from any supplied WKT representation. The difference is that, unlike the other static methods, `Parse()` does not require you to set an SRID; the spatial reference system is assumed based on the datatype being used. For the geography datatype, the `Parse()` method always uses SRID 4326, whereas for the geometry datatype it is SRID 0.

If you attempt to set the value of a geometry or geography column or variable directly from a character string, the string will be treated as WKT and passed to the `Parse()` method. As such, the following T-SQL code listing,

```
DECLARE @Delhi geography = 'POINT(77.25 28.5)';
```

produces exactly the same result as

```
DECLARE @Delhi geography = geography::Parse('POINT(77.25 28.5)');
```

which, in turn, is equivalent to

```
DECLARE @Delhi geography = geography::STGeomFromText('POINT(77.25 28.5)', 4326);
```

As long as you are dealing with the common cases of using the geography datatype with SRID 4326, or the geometry datatype with SRID 0, you can therefore use the `Parse()` method as a convenient way of shortening your code.

To demonstrate the same example using the static methods provided by the `SqlGeography` or `SqlGeometry` classes in a .NET application, you will probably find it easier to write:

```
SqlGeography Delhi = SqlGeography.Parse("POINT(77.25 28.5)");
```

compared to

```
SqlGeography Delhi = SqlGeography.STGeomFromText(
  new SqlChars("POINT(77.25 28.5)"), 4326);
```

One subtle difference worth noting from this example is that, although `STGeomFromText()` accepts the supplied WKT input as a `SqlChar` array, the `Parse()` method treats the WKT input as a `SqlString`. `SqlChar` values can be streamed, whereas a `SqlString` cannot. Using `Parse()` therefore requires a contiguous block of memory to be allocated for the entire supplied WKT string. This, combined with the fact that `Parse()` can only be used for creating instances defined using limited SRIDs, means that you will need to decide whether it is suitable for use in a particular scenario compared to the more verbose `STGeomFromText()` method.

▓ **Note** All of the static methods that operate on WKT input expect decimal coordinate values to be represented using a decimal point (.) to separate the integral and fractional parts of the coordinate, for example, 52.61. Depending on the regional settings of your database or operating system, you may find that coordinate values are instead displayed and represented using other coordinate separators, such as the comma in 52,61. When supplying WKT for any of the static methods listed in this section, be sure to check the culture settings of your application.

Retrieving the WKT Representation of an Instance

Well-Known Text is simply one format in which geometry and geography data can be represented. Remember that, internally, SQL Server actually stores spatial data in a binary format, not as a text string. If you want to retrieve the Well-Known Text of an existing geography or geometry instance, you can use one of the appropriate instance methods: STAsText(), AsTextZM(), or ToString().

STAsText() is the OGC-compliant method for retrieving the Well-Known Text of an instance. The returned nvarchar (or SqlChars) WKT string will only contain 2D coordinates (*x* and *y*, or latitude and longitude). It will not contain any *z*- or *m*-coordinate values associated with the geometry.

AsTextZM() is an extended method that returns the Well-Known Text of an instance as an nvarchar(max) or SqlChars value, including any *z*- and *m*-coordinate values defined by the geometry.

ToString() is a method defined by the Object base class in the .NET framework, and therefore is inherited and implemented by all classes, including the geometry and geography datatypes. The purpose of the ToString() method is to convert any object into a string value suitable for display purposes. When implemented by the geometry and geography datatypes, the ToString() method retrieves the WKT of an instance including *z*-and *m*-coordinate values as an nvarchar(max) value, just as AsTextZM() method does. When called on a SqlGeography or SqlGeometry instance in .NET code, ToString() returns a string rather than SqlChars returned by AsTextZM(). Apart from the datatype of the returned value, there is no difference between the AsTextZM() and ToString() methods.

The following code listing demonstrates the output of the STAsText(), AsTextZM(), and ToString() methods when called on a geometry Point instance containing *x*-, *y*-, and *z*-coordinate values.

```
DECLARE @Point geometry = geometry::STPointFromText('POINT(14 9 7)', 0);
SELECT
  @Point.STAsText() AS STAsText,
  @Point.AsTextZM() AS AsTextZM,
  @Point.ToString() AS ToString;
```

The results are shown as

STAsText	AsTextZM	ToString
POINT (14 9)	POINT (14 9 7)	POINT (14 9 7)

Creating Spatial Data from Well-Known Binary

The Well-Known Binary format, like the WKT format, is a standardized way of representing spatial data defined by the OGC. In contrast to the text-based WKT format, WKB represents a geometry or geography instance as a binary value. Every WKB representation begins with a header section that defines the type of geometry being represented, and the order in which bytes are expressed (big-endian or little-endian). Depending on the type of geometry, the header may also contain additional descriptive information such as the number of geometries contained within a multielement instance, or the number of rings contained in a Polygon geometry. Following the information in the header, a

WKB representation lists a stream of 8-byte values representing the coordinates of each point in the geometry.

Although SQL Server 2012 stores spatial data internally as a stream of binary data, it is not the same as the WKB binary data format. As a result, you cannot directly set the value of an item of geography or geometry data from a WKB representation. Instead, you must pass that WKB representation to one of the appropriate static methods. Likewise, if you directly select the internal binary value that SQL Server uses to store an item of spatial data, it will not be the same as the WKB representation of that feature. One difference between WKB and SQL Server's own internal binary format is that SQL Server serializes the spatial reference identifier and other properties related to the geometry not present in the WKB representation.

▨ **Note** The WKB format has some similarities with the internal binary format that SQL Server uses to store geometry and geography data, but they are not the same. As in WKT, creating spatial data from WKB requires passing that WKB representation to a suitable static method.

The following are some advantages of the WKB format.

- Creating objects from WKB is faster than using static methods based on a text-based representation such as WKT. Each x- and y- (or latitude and longitude) coordinate value in WKB is stored on 8-byte binary boundaries, as they are in SQL Server's own internal storage representation. The WKB static methods can therefore efficiently process and create the associated instance from WKB, rather than in WKT or GML where the parser must read in the whole text representation first.

- Because it is a binary format, WKB maintains the precision of floating-point coordinate values calculated from binary operations, without the rounding errors introduced in a text-based format.

However, WKB also has the following significant disadvantage.

- Binary values cannot be easily understood by a human reader; it can therefore be hard to detect errors in a WKB representation that could have been easily spotted from examining the equivalent WKT or GML representation.

Choosing a WKB Static Method

Just as for the WKT format, SQL Server 2012 provides a specific method for creating each type of geometry from a Well-Known Binary representation, as well as a generalized method STGeomFromWKB() for creating any type of object from valid WKB. The list of static methods that can be used to create geography or geometry data from WKB is shown in Table 4-2.

Table 4-2. Methods to Instantiate Spatial Data from Well-Known Binary

Geometry	Static Method
Point	STPointFromWKB()
LineString	STLineFromWKB()
Polygon	STPolyFromWKB()
MultiPoint	STMPointFromWKB()
MultiLineString	STMLineFromWKB()
MultiPolygon	STMPolyFromWKB()
GeometryCollection	STGeomCollFromWKB()
Any supported geometry	STGeomFromWKB()

To demonstrate the use of these methods, let's first take a look at an example WKB representation of a Point geometry:

```
0x00000000014001F5C28F5C28F6402524DD2F1A9FBE
```

The elements of this binary string are broken down in Table 4-3.

Table 4-3. Elements Contained Within an Example WKB Geometry Representation

Value	Description
0x	Hexadecimal notation identifier
00	Byte order marker. 0×00 indicates little-endian byte order
00000001	This geometry is a Point, denoted as type 1
4001F5C28F5C28F6	*x*-coordinate (10.572)
402524DD2F1A9FBE	*y*-coordinate (2.245)

To create a geometry Point instance from this WKB representation, using the Qatar National Grid (SRID 2099), you can use the STPointFromWKB() method as follows.

```
SELECT
geometry::STPointFromWKB(0x00000000014001F5C28F5C28F6402524DD2F1A9FBE, 2099);
```

Or, you can use the generic STGeomFromWKB() method, which can be used to create any type of geometry from WKB:

```
SELECT
geometry::STGeomFromWKB(0x00000000014001F5C28F5C28F6402524DD2F1A9FBE, 2099);
```

■ **Note** The spatial reference identifier is not serialized as part of the WKB binary string, so it must be provided as the second parameter to any static methods that instantiate geometries from WKB.

Representing an Existing Geometry as WKB

Just as SQL Server provides the STAsText() method to retrieve the WKT of a geometry, so too does it provide a method to retrieve the WKB representation of an instance. In order to retrieve the WKB representation of a geometry or geography instance you can use the STAsBinary() method, as follows.

```
DECLARE @g geometry = geometry::STPointFromText('POINT(14 9 7)', 0);
SELECT
  @g.STAsBinary();
```

The result is as follows.

0x01010000000000000000002C400000000000002240

Note that, like its WKT sister, STAsText(), the WKB representation produced by the STAsBinary() method specifies coordinates in two dimensions only: *x* and *y* for the geometry datatype, or latitude and longitude for the geography datatype. You can confirm this by converting the Well-Known Binary result above back to Well-Known Text:

```
-- Declare point containing x, y, and z coordinates
DECLARE @g geometry = geometry::STPointFromText('POINT(14 9 7)', 0);

-- Convert to WKB using STAsBinary()
DECLARE @WKB varbinary(max) = @g.STAsBinary();

-- Now create a new geometry instance from this WKB
DECLARE @h geometry = geometry::STPointFromWKB(@WKB, 0);

--Retrieve the Well-Known Text of the new geometry
SELECT @h.AsTextZM();
```

The geometry created from the WKB retrieved from the STAsBinary() method is now simply POINT(14 9), with no *z*-coordinate value. In order to create a WKB representation that retains the full fidelity of the original point supplied in this example, which has *x*-, *y*-, and *z*-coordinates, you can use the AsBinaryZM() method instead. This will serialize any geometry or geography instance into WKB format including *x*-, *y*-, *z*-, and *m*-coordinate values, as follows.

```
DECLARE @g geometry = geometry::STPointFromText('POINT(14 9 7)', 0);
SELECT @g.AsBinaryZM();
```

The WKB result produced by the AsBinaryZM() method in this example, which is a longer binary string containing three coordinate values, is:

0x01E903000000000000000002C4000000000000002240000000000000001C40

Creating Spatial Data from Geometry Markup Language

Geometry Markup Language is an XML-based language for representing spatial information. In common with all XML dialects, GML is a very explicit and highly structured format, where each property of the geometry is contained within specific element tags within the document structure.

The following code listing demonstrates an example of the GML representation of a Point located at a latitude of 47.6 degrees North, longitude 122.3 degrees West.

```
<Point xmlns="http://www.opengis.net/gml">
  <pos>47.6 -122.3</pos>
</Point>
```

Note that, unlike in WKT, the GML format states geographic coordinates in latitude–longitude order rather than longitude–latitude order (although geometric coordinates are listed in x–y order in both WKT and GML).

GML does not support z- or m-coordinates, so every coordinate pair is made up of exactly two values, separated by a space. To define a single coordinate pair, as used to create a Point geometry, those values are listed within the GML <pos> element. To define a LineString or Polygon containing more than one pair of coordinate points, the values of each coordinate pair are instead listed within the GML <posList> element, with each coordinate pair also separated by a space.

Note that GML uses a space both as the separator between individual values within a coordinate tuple, as well as to separate each coordinate tuple from the next. There is no need to differentiate these delimiters from each other because every GML coordinate tuple contains exactly two values; therefore the elements in a <posList> can be parsed into an array of points by breaking it apart following every other space.

The following code listing demonstrates the GML representation of a LineString connecting three points at (–6,4), (3,–5), and (10,8).

```
<LineString xmlns="http://www.opengis.net/gml">
  <posList>-6 4 3 -5 10 8</posList>
</LineString>
```

▓ **Tip** You can return the GML representation of any existing geography or geometry instance by calling the AsGml() method.

Some advantages of the GML format are as follows.

- GML is text-based, making it relatively easy to examine and understand the information contained within.

- The explicit structure of a GML document mirrors the structure of a geometry itself; a GML <Polygon> contains an <exterior> element, which specifies a <LinearRing> containing an array of coordinates in a <posList>, for example. This makes it easy to understand the structure of a complex geometry by examining the structure of the associated GML representation.

- GML is very verbose, explicitly stating all values within specific elements.

However, GML also has the following disadvantages.

- It is very verbose! Although both WKT and GML are text-based formats, the GML representation of a geometry requires substantially more space than the equivalent WKT representation

- Because GML is text-based, it too suffers from precision issues caused by rounding of binary floating-point values.

GML is most commonly used for representing spatial information in an XML-based environment, including when syndicating spatial data over the Internet.

▓ **Note** The GML methods implemented in SQL Server are based on a scaled-down version of the GML 3.1.1 schema. You can view the schema used in SQL Server at `http://schemas.microsoft.com/sqlserver/profiles /gml/` or you can find the full GML standards on the OGC website, located at `http://www.opengeospatial.org/standards/gml`.

GeomFromGml()—The Only GML Static Method

Unlike the WKT and WKB formats, SQL Server does not provide different methods for creating each type of geometry from GML; every geometry, whether Point, LineString, Polygon, or GeometryCollection, is created using the same generic static method, `GeomFromGml()`. The geometry returned by the `GeomFromGml()` method is determined by the structure and content of the GML representation supplied.

The `GeomFromGml()` method is implemented by both geometry and geography datatypes. The following code listing demonstrates its usage to create a geography Point instance at a latitude of 47.6, longitude of 122.3 West using the North American datum 1983 (SRID 4269):

```
DECLARE @gml xml =
'<Point xmlns="http://www.opengis.net/gml">
  <pos>47.6 -122.3</pos>
</Point>';

SELECT
geography::GeomFromGml(@gml, 4269);
```

The GML Namespace

The `xmlns` attribute of an XML element associates that element with a particular namespace. XML elements are unique only within a given namespace, so `<Point xmlns="http://www.opengis.net/gml">` is different from `<Point xmlns="http://www.someothernamespace.com">`, or just `<Point>` with no associated namespace.

In a GML representation, every element must belong to the GML namespace, `http://www.opengis.net/gml`. This unambiguously defines that element as being a GML element, rather than an element of the same name from any other XML namespace. To ensure that a GML representation is valid, you should always attach the `xmlns="http://www.opengis.net/gml"` attribute to the top-level tag of the GML document. This namespace will then be inherited by all of the child elements nested within that element.

Using the example of a LineString, the GML representation should therefore always be formed as follows.

```
<LineString xmlns="http://www.opengis.net/gml">
  <posList>-6 4 3 -5</posList>
</LineString>
```

If you omit the namespace, you will still have valid, well-formed XML, but it will no longer define a valid GML geometry. Attempting to create a geometry from such a representation using the GeomFromGml() method will result in an error as shown in the next example:

```
DECLARE @NoGMLNameSpace xml =
'<LineString>
  <posList>-6 4 3 -5</posList>
</LineString>';

SELECT geometry::GeomFromGml(@NoGMLNameSpace, 0);
```

The error received is rather confusing, with the FormatException message being given as

```
System.FormatException: 24129: The given XML instance is not valid because the top-
level tag is LineString. The top-level element of the input Geographic Markup
Language (GML) must contain a Point, LineString, Polygon, MultiPoint,
MultiGeometry, MultiCurve, MultiSurface, Arc, ArcString, CompositeCurve,
PolygonPatch or FullGlobe (geography Data Type only) object.
```

The text of the error message states that the GML representation passed to the GeomFromGml() method is invalid because the top-level tag is LineString. Instead, it helpfully suggests a list of possible valid elements, including... *LineString*?

As explained previously, XML elements are unique only within a particular namespace; what the preceding error message really should say is that the top-level element of the input GML must be one of the listed elements from the GML namespace. Declaring the GML namespace as an attribute on the parent element tag resolves the error, as shown in the following example.

```
DECLARE @WithGMLNameSpace xml =
'<LineString xmlns="http://www.opengis.net/gml">
  <posList>-6 4 3 -5</posList>
</LineString>';

SELECT geometry::GeomFromGml(@WithGMLNameSpace, 0);
```

```
(1 row(s) affected)
```

Representing an Existing Geometry as GML

The GML equivalent to the STAsText() and STAsBinary() methods is called AsGml(). The AsGml() method can be used to return the GML representation of any instance of geography or geometry data, as shown in the following code listing.

```
DECLARE @polygon geography = 'POLYGON((-4 50, 2 50, 2 60, -4 60, -4 50))';
SELECT @polygon.AsGml();
```

The result is:

```
<Polygon xmlns="http://www.opengis.net/gml">
  <exterior>
    <LinearRing>
      <posList>50 -4 50 2 60 2 60 -4 50 -4</posList>
    </LinearRing>
  </exterior>
</Polygon>
```

Note that, because this is an instance of the geography datatype, the latitude and longitude values of each coordinate pair in the resulting GML are listed in reverse order compared to that in the supplied WKT.

PRACTICAL USES OF GML IN SQL SERVER

GML is a widely accepted standard in the geospatial world, and it provides a rich set of elements capable of describing spatial features with all their associated metadata. It is used in many professional and industrial datasets. For example, GML is the native format in which data from the Ordnance Survey (the British government's national executive mapping agency) is distributed.

Unfortunately, SQL Server implements only a reduced subset of the full GML standard, and lacks many of its more advanced elements. What's more, the parser used by the GeomFromGml() method will fail to parse GML documents containing those GML elements not recognized by SQL Server, even if the document itself adheres to the full published GML schema.

For this reason, I find the GeomFromGml() method to be of little use to create geography or geometry data from GML documents found "in the wild," because there is no guarantee that SQL Server will be able to parse them. The best way of knowing that SQL Server will be able to parse a particular GML file is if that file were itself created from SQL Server's AsGml() method, but that of course implies that the data has already been successfully imported into the database!

Creating Spatial Data from Dynamically Generated WKT

The static methods introduced thus far in this chapter create instances of geometry or geography data from fully formed WKT, WKB, or GML representations. However, on many occasions we do not have, nor necessarily want, such predefined representations to hand. Instead of providing a static WKT or WKB string, you may want to create a geometry programmatically through code, for example. Creating geometries programmatically allows you to define spatial features based on a query of an underlying data source, or take advantage of programming logic such as conditional blocks and control-of-flow statements to determine the resulting geometry at runtime.

The first approach to creating such "dynamic" geography or geometry data is to consider methods that construct a WKT string in code before passing it to a static method. Because WKT is just a simple text string, we can CAST numeric coordinates into nvarchar values and then use the range of T-SQL string manipulation functions to construct the required WKT string.

To demonstrate this approach, suppose that you had a table containing the log data transmitted from the GPS device in a moving vehicle. The table records the latitude and longitude of the vehicle sampled at regular intervals in time, stored in two float columns, together with a timestamp record of when that measurement was made, stored in a datetime column. You can create a table illustrating this structure together with some sample data using the following code listing.

```
CREATE TABLE GPSLog (
  Latitude float,
  Longitude float,
  LogTime datetime
);
INSERT INTO GPSLog VALUES
  (51.868, -1.198, '2011-06-02T13:47:00'),
  (51.857, -1.182, '2011-06-02T13:48:00'),
  (51.848, -1.167, '2011-06-02T13:49:00'),
  (51.841, -1.143, '2011-06-02T13:50:00'),
  (51.832, -1.124, '2011-06-02T13:51:00');
```

Now suppose that we wanted to create Point instances corresponding to each record in the table. Because the coordinates were recorded from a GPS system, we know that the SRID is 4326, and because this is a geographic coordinate system we should use the geography datatype.

Therefore, we could use T-SQL string methods to concatenate the relevant elements of a WKT representation for each Point and pass them to the STGeomFromText() method:

```
SELECT geography::STGeomFromText(
  'POINT(' + CAST(Longitude AS varchar(32)) + ' ' + CAST(Latitude AS varchar(32)) + ')',
  4326
  )
FROM GPSLog;
```

The preceding code listing uses the CAST statement to convert each coordinate to a nvarchar value. It also concatenates the two coordinates, separated by a space, and appends round brackets and the POINT keyword around the outside. In other words, we've dynamically constructed the WKT representation of each row in the table, and then used this to create a Point instance using the STGeomFromText() method.

This example doesn't really provide much value; we could have achieved the same result more easily by supplying the numeric latitude and longitude values directly to the Point() method, as follows.

```
SELECT geography::Point(Latitude, Longitude, 4326) FROM GPSLog;
```

The Point() method is a static method that can be used to create Point geometries from three parameters: two float coordinate values and an integer SRID. Not only does using Point() make this code simpler to read than the previous example, but because it doesn't require unnecessary CASTing and string concatenation to create the WKT representation, it will almost certainly be faster too.

■ **Note** When using the geography Point() method, the coordinate parameters are supplied with latitude first, then longitude, which is opposite to the order in which they are stated in WKT.

But what if we wanted to create something a bit more complex? Suppose that, rather than create individual Point instances for each row in the GPSLog table, you wanted to create a LineString joining each of the points in order. There is no inbuilt function that accepts an array of coordinates and returns the LineString created from them, so dynamically constructing the WKT may be a better choice here.

The following code listing demonstrates one way of achieving this.

```
-- Declare an empty nvarchar to hold our constructed WKT string
DECLARE @WKT nvarchar(max) = '';

-- Build up the comma-delimited list of coordinate pairs
```

```
SELECT @WKT = @WKT + CAST(Latitude AS varchar(32)) + ' ' + CAST(Longitude AS varchar(32)) +
', '
FROM GPSLog
ORDER BY LogTime;

-- Remove the final trailing comma
SET @WKT = LEFT(@WKT, LEN(@WKT) - 1);

-- Append the LINESTRING keyword and enclose the coordinate list in brackets
SET @WKT = 'LINESTRING(' + @WKT + ')';

-- Pass the constructed WKT to the static method
SELECT geography::STGeomFromText(@WKT, 4326);
```

The preceding code listing creates the desired result, illustrated in the Spatial Results tab of SQL Server Management Studio as shown in Figure 4-1.

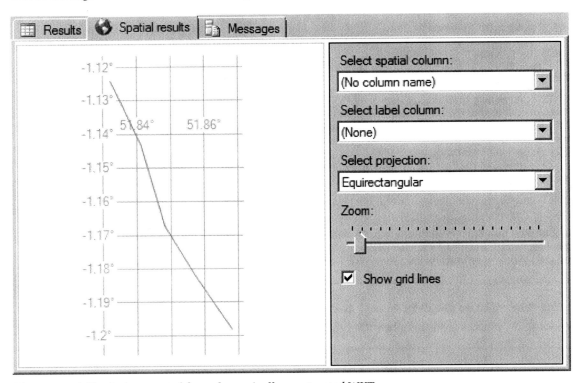

Figure 4-1. A LineString created from dynamically constructed WKT.

However, there are a couple of problems with this method. First, the code required to create it is pretty ugly. Ugly code is not only unappealing to look at, but it's also hard to maintain, and it's much more likely to conceal hidden bugs. Without the comments inserted, would it be obvious why you had to use the LEFT function to trim the last character from the list of coordinates? The code required to construct the WKT could arguably be cleaned up somewhat if implemented as a recursive CTE, but it would still involve a degree of manual string manipulation.

It's also slow: string manipulation functions are generally not known for being efficient, and this method requires both CASTing and concatenating of nvarchar values.

Finally, although this approach is somewhat dynamic, it's hard to include much control-of-flow or conditional operators. Consider how much more complicated the code would quickly become if the GPSLog table contained details of multiple vehicles that we wanted to plot as separate LineStrings, or if we were to try to construct more complicated geometries such as Polygons from the underlying data.

The fact is that, although you can use T-SQL string functions to create dynamic WKT strings, the primarily procedural-based T-SQL engine is not designed for this kind of operation. Fortunately, SQL Server provides us with an alternative in the form of the SqlGeometryBuilder and SqlGeographyBuilder classes available in SqlServer.Types.dll, which we examine in the next section.

Creating Spatial Data Using the Builder Classes

As explained in Chapter 3, the spatial functionality of SQL Server's geometry and geography datatypes is contained in a compiled .NET assembly, SqlServer.Types.dll. This assembly is installed by SQL Server, and located in the /100/SDK/Assemblies subdirectory of the directory in which SQL Server is installed.

In addition to the SqlGeometry and SqlGeography classes, which mirror the functionality of the geometry and geography datatypes in SQL Server, the SqlServer.Types.dll assembly also provides additional SqlGeometryBuilder and SqlGeographyBuilder classes, which are only accessible via .NET code.

The SqlGeometryBuilder and SqlGeographyBuilder classes provide a simple core set of methods that can be used to programmatically build geometry and geography instances, respectively. These can either be created in the application layer or, if exposed via a CLR UDF or stored procedure, in SQL Server itself.

This section demonstrates how to create spatial data using the SqlGeometryBuilder class in a C# console application, but the same procedure can be followed whatever the tier in which this code is used.

▓ **Tip** The SqlGeometryBuilder and SqlGeographyBuilder classes can be used in any .NET application that references the SqlServer.Types.dll library, and are not dependent on SQL Server being installed.

Configuring a .NET Console Application for Spatial Data

To demonstrate the basic approach required to use the Builder classes, we start by creating a simple C# console application that creates a geometry, and then prints the Well-Known Text of that geometry to the screen. To do so:

- Load up Visual Studio and, from the **File** menu, select **New ➤ Project**.

- In the following dialogue box, click to expand the set of Visual C# project types, and highlight **Console Application**.

- Choose a name and location for your project, and click **OK**.

These steps are illustrated in Figure 4-2.

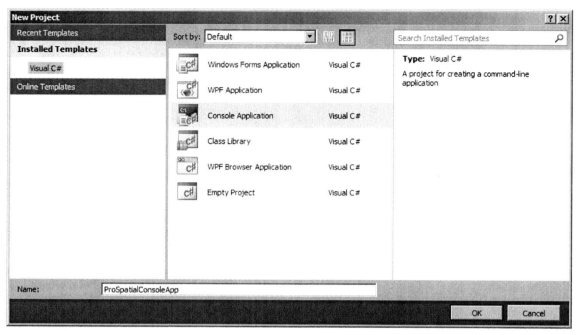

Figure 4-2. *Creating a new spatial console application.*

When your project is first created, you'll see the default `Program.cs` code file in which we insert the code for our application. But, before we do so, we need to include a reference to the `Microsoft.SqlServer.Types.dll` library.

- Select **Project ➤ Add Reference**.

- On the Add Reference dialogue box that appears, ensure that the .NET tab is selected. Scroll down the list until you find `Microsoft.SqlServer.Types` and click to highlight it.

- Click **OK**.

These steps are illustrated in Figure 4-3.

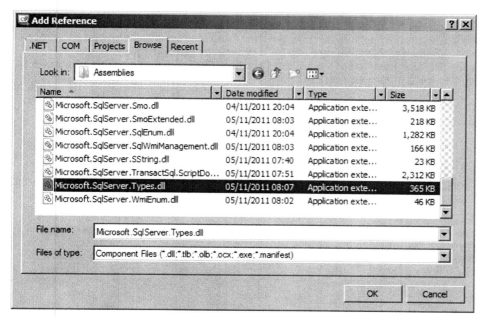

Figure 4-3. Adding a reference to the Microsoft.SqlServer.Types library.

■ **Note** Depending on your system configuration, the `Microsoft.SqlServer.Types` library might not automatically show up in the list of installed components under the Visual Studio .NET tab. In such cases, you can locate the library manually by clicking the Browse tab, navigating to `\Program Files (x86)\Microsoft SQL Server\110\SDK\Assemblies` and highlighting `Microsoft.SqlServer.Types.dll` in that directory.

Once the reference has been added to the project, we add a `using` directive so that we can easily reference the methods contained in the `Microsoft.SqlServer.Types` library without having to specify the namespace each time. Add the following line to the top of your `Program.cs` file,

```
using Microsoft.SqlServer.Types;
```

The project is now set up and ready to use the spatial datatypes, and we can get on with writing the body of our code.

Constructing a Simple Point

The first thing to do is to create a new instance of the appropriate builder class. There are two builder classes to choose from: `SqlGeographyBuilder` constructs `SqlGeography` instances, whereas `SqlGeometryBuilder`, unsurprisingly, constructs `SqlGeometry` instances.

For this first example, we will create a geometry Point instance, so we use the corresponding `SqlGeometryBuilder` class. Add the following code as the first line in the `Main` method of the application.

```
SqlGeometryBuilder gb = new SqlGeometryBuilder();
```

After instantiating the appropriate builder class, the next thing is to specify the spatial reference system in which the coordinates of this geometry will be defined. You do this by passing the appropriate SRID to the SetSrid() method of the builder instance. The following example illustrates how to set the spatial reference of the geometry to SRID 27700.

```
gb.SetSrid(27700);
```

■ **Caution** You must call SetSrid() to set the SRID of the builder immediately after it is created, and before adding any points.

The next step is to specify the type of geometry that will be created. For the SqlGeometryBuilder, you do this by passing a member of the OpenGisGeometryType enumeration to the BeginGeometry() method. The equivalent for the SqlGeographyBuilder class is to pass an OpenGisGeographyType to the BeginGeography() method. There is one enumeration for every type of geometry that can be created.

To begin creating a Point geometry using the SqlGeometryBuilder, you use the following code.

```
gb.BeginGeometry(OpenGisGeometryType.Point);
```

■ **Note** The SqlGeometryBuilder and SqlGeographyBuilder classes have a near identical set of methods, except that every occurrence of the word "geometry" becomes "geography". So, BeginGeometry() corresponds to BeginGeography(), EndGeometry() becomes EndGeography(), and ConstructedGeometry is equivalent to ConstructedGeography.

The first set of coordinates of the geometry are specified with a call to the BeginFigure() method. The following code listing creates a point at an x-coordinate of 300500 and y-coordinate of 600200.

```
gb.BeginFigure(300500, 600200);
```

If the geometry contains more than a single Point, then additional line segments are added by calling the AddLine() method. Because the Point we are defining in this example contains only one pair of coordinates, we do not need to use AddLine(), and we can now end the figure:

```
gb.EndFigure();
```

A SqlGeometry Point instance contains only a single figure, so at this point we can end the geometry:

```
gb.EndGeometry();
```

Having ended the geometry, we can then retrieve the constructed SqlGeometry Point via the ConstructedGeometry property of the SqlGeometryBuilder instance:

```
SqlGeometry Point = gb.ConstructedGeometry;
```

This is a simple demonstration application, therefore we then just print the WKT of the constructed geometry to the console window, using the ToString() method:

```
Console.WriteLine(Point.ToString());
```

Here's the full code listing for Program.cs:

```
using System;
using System.Collections.Generic;
using System.Linq;
using System.Text;
using System.Data.SqlTypes;
using Microsoft.SqlServer.Types;

namespace ProSpatial.Ch4
{
  class Program
  {
    static void Main(string[] args)
    {

      // Create a new instance of the SqlGeographyBuilder
      SqlGeometryBuilder gb = new SqlGeometryBuilder();

      // Set the spatial reference identifier
      gb.SetSrid(27700);

      // Declare the type of geometry to be created
      gb.BeginGeometry(OpenGisGeometryType.Point);

      // Add the coordinates of the first (and only) point
      gb.BeginFigure(300500, 600200);

      // End the figure
      gb.EndFigure();

      // End the geometry
      gb.EndGeometry();

      // Retrieve the constructed geometry
      SqlGeometry Point = gb.ConstructedGeometry;

      // Print WKT of the geometry to the console window
      Console.WriteLine(Point.ToString());

      // Wait for user input before exiting
      Console.ReadLine();
    }
  }
}
```

Hit F5 to debug the application, and you should see the WKT of the constructed geometry instance displayed as

---

```
POINT (300500 600200)
```

Building Polygons with Multiple Rings

Let's now look at some slightly more complex examples, the first of which is to create a geometry Polygon containing an interior ring. The steps involved are similar to the preceding example, except that each ring in the Polygon begins with a new call to the BeginFigure() method, stating the coordinates of the first point in that ring. Additional coordinates are added to each ring using the AddLine() method, which adds a straight line segment from the previous point to the given coordinates. Polygon rings must be closed, therefore the coordinates specified in the final call to AddLine() must always be the same as those provided to the BeginFigure() method used to commence that ring. The following code listing demonstrates this approach.

```
// Create a new instance of the SqlGeometryBuilder
SqlGeometryBuilder gb = new SqlGeometryBuilder();

// Set the spatial reference identifier
gb.SetSrid(0);

// Declare the type of geometry to be created
gb.BeginGeometry(OpenGisGeometryType.Polygon);

// Exterior ring
gb.BeginFigure(0, 0);
gb.AddLine(10, 0);
gb.AddLine(10, 20);
gb.AddLine(0, 20);
gb.AddLine(0, 0);
gb.EndFigure();

// Interior ring
gb.BeginFigure(3, 3);
gb.AddLine(7, 3);
gb.AddLine(5, 17);
gb.AddLine(3, 3);
gb.EndFigure();

// End the geometry and retrieve the constructed instance
gb.EndGeometry();
SqlGeometry Polygon = gb.ConstructedGeometry;
```

The Polygon instance created by this code listing is equivalent to the following WKT.

```
POLYGON ((0 0, 10 0, 10 20, 0 20, 0 0), (3 3, 7 3, 5 17, 3 3))
```

■ **Note** To construct a Polygon geometry using the SqlGeometryBuilder class, each ring requires a separate call to the BeginFigure() method. The exterior ring is the first to be created, and every subsequent figure defines an interior ring.

Creating Geometry Collections

To build a collection-type geometry, you begin with a call to BeginGeometry() (or BeginGeography()), specifying one of either the MultiPoint, MultiLineString, MultiPolygon, or GeometryCollection geometry types. Then, for each element within the collection you call BeginGeometry() (or BeginGeography()) again, specifying the type of that individual geometry.

To demonstrate, the following example creates a MultiPoint geometry containing three Points. This time, I use the SqlGeographyBuilder() class, so note that I use the corresponding geography method names and enumerations. Also note that the coordinates passed to the BeginFigure() method must be given in latitude–longitude order:

```
// Create a new instance of the SqlGeographyBuilder
SqlGeographyBuilder gb = new SqlGeographyBuilder();

// Set the spatial reference identifier
gb.SetSrid(4269);

// Declare the type of collection to be created
gb.BeginGeography(OpenGisGeographyType.MultiPoint);

// Create the first point in the collection
gb.BeginGeography(OpenGisGeographyType.Point);
gb.BeginFigure(40, -120);
gb.EndFigure();
gb.EndGeography();

// Create the second point in the collection
gb.BeginGeography(OpenGisGeographyType.Point);
gb.BeginFigure(45, -100);
gb.EndFigure();
gb.EndGeography();

// Create the third point in the collection
gb.BeginGeography(OpenGisGeographyType.Point);
gb.BeginFigure(42, -110);
gb.EndFigure();
gb.EndGeography();

// End the collection geometry and retrieve the constructed instance
gb.EndGeography();
SqlGeography MultiPoint = gb.ConstructedGeography;
```

The geometry created in this example is equivalent to the following WKT.

```
MULTIPOINT((-120 40), (-100 45), (-110 42))
```

■ **Caution** Be sure that all figures and geometries are closed (i.e., every BeginFigure() and BeginGeometry() have matching EndFigure() and EndGeometry() calls) before retrieving the constructed geometry from the Builder class.

Building Curved Geometries

To add curved segments that are used to define a CircularString, CompoundCurve, or CurvePolygon geometry, you use the AddCircularArc() method. This works in a similar way to AddLine(), except that it requires two sets of coordinates: an anchor point that the curve passes through and the final point of the arc. The following code listing demonstrates how to create a CompoundCurve geometry using the SqlGeometryBuilder class.

```
// Create a new instance of the SqlGeometryBuilder
SqlGeometryBuilder gb = new SqlGeometryBuilder();

// Set the spatial reference identifier
gb.SetSrid(0);

// Declare the type of geometry to be created
gb.BeginGeometry(OpenGisGeometryType.CompoundCurve);

// Add the first point of the geometry
gb.BeginFigure(50, 0);

// Define a straight line segment to the point at (50, 10)
gb.AddLine(50, 10);

// Create a circular arc segment that passes through (55,5) and ends at (60,0)
gb.AddCircularArc(55, 5, 60, 0);

// End the figure
gb.EndFigure();

// End the geometry
gb.EndGeometry();

// Retrieve the constructed instance
SqlGeometry Curve = gb.ConstructedGeometry;
```

The result is equivalent to the following WKT: a CompoundCurve consisting of a single straight line segment followed by a circular arc segment.

```
COMPOUNDCURVE((50 0, 50 10), CIRCULARSTRING(50 10, 55 2, 60 0))
```

Although the examples shown here have used hard-coded coordinate values for simplicity, it is easy to see how the SqlGeometryBuilder and SqlGeographyBuilder classes provide much more flexibility for defining dynamic spatial instances than the static methods provided by the geometry and geography datatypes within SQL Server.

Looking back at the earlier example of the table of GPS points, for example, you could create a CLR User-Defined Aggregate that used the SqlGeographyBuilder class to construct a LineString representing the route by reading the coordinate values of each point in the table and passing these to successive calls to the AddLine() method, returning the constructed geography instance once all points had been added.

Programmatically Defining Three- and Four-Dimensional Geometries

The `BeginFigure()`, `AddLine()`, and `AddCircularArc()` methods used to construct geometries with `SqlGeometryBuilder` or `SqlGeographyBuilder` require coordinate tuples containing x and y, or latitude and longitude values. These methods also provide overloads that will accept x-, y-, z-, and m-coordinates for the `SqlGeometryBuilder`, or latitude, longitude, z, and m for the `SqlGeographyBuilder`. This is demonstrated in the following code listing, which creates a SqlGeography Point instance containing a z-coordinate value.

```
// Create a new instance of the SqlGeographyBuilder
SqlGeographyBuilder gb = new SqlGeographyBuilder();

// Set the spatial reference identifier
gb.SetSrid(4326);

// Declare the type of geometry to be created
gb.BeginGeography(OpenGisGeographyType.Point);

// Specify latitude, longitude, z, m coordinate values
gb.BeginFigure(52, 0.15, 140, null);

// End the figure
gb.EndFigure();

// End the geography
gb.EndGeography();

// Return the constructed instance
SqlGeography PointZ = gb.ConstructedGeography;
```

■ **Note** There is no overload that accepts only latitude, longitude, and z-coordinate values, only one that accepts latitude, longitude, z-, and m-coordinates. If you do not require an m-coordinate value, simply pass a `null` parameter value as in this example.

Summary

In this chapter, you saw different methods of creating instances of the geometry and geography datatype in SQL Server.

- There are static methods dedicated to creating different types of geometries from Well-Known Text and Well-Known Binary, as well as generic methods to create any type of geometry.

- Static methods must be supplied with a fully formed representation of the geometry to be created, together with the spatial reference identifier in which the coordinates of that geometry are defined.

- It is possible to dynamically create WKT (or WKB) representations before passing them to the appropriate static method, but doing so can require some awkward string manipulation.

- You can use the `SqlGeometryBuilder` and `SqlGeographyBuilder` classes to programmatically create geometry or geography instances in .NET. This facilitates a much more manageable approach to creating dynamic spatial instances at runtime.

CHAPTER 5

Importing Spatial Data

In the last chapter, we examined various methods that can be used to create individual items of geography or geometry data, for example, using a static method that accepts WKT or WKB input, or using one of the SqlGeometryBuilder or SqlGeographyBuilder classes. Each of these methods creates only a single item of data at a time. So what if you wanted to import an entire set of spatial data?

In this chapter, I will introduce you to some of the sources from which you can obtain publicly available sets of spatial information, examine the formats in which those datasets are commonly supplied, and teach you some of the techniques you can use to import that information into SQL Server.

Sources of Spatial Data

There is a wealth of existing spatial information that you can purchase from various commercial data vendors, as well as an ever-increasing amount of data made freely available by educational institutions and government agencies. Table 5-1 provides details of a few sources of spatial data that you can download over the Internet.

Table 5-1. *Sources of Freely Downloadable Spatial Information*

Source[a]	Description
http://www.geonames.org	The GeoNames database contains over 8,000,000 place names across all countries and can be downloaded free of charge.
http://geodata.grid.unep.ch/	The United Nations Geo Data Portal includes global, national, regional, and subregional statistics and spatial data, covering themes such as freshwater, population, forests, emissions, climate, disasters, health, and GDP.
http://www.diva-gis.org/gData	This dataset, originally designed to support the study of biodiversity, contains a wealth of feature layers including inland water, administrative areas, altitude, and population density for almost every country in the world.

Source[a]	Description
http://www.census.gov	The U.S. Census Bureau Geography Division has lots of high-quality spatial information, including a gazetteer, Zip Code Tabulation Areas (ZCTAs), and the TIGER database of streets, rivers, railroads, and many other geographic entities (United States only).
http://earth-info.nga.mil/gns/html/	The U.S. National Geospatial-Intelligence Agency (NGA) GEOnet Names Server (GNS) is the official U.S. repository of all foreign place names, containing information about location, administrative division, and quality.
http://www.ordnancesurvey.co.uk/products/os-opendata.html	The Ordnance Survey is the executive mapping agency of Great Britain. Its range of OpenData products includes transportation, natural features, administrative, and postcode data for Great Britain.
http://www.openstreetmap.org	A collaboratively edited, openly available streetmap of the whole world (think of it as the "Wikipedia" of Web maps). The OSM planet database has over 250 Gb of vector data available for download in XML format.
http://geodata.gov/wps/portal/gos	The U.S. government "Geospatial One Stop" Web page of geographic data contains classified links to a variety of sources covering areas including ecology, geology, health, transportation, and demographics.

a There may be restrictions on the use of data obtained from these sources. Please refer to the respective providers for specific details.

Spatial datasets obtained from the sources listed in Table 5-1 may be provided in a variety of different formats, and may contain a significant volume of data. A full download of U.S. census data, for example, is several hundred gigabytes in size.

The remainder of this chapter describes some of the alternative formats in which spatial data is commonly supplied, and explains techniques that you can use to import this data into SQL Server 2012.

Importing Tabular Spatial Data

The most abundant (and also the simplest) source of freely available geographic information generally takes the form of a list of place names, together with separate columns containing the latitude and longitude coordinates of each location. These tabular sources may also contain other columns of related information, such as associated demographic or economic measures. Information presented in this format is commonly known as a *gazetteer*, a dictionary geographic information. Spatial information in gazetteer format resembles the index that can be found at the back of an atlas, which may list place names, or road names, for example, together with the location of that item on the map.

To demonstrate how to add a column of spatial data to a table containing columns of latitude and longitude (or Northing and Easting coordinates), let's consider an example using a file of earthquake data provided by the United States Geological Survey (USGS). The USGS makes a number of datasets freely available that you can download from their website at http://www.usgs.gov. One such dataset lists real-time, worldwide earthquakes from the past seven days, which you can download directly from http://earthquake.usgs.gov/eqcenter/catalogs/eqs7day-M1.txt. This file is a comma-separated list of data containing various attributes of each earthquake in columnar format, as listed and described in Table 5-2.

Table 5-2. Columns of Datae in the eqs7day-M1.txt File

Column	Description	ǝ	Length
Src	The two-character identifier of the source network that contributed the data	String [DT_STR]	2
Eqid	The unique identifier for this earthquake	String [DT_STR]	8
Version	The version number	String [DT_STR]	1
Datetime	A text string describing the date at which the recording was made	String [DT_STR]	50
Lat	The latitude of the earthquake epicenter, stated in the EPSG:4326 spatial reference system	Float [DT_R4]	-
Lon	The longitude of the earthquake epicenter, stated in the EPSG:4326 spatial reference system	Float [DT_R4]	-
Magnitude	The magnitude of the earthquake, determined by the strength of the seismic waves detected at each station	Float [DT_R4]	-
Depth	The depth of the earthquake's center, measured in kilometers	Float [DT_R4]	-
NST	The number of reporting stations	Two-byte signed integer [DT_I2]	-
Region	A text string description of the area in which the earthquake occurred	String [DT_STR]	255

To obtain a copy of this data, follow these steps.

1. Load your Web browser and, in the address bar, type the following URL address, http://earthquake.usgs.gov/eqcenter/catalogs/eqs7day-M1.txt. The browser will show the contents of the latest feed, as demonstrated in the example in Figure 5-1.

2. Save this file to an accessible location by choosing File ⌂ Save As (or Save Page As, depending on your browser). You will be prompted for a file name and location. For this example, it is assumed that you name the file eqs7day-M1.txt and save it to the C:\Spatial folder.

■ **Note** Because the eqs7day-M1.txt file contains a constantly updated feed of data from the last seven days, the actual content of the file you download will be different from that demonstrated in this chapter.

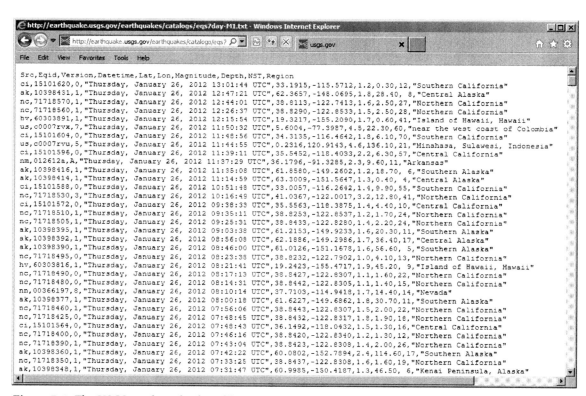

Figure 5-1. The USGS earthquake data file.

Importing the Text File

There are a number of different ways to import data into SQL Server 2012. This example uses the Import and Export Wizard, which allows you to step through the creation of a simple package to move data from a source to a destination. If you want to create a repeatable load process, or have more control over the way in which the data is imported, you may instead prefer to create a custom SSIS package, or use the BCP Bulk Copy tool.

The steps to import the earthquake file using the Import and Export Wizard follow.

1. From the Object Explorer pane in Microsoft SQL Server Management Studio, right-click the name of the database into which you would like to import the data, and select Tasks ➤ Import Data.

2. The Import and Export Wizard appears. Click Next to begin.

3. The first page of the wizard prompts you to choose a data source. Select Flat File Source from the Data Source drop-down list at the top of the screen.

4. Click the Browse button and navigate to the eqs7day-M1.txt text file that you saved earlier. Highlight the file and click Open.

5. By default, the Text Qualifier field for the connection is set to <none>. The text strings within the eqs7day-M1.txt file are contained within double quotes, so change this value to be a double quote character (") instead.

6. The eqs7day-M1.txt text file contains headings, so check the Column Names in the First Data Row check box.

7. Click the Advanced option in the left pane. Click each column in turn and, from the properties pane on the right side, amend the values of the DataType and OutputColumnWidth fields to match the values shown in Table 5-1.

8. Once you have made the appropriate changes, click the Next button. The wizard prompts you to choose a destination.

9. Enter any authentication details required to connect to the chosen SQL Server 2012 database, and then click Next.

10. The wizard prompts you to select source tables and views. By default, the wizard automatically creates a destination table called eqs7day-M1. You can leave this name if you like, but it's generally not a good idea to use table names that contain nonalphanumeric characters. Instead, I suggest you double-click on the table name in the destination column and edit it to remove the minus sign, making the destination table simply *eqs7dayM1*. Then click Next.

11. On the Save and Run Package screen, click Finish (depending on the edition of SQL Server 2012 you are using, this may be called Run Package). The package summary appears, and you are prompted to verify the details.

12. Click Finish again to execute the package.

You will receive a message informing you that the execution was successful, and stating the number of rows transferred from the text file into the destination table. You may now close the wizard by clicking the Close button.

Let's check the contents of the new table. You can do this by opening a new query window and issuing the following command against the database to which you just imported the earthquake data.

```
SELECT * FROM eqs7dayM1;
```

You will see the data inserted from the text file, as shown in Figure 5-2.

	Src	Eqid	Version	Datetime	Lat	Lon	Magnitude	Depth	NST	Region
1	nc	71717780	0	Wednesday, January 25, 2012 12:42:44 UTC	38.8195	-122.8527	1	1.8	20	Northern California
2	ak	10397758	1	Wednesday, January 25, 2012 12:23:00 UTC	60.4293	-151.5137	2.1	60.2	22	Kenai Peninsula, Alaska
3	ci	11058013	0	Wednesday, January 25, 2012 11:55:10 UTC	33.0345	-116.4323	1.5	9.2	67	Southern California
4	ci	11058005	0	Wednesday, January 25, 2012 11:44:35 UTC	33.9927	-116.9753	1.5	9.9	81	Southern California
5	uw	60389591	2	Wednesday, January 25, 2012 11:22:38 UTC	46.3403	-122.2337	1.2	8.8	29	Washington
6	ak	10397744	1	Wednesday, January 25, 2012 11:13:23 UTC	61.0066	-147.1444	2.1	20.4	19	Southern Alaska
7	nc	71717750	0	Wednesday, January 25, 2012 11:10:28 UTC	38.8272	-122.7818	1	2.4	10	Northern California
8	ak	10397736	1	Wednesday, January 25, 2012 10:53:39 UTC	59.7226	-152.8808	2.4	82.3	14	Southern Alaska
9	uw	60389576	5	Wednesday, January 25, 2012 10:51:30 UTC	46.3402	-122.2362	3.4	8.9	48	Washington
10	nn	00366024	8	Wednesday, January 25, 2012 10:27:08 UTC	37.2995	-114.833	1.6	12.1	17	Nevada
11	ak	10397726	1	Wednesday, January 25, 2012 10:12:27 UTC	64.5168	-147.2814	1.4	0.3	9	Central Alaska

Figure 5-2. The data inserted from the eqs7day-M1.txt file.

Creating a Computed Column

The location of each earthquake is currently described in the eqs7dayM1 table by latitude and longitude coordinate values stored in the Lat and Lon columns. In order to use any of the spatial methods provided by SQL Server, we need to use these coordinates to create a representation of each earthquake using the geography or geometry datatype instead. To do so, we can create a new computed column containing a Point geometry representing the epicenter of each earthquake using the Point() method of the geography datatype. This is demonstrated in the following code listing.

```
ALTER TABLE eqs7dayM1
ADD Epicenter AS geography::Point(Lat, Lon, 4326);
```

To test the contents of the Epicenter column, you can now run the following query,

```
SELECT TOP 5
  Eqid,
  Epicenter.STAsText() AS Epicenter
FROM
  eqs7dayM1;
```

The results are as follows.

```
Eqid          Epicenter
10325561      POINT (-150.3317 65.0131)
10325555      POINT (-152.2948 57.4106)
00349540      POINT (-119.8993 39.4092)
10325549      POINT (-149.6373 61.2189)
71655381      POINT (-121.287 36.6595)
```

Populating a Noncomputed Column

Using the `Point()` method, we have been able to populate the `Epicenter` column with Point geometries representing the latitude and longitude of each earthquake's epicenter, which lies on the surface of the earth. However, the origin of an earthquake (its *hypocenter*) normally lies deep within the earth, tens or hundreds of miles underground. In the eqs7day-M1 dataset, the depth of the hypocenter, in kilometers, is recorded in the `Depth` column. To be able to represent the position of the hypocenter of each earthquake instead, we need to define each Point with an additional z-coordinate based on the value of the `Depth` column.

The following code adds a new column, `Hypocenter`, to the eqs7dayM1 table. Rather than being computed like the `Epicenter` column, the `Hypocenter` column is populated with an `UPDATE` statement that sets the value of each row using a dynamically created WKT string based on the latitude, longitude, and depth of each earthquake. Note that, because the `Depth` column represents a distance *beneath* the earth's surface, the z-coordinate of each Point is set based on the negative value of the `Depth` column.

```
-- First, add a new column to the table
ALTER TABLE eqs7dayM1
ADD Hypocenter geography;
GO

-- Populate the column

UPDATE eqs7dayM1
SET Hypocenter =
  geography::STPointFromText(
    'POINT('
      + CAST(Lon AS varchar(255)) + ' '
      + CAST(Lat AS varchar(255)) + ' '
      + CAST (-Depth AS varchar(255)) + ')',
    4326);
```

You can now select the data contained in the eqs7dayM1 table, including the Point representations of both the epicenter and hypocenter of each earthquake, as follows.

```
SELECT TOP 5
  Eqid,
  Epicenter.ToString() AS Epicenter,
  Hypocenter.ToString() AS Hypocenter
FROM
  eqs7dayM1;
```

The results follow.

Eqid	Epicenter	Hypocenter
10325561	POINT(-150.3317 65.0131)	POINT(-150.332 65.0131 -0.1)
10325555	POINT(-152.2948 57.4106)	POINT(-152.295 57.4106 -30.1)
00349540	POINT(-119.8993 39.4092)	POINT(-119.899 39.4092 -6.8)
10325549	POINT(-149.6373 61.2189)	POINT(-149.637 61.2189 -33)
71655381	POINT(-121.287 36.6595)	POINT(-121.287 36.6595 -7.9)

Comparing Computed, Noncomputed, and Persisted Columns

The Epicenter and Hypocenter columns of the eqs7dayM1 table both appear to behave in the same way: you can include them in a SELECT statement, and apply the full range of geography methods on both. However, there are some important differences between them due to the way they were created.

> Epicenter is a computed column, and the Point instances it contains are calculated only at runtime of a query that involves that column. The epicenters are created using the Point() method based on the coordinates contained in the Lat and Lon columns of the eqs7dayM1 table, which creates a dependency on those columns remaining in the table schema. The values in the Epicenter column are not stored anywhere, and are disposed of following every query execution.

> Hypocenter is a regular noncomputed column in which the value of every geography Point instance is materialized and stored in the database. This eliminates the dependency on the Lat and Lon columns (and the Depth column), because the individual coordinate values of each earthquake can be retrieved from the Hypocenter column using the Lat, Lon, and Z properties if necessary.

There are are advantages and disadvantages of both methods. Using a computed column requires less storage in the database layer, because computed values are never physically stored in the table. However, they require more overhead in the execution phase in order to determine the value of each instance when used in a query. An advantage of computed columns is that when dealing with Point data as in this example, you might find it easier to manage separate columns of numeric coordinates than having to manage a single compound geography value, especially when dealing with spatial data in which coordinates are frequently changing. To update any single coordinate of a geography instance, for example, requires you to completely recreate the instance from a static method, which could be deferred until query time if using a computed column. However, a drawback of computed columns is that, because their value is only calculated at runtime, you cannot generally create an index on a computed column. Spatial indexes are crucial to creating efficient performant queries, as discussed later in this book.

A third option worth considering is the fact that computed columns can be *persisted*. A persisted computed column contains values that are defined according to a specified calculation, as in the case of the Epicenter column, but the values of which are materialized and stored in the database as is the Hypocenter column. The stored values of a persisted computed column are updated whenever the value of a column used as part of its calculation changes.

Persisted computed columns can be considered to represent the best of both worlds, allowing you to easily manage coordinate data in separate numeric columns while also seamlessly providing a geography Point instance based on those coordinates for use in any spatial queries. And, because the values are materialized in the database, indexes can be added to persisted computed columns.

The following code listing adds a new persisted computed column, Hypocenter_Persisted, using the PERSISTED option following the column definition.

```
ALTER TABLE eqs7dayM1
ADD Hypocenter_Persisted AS geography::STPointFromText(
  'POINT('
    + CAST(Lon AS varchar(255)) + ' '
    + CAST(Lat AS varchar(255)) + ' '
    + CAST (-Depth AS varchar(255)) + ')',
  4326) PERSISTED;
```

Note that, even though the Hypocenter_Persisted column is persisted, the values it contains still have a dependency on the Lat, Lon, and Depth columns, and you will not be able to drop any column from a table that is referenced by a computed column definition. Persisted computed columns are not necessarily the right option in every scenario, but it's certainly useful to be aware of them.

Importing Data Using OGR2OGR

OGR2OGR is a component of the Geospatial Data Abstraction Library, more commonly referred to as GDAL. GDAL is an open-source library and command-line toolkit that provides various utilities to read and write from different spatial data formats.

The core GDAL library provides raster data functionality for data sources such as GeoTIFF, MrSID, and JPEG2000, whereas the OGR sublibrary provides support for vector data, including ESRI shapefiles, MapInfo files, KML, GML, and various spatial databases including PostGIS, Oracle Spatial, and SQL Server.

The GDAL/OGR library is relatively mature, powerful, and has an active development community. It's also free, and licensed under a permissive MIT-style open source license. This section shows how to use OGR2OGR, the command-line component of the OGR library, to import data from various different sources into SQL Server.

Obtaining and Installing the GDAL/OGR Library

In common with much open source software, the GDAL/OGR library has been developed to work across many different operating environments and to be relatively platform-independent. Unfortunately, that means that it is not necessarily as simple to set up compared to an application that has been tailored specifically for the Windows operating system from the outset. Nevertheless, it is not too hard to get working, and there are two possible approaches you can follow.

One option is to download the latest GDAL source from http://download.osgeo.org/gdal and configure and compile it using Visual Studio (or another tool from which you can compile C++). This will give you the most flexibility to adjust some of GDAL's configuration options, such as linking in additional optional libraries. This is also the best route to take if you want to understand how GDAL works behind the scenes, or if you want to extend it or integrate its functionality into part of another application or larger workflow. However, you should expect to invest a little time and effort to understand the structure of the source code if you choose to take this route.

Alternatively, if you simply want to get hold of a working copy of the OGR2OGR executable so that you can follow along with the examples in this section, I suggest instead that you download the OSGeo4w package from http://osgeo4w.osgeo.org. OSGeo4w (Open Source Geospatial for Windows) is a package containing ready-compiled Windows binaries of a range of open source geospatial tools, including GDAL/OGR, MapServer, QGIS, and many more. I recommend OSGeo4W not only as a convenient way to get hold of GDAL/OGR itself, but you also might find that you can make use of many of the other included tools to integrate with spatial data in SQL Server.

Whatever option you choose, ensure that your version of the GDAL library corresponds to version 1.8.0 or greater because this is the version at which support for SQL Server was first introduced.

OGR2OGR—Basic Syntax

OGR2OGR is the command-line component of the GDAL/OGR library that can be used to convert vector data from one format to another. You can retrieve a full list of usage options by typing the following in a command prompt window (assuming that the directory in which OGR2OGR is installed is located in the command path).

```
ogr2ogr /?
```

The basic syntax to load data from a source to a destination is as follows.

```
ogr2ogr -f {OutputFormat}    {Destination}    {Source}    {Additional Options}
```

To import data into SQL Server you state the {OutputFormat} as "MSSQLSpatial", and specify the {Destination} using the connection string of the target SQL Server database. In the code listing below, the contents of the {Source} file will be loaded into a new table in the ProSpatial database of the default localhost SQL Server instance, for example:

```
ogr2ogr
  -f "MSSQLSpatial"
  "MSSQL:server=localhost;database=ProSpatial;trusted_connection=yes"
  {Source}
  {Additional Options}
```

The default OGR2OGR behavior is to create a new table in the destination database named with the same filename as the {Source} dataset. The data from a shapefile named MyData.shp will be imported into the SQL Server table MyData, for example. If a table with that name already exists then the command will fail. This behavior can be modified by specifying one of the following flags in the {Additional Options}.

-**append** appends new records into an existing table with the specified name.

-**overwrite** deletes the existing destination table and re-creates it.

-**nln** *"tablename"* inserts data into the named table rather than the default table named based on the {Source} dataset name.

There are further {Additional Options}, some of which vary depending on the nature of the source data. In the following sections we examine some practical scenarios that demonstrate these options, as well as the syntax required to load from {Source} datasets of several common formats.

Importing ESRI Shapefile Data

The shapefile format was designed and is maintained by Environmental Systems Research Institute, Inc. (ESRI). Originally developed for use in its ARC/INFO suite of GIS software, the shapefile is now a very common format used for exchanging spatial information between all kinds of systems, and is the format in which most commercial spatial data is supplied. Over time, a large body of spatial datasets has been created in ESRI shapefile format.

Although a set of data provided in shapefile format is commonly referred to as "*a*" shapefile (singular), this is a slight misnomer because a single shapefile actually consists of several files. Each file relating to a given shapefile dataset shares the same file name, with one of the following file extensions.

.shp: The SHP file contains the raw geometrical shape data. Each SHP file can contain items of only one kind of geometry shape: Points, LineStrings, or Polygons.

.shx: The SHX file maintains the shapefile index, which holds one index entry for every shape in the shapefile document. Each index entry describes the start position and length of the associated shape record in the SHP file.

.dbf: The DBF file contains additional nonspatial attributes of each shape. For instance, in a shapefile containing Polygons representing the states of America, the DBF file might contain the name of each state, its population, or the name of its state capital.

.prj: The PRJ file gives details about the projection in which the coordinates of the geometry data are represented, in the same format as used in the well_known_text column of the sys.spatial_reference_systems table. When importing a shapefile into SQL Server, this file contains the information that is required to determine the correct spatial reference identifier (SRID).

Shapefiles may contain coordinate data defined using either projected or geographic coordinate reference systems. The following sections show an example of each of these, imported into a column of the geometry and geography datatype, respectively.

Obtaining Sample Shapefile Data

For this example, we use a projected dataset of Polygons representing precinct outlines of the city of Boston, Massachussetts. As do many large U.S. cities, the City of Boston maintains a website from which you can download various spatial datasets related to the city.

To download the precinct dataset, go to the website at `http://hubmaps1.cityofboston.gov/datahub/` (you may be asked to accept a license agreement). From the left-hand menu, select GIS Data Downloads to display various layers, grouped by theme. Under the Political heading, click on the small blue icon to the right of the Precincts layer, which will bring up a popup window. Click on the link in the popup window to download the layer and metadata, as shown in Figure 5-3. Then having downloaded the Precincts.zip file, unzip it to extract the set of files for the Precincts shapefile.

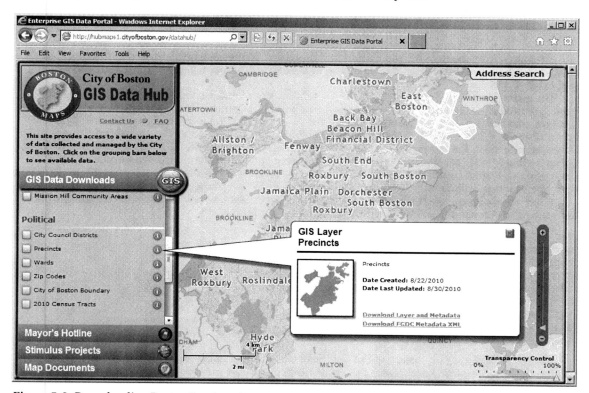

Figure 5-3. *Downloading Boston Precinct data.*

Loading the Data

To import the shapefile into SQL Server using the default OGR2OGR options, open a command prompt window, navigate to the folder in which you extracted the Precincts shapefile, and execute the following command (you need to change the SQL Server connection string as appropriate).

```
ogr2ogr
  -f "MSSQLSpatial"
  "MSSQL:server=localhost;database=ProSpatial;trusted_connection=yes"
  "precincts.shp"
```

■ **Note** For the purposes of clarity, I've separated the output format, destination, and source parameter values in this code listing onto separate lines. However, when executing OGR2OGR you should not insert carriage returns between parameters, but list them all on the same line with a space separating each.

After importing the dataset, you should find that three tables have been created in the specified destination database (the ProSpatial database, in my case): precincts, geometry_columns, and spatial_ref_sys.

The geometry_columns and spatial_ref_sys tables store metadata about any spatial data that has been imported by OGR2OGR into a destination database. If, at some point in the future, you were to use this same data as the source of another transformation (suppose you were to export the precincts dataset from SQL Server to KML) then OGR2OGR would refer to these tables to provide additional information used in the conversion. In essence, spatial_ref_sys is OGR2OGR's own version of SQL Server's sys.spatial_reference_systems table. However, such information is not essential and can always be re-created, so you can ignore these tables for now (or even delete them if you choose, although be aware that they will be re-created the next time you import any data).

What's more interesting to us right now is the precincts table, which contains the data imported from the precincts shapefile. The structure of the table is as follows.

```
[ogr_fid] [int] IDENTITY(1,1) NOT NULL,
[ogr_geometry] [geometry] NULL,
[objectid] [numeric](10, 0) NULL,
[prcnts_id] [float] NULL,
[id] [varchar](4) NULL,
[wdpct] [varchar](4) NULL,
[pct] [varchar](2) NULL,
[shape_area] [numeric](19, 11) NULL,
[shape_len] [numeric](19, 11) NULL
```

The polygon shapes representing the outline of each precinct have been imported into a geometry column of the table named ogr_geometry. The attributes from the precincts.dbf file have been used to populate additional columns in the table, containing various identifiers together with the length and area of each precinct shape. To ensure uniqueness of each row in the table, OGR2OGR has automatically added an IDENTITY column, ogr_fid, which contains a unique integer reference for each record.

To test out the data loaded into the table, we can plot the ogr_geometry column on the Management Studio Spatial Results Tab, as shown in Figure 5-4.

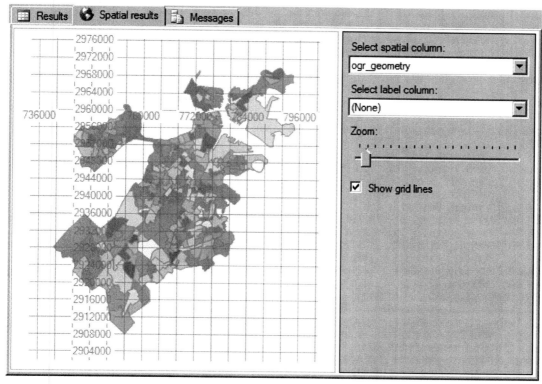

Figure 5-4. The precincts shapefile plotted using the Management Studio Spatial Results tab.

■ **Note** After importing a dataset, you may find that OGR2OGR creates additional tables in your database: geometry_columns and spatial_ref_sys. These tables are used by OGR2OGR to store additional metadata.

Assigning an Output SRID

The result displayed in Figure 5-4 seems pretty good, but there are still a few tweaks that you might want to make. You could, for example, use the -nln "NewTable" option to change the name of the table into which the data is inserted, or specify -select objectid,pct to copy only certain attribute fields from the shapefile to columns in the destination table.

The most important change to be made, however, is to correct a problem that might not yet be apparent but which can be demonstrated by executing the following code listing.

```
SELECT ogr_geometry.STSrid FROM precincts;
```

The STSrid property returns the spatial reference identifier of an instance, and the results of this query show that OGR2OGR has loaded every record in the precincts table using a spatial reference identifier of 32768. This value seems like a perfectly plausible SRID so it might not strike you as particularly odd, but it's not the correct spatial reference identifier for this data. In fact, it's not a valid

SRID at all; it's the code that OGR2OGR uses when the destination spatial reference system is undefined. (Perhaps a code of 99999 would have made this more obvious!)

To assign the correct SRID, we first need to examine the properties of the spatial reference system in which the coordinates were originally supplied, which is described in the `precincts.prj` file that accompanies the shapefile. The PRJ file is a simple text file, so you can load it up in any text editor to show the contents as follows.

```
PROJCS[
  "NAD_1983_StatePlane_Massachusetts_Mainland_FIPS_2001_Feet",
  GEOGCS[
    "GCS_North_American_1983",
    DATUM["D_North_American_1983",SPHEROID["GRS_1980",6378137.0,298.257222101]],
    PRIMEM["Greenwich",0.0],
    UNIT["Degree",0.0174532925199433]],
  PROJECTION["Lambert_Conformal_Conic"],
  PARAMETER["False_Easting",656166.6666666665],
  PARAMETER["False_Northing",2460625.0],
  PARAMETER["Central_Meridian",-71.5],
  PARAMETER["Standard_Parallel_1",41.71666666666667],
  PARAMETER["Standard_Parallel_2",42.68333333333333],
  PARAMETER["Latitude_Of_Origin",41.0],
  UNIT["Foot_US",0.3048006096012192]]
```

This preceding PRJ text should look familiar to you as the Well-Known Text representation of a projected spatial reference system, which we examined back in Chapter 1. This particular system is the state plane coordinate system for Massachussetts Mainland, which uses a Lambert Conformal Conic projection of the North American 1983 Datum, centered on a central meridian at 71.5 degrees West.

Because this is a projected coordinate system, we can't look for it in SQL Server's `sys.spatial_reference_systems` table. Instead, you can go to the EPSG registry website at `http://www.epsg-registry.org` and search for spatial reference systems using the name "Massachusetts Mainland". There will be a few matches returned, but the distinguishing properties of the system we're looking for is that it's based on the NAD83 datum, with the unit of measure being US Feet. This leads to only one possible spatial reference system: SRID 2249.

To correct the SRID of the records in the precincts table, you could execute a T-SQL UPDATE query after importing the data, as follows.

```
UPDATE precincts
SET ogr_geometry.STSrid = 2249;
```

A better approach, however, would be to make OGR2OGR assign the correct SRID at the point the data is inserted. This can be done by specifying the `-a_srs` parameter, together with the EPSG code of the spatial reference system to be used. The following example recreates the precincts table using the `-a_srs` parameter to populate every record with SRID 2249. Note that because I want to replace the existing precincts table, I've also included the `–overwrite` parameter:

```
ogr2ogr
  -f "MSSQLSpatial"
  "MSSQL:server=localhost;database=ProSpatial;trusted_connection=yes"
  "precincts.shp"
  -a_srs "EPSG:2249"
  -overwrite
```

■ **Tip** You can find the full list of OGR2OGR options by calling `ogr2ogr /?` or by looking at `http://www.gdal.org/ogr2ogr.html`.

Re-executing the previous code listing to retrieve the SRID of the values in the `ogr_geometry` column now shows that all the data have been imported with the correct SRID:

```
SELECT DISTINCT ogr_geometry.STSrid FROM precincts;
```

```
2249
```

Another Example: Specifying Layer Creation Options

To provide a further example of importing data from shapefile format into SQL Server, we will use data from the U.S. Census Bureau representing the Zip Code Tabulation Areas (ZCTAs) of the state of California. These ZCTAs were defined by the U.S. Census Bureau during the U.S. 2010 census, and are approximately equivalent to the delivery area for a five-digit ZIP code as used by the U.S. Postal Service. You can download the ESRI shapefile of the Californian ZCTA areas used in this example from the following URL: `http://www2.census.gov/geo/tiger/TIGER2010/ZCTA5/2010/tl_2010_06_zcta510.zip`.

■ **Tip** You can download many other interesting shapefile datasets from the U.S. Census by using the Web download interface at `http://www.census.gov/cgi-bin/geo/shapefiles2010/main`.

Download this ZIP file and extract its contents. You should see the familiar structure of a shapefile dataset: the `.shp` file that defines the coordinate data, the `.dbf` file containing the various attributes attached to each shape, the `.shx` index file, and the `.prj` file describing the projection parameters. Let's start by looking at the `tl_2010_06_zcta510.prj` file, the content of which is shown below:

```
GEOGCS[
  "GCS_North_American_1983",
  DATUM["D_North_American_1983",SPHEROID["GRS_1980",6378137,298.257222101]],
  PRIMEM["Greenwich",0],
  UNIT["Degree",0.017453292519943295]
]
```

Notice that, because the Well-Known Text definition in the `tl_2010_06_zcta510.prj` file begins with the keyword GEOGCS, we know that the coordinates of this shapefile are defined using a geographic coordinate system, and should be imported into a column of the geography datatype. Now, we just need to determine the appropriate SRID for the data in this column.

To find out the SRID, you could search for the parameters listed in the `tl_2010_06_zcta510.prj` file on the EPSG registry website, as we did to find the SRID of the Massachussetts Mainland projection in the preceding example. However, even though this would allow you to find the correct SRID, it wouldn't necessarily prove that this data could be imported into SQL Server. Remember that SQL Server only supports geographic coordinates defined using one of the spatial reference systems listed in the `sys.spatial_reference_systems` table. Therefore, instead of looking up the projection on a website, we'll search for a record in the `sys.spatial_reference_systems` table that matches the parameters given in the `tl_2010_06_zcta510.prj` file. That way, we can look up the corresponding SRID and check that it's a supported spatial reference system at the same time.

The `.prj` file states that the ZCTA coordinate data is defined using a geographic coordinate system based on the NAD 83 datum. We can search for the correct identifier for this spatial reference system in the `sys.spatial_reference_systems` table using the query:

```
SELECT
  spatial_reference_id
FROM
  sys.spatial_reference_systems
WHERE
  well_known_text LIKE 'GEOGCS%"NAD83"%';
```

The single result returned is as follows.

```
spatial_reference_id
4269
```

So, when importing the data contained in the ZCTA shapefile, we should use the `-a_srs` parameter to assign SRID 4269. Because SRID 4269 is a geographic coordinate reference system, we also need to tell OGR2OGR to import the data into a column using the `geography` datatype rather than the `geometry` datatype as used in the last example.

OGR2OGR settings that are specific to the destination data format, such as the choice between using the `geometry`/`geography` datatype, are known as *layer creation options*. You can specify one or more layer creation options using the `-lco` flag. In the following code listing, two layer creation options are given.

> `GEOM_TYPE="geography"` specifies that the shape data should be inserted into a column of the geography datatype (the alternative, and default value, is `GEOM_TYPE="geometry"`).

> `GEOM_NAME="geog4269"` sets the name of the geography column to geog4269 (I've chosen this column name following my convention of concatenating the datatype and SRID of the data it contains).

As in the preceding example, I use the `-a_srs` parameter to ensure that the created geometries are assigned the correct SRID of EPSG:4269. I also use the `-overwrite` option to specify that the requested destination table should be replaced should it already exist.

I also include two other options:

> `-nln "CaliforniaZCTA"` specifies the name of the destination table in SQL Server. Without this switch, the table would have been named tl_2010_06_zcta510 to match the input shapefile, but that's rather difficult to remember!

> `-progress` is a switch to tell OGR2OGR to display a simple progress bar in the console window as the data is uploaded. This is particularly useful when loading larger datasets to give an indication of how far along the import procedure has progressed (and how much farther it has to go).

Here's the full code listing to load the Californian ZCTA shapefile:

```
ogr2ogr
  -f "MSSQLSpatial"
  "MSSQL:server=localhost;database=ProSpatial;trusted_connection=yes"
  "tl_2010_06_zcta510.shp"
  -a_srs "EPSG:4269"
  -overwrite
  -lco "GEOM_TYPE=geography"
  -lco "GEOM_NAME=geog4269"
  -nln "CaliforniaZCTA"
  -progress
```

As the records are imported from the shapefile into SQL Server, OGR2OGR will update a percentage progress bar as illustrated in Figure 5-5.

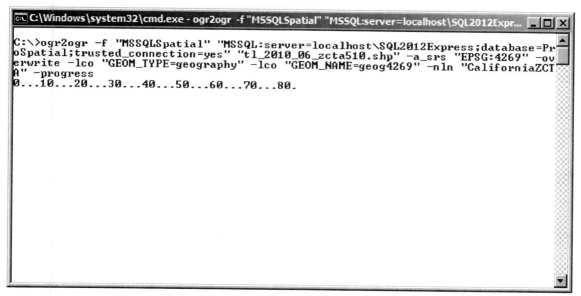

Figure 5-5. Displaying progress of OGR2OGR import from ESRI shapefile.

Once the progress bar has reached 100%, the import is complete and you can select the data from the CaliforniaZCTA table, the (partial) content of which is displayed in the SSMS Spatial Results tab as shown in Figure 5-6.

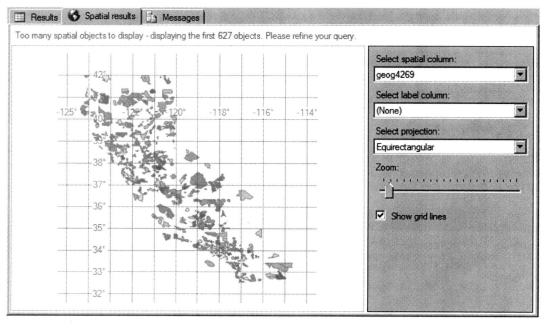

Figure 5-6. *Displaying the ZCTA areas of California.*

Importing MapInfo Data

MapInfo Professional is a GIS system for Windows platforms often used in public sector organizations. MapInfo datasets are saved in an ASCII text format, either using the native .tab file extension, or saved as a MapInfo Interchange File (MIF), which typically comes as a pair of files with .mif and .mid extensions. OGR2OGR can read and write MapInfo datafiles in either native (.tab) or interchange (.mid/.mif) format.

Obtaining Sample MapInfo Data

To demonstrate the process of importing MapInfo data into SQL Server, we will use a dataset from Geoscience Australia, a department of the Australian government responsible for various geoscientifc and environmental research and information management.

Starting from the homepage of the Geoscience Australia website at http://www.ga.gov.au/, use the search box to search for "*river basins data*". When the search results are displayed, clicking the top hit should take you to a page of metadata titled "Australia's River Basins 1997". This page tells you various useful information about this dataset and, around halfway down the page (under the heading "Access"), contains a link labeled "Free Data Download".

■ **Note** At the time of writing, the direct URL link for the river basins dataset is

https://www.ga.gov.au/products/servlet/controller?event=FILE_SELECTION&catno=42343.

On the File Selection page, click to select the MapInfo Interchange Format (MIF) checkbox in the Available Files column as shown in Figure 5-7, and then click Continue to File Download. Finally, click on the dataset title hyperlink to download the file.

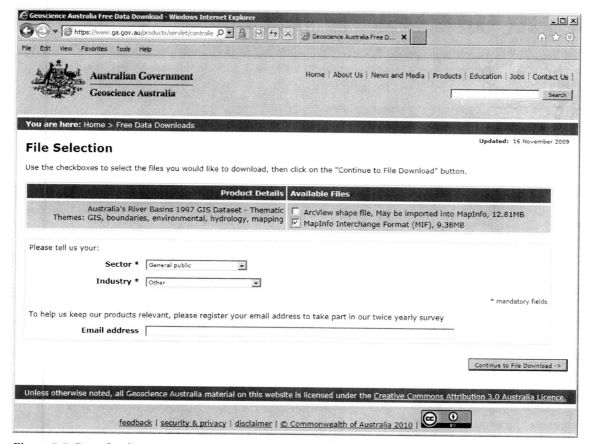

Figure 5-7. *Downloading a MapInfo dataset from the Geoscience Australia website.*

The file download consists of a single ZIP archive containing several files. Extract these files to find three datasets containing Point (rbasin_point), LineString (rbasin_chain), and Polygon (rbasin_polygon) features in MapInfo Interchange Format, each having an associated .mid and .mif file. There is also a copyright notice and a user guide to accompany the dataset.

Determining the SRID

Following the same steps as with the ESRI shapefile examples, before loading the data into SQL Server, we first need to determine what SRID is associated with the coordinates. But, unlike with the shapefile data sources, we don't have a .prj file to refer to and, although the header of a MapInfo file can contain details of the projection used, the river basin files obtained from Geoscience Australia don't have this information.

Fortunately, a quick glance through the user guide that accompanies the download reveals a passage in Section 2.3, Coordinate system, as follows.

Australia's River Basins 1997 data is available in geographical coordinates (latitude and longitude) in decimal degrees using the Australian Geodetic Datum (AGD66).

Perfect. Now, as we did with the U.S. Census data, we just need to take a look in the `sys.spatial_reference_systems` table to find the ID for a geographic coordinate system based on the AGD66 datum:

```
SELECT * FROM sys.spatial_reference_systems
WHERE well_known_text LIKE '%AGD66%';
```

There's a single matching result returned, with SRID 4202.

Loading the Data

That's all the information we need, so now we can use OGR2OGR to import the MapInfo data from the `RBasin_Polygon` dataset using the following command,

```
ogr2ogr
  -f "MSSQLSpatial"
  "MSSQL:server=localhost;database=ProSpatial;trusted_connection=yes"
  "RBasin_Polygon.mid"
  -a_srs "EPSG:4202"
  -lco "GEOM_TYPE=geography"
  -lco "GEOM_NAME=geog4202"
```

Note that this code listing follows exactly the same pattern as used to load data from ESRI shapefiles; the options set in this case specify that the data should be loaded into a new table in the `tempdb` database of the SQL Server instance running on `localhost`, using SRID 4202, with a geography column named geog4202. The only difference from the last example, in fact, is that instead of providing the name of the `.shp` shapefile, you provide the name of the MapInfo `.mid` file instead. There are no additional options to set regarding the input file format; this is determined dynamically from the structure of the input file itself.

Once the import has finished, select the data in the `RBasin_Polygon` table in SQL Server and you should see the familiar shape of Australia, as shown in Figure 5-8.

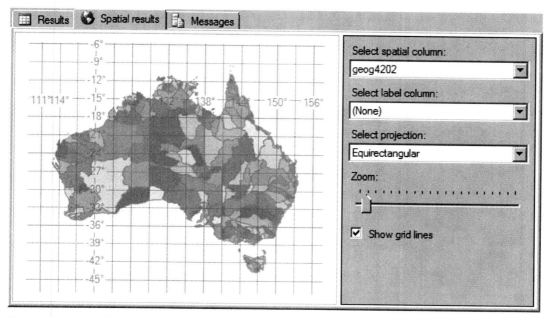

Figure 5-8. *Australian River Basins imported from MapInfo into SQL Server.*

Reprojecting Data During Import

In all the preceding examples we've used the -a_srs option to assign the SRID to the data in SQL Server to be the same as the spatial reference system in which the coordinates of the source dataset were defined. It's worth noting that OGR2OGR can also *reproject* data from the source coordinate system into another spatial reference system as it is imported into the destination. To do so, instead of using the -a_srs option to assign a spatial reference system to the output, you use -s_srs to specify the EPSG code of the source coordinate system and -t_srs to specify the coordinate system into which it should be transformed.

For example, the following code listing demonstrates how to import the Boston precincts shapefile dataset used previously but, this time, reprojects the data from SRID 2249 to SRID 4326 as it is loaded. This involves conversion from a projected coordinate system to a geographic coordinate system, therefore I've also used the GEOM_TYPE layer creation option to ensure that a geography column is used in the destination table, which I've called precincts_reprojected:

```
ogr2ogr
  -f "MSSQLSpatial"
  "MSSQL:server=localhost;database=ProSpatial;trusted_connection=yes"
  "precincts.shp"
  -s_srs "EPSG:2249"
  -t_srs "EPSG:4326"
  -overwrite
  -lco "GEOM_TYPE=geography"
  -lco "GEOM_NAME=geog4326"
  -nln "precincts_reprojected"
```

The resulting Polygons, now contained in the geography column geog4326, are illustrated in Figure 5-9.

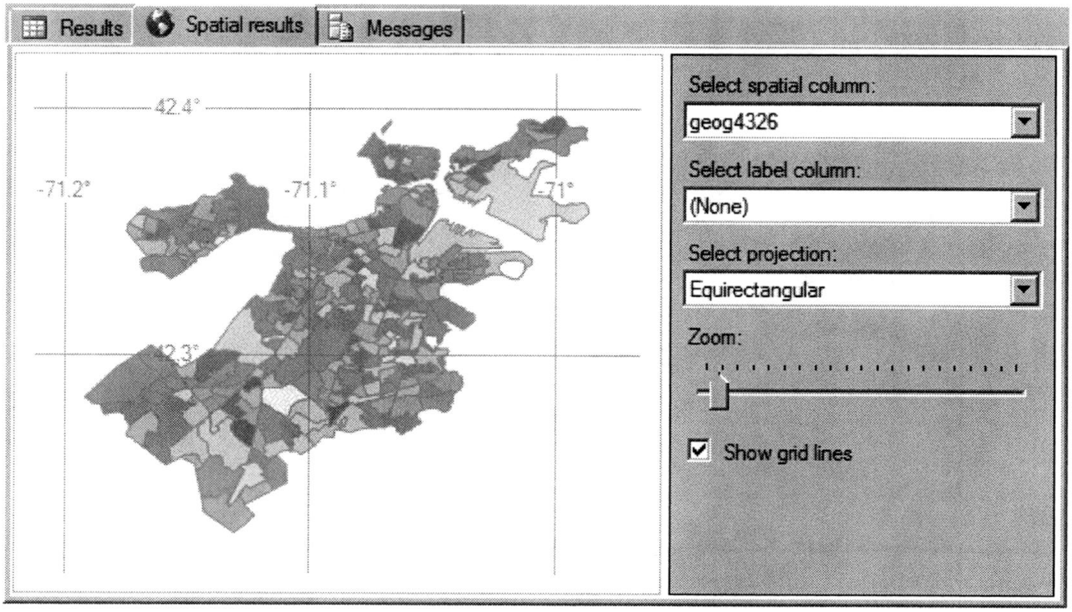

Figure 5-9. Massachussetts precinct polygons reprojected to SRID 4326 in the geography datatype.

Reprojection and transformation between different coordinate systems are covered in detail in Chapter 8.

Exporting Spatial Data from SQL Server

Although the main focus of this chapter is concerned with getting data from different sources into SQL Server, it is worth noting that OGR2OGR can just as easily be used to export data from SQL Server into another supported format.

To export data from SQL Server with OGR2OGR you follow the same basic pattern as when importing, except that you provide the SQL Server connection string as the {Source} for the transformation, and set the filename of the target file as the {Destination}. You also need to set the -f option to specify the format in which the output file should be written.

It is often the case that you don't want to export a complete single table, but possibly a subset of a table, or the results of a query that combines fields from multiple tables. To do this, you can specify the -sql option, supplying a SQL query to be executed that will return the relevant source data from the database.

To demonstrate, in the following sections we take the data from the precincts_reprojected table and export them to a KML file.

Keyhole Markup Language

Keyhole Markup Language, more commonly known as KML, is an XML-based language originally developed by Keyhole Inc. for use in its EarthViewer application. In 2004, Google acquired Keyhole, together with EarthViewer, which it used as the foundation on which to develop its popular Google Earth platform (http://earth.google.com). Although the KML format has undergone several revisions since then (at the time of writing, the latest version is KML 2.2), it continues to be the native format for storing spatial information used in Google Earth.

In 2008, KML was adopted by the Open Geospatial Consortium as a standard format for spatial information, and you can now find the latest implementation of the KML specification at the OGC website, at http://www.opengeospatial.org/standards/kml/.

KML has always been used within the Google Earth community to share user-created spatial data, however, the popularity and accessibility of the Google Earth platform among the wider Internet community means that KML is becoming increasingly used for educational and research purposes, as well as in critical applications such as emergency and disaster services. Coupled with its adoption as a standard by the OGC, KML is becoming an increasingly important format for the interchange of spatial data.

Exporting from SQL Server to KML with OGR2OGR

To use OGR2OGR to write spatial data to a KML file, you set the -f format flag as "KML", and set the name of the kml file as the {Destination}. Note that KML files can only contain coordinates defined using SRID 4326, so if your source data uses any other spatial reference system, you will also have to use the -t_srs option to transform the coordinates to SRID 4326 in the process. In this example, we export data from the precincts_reprojected table, in which the geog4326 column already contains coordinates in the correct spatial reference system (because they were transformed into SRID 4326 during import).

We use the -sql option to retrieve only the ID and shape of each precinct. The shape information itself is retrieved from the geog4326 column in Well-Known Binary format using the STAsBinary() method. Although OGR2OGR can read SQL Server's native binary format, I find it sometimes leads to problems, and using the industry-standard WKB format is a more reliable option.

Here's the code listing to export the relevant data from the precincts_reprojected table to a new precincts.kml file in the c:\spatial directory:

```
ogr2ogr
  -f "KML"
  "C:\spatial\precincts.kml"
  "MSSQL:server=localhost;database=tempdb;trusted_connection=yes;"
  -sql "SELECT prcnts_id, geog4326.STAsBinary() FROM precincts_reprojected"
  -overwrite
```

The resulting KML file begins as shown below. Notice how the KML structure of a Polygon, in which a space-separated list of coordinates is listed within a <coordinates> element contained within <outerBoundaryIs>, closely resembles the GML format in which space-separated Polygon coordinates are listed within the <posList> element contained within an <exterior> element:

```
<?xml version="1.0" encoding="utf-8" ?>
<kml xmlns="http://www.opengis.net/kml/2.2">
<Document><Folder><name>SELECT</name>
<Schema name="SELECT" id="SELECT">
  <SimpleField name="Name" type="string"></SimpleField>
  <SimpleField name="Description" type="string"></SimpleField>
  <SimpleField name="prcnts_id" type="float"></SimpleField>
</Schema>
  <Placemark>
    <Style>
      <LineStyle><color>ff0000ff</color></LineStyle>
      <PolyStyle><fill>0</fill></PolyStyle></Style>
    <ExtendedData>
      <SchemaData schemaUrl="#SELECT">
        <SimpleData name="prcnts_id">1</SimpleData>
      </SchemaData>
```

123

```
      </ExtendedData>
      <Polygon>
        <outerBoundaryIs>
          <LinearRing>
            <coordinates>-71.008036474492485,42.387093194669127
 -71.010502257322116,42.389034720949425 -71.011425746332051,42.38976473048055
-71.011931948239607,42.390174099511839 -71.01262223043183,42.390907499155361
-71.013103274784129,42.391509391490196 …
-71.008036474492485,42.387093194669127
            </coordinates>
          </LinearRing>
        </outerBoundaryIs>
      </Polygon>
    </Placemark>
    <Placemark>
…
    </Placemark>
</Folder></Document></kml>
```

When viewed in Google Earth, this KML file is displayed as shown in Figure 5-10.

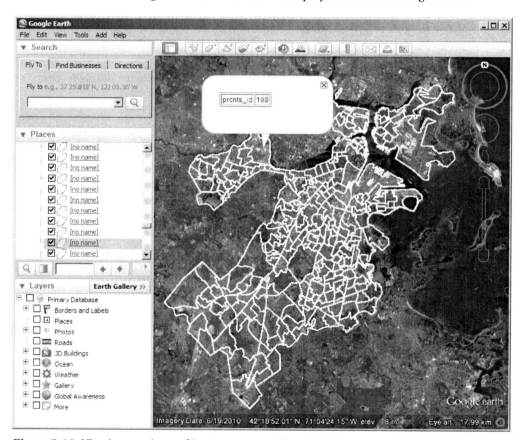

Figure 5-10. *Viewing precincts of Boston exported from SQL Server to a KML file in Google Earth.*

Spatial ETL Using SQL Server Integration Services

The techniques discussed thus far in this chapter demonstrate some simple methods that allow you to import spatial data in various formats into SQL Server 2012, but they cannot readily be automated or used as part of a robust extraction, transformation, and load (ETL) process.

Unfortunately, SQL Server Integration Services, Microsoft's own ETL tool for SQL Server, does not directly support transformations between spatial data formats such as the ESRI shapefile or MapInfo file format. However, there are still ways to use spatial data in SSIS, as is demonstrated in this section.

Importing Point Data Using a Custom Script Component

SQL Server does not provide any specific functionality for dealing with spatial data. However, because geography and geometry are CLR datatypes based on the .Net framework, you can import spatial data in an SSIS dataflow task by using a custom script component that references the Microsoft.SqlServer.Types.dll library and makes use of the SqlGeography and SqlGeometry classes.

To demonstrate this approach, we will create an SSIS package that loads the same eqs7day-M1 dataset used right at the beginning of this chapter, but instead of running a T-SQL script to populate a geography Point column representing the epicenter of each record after loading the table, we'll create this column as part of the SSIS load process itself.

▓ **Note** SQL Server Integration Services is not available as part of SQL Server Express. To follow this example you must be using SQL Server developer, standard or enterprise edition.

Creating a New SSIS Project

To begin, create a new SSIS project by following these steps.

1. From the main menu of Business Intelligence Development Studio (or Visual Studio), select **File ➤ New ➤ Project...**

2. In the New Project dialog box that appears, highlight Integration Services Project from the Business Intelligence Project types templates.

3. Choose a Name and Location for the new SSIS project, and then click **OK**.

Creating the Text File Connection

Once the new project has been created, define a connection to the eqs7day-M1.txt source file as follows.

1. From the Visual Studio main menu, click on **SSIS ➤ New Connection...**

2. In the Add SSIS Connection Manager dialog box that appears, select FLATFILE Connection manager for flat files, and then click the **Add...** button.

3. The Flat File Connection Manager Editor dialog will appear. Notice that this is exactly the same dialog as you used to set the file source for the Import/Export Wizard at the beginning of this chapter, and you need to choose exactly the

same settings as before. Start by giving a name to this connection. I use "*Earthquakes Text File*".

4. Click the **Browse** button, and navigate to the eqs7day-M1.txt text file. Highlight the file and click open.

5. Change the Text qualifier to be a double quote character (").

6. Click to enable the checkbox next to *Column names in the first data row*.

7. You now need to configure the datatype of each column in the textfile. Select the **Advanced** option from the left-hand pane of the Flat File Connection Manager Editor. As before, click each column in turn and, from the properties pane on the right-hand side, amend the values of the **Datatype** and **OutputColumnWidth** fields to match the values shown in Table 5-2.

8. Once you have made the appropriate changes as shown in Figure 5-11, click **OK** to close the Flat File Connection Manager Editor.

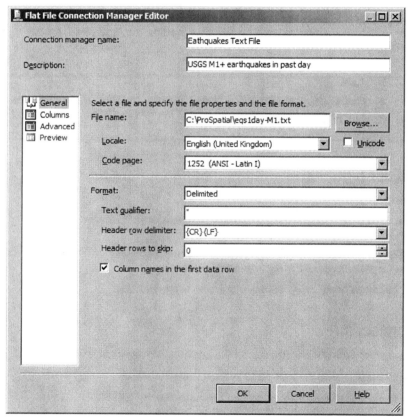

Figure 5-11. SSIS Flat File Connection Manager to the eqs7day-M1.txt file.

The new connection will appear in the Connection Managers pane at the bottom of the screen.

Creating the SQL Server Connection

Next you need to add the details of the SQL Server database that will be the destination into which the data are inserted. We will use an OLE DB connection to the database, which you can create by following these steps.

1. From the Visual Studio main menu, click on **SSIS ➤ New Connection…**

2. In the Add SSIS Connection Manager dialog box that appears, select OLEDB Connection manager for OLE DB connections, and then click the **Add…** button.

3. On the next screen, you will see a list of all available data connections. Click **New…**

4. From the Provider dropdown at the top of the form, ensure that SQL Server Native Client 11.0 is selected.

5. Enter the relevant details of the SQL Server instance to which you wish to upload the data, and click **OK**.

The connection manager settings that I use for connecting to the SQL Server 2012 instance running on my local machine are shown in Figure 5-12.

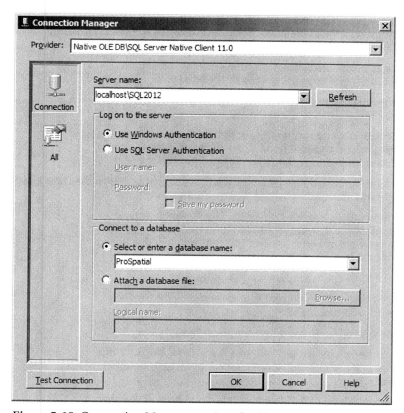

Figure 5-12. Connection Manager settings for SQL Server 2012.

We've now set up the relevant connections for our project, so it's time to add the task that will transform the data from our text file into SQL Server.

Adding a New Dataflow Task and Specifying the Data Source

The project will contain a single dataflow task that transforms data from the source text file into the destination SQL Server table. From the Toolbox on the left-hand side of the screen, drag a new Data Flow Task onto the Control Flow designer surface in the center of the screen, and then double-click on the Data Flow Task to edit it.

We will add a data source to the dataflow that uses the connection to our eqs7day-M1.txt file:

1. From the toolbox, under the Other Sources heading, select Flat File Source, and drag it into the designer surface.

2. Double-click the Flat File Source to bring up the Flat File Source Editor.

3. Select the Earthquakes Text File connection from the dropdown box, and click **OK**.

Creating the Script Component

Next we need to add a script component that will use the *lat* and *lon* columns from the text file source to create a new geography column containing a Point instance. Because this script will act upon input columns and create new output columns, we must use a *transformation* script.

1. Open the toolbox once again and, under the Common heading, select the Script Component item and drag it onto the dataflow workspace.

2. In the Select Script Component Type dialog window that appears, select Transformation, and click **OK**.

3. Now connect the flat file source as an input to the script component. To do this, first click once on the Flat File Source item. Then click and drag the green arrow that appears underneath to connect it to the Script Component item.

To configure the script, double-click on the Script Component item that you just added to the Data Flow window. This will bring up the Script Transformation Editor dialog window.

1. Click on the Input Columns tab on the left-hand side. The Available Input Columns table will show all of the columns available from our source text file. For this transformation, we need only the Lat and Lon columns, so click once to select the check boxes next to each of these items.

2. Next, click on the Inputs and Outputs item on the left-hand side.

3. Click once on the small [+] icon next to Output 0, and then click on the Output Columns item that appears underneath it.

4. Click on the **Add Column** button to create a new output column.

5. A new output column will be created. By default, this is named *Column*; while the name of the column is still highlighted, let's change it to something more informative, such as *Location*.

6. In the properties window on the right-hand side, set the DataType of the new Location column to image [DT_IMAGE].

The preceding steps are illustrated in Figure 5-13.

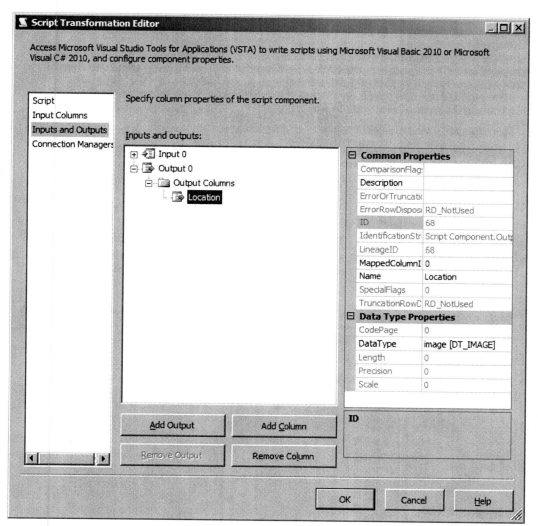

Figure 5-13. Configuring the Script Transformation Component.

■ **Note** Why do we specify the image [DT_IMAGE] datatype for a column that will contain geography data? SSIS datatypes are not specific to SQL Server, because SSIS can connect to many different data sources. The image [DT_IMAGE] datatype, named because it can be used to store image data in databases, can be used to represent any binary value up to a maximum size of 2^31-1 (2,147,483,647) bytes, including geography or geometry data.

To add the code that will be executed by the script task, click on the script tab on the left-hand side of the Script Editor Transformation dialog box. You can create SSIS custom scripts using either Microsoft Visual C# 2010 or Microsoft Visual Basic 2010. C# is the default, and that's what I use in this example. (If you prefer to write your own script in Visual Basic, you can do so by changing the ScriptLanguage property in the right-hand pane.)

Click the **Edit Script...** button. A new Visual Studio editor window will appear containing the skeleton template for a C# script component. We edit this script to create a geography Point item to populate the Location column as part of the dataflow.

Before we can create our new script, we first need to add the necessary references to the .NET libraries that contain the methods we want to use.

1.   From the main menu, select **Project ➤ Add Reference...**

2.   Scroll down the list of components under the .NET tab, and highlight the Microsoft.SqlServer.Types component (or Browse to the Program Files (x86)\Microsoft SQL Server\110\SDK\Assemblies directory and highlight it from there).

3.   Click **OK**. Microsoft.SQLServer.Types will appear in the References list in the Solution Explorer pane.

Having included a reference to Microsoft.SQLServer.Types in our project, we also need to include the corresponding namespace in our code so that we can easily reference the methods included in the assembly. To do so, add this line to the list of references at the top of main.cs, on the line immediately following using Microsoft.SqlServer.Dts.Runtime.Wrapper:

using Microsoft.SqlServer.Types;

We also use the BinaryWriter() and MemoryStream() methods from the System.IO namespace, so include a reference to that namespace by adding the following line,

using System.IO;

The main functionality of our script is contained within the ProcessInputRow() method. This method acts upon the data in each row of the source file as they pass through the script component. There is already an empty template for ProcessInputRow() method in the script, as follows.

```
public override void Input0_ProcessInputRow(Input0Buffer Row)
{
    /*
    Add your code here
    */
}
```

Edit this to be as follows.

```
public override void Input0_ProcessInputRow(Input0Buffer Row)
{
    // Instantiate a new geography object
    SqlGeography point = new SqlGeography();

    // Use the Point() method of the geography datatype to create a point from the lat and lon
    // values of this row
    point = SqlGeography.Point(Row.Lat, Row.Lon, 4326);

    // Instantiate a new memorystream
    MemoryStream ms = new MemoryStream();
```

```
// Instantiate a new binarywriter based on the memorystream
BinaryWriter bw = new BinaryWriter(ms);

// Write the result to the binarywriter
point.Write(bw);

// Insert the resulting object into the Location row
Row.Location.AddBlobData(ms.ToArray());
    }
}
```

We are not performing any postexecute() or preexecute() methods, so you can remove these empty methods from the file if you wish. When you have made these changes, the resulting main.cs file should look like that shown in the following code listing.

```
using System;
using System.Data;
using Microsoft.SqlServer.Dts.Pipeline.Wrapper;
using Microsoft.SqlServer.Dts.Runtime.Wrapper;
using Microsoft.SqlServer.Types;
using System.IO;

[Microsoft.SqlServer.Dts.Pipeline.SSISScriptComponentEntryPointAttribute]
public class ScriptMain : UserComponent
{
    public override void Input0_ProcessInputRow(Input0Buffer Row)
    {
        SqlGeography point = new SqlGeography();
        point = SqlGeography.Point(Row.Lat, Row.Lon, 4326);
        MemoryStream ms = new MemoryStream();
        BinaryWriter bw = new BinaryWriter(ms);
        point.Write(bw);
        Row.Location.AddBlobData(ms.ToArray());
    }
}
```

Save the script (Ctrl + Shift + S) and then select **File ➤ Exit** to close the script window and return to the Script Transformation Editor dialog window. Now Click **OK** to exit the Script Transformation Editor and return to the Data Flow tab of the main SSIS project.

Specifying the Destination

Now that we have added the source and the transformation of our dataflow task, we need to set the destination, the SQL Server table into which the task will insert the data.

1. From the toolbox, under Other Destinations, select and drag a new OLE DB Destination to the Data Flow workspace.

2. Click once on the Script Component item in the workspace, and drag the green output connector from the Script Component onto the new OLE DB destination item.

3. Double-click the OLE DB destination item to open the OLE DB Destination Editor dialog window.

4. On the Connection Manager tab, ensure that the OLE DB Connection manager dropdown shows the SQL Server connection that you added to the project earlier. To distinguish this set of data from the version loaded earlier through the SQL Server Import/Export Wizard, wewill create a new table for it, so click the New... button next to the *Name of the table or the view*.

   SSIS will generate a CREATE TABLE script for you based on the datatypes of the columns included in the dataflow; the only modification you need to make is to name the table and change the type of the Location column from IMAGE to geography. The modified script I used is as follows.

```
CREATE TABLE [eqs7dayM1_SSIS] (
  [Src] CHAR(2),
  [Eqid] VARCHAR(8),
  [Version] CHAR(1),
  [DateTime] VARCHAR(50),
  [Lat] REAL,
  [Long] REAL,
  [Magnitude] REAL,
  [Depth] REAL,
  [NST] SMALLINT,
  [Region] VARCHAR(255),
  [Location] GEOGRAPHY
)
```

   Then click OK.

5. Click "Mapping" from the left-hand pane of the OLE DB Connection Manager window. You should see that all of the columns from the original text file together with the new Location column that is created in the script component are automatically mapped to the appropriate columns in the destination table, as shown in Figure 5-14. Click **OK**.

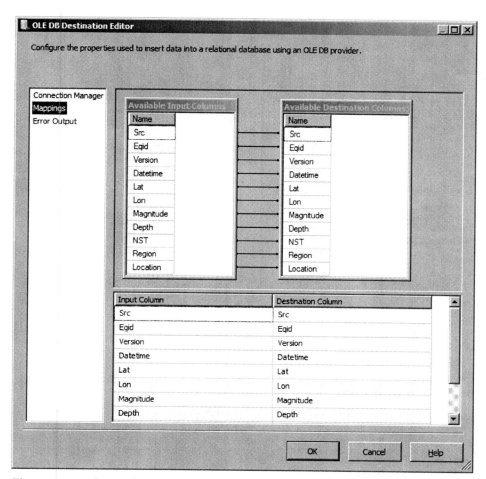

Figure 5-14. *Columns from the source text file and the Location column created by the script component mapped to columns in the SQL Server destination.*

The SSIS project is now finished and ready to run. The complete dataflow task is illustrated in Figure 5-15.

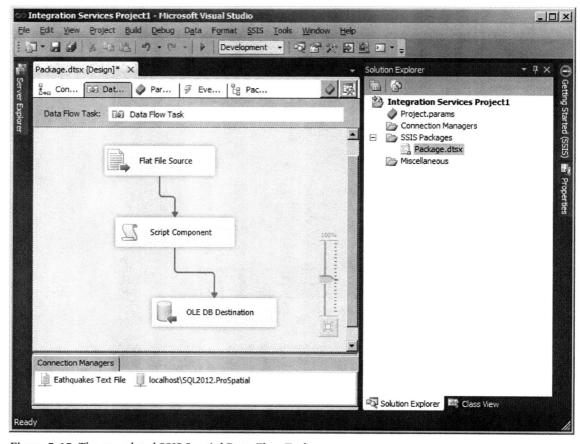

Figure 5-15. The completed SSIS Spatial Data Flow Task.

Running the SSIS package

We have now added all the components of the dataflow, so press F5 to run the project. Once the project has executed, you can go back to SQL Server Management Studio and run the following T-SQL statement in a query window.

```
SELECT
  Eqid,
  Region,
  Location.STAsText() AS WKT
FROM
  dbo.Eqs7dayM1_SSIS;
```

The results show the rows of data successfully imported from the Eqs7day-M1.txt text file, together with a new column, Location, containing the geography Point created by the SSIS script component, as follows.

Eqid	Region	WKT
51204068	Northern California	POINT (-122.8238 38.809)
10330433	Southern California	POINT (-116.1075 33.7415)
00048942	Central Alaska	POINT (-150.3075 63.0547)
2008taaw	Greece	POINT (21.4639 38.0295)

This end result is identical to that obtained from importing the text file using the SQL Server Import/Export Wizard and then manually adding and populating the geography column with an UPDATE query. The difference is that, in this case, the derived column was created by the script component in an SSIS package, which can be easily repeated as part of an automated load task.

Using Third-Party Source Components

The previous example was relatively simple because it sought only to create Point geometries from a pair of numeric coordinate columns in the source dataset. To extend this example to create more complex geometries, or to use SSIS to load data from sources such as ESRI shapefiles, we need a more flexible data source than a simple text file.

CodePlex SSIS Shapefile Source

There's a project on the CodePlex open source repository that aims to provide an SSIS data source for loading Points, LineStrings, or Polygons from ESRI shapefiles. You can find the project page at http://shapefilesource.codeplex.com/.

At the time of writing, this project is still very young, and only in beta release. It's also a little bit fiddly to set up; instead of being able to directly read shapefile data from the data source into a SQL Server destination, you still need to use an intermediate custom script transformation. The custom script must take the DT_IMAGE produced by the shapefile reader and turn it into a WKT string, which is then used as an input to the STGeomFromText() method on the destination server. Despite its current shortcomings, the project shows promise and is probably worth keeping an eye on for the future.

Safe FME

If you want to import an ESRI shapefile, MapInfo, or other spatial dataset into SQL Server in a production environment, another option is to use a commercial third-party component. The most popular tool for this purpose is the Feature Manipulation Engine (FME) from Safe Software (http://www.safe.com).

FME can convert data between a huge range of spatial formats (250+), and it can also transform and manipulate that data in various ways as part of a workflow. In addition to providing a stand-alone desktop application and server component, FME also provides a set of extensions that integrate with SQL Server Integration Services, providing additional source readers and destination writers for working with different formats of spatial data as part of an ETL process.

Figure 5-16 illustrates a simple FME workflow that takes geometry and attribute data from a shapefile and loads it directly into SQL Server.

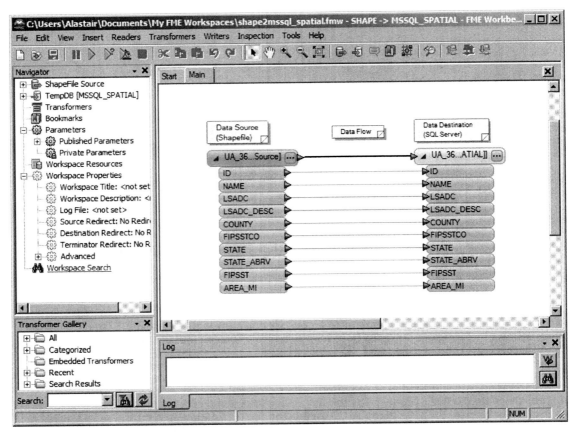

Figure 5-16. Loading data from a shapefile to SQL Server using Safe FME.

It is not my intention to describe Safe FME in any further detail here, but I do recommend that you check it out if you have need to load a large amount of spatial data from many different formats into SQL Server.

Summary

In this chapter, you learned about a variety of data formats in which existing spatial data may be provided, and how you can import those data into SQL Server 2012. Specifically, this chapter covered the following.

- There are many alternative file formats in which spatial information is commonly stored and shared, including tabular geographic information, the ESRI shapefile format, MapInfo files, KML, and many more.

- There are a number of sources from which you can obtain freely available spatial data over the Internet. The data obtained from these sources range in quality and in coverage. If you are downloading spatial data for use in a critical application, be sure to check the accuracy of that data first!

- Simple spatial information provided in tabular gazetteer format can be imported using the Import and Export Wizard. You can then create a computed column or use the T-SQL UPDATE statement in conjunction with the Point() static method to populate a geography or geometry column from the coordinate values of each row of data in the table.

- To construct an item of spatial data from tabular information containing a z-coordinate, you can manually construct the WKT representation of a geometry based on each coordinate value, and then pass that representation to the relevant WKT static method, such as STPointFromText().

- There are a number of other tools capable of converting and importing spatial data that are compatible with SQL Server. OGR2OGR is one such tool, which can read from and write to a variety of formats, and you saw examples of how to load ESRI shapefiles and MapInfo interchange files into SQL Server, and how to export data to KML format.

- SQL Server Integration Services does not directly support spatial data formats. To perform ETL of spatial data, you can write a custom script component, or use a commercial add-in such as FME from Safe Software.

CHAPTER 6

Geocoding

Even though the dedicated spatial datatypes, geometry and geography, are a relatively recent addition to SQL Server, almost every existing SQL Server database already contains some form of spatial information, that is, data that describes the location of some feature or other. This spatial information might not be of the sort we have considered so far in this book, being described using coordinates from a spatial reference system, but might instead be the addresses of customers or suppliers, postal codes, delivery routes, or the names of cities or regions for which a sales manager is responsible. Wouldn't it be useful if you could conduct spatial analysis based on this sort of common, unstructured spatial information? That is exactly what *geocoding* enables you to do.

The process of geocoding involves taking a text-based description of a location or place, such as a street address, the name of a landmark, or a postal code, and deriving a structured spatial representation of that feature. In practice, the representation returned by most geocoding methods is a single pair of coordinates representing the approximate center of the supplied address, but they may also return a bounding box representing the extent of a feature, or even a Polygon representing its precise shape.

To demonstrate the process of geocoding, let's consider an example. The address of the White House, the official residence of the president of the United States, is 1600 Pennsylvania Avenue NW, Washington DC, 20500. If you were to geocode this address, you might obtain the coordinates 38.8980 degrees latitude, –77.0365 degrees longitude, corresponding to a Point located in the WGS84 spatial reference system. The geocoding process is illustrated in Figure 6-1.

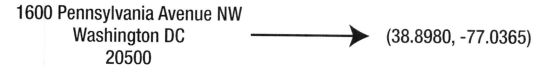

Figure 6-1. Geocoding an address into latitude and longitude coordinates

There are a number of different ways to provide geocoding functionality; some geocoding tools are desktop-based applications, whereas others are services that you access over the Web. In this chapter, I'll show you how to create a .NET geocoding function that calls into the Bing Maps REST geocoding service, and how to integrate this function into SQL Server. I'll then discuss some considerations for using geocoding in a batch or asynchronous environment, and introduce the concept of reverse-geocoding.

The Bing Maps Geocoding Service

Microsoft provides a number of online spatial services under the "Bing Maps" brand. One of these, the Bing Maps REST Locations API, exposes a representational state transfer (REST) interface into a

geocoding service. You can read more details about the Bing Maps REST Locations API at
`http://msdn.microsoft.com/en-us/library/ff701715.aspx`.

Because the Locations API is free for most applications, and simple to use, I use this service to provide geocoding functionality in this chapter. However, you could apply a similar approach to many other web-based geocoding services.

Obtaining a Bing Maps Key

In order to use the Bing Maps geocoding service, you must provide authenticatation in the form of an alphanumeric key. If you want to follow any of the code samples in this chapter, you'll therefore need to sign up for a key, which you can do by following the instructions at `https://www.bingmapsportal.com/`.

Registration is free and quick. You'll first need to log in to the Bing Maps portal site with a Windows Live ID and create a new account by filling in the form shown in Figure 6-2.

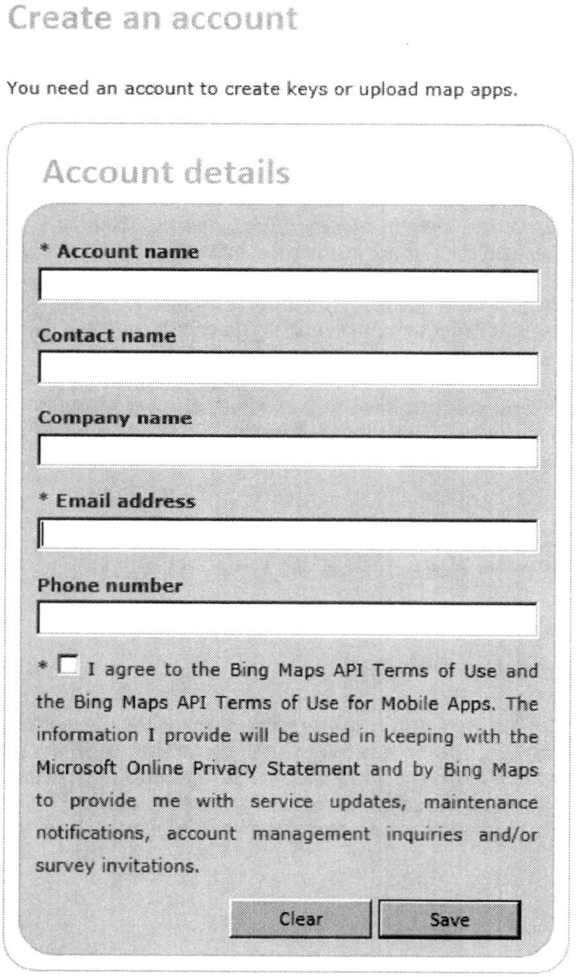

Create an account

You need an account to create keys or upload map apps.

Account details

* Account name

Contact name

Company name

* Email address

Phone number

* ☐ I agree to the Bing Maps API Terms of Use and the Bing Maps API Terms of Use for Mobile Apps. The information I provide will be used in keeping with the Microsoft Online Privacy Statement and by Bing Maps to provide me with service updates, maintenance notifications, account management inquiries and/or survey invitations.

| Clear | Save |

Figure 6-2. Creating a Bing Maps account

Having entered the required registration details, select the menu option to "Create or view keys". You'll be prompted to enter a name for your application, as well as the URL at which the application will be hosted. You'll also need to select the type of application for which the key will be used. For the purposes of this chapter, you can request a "Developer" application key, with an application URL pointing to a localhost address, such as http://127.0.0.1, as shown in Figure 6-3.

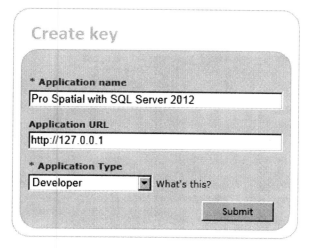

Figure 6-3. *Creating a Bing Maps key*

Keys are used to track usage of the Bing Maps service, and are also used for recording certain billable transactions, as described at http://msdn.microsoft.com/en-us/library/ff859477.aspx. However, you are only billed for production applications for which you have taken out an enterprise license agreement. You won't incur any costs for using Bing Maps in a development environment, or for any production applications that are not covered by an enterprise license. For the rest of this chapter, I'll assume that you've signed up for a developer key, which will be a 64-character alphanumeric string such as this:

At7aATG4p6LjyQha9TFGduTh15_i5N0t4R341k3y!Uvs3VIE2QhsOSRx_tFoKURkD5vOeRs

In any of the code samples in this chapter where you see the text ENTERYOURBINGMAPSKEY, be sure to substitute your key in the appropriate place to be able to access the Bing Maps service.

Calling the Bing Maps REST Locations API

You access the Bing Maps Locations API by making an HTTP request to the URL at http://dev.virtualearth.net/REST/v1/Locations (using a web browser, or via the .NET HttpWebRequest class, for example). This request is based on a template that contains a number of parameters for the elements of the address to be geocoded, as in the following example (be sure to enter your Bing Maps key where indicated):

```
http://dev.virtualearth.net/REST/v1/Locations?countryRegion=UK&adminDistrict=Norfolk
&locality=Norwich&postalCode=NR2 4TE&addressLine=27 Heigham Street&o=xml&key=
ENTERYOURBINGMAPSKEY
```

In this example, the service is called to geocode an address at 27 Heigham Street, Norwich, Norfolk, NR2 4TE, UK. The parameter o=xml is provided to specify that the result should be returned in XML format (the default is to return results as JSON). The results returned by the service when geocoding the preceding address with a valid Bing Maps key are as follows:

```
<Response>
<Copyright>Copyright © 2011 Microsoft and its suppliers. All rights reserved. This API
cannot be accessed and the content and any results may not be used, reproduced or
transmitted in any manner without express written permission from Microsoft
Corporation.</Copyright>
<BrandLogoUri>http://dev.virtualearth.net/Branding/logo_powered_by.png</BrandLogoUri>
<StatusCode>200</StatusCode>
<StatusDescription>OK</StatusDescription>
<AuthenticationResultCode>ValidCredentials</AuthenticationResultCode>
<TraceId>ece6495ca47a416f8dc4dad13b64f6a2</TraceId>
<ResourceSets>
  <ResourceSet>
    <EstimatedTotal>1</EstimatedTotal>
    <Resources>
      <Location>
        <Name>NR2 4TE, Norwich, Norfolk, United Kingdom</Name>
        <Point><Latitude>52.634046</Latitude><Longitude>1.286097</Longitude></Point>
        <BoundingBox>
          <SouthLatitude>52.630183282429321</SouthLatitude>
          <WestLongitude>1.2776115753233459</WestLongitude>
          <NorthLatitude>52.637908717570674</NorthLatitude>
          <EastLongitude>1.2945824246766542</EastLongitude>
        </BoundingBox>
        <EntityType>Postcode1</EntityType>
        <Address>
          <AdminDistrict>England</AdminDistrict>
          <AdminDistrict2>Norfolk</AdminDistrict2>
          <CountryRegion>United Kingdom</CountryRegion>
          <FormattedAddress>NR2 4TE, Norwich, Norfolk, United Kingdom</FormattedAddress>
          <Locality>Norwich</Locality>
          <PostalCode>NR2 4TE</PostalCode>
        </Address>
        <Confidence>High</Confidence>
      </Location>
    </Resources>
  </ResourceSet>
</ResourceSets>
</Response>
```

Most geocoding algorithms are approximate. This is because they rely on parsing a number of free-text user-supplied fields, and are therefore unlikely to find an exact match for the address entered.

Instead, they tend to separate out components of an address and find the best match (or matches) for the elements given.

In the example above, the value of the `<EntityType>` element, *Postcode1*, signifies that, in this case, the result is based on a match of the supplied postcode value only rather than the full street address. This might occur in situations when the full street address could not be located (because it was mistyped, for example). The result contains both an approximate center point for the geocode postcode match, provided in the `<Point>` element of the `<Location>`, as well as a `<BoundingBox>` representing the extent of this area.

Creating a .NET Geocoding Assembly

To access the Bing Maps Locations API from within SQL Server, we will use Visual Studio to build a custom .NET assembly that will be executed by the SQLCLR. This is another example of the benefits of the integration of the .NET CLR within SQL Server: it allows you to extend the functionality of SQL Server using any of the methods contained in the .NET Base Class Library, including using classes such as `HttpWebRequest` to access a web-based resource.

Because this is the first time I've described how to use spatial functionality from within an SQLCLR assembly, I'll explain the process in detail, step by step. In subsequent chapters, I'll assume that you're familiar with the basic process of assembly creation and deployment given here.

■ **Note** The following steps describe the creation of a .NET assembly using the freely available Visual C# 2010 Express Edition. You may use a different edition of Visual Studio, but be aware that you may find that some of the menu items appear under different headings than described here.

Creating a New Project

Your first task is to create a new class library project, by following these steps.

1. From the Visual Studio menu bar, select File ➤ New Project (or press Ctrl+N).

2. In the New Project dialog box, shown in Figure 6-4, select the Class Library template and type a name for the new project. For the assembly containing the code samples in this chapter, I named the project ProSpatialCh6.

3. Click OK.

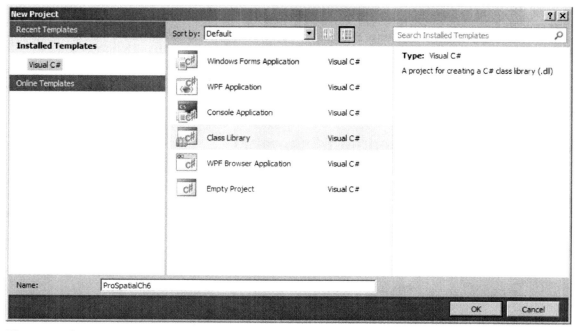

Figure 6-4. Creating a new project using Visual C# 2010 Express Edition

Once the project has been created, the project workspace will appear, and the main window will show the contents of the default class file within the project.

Configuring the Project

Before adding the geocoding function, we need to make a number of changes to configure the project. To make these changes, follow these steps.

1. Open the project properties page by selecting Project ➤ ProSpatialCh6 Properties from the main menu bar.

2. From the Application tab, ensure that the Target Framework is set to .NET Framework 3.5 or greater. If it is not already, then change the value (which might require you to save and reload the project).

3. Select Build from the list of tabs on the left side of the project properties page.

4. In the Output path field, enter the location in which you want the compiled geocoder assembly to be created. In this example, I set the output path to `C:\Spatial`

Theses steps are illustrated in Figure 6-5.

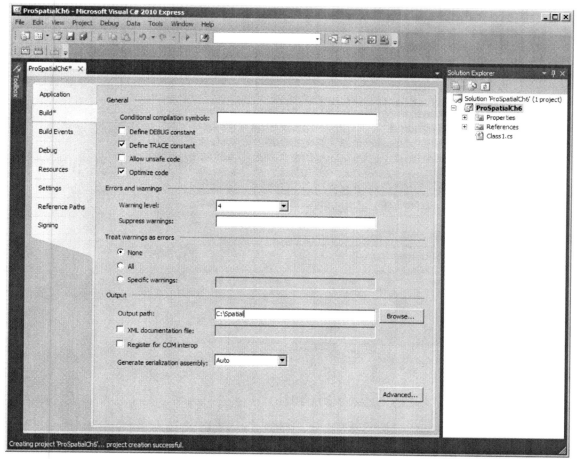

Figure 6-5. Setting the compile options for the Geocoder project

Adding a Reference to Microsoft.SqlServer.Types.dll

The coordinates returned from the Locations API are expressed in geographic coordinates measured using the EPSG:4326 spatial reference system. Our geocoding function will create a geography Point instance from these coordinates. To be able to do so, we must therefore include a reference to the `Microsoft.SqlServer.Types.dll` library that contains the methods of the `SqlGeography` and `SqlGeometry` classes.

1. From the Project menu, select Add Reference.

2. Click on the Browse tab and navigate to the folder in which the `Microsoft.SqlServer.Types.dll` assembly is installed. On my system, this is `/Program Files (x86)/Microsoft SQL Server/110/SDK/Assemblies`.

3. Highlight the `Microsoft.SqlServer.Types.dll` assembly and click OK.

These steps are illustrated in Figure 6-6.

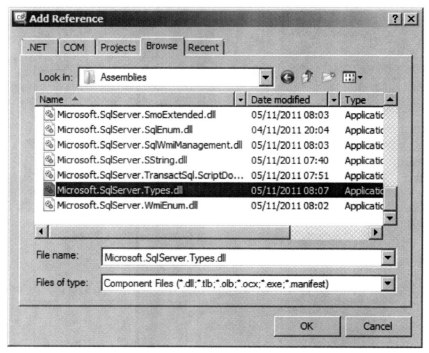

Figure 6-6. *Adding a reference to the Microsoft.SqlServer.Types.dll library*

Adding a Simple Geocoding Function

Now that the project is set up, it's time to add the method that will perform the geocoding itself. Add a new class file to the project by selecting Project ➤ Add new item ➤ Class. Name the new class file Geocoder.cs and click Add.

When the new class file is created, it will contain an empty template. Replace this with the following code listing, inserting the value of your Bing Maps key where indicated.

```
using System;
using System.Data;
using System.Data.SqlClient;
using System.Data.SqlTypes;
using Microsoft.SqlServer.Server;
using Microsoft.SqlServer.Types;
using System.Collections.Generic;
using System.Xml; // Used to manipulate XML response
using System.Net; // Used to make HTTP Request
using System.IO; // Used to read stream of data

namespace ProSpatial.Ch6
{
  public partial class UserDefinedFunctions
  {
```

```csharp
public static XmlDocument Geocode(
  string countryRegion,
  string adminDistrict,
  string locality,
  string postalCode,
  string addressLine
)
{
  // Variable to hold the geocode response
  XmlDocument xmlResponse = new XmlDocument();

  // Bing Maps key used to access the Locations API service
  string key = "ENTERYOURBINGMAPSKEY";

  // URI template for making a geocode request
  string urltemplate = "http://dev.virtualearth.net/REST/v1/Locations?countryRegion={0}
     &adminDistrict={1}&locality={2}&postalCode={3}&addressLine={4}&key={5}&output=xml";

  // Insert the supplied parameters into the URL template
  string url = string.Format(urltemplate, countryRegion, adminDistrict, locality,
                             postalCode, addressLine, key);

  // Attempt to geocode the provided address
  try {

    // Initialise web request
    HttpWebRequest webrequest = null;
    HttpWebResponse webresponse = null;
    Stream stream = null;
    StreamReader streamReader = null;

    // Make request to the Locations API REST service
    webrequest = (HttpWebRequest)WebRequest.Create(url);
    webrequest.Method = "GET";
    webrequest.ContentLength = 0;

    // Retrieve the response
    webresponse = (HttpWebResponse)webrequest.GetResponse();
    stream = webresponse.GetResponseStream();
    streamReader = new StreamReader(stream);
    xmlResponse.LoadXml(streamReader.ReadToEnd());

    // Clean up
    webresponse.Close();
    stream.Dispose();
    streamReader.Dispose();
  }
  catch(Exception ex)
  {
    // Exception handling code here;
  }

  // Return an XMLDocument with the geocoded results
  return xmlResponse;
```

```
      }
    }
  }
```

This code is pretty self-explanatory; It defines a single method, Geocode(), which accepts five string parameters, representing the different elements of the address to be geocoded. The Geocode() method constructs a URL template for the Locations API service including placeholders for each of the address elements, and inserts the supplied values in the appropriate places. An HttpWebRequest is used to call the service, and the response is read into an XmlDocument, which is then returned by the method.

Creating a Geocoding UDF Wrapper

You might have noticed that there's nothing in the preceding code listing that makes it specific to SQL Server; it's a regular C# method that accepts a number of string parameters (not SqlString parameters) representing the elements of an address. It returns an XMLDocument containing the response from the Bing Maps Locations API service, again, not anything unusual.

The reason for creating the code in this manner is to highlight an important fact about working with spatial functionality in .NET (and, in fact, SQLCLR procedures in general); wherever possible you should try to encapsulate your code and make it platform-independent rather than tying it to a particular tier. The geocoding function illustrated previously can be reused in a number of layers of the application architecture—in a SQL Server database, in an ASP.Net website, or in a client application, for example—with only a minimal amount of additional coding required. In fact, within this chapter I demonstrate the flexibility of this approach by creating two different functions that expose the geocoded result to SQL Server in different ways.

Before we can actually use this function in SQL Server, we therefore need to create an additional "wrapper" method around this base geocoding function. The wrapper will accept the address parameters in SQL Server's own SqlString format, pass these to the geocoder method, and construct and return a geography Point instance from the XML response returned. To keep this example simple, our wrapper function will return a single scalar value, representing the first matched location returned by the geocode service. (If no matching address can be found then an empty Point is returned.) Here's the code, which you should add in to the existing UserDefinedFunctions class in the Geocoder.cs file:

```
// Declare a UDF wrapper method
[Microsoft.SqlServer.Server.SqlFunction(DataAccess = DataAccessKind.Read)]
public static SqlGeography GeocodeUDF(
  SqlString addressLine,
  SqlString locality,
  SqlString adminDistrict,
  SqlString postalCode,
  SqlString countryRegion
  )
{
  // Document to hold the XML geocoded location
  XmlDocument geocodeResponse = new XmlDocument();

  // Attempt to geocode the requested address
  try
  {
    geocodeResponse = Geocode(
      (string)countryRegion,
      (string)adminDistrict,
      (string)locality,
      (string)postalCode,
```

```
        (string)addressLine
      );
    }
    // Failed to geocode the address
    catch (Exception ex)
    {
      SqlContext.Pipe.Send(ex.Message.ToString());
    }

    // Specify the XML namespaces
    XmlNamespaceManager nsmgr = new XmlNamespaceManager(geocodeResponse.NameTable);
    nsmgr.AddNamespace("ab","http://schemas.microsoft.com/search/local/ws/rest/v1");

    // Check that we received a valid response from the Bing Maps geocoding server
    if (geocodeResponse.GetElementsByTagName("StatusCode")[0].InnerText != "200")
    {
      throw new Exception("Didn't get correct response from geocoding server");
    }

    // Retrieve the list of geocoded locations
    XmlNodeList Locations = geocodeResponse.GetElementsByTagName("Location");

    // Create a geography Point instance of the first matching location
    double Latitude = double.Parse(Locations[0]["Point"]["Latitude"].InnerText);
    double Longitude = double.Parse(Locations[0]["Point"]["Longitude"].InnerText);
    SqlGeography Point = SqlGeography.Point(Latitude, Longitude, 4326);

    // Return the Point to SQL Server
    return Point;
}
```

Compiling the Assembly

Having added the necessary methods, you can now compile the assembly by selecting Build ➤ Build Solution, or press Ctrl+Shift+B. You should see the following message appear in the output window (if you cannot see the output window, select it from the View menu or press Ctrl+Alt+O).

```
------ Build started: Project: ProSpatialCh6, Configuration: Release Any CPU ------
ProSpatialCh6 -> C:\Spatial\ProSpatialCh6.dll
========== Build: 1 succeeded or up-to-date, 0 failed, 0 skipped ==========
```

That's all that is required from Visual Studio, so you can go back to SQL Server now.

Configuring the Database

Before we can use the geocoding function, we need to make a few configuration changes to the SQL Server Database Engine to allow it to use the assembly correctly.

Enabling CLR Support

We know that SQL Server runs the .NET CLR process; that's how the geometry and geography datatypes work. However, although the system-defined CLR datatypes require no additional CLR configuration, you cannot normally import and run *user*-defined CLR functions in SQL Server because this feature is disabled by default. This is a deliberate safety mechanism to ensure that a database administrator has allowed the use of these powerful (although potentially dangerous) features. In order to use the custom .NET geocoding function, you first need to configure the database to enable CLR support. You can do this by running the following T-SQL code.

```
EXEC sp_configure 'clr enabled', '1';
GO
```

If the configuration change is successful, you should receive the following message.

```
Configuration option 'clr enabled' changed from 0 to 1.

Run the RECONFIGURE statement to install.
```

To complete the change, we need to reconfigure the server to reflect the changed value, by issuing a T-SQL query with the RECONFIGURE statement as follows.

```
RECONFIGURE;
GO
```

The SQL Server configuration settings will now be updated to allow you to run user-defined CLR code, and you should receive the following message.

```
Command(s) completed successfully.
```

Setting Security Permissions

Because we will be using our .NET managed code to access information from a web service, we also need to set the appropriate security permissions on the database to enable access to external data. The simplest way of allowing this is to set the database to be trustworthy. This can be done by running the following T-SQL code (note that you should change the name ProSpatial to match the name of your database).

```
ALTER DATABASE ProSpatial SET TRUSTWORTHY ON;
GO
```

You should receive the following message.

```
Command(s) completed successfully.
```

The database is now configured and ready to import the geocoding assembly.

> ■ **Note** Although setting a database to be trustworthy might be the simplest way to grant access to external resources, it is not necessarily representative of security best practice in a production environment. Understanding the different security levels and permission sets for .NET assemblies within SQL Server can be complicated. If you'd like to learn more on this subject, try reading Chapter 7 of "Expert SQL Server 2008 Development" (by the author, Apress, 2009).

Importing the Assembly

Having created and compiled our .NET assembly and made the necessary configuration changes to our server, we can now import the assembly into the database. You can do this by executing the following T-SQL script.

```
CREATE ASSEMBLY ProSpatialCh6
FROM 'C:\Spatial\ProSpatialCh6.dll'
WITH PERMISSION_SET = EXTERNAL_ACCESS;
GO
```

This creates an assembly in the database called ProSpatialCh6, from the ProSpatialCh6.dll output file compiled by Visual Studio. You will need to change the file path specified from C:\Spatial\ProSpatialCh6.dll to match the build output location and assembly name that you set in Visual Studio earlier.

The PERMISSION_SET argument specifies the permission level granted to this assembly. By default, new SQL Server assemblies are marked as SAFE, which means that they can only access restricted, local resources. This is a security feature to ensure that any code cannot access external (potentially dangerous) resources to which it is not permitted access. For our geocoding function to work, we need to explicitly allow our code to access external resources, by specifying PERMISSION_SET = EXTERNAL_ACCESS.

Once the assembly has been created, it should appear in the SQL Server Management Studio Object Explorer, listed under Assemblies within the Programmability node of the database into which it was imported, as shown in Figure 6-7 (you may need to refresh the Object Explorer view before the assembly becomes visible, by right-clicking the Assemblies node and selecting Refresh).

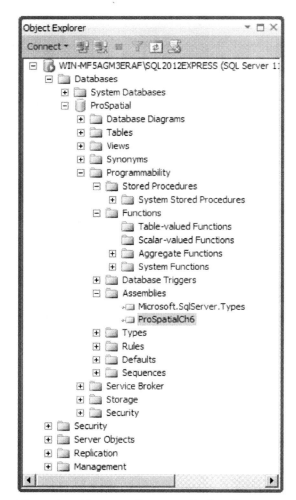

Figure 6-7. The geocoding assemby listed in SQL Server Management Studio Object Explorer

Creating the Geocode Function

Now that we have imported our assembly, we need to define a function so that we can access the geocoding method from within T-SQL code. The function will specify a number of input parameters containing different descriptive fields of an address, and return a geography Point instance representing that address, constructed from the coordinates returned from the Bing Maps geocode service.

To create the function, execute the following T-SQL code.

```
CREATE FUNCTION dbo.Geocode(
  @addressLine nvarchar(max),
  @locality nvarchar(max),
  @adminDistrict nvarchar(max),
  @postalCode nvarchar(max),
```

```
    @countryRegion nvarchar(max)
    ) RETURNS geography
AS EXTERNAL NAME
ProSpatialCh6.[ProSpatial.Ch6.UserDefinedFunctions].GeocodeUDF;
```

This code creates a T-SQL function called Geocode that provides an interface to the GeocodeUDF method contained within the ProSpatialCh6 assembly. It specifies that the parameters that must be provided when using the Geocode function are an address, the name of a city, the subdivision (i.e., county/state), the postal code (or ZIP code), and the country or region. These parameters correspond exactly to the parameters passed by the .NET method to the Locations API geocoding service. The return value of the function is a geography instance, containing a Point geometry associated with that address.

▓ **Note** When creating a function from a .NET assembly, the syntax for the AS EXTERNAL NAME clause is
AssemblyName.[Namespace.ClassName].FunctionName.

That's it! Congratulations, you've just used .NET to add a new function to SQL Server, extending the existing spatial functionality by allowing you to geocode address data.

Using the Geocode Function

Finally, we get to use our geocoding function. To test it out, let's try retrieving the latitude and longitude of a Point at the Apress head office, located at the following postal address:

Apress, Inc.
233 Spring Street
New York,
NY 10013

To retrieve the WKT representation of a Point based on the Apress office address, you can execute the following query in SQL Server Management Studio.

```
SELECT dbo.Geocode('233 Spring Street','New York','NY','10013','USA').ToString();
```

The result is as follows.

```
POINT (-74.004799 40.725906)
```

To check the accuracy of the function, we can plot this result against a road map of New York city using Bing Maps, as shown in Figure 6-8.

Figure 6-8. Plotting the geocoded address location of the Apress offices on Bing Maps

Creating a Geocoding TVF Wrapper

In the previous example, the geocoding wrapper function was created as a scalar UDF; you supply a single address, and you get a single geocoded result back. However, this approach has some limitations:

First, the Locations API service actually returns several columns of information about the matched geocoded result. As shown in the example given near the beginning of this chapter, the XML response may contain not only the coordinates of a single point at the center of the requested location, but also the bounding box describing the extent of a feature, and additional metadata about the match found. A UDF that returns only a single scalar Point value loses this additional information.

Second, geocoding is not a precise operation: frequently we may find that the source address is not completely and exactly specified, and there is some scope for ambiguity as to the exact location to which it refers. Consider the example from the beginning of this chapter, referring to the address of the White House. Suppose that we had omitted the fact that we were looking for 1600 Pennsylvania Avenue, *Washington D.C.* Knowing only the street number and name, and that this address was in the United States, we could have been referring to Pennsylvania Avenue in Baltimore, or Atlantic City, or one of two Pennsylvania Avenues in the state of West Virginia, or one of several others. In these cases, the Bing Maps Locations API could return multiple rows of results, representing each of the possible matching geocoded locations. Our current function automatically returns the first match, but it is not necessarily the correct one.

Because the result of a geocoding operation has the potential to return multiple rows and columns of data, it sounds like a suitable situation in which to use a table-valued function (TVF) that returns a table of several possible matched locations, allowing the user to choose which one they meant. Such a TVF is demonstrated in the following code listing:

```
[Microsoft.SqlServer.Server.SqlFunction(
        Name = "GeocodeTVF",
        FillRowMethodName = "GeocodeTVFFillRow",
        DataAccess = DataAccessKind.Read,
        TableDefinition = @"Name nvarchar(255),
                            Point geography,
                            BoundingBox geography")]
public static System.Collections.IEnumerable GeocodeTVF(
    SqlString addressLine,
    SqlString locality,
    SqlString adminDistrict,
    SqlString postalCode,
    SqlString countryRegion
)
{

    // Document to hold the XML geocoded location
    XmlDocument geocodeResponse = new XmlDocument();

    try
    {
        geocodeResponse = Geocode(
            (string)countryRegion,
            (string)adminDistrict,
            (string)locality,
            (string)postalCode,
            (string)addressLine
        );
    }
    // Failed to geocode the address
    catch (Exception ex)
    {
        SqlContext.Pipe.Send(ex.Message.ToString());
    }

    // Define the default XML namespace
    XmlNamespaceManager nsmgr = new XmlNamespaceManager(geocodeResponse.NameTable);
    nsmgr.AddNamespace("ab", "http://schemas.microsoft.com/search/local/ws/rest/v1");
```

```
// Create a set of all <Location>s in the response
XmlNodeList Locations = geocodeResponse.GetElementsByTagName("Location");

// Set up a list to hold results
List<object[]> items = new List<object[]>();

// Loop through each location in the response
foreach (XmlNode locationNode in Locations)
{
  // Create a new object for this result
  object[] item = new object[3];

  // Retrieve the name of this location
  string Name = locationNode["Name"].InnerText;
  item.SetValue(Name, 0);

  // Create a point for this location
  double Latitude = double.Parse(locationNode["Point"]["Latitude"].InnerText);
  double Longitude = double.Parse(locationNode["Point"]["Longitude"].InnerText);
  SqlGeography Point = SqlGeography.Point(Latitude, Longitude, 4326);
  item.SetValue(Point, 1);

  // Create a polygon for this location's bounding box
  if (locationNode.SelectSingleNode("ab:BoundingBox", nsmgr) != null)
  {
    // Retrieve the latitude/longitude extents of the box
    double BBSLatitude = double.Parse(
      locationNode.SelectSingleNode("ab:BoundingBox/ab:SouthLatitude", nsmgr).InnerText);

    double BBNLatitude = double.Parse(
      locationNode.SelectSingleNode("ab:BoundingBox/ab:NorthLatitude", nsmgr).InnerText);

    double BBWLongitude = double.Parse(
      locationNode.SelectSingleNode("ab:BoundingBox/ab:WestLongitude", nsmgr).InnerText);

    double BBELongitude = double.Parse(
      locationNode.SelectSingleNode("ab:BoundingBox/ab:EastLongitude", nsmgr).InnerText);

    // Build a geography polygon of the box
    SqlGeographyBuilder gb = new SqlGeographyBuilder();
    gb.SetSrid(4326);
    gb.BeginGeography(OpenGisGeographyType.Polygon);
    gb.BeginFigure(BBSLatitude, BBWLongitude);
    gb.AddLine(BBSLatitude, BBELongitude);
    gb.AddLine(BBNLatitude, BBELongitude);
    gb.AddLine(BBNLatitude, BBWLongitude);
    gb.AddLine(BBSLatitude, BBWLongitude);
    gb.EndFigure();
    gb.EndGeography();
    SqlGeography Polygon = gb.ConstructedGeography;
    item.SetValue(Polygon, 2);
  }

  // Add this result to the set of results
```

```
      items.Add(item);

  }

  return items;
}
public static void GeocodeTVFFillRow(
  object obj,
  out SqlString Name,
  out SqlGeography Point,
  out SqlGeography BoundingBox)
{
  object[] item = (object[])obj;
  Name = (SqlString)(item[0].ToString());
  Point = (SqlGeography)item[1];
  BoundingBox = (SqlGeography)item[2];
}
```

Note that this function still calls exactly the same underlying Geocode method as the scalar GeocodeUDF method described previously; it just handles the resulting XMLDocument in a different way, returning a table of possible results to SQL Server rather than only the first match. I haven't needed to change the actual code that calls the Bing Maps web service at all, which demonstrates the benefits of separating out your code into modular reusable units.

Having added the GeocodeTVF() method to the UserDefinedFunctions class of your geocoding project, recompile the assembly in Visual Studio by selecting Rebuild Solution from the Build menu. Then drop and re-create the ProSpatialCh6 assembly in SQL Server, and register the new function as follows:

```
CREATE FUNCTION dbo.GeocodeTVF(
  @addressLine nvarchar(255),
  @locality nvarchar(255),
  @adminDistrict nvarchar(255),
  @postalCode nvarchar(255),
  @countryRegion nvarchar(255)
  ) RETURNS table (Name nvarchar(255), Point geography, BoundingBox geography)
AS EXTERNAL NAME
  ProSpatialCh6.[ProSpatial.Ch6.UserDefinedFunctions].GeocodeTVF;
```

Table-valued functions return table result sets, so the syntax for their usage is a bit different than that used for inline UDF functions. To demonstrate, let's look at the example stated previously by looking for an address of "1600 Pennsylvania Avenue", somewhere in the United States:

```
SELECT * FROM dbo.GeocodeTVF('1600 Pennsylvania Avenue', '', '', '', 'USA');
```

The results from the table-valued function now contain not only a single result, but five matching results. What's more, we don't only have a single Point geometry associated with each matching record, but also a Polygon representing the extent of each instance:

Name	Point	BoundingBox
1600 Pennsylvania Ave, Colton, CA 92324	0xE610000…	0xE6100000010405…
1600 Pennsylvania Ave, Fairfield, CA 94533	0xE610000…	0xE6100000010405…
1600 Pennsylvania Ave, Los Angeles, CA 90033	0xE610000…	0xE6100000010405…

1600 Pennsylvania Ave, Richmond, CA 94801	0xE610000...	0xE6100000010405...
1600 Pennsylvania Ave, West Sacramento, CA 95691	0xE610000...	0xE6100000010405...

Asynchronous and Batch Geocoding

So far, we've manually called the geocoding function from a SELECT query to geocode a single address at a time. But suppose that you wanted to automatically geocode every new address record that was entered into an Addresses table, such as this simple example:

```
CREATE TABLE Addresses (
  AddressID int identity(1,1),
  Address nvarchar(255),
  Location geography
);
```

Ideally, every time a new address is inserted into the Address column of the table, we'd like the Location column to be updated with a geography Point record representing the location of that address. The logic to do this is not too hard; you could simply create an UPDATE trigger on the table, which calls the Geocode procedure and updates the corresponding value:

```
CREATE TRIGGER tgGeocodeAddress
ON Addresses
FOR INSERT, UPDATE AS
BEGIN
  SET NOCOUNT ON;
  UPDATE Addresses
  SET Location = dbo.Geocode(Address)
  WHERE AddressID IN (SELECT AddressID FROM inserted);
END;
```

However, there's a problem here: CLR UDFs in SQL Server can be slow at the best of times, but our Geocode function is going to suffer especially because it relies on waiting for a response from a network resource. Every single INSERT transaction is going to be forced to wait for that geocode function to return a result before completing, which, depending on the latency of the network, the load on the Bing Maps REST service, and other factors, could cause each INSERT transaction on the table to take a couple of seconds or more. Even on a database with only a few concurrent users issuing single row updates at a time, the potential for deadlocks, concurrency issues, and generally bringing the server to its knees is huge.

One possible solution is to employ an *asynchronous* trigger, one that will perform the geocoding task in the background and update the record in the Addresses table when the web service has returned its response. You can do this with SQL Server Service Broker by creating a procedure that listens for messages sent to a service queue. Details of addresses to be geocoded are sent to the queue and processed asynchronously, updating the corresponding record when a result is returned from the Locations API service rather than hold up the transaction waiting for a response at the point the INSERT or UPDATE operation is made. For more details on how you can set up such a queueing system using Service Broker, I recommend reading "Pro SQL Server 2008 Service Broker" (Apress, 2008).

Another point to bear in mind is that, if you are planning to geocode a lot of addresses, it would be quite inefficient to process each address one at a time through the Locations API. Instead, you can use a service that allows you to upload an entire set of address data and process it as a batch operation, downloading the geocoded data when the operation has completed. One such service is the Geocode

Dataflow API that is part of the Bing Spatial Data Services, described in more detail at
http://msdn.microsoft.com/en-us/library/ff701734.aspx.

Reverse Geocoding

So far, we've only looked at one-way geocoding, starting with an address and deriving the corresponding latitude/longitude coordinates, which enables us to create a geography Point representing that location. But what about performing the reverse operation: starting with a set of coordinates and returning a description of the closest matching point of interest?

There are several potential applications of such a function. Suppose that you had collected coordinates from a GPS system, or triangulated the location of a mobile phone call, and wanted to obtain a description of that location: in what town is this person, for example? Or to what address is this delivery vehicle closest?

The process of reverse-geocoding is illustrated in Figure 6-9.

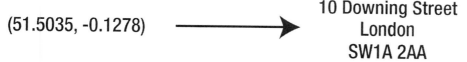

(51.5035, -0.1278) ⟶ **10 Downing Street London SW1A 2AA**

Figure 6-9. Reverse geocoding

Fortunately, the Bing Maps REST services also expose reverse-geocoding functionality. To perform a reverse-geocode, rather than providing the address to be looked up, you simply provide the (WGS84) latitude and longitude coordinates instead. The following code listing demonstrates the URL syntax required to reverse-geocode a Point located at a latitude of 47.64054 degrees and a longitude of 122.12934 west:

http://dev.virtualearth.net/REST/v1/Locations/47.64054,-122.12934?o=xml&key=YOURBINGMAPSKEY

This URL returns the following XML response

```
<Response xmlns:xsi="http://www.w3.org/2001/XMLSchema instance"
xmlns:xsd="http://www.w3.org/2001/XMLSchema"
xmlns="http://schemas.microsoft.com/search/local/ws/rest/v1">
  <Copyright>Copyright © 2010 Microsoft and its suppliers. All rights reserved. This API
cannot be accessed and the content and any results may not be used, reproduced or transmitted
in any manner without express written permission from Microsoft Corporation.</Copyright>
  <BrandLogoUri>http://dev.virtualearth.net/Branding/logo_powered_by.png</BrandLogoUri>
  <StatusCode>200</StatusCode>
  <StatusDescription>OK</StatusDescription>
  <AuthenticationResultCode>ValidCredentials</AuthenticationResultCode>
  <TraceId>fbfb8df89423415589eec14c8de7585e</TraceId>
  <ResourceSets>
    <ResourceSet>
      <EstimatedTotal>2</EstimatedTotal>
      <Resources>
        <Location>
          <Name>1 Microsoft Way, Redmond, Washington 98052, United States</Name>
          <Point>
            <Latitude>47.640568390488625</Latitude>
            <Longitude>-122.1293731033802</Longitude>
```

```
          </Point>
          <BoundingBox>
            <SouthLatitude>47.636705672917948</SouthLatitude>
            <WestLongitude>-122.137016420622</WestLongitude>
            <NorthLatitude>47.6444311080593</NorthLatitude>
            <EastLongitude>-122.1217297861384</EastLongitude>
          </BoundingBox>
          <EntityType>Address</EntityType>
          <Address>
            <AddressLine>1 Microsoft Way</AddressLine>
            <AdminDistrict>Washington</AdminDistrict>
            <AdminDistrict2>King</AdminDistrict2>
            <CountryRegion>United States</CountryRegion>
            <FormattedAddress>1 Microsoft Way, Redmond, Washington 98052, United
States</FormattedAddress>
            <Locality>Redmond</Locality>
            <PostalCode>98052</PostalCode>
          </Address>
          <Confidence>Medium</Confidence>
        </Location>
        <Location>
          <Name>1 Microsoft Way, Redmond, WA 98052 6399</Name>
          <Point>
            <Latitude>47.639747</Latitude>
            <Longitude>-122.129731</Longitude>
          </Point>
          <BoundingBox>
            <SouthLatitude>47.635884282429323</SouthLatitude>
            <WestLongitude>-122.13737419709076</WestLongitude>
            <NorthLatitude>47.643609717570676</NorthLatitude>
            <EastLongitude>-122.12208780290925</EastLongitude>
          </BoundingBox>
          <EntityType>Address</EntityType>
          <Address>
            <AddressLine>1 Microsoft Way</AddressLine>
            <AdminDistrict>WA</AdminDistrict>
            <AdminDistrict2>King County</AdminDistrict2>
            <CountryRegion>United States</CountryRegion>
            <FormattedAddress>1 Microsoft Way, Redmond, WA 98052 6399</FormattedAddress>
            <Locality>Redmond</Locality>
            <PostalCode>98052 6399</PostalCode>
          </Address>
          <Confidence>Medium</Confidence>
        </Location>
      </Resources>
    </ResourceSet>
  </ResourceSets>
</Response>
```

Because the response returned from the reverse-geocoding service follows exactly the same structure as for the geocoding service, this makes it easy to adapt the UDF and TVF functions introduced earlier this chapter to cater for reverse-geocoding if required as well.

Summary

In this chapter, you learned how to extend the functionality of SQL Server to geocode address data. Specifically, you learned the following:

- Geocoding can be used to derive a structured spatial representation of a feature on the Earth from descriptive information about that feature.

- The Bing Maps Web Services provide a method that can be used to geocode data, accessible via a REST interface over the Web.

- You can create a reusable .NET method to access the REST service, and then create one or more wrapper classes to expose geocoding functionality in SQL Server as a UDF or TVF. These methods can be called directly from T-SQL code to return geography data from a supplied address value.

- Reverse-geocoding is the opposite process to geocoding: taking a latitude/longitude coordinate pair, and deriving the corresponding street address or location. This functionality is also provided by the Bing Maps REST service, and can be incorporated into SQL Server using similar methods.

As a final note, bear in mind that, although I've demonstrated that it is possible to geocode address data directly from the database layer, it does not always make sense to do so. I've highlighted the benefits of creating modular reusable code, so that if you decide to perform geocoding in an application layer instead, you can do so using the same code base as described in this chapter.

CHAPTER 7

Precision, Validity, and Errors

Most software comes supplied with online technical documentation containing examples that describe and demonstrate all of that software's features, and SQL Server is no different. Microsoft Books Online includes a reference guide to all of the geography and geometry methods available in SQL Server 2012, including sample code listings illustrating their usage. You can view the full reference guide at http://msdn.microsoft.com/en-us/library/bb933790%28v=SQL.110%29.aspx.

It's all very well following the code samples provided by the software manufacturer, and Books Online is an excellent reference if all you want to know is the syntax required to use each method. However, many of the examples are quite artificial, demonstrating each function in isolation, using perfect, compact, fully formed datasets. In the real world, we must accept that the spatial data we are given to work with is frequently less perfect than in these idealistic examples. You'll often discover that the textbook samples start to fall down when they are applied to the gnarly ugly data that we, as developers, all face on a day-to-day basis.

In this chapter, we'll examine some of the issues that can affect the quality, accuracy, and reliability of spatial information. I'll also show you techniques to minimize or eliminate the negative effect of such issues, ultimately leading to more robust, useful spatial applications.

Precision

If you were to ask your bank manager how much money you had in your account and she replied "somewhere between $800 and $810," you'd probably be a bit concerned. We have come to expect that all data held in databases should have an exact known value. If that value can't be determined then we assume that there must be an error in the process used to gather the information or a bug in the system used to retrieve it. However, one important fact to remember is that *all* spatial data is only ever an approximation. The accuracy of that approximation depends on a number of factors:

Firstly, there are approximations and assumptions in the underlying theoretical approach used to define the data; as explained in Chapter 1, spatial data is defined relative to a geodetic model of the earth. That model provides only a rough fit around the true shape of the earth, and doesn't match it exactly. Projected coordinate systems can introduce further inaccuracies, as geodetic features must be distorted in order to be represented on a flat plane. Remember also that vector spatial data stores only simple geometric shapes, which fail to reflect the true, complex and organic shape of many features on the Earth.

Secondly, precision errors may be introduced as a result of practical limitations of the measuring systems and instruments used for collecting and recording spatial data. Location information gathered from consumer GPS devices, for example, is generally only accurate to within a few meters. More advanced scientific tools and surveying equipment have greater accuracy, but inevitably still possess a margin of error.

Finally, precision errors may be introduced as a result of the way in which spatial data is stored, retrieved, and manipulated in systems such as SQL Server, and at every subsequent stage at which data passes through layers of an application interface.

It is this last category of errors with which we are most concerned in this chapter, because these are generally the errors that we, as developers, are able to control (at least to some degree).

Storage Precision

SQL Server stores geography and geometry coordinates as binary values, adhering to the IEEE-754 standard for binary floating-point arithmetic. Based on this standard, each coordinate is represented as a double precision floating point number that is 64 bits (8 bytes) long. By storing coordinates as floating point values, SQL Server ensures that a large range of possible coordinate values can be accommodated, while requiring only a limited amount of storage.

Although SQL Server stores coordinates as binary floating point values, WKT, the format in which coordinate data is most commonly supplied, is a text-based format in which coordinates are stated in decimal format. Not all decimal numbers can be represented exactly in floating-point binary format. Whenever you use a static method to create an instance of geography or geometry data from WKT (or any other static method that accepts decimal input), the supplied coordinates are therefore implicitly converted to the closest equivalent binary floating point value. Essentially, each WKT coordinate value is CAST from nvarchar to binary(8). As with conversion of any other type of data between datatypes, this presents the possibility of truncation or rounding of the coordinate values.

The range of possible coordinate values that can be stored in an 8-byte binary value is roughly equivalent to 15 digits of decimal precision. So, for example, the x-coordinate of a geometry Point might be stored as 0x3FF3C0CA428C59F8, which corresponds to a decimal value of 1.234567890123456. Some of the geography and geometry static methods allow you to create instances from coordinate values with greater precision than this; the Point() method, for example, will accept decimal coordinate values with up to 38 digits of precision. However, those coordinates will ultimately be stored with the same fixed 64-bit binary precision, and supplying coordinates with greater precision will not lead to any greater precision of the stored geography or geometry value.

To demonstrate, consider the following code listing, which creates two geometry Point instances using the Point() static method. The y-coordinate of both instances is the same. The value of the x-coordinate differs, but only following the sixteenth decimal place:

```
DECLARE @Precise geometry;
SET @Precise = geometry::Point(10.23456789012345, 0, 0);

DECLARE @SuperPrecise geometry;
SET @SuperPrecise = geometry::Point(10.2345678901234567890123456789012345678901234567, 0, 0);

SELECT @Precise.STEquals(@SuperPrecise);
```

The additional decimal places of precision supplied for the @SuperPrecise Point cannot be represented in an 8-byte binary value. As a result, the x-coordinate values that SQL Server stores for both the @Precise and @SuperPrecise instances are exactly the same (0x3C8B514819782440). The STEquals() method, which compares whether two instances are equal, returns the value 1, which confirms that both Points are the same.

The preceding example demonstrated that supplying excess precision has no effect on the coordinate values of a geometry; they will always be stored in the database as 8-byte binary values.

Likewise, it is worth remembering that coordinates supplied with less decimal precision will still occupy a fixed 8-bytes when converted to binary and saved to the database. Thus, in the following example, even though @HighPrecision is instantiated from coordinates with greater precision than @LowPrecision, the two Points occupy exactly the same amount of space.

```
DECLARE @LowPrecision geometry;
SET @LowPrecision = geometry::STPointFromText('POINT(1 2)', 0);

DECLARE @HighPrecision geometry;
SET @HighPrecision = geometry::STPointFromText('POINT(1.23456789012345678901234567 89
2.3456789012345678)', 0);

SELECT
  DATALENGTH(@LowPrecision),
  DATALENGTH(@HighPrecision);
```

22	22

The result demonstrates that you do not create simpler geometries, or require less space to represent geometries created from less precise coordinates. Both Points in this example (and all Points created from a single coordinate pair) occupy exactly 22 bytes, as shown by the result of the DATALENGTH function.

Practical Implications of Fixed Binary Precision

What effect does the design decision to store coordinates as 8-byte binary values have on the accuracy of spatial data stored in SQL Server? The answer to this question depends on whether you are referring to the geometry or geography datatype.

geometry Precision

Firstly, let's consider the precision of coordinates defined in a planar coordinate system, stored using the geometry datatype. Suppose you were given the coordinates of a location measured in the EPSG:26913 spatial reference system. This is the spatial reference identifier corresponding to UTM Zone 13N, a projected spatial reference system based on the NAD83 datum. The unit of measurement for coordinates in this system is the meter.

Because geometry coordinates represent the distance of a point from an origin in a linear unit of measure, it is easy to see the correlation between the precision of the supplied coordinates and the accuracy of the stored position. Assuming that coordinates were supplied using the full precision capable of being represented in an 8-byte binary value, equivalent to 15 decimal places of accuracy, you can be sure that the stored location of any geometry data in SQL Server based on this SRID will be accurate to within 0.000000000000001 meters of the supplied value, in both the x- and y-axes.

geography Precision

What about the effects of fixed precision in coordinates of the geography datatype? In such cases it's less obvious what the magnitude of any error would be because, whereas geographic coordinates are expressed in angular degrees, we tend to think of the "accuracy" of a location in terms of meters away from its true position. So just how far, in terms of distance measured across the earth's surface, does 15 decimal places of one degree of latitude or longitude correspond? To answer this question, we have to consider the error in the longitude and latitude coordinates separately.

The distance on the Earth's surface represented by one degree of longitude or one degree of latitude varies depending on the corresponding latitude. This is illustrated in Figure 7-1.

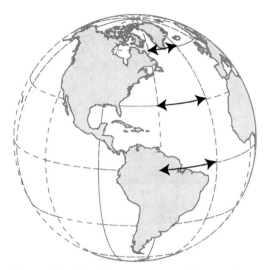

Figure 7-1. The distance covered by one degree of longitude varies with latitude

At the equator, where the distance represented by one degree of longitude is greatest, one degree of longitude corresponds to about 111.3 km. We can verify this using SQL Server's STDistance() method to measure the distance between two points on the equator separated by one degree of longitude, as follows:

```
DECLARE @EquatorA geography = geography::Point(0,0,4326);
DECLARE @EquatorB geography = geography::Point(0,1,4326);

SELECT @EquatorA.STDistance(@EquatorB);
```

The result is shown following. As the coordinate values in this case were stated using SRID 4326, this result is calculated relative to the WGS84 datum and expressed in meters:

```
111319.490735885
```

As you approach the poles, the meridian lines representing points of equally spaced longitude converge, and the distance represented by one degree of longitude decreases. At the Tropic of Cancer (the circle of latitude at which the sun appears directly overhead during the June Solstice), which lies at a latitude of approximately 23.5 degrees, the distance covered by one degree of longitude is reduced to about 102.1 km, which can be verified using the following code listing:

```
DECLARE @TropicOfCancerA geography = geography::Point(23.5,0,4326);
DECLARE @TropicOfCancerB geography = geography::Point(23.5,1,4326);

SELECT @TropicOfCancerA.STDistance(@TropicOfCancerB);
```

```
102140.828881171
```

At the Arctic circle, which lies at a latitude of approximately 66.5 degrees North, one degree of longitude covers only 44.5 km:

```
DECLARE @ArcticCircleA geography = geography::Point(66.5,0,4326);
DECLARE @ArcticCircleB geography = geography::Point(66.5,1,4326);

SELECT @ArcticCircleA.STDistance(@ArcticCircleB);
```

```
44513.5512918299
```

At the poles, one degree of longitude covers an infinitely small distance. Figure 7-2 depicts a graph illustrating the distance on the Earth's surface represented by one degree of longitude at any latitude.

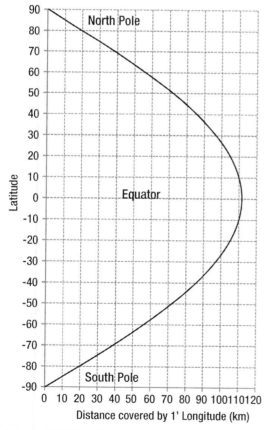

Figure 7-2. The distance on the Earth's surface covered by one degree of longitude at any latitude

Due to the oblate shape of the earth, the distance covered by one degree of latitude also varies with latitude, although the variance is much less than that of longitude. One degree of latitude at the equator corresponds to about 110.6 km whereas at the poles, where the distance is greatest, one degree of latitude corresponds to about 111.7 km.

So, assuming 15 decimal places of precision and a "worst-case" scenario in which one degree of latitude/longitude represents 111 km along the ground, coordinates of geography instances are capable of describing a location with a precision of 111 km/10E15, which still means that any supplied coordinate value can be stored with submillimeter precision, wherever it lies on the globe. It's probably safe to say that SQL Server therefore stores spatial data with sufficient accuracy for all but the most demanding of spatial applications.

Balancing Precision Against Transmission Size

As a general rule, you should always retain the maximum amount of precision possible throughout your spatial applications. When creating geometry and geography instances, for example, you should provide coordinates with the full, most precise value available from your data. As demonstrated previously, SQL Server will represent this as a 64-bit binary value, which will retain the maximum fidelity of your data.

However, when retrieving coordinate values for display purposes, or to pass to another application in decimal format, you may wish to deliberately limit the precision of those values. Unlike a fixed-width binary value, WKT strings (or any other text-based representation of decimal coordinates) vary in length depending on the number of decimal places with which coordinates are stated. There are occasions when you might deliberately want to reduce the precision of these coordinate values to reduce the size of data that needs to be transmitted between the database and other layers of your application. This is most likely to occur when sending data to an end-user UI system over a network, where extreme accuracy (e.g., at the submillimeter level) is not required, and performance gains can be made by reducing the transmission size of the data and reducing bandwidth.

Suppose that you have a web-based mapping application that plots a number of points of interest stored in SQL Server. The locations of these points are stored using the geography datatype, so each coordinate is natively stored as an 8-byte binary value. However, in order to pass this information to the web application, that data is to be represented as WKT, and exposed via a web service. To minimize bandwidth, it is decided to round the coordinate values in the WKT string to only display five decimal places of precision. The following code listing demonstrates a C# SQLCLR function to achieve this:

```
using System;
using System.Collections.Generic;
using System.IO;
using System.Text;
using Microsoft.SqlServer.Types;
using System.Data;
using System.Data.SqlTypes;
using Microsoft.SqlServer.Server;

namespace ProSQLSpatial.Ch7
{
  class RoundGeography : IGeographySink110
  {
    private readonly IGeographySink110 _target;  // the target sink
    private readonly int _precision;       // the number of fractional digits in the return
value

    public RoundGeography(int precision, IGeographySink110 target)
    {
```

```
      _target = target;
      _precision = precision;
   }

   public void SetSrid(int srid)
   {
      _target.SetSrid(srid);
   }

   public void BeginGeography(OpenGisGeographyType type)
   {
      _target.BeginGeography(type);
   }

   // Each BeginFigure call rounds the start point to the required precision.
   public void BeginFigure(double x, double y, double? z, double? m)
   {
      _target.BeginFigure(Math.Round(x, _precision), Math.Round(y, _precision), z, m);
   }

   // Each AddLine call rounds subsequent points to the required precision.
   public void AddLine(double x, double y, double? z, double? m)
   {
      _target.AddLine(Math.Round(x, _precision), Math.Round(y, _precision), z, m);
   }

   // Each AddCircularArc call rounds subsequent points to the required precision
   public void AddCircularArc(double x1, double y1, double? z1, double? m1, double x2,
                              double y2, double? z2, double? m2)
   {
      _target.AddCircularArc(Math.Round(x1, _precision), Math.Round(y1, _precision), z1, m1,
                     Math.Round(x2, _precision), Math.Round(y2, _precision), z2, m2);
   }

   public void EndFigure()
   {
      _target.EndFigure();
   }

   public void EndGeography()
   {
      _target.EndGeography();
   }
}

// Create a wrapper function
public partial class UserDefinedFunctions
{
   [Microsoft.SqlServer.Server.SqlFunction(DataAccess = DataAccessKind.Read)]
   public static SqlGeography RoundGeography(SqlGeography g, Int32 precision)
   {
      SqlGeographyBuilder constructed = new SqlGeographyBuilder();
      RoundGeography rounded = new RoundGeography(precision, constructed);
      g.Populate(rounded);
```

```
        return constructed.ConstructedGeography.MakeValid();
    }
  }
}
```

The preceding code listing makes use of an IGeographySink110 interface, which is populated with a supplied geography instance. When the first point is added to the geography instance (in the BeginFigure() method), and as each subsequent point is added (in the AddLine() or AddCircularArc() methods), the coordinate values are rounded to the specified number of decimal places. Finally, the MakeValid() method is called on the constructed geography instance to ensure that the rounded coordinate values have not caused the geometry to degenerate, and the resulting value is returned to the caller.

You can compile this method in an assembly and import it into SQL Server, then register a corresponding function as follows:

```
CREATE FUNCTION dbo.RoundGeography (
  @g geography,
  @precision int
) RETURNS geography
AS EXTERNAL NAME
ProSpatialCh7.[ProSpatial.Ch7.UserDefinedFunctions].RoundGeography;
```

To test the effectiveness of the new RoundGeography function, we'll use it to round the coordinates of a Point representing the location of the Eiffel Tower in Paris from 16 decimal places to 5 decimal places, as follows:

```
DECLARE @EiffelTower geography = 'POINT(2.2945117950439298 48.858259942745526)';
DECLARE @RoundedEiffelTower geography = dbo.RoundGeography(@EiffelTower, 5);

SELECT
  @EiffelTower.ToString() AS WKT,
  DATALENGTH(@EiffelTower.ToString()) AS Length
UNION ALL
SELECT
  @RoundedEiffelTower.ToString() AS WKT,
  DATALENGTH(@RoundedEiffelTower.ToString()) AS Length;
```

The results are as follows:

WKT	Length
POINT (2.2945117950439298 48.858259942745526)	90
POINT (2.29451 48.85826)	48

By rounding the coordinate values to 5 decimal places, we have nearly halved the size of the the WKT string to be transferred, from 90 bytes to 48 bytes. What effect has this had on the accuracy of the data? By executing the following query, we can see that we have shifted the location of the Eiffel Tower by just 13 cm:

```
SELECT @EiffelTower.STDistance(@RoundedEiffelTower);
```

```
0.13187268312192
```

Depending on the purpose of the application, this difference of 13 cm may or may not be significant. It will be a matter of deciding on an individual case-by-case basis the appropriate tradeoff between accuracy and datasize.

■ **Note** Reducing the number of decimal places in a coordinate value will not reduce the size of spatial data stored in SQL Server, but may reduce the size of data transferred to and from the database if transmitted in text format.

Calculation Precision

In the last section, we looked at issues relating to the precision with which coordinates are supplied, stored, and retrieved from SQL Server. In practice, it is relatively unlikely that you will encounter too many precision problems here; as long as you do not have a highly specialized application that requires greater than 64-bit coordinate accuracy, you can be fairly sure that SQL Server will be able to store and retrieve it with full fidelity.

A separate, and perhaps more important issue to consider relates to the precision with which SQL Server perform calculations on coordinates. Every time you use any method that creates or modifies a geometry or geography instance, or compares the relationship between two geometries, there is the potential for coordinates to be modified slightly, and this is very important to understand, especially if you are creating any application that relies on testing for strict equality between two geometries.

To demonstrate the issue, let's look at example. Consider the following two lines:

```
DECLARE @line1 geometry = 'LINESTRING(0 13, 431 310)';
DECLARE @line2 geometry = 'LINESTRING(0 502, 651 1)';
```

You can view these lines in SSMS Spatial Results tab as follows:

```
SELECT @line1
UNION ALL SELECT @line2;
```

The result is shown in Figure 7-3.

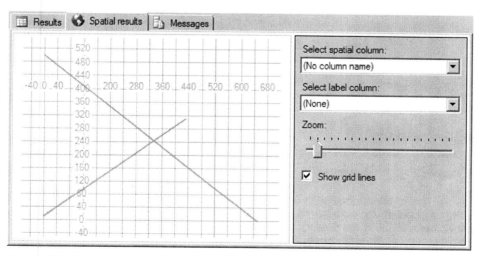

Figure 7-3. Two intersecting lines viewed in the SSMS spatial results tab

The two lines clearly cross each other, and SQL Server will calculate the point at which they intersect using the STIntersection() method:

```
SELECT
@line1.STIntersection(@line2).ToString();
```

The calculated result of the point of intersection is POINT (335.23450808497148 244.008466128158). So far, there's nothing unusual. But what about if we run the following query instead:

```
SELECT
  @line1.STIntersection(@line2).STIntersects(@line1),    --0
  @line1.STIntersection(@line2).STIntersects(@line2);    --0
```

The STIntersects() method returns 0 in both cases. When expressed in words, the result of this query suggests "The point at which line1 intersects line2 does not intersect line1 or line2." Huh?

Let's look at another example, this time involving two overlapping Polygons:

```
DECLARE @square geometry = 'POLYGON((0 0, 100 0, 100 100, 0 100, 0 0))';
DECLARE @rectangle geometry = 'POLYGON((-10 5, 10 5, 10 15, -10 15, -10 5))';

SELECT
  @rectangle.STIntersects(@square),
  @rectangle.STIntersection(@square).STArea();
```

The preceding code listing creates a simple square Polygon, one hundred units high by one hundred units wide, and a smaller rectangular Polygon that overlaps it on the left-hand side. These shapes are illustrated in Figure 7-4.

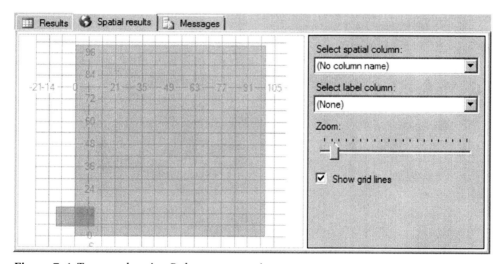

Figure 7-4. Two overlapping Polygon geometries

The region of the overlap between the two geometries is a square 10 units wide by 10 units high, exactly 100 units in area. However, the result returned by the STArea() method when used to calculate the area created by the intersection in the preceding code listing is 99.999999999995.

The numbers involved in this example are hardly complex, so you would probably expect the result to be exactly 100, right? What's interesting is that, if we increase the size of the large square by extending it further along the *x*- and *y*-axes without changing the region of overlap with the smaller rectangle, the calculated area of intersection between the two geometries becomes less and less precise. The following code listing demonstrates the calculated area of intersection between the rectangle and increasing-sized square Polygons which it overlaps (the true area of overlap maintained consistently at 100 units):

```
DECLARE @rectangle geometry = 'POLYGON((-10 5, 10 5, 10 15, -10 15, -10 5))';

DECLARE @square geometry = 'POLYGON((0 0, 1000 0, 1000 1000, 0 1000, 0 0))';
SELECT @rectangle.STIntersection(@square).STArea();
-- 99.9999999999713

DECLARE @square2 geometry = 'POLYGON((0 0, 100000 0, 100000 100000, 0 100000, 0 0))';
SELECT @rectangle.STIntersection(@square2).STArea();
-- 99.9999999962893

DECLARE @square3 geometry = 'POLYGON((0 0, 1e9 0, 1e9 1e9, 0 1e9, 0 0))';
SELECT @rectangle.STIntersection(@square3).STArea();
-- 99.9999690055833

DECLARE @square4 geometry = 'POLYGON((0 0, 1e12 0, 1e12 1e12, 0 1e12, 0 0))';
SELECT @rectangle.STIntersection(@square4).STArea();
-- 99.9691756255925

DECLARE @square5 geometry = 'POLYGON((0 0, 1e15 0, 1e15 1e15, 0 1e15, 0 0))';
SELECT @rectangle.STIntersection(@square5).STArea();
-- 67.03125
```

■ **Note** Because WKT is a parsed text format, you can state coordinates using scientific notation. In the preceding code listing, the coordinate value 1e9 is equal to 1,000,000,000.

So what's going on here? It's not the rounding issues caused by conversion from binary to decimal; as explained earlier, that only occurs when a new geometry is instantiated from, or retrieved as, WKT. It is, however, another kind of internal coordinate conversion. Although SQL Server stores coordinates as floating point binary values, it performs spatial calculations using integer arithmetic. Floating point coordinates are, by the very nature of any floating point system, approximate, and floating point arithmetic is not "robust;" calculating the difference between two similar floating point values, for example, can create results containing errors with large orders of magnitude. Integer arithmetic, in contrast, is always exact and reliable, whatever the integer values supplied.

Therefore, in order to perform spatial calculations in a robust fashion, SQL Server first snaps all coordinates to an integer grid. Note that coordinate values are not simply converted to the closest integer value (which would lose any fractional precision), but they are scaled to an integer value on a dynamically sized grid. This can be tricky to visualize, but I find a helpful analogy is to think back to mathematics lessons at school, in the days before MS Excel, when you had to draw graphs by hand on a piece of graph paper. The skill in drawing such graphs was to choose an appropriate scale, deciding how many units each cell on the grid should represent. The ideal scale is one in which all the data values can be plotted exactly on a grid cell boundary, but subject to the fact that you had to get the whole range of data to fit on a fixed size piece of paper.

SQL Server takes a similar approach; every spatial calculation takes place on an integer grid of fixed size, equivalent to the fixed size sheet of graph paper. The geometries involved in the calculation are scaled to fit onto this grid, which is equivalent to adjusting the size of the bars for a bar chart drawn on graph paper, say. Having achieved the optimum scaling possible considering the overall fixed grid size, each coordinate is then snapped to the closest cell on the grid. Some results will lie exactly on a grid cell boundary, in which case the results returned by SQL Server will be exact but, in other cases, the result will be subject to some error. Finally, the result of the integer calculation is then converted back into floating-point coordinates again, in the same scale as originally supplied.

The amount of error introduced in this process is determined by two main factors:

- The overall size of the grid on which calculations are performed.
- The extent of the geometries involved in a given calculation.

With regard to the first of these factors, all spatial calculations in SQL Server 2012 are performed on integer values with 42 bits of precision. This 42-bit precision is used across all SQL Server 2012 and SQL Azure instances, and represents a considerable increase in precision compared to the 27-bit integer grid used by SQL Server 2008/R2.

As for the second factor, the greater the range of coordinate values that must be covered by the integer grid, then the more coarse the grid resolution must become in order to accommodate the full set of data. As each cell becomes larger and the distance between cells increases, there is a greater distance that coordinates might potentially be snapped. This explains the effect demonstrated in the preceding code listing, in which the area of intersection between the square and rectangular Polygon became less and less precise as the overall size of the square became larger and larger, because the integer grid had to become ever more coarse to accommodate it, leading to less accurate results.

■ **Caution** Because SQL Server 2012 performs calculations using a more precise, 42-bit, integer grid than that used in SQL Server 2008/R2, the results of any spatial computations may differ from those obtained under a different version of the database server. This is especially important to consider when upgrading a database from a previous version, because executing a spatial query in SQL Server 2012 may lead to different results than those previously obtained from running exactly the same query under SQL Server 2008/R2.

Precision and Equality

The 42-bit integer grid is pretty high accuracy and it will only lead to fractional shifts in coordinates that are very unlikely to have any significant impact on all but very large, very detailed geometries. The preceding example deliberately used an exaggerated square geometry 1 quadrillion units (1e15) in height and width in order to emphasize the effect caused.

However, it does raise an important point: even if the coordinates have not shifted *much*, performing almost any type of operation can cause the coordinate values of an instance to shift *a little*. This means you must be incredibly careful with any operations that require you to test whether two instances are exactly equal (as in the STEquals() method). If one or both instances have been involved in a calculation requiring them to be snapped to the integer grid and back, their coordinates may have changed fractionally.

It is therefore best never to test for exact equality between two geometries, but to test whether two instances are "equal" within a certain acceptable tolerance. The method for determining an acceptable tolerance may differ depending on the geometry types being compared, and on the particular application in question. For example, to compare whether two LineStrings are "equal," you might check that the start points and end points lie within a certain distance of each other, that the length of each LineString is roughly the same, and that the path of one LineString never deviates by more than a certain amount from the path of the other. These checks can be incorporated in a function as follows:

```
CREATE FUNCTION CompareLineStrings (@l1 geometry, @l2 geometry)
RETURNS bit AS
BEGIN

-- Only test LineString geometries
IF NOT (@l1.STGeometryType() = 'LINESTRING' AND @l2.STGeometryType() = 'LINESTRING')
RETURN NULL

-- Startpoints differ by more than 1 unit
IF @l1.STStartPoint().STDistance(@l2.STStartPoint()) > 1
RETURN 0

-- Endpoints differ by more than 1 unit
IF @l1.STEndPoint().STDistance(@l2.STEndPoint()) > 1
RETURN 0

-- Length differs by more than 5%
IF ABS(@l1.STLength() - @l2.STLength() / @l1.STLength()) > 0.05
RETURN 0

-- Any part of l2 lies more than 0.1 units from l1
IF @l1.STBuffer(0.1).STDifference(@l2).STEquals('GEOMETRYCOLLECTION EMPTY') = 0
RETURN 0

-- All tests pass, so return success
RETURN 1
END
```

This function compares different aspects of similarity between two LineString geometries. If any of the tests fail then the function returns 0, otherwise the function returns 1.

An alternative method of comparing whether two geometries are equal is to use the STEquals() method but, rather than directly compare whether the points in two geometries are the same, use it in conjunction with the RoundGeography() method introduced earlier this chapter to compare whether the sets of coordinates are the same after having been rounded to a certain number of decimal places. Clearly, the fewer the number of decimal places to which values are rounded, the greater is the tolerance within which the instances will be considered equal.

Validity

Whenever you create a new geometry or geography instance from a static method, such as STGeomFromText(), SQL Server performs a number of checks on the created geometry. Examples of some of these checks are as follows:

- A LineString must have at least two distinct points.

- A Polygon must contain at least four points, and the start point and end point must be the same.

- The spatial reference system in which the coordinates of any geography instance are defined must correspond to one of the supported spatial reference systems in the sys.spatial_reference_systems table.

If any of these checks fail, SQL Server will throw an exception. Generally speaking, each rule has its own exception number and corresponding exception message. Some examples of specific error messages are demonstrated in the following code listings. Firstly, attempting to create a geometry LineString containing only one point:

```
DECLARE @LineMustHave2Points geometry;
SET @LineMustHave2Points = geometry::STLineFromText('LINESTRING(3 2)', 0);
```

```
System.FormatException: 24117: The LineString input is not valid because it does not have
enough distinct points. A LineString must have at least two distinct points.
```

The next code listing demonstrates a Polygon that only contains three points in its exterior ring:

```
DECLARE @PolygonMustHave4Points geometry;
SET @PolygonMustHave4Points = geometry::STPolyFromText('POLYGON((0 0, 10 2, 0 0))', 0);
```

```
System.FormatException: 24305: The Polygon input is not valid because the ring does not have
 enough distinct points. Each ring of a polygon must contain at least three distinct points.
```

And the following example attempts to create a Point from well-formed WKT, but using an invalid spatial reference identifier:

```
DECLARE @UnsupportedSRID geography;
SET @UnsupportedSRID = geography::STPointFromText('POINT(52 0)', 123);
```

```
System.FormatException: 24204: The spatial reference identifier (SRID) is not valid. The
specified SRID must match one of the supported SRIDs displayed in the
sys.spatial_reference_systems catalog view.
```

Each of the preceding examples generates an exception message, and the requested geometry is not created. Fortunately, the exception messages state pretty clearly what the problem is, so finding and fixing these errors is relatively easy.

However, even if you were to address these errors so that the static method executes successfully, it does not necessarily mean that the resulting geometry is valid. In other words, it is possible to create some geometries that do not cause any exceptions to be thrown, but which do not meet the OGC requirements for that type of geometry. For example, the following code listing creates a geometry Polygon in which the interior rings crosses the exterior ring. This code listing can be executed and will successfully create a geometry instance with no exception occurring:

```
DECLARE @SelfIntersectingPolygon geometry;
SET @SelfIntersectingPolygon = 'POLYGON((0 0, 6 0, 3 5, 0 0), (2 2, 8 2, 8 4, 2 4, 2 2))';
```

Another example of an invalid geometry is a LineString that retraces itself, defining certain segments of the LineString twice, as shown in the following code listing:

```
DECLARE @InvalidLinestring geometry;
SET @InvalidLinestring = 'LINESTRING(0 0, 10 0, 5 0)';
```

Once again, this geometry can be created and stored in SQL Server, even though it is not valid. However, although it is possible to define, store, and retrieve invalid geometries without receiving any exception messages, you will receive an exception if you attempt to use them in any spatial queries. For example, if you were to try to determine the area of the preceding Polygon using the STArea() method:

```
@SelfIntersectingPolygon.STArea();
```

you would get the following result:

```
System.ArgumentException: 24144: This operation cannot be completed because the instance is
not valid. Use MakeValid to convert the instance to a valid instance. Note that MakeValid
may cause the points of a geometry instance to shift slightly.
```

As the message contained within the exception suggests, in order to perform any operations on an invalid geometry, you must first make it valid.

Testing Whether a Geometry Is Valid

The first step in dealing with invalid geometry data is to identify those geometries that are invalid. To do so, you can use the STIsValid() method. The STIsValid() method tests whether a geometry or geography instance meets all the criteria required to ensure that instance is valid, based on the OGC definition of the type of geometry in question.

The STIsValid() method requires no parameters, and can be called as follows:

```
Instance.STIsValid()
```

If the instance is valid, this method returns a bit value of 1 and, if the instance is invalid, it returns 0. To demonstrate the STIsValid() method, consider the following example code:

```
DECLARE @Spike geometry
SET @Spike = geometry::STPolyFromText('POLYGON((0 0,1 1,2 2,0 0))', 0)
SELECT
  @Spike.STAsText(),
  @Spike.STIsValid().
```

```
POLYGON ((0 0, 1 1, 2 2, 0 0))  0
```

In this case, although SQL Server lets us create the Polygon geometry without exception, it is not valid according to the OGC specifications because the exterior ring consists of a single spike. Because the exterior ring intersects itself it is not simple, which is one of the requirements of the Polygon geometry.

Invalid geometries can only be created by supplying an invalid representation to a static method; all geometry instances returned by SQL Server's instance methods (such as the result of the STUnion(), STIntersection(), or STBuffer() methods) will always be valid. There is therefore no need to call STIsValid() on the results of any of these methods.

▦ **Note** All geometries returned as the result of a SQL Server method on an existing instance will be valid.

Finding Out Why a Geometry Is Invalid

Having identified that a geometry is invalid, the next logical step is to determine the cause of its invalidity. In a simple example such as in the preceding code listing, it is relatively easy to glance at the Well-Known Text and see the cause of the problem. However, this is not the case when dealing with invalid geometries constructed from thousands of points, represented in binary format or imported programmatically! This was a real headache in SQL Server 2008, when data imported from external sources (such as U.S. census TIGER data) would frequently be declared as "invalid," with no further information provided as to the cause.

Fortunately, SQL Server 2012 introduces a new method specifically intended to help diagnose problems with invalid geometries, IsValidDetailed(). Rather than simply returning a bit value representing if a geometry is valid or not, the IsValidDetailed() method returns a code and text description of the cause of any invalidity of a geometry, as demonstrated in the following code listing:

```
DECLARE @g geometry = 'LINESTRING(0 0, 5 10, 8 2)';
DECLARE @h geometry = 'LINESTRING(0 0, 10 0, 5 0)';
DECLARE @i geometry = 'POLYGON((0 0, 2 0, 2 2, 0 2, 0 0), (1 0, 3 0, 3 1, 1 1, 1 0))';

SELECT
  @g.STIsValid() AS STIsValid, @g.IsValidDetailed() AS IsValidDetailed
UNION ALL SELECT
  @h.STIsValid(), @h.IsValidDetailed()
UNION ALL SELECT
  @h.STIsValid(), @i.IsValidDetailed();
```

The results are as follows:

STIsValid	IsValidDetailed
1	24400: Valid
0	24413: Not valid because of two overlapping edges in curve (1).
0	24404: Not valid because polygon ring (2) intersects itself or some other ring.

Based on the output of IsValidDetailed(), you can then investigate further the particular problem identified with the geometry. For a full list of possible problems identified by IsValidDetailed(), please refer to the appendix.

A final point worth noting is that STIsValid() and IsValidDetailed() check only that a geometry is well-formed according to OGC definitions. They do not necessarily ensure that a geometry makes logical sense. In the following code listing, the STIsValid() method confirms that the Point geometry is valid, even though the coordinates lie outside the bounds of the area of use of the specified spatial reference system (the minimum x,y bounds of EPSG:27700 are at 0,0):

```
DECLARE @g geometry;
SET @g = geometry::STGeomFromText('POINT(-300412 -200123)', 27700);
SELECT @g.STIsValid();
```

Making an Object Valid

Having used STIsValid() to identify those geometries that are invalid, we can now set about making them valid. SQL Server 2012 comes with a dedicated method, MakeValid(), designed to "fix" invalid geometry or geography data. The MakeValid() method can be used on any type of geometry, and will return a valid geometry based on the set of points specified. However, in order to do so, the resulting geometry may be of a different type than that originally supplied, and the coordinate values of that geometry may also have shifted fractionally.

To understand how MakeValid() works, let's examine its output when called on the invalid geometries discussed in the previous section. Firstly, let's consider the case of the self-intersecting LineString:

```
DECLARE @InvalidLinestring geometry;
SET @InvalidLinestring = 'LINESTRING(0 0, 10 0, 5 0)';
SELECT @InvalidLinestring.MakeValid().ToString()
```

In this example, the reason for the invalidity is that the final coordinate (5,0) causes the path of the LineString to retrace itself. The valid geometry returned by the MakeValid() method therefore simply omits this line segment, as follows:

```
LINESTRING(0 0, 10 0)
```

Note that the result is still a LineString, and still represents exactly the same set of points, although the end point of the LineString is now different. Now let's consider the example of the Polygon consisting of a single spike.

```
DECLARE @Spike geometry = 'POLYGON((0 0,1 1,2 2,0 0))';
SELECT @Spike.MakeValid().ToString()
```

In this case, the appropriate geometry type to represent the three distinct points in the supplied WKT is not a Polygon as originally stated, but a LineString. The result of the MakeValid() method in this case is therefore a valid LineString, as follows:

```
LINESTRING (2 2, 1 1, 0 0)
```

■ **Caution** Note that in some cases (as demonstrated here), the MakeValid() method may return a different type of geometry than that originally supplied.

Finally, let's consider the case of the Polygon in which the interior ring crossed over the exterior ring:

```
DECLARE @SelfIntersectingPolygon geometry;
SET @SelfIntersectingPolygon = 'POLYGON((0 0, 6 0, 3 5, 0 0), (2 2, 8
2, 8 4, 2 4, 2 2))';
SELECT @SelfIntersectingPolygon.MakeValid().ToString();
```

In this example, the ambiguous areas of space defined by the rings of the original supplied Polygon have been divided into four separate Polygons, contained within a MultiPolygon collection. The segments of interior ring that lay outside the original exterior ring have been treated as defining new Polygons, as shown in Figure 7-5.

```
MULTIPOLYGON (
((2.4000000000000004 4, 3.6 4, 3 5, 2.4 4, 2.4000000000000004 4)),
((2 3.3333333333333335, 2.4 4, 2 4, 2 3.3333333333333335)),
((4.8 2, 8 2, 8 4, 3.6000000000000005 4, 4.8 2)),
((0 0, 6 0, 4.8 2, 2 2, 2 3.3333333333333335, 0 0))
)
```

Notice also that the result of this example demonstrates how precision issues can arise as a result of any spatial operations in SQL Server, including the result of the MakeValid() operation (the very first coordinate, if calculated using decimal arithmetic, would be 2.4 exactly, not 2.4000000000000004).

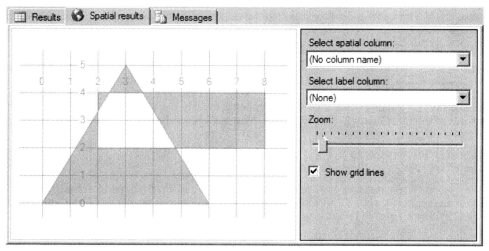

Figure 7-5. A MultiPolygon created as a result of calling MakeValid() on an invalid Polygon in which the interior ring intersects the exterior ring.

If called on a existing valid instance, MakeValid() has no effect. Therefore it is a very useful method that can be safely called to ensure geography or geometry data is valid before passing it on for further calculations.

INVALID GEOMETRY, OR THE WRONG SORT OF GEOMETRY?

Issues of invalid data generally only occur when you are creating geometry or geography from raw data imported into SQL Server 2012, or created programmatically through one of the builder classes. SQL Server will never return invalid geometries from one of its instance methods, so once you've got a set of clean valid data in your database, you can generally use it without too many worries as to issues of invalidity.

Sometimes, problems apparently caused by the requirement of validity are actually due to the fact that the wrong geometry type has been selected to represent an item of data. The most common example of this I see is when people use LineString geometries to represent routes using data gathered from GPS devices. The problem in such cases is that, as discussed previously, if any segment of a LineString geometry retraces itself, the LineString will be considered invalid.

Considering that the GPS data is recorded as a set of distinct readings at separate intervals in time, the most appropriate geometry to use in such a case is arguably a MultiPoint rather than a LineString (because there is no evidence to suggest that the vehicle actually followed the straight line route between each point in the log as indicated by the linear interpolation of a LineString geometry). The M-coordinate of each Point in the MultiPoint can be used to store the order in which those points were recorded. Alternatively, a route that retraces itself may have to be represented as a number of distinct LineString elements in a MultiLineString collection.

Handling Errors

The geometry and geography datatypes are CLR datatypes, so spatial operatons are executed within the SQLCLR environment, the .NET Framework Common Language Runtime process hosted by SQL Server. The .NET Framework provides its own exception-handling mechanism, which is quite separate from the mechanism used to deal with T-SQL exceptions typically encountered in SQL Server. So, how do the two systems interact when an exception occurs when dealing with geography or geometry data?

SQL Server automatically wraps an exception handler around any SQLCLR managed code executed from within SQL Server. This includes any user-defined CLR procedures or functions as well as the system-defined CLR methods used by the geography and geometry datatypes. The purpose of the wrapper is that, if any managed code throws an exception, it is caught by the wrapper, which then generates an error, rather than allowing the exception to bubble up further through the system. The error message created by the wrapper contains details of the SQLCLR exception, together with a stack trace of the point at which it occurred.

Dissecting a SQLCLR Exception

To understand the way in which SQLCLR errors are handled, let's look at an example by revisiting one of the code listings from the previous section:

```
DECLARE @LineMustHave2Points geometry;
SET @LineMustHave2Points = geometry::STLineFromText('LINESTRING(3 2)', 0);
```

This code listing raises an exception because the supplied WKT specifies a LineString containing only one point. Executing this code listing in SQL Server Management Studio produces the following message:

```
Msg 6522, Level 16, State 1, Line 2
A .NET Framework error occurred during execution of user-defined routine or aggregate
"geometry":
System.FormatException: 24117: The LineString input is not valid because it does not have
enough distinct points.
A LineString must have at least two distinct points.
System.FormatException:
   at Microsoft.SqlServer.Types.Validator.Execute(Transition transition)
   at Microsoft.SqlServer.Types.ForwardingGeoDataSink.EndFigure()
   at Microsoft.SqlServer.Types.OpenGisWktReader.ParseLineStringText()
   at Microsoft.SqlServer.Types.OpenGisWktReader.ParseTaggedText(OpenGisType type)
   at Microsoft.SqlServer.Types.OpenGisWktReader.Read(OpenGisType type, Int32 srid)
   at Microsoft.SqlServer.Types.SqlGeometry.GeometryFromText(OpenGisType type, SqlChars
text, Int32 srid)
```

There are several components to this error message, so let's dissect it into its separate elements, starting with the first line: Msg 6522, Level 16, State 1, Line 2. This line actually contains four pieces of information:

- The value immediately following Msg tells us the error number that has occurred; in this case, it is error number 6522.

- The Level tag informs us that the error in this case has been classified as a level 16 error. Every error in SQL Server is assigned a level in the range between 1 and 25, and this value can be used as an approximate indication of the severity of the error. A level 16 error falls into the category of "errors that can be corrected by the user," as described in Microsoft documentation. The majority of exceptions thrown by SQL Server are in this category, including constraint violations, parsing and compilation errors, and many other runtime exceptions.

- Each exception also has a State, which contains information about the exception that is used internally by SQL Server. This error has a State of 1, but because the values that SQL Server uses for this tag are not documented, this information is not very helpful!

- Line 2 informs us that the error occurred in the second line of the submitted batch of code, in the attempt to instantiate the geometry LineString.

The second line of the message contains the description of the error that has occurred. In this case, it informs us that A .NET Framework error occurred during execution of user-defined routine or aggregate. The important thing to note here is that this message, and the preceding error number, level, and state, relate to the generic error raised by SQL Server whenever any unhandled exception occurs within SQLCLR. This is exactly the same error as would be raised if an error were encountered in any user-defined CLR procedure, or when using the hierarchyid datatype (another system-deifned CLR datatype), for example.

It is only following the generic error description that we get on to the specific details of the SQLCLR exception that caused this error to be raised in this case. The next line of the error message reports that an exception (of type System.FormatException) 24117 was encountered, and we get an unusually verbose and helpful description of the particular error that occurred: The LineString input is not valid because it does not have enough distinct points. A LineString must have at least two distinct points.

Following the error message is the stack trace, which reveals where the error occurred in execution; in this case the exception originally occurred within the Execute() method of the Validator class, which had been called from the SqlGeometry GeometryFromText() method.

Let's now compare this to the message received from another one of the other earlier examples, which occurs when trying to use an unsupported SRID for the geography datatype:

```
DECLARE @UnsupportedSRID geography;
SET @UnsupportedSRID = geography::STPointFromText('POINT(52 0)', 123);
```

The message received is as follows:

```
Msg 6522, Level 16, State 1, Line 2
A .NET Framework error occurred during execution of user-defined routine or aggregate
"geography":
System.FormatException: 24204: The spatial reference identifier (SRID) is not valid. The
 specified SRID must match one of the supported SRIDs displayed in the
sys.spatial_reference_systems catalog view.
System.FormatException:
    at Microsoft.SqlServer.Types.GeographyValidator.ValidateSrid(Int32 srid)
    at Microsoft.SqlServer.Types.ForwardingGeoDataSink.SetSrid(Int32 srid)
    at Microsoft.SqlServer.Types.CoordinateReversingGeoDataSink.SetSrid(Int32 srid)
    at Microsoft.SqlServer.Types.OpenGisWktReader.Read(OpenGisType type, Int32 srid)
    at Microsoft.SqlServer.Types.SqlGeography.GeographyFromText(OpenGisType type, SqlChars
taggedText, Int32 srid)
```

Notice that the error number, level, and state, together with the initial part of the error message are identical to that received previously, even though the cause of the error in this case was completely different. It is only by examining the error message in full that we get to see the underlying CLR exception that caused the error to be triggered (in this case, System.FormatException 24204).

Error-Handling Mechanisms

Generally speaking, it is best to deal with any exceptions in code at the lowest level possible. In the case of user-defined CLR functions, this means adding code to handle the exception within the CLR function itself, in which case it never needs to be caught at the T-SQL level. However, this is not an option for system-defined CLR types; there is no way to add exception-handling code to the sealed Microsoft.SqlServer.Types.dll library, so any exceptions will inevitably bubble up and trigger the error handler in the SQLCLR wrapper demonstrated in the previous section.

How, then, should you create specific code paths to handle such exceptions? The general approach to error-handling in T-SQL (and in many other programming languages) is to use a TRY/CATCH construct, containing two blocks of code. The try block contains exception-prone code that is to be "tried." The second block of code, called the catch block, contains code that should be called in the event that the code in the try block fails. As soon as any exception occurs within the try block, execution immediately jumps into the catch block, which is known as "catching" the exception. Within the catch block, different courses of action can be taken depending on the nature of the exception that occurred, which can (generally) be determined by examining the value of the ERROR_NUMBER() function as shown in the following code listing:

```
BEGIN TRY
  SELECT geometry::STPolyFromText('POLYGON((0 0, 10 2, 0 0))', 0);
END TRY
BEGIN CATCH
  IF ERROR_NUMBER() = 123
    -- Code to deal with error 123 here
    SELECT 'Error 123 occurred'
  ELSE IF ERROR_NUMBER() = 456
    -- Code to deal with error 456 here
    SELECT 'Error 456 occurred'
  ELSE
    SELECT ERROR_NUMBER() AS ErrorNumber;
END CATCH
```

The problem is that this common approach to selecting conditional code paths based on T-SQL error number won't work for the geography and geometry datatypes, because every exception occurring within managed code will lead to the same T-SQL error: generic error 6522.

In order to create different code paths according to the CLR exception that occurred, we must parse the contents of ERROR_MESSAGE() to try to identify the original CLR exception number specified in the stack trace. The exceptions generated by the system-defined CLR types have five-digit exception numbers in the range 24000 to 24999, so can be distilled from the ERROR_MESSSAGE() string using the T-SQL PATINDEX function. The following code listing demonstrates this approach:

```
BEGIN TRY
  SELECT geometry::STPolyFromText('POLYGON((0 0, 10 2, 0 0))', 0);
END TRY
BEGIN CATCH
  -- Has a SQLCLR error occurred?
  IF ERROR_NUMBER() = 6522
  BEGIN
    -- Retrieve the error message
    DECLARE @errorMsg nvarchar(max) = ERROR_MESSAGE();
```

```
      DECLARE @exc int;
      -- Distil the SQLCLR exception number from the error message
      SET @exc = SUBSTRING(@errorMsg, PATINDEX('%: 24[0-9][0-9][0-9]%', @errorMsg) + 2, 5);
      IF @exc = 24305
        -- Code to deal with exception 24305 here
        SELECT 'Exception 24305 occurred';
      ELSE IF @exc = 24000
        -- Code to deal with exception 24000 here
        SELECT 'Exception 24000 occurred';
      ELSE
        SELECT '...';
   END
END CATCH
```

With this revised code, the catch block is able to dictate different courses of action depending on the nature of the SQLCLR exception that caused the try block to fail. In this case, the misformed Polygon in the try block generates a 24305 exception, and the appropriate code to deal with this is triggered in the catch block.

As an alternative approach to error-handling, you might choose to create your own custom wrapper methods around each of the system-defined methods in SqlServer.Types.dll, which check for and handle any CLR exceptions before passing the result back to SQL Server. An example of such a wrapper placed around the geography Parse() method is shown in the following code listing:

```
[Microsoft.SqlServer.Server.SqlFunction()]
public static SqlGeography GeogTryParse(SqlString Input)
{
  SqlGeography result = new SqlGeography();
  try
  {
    result = SqlGeography.Parse(Input);
  }
  catch
  {
    // Exception Handling code here

  }
  return result;
}
```

The preceding code listing wraps a call to the SqlGeography Parse() method in a try block, which allows the possibility to include appropriate exception handling code in the corresponding catch block. To use this approach, you could register the GeogTryParse() function in SQL Server and use it in place of the built-in geography Parse() method.

Table 7-1 lists some of the common exceptions you might want to create code paths to deal with, and their corresponding exception numbers. For a full list of all exceptions, please see the appendix of this book.

Table 7-1. Spatial exception numbers and messages

Exception Number	Description
24111	The well-known text (WKT) input is not valid.
24112	The well-known text (WKT) input is empty. To input an empty instance, specify an empty instance of one of the following types: Point, LineString, Polygon, MultiPoint, MultiLineString, MultiPolygon, or GeometryCollection.
24114	The label {0} in the input well-known text (WKT) is not valid. Valid labels are POINT, LINESTRING, POLYGON, MULTIPOINT, MULTILINESTRING, MULTIPOLYGON, or GEOMETRYCOLLECTION.
24117	The LineString input is not valid because it does not have enough distinct points. A LineString must have at least two distinct points.
24118	The Polygon input is not valid because the exterior ring does not have enough points. Each ring of a polygon must contain at least three distinct points.
24119	The Polygon input is not valid because the start and end points of the exterior ring are not the same. Each ring of a polygon must have the same start and end points.
24120	The Polygon input is not valid because the interior ring number {0} does not have enough points. Each ring of a polygon must contain at least three points.
24121	The Polygon input is not valid because the start and end points of the interior ring number {0} are not the same. Each ring of a polygon must have the same start and end points.
24306	The Polygon input is not valid because the start and end points of the ring are not the same. Each ring of a polygon must have the same start and end points.

Summary

In this chapter, you learned some of the issues that can affect the quality, accuracy, and robustness of spatial data in SQL Server, and some of the methods that can be used to prevent the negative effect of such issues.

- SQL Server stores coordinates as 8-byte floating-point binary values, according to the IEEE-754 specification.

- When you create a geography or geometry instance from a static method such as STGeomFromText(), the coordinate values are converted from nvarchar to binary(8). This has the possibility for truncation or rounding of the supplied values.

- When you perform calculations involving geometries, SQL Server uses integer arithmetic based on a dynamically scaled 42-bit grid. This introduces an element of approximation into the results of any spatial methods.

- You should avoid attempting to perform tests of exact equality between any two geometries, instead testing whether they lie within a certain tolerance of each other.

- It is possible to create invalid geometries, but these can only be stored and retrieved. In order to perform other operations, they must be made valid first.

- The process of making a geometry valid may cause it to change type (e.g., from a LineString to a MultiLineString) and may also cause its coordinates to shift slightly.

- Errors encountered when using the geography and geometry datatypes will initially trigger a CLR exception. This will in turn be caught by a wrapper and lead to a T-SQL error 6522.

- Although you cannot use ERROR_NUMBER() to switch between alternative code paths for CLR exceptions, you can distill the contents of ERROR_MESSAGE() to retrieve the number of the underlying CLR exception.

CHAPTER 8

Transformation and Reprojection

SQL Server supports spatial data defined in a wide variety of spatial reference systems used across the world. When you create an individual item of geography data, you can use any one of the 392 spatial reference systems listed in the sys.spatial_reference_systems table. And if you create geometry data, you can use any spatial reference system you like; you can even define your own coordinate system that uses coordinates measured from an origin somewhere in your living room.

Coordinate values are only valid for the spatial reference system in which they were defined, and you can only compare two coordinates if they were obtained from the same coordinate system. In SQL Server, this means that when you want to perform an operation involving two items of spatial data—to work out whether they intersect, to calculate the distance between them, or to join them together, for example—both items must be of the same data type (i.e., both geography or both geometry), and both must be defined using the same SRID. If you attempt to compare geometry data with geography data you will receive an exception. If you attempt to compare two instances of the same type defined using different SRIDs you will receive a NULL result.

The constraint that every item of data must use the same spatial reference system may not present too many difficulties if you source your own spatial data; simply choose a reference system that is appropriate for your application, and ensure that all coordinates are measured and consistently recorded using that system. Unfortunately, as developers we rarely have such control over how our data is gathered, and we frequently have to accommodate data provided in a variety of different SRIDs. For example, data from the U.S. Census bureau (http://www.census.gov) is provided using geographic coordinates based on the NAD83 datum (SRID 4269), but clearinghouses and GIS departments of individual states typically use the state plane coordinate system of that state. Government agencies of some other countries, such as Great Britain and Finland, use spatial reference systems based on the national grid of those particular countries. And then, of course, there is 4326, the most commonly used SRID for global applications.

SQL Server does not include any inbuilt methods to convert data between the two spatial datatypes, or to transform coordinates between different spatial reference systems of the same datatype. However, in this chapter I'll show you how you can integrate a freely available, open source projection library, Proj.NET, into SQL Server, and use the methods of this library to transform coordinates between different spatial reference systems suitable for both the geography and geometry datatypes. By transforming data from different sources into a common, consistent spatial format, you can then use the full range of spatial methods across your whole dataset.

Datum Transformation

Every spatial reference system used to define geospatial information is based on an underlying model of the Earth: the datum. The datum describes the size and shape of the ellipsoid used to approximate the shape of the Earth and the reference points on the surface of the Earth used to realize that model.

To compare the definitions of spatial reference systems based on different datums, let's retrieve the well-known text (WKT) representation of two geographic spatial reference systems listed in SQL Server's sys.spatial_reference_systems table.

■ **Note** The Classical scholars among you may suggest that the plural of datum, referred to in the preceding sentence, is *data*. Although this may be true of the Latin term from which the word is derived, when used in the context of a geodetic datum, the correct English plural is *datums*. Fortunately, this also prevents confusion with the more common use of the word "data" with which we are familiar in SQL Server!

First, let's look at the Luxembourg 1930 spatial reference system, SRID 4181. To retrieve the well-known text for this system, execute the following query:

```
SELECT well_known_text
FROM sys.spatial_reference_systems
WHERE spatial_reference_id = 4181;
```

The results are shown following (indents added):

```
GEOGCS[
  "Luxembourg 1930",
  DATUM[
    "Luxembourg 1930",
    ELLIPSOID["International 1924", 6378388,  297]
  ],
  PRIMEM["Greenwich", 0],
  UNIT["Degree", 0.0174532925199433]
]
```

Now let's compare this to the Deutches Hauptdreiecksnetz system used in Germany, which is SRID 4314. To retrieve the well-known text for this system, execute the following query:

```
SELECT well_known_text
FROM sys.spatial_reference_systems
WHERE spatial_reference_id = 4314;
```

Again, the results have been formatted and shown as follows:

```
GEOGCS[
  "DHDN",
  DATUM[
    "Deutsches Hauptdreiecksnetz",
    ELLIPSOID["Bessel 1841", 6377397.155, 299.1528128]
  ],
  PRIMEM["Greenwich", 0],
  UNIT["Degree", 0.0174532925199433]
]
```

Examining the preceding WKT output, we can see several similarities between the two spatial reference systems; they are both geographic coordinate systems, in which coordinates are stated in angular degrees measured from the Greenwich prime meridian. However, the datum on which those coordinates are applied is different in each system. The Luxembourg 1930 datum defines a set of points relative to the International 1924 ellipsoid, which has a radius of 6,378,388 meters at the equator, and 6,356,911.946 meters at the Poles. The Deutches Hauptdreiecksnetz system uses the Bessel 1841 ellipsoid, which is based on a more conservative estimate of the size of the earth, with an ellipsoid of equatorial radius 6,377,397.155 meters and polar radius of 6,356,078.965 meters.

■ **Note** Instead of giving the dimensions of both the equatorial and polar axes, the WKT definition of a spatial reference gives the length of the larger, semi-major axis together with the inverse flattening ratio. This ratio, which generally has a value of around 300, indicates how much larger the earth is assumed to be at the equator than at the poles, and can be used to derive the polar axis of the ellipsoid model.

The different ellipsoid models used in these datums are illustrated in Figure 8-1.

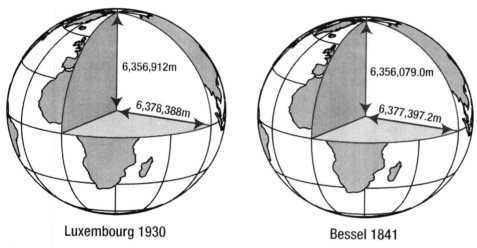

Luxembourg 1930   Bessel 1841

Figure 8-1. Comparing different geodetic datums

You cannot compare geography data defined using SRID 4181 to geography data defined using SRID 4314 without first transforming the sets of data to be based on a consistent datum. Failure to do so (i.e., treating geographic coordinates defined relative to one datum as if they had been defined on another) can lead to coordinate locations being incorrect by several hundred meters.

Datum transformation involves converting coordinate values defined using one geodetic datum into the equivalent coordinate values based on a different datum. In the context of the previous example, we could either transform the coordinates defined using the Luxembourg datum to the DHDN datum, or vice versa; the important thing is that all the resulting data should be defined relative to the same datum.

Transformation Algorithms

The process of datum transformation involves applying a mathematical function to adjust coordinate values based on a specified algorithm and set of parameters. There are several alternative transformation algorithms available, with varying degrees of complexity and accuracy. Generally speaking, the greater the number of parameters used in the transformation, the more complex the algorithm, and the greater the accuracy of the results.

In the following section, I'll examine three different algorithms that can be used to transform coordinates between geodetic datums, in increasing order of complexity.

Coordinate Offsets (Two Parameters)

The simplest form of transformation involves adding constant values to the latitude and longitude coordinate values defined relative to one datum to approximate the corresponding coordinates on a second datum. This sort of transformation algorithm can be expressed in generalized form as follows:

```
Latitude₂ = Latitude₁ + ΔLatitude
Longitude₂ = Longitude₁ + ΔLongitude
```

This algorithm is very simplistic and requires only two parameters: the ΔLatitude and ΔLongitude offsets to be added to each supplied coordinate value. For a transformation between any two given datums, the same latitude and longitude offsets are applied consistently to every coordinate value across the whole globe, as illustrated in Figure 8-2.

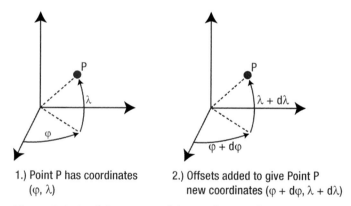

1.) Point P has coordinates (φ, λ)

2.) Offsets added to give Point P new coordinates (φ + dφ, λ + dλ)

Figure 8-2. Applying geographic coordinate offsets

As an example, the location of Cardiff, Wales, has coordinates of (51.4826, –3.18183) relative to the WGS84 datum. The same location expressed relative to the OSGB36 datum is (51.4821, –3.18057). Thus we can define a set of offsets to convert from WGS84 to OSGB36 as follows:

$\Delta\lambda$, The change in latitude between "from" datum and "to" datum = 0.0005 degrees.

$\Delta\varphi$, The change in longitude between "from" datum and "to" datum = 0.00126 degrees.

However, this method is unable to allow for any change in shape between the datums, and is only really suitable for low-precision applications in a limited area. The offsets calculated here are based on the differences between datums calculated at a single point and, as the geographic range of coordinates to be transformed increases, the accuracy of the results obtained by this method diminishes.

Molodensky Transformation (Five Parameters)

The Molodensky transformation, named after Russian geodesist Mikhail Molodensky, is an algorithm for converting coordinates between datums based on five parameters. These parameters describe the translation of the center of the ellipsoid between the two datums in x-, y-, and z-axes (Δx, Δy, and Δz), together with the difference in the length of the semi-major axis (Δa) and flattening ratio (Δf). Unlike the simple geographic coordinate offset approach described previously, the Molodensky transformation can account for a change in the shape, size, and position of the ellipsoid model between two datums.

The Molodensky transformation can be expressed in general form as follows:

```
Latitude₂ = f(Latitude₁, Δx, Δy, Δz, Δa, Δf)
Longitude₂ = f(Longitude₁, Δx, Δy, Δz, Δa, Δf)
```

Figure 8-3 illustrates the process of Molodensky transformation of a point between two datums.

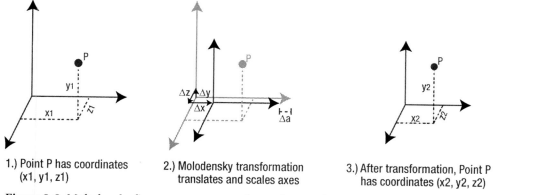

1.) Point P has coordinates (x1, y1, z1)

2.) Molodensky transformation translates and scales axes

3.) After transformation, Point P has coordinates (x2, y2, z2)

Figure 8-3. Molodensky five-parameter transformation applies translation and scaling of datum, but not rotation.

Molodensky transformations using an appropriate set of parameters can generally achieve results that are accurate to within a few meters. For example, the following set of parameters can be used to transform from the local datum used in the Bahamas to the WGS84 datum:

Δa, Difference in semi-major axis between "from" datum and "to" datum = – 69.4 meters

Δf, Difference in flattening ratio between datums = –0.000037264639

Δx, Translation along the x-axis = –4 meters

Δy, Translation along the y-axis = 154 meters

Δz, Translation along the z-axis = 178 meters

Because the Molodensky transformation only translates and scales parallel to the plane of the existing defined axes, it is not suitable for cases in which the orientation of the ellipsoid has been rotated.

Helmert Transformation (Seven Parameters)

The Helmert transformation, named after German geodesist Friedrich Helmert, requires seven parameters to describe the transformation from one datum to another. For this reason, it is also commonly known as the seven-parameter transformation. The parameters represent a translation along the three coordinate axes (x, y, and z), as well as a rotation about each of the three axes. A final parameter provides a scaling factor used across all three axes.

The process involved in the Helmert transformation is illustrated in Figure 8-4.

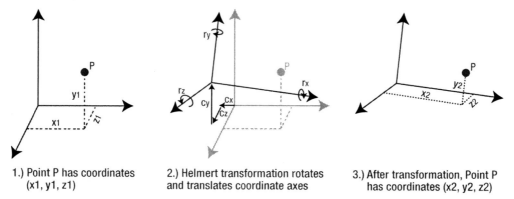

1.) Point P has coordinates
   (x1, y1, z1)

2.) Helmert transformation rotates
   and translates coordinate axes

3.) After transformation, Point P
   has coordinates (x2, y2, z2)

Figure 8-4. The Helmert transformation rotates and translates coordinate axes between datums

For example, the parameters required to perform a Helmert transformation from the Bessel 1841 datum to the WGS84 datum are as follows:

c_x, Translation along the x-axis = –582 meters

c_y, Translation along the y-axis = –105 meters

c_z, Translation along the z-axis = –414 meters

r_x, Rotation about the x-axis = –1.04 arcseconds

r_y, Rotation about the y-axis = –0.35 arcseconds

r_z, Rotation about the z-axis = 3.08 arcseconds

s, Scaling factor = –8.3 parts per million

■ **Note** The preceding section does not provide an exhaustive list of transformation algorithms, but describes some of those most commonly used in GIS applications. Other more complex algorithms are sometimes used, particularly in specialized scientific use, where the degree of accuracy required is much greater.

Transforming to and from WGS84

In theory, it would be possible to compile a list of the transformation parameters required to convert between any datum and any other datum, using any of the transformation algorithms listed previously. With this knowledge, we could apply the relevant parameters to transform coordinates defined using the Luxembourg 1930 datum directly into the DHDN datum, for example. However, to specify the explicit conversion between every combination of the 392 geodetic systems supported by SQL Server would require 153,272 sets of parameters. This would correspond to over one million individual Helmert transformation parameters!

Fortunately, this is not generally necessary, and there is a much more efficient way of defining the parameters required to convert between any two datums. The key to this approach is that all of the transformation algorithms described in the preceding section are *reversible*. That is, if applying a given set of parameters transforms from datum A to datum B, then applying the inverse set of parameters (i.e., supplying the negative value of each parameter) will transform from datum B back to datum A again. (Note that although this is true of all the algorithms described here, it is not true of every transformation algorithm. The Molodensky–Badekas algorithm, for example, is not reversible.)

Therefore, rather than determine the set of parameters to convert from any datum directly into any other datum, we need only define the parameters required to convert from any datum to a single common datum. We can then transform coordinates between any two datums using a two-step process: first applying the parameters to convert from the source datum into the common datum, and then applying the inverse set of parameters associated with the target datum to convert from the common datum to the target. Of course, if the common datum happens to be the source or target datum desired, then one of these steps can be omitted.

The single common intermediate datum into which datums are generally transformed is, as you may have guessed, WGS84, and the transformation most commonly used is the seven-parameter Helmert transformation. The seven parameters required to transform into the WGS84 datum are commonly included in the WKT definition of a datum, following the TOWGS84 keyword. This is demonstrated in the following code listing, which restates the WKT representation of the Luxembourg 1930 spatial reference system given earlier but now includes the TOWGS84 parameters required to convert coordinates from this system to WGS84 (highlighted in bold):

```
GEOGCS[
  "Luxembourg 1930",
  DATUM[
    "Luxembourg_1930",
    ELLIPSOID["International 1924", 6378388, 297],
    TOWGS84[-193, 13.7, -39.3, -0.41, -2.933, 2.688, 0.43],
    ],
  PRIMEM["Greenwich", 0],
  UNIT["Degree",0.01745329251994328]
]
```

The first three values following the TOWGS84 keyword represent the translation in the x-, y-, and z-axes, measured in meters. The next three parameters represent the rotation around the x-, y-, and z-axes, measured in seconds of an arc, and the final parameter represents the scale change, measured in parts per million. Taken together, these parameters provide all the information required to convert from this datum to the WGS84 datum.

The seven parameters required to perform a Helmert transformation from the Deutsches Hauptdreiecksnetz system to WGS84 may be stated as part of the following WKT:

```
GEOGCS[
  "DHDN",
  DATUM[
    "Deutsches Hauptdreiecksnetz",
```

```
    ELLIPSOID["Bessel 1841", 6377397.155, 299.1528128]
    TOWGS84[582, 105, 414, -1.04, -0.35, 3.08, 8.3],
    ],
  PRIMEM["Greenwich", 0],
  UNIT["Degree", 0.0174532925199433]
]
```

Knowing the additional TOWGS84 parameters just given, we can now convert from Luxembourg to DHDN using two transformations: first applying the TOWGS84 parameters of the Luxembourg datum to convert from Luxembourg to WGS84, and then applying the inverse TOWGS84 parameters from the DHDN datum to convert from WGS84 to DHDN. This process is illustrated in Figure 8-5.

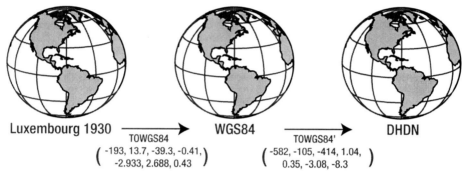

Figure 8-5. Applying datum transformation parameters to convert between any two datums via WGS84

■ **Note** There are different conventions regarding how to define the three rotation parameters supplied to the Helmert transformation, which essentially differ in their interpretation of what is being rotated. In a position vector rotation, the axes remain constant and the frame of points is rotated around the axes. In a coordinate frame rotation, the points remain constant while the axes themselves are rotated. The practical difference between these two definitions is that the rotation parameters have changed sign. If you obtain Helmert transformation parameters it's best to check which convention was used, and reverse the rotation parameters as necessary.

Projection, Unprojection, and Reprojection

In the preceding section, we considered how to transform coordinates defined relative to different geodetic datums. In SQL Server terminology, this relates to converting geography data defined using one spatial reference system to geography data using a different spatial reference system. Let's now turn our attention to consider the process involved in converting geometry data between different spatial reference systems.

Remember that while geography data is defined using geographic coordinates of latitude and longitude, geometry data uses Cartesian coordinates, which are generally based on a projected spatial reference system. You do not normally convert coordinates directly from one projected system into another; instead, you first convert projected coordinates back to 3D geographic coordinates on their underlying geodetic model (i.e., you "unproject" them, also known as an inverse projection). Then, you reproject them back onto a two-dimensional plane using the set of parameters required by the destination coordinate system (known as a forward projection).

To illustrate these concepts, let's consider the NAD83 geographic coordinate reference system, SRID 4269, which is widely used across North America. The well-known text representation of this spatial reference system is as follows:

```
GEOGCS["NAD83",
  DATUM["North American Datum 1983",
    SPHEROID["GRS 1980", 6378137.0, 298.257222101,  AUTHORITY["EPSG","7019"]],
    AUTHORITY["EPSG","6269"]],
  PRIMEM["Greenwich", 0.0, AUTHORITY["EPSG","8901"]],
  UNIT["degree", 0.017453292519943295],
  AUTHORITY["EPSG","4269"]]
```

The Massachusetts Mainland spatial reference system (EPSG:2249) is a projected spatial reference based on a Lambert Conic Conformal projection of the NAD83 datum. The well-known text representation of this system is as follows:

```
PROJCS["NAD83 / Massachusetts Mainland",
  GEOGCS["NAD83",
    DATUM["North_American_Datum_1983",
      SPHEROID["GRS 1980", 6378137.0, 298.257222101, AUTHORITY["EPSG","7019"]],
      AUTHORITY["EPSG","6269"]],
    PRIMEM["Greenwich", 0.0, AUTHORITY["EPSG","8901"]],
    UNIT["degree", 0.017453292519943295],
    AUTHORITY["EPSG","4269"]],
  PROJECTION["Lambert Conic Conformal (2SP)", AUTHORITY["EPSG","9802"]],
  PARAMETER["central_meridian", -71.5],
  PARAMETER["latitude_of_origin", 41.0],
  PARAMETER["standard_parallel_1", 42.68333333333334],
  PARAMETER["false_easting", 200000.0],
  PARAMETER["false_northing", 750000.0],
  PARAMETER["standard_parallel_2", 41.71666666666667],
  UNIT["US survey foot", 0.3048006096012192, AUTHORITY["EPSG","9003"]],
  AXIS["Easting", EAST],
  AXIS["Northing", NORTH],
  AUTHORITY["EPSG","2249"]
]
```

The NAD83 Universal Transverse Mercator Zone 18N, SRID 26918, is another projected spatial reference system based on the NAD83 datum. It shares the same underlying geodetic model of the Earth as the Massachusetts Mainland system. However, it uses a transverse Mercator projection rather than a conic projection in which coordinate values are measured in meters rather than feet.

The well-known text for SRID 26918 is as follows:

```
PROJCS["NAD83 / UTM zone 18N",
  GEOGCS["NAD83",
    DATUM["North_American_Datum_1983",
      SPHEROID["GRS 1980", 6378137, 298.257222101, AUTHORITY["EPSG","7019"]],
      AUTHORITY["EPSG","6269"]],
    PRIMEM["Greenwich",0, AUTHORITY["EPSG","8901"]],
    UNIT["degree",0.01745329251994328],
    AUTHORITY["EPSG","4269"]],
  PROJECTION["Transverse_Mercator"],
  PARAMETER["latitude_of_origin",0],
```

```
    PARAMETER["central_meridian",-75],
    PARAMETER["scale_factor",0.9996],
    PARAMETER["false_easting",500000],
    PARAMETER["false_northing",0],
    UNIT["metre",1, AUTHORITY["EPSG","9001"]],
    AXIS["Easting",EAST],
    AXIS["Northing",NORTH],
    AUTHORITY["EPSG","26918"]
]
```

To convert coordinate data from the Masachussets State Plane projected system into UTM Zone 18N projection first requires unprojection into NAD83, the underlying geodetic model on which both projections are based, and then reprojection into UTM Zone 18N. This is illustrated in Figure 8-6.

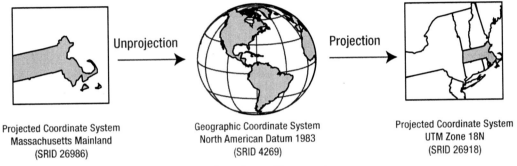

Projected Coordinate System
Massachusetts Mainland
(SRID 26986)

Geographic Coordinate System
North American Datum 1983
(SRID 4269)

Projected Coordinate System
UTM Zone 18N
(SRID 26918)

Figure 8-6. Converting between two projected coordinate systems

In the preceding example, the source and target projected spatial reference systems were both based on the same underlying geodetic datum: the North American Datum 1983. But what if you wanted to convert between projected spatial reference systems based on different datums?

To do this, you need to add an additional step to perform a datum conversion. The process is as follows:

- First, unproject from the source projection to geodetic coordinates based on the source datum.

- Then, perform a datum conversion from the source datum to the target datum using, for example, the Helmert transformation discussed earlier this chapter.

- Finally, reproject geographic coordinates from the target datum into the target projected spatial reference system.

To demonstrate, suppose that you wanted to convert coordinates from the Massachussets Mainland spatial reference system based on the NAD1983 datum into the CONUS Albers projection based on the NAD1927 datum. The process required to perform this conversion is illustrated in Figure 8-7.

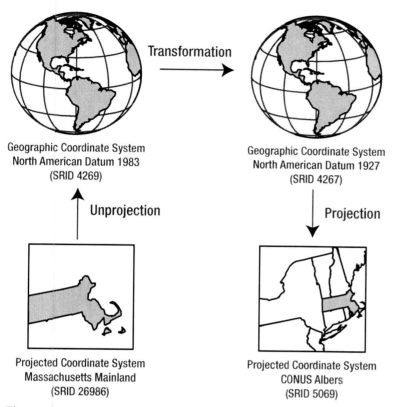

Figure 8-7. *Unprojection, datum transformation, and reprojection from one projected spatial reference system to another.*

Performing Manual Calculations

The processes of datum transformation and projection described previously involve nothing more than a series of deterministic mathematical conversions. You could, if you wanted, write your own functions to perform the necessary calculations to convert coordinates between any spatial reference system of the geography or geometry datatype.

However, converting between geographic coordinates on a three-dimensional, round model and projected coordinates on a two-dimensional flat surface can involve some pretty tricky mathematics. For example, the following formulae describe the calculations necessary to project latitude and longitude coordinates into x- and y-coordinates in a Lambert conformal conic projection, as used in the Massachussetts Mainland system described in the preceding example:

$$x = \rho \sin[n(\lambda - \lambda_0)]$$
$$y = \rho_0 - \rho \cos[n(\lambda - \lambda_0)]$$

where

$$n = \frac{\ln(\cos\phi_1 \sec\phi_2)}{\ln[\tan(\frac{1}{4}\pi + \frac{1}{2}\phi_2)\cot(\frac{1}{4}\pi + \frac{1}{2}\phi_1)]}$$

$$\rho = F\cot^n\left(\frac{1}{4}\pi + \frac{1}{2}\phi\right)$$

$$\rho_0 = F\cot^n\left(\frac{1}{4}\pi + \frac{1}{2}\phi_0\right)$$

$$F = \frac{\cos\phi_1 \tan^n(\frac{1}{4}\pi + \frac{1}{2}\phi_1)}{n}$$

Fortunately, understanding and implementing these detailed formulae is completely unnecessary. Because clever people have already done the hard work for us, rather than reinvent the wheel, we can use one of the many available spatial libraries that handle the conversion between datums and projections. This is exactly what we'll do in the next section.

Creating a Reusable Spatial Conversion Library

There are several libraries available that provide the necessary algorithms for transforming and projecting coordinates between spatial references systems. In this section, I'll show you how to use the Proj.NET library, which is an open source project available on the codeplex website at `http://www.codeplex.com/ProjNET`. The Proj.NET library contains all the necessary functions to support datum transformations and projection between a number of common map projections, including Mercator, Albers, and Lambert Conformal.

Storing Transformation Parameters

Before we get onto the issue of the transformation function itself, we need to define a structure in which to store the parameters necessary to convert between different spatial reference systems. Although SQL Server already contains details of many spatial reference systems in the `sys.spatial_reference_systems` table, this information is not sufficient for transformation and projection purposes. Why? Well, firstly, this table stores only those geodetic spatial reference systems supported by the geography datatype; it does not contain any details of projected spatial reference systems that can be used by the geometry datatype. Secondly, even those spatial reference systems that are listed in `sys.spatial_reference_systems` do not contain the `TOWGS84` parameters required to transform coordinates into a different geodetic datum.

We can't modify or insert additional rows into `sys.spatial_reference_systems`, so instead we'll simply create a new table to store this information using a simple structure as follows:

```
CREATE TABLE prospatial_reference_systems (
  spatial_reference_id int,
  well_known_text nvarchar(max)
);
```

To populate this table, you need to provide the EPSG spatial reference identifier and the well-known text definition of each spatial reference system between which you want to convert data. You can find details of spatial reference systems on the Internet, including from http://www.epsg-registry.org or http://www.spatialreference.org. Once you've obtained the SRID and WKT (including the TOWGS84 parameter) of the systems you'd like to support, you can insert them into the prospatial_reference_systems table.

To demonstrate the range of possible conversions between coordinate systems, the following code listing inserts three records into the prospatial_reference_systems table:

- WGS84, a geographic coordinate system based on the WGS84 datum

- UTM Zone 31N, a projected coordinate system also based on the WGS84 datum

- The British National Grid, a projected coordinate system based on the OSGB36 datum.

```
INSERT INTO prospatial_reference_systems (
  spatial_reference_id,
  well_known_text
)
VALUES
(4326,
'GEOGCS["WGS 84",
  DATUM[
    "World Geodetic System 1984",
    SPHEROID["WGS 84", 6378137.0, 298.257223563, AUTHORITY["EPSG","7030"]],
    AUTHORITY["EPSG","6326"]
  ],
  PRIMEM["Greenwich", 0.0, AUTHORITY["EPSG","8901"]],
  UNIT["degree", 0.017453292519943295],
  AXIS["Geodetic longitude", EAST],
  AXIS["Geodetic latitude", NORTH],
  AUTHORITY["EPSG","4326"]
]'),
(32631,
'PROJCS["WGS 84 / UTM zone 31N",
  GEOGCS["WGS 84",
    DATUM[
      "WGS_1984",
      SPHEROID["WGS 84", 6378137, 298.257223563, AUTHORITY["EPSG","7030"]],
      AUTHORITY["EPSG","6326"]
    ],
    PRIMEM["Greenwich", 0, AUTHORITY["EPSG","8901"]],
    UNIT["degree", 0.01745329251994328, AUTHORITY["EPSG","9122"]],
    AUTHORITY["EPSG","4326"]
  ],
  PROJECTION["Transverse_Mercator"],
  PARAMETER["latitude_of_origin",0],
  PARAMETER["central_meridian",3],
  PARAMETER["scale_factor",0.9996],
  PARAMETER["false_easting", 500000],
  PARAMETER["false_northing",0],
  UNIT["metre", 1, AUTHORITY["EPSG","9001"]],
  AUTHORITY["EPSG","32631"]
]'),
```

```
(27700,
'PROJCS["OSGB 1936 / British National Grid",
  GEOGCS["OSGB 1936",
    DATUM[
      "OSGB 1936",
      SPHEROID["Airy 1830", 6377563.396, 299.3249646, AUTHORITY["EPSG","7001"]],
      TOWGS84[446.448, -125.157, 542.06, 0.15, 0.247, 0.842, -4.2261596151967575],
      AUTHORITY["EPSG","6277"]
    ],
    PRIMEM["Greenwich", 0.0, AUTHORITY["EPSG","8901"]],
    UNIT["degree", 0.017453292519943295],
    AXIS["Geodetic longitude", EAST],
    AXIS["Geodetic latitude", NORTH],
    AUTHORITY["EPSG","4277"]
  ],
  PROJECTION["Transverse Mercator"],
  PARAMETER["central_meridian", -2.0],
  PARAMETER["latitude_of_origin", 49.0],
  PARAMETER["scale_factor", 0.9996012717],
  PARAMETER["false_easting", 400000.0],
  PARAMETER["false_northing", -100000.0],
  UNIT["m", 1.0],
  AXIS["Easting", EAST],
  AXIS["Northing", NORTH],
  AUTHORITY["EPSG","27700"]
]');
```

The code samples that accompany this book contain a script to populate this table with details of many other commonly used spatial reference systems.

Compiling the Proj.NET Assembly for SQL Server

To perform the transformation and conversion of coordinates between any two systems based on the parameters defined in the prospatial_reference_systems table, we'll leverage the Proj.NET library.

Because the Proj.NET library is coded in C#, it can be compiled into a .dll assembly that can be imported into SQL Server, and its methods exposed via user-defined functions. This is the approach we'll follow in the following section. To begin, follow these steps:

1. First, download the *Source Code* of the latest Proj.Net build from the codeplex website at http://www.codeplex.com/ProjNET. At the time of writing, the latest version is changeset 34175, dated May 26th, 2009. Note that you must download the source code, not the precompiled binary .dll library, as we must first make a few modifications to the code to make it suitable for use in SQL Server.

2. Unzip the downloaded Proj.NET archive, projnet-34175.zip, and load the solution file, ProjNET.sln, in Visual Studio. This is a Visual Studio 2008 solution so, if you open the file in a more recent edition, the Visual Studio Conversion Wizard dialog may appear to upgrade the solution. If prompted, do so.

The solution contains a number of different projects, including a demo website, a test framework, and a Silverlight-compatible library. However, the project that is of interest to us is the ProjNET project, highlighted in the Visual Studio Solution Explorer pane shown in Figure 8-8.

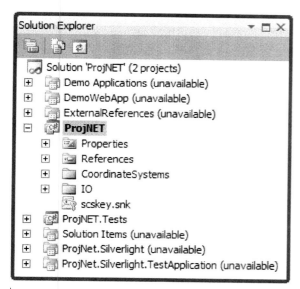

Figure 8-8. The ProjNET project highlighted in the Visual Studio Solution Explorer pane

The ProjNET project is the core assembly containing all the methods required for coordinate transformation and conversion. We will create an additional separate assembly that calls into the methods of the ProjNET assembly and exposes them in a format suitable for geometry and geography data. However, there is a small issue to address before we do so: SQLCLR assemblies do not generally allow their methods to be called by any other code, unless they are trusted. There are two possible solutions to this problem:

> We could register the calling assembly as an UNSAFE assembly, one that is granted full trust to perform pretty much any action in the database. This would achieve the objective of allowing it to access the methods in the ProjNET assembly, but it would also introduce an unnecessary level of risk. Code in an assembly with the UNSAFE permission set has permission to do all sorts of things, including accessing the file system and network resources, and registering assemblies as UNSAFE should be avoided if at all possible.

> The second, better option is to alter the ProjNET assembly itself to allow partially trusted callers. Microsoft recommends that all assemblies registered in SQL Server (except those added to the Global Assembly Cache) should be decorated with the System.Security.AllowPartiallyTrustedCallers attribute, so that they can be accessed from other SAFE or EXTERNAL_ACCESS assemblies, preventing the need to grant full trust where it is not required.

■ **Note** For more information about using SQLCLR libraries from partially trusted callers, refer to
http://msdn.microsoft.com/en-us/library/ms345097%28v=SQL.110%29.aspx

---

Fortunately, implementing the necessary change to the Proj.NET library to allow partially trusted callers is very simple:

1. From the Solution Explorer pane, click to expand the ProjNET Properties folder, and then double-click to edit the *AssemblyInfo.cs* file contained inside.

2. Decorate the assembly with the `AllowPartiallyTrustedCallers` attribute, by adding the line shown below onto the end of the AssemblyInfo.cs file (immediately after the existing attribute declarations):

   `[assembly: System.Security.AllowPartiallyTrustedCallers]`

3. Now, right-click on the ProjNET project in the Solution Explorer pane and select "Build" to recompile the assembly.

4. That's it! A message in the output window should report that the build succeeded, and you can now close the ProjNET solution by clicking on the Visual Studio File menu and selecting "Close Solution".

Creating Transformation Sinks

Having compiled the ProjNET library to allow partially trusted callers, we'll now create methods that will call into the ProjNET transformation functions and wrap them in a manner suitable for SQL Server's geography and geometry datatypes. These will be contained in a separate project, so begin by creating and configuring the new project, as follows:

1. From the Visual Studio menu bar, select File ➤ New Project. Highlight the Class Library template and name the new library, as shown in Figure 8-9.

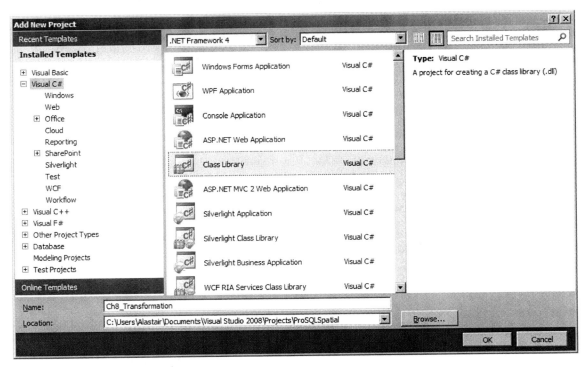

Figure 8-9. Adding a new project

2. Once the project has been created, go to the Project menu and select Add Reference.

3. In the Add Reference dialog box, click on the Browse tab and navigate to the directory in which the recompiled ProjNet.dll library was just created. (By default this is in the /SharpMap.CoordinateSystems/Bin/Debug subdirectory of the directory in which Proj.NET was unarchived.) Highlight the ProjNET.dll and click OK.

4. Click Add Reference again, and this time add a reference to the Microsoft.SqlServer.Types.dll library. By default, this is installed in the /SDK/Assemblies subdirectory of your SQL Server installation folder. Highlight the SQLServer.Types.dll library and click OK.

Having configured the project, the next step is to create the sink interfaces. There are four sink interfaces required to cover each combination of possible conversions between the geometry and geography datatypes:

- geography to geometry
- geography to geography
- geometry to geography
- geometry to geometry

The sinks will all follow essentially identical structures, with the exception of the expected input and return types. The following code listing demonstrates the sink to convert coordinates from the geography datatype to the geometry datatype, so it implements the IGeographySink110 interface. For each method in the sink, the parameter values passed in are used to populate a corresponding IGeometrySink110 interface. So, for example, the OpenGisGeographyType used to denote the type of geography instance passed to the sink (in the BeginGeography() method) is converted to the corresponding OpenGisGeometryType and passed through to the BeginGeometry() method of the IGeometrySink110. As each point is passed to the IGeographySink110 BeginFigure() and AddLine() methods, the latitude and longitude coordinates are converted using a Proj.NET ICoordinateTransformation class into the corresponding x- and y-coordinates, and these are then provided to the equivalent IGeometrySink110 BeginFigure() and AddLine() methods.

Here's the code listing:

```
using System;
using Microsoft.SqlServer.Types; // SqlGeometry and SqlGeography
using ProjNet.CoordinateSystems.Transformations; // Proj.NET

namespace ProSpatial.Ch8
{
  class TransformGeographyToGeometrySink : IGeographySink110
  {

    private readonly ICoordinateTransformation _trans;
    private readonly IGeometrySink110 _sink;

    public TransformGeographyToGeometrySink(
      ICoordinateTransformation trans,
      IGeometrySink110 sink
    )
    {
      _trans = trans;
      _sink = sink;
```

```csharp
}

public void BeginGeography(OpenGisGeographyType type)
{
  // Begin creating a new geometry of the type requested
  _sink.BeginGeometry((OpenGisGeometryType)type);
}

public void BeginFigure(double latitude, double longitude, double? z, double? m)
{
  // Use ProjNET Transform() method to project lat,lng coordinates to x,y
  double[] startPoint = _trans.MathTransform.Transform(new double[]
                        { longitude, latitude });

  // Begin a new geometry figure at corresponding x,y coordinates
  _sink.BeginFigure(startPoint[0], startPoint[1], z, m);
}

public void AddLine(double latitude, double longitude, double? z, double? m)
{
  // Use ProjNET to transform end point of the line segment being added
  double[] toPoint = _trans.MathTransform.Transform(new double[]
                     { longitude, latitude });

  // Add this line to the geometry
  _sink.AddLine(toPoint[0], toPoint[1], z, m);
}

public void AddCircularArc(double latitude1, double longitude1, double? z1, double? m1,
                           double latitude2, double longitude2, double? z2, double? m2
)
{
  // Transform both the anchor point and destination of the arc segment
  double[] anchorPoint = _trans.MathTransform.Transform(new double[]
                         { longitude1, latitude1 });
  double[] toPoint = _trans.MathTransform.Transform(new double[]
                     { longitude2, latitude2 });

  // Add this arc to the geometry
  _sink.AddCircularArc(anchorPoint[0], anchorPoint[1], z1, m1,
                       toPoint[0], toPoint[1], z2, m2);
}

public void EndFigure()
{
  _sink.EndFigure();
}

public void EndGeography()
{
  _sink.EndGeometry();
}

public void SetSrid(int srid)
```

```
      {
        // Just pass through
      }
    }
  }
}
```

For the code listings of the corresponding geometry to geography, geometry to geometry, and geography to geography sinks, please see the code samples accompanying this book.

To actually make use of the interfaces, each sink will have a corresponding function, which we will expose in SQL Server. The function to accompany the TransformGeographyToGeometrySink interface requires two inputs: an item of geography data and the SRID of a projected coordinate system, whose parameters are listed in the prospatial_reference_systems table created earlier. The method projects the supplied geography input into the appropriate coordinate system and returns the corresponding geometry value.

The method will read the parameters associated with both the source and destination systems from the prospatial_reference_systems table, so we need to decorate the function with the DataAccessKind.Read attribute. Here's the function signature:

```
[Microsoft.SqlServer.Server.SqlFunction(DataAccess = DataAccessKind.Read)]
    public static SqlGeometry GeographyToGeometry(SqlGeography geog, SqlInt32 toSRID)
```

Once called, the first thing the method must do is to determine the parameters of the source and destination reference systems. The source spatial reference identifier is retrieved from the STSrid property of the supplied geography instance. The target SRID is the integer value supplied as the second parameter to the function.

The function then retrieves the corresponding WKT for these systems by querying the prospatial_reference_systems table via the context connection (if you named your spatial reference table something else then be sure to change the query appropriately).

The well-known text representation of the source and destination systems is used to create a CoordinateTransformation instance. This instance is then passed to the appropriate sink interface in order to populate a SqlGeometryBuilder instance with transformed values. Finally, the ConstructedGeometry instance created by the SqlGeometryBuilder is returned to the client.

The code listing for the GeographyToGeometry function is shown following:

```
using System;
using System.Collections.Generic;
using System.Text;
using System.Data.SqlTypes;
using System.Data.SqlClient; // Required for context connection
using Microsoft.SqlServer.Server; // SqlFunction Decoration
using Microsoft.SqlServer.Types; // SqlGeometry and SqlGeography
using ProjNet.CoordinateSystems; // ProjNET coordinate systems
using ProjNet.CoordinateSystems.Transformations; // ProjNET transformation functions
using ProjNet.Converters.WellKnownText; //ProjNET WKT functions

namespace ProSpatial.Ch8
{
  public partial class UserDefinedFunctions
  {

    [Microsoft.SqlServer.Server.SqlFunction(DataAccess = DataAccessKind.Read)]
    public static SqlGeometry GeographyToGeometry(SqlGeography geog, SqlInt32 toSRID)
    {
      // Use the context connection to the SQL Server instance on which this is executed
      using (SqlConnection conn = new SqlConnection("context connection=true"))
```

```
{
  // Open the connection
  conn.Open();

  // Retrieve the parameters of the source spatial reference system
  SqlCommand cmd = new SqlCommand("SELECT well_known_text FROM
            prospatial_reference_systems WHERE spatial_reference_id = @srid", conn);
  cmd.Parameters.Add(new SqlParameter("srid", geog.STSrid));
  object fromResult = cmd.ExecuteScalar();

  // Check that details of the source SRID have been found
  if (fromResult is System.DBNull || fromResult == null)
  { return null; }

  // Retrieve the WKT
  String fromWKT = Convert.ToString(fromResult);

  // Create the source coordinate system from WKT
  ICoordinateSystem fromCS = CoordinateSystemWktReader.Parse(fromWKT) as
                        ICoordinateSystem;

  // Retrieve the parameters of the destination spatial reference system
  cmd.Parameters["srid"].Value = toSRID;
  object toResult = cmd.ExecuteScalar();

  // Check that details of the destination SRID have been found
  if (toResult is System.DBNull || toResult == null)
  { return null; }

  // Execute the command and retrieve the WKT
  String toWKT = Convert.ToString(toResult);

  // Clean up
  cmd.Dispose();

  // Create the destination coordinate system from WKT
  ICoordinateSystem toCS = CoordinateSystemWktReader.Parse(toWKT) as
                        ICoordinateSystem;

  // Create a CoordinateTransformationFactory instance
  CoordinateTransformationFactory ctfac = new CoordinateTransformationFactory();

  // Create the transformation between the specified coordinate systems
  ICoordinateTransformation trans = ctfac.CreateFromCoordinateSystems(fromCS, toCS);

  // Create a geometry instance to be populated by the sink
  SqlGeometryBuilder b = new SqlGeometryBuilder();

  // Set the SRID to match the destination SRID
  b.SetSrid((int)toSRID);

  // Create a sink for the transformation and plug it in to the builder
  TransformGeographyToGeometrySink s = new TransformGeographyToGeometrySink(trans, b);
```

```
            // Populate the sink with the supplied geography instance
            geog.Populate(s);

            // Return the transformed geometry instance
            return b.ConstructedGeometry;
        }
      }
    }
}
```

As with the sink interfaces, the functions required for the other conversions from geometry to geography, geometry to geometry, and geography to geography, are included in the code listings that accompany this book, which can be downloaded from the Apress website at http://www.apress.com.

Having added all the necessary sinks and functions, save the project and compile the assembly by selecting Project ➤ Build Solution.

Registering the Transformation Assembly and Functions

At this stage, you should have two compiled .dll assemblies:

- The ProjNET project library (modified to allow partially trusted callers)
- An assembly containing SqlFunction methods that expose the ProjNET transformations, operating on geometry and geography data

Before registering the assemblies in SQL Server, if you have not already done so, ensure that your SQL Server instance is configured to enable user-defined CLR routines by executing the following T-SQL code in SQL Server Management Studio:

```
EXEC sp_configure 'clr enabled', '1';
GO
```

To complete the configuration change, reconfigure the server to reflect the new value, by issuing a T-SQL query with the RECONFIGURE statement as follows:

```
RECONFIGURE;
GO
```

You can then register the transformation assemblies into your chosen database by issuing the following T-SQL command, substituting the name and location where you compiled the custom dll library:

```
CREATE ASSEMBLY ProSpatialCh8
FROM 'C:\ProSQLSpatial\Ch8_Transformation\bin\Release\Ch8_Transformation.dll'
WITH PERMISSION_SET = SAFE;
GO
```

■ **Note** You do not need to explicitly register the ProjNET library in SQL Server, only the library containing the custom SQL functions. Since the ProjNET library is referenced from this assembly, SQL Server will automatically locate and import the ProjNET assembly at the same time. You only need to make sure that both dlls are present in the same folder on the server, or deployed to the Global Assembly Cache.

Having imported the assembly, the next step is to register the corresponding function. Here's the T-SQL code required to create the GeographyToGeometry function:

```
CREATE FUNCTION dbo.GeographyToGeometry(@geog geography, @srid int)
RETURNS geometry
EXTERNAL NAME ProSpatialCh8.[ProSpatial.Ch8.UserDefinedFunctions].GeographyToGeometry;
GO
```

Transforming Spatial Data in T-SQL

With the assemblies and functions registered, our transformation functionality is ready to go. To transform any item of geography or geometry data into another spatial reference system, first ensure that the prospatial_reference_systems table is populated with the correct parameters corresponding to both the source and target spatial reference systems. Then call the transformation method, supplying the instance to be transformed, and the SRID of the desired target system.

For example, the following code listing demonstrates how to convert a geography Point defined using the EPSG:4326 system into a geometry Point defined using UTM Zone 31N (EPSG:32631):

```
DECLARE @Norwich geography;
SET @Norwich = geography::STPointFromText('POINT(1.369338 53.035498)', 4326);

SELECT dbo.GeographyToGeometry(@Norwich, 32631).ToString();
```

The GeographyToGeometry() method reads in the parameters of the source and target spatial reference system from the well_known_text column of the prospatial_reference_systems table. In this example, the requested destination system, 32631, is based on a projection of the same datum used by the source reference system, 4326. Therefore, no datum conversion is necessary, and conversion involves only projecting the coordinates based on a transverse Mercator projection. The coordinates of each point in the supplied geography instance (in this case, there is only one) are projected to the destination reference system, and the well-known text of the resulting geometry instance is returned as follows:

```
POINT (390659.51922243327 5877462.7522814982)
```

We can also try another example, this time converting a point from WGS84 to the British National Grid system, which is based on the OSGB36 datum. In this case, conversion involves both a datum transformation and also projection. Fortunately, ProjNET determines and performs the required actions automatically behind the scenes, so no further steps need be added to the code listing:

```
DECLARE @Oxford geography;
SET @Oxford = geography::STPointFromText('POINT(-1.256804 51.752143)', 4326);

SELECT dbo.GeographyToGeometry(@Oxford, 27700).ToString();
```

```
POINT (451400.00276604667 206200.52991363779)
```

You can confirm both of the preceding results using one of a number of online coordinate conversion tools, such as that available at http://nearby.org.uk.

As a graphical demonstration of this transformation function, Figure 8-10 illustrates a side-by-side comparison of three versions of the same MultiPolygon geometry representing Great Britain and

Northern Ireland. The left image shows the original geography instance using SRID 4326, displayed in the Management Studio Spatial Results tab using a Bonne projection; the center image displays the result of the GeographyToGeometry() method when used to transform into a geometry MultiPolygon using SRID 32631; the right image displays the same MultiPolygon when transformed into SRID 27700.

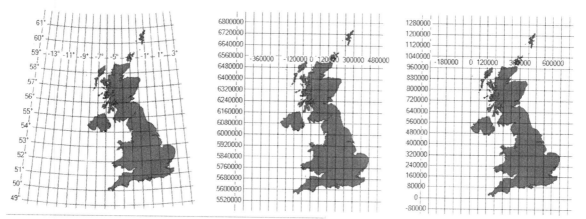

Figure 8-10. *Three different projections of Great Britain. From left to right: geographic (EPSG:4326) using Bonne projection, UTM Zone 31N (EPSG:32631), Ordnance Survey National Grid of Great Britain (EPSG:27700)*

Architecture and Design Considerations

So far in this chapter I've shown you both the theory behind spatial transformation and reprojection, and also demonstrated a technical solution enabling you to convert spatial data between spatial reference systems directly in SQL Server. In this final section, I'd like briefly to discuss some practical considerations to bear in mind when dealing with spatial transformations in a real-world application.

The first thing I'd like to point out is that reprojection or conversion of spatial data, particularly of complex geometries comprised of many points, is a computationally intensive operation. I therefore do not recommend that you try to convert data on the fly at runtime, but rather precalculate and store reprojected versions of each shape in the database in all those systems in which it is likely to be used.

The second fact is that reprojection and transformation inevitably cause a slight loss in fidelity of the original coordinate data, and each subsequent conversion degrades the accuracy still further. Therefore, if you are supplied with data that uses a different spatial reference system from the rest of your data, and therefore needs converting, there may be some value in also retaining the full fidelity original data (for performing isolated calculations of STArea(), for example), alongside a reprojected version that is consistent with the spatial reference system used by the rest of your application.

So, you may have several versions of the same geometry: one in the geography datatype, using the North American Datum 1983 (SRID 4269), and one in the geometry datatype, using the New York Long Island State Plane Coordinate System (SRID 2263), for example. When using this approach, I tend to maintain separate columns in my table for each datatype/SRID combination, only storing instances of the same SRID in that column, and name them according to the pattern <datatype><srid>. For the example given previously, I might therefore use a table structure such as this:

```
CREATE TABLE SampleSpatialData (
  Id int,
  Geog4326 geography,
```

```
  Geom2263 geometry
);
```

By adding triggers to the table that call the necessary transformation functions you can ensure that, should any of the spatial columns be updated, all of the other spatial columns are updated with transformed versions of the updated geometry, keeping the data in sync. Different stored procedures can utilize different spatial columns as appropriate, and separate indexes can be added to the columns to optimize performance.

The final point to note is that, while the SQLCLR makes it possible to perform spatial transformations within SQL Server, you should always consider whether this is the most appropriate place at which to do so. CLR procedures are easily moved between tiers of the application hierarchy, and the Proj.NET library used in this chapter could be leveraged just as readily in a front-end Silverlight application, or in a middle-tier web service, for example, rather than directly in the database layer.

If the only time at which you find it necessary to convert data is at the point it is first imported into SQL Server, you might want to investigate one of the ETL tools that can perform conversion and reprojection of spatial data as an integrated part of a load process, such as Safe FME or OGR2OGR discussed in Chapter 5, or create a custom component that calls Proj.NET as part of an SSIS data transformation instead.

Summary

In this chapter, you learned about the process involved in transforming coordinate data between different spatial reference systems.

- Converting data between spatial reference systems based on different underlying geodetic models of the earth requires datum transformation.

- There are various algorithms used for datum transformation. The most common method is the Helmert transformation, which requires seven parameters.

- Helmert transformation parameters that convert to the WGS84 datum can be included with the well-known text representation of a datum, following the TOWGS84 keyword.

- By applying the inverse set of TOWGS84 parameters, you can convert from WGS84 into the target datum.

- Proj.NET is an open source projection library that implements a variety of projections and can create transformations between any two datums given the corresponding WKT.

- Custom CLR functions can be written that call into the Proj.NET library, and expose its functionality to create transformation functions for the geometry and geography datatypes in SQL Server.

- These functions can also be called from CLR code in other layers of an application: in the client, a web layer, or as part of an SSIS ETL load, for example.

CHAPTER 9

Examining Spatial Properties

There are many questions that we might ask about an individual item of spatial data: Where is it? How big is it? What sort of object is it? Where does it start and end? Where does its center lie? In this chapter, you'll learn about the methods that SQL Server provides to answer questions such as these. Note that all of the content in this chapter relates to examining individual items of spatial data, considered in isolation. Methods that analyze the properties of, or relationship between, two or more items of data will be covered in later chapters.

Property and Method Syntax—A Reminder

Before examining any specific methods or properties, it's worth having a quick reminder about the general syntax used when writing queries involving the geography and geometry datatypes. All of the topics in this chapter involve instance methods or properties that are applied directly to an individual item or column of data. Some can be retrieved directly using property syntax, as follows:

```
SELECT Instance.Property;
```

Examples of such properties include STX, Lat, and STSrid. However, other aspects of information must be retrieved via a method, in which case the appropriate syntax is:

```
SELECT Instance.Method();
```

Methods that use this syntax include STNumPoints() and STGeometryType(). Some methods require one or more parameters, which should be supplied in parentheses following the method name:

```
SELECT Instance.Method( parameter );
```

One example of a method that requires a parameter is STPointN(n), which returns the nth point from a geometry. I'll include code listings in each section that demonstrate the appropriate syntax to use when retrieving a specific piece of information.

As with the static methods discussed in Chapter 4, many of the instance methods discussed in this chapter are based on the standards defined by the Open Geospatial Consortium. For such methods, the name of the method is prefixed by the latters "ST", as in STX, STLength(), and STCentroid(). Additional methods that SQL Server implements on top of the OGC standards are called extended methods, and have no prefix before the method name.

Some OGC methods describe particular aspects of a geometry by asking a single question that leads to a yes/no answer: "Is a geometry simple?", "Is it closed?" or "Is it empty?", for example. Methods that test these sorts of question follow the naming convention STIsXXX(), where XXX is the property or behavior being tested. The preceding questions can be asked using the methods STIsSimple(), STIsClosed(), and STIsEmpty(), for example. The result returned is a Boolean value: either 0 (i.e., false, the instance does not exhibit the behavior in question) or 1 (i.e., true, the instance does exhibit the behavior in question).

■ **Caution** Although many of the methods and properties discussed in this chapter apply to both the `geometry` and `geography` datatypes, some methods are implemented by only one type. For each method I introduce, I'll tell you which datatype (or datatypes) implements it and how it can be used on instances of that type.

Examining the Type of Geometry Used to Represent a Feature

Every item of geography or geometry data is based on an underlying geometry: Point, LineString, Curve, Polygon, or a collection containing combinations of these. The type of geometry used dictates not only the accuracy with which that instance approximates the feature it represents, but also affects the behavior of certain methods when called on that instance. The STX and STY properties discussed later in this chapter, for example, can only be used on Point instances of the `geometry` datatype, and will return NULL if used on an instance of any other type of geometry. Likewise, `STIsRing()` returns NULL if called on any type of geometry other than a LineString or other type of Curve.

One of the basic facts you might want to establish, therefore, is what type of geometry is used to represent a feature. This might appear obvious from a visual examination of a WKT or GML string, however, it is certainly not obvious from the WKB representation or SQL Server's own binary format.

SQL Server 2012 provides three methods that can be used to describe programmatically the type of geometry used to represent an instance:

- `STGeometryType()`
- `InstanceOf()`
- `STDimension()`

All three of these methods can be used on either the `geometry` or the `geography` datatype.

Returning the Type of Geometry

`STGeometryType()` can be used to return a text description of the type of geometry used to represent an instance of data. `STGeometryType()` requires no parameters and can be called on an item of geography or geometry data as follows:

`Instance.STGeometryType()`

The value returned by the `STGeometryType()` method is an `nvarchar(4000)` string that contains the name of the type of geometry represented by the instance in question. The possible values returned by `STGeometryType()` are as follows:

- `Point`
- `LineString`
- `CircularString`
- `CompoundCurve`
- `Polygon`
- `CurvePolygon`
- `MultiPoint`
- `MultiLineString`

- MultiPolygon
- GeometryCollection
- FullGlobe

To demonstate, the following code listing creates a LineString geometry instance, @Line, and then uses the STGeometryType() method to return the name of the type of geometry it represents:

```
DECLARE @Line geometry;
SET @Line = 'LINESTRING(0 0, 5 2, 8 3)';
SELECT @Line.STGeometryType();
```

The result follows:

```
LineString
```

Testing the Type of Geometry

The InstanceOf() method complements the functionality of the STGeometryType() method. Whereas STGeometryType() is used as a descriptive method to return the name of the type of geometry, the InstanceOf() method is used to test whether an instance is a specified type of geometry.

The syntax for using the InstanceOf() method is as follows:

```
Instance.InstanceOf(geometry_type)
```

The parameter geometry_type, which is an nvarchar(4000) string, specifies a type of geometry to which Instance is compared. The list of possible geometry_type parameter values that can be supplied to InstanceOf() is similar to the list of possible values returned by the STGeometryType() method, although not identical. One of the reasons why the set of values does not match exactly is because InstanceOf(geometry_type) can not only be used to determine if an instance is the exact type of geometry specified by geometry_type, but also if it is any of the types of geometry descended from geometry_type. Therefore, the set of geometry_type values against which an instance can be tested includes not only the 11 instantiable object types returned by STGeometryType(), but also the abstract Curve, Surface, MultiCurve, and MultiSurface geometry types from which LineStrings, Polygons, MultiLineStrings, and MultiPolygons are descended, respectively. You can also specify the generic Geometry type from which all other geometry types are descended.

The full list of possible values for the geometry_type parameter supplied to the InstanceOf() method is as follows:

- Geometry
- Point
- Curve
- LineString
- CircularString
- CompoundCurve
- Surface
- Polygon
- CurvePolygon
- MultiPoint

213

- MultiCurve
- MultiLineString
- MultiSurface
- MultiPolygon
- GeometryCollection
- FullGlobe

The following code listing creates a CircularString geometry, and then tests whether that geometry is an instance of a Curve, a CircularString, and a LineString.

```
DECLARE @CircularString geometry;
SET @CircularString = 'CIRCULARSTRING(0 0, 3 5, 6 1)';

SELECT
  @CircularString.InstanceOf('Curve'),            -- 1
  @CircularString.InstanceOf('CircularString'),   -- 1
  @CircularString.InstanceOf('LineString');       -- 0
```

The results confirm that @CircularString is a CircularString geometry (which is derived from the Curve geometry type), and not an instance of a LineString.

Determining the Number of Dimensions Occupied by a Geometry

Rather than determining the specific type of geometry represented by a geography or geometry instance, as returned by STGeometryType() or tested by InstanceOf(), it is sometimes helpful to consider only the number of dimensions occupied by a geometry. For example, when creating an application that draws features on a map, we may want to create a section of code that determines the fill color with which different items of data should be shaded. This code path is only relevant to two-dimensional features—Polygons, CurvePolygons, and MultiPolygons (or a GeometryCollection containing any of these elements)—because only two-dimensional objects contain an area that can be filled. Likewise, zero-dimensional features—Points and MultiPoints—commonly represent points of interest on a map and may be plotted using pushpin icons that are only relevant to these types of features.

In order to switch between code paths in an application such as this, you can use the STDimension() method, which returns an integer value representing the number of dimensions occupied by a particular item of geometry or geography data. The STDimension() method does not require any parameters and can be used against an item of geography or geometry data as follows:

```
Instance.STDimension()
```

The result of the STDimension() method is an integer value representing the number of dimensions occupied by Instance, as follows:

- For a Point or MultiPoint, STDimension() returns 0.

- For a LineString, CircularString, CompoundCurve, or MultiLineString, STDimension() returns 1.

- For a Polygon, CurvePolygon, MultiPolygon, or FullGlobe, STDimension() returns 2.

- For empty geometries of any type (i.e., a geometry that contains no points in its definition), STDimension() returns –1.

- For a Geometry Collection containing several different types of geometry, STDimension() returns the maximum number of dimensions of any element contained within that collection.

▓ **Note** Single-element and multielement instances of the same type of geometry occupy the same number of dimensions.

Table 9-1 illustrates a comparison of the results obtained from the STGeometryType(), STDimension(), and InstanceOf() methods for various types of geometry. The STGeometryType() and STDimension() columns show the result obtained from calling each method on instances of the type of geometry shown in the Geometry column. The InstanceOf() column shows the values of geometry_type that will return a value of 1 (true) when called on that type of geometry.

Table 9-1. Comparing the Results of STGeometryType(), InstanceOf(), and STDimension()

Geometry	STGeometryType()	STDimension()	InstanceOf()
Point	Point	0	Geometry, Point
LineString	LineString	1	Geometry, Curve, LineString
CircularString	CircularString	1	Geometry, Curve, CircularString
CompoundCurve	CompoundCurve	1	Geometry, Curve, CompoundCurve
Polygon	Polygon	2	Geometry, Surface, Polygon
CurvePolygon	CurvePolygon	2	Geometry, Surface, CurvePolygon
MultiPoint	MultiPoint	0	Geometry, GeometryCollection, MultiPoint
MultiLineString	MultiLineString	1	Geometry, GeometryCollection, MultiCurve, MultiLineString
MultiPolygon	MultiPolygon	2	Geometry, GeometryCollection, MultiSurface, MultiPolygon
GeometryCollection	GeometryCollection	−1, 0, 1, 2[a]	Geometry, GeometryCollection
FullGlobe	FullGlobe	2	Geometry, FullGlobe
Empty Point	Point	−1	Geometry, Point
Empty LineString	LineString	−1	Geometry, Curve, LineString
Empty Polygon	Polygon	−1	Geometry, Surface, Polygon

[a] *When you use the STDimension() method on a GeometryCollection instance, it returns the greatest number of dimensions of any element in that particular collection. For instance, for a Geometry Collection containing only Point and LineString elements, the result of STDimension() would be 1.*

An illustration of the results of some common geometry types is shown in Figure 9-1.

STGeometryType() = Point
STDimension() = 0
InstanceOf('Geometry') = 1
InstanceOf('Point') = 1

STGeometryType() = MultiPoint
STDimension() = 0
InstanceOf('Geometry') = 1
InstanceOf('GeometryCollection') = 1
InstanceOf('MultiPoint') = 1

STGeometryType() = LineString
STDimension() = 1
InstanceOf('Geometry') = 1
InstanceOf('Curve') = 1
InstanceOf('Linestring') = 1

STGeometryType() = MultiLineString
STDimension() = 1
InstanceOf('Geometry') = 1
InstanceOf('GeometryCollection') = 1
InstanceOf('MultiCurve') = 1
InstanceOf('MultiLinestring') = 1

STGeometryType() = Polygon
STDimension() = 2
InstanceOf('Geometry') = 1
InstanceOf('Surface') = 1
InstanceOf('Polygon') = 1

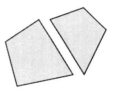

STGeometryType() = MultiPolygon
STDimension() = 2
InstanceOf('Geometry') = 1
InstanceOf('GeometryCollection') = 1
InstanceOf('MultiSurface') = 1
InstanceOf('MultiPolygon') = 1

STGeometryType() = CircularString
STDimension() = 1
InstanceOf('Geometry') = 1
InstanceOf('Curve') = 1
InstanceOf('CircularString') = 1

STGeometryType() = GeometryCollection
STDimension() = 2
InstanceOf('Geometry') = 1
InstanceOf('GeometryCollection') = 1

Figure 9-1. Comparing results of the STGeometryType(), STDimension(), and InstanceOf() methods

▓ **Note** You can download the code sample to create and test the geometries shown in Figure 9-1 (and all the remaining examples in this chapter) from the Apress website, http://www.apress.com

Testing for OGC Properties

The Open Geospatial Consortium specifications define attributes that can be assigned to types of geometry: they may be *simple* or *closed*. These attributes may be tested using the STIsSimple() and STIsClosed() methods, respectively.

Testing for Simplicity

The requirement for simplicity is essentially that a geometry cannot self-intersect; that is, it cannot contain the same point more than once (except in the case of the start/end point of a LineString or other curve). Some specific examples are as follows:

- Point geometries are always simple. MultiPoints are simple, so long as they do not contain the same Point more than once.

- LineStrings, Curves, and MultiLineStrings are simple so long as the path drawn between the points does not cross itself.

- Polygons, CurvePolygons, and MultiPolygons are always simple. (Assuming that they are valid; see Chapter 7 for information about validity)

- GeometryCollections are simple if all of the elements contained within the collection are themselves simple, and that no two elements within the collection intersect each other (other than touching at their boundaries).

The STIsSimple() method can be used to test whether a given geometry instance meets the criteria for simplicity. If the geometry represented by the instance is simple, the STIsSimple() method returns the value 1. If the geometry fails to meet the criteria required for simplicity, then the method returns 0. Figure 9-2 illustrates the results obtained from the STIsSimple() method when used on different types of geometries.

217

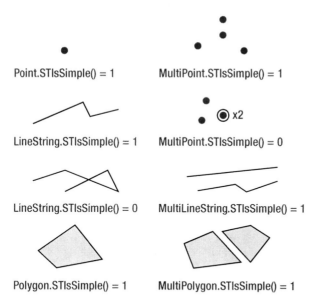

Point.STIsSimple() = 1   MultiPoint.STIsSimple() = 1

LineString.STIsSimple() = 1   MultiPoint.STIsSimple() = 0

LineString.STIsSimple() = 0   MultiLineString.STIsSimple() = 1

Polygon.STIsSimple() = 1   MultiPolygon.STIsSimple() = 1

Figure 9-2. *Testing whether a geometry is simple by using STIsSimple()*

To demonstrate the usage of STIsSimple() consider the following code listing, which creates a LineString geometry representing the route taken by a delivery van through the center of New York City. The LineString contains six points, representing the individual locations at which the van stops to make a delivery (for the purposes of illustration, we'll assume that the van takes the shortest straight-line journey between each location). The STIsSimple() method is then used to test whether the LineString geometry is simple.

```
DECLARE @DeliveryRoute geometry;
SET @DeliveryRoute = geometry::STLineFromText(
  'LINESTRING(586960 4512940, 586530 4512160, 585990 4512460,
  586325 4513096, 587402 4512517, 587480 4512661)', 32618);
SELECT
  @DeliveryRoute AS Shape,
  @DeliveryRoute.STIsSimple() AS IsSimple;
```

The STIsSimple() method in this example returns the value 0, indicating that the LineString geometry @DeliveryRoute is not simple; during its journey, the van must cross back over part of the route it has previously traveled. This might be an indication that the route represented by @DeliveryRoute is not the optimal route between the destinations. Now suppose that the van had started from the same point as before, but then had taken a different route between the remaining points, as follows:

```
DECLARE @DeliveryRoute geometry;
SET @DeliveryRoute = geometry::STLineFromText(
  'LINESTRING(586960 4512940, 587480 4512661, 587402 4512517,
  586325 4513096, 585990 4512460, 586530 4512160)', 32618);
SELECT
  @DeliveryRoute AS Shape,
  @DeliveryRoute.STIsSimple() AS IsSimple;
```

In this case, the LineString connects the same six points, but does not cross back on itself. The result of the STIsSimple() method used on this geometry is therefore 1.

By making the route simple, we have eliminated the need for the van to recross its path, reducing the total distance traveled from 3.6 km to 3.3 km (you can confirm the distance traveled using the STLength() method, which is introduced later in this chapter).

▨ **Note** The STIsSimple() method applies to the geometry datatype only. There is no equivalent method for the geography datatype.

Testing if a Geometry Is Closed

A geometry can be defined as *closed* based on the following rules:

- A Point geometry is not closed.
- A LineString, CircularString, or CompoundCurve is closed only if the start and end points are the same.
- All Polygon instances are closed.
- A Geometry Collection or multi-element geometry in which every individual geometry is closed is, itself, closed. A Geometry Collection or multi-element geometry containing any unclosed geometry (a Point, or an unclosed LineString) is not closed.

The STIsClosed() method can be used to test whether a geometry or geography instance meets the criteria specified above. The STIsClosed() method requires no parameters, and returns the value 1 if the instance is closed, or 0 if the instance is not closed. Figure 9-3 illustrates the results of the STIsClosed() method when used on examples of different types of geometry.

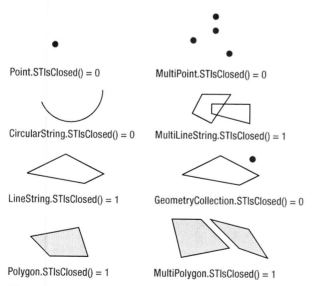

Figure 9-3. Comparing closed and not closed geometries using STIsClosed()

To demonstrate the STIsClosed() method in a real-life context, consider the following example. The summit of Mount Snowdon (*Yr Wyddfa*, in Welsh) is the highest mountain peak in Wales, at an altitude of just over 3,500 ft above sea level. To model the terrain of the mountain, we could create a MultiLineString geometry representing contour lines around the summit. A contour line is a line that connects points of equal elevation, so, in addition to stating longitude and latitude coordinates, the points of each LineString contain a *z*-coordinate value equal to the height of the contour which that LineString represents (measured in feet above sea level). The STIsClosed() method is then used to test whether the MultiLineString instance is closed.

```
DECLARE @Snowdon geography;
SET @Snowdon = geography::STMLineFromText(
'MULTILINESTRING(
 (-4.07668 53.06804 3445,  -4.07694 53.06832 3445,  -4.07681 53.06860 3445,
  -4.07668 53.06869 3445,  -4.07651 53.06860 3445,  -4.07625 53.06832 3445,
  -4.07661 53.06804 3445,  -4.07668 53.06804 3445),
 (-4.07668 53.06776 3412,  -4.07709 53.06795 3412,  -4.07717 53.06804 3412,
  -4.07730 53.06832 3412,  -4.07730 53.06860 3412,  -4.07709 53.06890 3412,
  -4.07668 53.06898 3412,  -4.07642 53.06890 3412,  -4.07597 53.06860 3412,
  -4.07582 53.06832 3412,  -4.07603 53.06804 3412,  -4.07625 53.06791 3412,
  -4.07668 53.06776 3412),
 (-4.07709 53.06768 3379,  -4.07728 53.06778 3379,  -4.07752 53.06804 3379,
  -4.07767 53.06832 3379,  -4.07773 53.06860 3379,  -4.07771 53.06890 3379,
  -4.07728 53.06918 3379,  -4.07657 53.06918 3379,  -4.07597 53.06890 3379,
  -4.07582 53.06879 3379,  -4.07541 53.06864 3379,  -4.07537 53.06860 3379,
  -4.07526 53.06832 3379,  -4.07556 53.06804 3379,  -4.07582 53.06795 3379,
  -4.07625 53.06772 3379,  -4.07668 53.06757 3379,  -4.07709 53.06768 3379))',
  4326);
SELECT
  @Snowdon AS Shape,
  @Snowdon.STIsClosed() AS IsClosed;
```

The shape of the @Snowdon MultiLineString geometry, as displayed in SQL Server Management Studio's Spatial Results tab, is illustrated in Figure 9-4.

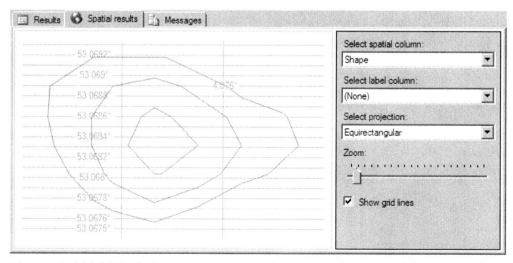

Figure 9-4. *A MultiLineString geometry representing contour rings around the summit of Mount Snowdon.*

Because each LineString element contained within the MultiLineString ends at the same point from which it started, @Snowdon is a closed geometry, and the result returned by the STIsClosed() method is 1.

▨ **Tip** Remember that you can use the optional z-coordinate to state the elevation, or height, of each point in a geometry.

Testing Whether a LineString or Curve Is a Ring

Rings are Curve geometries that are both simple and closed. The STIsRing() method is the OGC-compliant method for testing whether a geometry instance is an example of a ring.

When used on a LineString, CircularString, or CompoundCurve instance, STIsRing() returns a value of 1 if the instance meets the criteria for a ring, or 0 if the instance is not a ring. When used against any sort of geometry other than a Curve, the method returns NULL.

▨ **Tip** Since a ring is a closed simple LineString, STIsRing() = 1 is logically equivalent to InstanceOf('Curve') = 1 AND STIsClosed() = 1 AND STIsSimple() = 1.

To demonstrate the usage of STIsRing(), the following code listing creates a LineString geometry representing the track of the Indianapolis Motor Speedway, home of the Indy 500 race. It then uses the STIsRing() method to test whether the geometry created is a ring.

```
DECLARE @Speedway geometry;
SET @Speedway = geometry::STLineFromText(
  'LINESTRING(565900 4404737, 565875 4405861, 565800 4405987, 565670 4406055,
    565361 4406050, 565222 4405975, 565150 4405825, 565170 4404760, 565222 4404617,
    565361 4404521, 565700 4404524, 565834 4404603, 565900 4404737)', 32616);
SELECT
  @Speedway AS Shape,
  @Speedway.STIsRing() AS IsRing;
```

The result of the STIsRing() method is 1, which confirms that the geometry representing the oval-shaped track is a ring; it starts and ends at the same point, and does not cross itself.

Counting the Number of Points in a Geometry

Having established the type of geometry used to represent a feature, and the OGC properties of that geometry, another common requirement is to count the number of points used to define that geometry. There are two methods that return information relating to the number of points in a geometry definition – STNumPoints() and STIsEmpty().

Returning the Number of Points in a Geometry

The STNumPoints() method returns the number of points used to define a geography or geometry instance. Every point listed in the geometry definition is counted; if the geometry definition includes the same point several times, it will be counted multiple times. For example, the start and end point of each ring in a Polygon are the same. Because these points are duplicated, when used against a Polygon geometry, the result of STNumPoints() will always be greater than the number of sides of the shape.

The STNumPoints() method does not take any parameters and can be used on an item of geography or geometry data as follows:

```
Instance.STNumPoints()
```

The result of the method is an integer value representing the number of points used to define the instance. Figure 9-5 illustrates the results of the STNumPoints() method when used against a variety of geometry types.

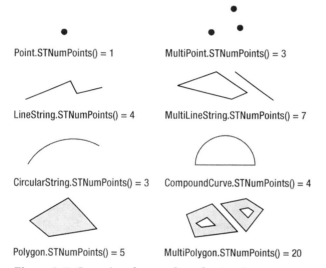

Point.STNumPoints() = 1   MultiPoint.STNumPoints() = 3

LineString.STNumPoints() = 4   MultiLineString.STNumPoints() = 7

CircularString.STNumPoints() = 3   CompoundCurve.STNumPoints() = 4

Polygon.STNumPoints() = 5   MultiPolygon.STNumPoints() = 20

Figure 9-5. *Counting the number of points in a geometry using STNumPoints()*

As an example of the STNumPoints() method, consider the Bermuda Triangle, an area of the Atlantic Ocean famed for causing the unexplained disappearance of ships and aircraft that pass through it. Although the exact location of the triangle varies between different sources, it is popularly defined as being the area contained within the points of Miami, Florida; San Juan, Puerto Rico; and the island of Bermuda. The following code listing creates a geography Polygon representing the Bermuda Triangle based on these points, and then calls the STNumPoints() method on the resulting instance:

```
DECLARE @BermudaTriangle geography;
SET @BermudaTriangle = geography::STPolyFromText(
  'POLYGON((-66.07 18.45, -64.78 32.3, -80.21 25.78, -66.07 18.45))',
  4326);

SELECT
  @BermudaTriangle AS Shape,
  @BermudaTriangle.STNumPoints() AS NumPoints;
```

The result of the STNumPoints() method in this example is 4.

▦ **Caution** The definition of a three-sided Polygon, such as the Bermuda Triangle, contains four points, not three, as you might think! This is because the STNumPoints() method counts the point at the start and end of each Polygon ring twice.

Testing Whether a Geometry Is Empty

An *empty* geometry is one that does not contain any points. Empty geometries are not generally created directly, but are often returned in the results of a spatial query. In such cases, they can be thought of as meaning "No location exists that matches the criteria of this query." For example, the STIntersection() method can be used to return a geometry that represents the set of points shared between two geometries. If those instances have no points in common (they are *disjoint*), then the result returned by the STIntersection() method will be an empty geometry.

▦ **Note** An empty geometry is not the same as NULL. A NULL value in a geometry or geography column suggests that a result has not been evaluated. An empty geometry suggests that a result has been evaluated, but the corresponding location does not exist on the earth.

The STIsEmpty() method can be used to test whether a given geometry is empty. It does not require any parameters and can be used against an instance of either the geometry or geography datatype as follows:

Instance.STIsEmpty()

If the geometry represented by Instance does not contain any points, then the result of STIsEmpty() will be 1. Otherwise, the result will be 0.

▦ **Tip** STIsEmpty() = 1 is logically equivalent to STNumPoints() = 0.

To demonstrate, the following example creates two parallel LineString geometries, @LineString1 and @LineString2. It then uses the STIntersection() method to create the geometry formed from the intersection of the two LineStrings, before calling the STIsEmpty() method on the resulting geometry.

```
DECLARE @LineString1 geometry;
DECLARE @LineString2 geometry;
SET @LineString1 = geometry::STLineFromText('LINESTRING(2 4, 10 6)', 0);
SET @LineString2 = geometry::STLineFromText('LINESTRING(0 2, 8 4)', 0);
SELECT
  @LineString1.STUnion(@LineString2) AS Shape,
  @LineString1.STIntersection(@LineString2).STIsEmpty() AS IsEmpty;
```

The result of the STIsEmpty() method is 1, which shows that the geometry created by the STIntersection() method in this case is an empty geometry, containing no points. In other words, @LineString1 and @LineString2 do not have any points in common with each other.

Returning Individual Points from a Geometry

With the exceptions of an empty geometry (which has no points) and a Point geometry (which contains only one point), every other geometry or geography instance is defined by a set of many individual points. It is often the case that we want to identify or retrieve these points individually from the geometry. SQL Server provides several methods that return individual points from a geometry, which we'll examine in this section.

Retrieving a Point by Index

The STPointN() method can be used to isolate and return any individual point from the definition of a geometry. STPointN() must be supplied with an integer parameter n, which specifies the ordinal number of the point that should be returned from the geometry. The syntax is as follows:

```
Instance.STPointN(n)
```

Instance.STPointN(n) returns the nth point of the geometry defined by Instance. Valid values for the parameter n range from 1 (the first point of the geometry) to the result returned by STNumPoints() (the final point in the geometry). The return value of the STPointN() method is a geography or geometry Point, matching the datatype of the instance on which the method was called.

PointN() is frequently used inside a loop construct in which the iterator ranges from 1 to the value of STNumPoints(), to loop through and perform some action with every point in a geometry as shown in the following C# code listing:

```
for (int n = 1; n <= geometry.STNumPoints(); n++) {

  SqlGeometry x = geometry.STPointN(n);

  // Do something with Point x…
}
```

Figure 9-6 illustrates the results of the STPointN() method when used on a variety of different types of geometry.

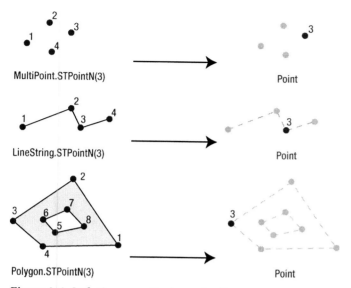

Figure 9-6. *Isolating a particular point from a geometry using STPointN()*

▧ **Note** To use the STPointN() method effectively, you must understand the order in which the points of a geometry are defined. If the geometry was created by a user, the points are listed in the order in which they were passed to the static method that created the instance. If the geometry was created by SQL Server (from the result of another method), points are ordered first by instance, then by ring within the instance, and then by point within each ring.

To demonstrate the usage of STPointN(), the following example creates a MultiPoint geography instance, in which each point represents the location of a mile marker spaced equally at every mile along the course of the London Marathon. The STPointN() method is used to select the fourteenth point in the MultiPoint, which represents the approximate halfway point of the race.

```
DECLARE @LondonMarathon geography;
SET @LondonMarathon = geography::STMPointFromText(
  'MULTIPOINT(0.0112 51.4731, 0.0335 51.4749, 0.0527 51.4803, 0.0621 51.4906,
  0.0448 51.4923, 0.0238 51.4870, 0.0021 51.4843, -0.0151 51.4814,
  -0.0351 51.4861, -0.0460 51.4962, -0.0355 51.5011, -0.0509 51.5013,
  -0.0704 51.4989, -0.0719 51.5084, -0.0493 51.5098, -0.0275 51.5093,
  -0.0257 51.4963, -0.0134 51.4884, -0.0178 51.5003, -0.0195 51.5046,
  -0.0087 51.5072, -0.0278 51.5112, -0.0472 51.5099, -0.0699 51.5084,
  -0.0911 51.5105, -0.1138 51.5108, -0.1263 51.5010, -0.1376 51.5031)',
  4326);

SELECT
  @LondonMarathon AS Shape,
```

```
@LondonMarathon.STPointN(14) AS Point14,
@LondonMarathon.STPointN(14).STAsText() AS WKT;
```

The WKT representation of the result returned by the STPointN() method is as follows:

```
POINT (-0.0719 51.5084)
```

Returning the Start and End Point of a Geometry

STStartPoint() and STEndPoint() are "shortcut" methods that provide the same result as STPointN() when used in the specific cases of returning the first point and the last point of a geometry, respectively:

- Instance.STStartPoint() is equivalent to Instance.STPointN(1)

- Instance.STEndPoint() is equivalent to
  Instance.STPointN(Instance.STNumPoints())

STStartPoint() and STEndPoint() can be used on any geography or geometry instances, although they are most useful when applied to nonclosed LineStrings or Curves, because these have separate and distinct endpoints, and are commonly directed (i.e., they have a logical "start" and "end"). The result of the STStartPoint() and STEndPoint() methods is a Point instance of either geography or geometry datatype, matching the type of the instance on which the method was called.

To demonstrate the use of these methods, let's consider an example. In May 1919, a crew of five aviators completed the first successful transatlantic flight, under the command of Lieutenant Commander Albert Read. Starting in Rockaway Naval Air Station, Read first piloted his NC-4 aircraft to Halifax, Nova Scotia, then on to Trepassey, Newfoundland, before crossing to the island of Horta in the Azores. From the Azores, the crew then set off to Lisbon, Portugal, and made a short stop in Spain before finally completing the journey at Plymouth, England. The following code listing creates a LineString geometry representing the approximate route taken, and then uses the STStartPoint() and STEndPoint() methods to return the points at the start and end of the journey.

```
DECLARE @TransatlanticCrossing geography;
SET @TransatlanticCrossing = geography::STLineFromText('
LINESTRING(
  -73.88 40.57, -63.57 44.65, -53.36 46.74, -28.63 38.54,
  -28.24 38.42, -9.14 38.71,  -8.22 43.49,  -4.14 50.37)',
  4326
);
SELECT
  @TransatlanticCrossing AS Shape,
  @TransatlanticCrossing.STStartPoint().STAsText() AS StartPoint,
  @TransatlanticCrossing.STEndPoint().STAsText() AS EndPoint;
```

The results, two Point geometries representing the locations of Rockway Naval Air Station and Plymouth, are as follows:

```
StartPoint              EndPoint
POINT (-73.88 40.57)    POINT (-4.14 50.37)
```

Determining the Center of a Geometry

There are many ways to define the "center" of a shape. In SQL Server, different methods are provided for determining the center of a geometry instance and for a geography instance.

Calculating the Centroid of a geometry Instance

For determining the center of a geometry Polygon, CurvePolygon, or MultiPolygon instance, you can use the STCentroid() method to calculate its *centroid*. The centroid of a Polygon can be thought of as its "center of gravity," the point around which the area contained by the Polygon is evenly distributed. The position of the centroid is derived mathematically from a calculation based on the overall shape of the geometry.

The STCentroid() method requires no parameters and can be used on any geometry instance that contains at least one Polygon or CurvePolygon element, as follows:

```
Instance.STCentroid()
```

The result is a single geometry Point instance, defined using the same SRID as the instance on which it was called. Note that STCentroid() can be used only on Polygon or MultiPolygon geometries; if used on a Point or LineString, the method will return NULL. Figure 9-7 illustrates the centroid of several Polygons of the geometry datatype.

▒ **Caution** The centroid of a Polygon is not necessarily contained inside the Polygon itself; it is the point around which the Polygon is evenly distributed.

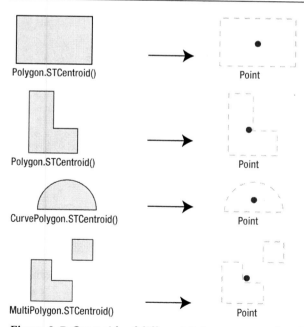

Polygon.STCentroid()   Point

Polygon.STCentroid()   Point

CurvePolygon.STCentroid()   Point

MultiPolygon.STCentroid()   Point

Figure 9-7. Centroids of different Polygon geometries obtained using STCentroid()

The following example creates a Polygon geometry representing the state of Colorado, and then uses the STCentroid() method to determine the centroid of that Polygon:

```
DECLARE @Colorado geometry;
SET @Colorado = geometry::STGeomFromText('POLYGON((-102.0423 36.9931, -102.0518
41.0025, -109.0501 41.0006, -109.0452 36.9990, -102.0423 36.9931))', 4326);
SELECT
  @Colorado AS Shape,
  @Colorado.STCentroid() AS Centroid,
  @Colorado.STCentroid().STAsText() AS WKT;
```

The WKT representation of the result of the STCentroid() method in this example is as follows:

```
POINT (-105.54621375420314 38.998581021101813)
```

In this example, I've used the geometry datatype, but supplied WGS84 geographic coordinates (SRID 4326). The centroid is therefore calculated by treating longitude and latitude as mapped directly to the *x*- and *y*-axis of a two-dimensional plane, and the resulting location is calculated as being a few miles north of Elevenmile Canyon Reservoir, in the geometric center of the state. This is illustrated in Figure 9-8.

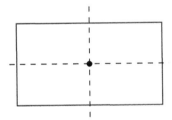

Figure 9-8. Calculating the geometric center of a Polygon using STCentroid().

Calculating the Envelope Center of a geography Instance

The STCentroid() method cannot be applied to the geography datatype. However, similar functionality is provided by the EnvelopeCenter() method. EnvelopeCenter() averages the position vectors that describe the location of each point in the geometry from the center of the earth, and returns a Point geometry plotted at the resulting position. This is a very simple approximation of the center point of any type of geometry. In contrast to the STCentroid() method of the geometry datatype, which can be used only on Polygon instances, the EnvelopeCenter() method can be used on any instance of the geography datatype, as follows:

```
Instance.EnvelopeCenter()
```

The result of the method is a geography Point instance, defined using the same spatial reference system as that in which the original instance was supplied.

▩ **Note** The result of the EnvelopeCenter() method is based on the average of each *unique* point in a geometry. If the same point is defined twice in a geography instance, such as the start point and end point of a closed ring, this point is included only once in the calculation.

Figure 9-9 illustrates the method by which the result of EnvelopeCenter() is calculated for a geography Polygon defined by the points P1, P2, P3, and P4. The position vectors describing the location of each point from the center of the earth are averaged (with the point P1, which represents both the start and end points of the Polygon ring, included only once), and the method returns the Point located at the resulting position.

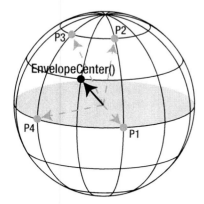

Figure 9-9. Using the EnvelopeCenter() method to calculate the center point of a geography instance

The following example creates a geography Polygon representing the state of Utah, and then uses the EnvelopeCenter() method to return the point at the center of the Polygon:

```
DECLARE @Utah geography;
SET @Utah = geography::STPolyFromText(
  'POLYGON((-109 37, -109 41, -111 41, -111 42, -114 42, -114 37, -109 37))', 4326);
SELECT
  @Utah AS Shape,
  @Utah.EnvelopeCenter() AS EnvelopeCenter,
  @Utah.EnvelopeCenter().STAsText() AS WKT;
```

The WKT representation of the Point returned by the EnvelopeCenter() method is as follows:

```
POINT (-111.33053985766453 40.018634026864916)
```

Figure 9-10 illustrates the location of this point relative to the Polygon representing the overall shape of Utah state, projected using the Mercator projection. Unlike STCentroid(), the centerpoint obtained from EnvelopeCenter() lies slightly to the northeast of the simple geometric center obtained from averaging the minimum and maximum coordinate values. This is due to the fact that the Polygon definition contains a greater density of points defining the concave corner at the northeast of the state than the single point at each of the other three corners. This causes the average vector calculated by EnvelopeCenter() to be weighted to the northeast.

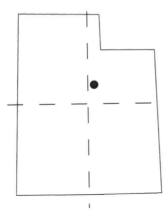

Figure 9-10. Using the EnvelopeCenter() method on a Polygon representing the state of Utah

Returning an Arbitrary Point from a Geometry

STPointN(), STStartPoint(), and STEndPoint() return one of the points used to define a geometry. By definition, the result of any of these methods will therefore be a point that lies on the edge of the geometry in question (because the shape of a geometry is defined by its edges). Sometimes, however, you might want to return a point that lies somewhere inside a geometry, not at its extremes. One example of this might be when determining the appropriate location to place a label on a map describing a feature. You wouldn't want the label to appear on the edge of the Polygon representing an area, but somewhere inside it. In these circumstances, you might want to use the STPointOnSurface() method.

The STPointOnSurface() method can be used on any instance of the geometry datatype to return an arbitrary point that lies within the interior of that geometry. The result of the STPointOnSurface() method depends on the type of geometry on which the method is called:

- For LineStrings, Curves, or MultiLineStrings, the result is a Point that lies somewhere on the path of the LineString / Curve.

- For Polygons and CurvePolygons, the result is a Point within the exterior ring (and not contained within an interior ring).

- For Points, the result is the Point itself, or in the case of MultiPoints, any one Point contained within the MultiPoint collection.

- For empty geometries, the STPointOnSurface() method returns NULL.

"Why would you want to return a single arbitrary point from a geometry?" you might be wondering. "Surely, if you wanted to choose a single location to represent the overall shape of a Polygon geometry you'd be better off determining the center of the shape using the STCentroid() method, because that will return a point in the middle of the shape?" The answer to this question is that, although the STCentroid() method can be used to determine the point representing the centroid of a geometry, the resulting Point is not necessarily contained within the geometry itself. In contrast, the result of the STPointOnSurface() method will always be a single Point that is guaranteed to lie in the interior of the geometry on which the method is called.

The STPointOnSurface() method can be used only with instances of the geometry datatype as follows:

```
Instance.STPointOnSurface()
```

The following example creates a Polygon geometry, and then uses the STPointOnSurface() method to return an arbitrary point contained within that Polygon:

```
DECLARE @Polygon geometry;
SET @Polygon = geometry::STGeomFromText('POLYGON((10 2,10 4,5 4,5 2,10 2))',0);
SELECT
  @Polygon AS Shape,
  @Polygon.STPointOnSurface() AS PointOnSurface,
  @Polygon.STPointOnSurface().STAsText() AS WKT;
```

The WKT representation of the result of the STPointOnSurface() method in this example is as follows:

```
POINT (8.3333333333333339 3.3333333333333335)
```

■ **Note** The STPointOnSurface() method returns an *arbitrary* point, not a *random* point. If you were to execute the preceding code listing several times, you would receive the same result on each occasion.

Returning Coordinate Values

Having used one of the methods in the preceding section to isolate an individual point from a geometry (or, in the case of a Point geometry, the point itself), we can then examine the coordinate values assigned to that point.

Coordinate values for instances of the geometry and geography datatypes are defined using different sorts of coordinate system: planar and geographic, respectively. This difference is also reflected in different methods you use to access those coordinate values between the two datatypes.

Returning geometry Coordinates

To retrieve the x and y Cartesian coordinates used to define a geometry instance, you use the STX and STY properties, respectively. These properties both return a floating-point number representing the appropriate coordinate value.

For example, the following example creates a Point geometry from projected coordinates representing the location of Johannesburg, South Africa, using the UTM projection (Zone 35, Southern Hemisphere). It then uses the STX and STY properties to retrieve the x- (Easting) and y- (Northing) coordinates of that Point.

```
DECLARE @Johannesburg geometry;
SET @Johannesburg = geometry::STGeomFromText('POINT(604931 7107923)', 32735);
SELECT
  @Johannesburg.STX AS X,
  @Johannesburg.STY AS Y;
```

The results are as follows:

```
X        Y
604931   7107923
```

Returning geography Coordinates

When using the geography datatype, the equivalent functionality of the STX and STY properties is provided by the Lat and Long properties. These properties work in exactly the same way as STX and STY, except that, instead of relating to *x* and *y* planar coordinate values of a geometry Point, they retrieve the geographic coordinates of latitude and longitude from a geography Point.

The following example creates a Point using the geography datatype from a well-known binary representation, corresponding to the location of Colombo, Sri Lanka. It then uses the Long and Lat properties to retrieve the longitude and latitude coordinates of that Point.

```
DECLARE @Colombo geography;
SET @Colombo =
  geography::STGeomFromWKB(0x01010000006666666666F65340B81E85EB51B81B40, 4326);
SELECT
  @Colombo.Long AS Longitude,
  @Colombo.Lat AS Latitude;
```

The results are as follows:

```
Longitude    Latitude
79.85          6.93
```

Returning Extended Coordinate Values

In addition to the required *x*- and *y*-coordinates of every point in a geometry instance, or the equivalent longitude and latitude coordinates in the geography datatype, each point may also be defined as having optional *z*- and *m*-coordinates. The *z*-coordinate is used to store the height, or elevation, of a point. The *m*-coordinate is any measure that can be associated with the point, expressed as a floating-point number.

To test whether a geometry contains *z*- or *m*-coordinate values, you can examine the HasZ and HasM properties of the instance. These properties return 1 if the instance contains at least one *z*- or *m*-coordinate, respectively, or 0 if they do not. Then to retrieve these additional coordinate values for either a geometry or geography instance, you can use Z and M properties of a Point geometry. The result is a floating-point number representing the appropriate *z*- or *m*-coordinate value. If no coordinate value is defined, the result is NULL. These properties apply to both the geography and geometry datatype.

For example, The Federal Communications Commission maintains a database of antenna structures registered for wireless telecommunications communication within the United States. The database contains a variety of fields, including the latitude and longitude of each antenna and the overall height above ground level. You can search the database online at http://wireless2.fcc.gov/UlsApp/AsrSearch/asrRegistrationSearch.jsp. The following code listing creates a Point geometry representing one such antenna, located at a latitude of 39°49'54"N and a longitude of 89°38'52"W, using the EPSG:4269 spatial reference system. The antenna extends to 34.7 m above ground level, which is represented by the *z*-coordinate of the point. The *m*-coordinate is assigned a value of 1000131, which represents a reference number assigned to this antenna. The example then demonstrates how the Z and M properties can be used to retrieve the corresponding coordinate values of the Point.

```
DECLARE @Antenna geography;
SET @Antenna =
  geography::STPointFromText('POINT(-89.64778 39.83167 34.7 1000131)', 4269);
SELECT
  @Antenna.HasM AS HasM,
  @Antenna.M AS M,
  @Antenna.HasZ AS HasZ,
  @Antenna.Z AS Z;
```

The results are as follows:

HasM	M	HasZ	Z
1	1000131	1	34.7

For a dataset where each record has only a single associated z- or m-value (such as a dataset containing only Point geometries, or a set of Polygons in which every point of a given Polygon is at a constant elevation), you may prefer to store those z- and m-coordinate values as separate numeric columns in your table rather than using the Z and M properties of a geometry/geography instance. Storing the additional coordinate values in separate columns makes it easier to set and retrieve those coordinate values without having to address the entire geometry instance. Adding indexes to those columns then allows you to query, say, all those antennae that are between 40 m and 50 m in height more efficiently than trying to query the Z and M properties of instances in a spatial column directly.

However, you may need to deal with more complex geometries such as LineStrings or MultiPoints where the z- and m-coordinates vary with each point in the geometry; in this case, it is more convenient to use the Z and M properties to serialize the additional coordinates of each point as part of the geometry/geography instance itself. Using Z and M properties ensures that all the coordinate values of a feature are serialized as part of a single contained instance, which might also enhance portability when you come to export that data from SQL Server into another system.

Properties Describing the Extent of a Geometry

So far, we have considered a number of properties that describe aspects of a geometry as a single Point—its center, start, end, or nth point—and the methods to retrieve the individual coordinate values associated with each of those points. Certain other properties are best described not by Points, but by Polygons or LineStrings describing the geographic extent of a feature. In this section, we'll examine some of these methods used to calculate the boundary and envelope of a geometry.

Calculating the Boundary of a Geometry

The STBoundary() method returns the geometry representing the boundary of a geometry instance. In spatial data, the word *boundary* does not mean the outer perimeter of the geometry, as you might expect, but has a specific definition depending on the type of geometry in question:

- Point and MultiPoint instances do not have a boundary.

- LineStrings and MultiLineStrings have a boundary formed from the start points and end points of the geometry, removing any points that occur an even number of times.

- The boundary of a Polygon is formed from the LineStrings that represent each of its rings.

The STBoundary() method does not require any parameters, so it can be invoked on an instance of the geometry datatype as follows:

```
Instance.STBoundary()
```

The result will be a geometry instance, the exact type of which will depend on the type of geometry of the instance on which it was called. Figure 9-11 illustrates the result of the STBoundary() method when used on a variety of different types of geometry.

■ **Tip** If used against a Polygon containing no interior rings, the geometry created by STBoundary() is the same as the ExteriorRing() method. However, whereas STExteriorRing() returns the points of the ring in the order they were defined, STBoundary() returns points starting with the smallest coordinate value.

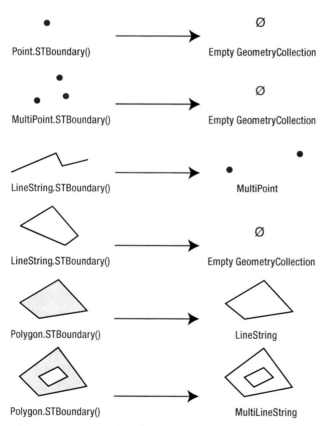

Figure 9-11. Examples of geometries created by the STBoundary() method

To demonstrate, the following example creates a Polygon geometry in the shape of a capital letter *A*, and then uses the STBoundary() method to identify the boundary of the Polygon:

```
DECLARE @A geometry;
SET @A = geometry::STPolyFromText(
  'POLYGON((0 0, 4 0, 6 5, 14 5, 16 0, 20 0, 13 20, 7 20, 0 0),
    (7 8,13 8,10 16,7 8))', 0);
SELECT
  @A AS Shape,
  @A.STBoundary() AS Boundary,
  @A.STBoundary().STAsText() AS WKT;
```

The following is the WKT representation of the result of the STBoundary() method in this example, which is illustrated in Figure 9-12.

```
MULTILINESTRING ((7 8, 10 16, 13 8, 7 8), (0 0, 4 0, 6 5, 14 5, 16 0, 20 0, 13 20,
7 20, 0 0))
```

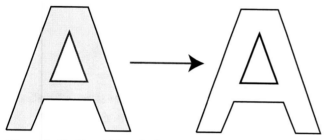

Figure 9-12. Identifying the boundary of a Polygon geometry of the capital letter A using STBoundary()

Calculating the Envelope of a Geometry

The envelope of a geometry represents the smallest axis-aligned rectangle that completely encompasses every part of the geometry. It is also referred to as a *bounding box*, although care should be taken not to confuse the "bounding box" of a geometry with its "boundary" as described in the preceding section.

If MinX, MaxX, MinY, and MaxY are the minimum and maximum x- and y-coordinates of any point contained in the geometry, then the bounding box is the Polygon defined by the following WKT representation:

```
POLYGON((MinX MinY, MaxX MinY, MaxX MaxY, MinX MaxY, MinX MinY))
```

The STEnvelope() method can be used to return the bounding box of any type of instance of the geometry datatype. It requires no parameters and can be called as follows:

```
Instance.STEnvelope()
```

The result of the STEnvelope() method will always be a Polygon, defined using the same SRID as the geometry instance on which it was invoked. Figure 9-13 illustrates the bounding boxes created by the STEnvelope() method when used on a variety of geometry instances.

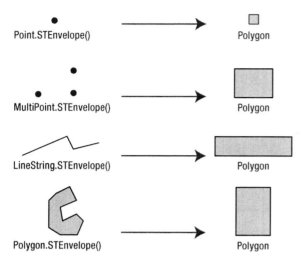

Figure 9-13. *Creating envelopes of different types of geometry using STEnvelope()*

■ **Note** If you use the STEnvelope() method on a Point instance, SQL Server will create the Polygon of smallest area around that point. For example, the result of STEnvelope() around a Point at POINT(30 20) is POLYGON ((29.999999 19.999999, 30.000001 19.999999, 30.000001 20.000001, 29.999999 20.000001, 29.999999 19.999999)).

The following code creates a Polygon geometry in the shape of a capital letter *A*, and then creates the bounding box around the Polygon using the STEnvelope() method:

```
DECLARE @A geometry;
SET @A = geometry::STPolyFromText(
  'POLYGON((0 0, 4 0, 6 5, 14 5, 16 0, 20 0, 13 20, 7 20, 0 0),
  (7 8,13 8,10 16,7 8))', 0);
SELECT
  @A AS Shape,
  @A.STEnvelope() AS Envelope,
  @A.STEnvelope().STAsText() AS WKT;
```

The following is the result of the STEnvelope() method in WKT format, which is illustrated in Figure 9-14:

```
POLYGON ((0 0, 20 0, 20 20, 0 20, 0 0))
```

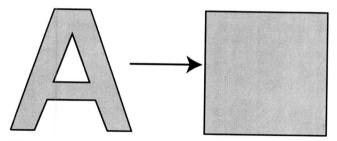

Figure 9-14. Creating a bounding box of a geometry Polygon of the capital letter A using STEnvelope()

Calculating the Bounding Circle of a geography Instance

The STEnvelope() method cannot be used on instances of the geography datatype, since the straight axis-aligned lines of a simple rectangular bounding box cannot be applied to an elliptical model of the earth. However, SQL Server provides an alternative method to describe the extent of a geography instance, through the use of the EnvelopeCenter() and EnvelopeAngle() methods.

You have already been introduced to the EnvelopeCenter() method earlier in this chapter, where it was used to determine the Point calculated from the vector average of all the points in a geography instance as an approximation of the center of any type of geometry. The EnvelopeAngle() method returns the angle between the point obtained from the EnvelopeCenter() method and the point in the geometry that lies furthest from the EnvelopeCenter() point. The resulting value is a measure of the maximum extent to which a geography instance spreads out from its central point. Figure 9-15 illustrates the method by which EnvelopeCenter() is calculated.

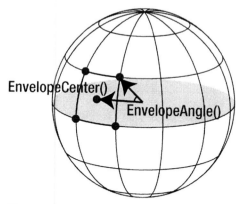

Figure 9-15. Calculating the extent of a geography instance using EnvelopeAngle()

The EnvelopeAngle() method does not require any parameters and can be called on an instance of the geography datatype as follows:

Instance.EnvelopeAngle()

The result of the EnvelopeAngle() method is a floating-point number. For geography instances that occupy less than a hemisphere, the value will be between 0 and 90, representing an angle measured in degrees. For any instances larger than a hemisphere, EnvelopeAngle() always returns 180 rather than the true obtuse angle.

The following example creates a geography Polygon, @NorthernHemisphere, representing the Northern Hemisphere. @NorthernHemisphere is defined as the area contained within an exterior ring of points lying just above the equator, at a latitude of 0.1 degrees north. The example then uses the EnvelopeAngle() method to calculate the greatest angle between any point in the @NorthernHemisphere Polygon and the center of the envelope.

```
DECLARE @NorthernHemisphere geography
SET @NorthernHemisphere =
  geography::STGeomFromText('POLYGON((0 0.1,90 0.1,180 0.1, -90 0.1, 0 0.1))',4326)
SELECT
  @NorthernHemisphere AS Shape,
  @NorthernHemisphere.EnvelopeAngle() AS EnvelopeAngle;
```

Since as the center of the envelope is the North Pole, and the Polygon extends to just above the equator, the result shows an angle close to 90°:

```
89.90000000000014
```

If we were to repeat this code listing, but moving the ring of points to lie exactly on the equator, the Polygon would no longer be contained within a single hemispehere and EnvelopeAngle() would instead return 180:

```
DECLARE @NorthernHemisphere geography
SET @NorthernHemisphere =
  geography::STGeomFromText('POLYGON((0 0,90 0,180 0, -90 0, 0 0))',4326)
SELECT
  @NorthernHemisphere AS Shape,
  @NorthernHemisphere.EnvelopeAngle() AS EnvelopeAngle;
```

```
180
```

▓ **Note** The result of the EnvelopeAngle() method for any geography instance larger than a hemisphere will always be 180.

I hope by now that you have a good appreciation of the difference between the geometry and geography datatypes, and understand the reason that you cannot calculate a simple bounding box on the ellipsoidal surface of the geography datatype. However, calculating the center and angle of a bounding circle using the alternative EnvelopeCenter() and EnvelopeAngle() methods provided by the geography datatype often don't give us the information we're after either.

A common requirement is to calculate a simple, four-sided Polygon that encompasses the extent of a geography instance, without worrying too much about the strict technicalities of defining straight lines on a smooth surface. In such cases, one approach is to treat the geographic coordinates of an instance as geometric coordinates, calculate the bounding box using the geometry STEnvelope() method, and then interpret the results back as a geography instance again. Here's an example:

```
-- Declare a geography instance
DECLARE @geog geography;
SET @geog = geography::STPolyFromText('POLYGON((-4 50, 2 52, -1 60, -4 50))', 4326);

-- Interpret as a geometry instance
DECLARE @geom geometry;
SET @geom = geometry::STPolyFromWKB(@geog.STAsBinary(), @geog.STSrid);

-- Create the (geometry) bounding box
DECLARE @geomboundingbox geometry;
SET @geomboundingbox = @geom.STEnvelope();

-- Interpret results as geography
DECLARE @geogboundingbox geography;
SET @geogboundingbox = geography::STPolyFromWKB(@geomboundingbox.STAsBinary(),
@geomboundingbox.STSrid);

SELECT @geogboundingbox.ToString();
```

The result is as follows:

```
POLYGON ((-4 50, 2 50, 2 60, -4 60, -4 50))
```

Note that this result is only an approximation, and the method will fail in certain cases (such as geometries that cross the 180th meridian of the poles). Nevertheless, this approach can still be used to provide a reasonable "bounding box" for geography instances in many circumstances.

Properties Related to Surfaces

Polygons and CurvePolygons, which are both descended from the abstract Surface type, are formed from one or more rings. These rings define the boundaries of the areas of space either included by or excluded from the geometry. There are a number of properties specific to working with the rings of surfaces, which will be discussed in this section.

Isolating the Exterior Ring of a Geometry Polygon

As previously discussed, Polygons and CurvePolygons may contain a number of internal rings that define *holes*: areas of space cut out of the main geometry. Sometimes, however, it can be useful to consider just the exterior ring of a Polygon, ignoring any interior rings that might be defined within it. The STExteriorRing() method can be used in this case.

STExteriorRing() returns a LineString or Curve geometry representing the exterior perimeter boundary of a Polygon or CurvePolygon. Figure 9-16 illustrates the results of the STExteriorRing() method when used against different geometry Polygon instances.

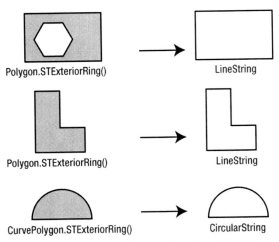

Figure 9-16. Isolating the exterior ring of a Polygon geometry

The following code listing creates a geometry Polygon in the shape of a capital letter *A*. The STExteriorRing() method is then used to return the exterior ring of the Polygon.

```
DECLARE @A geometry;
SET @A = geometry::STPolyFromText(
  'POLYGON((0 0, 4 0, 6 5, 14 5, 16 0, 20 0, 13 20, 7 20, 0 0),
         (7 8,13 8,10 16,7 8))',
    0);
SELECT
  @A AS Shape,
  @A.STExteriorRing() AS ExteriorRing,
  @A.STExteriorRing().STAsText() AS WKT;
```

The following WKT representation of the STExteriorRing() method is illustrated in Figure 9-17:

LINESTRING (0 0, 4 0, 6 5, 14 5, 16 0, 20 0, 13 20, 7 20, 0 0)

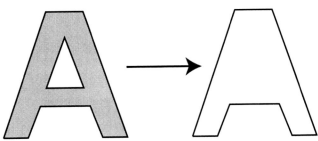

Figure 9-17. Using STExteriorRing() to isolate the exterior ring of the capital letter A

■ **Note** The STExteriorRing() method returns a LineString or Curve geometry of the exterior ring itself, not the Polygon that encloses the area within that ring. It does not simply "fill in the holes" created by the internal rings within a Polygon.

Counting the Interior Rings of a geometry

The STNumInteriorRing() method is used to return an integer value that represents the total number of internal rings defined within a Polygon or CurvePolygon geometry. If a Polygon contains no interior rings, then the result of the method is 0. STNumInteriorRing() requires no parameters and can be used against a geometry Polygon or CurvePolygon instance as follows:

Instance.STNumInteriorRing()

The result is an integer value, equal to or greater than zero, representing the number of interior rings defined by the geometry.

■ **Caution** Unlike the naming convention used for similar methods that count the number of geometries or number of points in an instance (STNumGeometries() and STNumPoints(), respectively), the method to count the number of interior rings is named STNumInteriorRing() (not the plural *STNumInteriorRings()*, as you may expect). This seems to be an oversight of the OGC rather than of Microsoft, as this is the way in which the method is defined in the OGC specifications.

Figure 9-18 illustrates the results of the STNumInteriorRing() method when used on two different MultiPolygon instances.

Polygon.STNumInteriorRing() = 1   MultiPolygon.STNumInteriorRing() = 3

Figure 9-18. Counting the number of interior rings in a Polygon geometry

To demonstrate, the following code listing creates a Polygon and then uses the STNumInteriorRing() method to confirm the number of interior rings contained within the Polygon:

```
DECLARE @Polygon geometry;
SET @Polygon = geometry::STPolyFromText('
  POLYGON(
    (0 0, 20 0, 20 10, 0 10, 0 0),
    (3 1,3 8,2 8,3 1),
    (14 2,18 6, 12 4, 14 2))',
```

```
    0);
SELECT
  @Polygon AS Shape,
  @Polygon.STNumInteriorRing() AS NumInteriorRing;
```

The result of the STNumInteriorRing() method is as follows:

2

Isolating an Interior Ring from a geometry Polygon

The STInteriorRingN() method isolates the *n*th interior ring from a Polygon or CurvePolygon. Because the rings of a Polygon are made up of closed LineStrings or Curves, the result of the method will always be a simple closed LineString or Curve. The syntax for the STInteriorRingN() method, used on an instance of a geometry Polygon, is as follows:

Instance.STInteriorRingN(n)

This will return the geometry that represents the *n*th ring of Instance. Valid values for n range from 1 (the first interior ring) to the result of STNumInteriorRing() (the final interior ring).

Figure 9-19 illustrates the resulting geometry created by the STInteriorRingN() method when used on a variety of different geometry instances.

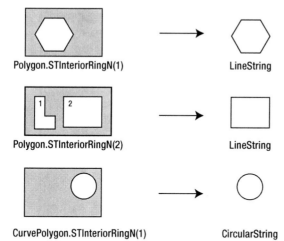

Figure 9-19. Isolating an interior ring from a Polygon geometry

To demonstrate the use of the STInteriorRingN() method, the following example creates a geometry Polygon in the shape of a capital letter *A*. It then uses the STInteriorRingN() method to isolate the first (and only) interior ring from the geometry.

```
DECLARE @A geometry;
SET @A = geometry::STPolyFromText(
  'POLYGON((0 0, 4 0, 6 5, 14 5, 16 0, 20 0, 13 20, 7 20, 0 0),
    (7 8,13 8,10 16,7 8))', 0);
```

```
SELECT
  @A AS Shape,
  @A.STInteriorRingN(1) AS InteriorRing1,
  @A.STInteriorRingN(1).STAsText() AS WKT;
```

The result of the STInteriorRingN() method, expressed in WKT here, is illustrated in Figure 9-20:

LINESTRING (7 8, 13 8, 10 16, 7 8)

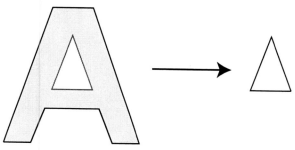

Figure 9-20. Isolating the interior ring from a geometry Polygon of the capital letter A

Counting the Rings in a geography Polygon

When using the geography datatype, which defines positions on a round model of the Earth, you cannot sensibly assign the rings of a Polygon into the categories of "interior" and "exterior;" every ring divides space into those areas contained within the Polygon and those excluded from it. For this reason, the geography datatype does not implement the STNumInteriorRing() method, but rather has a separate method, NumRings(). The NumRings() method counts the total number of rings in a geography Polygon instance, without making any distinction between whether they are "interior" or "exterior."

The NumRings() method can be used on a geography Polygon instance as follows:

Instance.NumRings()

The result is an integer value representing the total number of defined rings for the Polygon. Figure 9-21 illustrates the results of the NumRings() method on two different geography Polygons.

Polygon.NumRings() = 1   Polygon.NumRings() = 2

Figure 9-21. Counting the total number of rings in a geography Polygon using NumRings()

To demonstrate, the following code creates a geography Polygon containing two rings, representing the U.S. Department of Defense Pentagon building. It then uses the NumRings() method to count the number of rings in the instance.

```
DECLARE @Pentagon geography;
SET @Pentagon = geography::STPolyFromText(
  'POLYGON(
    (
      -77.0532 38.87086,
      -77.0546 38.87304,
      -77.0579 38.87280,
      -77.0585 38.87022,
      -77.0555 38.86907,
      -77.0532 38.87086
    ),
    (
      -77.0558 38.87028,
      -77.0569 38.87073,
      -77.0567 38.87170,
      -77.0554 38.87185,
      -77.0549 38.87098,
      -77.0558 38.87028
    )
  )',
  4326
);
SELECT
  @Pentagon AS Shape,
  @Pentagon.NumRings() AS NumRings;
```

The result of the NumRings() method confirms that the Polygon, @Pentagon, contains two rings:

2

Isolating a Ring from a geography Polygon

Just as the geography datatype implements the NumRings() method rather than STNumInteriorRing(), it also defines its own method for isolating any given ring from a Polygon, without classification of "interior" or "exterior." The method used to isolate any ring from a geography Polygon is RingN().

The RingN() method must be supplied with a parameter n, which specifies the ring to return from the geography instance, as follows:

```
Instance.RingN(n)
```

The value of n must be an integer between one and the total number of rings contained by the instance (which can be determined using the NumRings() method). The result of the method will be a LineString of the geography datatype, defined using the SRID of Instance.

Figure 9-22 illustrates the result of the RingN() method when used on a Polygon of the geography datatype.

Figure 9-22. *Isolating a particular ring from a geography Polygon using RingN()*

To demonstrate, the following code creates a geography Polygon containing two rings, once again representing the U.S. Department of Defense Pentagon building. It then uses the RingN() method to isolate just the first ring from the definition, before returning the WKT representation of the result.

```
DECLARE @Pentagon geography;
SET @Pentagon = geography::STPolyFromText(
  'POLYGON(
    (
      -77.05322 38.87086,
      -77.05468 38.87304,
      -77.05788 38.87280,
      -77.05849 38.87022,
      -77.05556 38.86906,
      -77.05322 38.87086
    ),
    (
      -77.05582 38.87028,
      -77.05693 38.87073,
      -77.05673 38.87170,
      -77.05547 38.87185,
      -77.05492 38.87098,
      -77.05582 38.87028
    )
  )',
  4326
);
SELECT
  @Pentagon AS Shape,
  @Pentagon.RingN(1) AS Ring1,
  @Pentagon.RingN(1).STAsText() AS WKT;
```

The WKT representation of the result of the RingN() method is as follows:

```
LINESTRING (-77.05322 38.87086, -77.05468 38.87304, -77.05788 38.8728, -77.05849 38.87022,
-77.05556 38.86906, -77.05322 38.87086)
```

Properties Related to GeometryCollections

There are two properties specifically used when dealing with geometry collections: STNumGeometries() and STGeometryN(). Conceptually, they mirror the behavior of STNumPoints() and STPointN() but, rather than counting or retrieving a particular point from a geometry, they count and retrieve a particular geometry from a geometry collection.

Counting the Number of Geometries in a Collection

The STNumGeometries() method operates in much the same way as the STNumPoints() method introduced earlier in this chapter, except that instead of counting the number of points within a geometry, STNumGeometries() returns an integer value equal to the number of geometries contained within a geometry or geography instance. When used against a GeometryCollection, the result will be the number of elements contained within the collection. If used against a single-element instance—Point, LineString, or Polygon—the result of STNumGeometries() will be 1. If used on an empty instance of any type, the result will be 0.

Figure 9-23 illustrates the results of the STNumGeometries() method when used on a variety of geometry instances.

Point.STNumGeometries() = 1   MultiPoint.STNumGeometries() = 4

   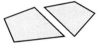

MultiLineString.STNumGeometries() = 2   MultiPolygon.STNumGeometries() = 2

GeometryCollection.STNumGeometries() = 2

Figure 9-23. *Counting the number of geometries in an instance using STNumGeometries()*

The STNumGeometries() method does not require any parameters and can be called on a geography or geometry instance as follows:

```
Instance.STNumGeometries()
```

In the following example, a GeometryCollection is created that contains a MultiPoint element (consisting of two Points), a LineString, and a Polygon. The STNumGeometries() method is then used to count the total number of elements in the collection.

```
DECLARE @Collection geometry;
SET @Collection = geometry::STGeomFromText('
  GEOMETRYCOLLECTION(
    MULTIPOINT((32 2), (23 12)),
    LINESTRING(30 2, 31 5),
    POLYGON((20 2, 23 2.5, 21 3, 20 2))
  )',
  0);

SELECT
  @Collection AS Shape,
  @Collection.STNumGeometries() AS NumGeometries;
```

The result of the STNumGeometries() method is three. Note that, even though the MultiPoint element contains two Point geometries, the result of STNumGeometries() for the entire collection is three, because the MultiPoint geometry is counted as only one element in the GeometryCollection. STNumGeometries() counts single-element geometries (Point, LineString, and Polygon), multielement geometries (MultiPoint, MultiLineString, and MultiPolygon), and empty geometries of any type contained within a collection as single items.

Retrieving an Individual Geometry from a Collection

The STGeometryN() method returns the *n*th geometry from a Geometry Collection. It can be used on either the generic Geometry Collection object or one of the specific subtypes of collection: MultiPoint, MultiLineString, or MultiPolygon.

The STGeometryN() method must be supplied with a single parameter n, using the following syntax,

```
Instance.STGeometryN(n)
```

where n is the ordinal number of the geometry from the collection that you want to retrieve. The value of n must be between one and the total number of elements in the Geometry Collection (which you can obtain from the value of STNumGeometries()).

Figure 9-24 illustrates the use of the STGeometryN() method to isolate individual elements from a range of geometries.

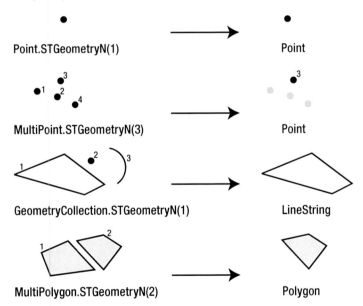

Figure 9-24. Isolating an individual geometry from a collection

---

■ **Note** You can use STGeometryN(1) on a single-element geometry, in which case the result of the method is the geometry itself.

The following example creates a MultiLineString geometry representing the seven runways at Dallas/Fort Worth International Airport, which has the greatest number of runways of any airport in the world. It then uses the STGeometryN() method to isolate and return a LineString geometry representing a single runway.

```
DECLARE @DFWRunways geography;
SET @DFWRunways = geography::STMLineFromText(
  'MULTILINESTRING(
    (-97.0214781 32.9125542, -97.0008442 32.8949814),
    (-97.0831328 32.9095756, -97.0632761 32.8902694),
    (-97.0259706 32.9157078, -97.0261717 32.8788783),
    (-97.0097789 32.8983206, -97.0099086 32.8749594),
    (-97.0298833 32.9157222, -97.0300811 32.8788939),
    (-97.0507357 32.9157992, -97.0509261 32.8789717),
    (-97.0546419 32.9158147, -97.0548336 32.8789861)
  )', 4326);
SELECT
  @DFWRunways AS Shape,
  @DFWRunways.STGeometryN(3) AS Geometry3,
  @DFWRunways.STGeometryN(3).STAsText() AS WKT;
```

The WKT representation of the result of the STGeometryN() method is as follows:

```
LINESTRING (-97.0259706 32.9157078, -97.0261717 32.8788783)
```

Calculating Metrics

There are two broad metrics that can be defined for a geometry: namely, how long is the geometry, and what area does it contain? SQL Server provides methods to answer both of these questions.

Measuring the Length of a Geometry

STLength() returns the length of a geometry. When used on a LineString or Curve, this gives the total length of the line or curve segments joining the points. When used on a Polygon, this represents the total length of all defined rings of the Polygon. For a Polygon or CurvePolygon containing only one ring, STLength() therefore returns the length of the perimeter of the Polygon. If used on a multielement type such as MultiLineString, the STLength() method returns the total length of all elements in an instance, or of all the instances within a GeometryCollection.

The STLength() method can be used on any type of geometry or geography instance as follows:

```
Instance.STLength()
```

The result is a floating-point number representing the length of the geometry in question. For geography instances, the result will be stated in the units in the unit_of_measure column of the sys.spatial_reference_systems table corresponding to the SRID in which the coordinates were stated. For geometry instances, the result will be stated in the same units of measure as the coordinates of the geometry themselves.

Figure 9-25 illustrates the result of the STLength() method when used on different types of geometry.

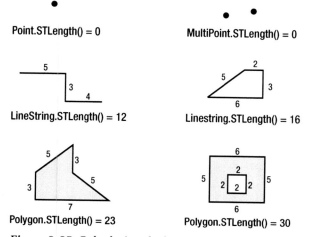

Figure 9-25. *Calculating the length of various types of geometry*

To demonstrate the use of STLength(), consider the following example; the Royal Mile is the straight route connecting Edinburgh Castle with the Palace of Holyrood House, which runs along some of the oldest streets in Edinburgh. The following code listing creates a LineString geometry representing the Royal Mile, and then uses the STLength() method to determine its length:

```
DECLARE @RoyalMile geography;
SET @RoyalMile = geography::STLineFromText(
  'LINESTRING(-3.20001 55.94821, -3.17227 55.9528)', 4326);
SELECT
  @RoyalMile AS Shape,
  @RoyalMile.STLength() AS Length;
```

The result of the STLength() method is as follows:

```
1806.77067641223
```

Because the coordinates of the @RoyalMile LineString were defined using the EPSG:4326 spatial reference system, the result is stated in the unit of measurement for that system, which is the meter. Prior to 1824, the result of 1,807 meters, as measured along the length of the Royal Mile, was the definition of a *Scottish mile*. This is longer than the mile in common usage today, which is equal to approximately 1,609 meters.

Calculating the Area Contained by a Geometry

The STArea() method is used to calculate and return the total area occupied by an object. If used on a zero- or one-dimensional object (i.e., a Point or a LineString), then the STArea() method will return 0.

When used with the geography datatype, the results of the STArea() method will be returned in the square of the unit of measure defined by the spatial reference system of the geography instance. For example, when used against a geography object specified with SRID 4326, the result returned by STArea() will be expressed in square meters, whereas when using SRID 4157, the unit of measure will be square feet.

When used against a geometry object, the unit of measure will be the square of the unit in which the coordinates were supplied.

The STArea() method can be called on any item of geography or geometry as follows:

```
Instance.STArea()
```

Figure 9-26 illustrates the result of the STArea() method when used against different types of geometry.

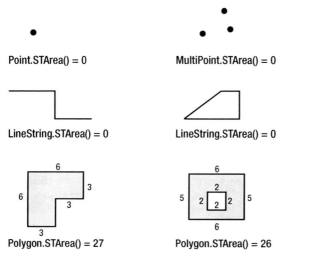

Figure 9-26. Calculating the area of various types of geometry using STArea()

▓ **Note** The result of STArea() will be 0 for any geometry unless it contains at least one Polygon or CurvePolygon geometry.

To demonstrate, the following code listing creates a geometry Polygon representing a plot of land in the south of France, using the UTM Zone 31N projection (EPSG:32631). The plot has an associated cost, represented by the variable @Cost. By dividing the total cost of the plot by the result of the STArea() method applied to the geometry, we can work out the cost per square meter of land.

```
DECLARE @Cost money = 80000;
DECLARE @Plot geometry;
SET @Plot = geometry::STPolyFromText(
  'POLYGON((633000 4913260, 633000 4913447, 632628 4913447, 632642 4913260,
    633000 4913260))',
  32631);
SELECT
  @Plot AS Shape,
  @Cost / @Plot.STArea() AS PerUnitAreaCost;
```

Because the coordinate values supplied in EPSG:32631 are measured in meters, the result represents the cost per square meter of land, as follows:

1.1720753058384

Setting or Retrieving the Spatial Reference Identifier (SRID)

Every instance of either the geography or geometry datatype has an associated spatial reference identifier. This specifies the system in which the coordinates are defined, enabling them to identify a unique location on the earth. The STSrid property can be used to return, or set, the SRID of any instance.

STSrid is unusual in that, whereas every other property discussed in this chapter is read-only, STSrid can be used to retrieve the current SRID assigned to an instance *or* set it to a new value.

For example, suppose you wanted to import some spatial data stated in projected coordinates from an unknown source, for which you did not know the spatial reference system in which the coordinates had been defined. Because projected coordinates operate on a flat plane, you can initially import the data into a field of geometry datatype using SRID 0, as follows:

```
CREATE TABLE #Imported_Data (
  Location geometry
);
```

```
INSERT INTO #Imported_Data VALUES
  (geometry::STGeomFromText('LINESTRING(122 74, 123 72)', 0)),
  (geometry::STGeomFromText('LINESTRING(140 65, 132 63)', 0));
```

You can check the SRID of the items contained in the Location column of the #Imported_Data table by selecting the STSrid property, as follows:

```
SELECT
  Location.STAsText(),
  Location.STSrid
FROM #Imported_Data;
```

The following are the results:

```
LINESTRING (122 74, 123 72)    0
LINESTRING (140 65, 132 63)    0
```

Now suppose that, having inserted the data, you discover that it relates to projected coordinates based on the EPSG:32731 reference system. You therefore want to update the SRID of all your records to reflect this. To do so, you can set the value of the STSrid property using an UPDATE statement, as follows:

```
UPDATE #Imported_Data
  SET Location.STSrid = 32731;
```

If you now select the value of the STSrid property once more, you find that the SRID of each geometry in the table has been updated to the correct value:

```
SELECT
  Location.STAsText(),
  Location.STSrid
FROM #Imported_Data;
```

The results are as follows:

```
LINESTRING (122 74, 123 72)     32731
LINESTRING (140 65, 132 63)     32731
```

■ **Note** Specifying a different SRID does not cause the coordinate values of a geometry to be reprojected into that system. It only provides the description of the system in which those coordinates have been defined.

Summary

In this chapter, you learned about various properties of the geometry and geography datatypes, and the methods used to access them.

- Some methods are used to isolate and retrieve individual parts of a geometry; they return geography or geometry instances matching the datatype and SRID of the instance on which the method was called. Examples include STStartPoint() (which returns a Point), STRingN() (which returns a Curve or LineString ring), and STEnvelope() (which returns a Polygon).

- Other methods return text or numeric values that describe some aspect of a geometry: the name of the type of geometry used to represent a feature (STGeometryType()), or the number of points it contains (STNumPoints()), for example.

- Some methods can only be applied to instances of either the geometry or geography datatype. In most cases, similar functionality is available in the other datatype using a different method.

Having a solid understanding of the properties available for each datatype and how to access them will help you to create spatial applications that analyze spatial data appropriately.

CHAPTER 10

Modification and Simplification

In this chapter, we'll examine the methods that can be used to create new geometries by modifying existing instances of geography or geometry data. Such modifications include enlarging or shrinking a geometry (STBuffer()), inverting it (ReorientObject()), straightening its curved edges (STCurveToLine()), or simplifying it (Reduce()).

Each of the methods discussed in this chapter acts upon only a single instance. Some methods, such as STConvexHull() and ReorientObject(), require no parameters. Others require one or more parameters, such as STBuffer() and Reduce(). As is the case with all the spatial functionality in SQL Server, the geometry and geography datatypes do not necessarily have the same set of methods available, or are implemented in exactly the same way. For each method introduced in this chapter, I'll show you how and when it can be used.

Note The methods discussed in this chapter do not alter the original instance on which they are invoked. Rather, they create a new instance based on a modification of that geometry.

Simplifying a Geometry

Spatial data is frequently complex; a single Polygon or LineString geometry may be constructed from tens of thousands of individual points. While possessing a large number of points increases the detail and accuracy of a shape, it also makes it cumbersome to deal with, and makes any queries involving that geometry less efficient.

In many cases, we may prefer to generalize spatial data so that it can be analyzed at a macro level without unnecessary detail. When considering a Polygon representing an entire country, for example, we rarely need to take account of every individual crag and cove that lies along its coastline. For large countries, a simple shape that approximates the national border to within 10, or even 100, meters may be sufficient for many purposes, and may lead to significant performance benefits compared to a more detailed geometry, accurate to the nearest millimeter.

One particular situation in which simplification should be considered is when retrieving spatial data for visual display, either on a screen or in print. As noted in Chapter 7, the coordinates of each point in a geometry or geography instance are stored with highly accurate, 64-bit precision. But, when you come to plot those coordinates on a display, you are generally limited to a fixed resolution; 72 or 96 dots per inch (DPI) are common resolutions for computer displays, while 300 DPI is a common standard for print.

When displayed, each point in the geometry must be plotted exactly at one of those dot locations; it is not possible to subdivide a pixel on a monitor, for example, and, depending on the scale at which it is displayed, the pixel location of coordinates in a highly detailed shape can coincide.

It is clearly a waste of computational resources to plot multiple overlapping points on the same pixel location, since they will not be distinguishable by the viewer, and rendering them will not lead to any greater detail in the displayed image. When retrieving spatial data for display with a small resolution (i.e., "zoomed out" from the shape), simpler features will therefore contain just as much visual detail as more complex features.

SQL Server's Reduce() method can be used to simplify a geometry: reducing the number of points in its definition, while still attempting to maintain its overall shape. The resulting simplified shape is useful both for performing fast approximate calculations, and also for displaying geometries at low resolutions. The Reduce() method uses a standard mathematical algorithm called the Douglas–Peucker algorithm, which is described in the following section.

The Douglas–Peucker Algorithm

The Douglas–Peucker algorithm, first published in an article in *Canadian Cartographer* in 1973 and named after its authors, David Douglas and Thomas Peucker, is an iterative algorithm that simplifies a shape based on a single parameter, *tolerance*. On its first iteration, the algorithm creates a very basic approximation of a shape by simply joining the start and end points directly with a straight line. On the second iteration, the points of the original geometry are examined to determine whether any lie farther away from this line than the specified tolerance value. If so, the point that lies farthest away is added back to the simplified geometry, creating a more refined approximation. On subsequent iterations this process is repeated: examining the remaining original points and, if any lie outside the stated tolerance, adding them back to refine the approximation further until, eventually, all of the points contained within the original geometry lie within the accepted tolerance from the approximation created. At this point the algorithm stops, and the approximation created by the last iteration is returned.

Figure 10-1 depicts the process by which the Douglas–Peucker algorithm simplifies a LineString geometry. In the example depicted, the algorithm requires three iterations before all the points in the simplified approximation lie with the specified tolerance value of the original LineString geometry.

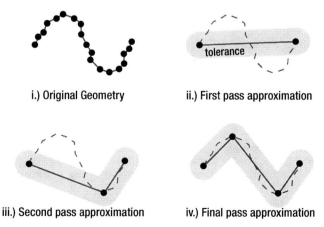

i.) Original Geometry   ii.) First pass approximation

iii.) Second pass approximation   iv.) Final pass approximation

Figure 10-1. The Douglas–Peucker reduction algorithm

The Reduce() Method

The Reduce() method allows you to apply the Douglas–Peucker algorithm to simplify any item of either geography or geometry data. The simplified approximation returned by the Reduce() method depends on the type of geometry on which it is used:

- For Point geometries, the algorithm has no effect. The result returned by Reduce() is exactly the same as the original supplied geometry.

- For LineString, CircularString, and CompoundCurve geometries, the algorithm maintains the direction of the geometry; that is, it retains the original start and end points. However, the coordinates of any other points in the simplified geometry may differ from those in the original supplied geometry due to rounding occurring during calculation.

- For Polygon and CurvePolygon geometries, neither the exact location of any of the points, nor the direction of the simplified instance will necessarily be maintained.

- For GeometryCollections, the Reduce() method acts on each element contained within the collection in isolation, and returns a collection consisting of the individual simplified geometries.

The Reduce() method can be used on an instance of either the geometry or geography datatype, using syntax as follows:

Instance.Reduce(tolerance)

The single parameter, tolerance, is applied by the Douglas–Peucker algorithm. This value represents the maximum allowed deviation between any point in the resulting simpler geometry compared to the original geometry. tolerance must be a positive, floating-point value, measured in linear units. When used on an instance of the geography datatype, tolerance is measured in the units defined by the unit_of_measure column of the sys.spatial_reference_systems table corresponding to the SRID in which the instance is defined. When used on an instance of the geometry datatype, tolerance is measured in the same unit of measure as the coordinate values of the instance.

The greater the tolerance, the greater is the degree of simplification in the geometry returned by the Reduce() method. Figure 10-2 illustrates the effect of supplying different tolerance values to the Reduce() method acting upon a MultiPolygon geometry representing Australia.

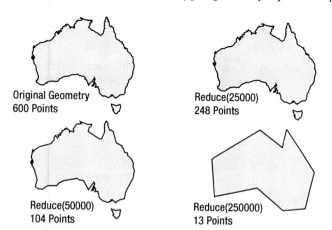

Figure 10-2. Comparing the geometry created by the Reduce() method with different levels of tolerance

> ▪ **Note** Point and MultiPoint geometries cannot be simplified. When used on an instance of these types of geometries, the Reduce() method returns a copy of the original unmodified geometry.

The following code listing creates a LineString geometry containing eight points, and then uses the Reduce() method to obtain a simplified reduction of that geometry that deviates by no more than one unit from any point in the original geometry:

```
DECLARE @LineString geometry;
SET @LineString =
'LINESTRING(130 33, 131 33.5, 131.5 32.9, 133 32.5, 135 33, 137 32, 138 31, 140 30)';

SELECT
  @LineString.Reduce(1).ToString() AS SimplifiedLine;
```

The simpler geometry obtained from the Reduce() method contains only three points, as represented by the following well-known text:

```
LINESTRING (130 33, 135 33, 140 30)
```

Converting Curves to Lines

When representing a curved feature—a meandering river, a bend in a road, or other arc, for example—the most suitable geometry type is generally the CircularString or, for an area contained by such an arc, a CurvePolygon. These geometries are capable of representing the shape of smoothly curved features with maximum accuracy, while requiring only a relatively small number of points to do so.

However, curved geometries were only introduced in SQL Server 2012 and are not supported by many other spatial systems or previous editions of SQL Server. To ensure that your data is portable to other spatial applications, and to maintain backward compatability with SQL Server 2008/R2, you may want to convert curved geometries to an approximation based on the equivalent linear geometry type; that is:

- CircularStrings and CompoundCurves can be approximated by LineStrings.
- CurvePolygons can be approximated by Polygons.

In order to maintain the shape of curved geometries, additional points need to be inserted along each arc segment, with the straight line segments between them approximating the smooth path of the curve. SQL Server provides two methods that can be used to perform these conversions to linear geometry types: STCurveToLine() and CurveToLineWithTolerance().

Linearization with STCurveToLine()

The OGC-compliant method for converting curved geometries to their equivalent linear geometry type is STCurveToLine(). It requires no parameters, and can be used on instances of either the geography or geometry datatype.

If used on geometry types other than a CircularString, CompoundCurve, or CurvePolygon, STCurveToLine() returns the unchanged instance on which it was called. Otherwise, it returns a LineString or Polygon (or collection of those types) representing a straight-edged approximation of the supplied curved geometry.

The following code listing creates a CircularString that forms a complete circle of radius 10 units about an origin at (0, 0). It then creates a linear approximation of that circle using the STCurveToLine() method.

```
DECLARE @CircularString geometry;
SET @CircularString = 'CIRCULARSTRING(10 0, 0 10, -10 0, 0 -10, 10 0)';

DECLARE @LineString geometry;
SET @LineString = @CircularString.STCurveToLine();

SELECT
  @CircularString.STLength(),
  @LineString.STLength(),
  @CircularString.STNumPoints(),
  @LineString.STNumPoints();
```

The results demonstrate that the length of the original curve and the corresponding LineString approximation created by STCurveToLine() are very similar (62.8318530717959 compared to 62.806623139095). However, whereas the CircularString required only 5 points, the LineString definition contains 65.

Approximate Linearization

While the STCurveToLine() method achieves the objective of creating a linear approximation of a curved geometry, there is no control over the accuracy of the resulting approximation. In the example demonstrated previously, the LineString returned by STCurveToLine() contained 65 points, a 1,200% increase on the number of points in the original CircularString instance!

On some occasions you may want to retain all of the points in the resulting geometry in order to create the closest approximation of the original curved feature. However, in other situations you may prefer to make a tradeoff, sacrificing some of that accuracy for a simpler linear approximation. One method of doing so would be to use a two-step process: first, using STCurveToLine() to create a detailed linear approximation of the feature, and then using the Reduce() method (described earlier this chapter) to remove some of the points from the resulting LineString or Polygon. However, SQL Server also provides a way to combine both these steps in one go, by using CurveToLineWithTolerance().

The CurveToLineWithTolerance() method can be used to create a linear approximation of a curved geometry in much the same way as STCurveToLine(), except that it requires two additional parameters — tolerance and relative — that affect how closely the resulting geometry matches the shape of the original geometry. The syntax is as follows:

`Instance.CurveToLineWithTolerance(tolerance, relative)`

The parameters are as follows:

- tolerance is the maximum allowed deviation between the resulting linear geometry and the original curved geometry. It is conceptually the same as the tolerance parameter supplied to the Reduce() method.

- relative is a Boolean flag that specifies whether the tolerance used to determine the simplified result should be treated as an absolute value, or whether the degree of simplification should be relative to the size of the geometry. If relative is set to false, the supplied tolerance is considered to be an absolute tolerance, expressed in the same unit of measurement as the coordinates themselves (or the linear unit of measurement corresponding to geographic coordinates). If relative is set to true, the allowed tolerance is calculated as the product of the supplied tolerance value and the diameter of the bounding box of the original instance. Thus, when relative is true, the result of CurveToLineWithTolerance() when called on geographically larger shapes will be allowed to deviate more than for smaller, more precise geometries.

Figure 10-3 compares the results of STCurveToLine() and LineToCurveWithTolerance() when invoked on a CircularString instance.

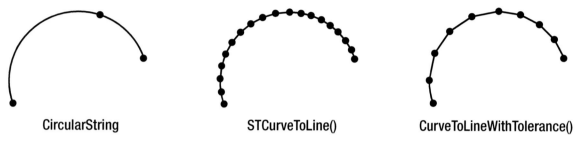

CircularString   STCurveToLine()   CurveToLineWithTolerance()

Figure 10-3. Linear approximations of a CircularString created using STCurveToLine() and CurveToLineWithTolerance()

Reorienting a geography Polygon

For the geography datatype, the order of the vertices in a Polygon ring determines the area of space contained within the Polygon. SQL Server applies the "left-hand rule" (or "left-foot rule"), so that areas lying to the left-hand side of the line drawn between the points are considered to be inside the Polygon, whereas areas to the right of the line are excluded.

Unfortunately, not all spatial systems follow this convention; some systems and spatial data formats employ the "right-hand rule" instead, which applies exactly the same logic as the left-hand rule but in reverse. Under the right-hand rule, areas on the right-hand side of the path between the points of a Polygon ring are included, whereas areas on the left are excluded.

In order to import data into SQL Server that has been defined using the right-hand rule convention, you need to reverse the order in which the points are defined. This will change the orientation of each ring and have the effect of inverting the Polygon; any area previously included will be excluded, and any area previously in the exterior of the Polygon will now be in the interior.

To perform this inversion operation, you can use the ReorientObject() method. ReorientObject() can be invoked only on instances of the geography datatype (since ring orientation is not significant for the geometry datatype), as follows:

```
Instance.ReorientObject()
```

ReorientObject() affects only two-dimensional geometries: Polygons, CurvePolygons, or collections containing either of those geometry types (Points, LineStrings, and other curves are returned by the ReorientObject() method as-is). The rings of each Polygon or CurvePolygon supplied are reversed, so that the resulting geometry represents the complementary shape on the Earth's surface. Logically, for an individual geography Polygon, @polygon:

```
DECLARE @polygon geography = 'POLYGON((-2 50, 4 52, -1 60, -2 50))';
SELECT @polygon.ReorientObject();
```

gives the same result as:

```
DECLARE @polygon geography = 'POLYGON((-2 50, 4 52, -1 60, -2 50))';
DECLARE @world geography = geography::STGeomFromText('FULLGLOBE', @polygon.STSrid);
SELECT @world.STDifference(@polygon);
```

Figure 10-4 illustrates a geography Polygon containing an interior ring, and the corresponding inverted Polygon created by the ReorientObject() method.

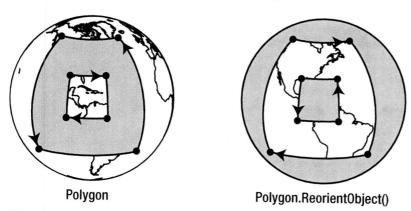

Polygon   **Polygon.ReorientObject()**

Figure 10-4. Inverting a geography Polygon with ReorientObject()

Sometimes, you might have a set of data that has been created with a mixture of rules regarding ring orientation. For example, suppose that you had a front-end application that allowed users to define areas by clicking on a map to place the vertices of a Polygon. Some users may have encompassed an area by placing points in a counterclockwise direction (following the "left-hand rule"), whereas others may have placed the points in a clockwise fashion (following the "right-hand rule"). How do you know whether these instances should be reoriented?

One useful technique for dealing with such cases is to combine ReorientObject() with EnvelopeAngle() (discussed in Chapter 9). Assuming that, as in most applications, the areas of interest defined by users of the application are always smaller than a hemisphere, the value of EnvelopeAngle() for those geometries should always be less than 90. If the Polygon defined by a user is greater than a hemisphere (i.e., EnvelopeAngle() returns 180), then we assume that the ring orientation is incorrect, and call ReorientObject() to invert the geometry. The following code listing demonstrates this approach in a simple SELECT statement, although this same logic could easily be applied to a stored procedure called at the point that user-created data was inserted into a table:

```
DECLARE @g geography;
-- SET @g to be polygon defined by user

-- Reorient the polygon if it has been defined as larger than a hemisphere
-- Assume that this indicates incorrect ring orientation
SELECT
CASE
  WHEN @g.EnvelopeAngle() <= 90 THEN @g
  ELSE @g.ReorientObject()
END AS Oriented;
```

Densification

Densification can be thought of as the opposite of simplification. Whereas simplification seeks to remove points from the definition of a geometry while maintaining its overall general shape, densification inserts additional points that lie on the path of the existing shape.

For example, the geometry LineString LINESTRING(0 0, 10 0) can be densified by inserting additional points that lie along the *x*-axis between the two points, such as LINESTRING (0 0, 4 0, 8 0, 10 0). This is illustrated in Figure 10-5.

LINESTRING(0 0, 10 0)   **LINESTRING(0 0, 2 0, 6 0, 10 0)**

Figure 10-5. Additional points inserted as a result of densifiying a LineString geometry

Inserting these additional points does not change the shape of the geometry, nor does it have any effect on the length or area contained by the shape, so why do it?

Densification of a geometry, in isolation, isn't very useful. However, it becomes important when you want to reproject that geometry into a different spatial reference system. In Chapter 8, I showed you how to create functions that could convert coordinates between different spatial reference systems. These functions can convert individual coordinate values, making them suitable for use in either the geometry or geography datatype. However, simply converting the coordinates of each point to a suitable spatial reference system does not create a logically equivalent geometry; the geometry and geography datatypes operate on different types of surfaces, with different assumptions about the shape of the earth. Although you can convert the individual points that form the vertices of a Polygon, say, the path followed between those points differs in different spatial reference systems. In the geometry datatype, for example, the path between any two points is a straight line. Using the geography datatype, in contrast, the path between any two points is a great elliptic arc. Therefore, the midpoint of a LineString calculated between two points on the Earth's surface using the geometry datatype is not the same as the midpoint of the LineString between those same two points in the geography datatype (even after accounting for coordinate conversion).

To demonstrate this concept, consider the border between the United States and Canada, which was defined in the Anglo-American Treaty of 1818 as the ". . . line drawn from the most northwestern point of the Lake of the Woods, along the 49th parallel of north latitude . . . to the Stony Mountains." The 49th parallel is the circle around the Earth formed from all those points at a latitude of 49 degrees North of the equator. You can see the section of the 49th parallel drawn as a straight line on Microsoft Bing Maps, as shown in Figure 10-6.

Figure 10-6. The straight line path between two points on the 49th parallel

Bing Maps uses a projected spatial reference system, EPSG: 3857, in which coordinates are measured in meters on a spherical Mercator projection of the WGS84 datum. Using this system, the section of the 49th parallel highlighted in Figure 10-6 can be represented as a single LineString between two points of the geometry datatype, as follows:

```
DECLARE @49thParallel geometry;
SET @49thParallel = geometry::STLineFromText('LINESTRING (-13727919 6274861, -10592049
6274861)', 3857);
```

However, since the American–Canadian border is defined with respect to a latitude coordinate, you might find it more natural to use the geography datatype instead. Using the coordinate conversion function described in Chapter 6, we can convert the coordinates of this LineString to EPSG:4326 suitable for the geography datatype. This results in the following:

```
DECLARE @49thParallel_geo geography;
SET @49thParallel_geo = geography::STLineFromText('LINESTRING (-123.32 49, -95.15 49)', 4326);
```

As you might expect, the geography LineString connects two points with a latitude of 49 degrees. The problem is that the resulting shape drawn between these two points is actually quite different from that in the preceding example. The path between two points in the geography datatype does not follow the straight line of constant latitude shown in Figure 10-6, but rather follows the great elliptic arc between the points. Since the two points at either end of this LineString lie north of the equator, the shortest path between them does not follow a line of constant latitude 49 degrees, but bends up towards the North Pole. In fact, if the United States–Canada border were defined using this geography LineString, the new border between Canada and the United States would look something like that shown in Figure 10-7.

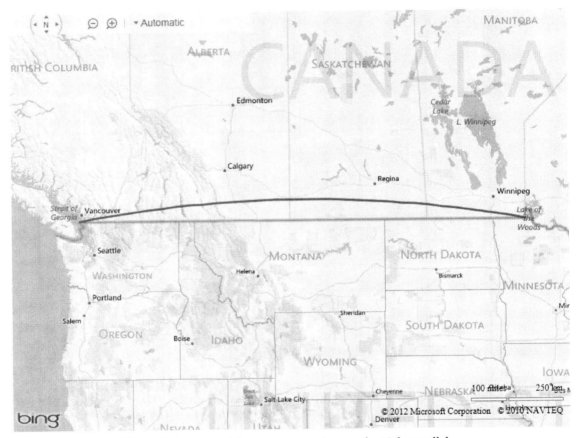

Figure 10-7. The geodesic LineString path between two points on the 49th parallel

In order to define a geography LineString that follows a straight line on a Mercator projected map (a "rhumb line," or *loxodrome*), as in Figure 10-6, the LineString should first be densified, creating additional anchor points that lie along the 49th parallel to fix the geography LineString to the appropriate path. Likewise, if you define a geography LineString representing the great elliptic arc between two points and want to maintain that geodesic property when converting to the geometry datatype, you should first densify the geography instance.

SQL Server does not include a built-in method to densify geometry or geography instances, but there is a densification sink included as part of the SQLSpatialTools codeplex project available at http://sqlspatialtools.codeplex.com. The logic for calculating where to place the additional points in the densified instance is contained in the AddLine() method, which converts the start and end points of each line segment in the supplied geography instance into a unit vector on a plane. If the angle between the vectors exceeds a stated minimum angle then additional points are inserted until the angle between each subsequent line segment is less than the chosen value. This process is illustrated in the following code listing:

```
public void AddLine(double latitude, double longitude, double? z, double? m)
{
  // Transform from geodetic coordinates to a unit vector
  Vector3 endPoint = Util.SphericalDegToCartesian(latitude, longitude);

  double angle = endPoint.Angle(_startPoint);
  if (angle > MinAngle)
  {
    // _startPoint and endPoint are the unit vectors that correspond to the input
    // start and end points. In their 3D space we operate in a local coordinate system
    // where _startPoint is the x axis and the xy plane contains endPoint. Every
    // point is now generated from the previous one by a fixed rotation in the local
    // xy plane, and converted back to geodetic coordinates.

    // Construct the local z and y axes
    Vector3 zAxis = (_startPoint + endPoint).CrossProduct(_startPoint - endPoint).Unitize();
    Vector3 yAxis = (_startPoint).CrossProduct(zAxis);

    // Calculate how many points are required
    int count = Convert.ToInt32(Math.Ceiling(angle / Util.ToRadians(_angle)));

    // Scale the angle so that points are equally placed
    double exactAngle = angle / count;

    double cosine = Math.Cos(exactAngle);
    double sine = Math.Sin(exactAngle);

    // Set the first x and y points in the local coordinate system
    double x = cosine;
    double y = sine;

    for (int i = 0; i < count - 1; i++)
    {
      Vector3 newPoint = (_startPoint * x + yAxis * y).Unitize();

      // Add the point
      _sink.AddLine(Util.LatitudeDeg(newPoint), Util.LongitudeDeg(newPoint), null, null);

      // Rotate to get next point
      double r = x * cosine - y * sine;
      y = x * sine + y * cosine;
      x = r;
    }
  }
  _sink.AddLine(latitude, longitude, z, m);

  // Remember last point we added
  _startPoint = endPoint;
}
```

To register the DensifyGeography function that utilizes this sink interface, you can download and install the SqlSpatialTools package from http://sqlspatialtools.codeplex.com.

Buffering

In addition to identifying points that are completely contained within the interior of a geometry or those that lie on its boundary, there are often situations in which you want to consider those points that lie in the area of space immediately surrounding a particular object. To do so, you can create a "buffer." A buffer, in this context, refers to the area formed from all of the points that lie within a given distance of a geometry. There are several methods for creating buffers around a geometry, as will be discussed in the following sections.

Creating a Buffer

The STBuffer() method is the OGC standard method for buffering a geometry. When used on a single-element instance—a Point, LineString, CircularString, CompoundCurve, or Polygon—the result of STBuffer() is a Polygon geometry whose perimeter is defined by all those points that lie a given distance away from the original geometry. When creating the buffer of a multielement instance, the buffer of each element in the collection is calculated separately, and then the union of all the individual buffered geometries is returned. Figure 10-8 illustrates the buffered geometries created by calling STBuffer() on a range of different types of geometry.

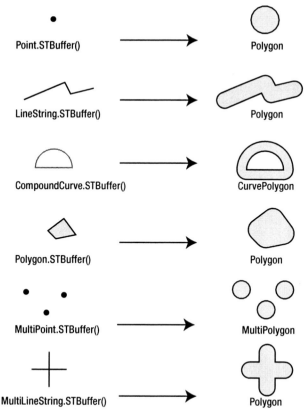

Figure 10-8. Buffers created around different types of geometries

The STBuffer() method can be invoked on any instance of the geography or geometry datatype, supplying a single parameter, distance, as follows:

```
Instance.STBuffer(distance)
```

The distance parameter is a floating-point value that represents the radius of the buffer zone to be created. When used on items of the geography datatype, the value of this parameter is specified in the linear unit of measurement defined by the spatial reference of the instance on which the method is called. For example, the radius of the buffer zone for any instance of the geography datatype defined with SRID 4296 must be specified in meters. When used on items of geometry data, the distance parameter is specified in the same unit of measure as the coordinate values of the geometry itself.

■ **Tip** To check the linear unit of measure used by any geographic spatial reference system, you can look at the value in the unit_of_measure column of the sys.spatial_reference_systems table.

The result of the STBuffer() method is a geometry or geography instance, using the same datatype and SRID as the original instance, enlarged to contain all those points that lie within the provided distance. Alternatively, if you provide a negative value for the distance parameter the resulting geometry created by STBuffer() removes all those points lying within the stated distance from the geometry. By providing different values for distance, you can vary the amount by which a geometry is enlarged or contracted.

To demonstrate, suppose that you run a pizza delivery business that offers a free home-delivery service to all customers who live within a 5 km distance from the restaurant. You could use the STBuffer() method to define the area within which customers are entitled to receive free delivery. The following code illustrates this example, creating a 5 km buffer around a Point representing a restaurant located at a latitude of 52.6285N, longitude of 1.3033E, using SRID 4326:

```
DECLARE @Restaurant geography;
SET @Restaurant = geography::STGeomFromText('POINT(1.3033 52.6285)', 4326);

DECLARE @FreeDeliveryZone geography;
SET @FreeDeliveryZone = @Restaurant.STBuffer(5000);

SELECT
    @FreeDeliveryZone,
    @FreeDeliveryZone.STAsText() AS WKT;
```

Since @Restaurant is a Point geometry defined using EPSG:4326, the size of the buffer zone created in this example is 5,000 meters, the 5 km radius zone in which we are interested. Executing this query gives the following results (truncated):

```
POLYGON ((
  1.2295142928970047 52.630278502274521, 1.2295472461369081 52.638137614778167,   ...
1.2295142928970047 52.630278502274521))
```

This represents an approximately circular Polygon of radius 5 km, centered on the location of the restaurant.

Creating a Simpler Buffer

In the last example, the STBuffer() method was used to create a "circular" Polygon around a Point geometry. The resulting geometry contained a lot of points, too many to count. Fortunately, we don't need to count them; we can use the STNumPoints() method to do that for us, by adding the following line to the end of the code:

```
SELECT @FreeDeliveryZone.STNumPoints()
```

The result is as follows:

72

The buffer object created by the STBuffer() method centered around the restaurant contains 72 points, defining a regular 71-sided polygon (a *heptacontakaihenagon*!). If you needed to maintain the maximum accuracy of the buffer around any geometry, you could use this Polygon shape definition as it is. However, for the particular application demonstrated in this example—offering free pizza delivery—we probably don't need our buffer to be that accurate. Performing computations on a complex geometry takes more processing resources than doing so on a simpler shape with fewer point definitions, and in this case we could obtain sufficient accuracy of the free delivery zone from a "circular" Polygon containing many fewer points.

To create a simpler buffered shape, you can subsequently use Reduce() on the buffered geometry created by STBuffer(). However, similar to the CurveToLineWithTolerance() method discussed earlier this chapter, SQL Server provides an extended method that will create a simple buffer all in one process. In this case, the method is BufferWithTolerance().

You can use the BufferWithTolerance() method on any item of geography or geometry data as follows:

```
Instance.BufferWithTolerance(distance, tolerance, relative)
```

This method requires the following three parameters:

- The distance parameter is a floating-point value defining the radius of the created buffer, measured using the linear unit of measure for the spatial reference system of a geography instance, or using the same unit of measure as the coordinate values of a geometry instance. This is the same as required by the distance parameter of the STBuffer() method.

- The tolerance parameter is a floating-point value that specifies the maximum variation allowed between the "true" buffer distance as calculated by STBuffer() and the simpler approximation of the buffer returned by the BufferWithTolerance() method. In the example of creating a buffer around a Point, this represents how closely the buffer created by BufferWithTolerance() resembles a true circle around the point. The smaller the tolerance value, the more closely the resulting Polygon buffer will resemble the actual buffer, but also the more complex it will be.

- The relative parameter is a bit value specifying whether the supplied tolerance parameter of the buffer is relative or absolute. If relative is "true" (or 1), then the tolerance of the buffer is determined relative to the extent of the geometry in question. For the geometry datatype, this means that the buffer is calculated from the product of the tolerance parameter and the diameter of the bounding box of the instance. For geography instances (where bounding boxes do not apply), the relative tolerance is instead calculated as the product of the tolerance parameter and the angular extent of the object multiplied by the equatorial radius of the reference ellipsoid of the spatial reference system. If relative is "false" (or 0), then the value of the tolerance parameter is treated as an absolute value and applied uniformly as the maximum tolerated variation in the buffer created.

The tolerance and relative parameters, used together, define the acceptable level of tolerance by which the simpler buffer created by BufferWithTolerance() may deviate from the "true" buffer as created by STBuffer(). Only those points that deviate by more than the accepted tolerance are included in the resulting geometry. When determining an appropriate tolerance value to use with the BufferWithTolerance() method, remember that a greater tolerance will lead to a simpler geometry, but will result in a loss of accuracy. A lower tolerance will lead to a more complex, but more accurate, buffer.

Let's recalculate the free delivery area from the STBuffer() example using the BufferWithTolerance() method instead. We will keep the same buffer radius of 5 km around the restaurant, but this time we will specify an absolute tolerance of 250 m; any points from the "true" buffer that deviate by less than this accepted tolerance will not be included in the resulting geometry.

```
DECLARE @Restaurant geography;
SET @Restaurant = geography::STGeomFromText('POINT(1.3033 52.6285)', 4326);

DECLARE @FreeDeliveryZone geography;
SET @FreeDeliveryZone = @Restaurant.BufferWithTolerance(5000, 250, 'false');

SELECT
  @FreeDeliveryZone,
  @FreeDeliveryZone.STAsText() AS WKT;
```

The result of the BufferWithTolerance() method is represented by the following WKT:

```
POLYGON ((1.2334543773235034 52.643101987508025, 1.232677160061811
52.615398722587805, 1.2587899052764109 52.592656472913966, 1.3019631745506761
52.583575201434648, 1.3456512565414915 52.591700111972628, 1.3730991328944517
52.613856932852478, 1.3739649138786716 52.641559233221273, 1.3478827812694929
52.664326601552453, 1.3046395628365322 52.673424441701911, 1.2608777319130935
52.665284532304732, 1.2334543773235034 52.643101987508025))
```

It is clear from examining the WKT representation that the Polygon geometry created using BufferWithTolerance() contains fewer points than the geometry previously created using the STBuffer() method. Using STNumPoints(), we can confirm that the simpler geometry created using BufferWithTolerance() actually contains 11 points, which define a regular decagon. This still provides a reasonable approximation of the circular zone we are interested in for this application, and has the benefit that any methods that operate on the simpler resulting geometry will perform more efficiently.

Creating a Curved Buffer

The buffered geometry created by either the STBuffer() and BufferWithTolerance() methods always results in a Polygon or MultiPolygon instance. However, as can be seen in Figure 10-8, buffering the edges of a geometry normally results in a shape with round edges. The reason why the result of STBuffer() representing the free delivery area of our pizza restaurant calculated previously contained so many points was because it required a large number of small line segments, attempting to approximate the shape of a circle. Given that buffering leads to round edges, would it not be better to return a curved geometry as the result of a buffering operation? That is exactly what the BufferWithCurves() method does.

BufferWithCurves(), like STBuffer(), requires only a single parameter, distance. As with the STBuffer() method, this parameter represents the absolute distance away from original geometry to which the buffer should extend. Unlike the STBuffer() and BufferWithTolerance() methods, which return only linear geometry types, the result of BufferWithCurves() is a set of one or more CurvePolygons.

In the following code listing, the BufferWithCurves() method is used to create a curved buffer area of radius 5 km around the Point geometry representing the restaurant:

```
DECLARE @Restaurant geography;
SET @Restaurant = geography::STGeomFromText('POINT(1.3033 52.6285)', 4326);

DECLARE @FreeDeliveryZone geography;
SET @FreeDeliveryZone = @Restaurant.BufferWithCurves(5000);
```

The result is a CurvePolygon, as follows:

```
CURVEPOLYGON (CIRCULARSTRING (1.2294685878974647 52.629287128767807, 1.2501759176720646
52.597333781891479, 1.3019631745281746 52.583575200673891, 1.377128678068027
52.627666637068607, 1.3046395628322454 52.673424441557223, 1.2519903734599585
52.660789017463344, 1.2294685878974647 52.629287128767807))
```

■ **Tip** When you use the BufferWithCurves() method on a Point geometry, you create a CurvePolygon with a fixed radius, centered about that point. This is a useful way of quickly creating circular CurvePolygons.

Figure 10-9 compares the results obtained using the STBuffer(), BufferWithTolerance(), and BufferWithCurves() methods to create a buffer zone of set radius around a Point geometry.

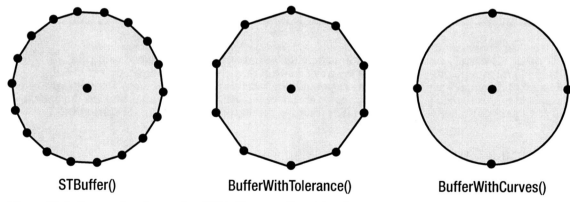

| STBuffer() | BufferWithTolerance() | BufferWithCurves() |

Figure 10-9. Comparing the resultsof STBuffer() , BufferWithTolerance(), and BufferWithCurves() when creating a buffer around a Point geometry

Creating the Convex Hull of a Geometry

The STConvexHull() method returns the smallest *convex* geometry that completely encompasses all the points in a given instance. A convex geometry is one in which no interior angle is greater than 180 degrees, so that the sides do not ever bend inwards or contain indentations. Convex hulls are useful in describing the geographic extent of a geometry since they generally offer a more precise fit than a simple bounding box and yet, unlike concave hulls, there is only one, unique convex hull around any given shape. Figure 10-10 illustrates the convex hull of a variety of different types of geometries.

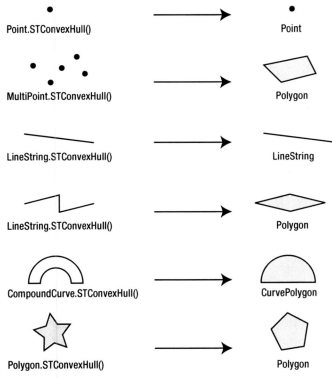

Figure 10-10. Creating the convex hull of a geometry

▓ **Tip** To help visualize a convex hull, consider an elastic band stretched around the outside of a geometry. When the elastic band is released, the shape that it snaps back into represents the convex hull of that geometry.

The STConvexHull() method requires no parameters, and can be invoked on any instance of geography or geometry datatype as follows:

```
Instance.STConvexHull()
```

The type of geometry returned by STConvexHull() will be the smallest convex geometry that contains all of the points contained in an instance. If used on a single Point instance, the convex hull will be the Point itself. If used on a MultiPoint or LineString in which all the individual points lie in a straight line, the convex hull will be a LineString. In all other cases, the convex hull of a geometry will be a Polygon.

Creating and analyzing the convex hull of a geometry can be a useful way of examining the geographical spread of an object on the Earth. To demonstrate this, the following example creates a convex hull representing the spread of reported cases of the H5N1 virus (commonly known as "bird flu").

In the following code listing, @H5N1 is a MultiPoint geometry, containing a point at each location where a case of the H5N1 virus had been recorded in humans, as reported by the World Health Organization between September 2003 and December 2004. We then use the STConvexHull() method of the geography datatype to create the convex hull Polygon that encompasses each point in the MultiPoint geometry to describe the overall spread of the disease.

```
DECLARE @H5N1 geography;
SET @H5N1 = geography::STMPointFromText(
  'MULTIPOINT(
    105.968 20.541, 105.877 21.124, 106.208 20.28, 101.803 16.009, 99.688 16.015,
    99.055 14.593, 99.055 14.583, 102.519 16.215, 100.914 15.074, 102.117 14.957,
    100.527 14.341, 99.699 17.248, 99.898 14.608, 99.898 14.608, 99.898 14.608,
    99.898 14.608, 100.524 17.75, 106.107 21.11, 106.91 11.753, 107.182 11.051,
    105.646 20.957, 105.857 21.124, 105.867 21.124, 105.827 21.124, 105.847 21.144,
    105.847 21.134, 106.617 10.871, 106.617 10.851, 106.637 10.851, 106.617 10.861,
    106.627 10.851, 106.617 10.881, 108.094 11.77, 108.094 11.75, 108.081 11.505,
    108.094 11.76, 105.899 9.546, 106.162 11.414, 106.382 20.534, 106.352 20.504,
    106.342 20.504, 106.382 20.524, 106.382 20.504, 105.34 20.041, 105.34 20.051,
    104.977 22.765, 105.646 20.977, 105.646 20.937, 99.688 16.015, 100.389 13.927,
    101.147 16.269, 101.78 13.905, 99.704 17.601, 105.604 10.654, 105.817 21.124,
    106.162 11.404, 106.362 20.504)',
  4326);

SELECT
  @H5N1 AS Shape
UNION ALL SELECT
  @H5N1.STConvexHull() AS Shape;
```

The resulting convex Polygon of the STConvexHull() method and the MultiPoint @H5N1 geometry from which it was created are illustrated in Figure 10-11, overlaid onto a map illustrating the affected area.

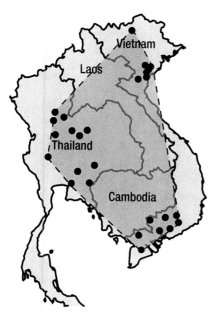

Figure 10-11. Using a convex hull to illustrate the spread of the H5N1 virus

One interesting fact to note is that, for the period of time that this data represents (from September 2003 through December 2004), individual cases of H5N1 had only been reported in the countries of Thailand and Vietnam. However, as shown in Figure 10-9, the convex hull around those points also covers most of Laos and Cambodia, which indicates that they lie within the area in which the disease had spread, and were at significant risk of exposure to the disease. Indeed, by January 21, 2005, less than one month after the last date recorded in this dataset, the first case of human infection of H5N1 had been reported in Cambodia itself.

■ **Note** In SQL Server 2008/R2, the STConvexHull() method could be applied only to instances of the geometry datatype. In SQL Server 2012, this method is now implemented by both the geometry and geography datatypes.

Summary

In this chapter, you have learned various methods of constructing new geometries by altering existing geography or geometry instances. Every method introduced in this chapter acts upon only a single instance, and returns an instance of the same datatype and SRID as the instance on which they are called.

CHAPTER 11

Aggregation and Combination

In this chapter, we'll look at various ways of combining spatial data. This could be, for example, collating a column of Points together into a single MultiPoint geometry (using UnionAggregate()) or joining two touching LineStrings together into a single LineString (using STUnion()). Combinations do not have to be additive; you can also, for example, subtract the area of space occupied by one Polygon from another, using STDifference(), or obtain the unique parts of two geometries using STSymDifference(). The common feature of all the methods discussed in this chapter is that they take two or more inputs and combine them in some way to produce a single output.

Creating a Union of Two Items of Spatial Data

To start with, let's consider combining just two individual items of geography or geometry data. The most common way of combining two geometries is to create the *union* between them, which defines the shape formed from all those points contained by the first geometry together with all those points contained by the second geometry.

The STUnion() method returns the union of two geometry or two geography instances. The method is invoked on one instance, GeomA, and the other instance with which it should be united, GeomB, must be supplied as a parameter to the method, as in GeomA.STUnion(GeomB). Since the union of two geometries contains the pointset of each geometry added together, you can think of the STUnion() method as being roughly equivalent to the plus (+) operator that adds together two numerical values, or concatenates two strings.

In other words,

```
SELECT geometry::Point(51, 1, 4326).STUnion(geometry::Point(52, 2, 4326));
```

Is conceptually similar to:

```
SELECT 1 + 3;
```

Or:

```
SELECT 'foo' + 'bar';
```

STUnion() can be used to combine two instances of the geometry datatype or two instances of the geography datatype but, as with all other spatial methods, cannot operate on instances of different types. Both geometries must be of the same datatype and be defined using the same SRID. If the two instances are defined using different spatial reference identifiers, STUnion() will return NULL.

To demonstrate, the following code listing creates two simple Polygon geometries representing the approximate shape of North Island and South Island of New Zealand. The STUnion() method is then used to create a MultiPolygon instance representing the combined landmasses:

```
DECLARE @NorthIsland geography;
SET @NorthIsland = geography::STPolyFromText(
  'POLYGON((175.3 -41.5, 178.3 -37.9, 172.8 -34.6, 175.3 -41.5))',
  4326);

DECLARE @SouthIsland geography;
SET @SouthIsland = geography::STPolyFromText(
  'POLYGON((169.3 -46.6, 174.3 -41.6, 172.5 -40.7, 166.3 -45.8, 169.3 -46.6))',
  4326);

DECLARE @NewZealand geography = @NorthIsland.STUnion(@SouthIsland);

SELECT @NewZealand;
```

The result returned by GeomA.STUnion(GeomB) is the simplest geometry that contains all of the points from both GeomA and GeomB, which, in this example, is a MultiPolygon as follows:

```
MULTIPOLYGON (((172.8 -34.6, 175.3 -41.5, 178.3 -37.9, 172.8 -34.6)),
((166.3 -45.8, 169.3 -46.6, 174.3 -41.6, 172.5 -40.7, 166.3 -45.8)))
```

Now let's consider some other situations: the following code listing creates a table containing two geometry columns containing a range of different geometry types. The SELECT statement returns the union created from the geometries in both columns:

```
DECLARE @table TABLE (
  geomA geometry,
  geomB geometry
);
INSERT INTO @table VALUES
('POINT(0 0)', 'POINT(2 2)'),
('POINT(0 0)', 'POINT(0 0)'),
('POINT(5 2)', 'LINESTRING(5 2, 7 9)'),
('LINESTRING(0 0, 5 2)', 'CIRCULARSTRING(5 2, 6 3, 9 2)'),
('POLYGON((0 0, 3 0, 3 3, 0 3, 0 0))', 'POLYGON((0 3, 3 3, 1 5, 0 3))'),
('POINT(0 0)', 'LINESTRING(2 2, 5 4)');

SELECT
  geomA.ToString(),
  geomB.ToString(),
  geomA.STUnion(geomB).ToString()
FROM @table;
```

Remember that STUnion() always returns the simplest geometry type that contains all of the points from the input geometries. For the examples above, the results are as follows:

```
MULTIPOINT ((2 2), (0 0))
POINT (0 0)
LINESTRING (7 9, 5 2)
COMPOUNDCURVE (CIRCULARSTRING (9 2, 6 3, 5 2), (5 2, 0 0))
POLYGON ((0 0, 3 0, 3 3, 1 5, 0 3, 0 0))
GEOMETRYCOLLECTION (LINESTRING (5 4, 2 2), POINT (0 0))
```

These results can be explained as follows:

1. The two points are distinct, and so require a MultiPoint collection to contain them both.

2. The two points are coincident, and so the resulting union is equal to the single Point itself.

3. The Point lies on the LineString (it is the start point of the LineString), and so the union returns just the LineString.

4. The LineString and CircularString share a boundary point at (5 2), and so can be combined into a single CompoundCurve.

5. The two Polygons share a common edge, and can be combined into a single Polygon.

6. The two geometries are of different types, and are physically disjoint from each other, so their union can only be represented by the least specific geometry type: a GeometryCollection.

The result of STUnion() when called on a range of different types of geometry is graphically illustrated in Figure 11-1.

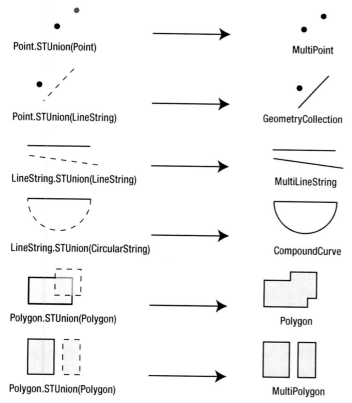

Figure 11-1. *Using STUnion() to create the union of two geometries.*

Appending One Geometry onto Another

Note that, while the result of STUnion() contains the combined set of points from two geometries, it does not simply append one geometry onto the other, and any sense of orientation in the original geometries is not necessarily preserved.

For example, suppose that you had one LineString, a_to_b, that connected the points from A to B, and another, b_to_c, that went from B to C; you might reasonably then expect that the result of a_to_b.STUnion(b_to_c) would be a single LineString that started at A and went, via B, to C. However, this is not necessarily the case, as demonstrated in the following code listing.

```
DECLARE @a_to_b geometry = geometry::STLineFromText('LINESTRING(0 0, 5 2)', 0);
DECLARE @b_to_c geometry = geometry::STLineFromText('LINESTRING(5 2, 8 6)', 0);
SELECT @a_to_b.STUnion(@b_to_c).ToString();
```

```
LINESTRING (8 6, 5 2, 0 0)
```

The result in this case is a LineString that starts at C and goes to A. This result conforms to the expected behavior of the STUnion() method, since it does indeed contain all of the points from both supplied LineStrings, but, as in this case, they may not be listed in the desired order.

To solve this problem, you can create a SQLCLR function that loops through and appends each of the points from the second geometry onto the first, retaining the order in which they were originally specified. While you could apply this method for any type of geometry, it has the greatest practical use in appending new line segments onto the end of a LineString or other Curve, since these are the geometries for which maintaining a sense of direction is generally most important.

The following C# code listing demonstrates a method, Extend, that requires three parameters: Segment1, Segment2, and Offset. The method uses the SqlGeometryBuilder() class to build a new LineString geometry, first adding all of the points from Segment1, and then appending all of the points from Segment2, in order, skipping the number of points specified in the Offset parameter from the beginning of the second segment. The Offset parameter can be used if, say, the end point of Segment1 coincides with the start point of Segment2, to avoid that point being duplicated in the constructed LineString.

```
public static SqlGeometry Extend(
  SqlGeometry @Segment1,
  SqlGeometry @Segment2,
  SqlInt32 @Offset)
  {
    SqlGeometryBuilder gb = new SqlGeometryBuilder();
    gb.SetSrid((int)(@Segment1.STSrid));
    gb.BeginGeometry(OpenGisGeometryType.LineString);
    gb.BeginFigure(
      (double)@Segment1.STStartPoint().STX,
      (double)@Segment1.STStartPoint().STY
    );
    for (int x = 2; x <= (int)@Segment1.STNumPoints(); x++) {
      gb.AddLine((double)@Segment1.STPointN(x).STX, (double)@Segment1.STPointN(x).STY);
    }
    for (int x = 1 + (int)@Offset; x <= (int)@Segment2.STNumPoints(); x++) {
      gb.AddLine((double)@Segment2.STPointN(x).STX, (double)@Segment2.STPointN(x).STY);
    }
    gb.EndFigure();
```

```
    gb.EndGeometry();
    return gb.ConstructedGeometry;
}
```

When imported and registered in the database, this function can be called as follows:

```
SELECT dbo.Extend(@a_to_b, @b_to_c, 1);
```

The result creates a single LineString, joining all those points from @a_to_b and @b_to_c in the order in which they were defined in the original geometries. The Offset parameter is set to 1 in order to avoid double counting the shared point at which the two LineStrings touch. The result is as follows:

```
LINESTRING (0 0, 5 2, 8 6)
```

Subtracting One Geometry from Another

If STUnion() provides the union created by two instances—the conceptual equivalent of adding two geometries together—you may be wondering what the reverse operation is. That is, how do we subtract one geometry instance from another? For this type of operation, we can use the STDifference() method.

STDifference() can be used with two instances of either the geometry or geography datatype, using syntax as follows:

```
GeomA.STDifference(GeomB);
```

The result is a geometry, of the same datatype and spatial reference system as both GeomA and GeomB, formed from all those points contained in GeomA that are not also in GeomB.

■ **Note** Unlike STUnion(), STDifference() is not a symmetric method. That is to say, GeomA.STDifference(GeomB) is not the same as GeomB.STDifference(GeomA).

The effect of calling STDifference() on different types of geometry is shown in Figure 11-2.

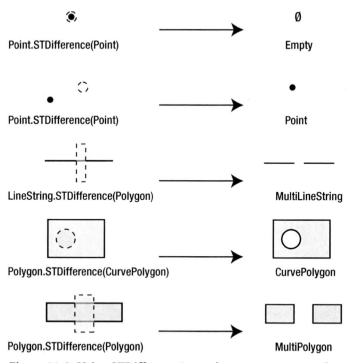

Point.STDifference(Point) → Empty

Point.STDifference(Point) → Point

LineString.STDifference(Polygon) → MultiLineString

Polygon.STDifference(CurvePolygon) → CurvePolygon

Polygon.STDifference(Polygon) → MultiPolygon

Figure 11-2. Using STDifference() to subtract one geometry from another

As an example demonstrating the use of the STDifference() method, the British Meteorological Office (commonly referred to as the "Met Office") operates a network of 16 radars used to continuously monitor and predict weather throughout the British Isles. Each radar is capable of providing high-quality qualitative rainfall and hydrological data within a range of approximately 75 km. The coverage provided by this radar network is illustrated in Figure 11-3.

Figure 11-3. *Weather radar coverage of the British Isles (one radar station, located on the island of Jersey, is not shown on the map)*

To demonstrate the use of the STDifference() method, the following code listing defines a MultiPoint instance representing the location of all the Met Office radars. It then uses BufferWithCurves() to create a set of circular CurvePolygons of radius 75 km centered around each radar station, representing the area covered by that radar. Finally, it uses the STDifference() method to calculate the difference between a MultiPolygon representing the British Isles and the GeometryCollection representing the area covered by radar.

```
-- Set the point locations of each weather radar station
DECLARE @Radar geography;
SET @Radar = geography::STMPointFromText(
  'MULTIPOINT(
    -2.597 52.398, -2.289 53.755, -0.531 51.689, -6.340 54.500, -5.223 50.003,
    -0.559 53.335, -4.445 51.980, -4.231 55.691, -2.036 57.431, -6.183 58.211,
    -3.453 50.963, 0.604 51.295,  -1.654 51.031, -2.199 49.209, -6.259 53.429,
    -8.923 52.700)', 4326);
-- Buffer each station to obtain the 75km coverage area
DECLARE @RadarCoverage geography
SET @RadarCoverage = @Radar.BufferWithCurves(75000);
```

```
-- Declare an approximate shape of the British Isles
DECLARE @BritishIsles geography;
SET @BritishIsles = geography::STMPolyFromText(
  'MULTIPOLYGON(
    ((0.527 52.879, -3.164 56.0197, -1.626 57.631, -4.087 57.654, -2.989 58.582,
    -5.0977 58.514, -6.504 56.240, -4.746 54.670, -3.516 54.848, -3.252 53.432,
    -4.614 53.301, -4.922 51.697, -3.12 51.505, -5.625 50.032, 1.626 51.286,
    0.791 51.423, 1.890 52.291, 1.274 52.959, 0.527 52.879)),
    ((-6.548 52.123, -5.317 54.518, -7.734 55.276, -9.976 53.354, -9.888 51.369,
    -6.548 52.123)))', 4326);

-- Calculate the difference between the British Isles and the area of radar coverage
SELECT
  @BritishIsles.STDifference(@RadarCoverage);
```

The resulting GeometryCollection returned by the STDifference() method in this example represents the area of land in the British Isles not covered by radars operated by the Met Office, as illustrated in Figure 11-4.

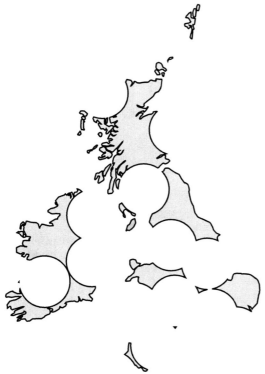

Figure 11-4. The area of the British Isles not covered by Met Office radar, created using the STDifference() method

Note that order is important; the geometry supplied as a parameter to the STDifference() method is subtracted from the geometry instance on which it is called. If you were to calculate @RadarCoverage.STDifference(@BritishIsles), you would instead obtain the area covered by radar that was not part of the British Isles.

Determining the Unique Parts of Two Geometries

Whereas GeomA.STDifference(GeomB) calculates the difference between GeomA and GeomB, GeomA.STSymDifference(GeomB) returns the *symmetric* difference between two geometries. This is the set of all those points that lie in either GeomA or GeomB, but not in both.

GeomA.STSymDifference(GeomB)

is logically equivalent to:

GeomA.STDifference(GeomB).STUnion(GeomB.STDifference(GeomA))

Because STSymDifference() calculates the symmetric difference between two geometries, it does not matter which is supplied as GeomA and which is GeomB. Figure 11-5 illustrates the results of calling STSymDifference() on different combinations of geometry types.

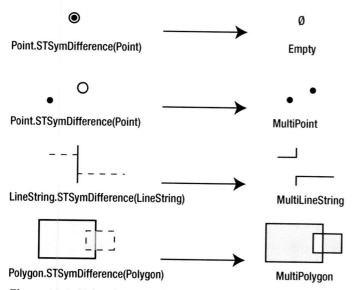

Figure 11-5. *Using STSymDifference() to determine the unique parts of two geometries.*

STSymDifference() can be used to compare and isolate the unique point sets of any two geometry or geography instances defined using the same spatial reference system. As an example, consider a city that has two competing radio stations, KWEST and KEAST. Each station is broadcast from its own transmitter, located in different parts of the city. The KWEST transmitter is located at a longitude of –87.88 and a latitude of 41.86 (using the EPSG:4269 spatial reference system). It broadcasts over a range of 10 km. The KEAST transmitter is located at longitude –87.79, latitude 41.89, and transmits over a range of 8 km.

By creating a circular buffer zone around each transmitter to represent the area of coverage of each station and using the STSymDifference() method to calculate their symmetric difference, we can determine those parts of the city that can receive one station or the other, but not both. This is demonstrated in the following code listing:

```
DECLARE @KWEST geography, @KEAST geography;
SET @KWEST = geography::Point(41.86, -87.88, 4269).BufferWithCurves(10000);
SET @KEAST = geography::Point(41.89, -87.79, 4269).BufferWithCurves(8000);

SELECT
  @KEAST.STSymDifference(@KWEST);
```

This symmetric difference of the two broadcasting coverage areas is illustrated by the region shaded gray in Figure 11-6.

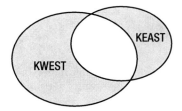

Figure 11-6. Visualizing the coverage areas of two radio stations

Defining the Intersection Between Two Geometries

The intersection of two geometries is defined as those points that both instances share in common. It is the logical opposite to their symmetric difference, as returned by the STSymDifference() method, which identifies those parts that exist in only one geometry or the other.

If the points contained within the intersection of two geometries lie in a single congruous area then the intersection can be represented as a single-element geometry, such as a Polygon. However, if the intersecting points are physically separate then the resulting intersection will be a multielement instance or geometry collection.

Figure 11-7 illustrates the intersection created between various types of geometry.

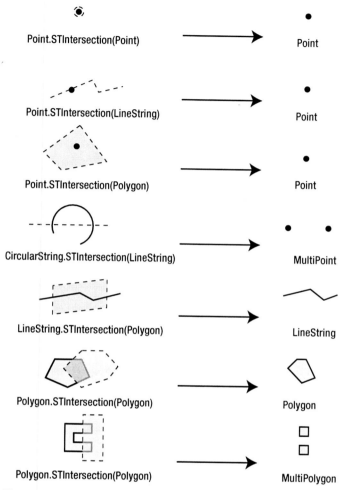

Figure 11-7. The intersection created between different types of geometry

The STIntersection() method can be used to return the intersection between any two geometry or geography instances of the same datatype and SRID. The resulting value will be a geometry of matching datatype and spatial reference system.

As an example, consider the Appian Way (or *Via Appia*), which was an ancient Roman road that ran from Rome to the city of Brindisi in southeast Italy. It is arguably one of the most important roads in world history because the Roman army used the route to quickly deploy men and supplies throughout Italy, and it undoubtedly contributed to their consequent military success. Along the route, the Via Appia passed through the Pontine Marshes, which were infested with mosquitoes carrying the deadly malaria disease.

The following code listing creates a LineString representing the Via Appia, and a Polygon representing the malaria-infested marsh area. It then uses the STIntersection() method to determine the treacherous section of route that intersects the marsh area.

```
-- Create the Pontine marshes
DECLARE @Marshes geography;
SET @Marshes = geography::STPolyFromText(
  'POLYGON((
    12.94 41.57, 12.71 41.46, 12.91 41.39, 13.13 41.26, 13.31 41.33, 12.94 41.57))',
  4326);
-- Declare the road
DECLARE @ViaAppia geography;
SET @ViaAppia = geography::STLineFromText(
  'LINESTRING(
    12.51 41.88, 13.25 41.28, 13.44 41.35, 13.61 41.25, 13.78 41.23, 13.89 41.11,
    14.22 41.10, 14.47 41.02, 14.79 41.13, 14.99 41.04, 15.48 40.98, 15.82 40.96,
    17.19 40.51, 17.65 40.50, 17.94 40.63)',
  4326);

-- Determine that section of road that passes through the marshes
SELECT @ViaAppia.STIntersection(@Marshes);
```

Figure 11-8 illustrates the features used in this example superimposed on a map of Italy. The result of the STIntersection() method corresponds to the section of LineString that passes through the Polygon representing the marshes.

Figure 11-8. Using STIntersection() to determine the section of the Appian Way that intersects the Pontine marshes

Aggregating Columns of Spatial Data

STUnion(), STDifference(), STIntersection(), and STSymDifference() are instance methods that can be applied to combine two variables, or perform a row-wise operation using the values contained in two columns of a table. However, what if you wanted to calculate the union of all the values in a single column of spatial data? In other words, if SELECT GeomA.STUnion(GeomB) is conceptually equivalent to SELECT A + B, then what is the spatial equivalent of SELECT SUM(A)?

In previous versions of SQL Server, the only way to calculate such an aggregate was to make use of some kind of loop that iterated through each value in the column and joined them onto the previous result one at a time, using STUnion(). For example, consider the following code listing, which creates a table containing four geography LineStrings:

```
CREATE TABLE #BunchOLines (
  line geography
);
INSERT INTO #BunchOLines VALUES
  ('LINESTRING(0 52, 1 53)'),
  ('LINESTRING(1 53, 1 54, 2 54)'),
  ('LINESTRING(2 54, 4 54)'),
  ('LINESTRING(2 54, 0 55, -1 55)');
```

These LineStrings are shown in the Spatial Results tab of SQL Server Management Studio, buffered by 5,000 for ease of display, as shown in Figure 11-9:

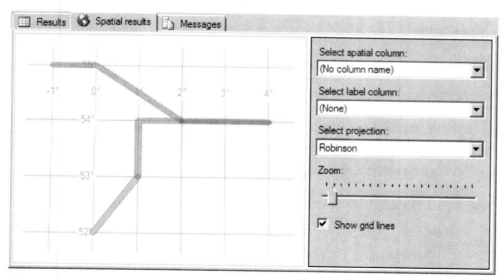

Figure 11-9. *Visualizing four geography LineStrings from a table*

To create a union aggregating all of the values in the line column in SQL Server 2008, one could first declare a variable as an empty geometry, and then STUnion() each row from the table to that geometry as part of an SELECT statement, as follows:

```
DECLARE @g geography = 'LINESTRING EMPTY';
SELECT @g = @g.STUnion(line) FROM #BunchOLines;

SELECT @g.STAsText();
```

```
MULTILINESTRING ((4 54, 2 54), (0 52, 1 53, 1 54, 2 54, 0 55, -1 55))
```

However, this approach quickly ran into difficulties if you attempted to use it on anything but the most basic table containing a small number of values. Other solutions, such as those involving cursors, also had their own difficulties. Fortunately, SQL Server 2012 provides a much more robust alternative, in the form of spatial aggregate functions.

You are probably familiar with the concept of an aggregate function, one that performs a calculation on a column of data or a set of values and returns a single result. Common T-SQL aggregate functions include SUM, MAX, and AVG, which are generally used to summarize columns of numeric data. Aggregate functions are frequently used together with a GROUP BY clause, to calculate subtotals based on different dimensions of the data. However, these common aggregate functions do not apply to the spatial datatypes. You cannot AVG a set of Points to find the midpoint. Nor can you SUM a set of touching Polygons together to create a single large Polygon. Instead, you must use one of the dedicated spatial aggregate functions, as follows:

- UnionAggregate()

- EnvelopeAggregate()

- CollectionAggregate()

- ConvexHullAggregate()

All of these aggregate methods act upon a column of geography or geometry data, and return a single geometry defined using the same datatype and SRID as the values in that column (if the column contains values of mixed spatial reference identifiers, the method will return NULL.

The syntax for calling these methods differs from those we have looked at so far this chapter since, unlike STUnion(), STDifference(), or STSymDifference(), aggregate functions are not instance methods; rather they are static methods and therefore must be invoked on the geography or geometry datatypes themselves, using syntax as follows (for a column of geography data):

```
SELECT geography::UnionAggregate(GeogColumn);
```

or, to aggregate a column of geometry data:

```
SELECT geometry::UnionAggregate(GeomColumn);
```

None of the aggregate methods require any parameters, but their results differ because they create different kinds of aggregate. In the following sections we'll look at each in turn:

UnionAggregate

The UnionAggregate() returns the simplest geometry that contains every point of every item in a column of geometry or geography data. As such, it is the column-wise operator that logically complements STUnion()'s row-wise functionality.

It can be used to determine the union aggregate of the LineStrings created in the earlier example as follows:

```
SELECT
  geography::UnionAggregate(line).STAsText()
FROM
  #BunchOLines;
```

And the result is exactly the same as created by using STUnion() to union each geometry together in turn:

```
MULTILINESTRING ((4 54, 2 54), (0 52, 1 53, 1 54, 2 54, 0 55, -1 55))
```

EnvelopeAggregate

EnvelopeAggregate() is a simpler aggregate than UnionAggregate() in that, rather than returning the geometry created from the union of all the points of every geometry in a column, EnvelopeAggregate() merely returns the envelope that encompasses all those points. When used on a column of geometry data, the resulting envelope will be an axis-aligned, rectangular Polygon. When used on a column of the geography datatype (which, remember, operates on a curved ellipsoidal surface), the resulting envelope will instead be a CurvePolygon.

Used against the preceding table of LineStrings, EnvelopeAggregate() returns the following:

```
SELECT
 geography::EnvelopeAggregate(line).STAsText()
FROM
 #BunchOLines;
```

```
CURVEPOLYGON (CIRCULARSTRING (3.8133501948535957 55.3015861207065, -1.5641318684829271
 55.301586120706496, -1.3755694169916859 52.242811272182934, 3.6247877433623552
 52.242811272182934, 3.8133501948535957 55.3015861207065))
```

CollectionAggregate

The CollectionAggregate() aggregate returns a GeometryCollection containing each of the values contained in the source column of data. Note that, unlike some other methods, the CollectionAggregate() does not attempt to choose the simplest geometry type to represent the combined set of geometries; it always returns a GeometryCollection type. This is the case even when the column of values being aggregated represents a set of homogeneous geometry types that could have been represented as a MultiPoint, or MultiPolygon, say.

You can create a CollectionAggregate() on the preceding table of LineStrings as follows:

```
SELECT
  geography::CollectionAggregate(line)
FROM
  #BunchOLines;
```

The result is as follows:

```
GEOMETRYCOLLECTION (
   LINESTRING (0 52, 1 53),
   LINESTRING (1 53, 1 54, 2 54),
   LINESTRING (2 54, 4 54),
   LINESTRING (2 54, 0 55, -1 55)
)
```

■ **Note** Even when aggregating a column of data in which every value is of a homogeneous geometry type, CollectionAggregate() will always return a generic Geometry Collection rather than the more specific multilelement collection.

ConvexHullAggregate

The final type of aggregate is the `ConvexHullAggregate()`. The `ConvexHullAggregate()` returns the smallest convex Polygon that encompasses all the geometry or geography objects in a given column. Just as the `UnionAggregate()` aggregate provides the column-wise equivalent of the `STUnion()` method, the `ConvexHullAggregate()` provides the column-wise equivalent of the `STConvexHull()` method discussed in the last chapter.

You can create the convex hull of the set of LineStrings in the preceding table as follows:

```
SELECT
  geography::ConvexHullAggregate(line)
FROM
  #BunchOLines;
```

The result, in this case, is a four-sided Polygon:

```
POLYGON ((0 52, 4 54, 0 55, -1 55, 0 52))
```

Note that the same result could have been achieved by first creating a `UnionAggregate()` of the geometries in the column, and then creating the convex hull of this union:

```
SELECT
  geography::UnionAggregate(line).STConvexHull()
FROM
  #BunchOLines;
```

```
POLYGON ((0 52, 4 54, 0 55, -1 55, 0 52))
```

However, this is a more resource-intensive method. If you require only to know the convex hull of a column of data you should use the dedicated `ConvexHullAggregate()` instead.

Combining Spatial Result Sets

In this chapter, we first looked at instance methods that combined two items of spatial data; then, we examined aggregates that operated on a column of the geography or geometry datatype. But what about combining two or more entire result sets containing spatial data? It is a fairly common requirement to merge the output of two or more SELECT statements into a single result set, or to create a view that combines data from two or more tables, for example. In these cases, there are a few special considerations to bear in mind with relation to spatial data.

To demonstrate, suppose that you had two tables of data: the first containing the names and locations of cities that have hosted the Olympic Games, while the second contained the names and locations of cities that hold annual marathons. The following code listing creates such tables and populates them with some sample data:

```
DECLARE @MarathonCities table(
  City varchar(32),
  Location geography
);

INSERT INTO @MarathonCities VALUES
```

```
('Amsterdam', 'POINT(4.9 52.4)'),
('Athens', 'POINT(23.7 38)'),
('Berlin', 'POINT(13.4 52.5)'),
('Boston', 'POINT(-71.1 42.4)'),
('Chicago', 'POINT(-87.7 41.9)'),
('Honolulu', 'POINT(-157.85 21.3)'),
('London', 'POINT(-0.15 51.5)'),
('New York', 'POINT(-74 40.7)'),
('Paris', 'POINT(2.34 48.8)'),
('Rotterdam', 'POINT(4.46 4.63)'),
('Tokyo', 'POINT(139.7 35.7)');

DECLARE @OlympicCities table(
  City varchar(32),
  Location geography
);


INSERT INTO @OlympicCities VALUES
('Sydney', 'POINT(151.2 -33.8)'),
('Athens', 'POINT(23.7 38)'),
('Beijing', 'POINT(116.4 39.9)'),
('London', 'POINT(-0.15 51.5)');
```

Clearly, these are not exhaustive lists, but they should provide sufficient data for this demonstration! Now, suppose that you wanted to write a query to select the names and locations of all those cities that either hold an annual marathon, or had been host to the Olympic Games. To do so, you might try the following query:

```
SELECT City, Location FROM @MarathonCities
UNION
SELECT City, Location FROM @OlympicCities;
```

Unfortunately, attempting to execute this query results in the following error:

```
Msg 421, Level 16, State 1, Line 30
The geography data type cannot be selected as DISTINCT because it is not comparable.
```

The problem here is that the default behavior of the UNION operator is to select distinct values in the result set. However, as the error message states, geography data is not comparable (and nor is geometry data).

As you have found out in recent chapters, you can't use normal operators to compare spatial instances; it doesn't make sense to say whether one geometry is bigger or smaller than another, for example. You can't even use the equals operator (=) to compare whether two geometries are the same; instead you have to use the dedicated STEquals() method of the geometry or geography datatype. So, when you try to perform a UNION between two result sets, you will get an error because SQL Server cannot make the comparison between the values in the result set to identify only those unique records. The same is true if you try to SELECT DISTINCT values from a geography or geometry column.

One alternative is to use UNION ALL, which will select all records from both SELECT statements as follows:

```
SELECT City, Location FROM @MarathonCities
UNION ALL
SELECT City, Location FROM @OlympicCities;
```

The query now executes, returning the following results:

```
Amsterdam    0xE6100000010C3333333333334A409A99999999991340
Athens       0xE6100000010C00000000000043403333333333B33740
Berlin       0xE6100000010C0000000000404A40CDCCCCCCCCCC2A40
Boston       0xE6100000010C333333333333345406666666666C651C0
Chicago      0xE6100000010C3333333333F34440CDCCCCCCCCEC55C0
Honolulu     0xE6100000010CCDCCCCCCCC4C35403333333333BB63C0
London       0xE6100000010C0000000000C04940333333333333C3BF
New York     0xE6100000010C9A9999999959444000000000008052C0
Paris        0xE6100000010C666666666664840B81E85EB51B80240
Rotterdam    0xE6100000010C85EB51B81E851240D7A3703D0AD71140
Tokyo        0xE6100000010C9A99999999D941406666666666766140
Sydney       0xE6100000010C6666666666E640C06666666666E66240
Athens       0xE6100000010C00000000000043403333333333B33740
Beijing      0xE6100000010C3333333333F343409A99999999195D40
London       0xE6100000010C0000000000C04940333333333333C3BF
```

Note that, because the result set of a UNION ALL query contains every row from both SELECT statements, London is included twice in the results since it is both an Olympic host city and holds an annual marathon. However, this is not the behavior we really want. In order to be able to present a distinct list of cities together with their location, you need to structure your tables slightly differently, so as to prevent the need ever to try to determine distinct geography or geometry data.

For example, you can normalize your table structure, maintaining geography or geometry data of each city in a separate table referenced by key, and having the @OlympicCities and @MarathonCities tables store only those keys of the cities in question. You can then determine the unique list of cities by performing a UNION join on the keys field, and only bringing in the corresponding spatial fields after the UNION operation has been performed. One such structure is demonstrated in the following code listing:

```
DECLARE @Cities table (
 CityId int,
 CityName varchar(32),
 CityLocation geography
 );
 INSERT INTO @Cities VALUES
(1, 'Amsterdam', 'POINT(4.9 52.4)'),
(2, 'Athens', 'POINT(23.7 38)'),
(3, 'Berlin', 'POINT(13.4 52.5)'),
(4, 'Boston', 'POINT(-71.1 42.4)'),
(5, 'Chicago', 'POINT(-87.7 41.9)'),
(6, 'Honolulu', 'POINT(-157.85 21.3)'),
(7, 'London', 'POINT(-0.15 51.5)'),
(8, 'New York', 'POINT(-74 40.7)'),
(9, 'Paris', 'POINT(2.34 48.8)'),
(10, 'Rotterdam', 'POINT(4.46 4.63)'),
(11, 'Tokyo', 'POINT(139.7 35.7)'),
(12, 'Sydney', 'POINT(151.2 -33.8)'),
(13, 'Athens', 'POINT(23.7 38)'),
(14, 'Beijing', 'POINT(116.4 39.9)');

DECLARE @MarathonCities table(
  CityId int
```

```
);
INSERT INTO @MarathonCities(CityId) VALUES
(1), (2), (3), (4), (5), (6), (7), (8), (9), (11);

DECLARE @OlympicCities table(
  CityId int
);
INSERT INTO @OlympicCities(CityId) VALUES
(12), (13), (14), (7);

SELECT
  CityName,
  CityLocation
FROM
  (SELECT CityId FROM @MarathonCities
  UNION
  SELECT CityId FROM @OlympicCities) AS DistinctList
JOIN @Cities c ON DistinctList.CityId = c.CityId;
```

The results now correctly list each distinct city that either holds an annual marathon or has hosted the Olympic Games.

Joining Tables Using a Spatial Column

Just as geometry and geography data is not comparable when used in a SELECT DISTINCT statement, nor can you define a JOIN between two tables using a column of the geometry or geography datatype. Attempting to execute a query such as this:

```
SELECT * FROM TableA JOIN TableB ON TableA.GeomField = TableB.GeomField;
```

will result in the following error:

```
Msg 403, Level 16, State 1, Line 34
Invalid operator for data type. Operator equals equal to, type equals geography.
```

Instead, you can join tables based on a comparison between two spatial columns, but you must use one of the dedicated spatial methods. For the example above, the equivalent operator to test the equality of two geometries is provided by the STEquals() method, so you can rewrite the query as follows:

```
SELECT * FROM TableA JOIN TableB ON TableA.GeomField.STEquals(TableB.GeomField) = 1;
```

However, joining two tables in this manner is rarely a good idea. As discussed in Chapter 7, you should avoid comparing exact equality between two spatial instances. But this is not the only join type possible: you can join two tables on a spatial column using any spatial method that acts upon two geometry or geography instances. For example, let's create a new table that divides the earth's surface into four quadrants: north-west, north-east, south-west, and south-east relative to an origin at (0,0). You can create such a table using the following code listing:

```
DECLARE @Quadrants table (
  Quadrant varchar(32),
  QuadrantLocation geography
);
```

```
INSERT INTO @Quadrants VALUES
('NW', 'POLYGON((0 0, 0 90, -179.9 90, -179.9 0, 0 0))'),
('NE', 'POLYGON((0 0, 179.9 0, 179.9 90, 0 90, 0 0))'),
('SW', 'POLYGON((0 0, -179.9 0, -179.9 -90, 0 -90, 0 0))'),
('SE', 'POLYGON((0 0, 0 -90, 179.9 -90, 179.9 0, 0 0))');
```

Now suppose that we wanted to obtain a set of results stating in which quadrant each of the cities in our previous @Cities table was located. To do so, we can join the tables together using the STIntersection() method to determine the QuadrantLocation in which each CityLocation lies:

```
SELECT
  CityName,
  Quadrant
FROM
  @Cities
  JOIN @Quadrants ON CityLocation.STIntersects(QuadrantLocation) = 1;
```

Because every city lies in one and only one quadrant, the results contain exactly the same number of rows as in the original @Cities table, with the Quadrant column showing the respective quadrant of the earth in which each city is located:

```
Boston      NW
Chicago     NW
Honolulu    NW
London      NW
New York    NW
Amsterdam   NE
Athens      NE
Berlin      NE
Paris       NE
Rotterdam   NE
Tokyo       NE
Athens      NE
Beijing     NE
Sydney      SE
```

Summary

In this chapter, you learned about various methods to combine two or more items, columns, or tables of spatial data. Combining geometries frequently involves an additive operation—creating a merged geometry that is greater than the sum of its parts—but this does not always have to be the case; it is also possible to subtract one geometry from another, or to select only those elements that exist in one geometry but not another.

The methods discussed in this chapter can be applied to either the geometry or geography datatypes, but all inputs to a given function must be of the same datatype. It is not possible to create the union of a geometry and geography instance together, for example.

CHAPTER 12

Testing Spatial Relationships

The key objective for most spatial queries is to try to understand the relationship between two or more features on the Earth in order to answer specific questions: for example, how far is it from a to b? Does the route between x and y pass through z? Does p share a common border with q? In this chapter, I'll introduce the methods that SQL Server provides to answer these questions by comparing different aspects of the relationship between two items of spatial data.

Calculating the Distance Between Two Geometries

The STDistance() method can be used to calculate the shortest distance between any two geometries. When used on instances of the geometry datatype, this is the length of the shortest straight line that can be drawn between the two instances. For the geography datatype, it is instead the length of the shortest great elliptic arc drawn between any two points contained in the two geometries, following the surface of the reference ellipsoid between them. Figure 12-1 illustrates the distance d returned by the STDistance() method when called on a variety of different types of geometries.

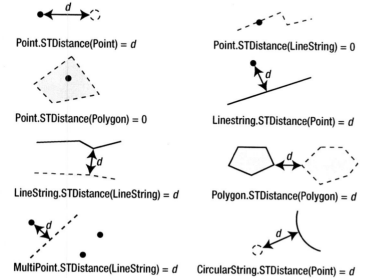

Point.STDistance(Point) = d Point.STDistance(LineString) = 0

Point.STDistance(Polygon) = 0   Linestring.STDistance(Point) = d

LineString.STDistance(LineString) = d Polygon.STDistance(Polygon) = d

MultiPoint.STDistance(LineString) = d CircularString.STDistance(Point) = d

Figure 12-1. Calculating the distance d between two geometries

The STDistance() method may be used to calculate the distance between two items of either the geometry or geography datatype, using syntax as follows:

```
Instance1.STDistance(Instance2);
```

Instance1 and Instance2 may be any type of geometry, but both must be instances of the same datatype, and defined using the same SRID. When used to calculate the distance between two instances of the geometry datatype, the result of the STDistance() method is returned in the same unit of measurement in which the coordinates were defined. When used to calculate the distance between two instances of the geography datatype, the result is expressed in the linear unit of measure defined in the unit_of_measure column of the sys.spatial_reference_systems table for the spatial reference system in question. Note that, for intersecting geometries, the result of STDistance() will always be 0.

One common use case for the STDistance() method is to identify the feature that lies closest to a given location or, in the more general case, to find the nearest n features to a location. This type of query is commonly called a "nearest-neighbor" query. To demonstrate how you might use the STDistance() method to perform a nearest-neighbor query in SQL Server, let's suppose that you are operating a disaster response service based in the state of Massachusetts. When you are notified of a major fire, you need to identify and contact the closest fire station to the incident so that it can send out a response unit. For this example, let's first create a table containing details of fire stations in the state of Massachusetts:

```
CREATE TABLE MA_Firestations(
  Id int IDENTITY(1,1) NOT NULL,
  Name varchar(255) NULL,
  Address varchar(255) NULL,
  City varchar(255) NULL,
  Location geometry NULL,
  CONSTRAINT [PK_MA_Firestations] PRIMARY KEY CLUSTERED
  ( Id ASC )
);
```

▓ **Note** I've added a unique integer id to each record in the MA_Firestations table, and then created a clustered primary key on the Id column. Having a clustered primary key on a table is a prerequisite for creating a spatial index, which we'll be doing shortly.

To populate the MA_Firestations table, let's create a few records representing individual fire stations. The location of each fire station is represented by a Point geometry defined using the Massachusetts State Plane Coordinate System, which is a projected coordinate system denoted by the SRID 26986:

```
INSERT INTO MA_Firestations (Name, Address, City, Location) VALUES
('SANDWICH FIRE DEPARTMENT',
'115 Rt. 6A',
'SANDWICH',
geometry::STPointFromText('POINT(283441 835235)', 26986)),

('BROCKTON FIRE DEPARTMENT',
'560 West Street',
'BROCKTON',
geometry::STPointFromText('POINT(237729 869074)', 26986)),
```

```
('SWANSEA FIRE DEPARTMENT',
'50 New Gardner Neck Road',
'SWANSEA',
geometry::STPointFromText('POINT(225000 831055)', 26986)),

('ASHLAND FIRE DEPARTMENT',
'70 Cedar Street',
'ASHLAND',
geometry::STPointFromText('POINT(205108 889508)', 26986));
```

Although you can test out the following example using just these four records, it is easier to see how a nearest-neighbor query works when selecting records from a dataset containing thousands, or millions, of records. If you want to add more records to the MA_Firestations table, you can download the full dataset of fire stations in Massachusetts as part of the code archive accompanying this book, available in the Source Code/Download area of the Apress web site (http://www.apress.com).

For this example, suppose that we have been informed of a fire at coordinates (210000, 890000), these coordinates being defined, like the location of the fire stations, using EPSG:26986. This corresponds to a point about 15 miles southwest of Boston. Now that we have a table detailing the location of every fire station, and we know the whereabouts of the fire, how do we go about identifying the nearest station to respond to the incident? In the following sections, we'll look at a few different approaches for this common scenario.

Finding Nearest Neighbors: Basic Approach

The most straightforward method of identifying the nearest neighbor is to use the STDistance() method in the ORDER BY clause of a SELECT statement to sort all of the fire stations in ascending order of their distance from the fire. Once the records have been sorted, you can use the SELECT TOP n syntax to return only the top *n* nearest neighbors. This approach is demonstrated in the following code listing:

```
-- Set the location of the fire
DECLARE @Fire geometry;
SET @Fire = geometry::STPointFromText('POINT (210000 890000)', 26986);

-- Sort all records and select the closest
SELECT TOP 1
  Name,
  Address,
  City,
  Location.STDistance(@Fire) AS Distance
FROM
  MA_Firestations
ORDER BY
  Location.STDistance(@Fire) ASC;
```

The single result is as follows:

Name	Address	City	Distance
ASHLAND FIRE DEPARTMENT	70 Cedar Street	ASHLAND	4916.60186549405

Although this query will correctly identify and return the nearest *n* neighboring fire stations to the fire (in this example, just the single nearest fire station is chosen), there is a problem with this approach. Consider the execution plan for this query, as shown in Figure 12-2:

Figure 12-2. Execution plan for a basic nearest-neighbor query

In order to find the single nearest neighbor, SQL Server must perform a scan, compute the result of STDistance(), and then sort every row in the table. When performing a nearest-neighbor search like this on a table containing millions of rows, the sort operation will become very expensive and yet all but one of the records will be subsequently discarded. This approach can therefore only be practically applied for the smallest of datasets.

■ **Note** The execution plans for the queries shown in this section are based on those calculated on my test server. The plan chosen by SQL Server's query optimizer depends on a number of factors, and you may get slightly different execution plans than me. Don't worry about this; the discussion here is still relevant.

Finding Nearest Neighbors Using a Spatial Index

In versions of SQL Server prior to SQL Server 2012, there was no way to increase the efficiency of the previous query; a simple nearest-neighbor search always involved a full scan and sort operation. However, SQL Server 2012 introduces a new query plan that can significantly improve the speed of a nearest-neighbor query by making use of a spatial index. Spatial indexes will be discussed in more detail in a later chapter but, for now, create an index on the Location column of the MA_Firestations table by executing the following code listing:

```
CREATE SPATIAL INDEX idx_Spatial
  ON MA_Firestations ( Location )
  USING GEOMETRY_GRID
  WITH (
    BOUNDING_BOX =(40000, 780000, 330000, 960000)
  );
```

In order to utilize the index in a nearest-neighbor search, your query must be structured according to a particular pattern. In order to conform to this pattern, modify the previous SELECT query to include a new condition in the WHERE clause to filter only those records where the result of STDistance() IS NOT NULL, as highlighted in the following code listing:

```
SELECT TOP 1
  Name,
  Address,
  City,
  Location.STDistance(@Fire) AS Distance
```

```
FROM
  MA_Firestations
WHERE
  Location.STDistance(@Fire) IS NOT NULL
ORDER BY
  Location.STDistance(@Fire) ASC;
```

▓ **Note** The only situations in which STDistance() returns NULL is where either one of the geometries involved is an empty geometry, or where the two geometries between which the distance is being calculated are defined using different SRIDs. Adding the condition WHERE Location.STDistance(@Fire) IS NOT NULL will therefore not change the results of the query in this case (nor in most other situations), but will prompt SQL Server to use the optimized nearest-neighbor execution plan.

The execution plan for this query now appears substantially more complicated, as illustrated in Figure 12-3. You should notice that the plan includes an element called *Clustered Index Seek (Spatial)*, which indicates that instead of scanning the entire table, the query processor now makes use of the spatial index to identify nearest neighbors. This should lead to better query performance, especially when dealing with large datasets, when a table scan would be very costly.

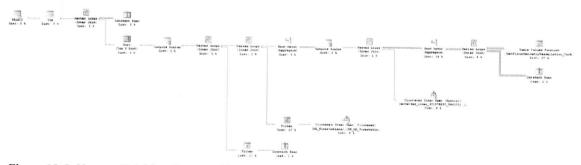

Figure 12-3. Nearest Neighbor Query utilizing a spatial index. The Clustered Index Seek (Spatial) is shown towards the right-hand side, feeding into a nested loop.

If the query plan you obtain from executing this code listing doesn't contain an item called *Clustered Index Seek (Spatial)* then you may have to add an explicit index hint to tell SQL Server to use the spatial index. You can do so by modifying the query as follows:

```
SELECT TOP 1
  Name,
  Address,
  City,
  Location.STDistance(@Fire) AS Distance
FROM
  MA_Firestations WITH(index(idx_Spatial))
WHERE
```

```
Location.STDistance(@Fire) IS NOT NULL
ORDER BY
  Location.STDistance(@Fire) ASC;
```

This new query plan for nearest-neighbor queries was only introduced in SQL Server 2012, so basic nearest-neighbor queries in SQL Server 2008/R2 could not make use of a spatial index even using this query template. Consequently, inventive users of previous versions of SQL Server developed a number of alternative ways to write efficient nearest-neighbor queries. While the need for these alternative methods has largely been deprecated in SQL Server 2012, it is still worthwhile understanding the logic behind these earlier approaches, which is described in the following sections.

Finding Nearest Neighbors Within a Fixed Search Zone

One way of refining the basic nearest-neighbor query described previously is to try to reduce the number of rows that need to be sorted. This can be done by using a two-stage approach: firstly, identifying a set of likely nearest-neighbor candidates by selecting only those records that lie within a predetermined radius of the feature in question; then, calculating the *n* nearest neighbors from this candidate subset only, which prevents the need to sort the entire dataset.

To determine the subset of candidate nearest neighbors, a search area can be created using the STBuffer() method (or BufferWithTolerance() or BufferWithCurves()). The size of the buffer should be chosen to be sufficiently large so that it contains the required number of nearest neighbors, but not so large that it includes many additional rows of data that exceed the desired number of results. Features lying within the search area are selected in a CTE using the efficient Filter() method, which uses a spatial index to identify the set of possible candidates. The STDistance() method is then used to calculate the distance associated with only those candidate records, rather than processing and sorting the whole table.

The following code listing demonstrates this approach, using STBuffer(25000) to identify candidate records that lie within a 25 km search area around the fire in which to search for nearest neighbors:

```
DECLARE @Fire geometry;
SET @Fire = geometry::STPointFromText('POINT (210000 890000)', 26986);

DECLARE @SearchArea geometry;
SET @SearchArea = @Fire.STBuffer(25000);

WITH Candidates AS (
  SELECT
    Name,
    Address,
    City,
    Location.STDistance(@Fire) AS Distance
  FROM
    MA_Firestations
  WHERE
    Location.Filter(@SearchArea) = 1
)
SELECT TOP 1 * FROM Candidates ORDER BY Distance;
```

As in the last example, this query correctly identifies the closest fire station as follows:

Name	Address	City	Distance
ASHLAND FIRE DEPARTMENT	70 Cedar Street	ASHLAND	4916.60186549405

The advantage of the fixed search zone approach is that the initial Filter() operation, which identifies those candidate records that lie within the vicinity of the fire, can make use of a spatial index seek. Once the candidate records are retrieved, STDistance() is called fewer times, and the dataset requiring sorting is much smaller, making the query significantly faster than the basic nearest-neighbor approach described previously. The execution plan for this query, shown in Figure 12-4, is similar to the dedicated nearest-neighbor query plan described earlier:

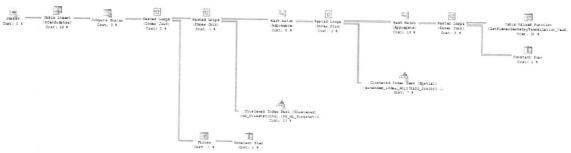

Figure 12-4. Execution plan for a nearest-neighbor query within a fixed search radius

However, the problem with this approach is that you must choose an appropriate fixed value to pass to the STBuffer() method as the radius of the search area. If you set the value too high, then there will be too many possible candidates returned and the filter will not be efficient. If you set the buffer size too small, then there is a risk that the search area will not contain any candidates, resulting in the query failing to identify any nearest neighbors at all.

For example, the fire station located the shortest distance from the fire in this example is Ashland Fire Department, which lies 4.9 km away. If we had narrowed our nearest-neighbor query to search only for candidates lying within a 4 km distance, using SET @SearchArea = @Fire.STBuffer(4000), the query would not have returned any results.

The fixed search zone approach is most useful in situations where you are able to reliably set an appropriate buffer size in which to select a set of candidate nearest neighbors. This might be based on known uniform distribution of your data; for example, you know that any item in the dataset will never lie more than 25 km from its nearest neighbor. Alternatively, you might want to obtain nearest neighbors within a particular distance constraint, for example, to answer the query "Show me the three closest gas stations within 10 miles of this location."

Finding Nearest Neighbors with an Expanding Search Zone

This method, like the previous one, uses a two-stage approach to identify nearest neighbors, where a set of possible nearest-neighbor candidates is first identified before selecting the actual nearest neighbor from the set of possible candidates. However, rather than identifying candidates that lie within a fixed buffer search zone (which faces the risk of failing to identify any nearest neighbors at all), this approach creates a series of expanding search ranges, which is ultimately guaranteed to find the nearest neighbor.

▓ **Note** The approach described here was first proposed by Isaac Kunen, a program manager on the SQL Server team. You can read the blog entry in which he describes this method at:

http://blogs.msdn.com/b/isaac/archive/2008/10/23/nearest-neighbors.aspx

To create the expanding ranges, an additional numbers table (or "tally table") is used, containing a single column of consecutive integers. Although at first it may seem unnecessary to create a table containing nothing more than a sequential list of numbers, numbers tables can prove very useful when it comes to solving certain problems in a set-based environment, as you will see in this example. To create and populate a numbers table with the integers between 0 and 1,000, execute the following code:

```
CREATE TABLE Numbers (
  Number int PRIMARY KEY CLUSTERED
);
SET NOCOUNT ON;
DECLARE @i int = 0;
WHILE @i <= 1000
BEGIN
  INSERT INTO Numbers VALUES (@i);
  SET @i = @i + 1;
END;
```

■ **Note** There are many different ways to populate a numbers table; a quick search of the Internet will reveal endless debates about the relative performance of methods using a CROSS JOIN versus an IDENTITY column, a CTE or the CLR. Seeing as this table contains only 1,000 rows, I'm opting for the most straightforward—a simple WHILE loop—and then we can get on with the matter at hand!

The Numbers table will be joined to the MA_Firestations table to create a series of expanding search ranges. The distance to which each successive search extends increases exponentially until a search area of sufficient size is found that contains the requisite number of nearest neighbors. All of the features in this search area are returned as candidates, and then the TOP 1 is selected as the true nearest neighbor. This approach is demonstrated in the following code:

```
DECLARE @Fire geometry;
SET @Fire = geometry::STPointFromText('POINT (210000 890000)', 26986);

WITH Candidates AS (
  SELECT TOP 1 WITH TIES
    Name,
    Address,
    City,
    Location.STDistance(@Fire) AS Distance,
    1000*POWER(2, Number) AS Range
  FROM
    MA_Firestations
    INNER JOIN Numbers
    ON MA_Firestations.Location.STDistance(@Fire) < 1000*POWER(2, Numbers.Number)
    ORDER BY Number
)
SELECT TOP 1 * FROM Candidates ORDER BY Range DESC, Distance ASC;
```

The result obtained is as follows:

Name	Address	City	Distance	Range
ASHLAND FIRE DEPARTMENT	70 Cedar Street	ASHLAND	4916.60186549405	8000

This query is a little more complicated than the last, and probably warrants some more explanation. Remember that the Numbers table contains consecutive integers, starting at zero. So, the condition MA_Firestations.Location.STDistance(@Fire) < 1000*POWER(2,Numbers.Number) specifies that the initial criterion for a feature to be considered a nearest-neighbor candidate is that the distance to that feature is less than 1000 * 2^0. Since the EPSG:26986 spatial reference system defines distances in meters, this equates to a 1 km search area; if you want to specify an alternative starting search radius, you may do so by changing the value of 1000 to another value (remember to use the unit of measure appropriate to the datatype and SRID of the data in question).

If the requisite number of neighbors (in this case, we are searching only for the TOP 1) are not found within the specified distance, then the search range is increased in size. Successive search ranges are obtained by raising 2 to the power of the next number in the Numbers table. Thus, the first range extends to 1 km around the fire, the second range extends to 2 km, then 4 km, 8 km, 16 km, and so on. By adopting an exponential growth model, this method is guaranteed to find the nearest neighbor within a relatively short number of iterations, however dispersed the distribution of the underlying features.

Once the search range has been sufficiently increased to contain at least the required number of candidate nearest neighbors, all of the features lying within that range are selected as candidates, by using a SELECT statement with the WITH TIES argument. Finally, the candidates are sorted by ascending distance from the fire, and the TOP 1 record is selected as the true nearest neighbor. The Range column included in the results states the distance to which the search range was extended to find the nearest neighbor, in this case, 8 km.

A typical execution plan for this query is as shown in Figure 12-5:

Figure 12-5. Execution plan for a nearest-neighbor query within an expanding search range

While it is slightly more complex to implement, this approach generally provides a consistently fast-performing solution (faster, often, than the dedicated nearest-neighbor query plan introduced earlier). Although it is sometimes not quite as fast as the fixed search area technique, it does not suffer from the limitations associated with having to specify a fixed search radius.

Nearest Neighbor Query Plan Comparison

In order to compare the efficiency of the various approaches to nearest-neighbor queries described previously, I decided to run a few tests. While I hope the previous scenario of firestations in Massachussetts provided a real-world example of when you might want to use a nearest-neighbor query, in order to conduct controlled performance tests I decided that an artificial dataset might be more appropriate. So I created a simple test table as follows:

```
CREATE TABLE TestNearestNeighbors (
  id int IDENTITY(1,1),
  point geometry,
```

```
    CONSTRAINT [PK_TestNearestNeighbors] PRIMARY KEY CLUSTERED
  ( id ASC )
);
```

A set of geometry Points would be inserted into this table, ranging between coordinates at (0, 0) and (100000, 100000). Therefore, I created the following spatial index, with a bounding box of sufficient size to ensure that all the points would be covered by the index:

```
CREATE SPATIAL INDEX sidx_point
  ON TestNearestNeighbors ( point )
  USING GEOMETRY_GRID
  WITH (
    BOUNDING_BOX =(0, 0, 100000, 100000)
  );
```

To start with, I added 10,000 random points to the table:

```
SET NOCOUNT ON;
DECLARE @i int = 0;
WHILE @i < 10000 BEGIN
  INSERT INTO TestNearestNeighbors(point)
  VALUES (geometry::Point(RAND()*100000, RAND()*100000, 0));

  SET @i = @i + 1;
END;
```

Now, with the test data primed, I created generic versions of each of the methods described above into stored procedures, as follows:

```
-- Basic Nearest Neighbor
CREATE PROCEDURE uspBasicNearestNeighbor (
  @Point geometry
)
AS BEGIN
SELECT TOP 1
  id
FROM
  TestNearestNeighbors
ORDER BY
  Point.STDistance(@Point) ASC;
END;
GO


-- Nearest Neighbor With Index
CREATE PROCEDURE uspNearestNeighborWithIndex (
  @Point geometry
)
AS BEGIN
SELECT TOP 1
  id
FROM
  TestNearestNeighbors WITH(index(sidx_point))
WHERE
  Point.STDistance(@Point) IS NOT NULL
ORDER BY
  Point.STDistance(@Point) ASC;
```

```
END;
GO

-- Fixed Search Area
CREATE PROCEDURE uspNearestNeighborFixedSearchRadius (
  @Point geometry,
  @Radius float
)
AS BEGIN
DECLARE @SearchArea geometry;
SET @SearchArea = @Point.STBuffer(@Radius);

WITH Candidates AS (
  SELECT
    id,
    Point.STDistance(@Point) AS Distance
  FROM
    TestNearestNeighbors
  WHERE
    Point.Filter(@SearchArea) = 1
)
SELECT TOP 1 * FROM Candidates ORDER BY Distance;
END;
GO

-- Expanding Search Area
CREATE PROCEDURE uspNearestNeighborExpandingSearchRadius (
  @Point geometry
)
AS BEGIN
WITH Candidates AS (
  SELECT TOP 1 WITH TIES
    Id,
    Point.STDistance(@Point) AS Distance,
    1000*POWER(2, Number) AS Range
  FROM
    TestNearestNeighbors
    INNER JOIN Numbers
    ON TestNearestNeighbors.Point.STDistance(@Point) < 1000 * POWER(2, Numbers.Number)
    ORDER BY Number
)
SELECT TOP 1 * FROM Candidates ORDER BY Range DESC, Distance ASC;
END;
GO
```

Each procedure was called repeatedly, and the time taken for each query recorded. After completing the batch of tests, I increased the number of rows in the base table to 100,000 and then 1,000,000, repeating the series of tests each time.

The results I obtained (on a fairly humble, dual-core laptop) are shown in Table 12-1.

Table 12-1. Comparing Performance of Nearest-Neighbor Queries

Method	Number of Rows in Base Table	Average Execution Time (ms)
Basic	10,000	389
Spatial Index	10,000	24
Fixed Search Zone	10,000	17
Expanding Search Zone	10,000	326
Basic	100,000	1,789
Spatial Index	100,000	74
Fixed Search Zone	100,000	22
Expanding Search Zone	100,000	30
Basic	1,000,000	18,360
Spatial Index	1,000,000	13
Fixed Search Zone	1,000,000	45
Expanding Search Zone	1,000,000	32,000

For this particular sample of data, the most consistently fast performing solution is the fixed search zone. However, the marginal speed advantage it offers over the nearest neighbor spatial index plan is probably more than offset by the risk of not finding any results. The Expanding Search Zone can produce good performance, but it is unreliable and difficult to maintain. These results should only be considered as illustrative: the actual performance times will depend on many factors, including the hardware configuration of your server, the nature and distribution of data in your base table, and the exact results required from your query. Having seen the different approaches available, I highly encourage you to perform your own tests to determine what is best for your particular circumstances.

Calculating the Shortest Path Between Two Geometries

STDistance(), as described in the preceding section, will give you a linear value representing the shortest distance between any two geometries. For nearest-neighbor queries, this is generally all that is required. We don't care exactly where, or in what direction the nearest neighbor is located relative to our chosen feature, as long as it is the shortest distance away.

In certain situations, however, we may want to know not only the shortest distance between two geometries but also the path along which that distance is measured. In other words, referring back to Figure 12-1, what is the line along which length *d* was calculated? For this, we can use the ShortestLineTo() method.

ShortestLineTo() returns the line segment of the shortest distance between any two points of two geometries. For two Point geometries, this is pretty intuitive: the shortest path between two points is the straight LineString that starts and ends at the two points in question. For example, in the following code listing, two geography Points are created representing the locations of Warsaw, Poland, and Kiev, in Ukraine. The ShortestPathTo() method is then used to return the shortest path between the two locations:

```
DECLARE @Warsaw geography = 'POINT(17 51.1)';
DECLARE @Kiev geography = 'POINT(30.5 50.5)';

SELECT
@Warsaw.ShortestLineTo(@Kiev).ToString();
```

The result is as follows (notice the effect that computation has had on the precision of the supplied coordinate values):

```
LINESTRING (17.000000000000007 51.100000000000009, 30.499999999999993 50.5)
```

As expected, the shortest line between the two cities is the LineString that directly connects them. Since, in the example above, the two points are of the geography datatype, this LineString is an elliptic arc. To visualize the results, you can add a buffer around each geometry and label them as follows:

```
DECLARE @Warsaw geography = 'POINT(17 51.1)';
DECLARE @Kiev geography = 'POINT(30.5 50.5)';

SELECT
  @Warsaw.STBuffer(40000), 'Warsaw'
UNION ALL SELECT
  @Kiev.STBuffer(40000), 'Kiev'
UNION ALL SELECT
  @Warsaw.ShortestLineTo(@Kiev).STBuffer(1000), 'ShortestLineTo';
```

The result of this query is displayed in the SSMS Spatial Results tab as shown in Figure 12-6.

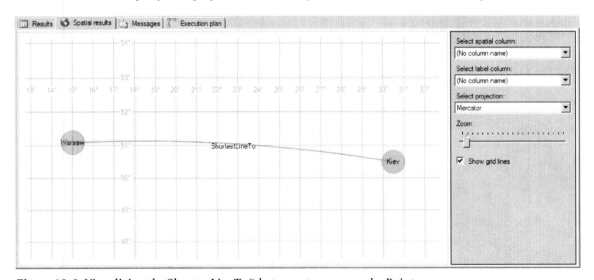

Figure 12-6. Visualizing the ShortestLineTo() between two geography Points

A situation in which ShortestLineTo() becomes more useful is where one or both of the geometries involved is of a more complex type than a simple Point. To demonstrate this, let's consider a practical example: trying to escape from the island of Alcatraz. Alcatraz Island was the site of one of the world's most famous prisons, which housed many notorious criminals, including Al Capone and Robert Stroud (the "Birdman of Alcatraz"), and has featured in many films, books, and other popular culture. In its 29 years of operation, it is claimed that no prisoner ever successfully escaped from the prison. One of the reasons for this is that the island itself stands isolated in San Francisco Bay, surrounded by freezing cold, hazardous ocean currents. Any escapees who did manage to escape from the prison were almost certain to drown before they made it to the mainland.

But let's suppose that you were going to make that escape attempt, that you'd evaded the guards, and were going to swim to freedom. To have the best chance of survival, you'd probably want to take the shortest direct line route across the water to the mainland. The following code listing recreates this situation, using a Polygon to represent Alcatraz Island, and a MultiLineString to represent various sections of the nearby mainland coastline, defined using the UTM Zone 10N spatial reference system, EPSG:32610. The ShortestLineTo() method is used to determine the shortest path from the island to safety:

```
DECLARE @Alcatraz geometry;
SET @Alcatraz = geometry::STPolyFromText('POLYGON ((550601 4186887, 550725 4186710,
550717 4186666, 550885 4186556, 551042 4186668, 550813 4186777, 550724 4186921, 550601
4186887))', 32610);

DECLARE @Mainland geometry;
SET @Mainland = geometry::STMLineFromText('MULTILINESTRING (
  (543439 4176527, 542823 4181517, 545168 4182528, 546212 4184864, 547360 4184205,
  552814 4184793, 554797 4177926),
  (542209 4192942, 546636 4187640, 544006 4185850, 541366 4185837, 536416 4190584,
  536063 4190804),
  (559959 4194939, 562216 4187077, 559076 4183237, 558998 4181794, 567307 4178019))',
32610);

SELECT @Alcatraz, 'Alcatraz'
UNION ALL SELECT @Alcatraz.ShortestLineTo(@Mainland), 'Escape Route'
UNION ALL SELECT @Mainland, 'Freedom';
```

The route is shown in the Spatial Results tab as illustrated in Figure 12-7.

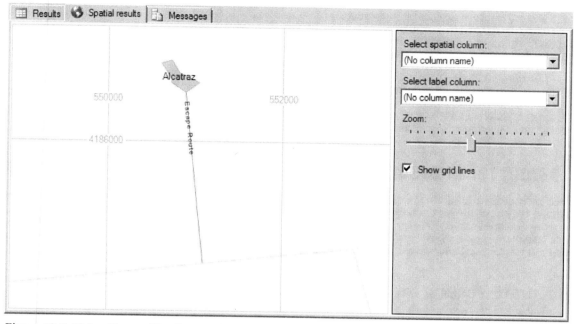

Figure 12-7. Using ShortestLineTo() to plot an escape from Alcatraz Island

Having determined the shortest path, we can also deduce some other useful information. The point at which we need to leave the island, for example, is given by `@Alcatraz.ShortestLineTo(@Mainland).STStartPoint()`, which is located at POINT (550885 4186556). The point at which we expect to reach freedom as we arrive on the mainland is `@Alcatraz.ShortestLineTo(@Mainland).STEndPoint()`, which is at approximately POINT (551095 4184607). Applying a bit of high school trigonometry to these points, we can also work out the bearing at which we'd have to travel across the sea:

```
DECLARE @Alcatraz geometry;
SET @Alcatraz = geometry::STPolyFromText('POLYGON ((550601 4186887, 550725 4186710,
550717 4186666, 550885 4186556, 551042 4186668, 550813 4186777, 550724 4186921, 550601
4186887))', 32610);

DECLARE @Mainland geometry;
SET @Mainland = geometry::STMLineFromText('MULTILINESTRING (
  (543439 4176527, 542823 4181517, 545168 4182528, 546212 4184864, 547360 4184205,
   552814 4184793, 554797 4177926),
  (542209 4192942, 546636 4187640, 544006 4185850, 541366 4185837, 536416 4190584,
   536063 4190804),
  (559959 4194939, 562216 4187077, 559076 4183237, 558998 4181794, 567307 4178019))',
32610);

DECLARE @Start geometry = @Alcatraz.ShortestLineTo(@Mainland).STStartPoint();
DECLARE @End geometry = @Alcatraz.ShortestLineTo(@Mainland).STEndPoint();

DECLARE @dx float = @End.STX - @Start.STX;
```

```
DECLARE @dy float = @End.STY - @Start.STY;

DECLARE @Bearing decimal(18,9) = ATN2(@dx, @dy);
SELECT (DEGREES(@Bearing) + 360) % 360;
```

The result, 173.85, represents a compass direction in degrees (in which North is 0, East is 90, South is 180 and West is 270). In other words, we would need to set off from the island at an angle just east of due south. The distance that we would have to swim is @Alcatraz.ShortestLineTo(@Mainland).STLength(), which is the same result as would be obtained by @Alcatraz.STDistance(@Mainland): 1,959.61 (meters).

Testing for Intersection

Two geometries are said to *intersect* if they share at least one point in common. That common point (or points) may lie either on the boundary or the interior of the geometries concerned. Testing to see whether one geometry intersects another is one of the most commonly used methods to identify objects that have some generalized spatial relationship to each other, for instance, identifying all the features that intersect a particular area of interest.

Accurate Testing for Intersection

The STIntersects() method tests whether two instances have at least one point in common. It is not specific as to how much of each geometry intersects the other, or in what manner they do so, just that one or more points is shared between the geometries. Figure 12-8 illustrates the results of the STIntersects() method when used to test the intersection between different types of geometries.

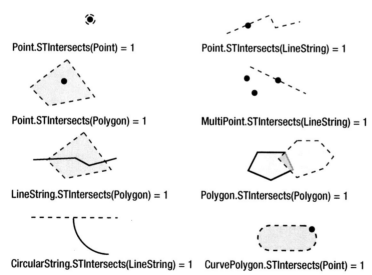

Point.STIntersects(Point) = 1   Point.STIntersects(LineString) = 1

Point.STIntersects(Polygon) = 1   MultiPoint.STIntersects(LineString) = 1

LineString.STIntersects(Polygon) = 1   Polygon.STIntersects(Polygon) = 1

CircularString.STIntersects(LineString) = 1   CurvePolygon.STIntersects(Point) = 1

Figure 12-8. *Results of the STIntersects() method when testing the intersection of different geometries*

▨ **Note** STIntersects() is used to test whether two geometries intersect. If you want to return the shape created by the intersection of two geometries, you should use the STIntersection() method instead.

STIntersects() can be used to test whether two instances of the geometry or geography datatype intersect as follows:

Instance1.STIntersects(Instance2)

The result of the STIntersects() method is 1 if the instances share any point in common, or 0 if they do not. To demonstrate, the following example code creates a table containing a Point, a LineString, and a Polygon geometry representing three well-known landmarks in Sydney: the Sydney Opera House, the Sydney Harbour Bridge, and the Royal Botanic Gardens. It then defines a Polygon geometry representing a 1 km square area of interest in the center of the city, and determines which of the geometries in the table intersect that area.

```
DECLARE @SydneyFeatures TABLE (
  Name varchar(32),
  Shape geometry
  );

INSERT INTO @SydneyFeatures VALUES
('Sydney Opera House', geometry::STPointFromText('POINT(334900 6252300)', 32756)),
('Sydney Harbour Bridge', geometry::STLineFromText(
  'LINESTRING(334300 6252450, 334600 6253000)', 32756)),
('Royal Botanic Garden', geometry::STPolyFromText('
  POLYGON ((334750 6252030, 334675 6251340, 335230 6251100, 335620 6251700,
  335540  6252040,335280 6251580, 335075 6251650, 335075 6251960, 334860 6252120,
  334750 6252030))', 32756));

DECLARE @AreaOfInterest geometry = geometry::STPolyFromText('
  POLYGON((334400 6252800, 334400 6251800, 335400 6251800, 335400 6252800,
  334400 6252800))', 32756);

SELECT
  Name
FROM
  @SydneyFeatures
WHERE
  Shape.STIntersects(@AreaOfInterest) = 1;
```

Executing this code listing gives the following results:

```
Sydney Opera House
Sydney Harbour Bridge
Royal Botanic Garden
```

All three features are returned, since they all intersect the area of interest in some way. Note that STIntersects() does not require the features to be completely contained within the area of interest; they simply need to intersect some part of it (this contrasts with the STWithin() method, discussed later in this chapter). To visualize the relationship between the particular features in this example, add the following code immediately after the end of the previous query:

```
SELECT Shape FROM @SydneyFeatures
UNION ALL SELECT @AreaOfInterest;
```

After executing the query, click the Spatial Results tab and you will see the results illustrated in Figure 12-9.

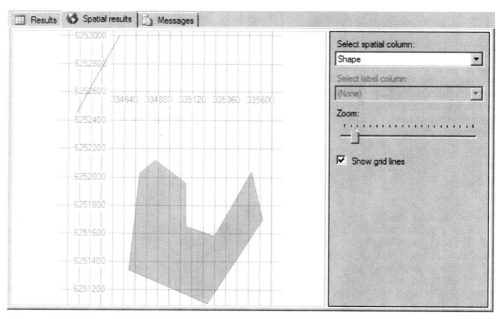

Figure 12-9. *Using the Spatial Results tab to confirm the intersection of geometries representing features in Sydney*

The large square geometry represents the area of interest. The Point geometry representing the Sydney Opera House is fully contained and located roughly in the center of the square. The LineString geometry representing the Sydney Harbour Bridge crosses the northwest corner of the area, and the Polygon geometry representing the Royal Botanic Gardens overlaps on the south side. All three geometries intersect the area of interest in some way, and are therefore included in the results returned by the condition STIntersects(@AreaOfInterest) = 1.

Approximate Testing for Intersection

The Filter() method provides similar functionality to the STIntersects() method; it too is used to test for any kind of intersection between two geometry or geography instances, returning the value 1 if intersection occurs, or 0 if no intersection occurs. However, instead of directly testing the two geometries in question to establish whether they share any points in common (as STIntersects() does), the Filter() method tests whether the two geometries intersect any common grid cells defined by the spatial index placed on one of the columns of data. Depending on the complexity of the geometries in question, this means that testing for the intersection between two geometries using the Filter() method can be much faster than using the STIntersects() method.

■ **Note** Spatial indexes store a record of the generalized extent of a geometry by creating a grid of cells, and recording those cells in the grid required to completely cover each geometry. This can be used as a primary filter to approximate the area of space that the geometry itself occupies. The topic of spatial indexes is covered fully in Chapter 18.

The `Filter()` method can be applied to perform a quick test of intersection between two instances of the geometry or geography datatype as follows:

```
Instance1.Filter(Instance2)
```

In order for `Filter()` to be effective, either `Instance1` or `Instance2` must be a column of spatial data on which a spatial index has been created. If no spatial index is present, the behavior of the `Filter()` method reverts to match that of the `STIntersects()` method.

THE FILTER() METHOD AND INDEX-DEPENDENCY

The behavior of the `Filter()` method is rather unusual, in that it operates differently in the presence of a spatial index than without; When an index exists, `Filter()` performs only a primary filter of the results, whereas in the absence of an index, `Filter()` performs a secondary filter just like `STIntersects()`.

This creates an interesting situation in which the results returned by a query that uses `Filter()` can be made to change through nothing more than the addition or modification of an index on that table.

If you want to perform a fast, approximate test of intersection then you may find `Filter()` useful. If, however, you want accurate results that remain consistent regardless of the presence or configuration of a spatial index, you should use `STIntersects()` instead.

Like the `STIntersects()` method, the `Filter()` method returns the value 1 if the instances intersect, or 0 if they do not. Although `Filter()` may be faster than `STIntersects()`, one disadvantage of the `Filter()` method is that there is a risk of returning false positive results; that is, the `Filter()` method might return the value 1 in some cases where the cell in the spatial index intersects the geometry in question, even if the instance itself does not.

One of the most useful applications of the `Filter()` method is therefore when you want to perform a fast approximate query of all those geometries that intersect a particular instance, in order to pass the data to a client that can then perform more detailed analysis of those geometries.

■ **Note** If used on a column of data that does not have a defined spatial index, the `Filter()` method defaults to exactly the same behavior as the `STIntersects()` method.

To demonstrate the `Filter()` method, you first need to create a table with a spatial index as follows:

```
CREATE TABLE #Geometries (
  id int IDENTITY(1,1) PRIMARY KEY,
```

```
  geom geometry
  );
CREATE SPATIAL INDEX [idx_Spatial]
  ON [dbo].[#Geometries] ( geom )
  USING GEOMETRY_GRID
  WITH (
    BOUNDING_BOX =(-180, -90, 180, 90),
    GRIDS =(
      LEVEL_1 = MEDIUM,
      LEVEL_2 = MEDIUM,
      LEVEL_3 = MEDIUM,
      LEVEL_4 = MEDIUM),
    CELLS_PER_OBJECT = 4 );
```

Then, execute the following code to insert two Polygon geometries into the table:

```
INSERT INTO #Geometries (geom) VALUES
('POLYGON((52.09 -2.14, 51.88 -2.15, 51.89 -1.89,52.12 -1.99, 52.09 -2.14))'),
('POLYGON((52.1 -2, 52.05 -2.01, 51.9 -1.9, 52.11 -2.15, 52.15 -1.9, 52.1 -2))');
```

Let's try to find out which Polygons in the #Geometries table intersect a Point geometry at coordinates (52.07, –2). First, we'll try using the Filter() method. To ensure that the Filter() method performs only an approximate test based on a primary filter, we'll add an explicit query hint to use the idx_Spatial index, as follows:

```
DECLARE @Point geometry = geometry::STGeomFromText('POINT(52.07 -2)', 0);

SELECT id
FROM #Geometries
WITH(INDEX(idx_Spatial))
WHERE geom.Filter(@Point) = 1;
```

The results of the Filter() method suggest that both Polygons contain this Point:

```
1
2
```

Now let's ask the same question using the STIntersects() method. To do so, we'll simply amend the query predicate, replacing the Filter() method with the STIntersects() method:

```
DECLARE @Point geometry = geometry::STGeomFromText('POINT(52.07 -2)', 0);

SELECT id
FROM #Geometries
WITH(INDEX(idx_Spatial))
WHERE geom.STIntersects(@Point) = 1;
```

In this case, the result of STIntersects() correctly shows that the Point is contained only in the first Polygon:

```
1
```

Why do the `Filter()` method and the `STIntersects()` method give different results in this example? Although the Point `@Point` lies very close to the edge of the second Polygon, it is not contained within it. However, the index grid cells provide only a loose fit around the shape of the Polygon, so they do contain the Point in question. Since the `Filter()` method obtains an approximate answer based on the cells representing each object in the spatial index, it can therefore create false positive results, as in this case.

■ **Note** The degree of accuracy with which the results of the `Filter()` method represents the actual intersection between two geometries depends on the properties of the spatial index that it uses, such as the bounding box, number of cells per object, and resolution of each grid level. These concepts will be discussed in detail in Chapter 18.

Testing for Disjointness

Whereas `STIntersects()` tests whether two instances intersect each other, `STDisjoint()` tests whether two instances are disjoint: that is, they have no points in common. `STIntersects()` and `STDisjoint()` are complementary methods, so that, for any given pair of geometries, if the result of one of these methods is true, the result of the other must be false. `A.Intersects(B) = 1` is logically equivalent to `A.Disjoint(B) = 0`.

■ **Tip** `STIntersects()` returns 1 if the instances intersect, and 0 if they are disjoint. `STDisjoint()` returns 1 if the instances are disjoint, and 0 if they intersect.

Figure 12-10 illustrates the results of the `STDisjoint()` method when used to test whether various geometries are disjoint.

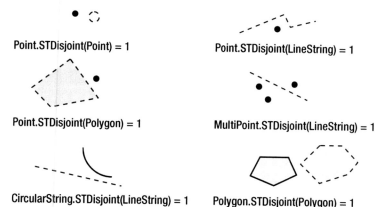

Point.STDisjoint(Point) = 1   Point.STDisjoint(LineString) = 1

Point.STDisjoint(Polygon) = 1   MultiPoint.STDisjoint(LineString) = 1

CircularString.STDisjoint(LineString) = 1   Polygon.STDisjoint(Polygon) = 1

Figure 12-10. Testing whether different geometries are disjoint by using STDisjoint()

The STDisjoint() method can be used on any two instances of the geometry or geography datatype as follows:

```
Instance1.STDisjoint(Instance2)
```

If the two instances are disjoint (i.e., they share no points in common), then the result of the STDisjoint() method is 1. If the two instances have any point in common, the STDisjoint() method returns the value 0.

Let's consider an example to demonstrate the STDisjoint() method. In order to protect and preserve the natural environment, many countries designate specific areas of outstanding natural beauty, such as national parks, which are governed by special planning restrictions that prevent industrial development in those areas. In the following code listing, a Polygon geometry is created representing an area of protected countryside in Dorset, England. A LineString geometry is then defined representing the proposed route of a new road being developed in the area. The STDisjoint() method is used to test whether the road avoids the designated area of countryside.

```
DECLARE @Countryside geography;
SET @Countryside = geography::STPolyFromText(
  'POLYGON((-2.66 50.67, -2.47 50.59, -2.39 50.64, -1.97 50.58,
  -1.94 50.66, -2.05 50.69, -2.02 50.72, -2.14 50.75, -2.66 50.67))',  4326);

DECLARE @Road geography;
SET @Road = geography::STGeomFromText(
  'LINESTRING(-2.44 50.71, -2.46 50.66, -2.45 50.61 )', 4326);

SELECT
@Road.STDisjoint(@Countryside);
```

The result of the STDisjoint() method is as follows:

0

This indicates that, in this case, the road is not disjoint to the protected countryside area, and the proposed route must be reconsidered.

Identifying Specific Types of Intersection

STIntersection(), Filter(), and STDisjoint() are all generalized tests of intersection between two geometries. They do not distinguish the manner or degree in which the geometries intersect; only whether they have at least one point in common. In this section, we'll examine methods that test for specific types of intersection that can occur between two geometries.

Determining Whether One Geometry Crosses Another

The STCrosses() method can be used to test the specific case of intersection where one geometry crosses another. In spatial terms, geometry A crosses geometry B when either of the following conditions is met:

- Geometry B is a Polygon (or CurvePolygon) and geometry A intersects both the interior and exterior of that Polygon. Note that this only applies when geometry A is a MultiPoint, LineString, Curve, or MultiLineString. If geometry A is also a Polygon or CurvePolygon, then this condition would be described as the two geometries *overlapping*.

- Geometry A and geometry B are both either LineStrings, Curves, or MultiLineStrings, and the geometry created by their intersection occupies zero dimensions (i.e., the two geometries intersect each other at a single point, or at multiple points, but do not follow each other along a continuous stretch).

■ **Note** A Point cannot cross any object. Two Polygons cannot cross each other, but they may overlap (for more information, see the discussion of the STOverlaps() method, later in this chapter).

Figure 12-11 illustrates a number of scenarios where one geometry crosses another, as tested by the STCrosses() method.

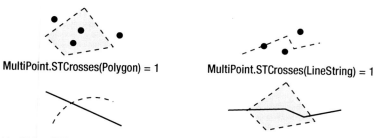

MultiPoint.STCrosses(Polygon) = 1   MultiPoint.STCrosses(LineString) = 1

LineString.STCrosses(CircularString) = 1   LineString.STCrosses(Polygon) = 1

Figure 12-11. Testing cases where one geometry crosses another by using STCrosses()

■ **Caution** The STCrosses() method is not symmetric. For example, a LineString can cross a Polygon, but a Polygon cannot cross a LineString. Be sure to specify the instances in the correct order when using the STCrosses() method.

The STCrosses() method can only be used to test whether one geometry instance crosses another. It cannot be used to compare two instances of the geography datatype. The syntax for its usage is as follows:

`Instance1.STCrosses(Instance2)`

If the two geometry instances satisfy the conditions described previously, then they are deemed to cross, and the STCrosses() method returns the value 1. Otherwise, the STCrosses() method returns the value 0.

To demonstrate the use of the STCrosses() method, consider the following example based on the London congestion charging zone. In order to reduce traffic in the city, in 2003 the mayor of London introduced a congestion zone covering an area in the center of London. Any vehicles entering the zone between 07:00 and 18:00 on a weekday are subject to a charge.

In this example, we will define a Polygon representing the zone in which the charge applies. Then we will create a LineString representing the route that a delivery van takes across the city, such as might be recorded by a GPS tracking system. We will then use the STCrosses() method to determine whether the route taken by the vehicle crosses the congestion zone and thus is subject to the charge.

```
DECLARE @LondonCongestionZone geometry;
SET @LondonCongestionZone = geometry::STPolyFromText(
  'POLYGON ((-0.12367 51.48642, -0.07999 51.49773, -0.07256 51.51593,
             -0.08115 51.52472, -0.10977 51.53168, -0.17644 51.51512,
             -0.21495 51.52631, -0.22672 51.51943, -0.18149 51.48174,
             -0.12367 51.48642))',
  4326);

DECLARE @DeliveryRoute geometry;
SET @DeliveryRoute = geometry::STLineFromText(
  'LINESTRING(
    -0.1428  51.5389, -0.1209 51.5190, -0.1171 51.5129, -0.1187 51.5112,
    -0.1136 51.5047, -0.1059 51.4983, -0.1043 51.4986, -0.1003 51.4946,
    -0.0935 51.4850, -0.0945 51.4827, -0.0929 51.4713
  )', 4326);

SELECT
@DeliveryRoute.STCrosses(@LondonCongestionZone);
```

The result of the STCrosses() method, confirming that the route does cross the congestion charging zone, is as follows:

1

To illustrate the geometries used in this example, you can add the following statement to the end of the query:

```
SELECT @LondonCongestionZone
UNION ALL SELECT @DeliveryRoute;
```

Switching to the Spatial Results tab displays the illustration shown in Figure 12-12. The LineString representing the route taken by the delivery van clearly crosses the Polygon representing the congestion charging zone.

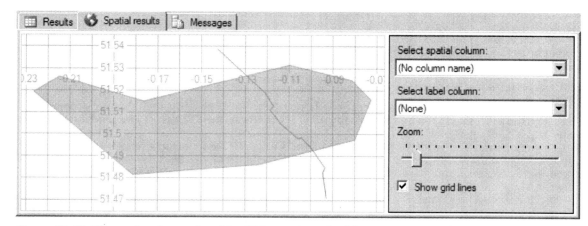

Figure 12-12. *Illustrating the results of the STCrosses() method for a route across the London congestion charging zone*

Finding Out Whether Two Geometries Touch

In order for two geometries to *touch* each other, the intersection between them must contain at least one point from the boundary of the geometries in question, but no interior points. You can test whether two geometries touch each other by using the STTouches() method. Figure 12-13 illustrates some examples of touching geometries.

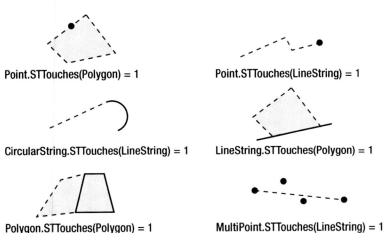

Point.STTouches(Polygon) = 1   Point.STTouches(LineString) = 1

CircularString.STTouches(LineString) = 1   LineString.STTouches(Polygon) = 1

Polygon.STTouches(Polygon) = 1   MultiPoint.STTouches(LineString) = 1

Figure 12-13. *Examples of different geometries that touch each other, confirmed by the STTouches() method*

Like STCrosses(), the STTouches() method can be used only to compare two instances of the geometry datatype, using the following syntax:

```
Instance1.STTouches(Instance2)
```

If Instance1 touches Instance2, then the STTouches() method returns the value 1, otherwise it returns the value 0.

■ **Note** STTouches() is a symmetric method; that is, for any two given instances,

```
Instance1.STTouches(Instance2) = Instance2.STTouches(Instance1).
```

As an example, Metropolitan France is divided into 21 administrative *regions* (not including the island of Corsica). In the following code listing, Polygon geometries are created to represent the regions of Aquitaine and Limousin, using coordinates defined in the Réseau Géodésique Français (RGF) spatial reference system, EPSG:2154. The STTouches() method is then used to test whether the two regions touch each other.

```
DECLARE @Aquitaine geometry;
SET @Aquitaine = geometry::STPolyFromText('POLYGON ((312120 6262629, 422584 6195898,
457270 6257031, 435167 6283717, 441086 6321733, 529746 6342627, 539728 6388817,
568689 6410364, 575744 6438769, 553092 6499585, 523687 6505245, 507807 6508498,
```

```
459341 6450634, 377913 6498699, 341793 6294740, 312120 6262629))', 2154);

DECLARE @Limousin geometry;
SET @Limousin = geometry::STPolyFromText('POLYGON ((523687 6505245, 553092 6499585,
575744 6438769, 605180 6427143, 630819 6434136, 659392 6477532, 653597 6528547,
668822 6546774, 645133 6588032, 609788 6593674, 537447 6579630, 541419 6542754,
523687 6505245))', 2154);

SELECT
@Aquitaine.STTouches(@Limousin);
```

The result of the STTouches() method is as follows:

1

The geometries created in this example do touch each other, and are illustrated in Figure 12-14, shown in relation to an outline map of France.

Figure 12-14. *Illustrating the touching French regions of Limousin and Aquitaine*

Testing for Overlap

Two geometries, A and B, are considered to *overlap* if the following criteria are all met:

- Both A and B are the same type of geometry.
- A and B share some, but not all, interior points in common.
- The geometry created by the intersection of A and B occupies the same number of dimensions as both A and B themselves.

Figure 12-15 illustrates some scenarios of overlapping geometries.

MultiPoint.STOverlaps(MultiPoint) = 1

LineString.STOverlaps(LineString) = 1

Polygon.STOverlaps(Polygon) = 1

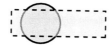

CurvePolygon.STOverlaps(Polygon) = 1

Figure 12-15. Examples of geometries that overlap one another, as confirmed using the STOverlaps() method

The STOverlaps() method can be used to test whether two instances of the geography datatype or geometry datatype overlap, using the following syntax:

Instance1.STOverlaps(Instance2)

The result is a value of 1 (true) if the instances do overlap, or 0 (false) if they do not.

To demonstrate the STOverlaps() method, consider the U.S. states of Arizona, Colorado, Utah, and New Mexico, which all meet at a single point known as the Four Corners. The Four Corners Monument is located at this spot, marked by a large circular bronze disk that lies partially in each of the four states, the only location in the United States where it is possible to do so. In this example, Polygon instances are created to represent each of the four states, and a further CurvePolygon instance is used to represent the circular Four Corners Monument (defined by creating a circular buffer of radius 1 meter about a Point). The STOverlaps() method is then used to test whether the monument overlaps each of the states.

```
DECLARE @States TABLE (
  Name varchar(32),
  Shape geometry
);
INSERT INTO @States(Name, Shape) VALUES
  ('Arizona', geometry::STPolyFromText('POLYGON((500000 4094872, 54963 4106576,
  -45243 3610718, 309650 3464577, 500000 3462850, 500000 4094872))', 9999)),
  ('Colorado', geometry::STPolyFromText('POLYGON((500000 4094872, 1123261 4117851,
  1088915 4562422, 500000 4538757, 500000 4094872))', 9999)),
  ('Utah', geometry::STPolyFromText('POLYGON((500000 4094872,500000 4538757,
  331792 4540684, 334361 4651711,85856 4661884, 54963 4106576, 500000 4094872))',
  9999)),
  ('New Mexico', geometry::STPolyFromText('POLYGON((500000 4094872, 500000 3462850,
  576134 3463126, 575729 3518546, 736683 3520990, 726722 3542965, 1067189 3556209,
  1034127 4111739, 500000 4094872))', 9999));

DECLARE @Monument geometry
  SET @Monument = geometry::STPointFromText('POINT(500000 4094872)',
  9999).BufferWithCurves(1);

SELECT
Name FROM @States WHERE
@Monument.STOverlaps(Shape) = 1;
```

The result confirms that the monument does overlap all four states:

```
Arizona
Colorado
Utah
New Mexico
```

■ **Note** It is not easy to choose a projection that can accurately portray the combined areas of Arizona, Colorado, Utah, and New Mexico; they do not lie in the same UTM zone, and each one has its own state plane projection system. In order to portray the four states with the least amount of distortion, the coordinates in this example are based on a transverse Mercator projection as used in the UTM system, but centered on a central meridian of 109° west longitude, the line of longitude on which the Four Corners point itself lies. This projection lies between UTM Zones 12N and 13N and is not a recognized EPSG spatial reference system. Since it does not have an associated spatial reference identifier, the SRID 9999 is used instead.

Testing Whether One Geometry Is Contained Within Another

Geometry A is said to be *within* geometry B if the interior of A is completely contained within B. Specifically, the two geometries must meet the following criteria:

- The interiors of both geometries must intersect.
- No point from geometry A may lie in the exterior of geometry B (although points from geometry A may lie in the boundary of B).

You can use the STWithin() method to test whether one geometry is contained within another geometry, as illustrated in the examples in Figure 12-16.

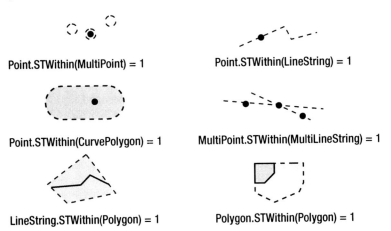

Point.STWithin(MultiPoint) = 1 Point.STWithin(LineString) = 1

Point.STWithin(CurvePolygon) = 1 MultiPoint.STWithin(MultiLineString) = 1

LineString.STWithin(Polygon) = 1 Polygon.STWithin(Polygon) = 1

Figure 12-16. Examples of geometries contained within other geometries, as tested using the STWithin() method

The syntax for the STWithin() method is as follows:

Instance1.STWithin(Instance2)

Instance1 and Instance2 may be instances of either the geometry or geography datatype, but they both must be of the same type, and defined using the same SRID. The result is the value 1 if Instance1 lies within Instance2, or 0 if it does not.

The following example uses a Polygon geometry representing the political ward of Stormont, Belfast. A ward is a district of local government in Northern Ireland, for which an individual councilor is elected. The points of the Polygon representing the Stormont ward are defined using the Irish National Grid system (SRID 29901). The example then demonstrates how the STWithin() method can be used to test whether the residents of a particular house represented by a Point, @Constituents, are constituents within that ward.

```
DECLARE @Stormont geometry;
SET @Stormont = geometry::STPolyFromText('POLYGON ((338109 373760, 341057
373912, 341208 375079, 338560 376107, 338109 373760))', 29901);

DECLARE @Constituents geometry;
SET @Constituents = geometry::STPointFromText('POINT(340275 375032)', 29901);

SELECT @Constituents.STWithin(@Stormont);
```

The result indicates that the Point representing the house does lie within the Polygon geometry representing the Stormont ward. The residents of that house are therefore constituents of that ward.

1

Testing Whether One Geometry Contains Another

STContains() can be used to test whether one geometry *contains* another geometry. Geometry A contains geometry B if the following criteria are met:

- The interior of both geometries intersects.
- None of the points of geometry B lies in the exterior of geometry A.

The STContains() method provides complementary functionality to the STWithin() method, such that a.STContains(b) is logically equivalent to b.STWithin(a).

■ **Caution** In order for geometry A to contain geometry B, it is not sufficient that no point of geometry B lies outside of geometry A; to suffice, *at least one point* of the interior of B must lie in the interior of A. For example, the LineString geometry that defines the exterior ring of a Polygon is not contained within that Polygon, since none of the points in the LineString lies in the interior of the Polygon, only in its boundary.

Figure 12-17 illustrates a variety of examples of spatial objects that contain other objects.

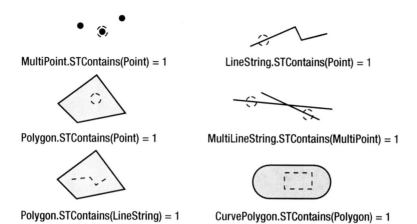

MultiPoint.STContains(Point) = 1

LineString.STContains(Point) = 1

Polygon.STContains(Point) = 1

MultiLineString.STContains(MultiPoint) = 1

Polygon.STContains(LineString) = 1

CurvePolygon.STContains(Polygon) = 1

Figure 12-17. Testing whether one object contains another by using STContains()

The STContains() method can be used to test whether one instance of the geometry or geography datatype, Instance1, contains another geometry of the same datatype and SRID, Instance2, as follows:

```
Instance1.STContains(Instance2)
```

The result is the value 1 if Instance1 contains Instance2, or 0 if it does not.

The following example creates a Polygon geometry representing the jurisdiction of the Oxfordshire Local Education Authority (LEA)—the local authority responsible for education and library services within the county of Oxfordshire, England. It then creates a Point geometry representing a school, and uses the STContains() method to determine whether or not the area for which the LEA has responsibility contains the school.

```
DECLARE @OxfordshireLEA geometry;
SET @OxfordshireLEA = geometry::STPolyFromText('POLYGON ((478150 178900, 446250
252400, 419900 209050, 428200 180250, 478150 178900))', 27700);

DECLARE @School geometry;
SET @School = geometry::STPointFromText('POINT(431400 214500)', 27700);

SELECT @OxfordshireLEA.STContains(@School);
```

The result of the STContains() method, confirming that the area for which the authority is responsible does contain the school, is as follows:

```
1
```

Defining Custom Relationships Between Geometries

For the majority of spatial applications, all of the necessary functionality to compare the relationships between two items of spatial data can be provided using the predefined SQL Server methods already discussed: STIntersects(), STContains(), STCrosses(), and so on. However, some applications require you to define and test for specific, custom spatial relationships between two instances that are not catered for by existing methods. In such cases, you can use STRelate().

The STRelate() method allows you to test for a user-defined relationship between two geometry instances, using a Dimensionally Extended 9-Intersection Model (DE-9IM) pattern. The DE-9IM model is a mathematical matrix that represents each of the possible intersections that can occur between the points located in the interior, boundary, and exterior of two geometries. A pattern from the DE-9IM model defines the relationship between two geometries based on whether intersection occurs between the geometries at each possible intersection and, if so, what the dimension of the resulting intersection is. By using one or more of these patterns, it is possible to reproduce the functionality of any of the other methods introduced in this chapter, as well as define your own custom relationships.

The STRelate() function can be used only to compare two instances of the geometry datatype, using the following syntax::

Instance1.STRelate(Instance2, Pattern)

Instance1 and Instance2 are instances of the geometry datatype. Pattern is a nine-character string pattern from the DE-9IM model that describes the relationship that you want to test. Each character in the Pattern string represents the type of intersection allowed at one of the nine possible intersections between the interior, boundary, and exterior of the two geometries. The values used in the pattern are as follows:

- T: An intersection must occur between the geometries.

- F: An intersection must not occur.

- 0: An intersection must occur that results in a zero-dimensional geometry (i.e., a Point or MultiPoint).

- 1: An intersection must occur that results in a one-dimensional geometry (i.e., a LineString, Curve, or MultiLineString).

- 2: An intersection must occur that results in a two-dimensional geometry (i.e., a Polygon, CurvePolygon, or MultiPolygon).

- *: It does not matter whether an intersection occurs or not.

To demonstrate how to construct a DE-9IM pattern for use with the STRelate() method, consider the intersections between two geometries that must exist for the STWithin() method to return true:

- The interior of geometry 1 must intersect the interior of geometry 2. It does not matter what the dimensions of this intersection are.

- Neither the interior nor the boundary of geometry 1 is allowed to intersect the exterior of geometry 2.

Using the DE-9IM model, this relationship can be represented by the matrix shown in Table 12-2.

Table 12-2. DE-9IM Matrix Representing the STWithin() Method

	Geometry 2 Interior	Geometry 2 Boundary	Geometry 2 Exterior
Geometry 1 Interior	T	*	F
Geometry 1 Boundary	*	*	F
Geometry 1 Exterior	*	*	*

In order to use the relationship stated in this matrix in combination with the STRelate() method, we first need to express the values contained in the cells of the matrix as a nine-character string. To do this, start at the top-left cell of the matrix and read the values from left to right and from top to bottom. For the relationship shown in the matrix in Table 12-2, this produces the pattern: T*F**F***.

You can test two geometries to see if they exhibit the relationship specified by supplying this pattern to the STRelate() method as follows:

```
Instance1.STRelate(Instance2, 'T*F**F***')
```

If the relationship of the two geometries meets the criteria specified in the pattern, then the STRelate() method returns 1. Otherwise, the method returns 0. In this example, the pattern T*F**F*** represents the intersections that must exist for one geometry to be contained within another, so Instance1.STRelate(Instance2, 'T*F**F***') is equivalent to Instance1.STWithin(Instance2).

As a practical example, suppose that we want to define and test for a specific type of intersection between two geometries, whether two instances are "connected," let's say. We'll define the conditions for two geometries to be connected as follows:

- The boundaries of the two geometries must intersect at one or more points, but they must not share a common side. In other words, the intersection between the two boundaries must be zero-dimensional.

- No parts of the interior of either geometry may intersect the other.

This relationship can be expressed in the DE-9IM matrix shown in Table 13-3.

Table 12-3. DE-9IM Matrix to Determine Whether Two Geometries Are Connected

	Geometry 2 Interior	Geometry 2 Boundary	Geometry 2 Exterior
Geometry 1 Interior	F	F	*
Geometry 1 Boundary	F	0	*
Geometry 1 Exterior	*	*	*

From this matrix, we can obtain the following DE-9IM pattern: FF*F0****. To demonstrate a situation in which you might use this pattern to test whether two geometries are connected, the following example creates two LineString geometries representing gas pipelines in Utah, expressed using the UTM Zone 12N projection based on the NAD 83 datum (SRID 26912). By supplying the DE-9IM pattern FF*F0**** to the STRelate() method, the example then checks whether the two pipelines are connected or not.

```
DECLARE @Pipe1 geometry;
SET @Pipe1 = geometry::STLineFromText('LINESTRING (446683 4441938, 446878 4442269,
    447236 4447851, 448057 4448802, 448060 4449019, 447303 4450244, 446746 4450760)',
    26912);

DECLARE @Pipe2 geometry;
SET @Pipe2 = geometry::STLineFromText('LINESTRING (437751 4438849, 443022 4438830,
    444164 4439588, 445240 4439580, 446683 4441938)', 26912);

SELECT
    @Pipe1.STRelate(@Pipe2,'FF*F0****');
```

The result of the STRelate() method is as follows:

1

This result confirms that, in this case, the two geometries satisfy the conditions specified by the pattern FF*F0****: the boundaries of both geometries intersect each other, leading to a zero-dimensional (Point) geometry, and neither the interior nor the boundary of either geometry intersects the interior of the other.

Summary

In this chapter, you learned about the various methods that can be used to define and test relationships between spatial features, including intersection- and proximity-based queries. Most of these methods are implemented by both the geometry and geography datatype, but some methods that test for specific sorts of intersection, such as STCrosses(), STTouches(), and STRelate(), are implemented only by the geometry datatype.

Remember that, even if a method is implemented in both the geography and geometry datatypes, you cannot test the spatial relationships between objects using a different datatype. For example, the STDistance() method can be used to calculate the distance between two geometry instances, or between two geography instances, but not the distance between a geography and a geometry instance.

CHAPTER 13

Clustering and Distribution Analysis

When dealing with large sets of spatial data (as with other sorts of data) we frequently don't want to consider each individual item at its most granular level. A dataset containing the details of hundreds of thousands of individual points is not particularly useful for business intelligence or analysis purposes, for example. Instead, what is generally required is a way of understanding trends in that data, by identifying patterns in the geographic spread and distribution of the underlying items.

In this chapter, we'll consider ways in which you can create such a summarized view of the distribution of a set of spatial data, and also look at methods to cluster that data. Clustering is a technique used to collate elements based on their physical proximity and other common attributes so that they may be assigned to a discrete collection, or "cluster." Having grouped a set of data, you can then analyze the properties and distribution of clusters rather than the individual items of data contained within the clusters. This is one way of facilitating distribution analysis.

Figure 13-1 illustrates an example of clustering. In the case illustrated, a set of 12 individual points is grouped into 4 clusters.

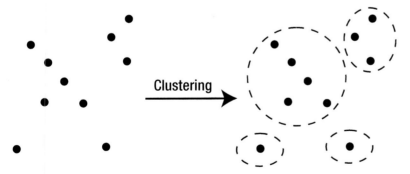

Figure 13-1. Clustering a set of points.

▓ **Tip** In Chapter 11, we considered spatial aggregates such as UnionAggregate(), which I likened to the SUM operator. Using a similar analogy, you can think of clustering as a way to GROUP a set of points.

Generally speaking, clustering is performed only on Point data. Since a Point represents a singular location in space, every Point in a given set of data can be assigned to one, and only one, cluster. However, clustering algorithms can theoretically be applied to any type of geometry, so long as care is taken to handle cases where a single item of data might be placed into two or more clusters.

There are many different clustering algorithms and methods of distribution analysis, with varying degrees of complexity and suitability for different datasets. In this chapter we'll consider just a few common algorithms and show some of the situations in which they can be used.

░ **Note** "Clustering" referred to in this chapter concerns the allocation of spatial features to distinct groups. It has nothing to do with clustering of SQL Server instances!

SQL Server's Spatial Histogram Procedures

Let's start off by considering the tools that come supplied with SQL Server "out-of-the-box." SQL Server includes two system stored procedures that can be used to analyze the physical distribution of a set of values of spatial data; these procedures are sp_help_spatial_geography_histogram and its sister, sp_help_spatial_geometry_histogram.

sp_help_spatial_geometry_histogram

The sp_help_spatial_geometry_histogram procedure can be used to analyze the data contained in a specified geometry column of a table. The process it uses is as follows:

1. Create a rectangular, axis-aligned grid. The extents of the grid are specified by the xmin, ymin, xmax, and ymax parameters supplied to the procedure. The size of the grid can be chosen to cover the entire geographic extent of a set of data, or it can instead be chosen to focus only on just a particular area of interest.

2. Divide the grid into a number of cells based on the supplied resolution parameter. resolution may be any value between 10 and 5,000, and represents the number of times the grid will be divided in both the x- and y-dimensions. Supplying a resolution parameter of 16 will divide the grid into 256 cells, for example. Each resulting cell is a regular-sided geometry Polygon.

3. Compare the grid of cells to the elements contained in the geometry column of a particular table, as specified by the colname and tabname parameters.

4. Return a table of results in which each row contains the shape of a grid cell and an associated cell identifier, together with the count of items from the chosen table that intersect the cell in question.

To consider this process in more detail, let's look at a practical example. Consider what happens when you call the sp_help_spatial_geometry_histogram procedure to analyze the distribution of a small number of points in a table, as created in the following code listing:

```
CREATE TABLE HistogramPoints (
  Location Geometry
);
INSERT INTO HistogramPoints VALUES
```

```
('POINT(1.5 2.5)'),
('POINT(3 7)'),
('POINT(4 5)'),
('POINT(4.5 5.2)'),
('POINT(4 6)'),
('POINT(5 5)'),
('POINT(9 8)'),
('POINT(7.5 2.5)'),
('POINT(8.2 7.5)'),
('POINT(8.5 6.5)');
```

To visualize the distribution of these Points in the SQL Server Spatial Results tab, add a small buffer around each as follows:

```
SELECT Location.STBuffer(0.1) FROM HistogramPoints;
```

The result is shown in Figure 13-2.

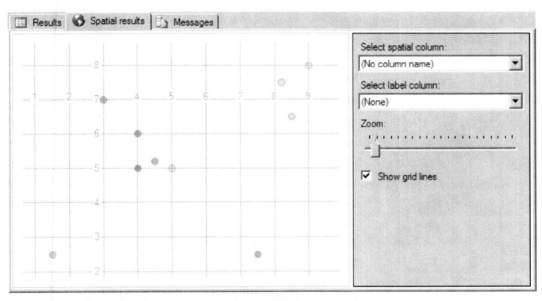

Figure 13-2. *Visualizing the distribution of a set of Point geometries*

We can use the sp_help_spatial_geometry_histogram procedure to analyze the distribution of the Points in the HistogramPoints table, using a grid that extends between (0,0) and (10,10), divided into 100 cells as follows:

```
EXEC sp_help_spatial_geometry_histogram
  @tabname = HistogramPoints,
  @colname= Location,
  @resolution = 10,
  @xmin=0,
  @ymin=0,
  @xmax=10,
  @ymax=10;
```

The `sp_help_spatial_geometry_histogram` procedure will return a table of results containing three columns: a unique CellId and geometry Polygon representing the shape of each cell, and a tally of the number of elements from the `Location` column of the `HistogramPoints` table that intersect that cell. An extract of the results follows:

CellId	Cell	IntersectionCount
63	0x00000000010405...	1
73	0x00000000010405...	1
44	0x00000000010405...	1
54	0x00000000010405...	2
64	0x00000000010405...	2

Having obtained the results, switch to the Spatial Results tab and choose the `IntersectionCount` field to label each Polygon. This allows you to quickly visualize the distribution of data in each grid cell, as shown in Figure 13-3.

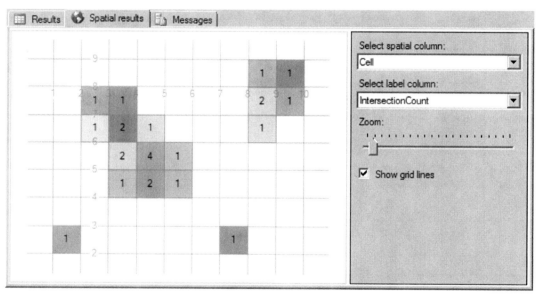

Figure 13-3. Visualizing the distribution of a set of points using sp_help_spatial_geometry_histogram

There are a couple of points to note about the output created by `sp_help_spatial_geometry_histogram`

Firstly, although the grid in Figure 13-3 has been divided into 10 columns and 10 rows (as requested), only those cells that intersect one or more features are returned in the results. In this example, the result set contains only 17 out of a possible 100 cells.

Secondly, the count returned for each cell is the count of *intersecting* features: the number of items in the `Location` column that touch, overlap, or cross, are contained within, or completely contain each grid cell. A Point geometry placed at the corner where four cells meet will be included in the intersection count of all four cells that it touches. This is demonstrated in this example by the four cells at the top right corner of Figure 13-3, all of which intersect the same single Point located at (9,8). Therefore, even when dealing with a column of only Point data, the sum of the IntersectionCount column returned by sp_help_spatial_geometry_histogram may differ from the number of rows in the base table.

The sp_help_spatial_geometry_histogram procedure is helpful in providing a quick overview of the distribution of a set of geometry data. The results can also be used as the basis for visualization of the distribution; imagine, for example, creating a heatmap from the data shown in Figure 13-3, in which cells were colored different shades depending on the count of intersecting items. This would be a very effective way of presenting, at a glance, those areas where data was most concentrated.

Another application where this function can be useful is when analyzing and performance-tuning a spatial index placed on a geometry column. By setting the xmin, xmax, ymin, and ymax properties to match that of the index bounding box, and setting the resolution parameter to match the grid resolution at a particular level of the index grid, you can determine exactly how many items of data fall into each grid cell, which is a key principle in creating an effective selective index. Spatial indexes are discussed in more detail in Chapter 18.

sp_help_spatial_geography_histogram

The sp_help_spatial_geography_histogram procedure, as you've probably guessed, fulfills the same purpose as the preceding sp_help_spatial_geometry_histogram procedure, except that it operates on a column of geography data. This necessitates a few changes in behavior:

> You do not supply explicit xmin, ymin, xmax or ymax parameters to specify the geographic extents of the histogram. Instead, the grid of cells is implicitly assumed to cover the entire globe.

> Like with sp_help_spatial_geometry_histogram, you supply a resolution parameter that determines how the grid will be divided into a set of cells. However, unlike its geometry sister, the grid cells created by sp_help_spatial_geography_histogram are not simple rectangular Polygons. Owing to the ellipsoidal nature of the geography datatype, before a grid can be created the surface of the ellipsoid must be projected onto a plane. The method of projection used by sp_help_spatial_geography_histogram first divides the globe into two hemispheres. The hemispheres are projected onto separate quadrilateral pyramids. These pyramids are then flattened and joined together to make a single planar surface, and it is on this surface that the grid of cells is created. This process of projection is illustrated in Figure 13-4. It is worth noting that, if you then display these cells using another projection of the geography datatype, such as a Mercator or Equirectangular projection, they will not appear to form a regular grid.

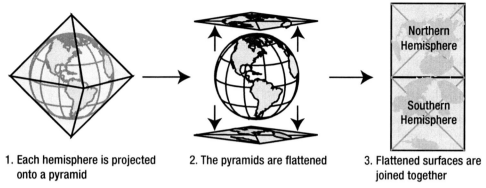

1. Each hemisphere is projected onto a pyramid   2. The pyramids are flattened   3. Flattened surfaces are joined together

Figure 13-4. Projecting the ellipsoidal surface of the geography datatype onto a plane in order to create a grid of cells.

■ **Note** The projection process described here is exactly the same process by which SQL Server creates cells used in a spatial index of a column of geography data, which makes sp_help_spatial_geography_histogram a useful function for performance-tuning of geography indexes.

To demonstrate the sp_help_spatial_geography_histogram method, let's consider another practical example. *Pongamia Pinnata* is a species of tree related to the pea family. Unlike its familiar legume cousin, the *Pongamia Pinnata* is highly toxic, although its seeds and fruits are used for other purposes including soap-making and the manufacture of oils and other lubricants.

The following table records a subset of occurrences of *Pongamia Pinnata*, as published by the LifeMapper biodiversity research site (http://www.lifemapper.org). The locations are recorded as geography Points, with coordinates measured using the EPSG:4326 spatial reference system.

```
CREATE TABLE LifeMapper_PongamiaPinnata (
  localId int,
  location geography
);

INSERT INTO LifeMapper_PongamiaPinnata VALUES
(122991120, 'POINT(-81.8266 26.693)'),
(217094166, 'POINT(-159.8 22.2)'),
(98482948, 'POINT(143.3 -13.8)'),
(94907937, 'POINT(143.333 -4.75)'),
(238638940, 'POINT(121.873 24.9125)'),
(207685693, 'POINT(121.873 24.9125)'),
(217095748, 'POINT(-66.0469 18.4065)'),
(217095749, 'POINT(-66.0469 18.4065)');
```

■ **Note** The full LifeMapper dataset for this species is included in the code samples that accompany this book, available from the downloads section of the Apress website, http://www.apress.com

---

To analyze the global geographic distribution of the *Pongamia Pinnata* species as recorded in the preceding table, you can use the sp_help_spatial_geography_histogram procedure, as follows:

```
EXEC sp_help_spatial_geography_histogram
    @tabname=LifeMapper_PongamiaPinnata,
    @colname=location,
    @resolution=10;
```

As with the sp_help_spatial_geometry_histogram procedure, the sp_help_spatial_geography_histogram procedure requires the name of the table and column to be examined, together with the resolution of the created grid. Notice that you do not supply parameters for the extent of the grid; it will always cover the entire globe. Also notice that, as in the example earlier, in this code listing I've set the resolution parameter to be 10. The abridged set of results obtained from executing this procedure against the full set of *Pongamia Pinnata* data are as follows:

CellId	Cell	IntersectionCount
1	0xE61000...	7
2	0xE61000...	9
94	0xE61000...	1
56	0xE61000...	4
12	0xE61000...	10
...		

As with the sp_help_spatial_geometry_histogram procedure, only those cells that intersect at least one feature are included in the results. In this case, that's 15 cells. Considering that the grid covers the whole globe, and the stated resolution of the grid was set to 10, you might therefore expect each of these cells to span (180/10) = 18 degrees of longitude and (90/10) = 9 degrees of latitude. However, switching to the Spatial Results tab quickly reveals that this is not the case, as shown in Figure 13-5.

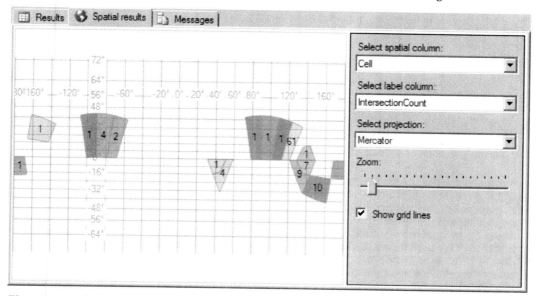

Figure 13-5. *The Spatial Results tab view of the distribution analysis created by* sp_help_spatial_geography_histogram

As can clearly be seen in Figure 13-5, when viewed using the Mercator projection the size of the cells created by sp_help_spatial_geography_histogram are neither regularly sized nor regularly spaced. In fact, because only those cells that intersect features are included in the output, it is quite hard to see any pattern in how the cells are arranged at all.

In order to make sense of the output, it would be helpful if we could visualize the complete grid of cells considered by the histogram procedure, even those that did not contain any occurrences of *Pongamia Pinnata*. To do this, we can insert an extra dummy record into the LifeMapper_PongamiaPinnata table, containing a single FullGlobe geometry. Since every geography Polygon is guaranteed to intersect the FullGlobe, this will ensure that every cell is included in the output. The following T-SQL will insert a new record into the LifeMapper_PongamiaPinnata table:

```
INSERT INTO LifeMapper_PongamiaPinnata VALUES
(-1, 'FULLGLOBE');
```

Calling the sp_help_spatial_geography_histogram as before now reveals all 100 of the cells as shown in Figure 13-6 (remember also that the count of intersecting items for every cell will now be one greater than the true count!):

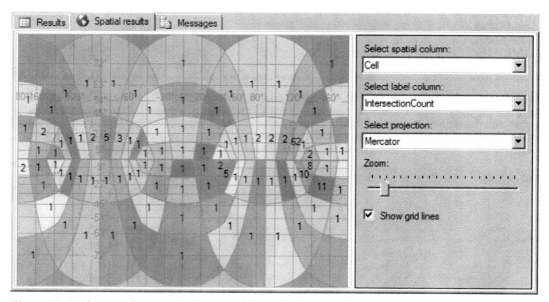

Figure 13-6. The complete set of cells created by sp_help_spatial_geography_histogram

It is now much easier to see the geometric pattern of cells created by sp_help_spatial_geography_histogram, with the IntersectionCount of each cell giving an indication of the geographic spread of the Pongami Pinnata species.

However, because of the specific nature of the way the grid is created, the results are not necessarily of that much use for general distribution analysis because the area covered by each grid cell varies. Using a resolution of 10, as in this case, the smallest grid cell occupies 2,481,819 km^2 while the largest occupies 7,958,745 km^2. When performing geographic distribution analysis, we generally want to ensure that we quantize the data to a regular-sized set of areas, or else risk skewing the results of any analysis.

One particular application where sp_help_spatial_geography_histogram is useful (and, in fact, the principal reason it was added to SQL Server) is in understanding indexes placed on geography columns. The cells in an index of a column of geography data are created using the same technique as used by sp_help_spatial_geography_histogram. By setting the resolution parameter to match the resolution of the grids of an index, you can create and visualize each individual cell, which aids in performance tuning, as will be discussed in a later chapter.

Creating a Customized Distribution Analysis

The histogram functions described in the preceding section are helpful for giving a broad overview of the distribution of the values in a column of spatial data, but they offer little ability to customize that analysis. The only way to customize the grid cells used by sp_help_spatial_geometry_histogram and sp_help_spatial_geography_histogram is the single resolution parameter, so there is no way to specify separate widths and heights for each cell, or to define irregularly shaped grid cells, for example. What's more, the only metric returned is the count of items that intersect each cell, and there is no way to link the results back to identify the source geometries included in each cell's count.

In this section, I'll attempt to overcome these shortcomings by creating a custom distribution analysis procedure. Rather like sp_help_spatial_geometry_histogram or sp_help_spatial_geography_histogram, this function will examine the distribution of values in a column of a specified table. However, in order to make the function more customizable and reusable, I'll allow the user to specify any pattern of cells against which to tessellate the values in the column.

The pattern of cells against which the data will be analyzed will be supplied as a Table Valued Parameter (TVP) to the procedure. The first step is to define a simple structure for this parameter, as follows:

```
CREATE TYPE dbo.CellPattern AS TABLE (
  CellID int NOT NULL,
  Cell geometry NOT NULL,
  PRIMARY KEY(CellID)
);
```

To analyze the distribution of features relative to the supplied pattern of cells, we'll create a procedure that uses the STIntersects() method to join from the geometry column of the selected table to the table of grid cells. Since the table name and column name will be supplied as parameters to the procedure, we'll construct the SQL statement dynamically in the procedure and then execute the query using sp_executesql. Dynamically generated SQL statements are very useful when you want to allow the flexibility to reuse the same procedure against different columns and tables but they do pose some risks, especially if, as in this case, the statement is generated from user-supplied input. In order to prevent accidental (or deliberate!) misuse, I've inserted a check that looks into the Information_Schema.Columns system view to ensure that the specified table and column exists and is of the geometry type, and that the current user has sufficient access to that column. Here's the full procedure:

```
CREATE PROCEDURE usp_geometry_distribution_analysis (
  @tablename sysname,
  @columnname sysname,
  @grid dbo.CellPattern READONLY
)
AS
BEGIN
  SET NOCOUNT ON;

  -- Ensure the specified geometry column exists in the table
  IF NOT EXISTS(SELECT 1 FROM Information_Schema.Columns
    WHERE Table_Name = @TableName
    AND Column_Name = @ColumnName
    AND DATA_TYPE = 'geometry'
```

```
)
BEGIN
  RAISERROR('Cannot access geometry column %s in table %s',16,1, @ColumnName, @TableName)
  RETURN -1;
END

-- Construct a dynamic SQL statement to count the number of items intersecting each
-- grid cell
DECLARE @sql nvarchar(max) = '';
SET @sql = 'SELECT g.CellId,
              g.Cell,
              count.IntersectionCount
            FROM (
              SELECT g.CellId,
              COUNT(c.' + QUOTENAME(@ColumnName) + ') AS IntersectionCount
              FROM ' + QUOTENAME(@TableName) + ' c
              JOIN @grid g ON c.' + QUOTENAME(@ColumnName) + '.STIntersects(g.Cell) = 1
              GROUP BY g.CellId) count
            JOIN @grid g ON count.CellId = g.CellId;';

-- Execute the statement
EXEC sp_executesql @sql, N'@grid dbo.CellPattern READONLY', @grid;

END;
```

To use the usp_geometry_distribution_analysis function, you provide three parameters: the name of an existing geometry column in a table to be analyzed, and a table parameter containing the cells against which you want the distribution to be compared. The example above is for the geometry datatype, but it could easily be adapted for the geography datatype as well.

Before we use the function, we now need a method to create the pattern of cells against which features in the table will be compared. This can be a regular grid of cells, such as that used by the sp_help_spatial_geometry_histogram procedure, or it could be something more complicated. In the following sections, we'll look at a couple of different examples of cell patterns that work well in different situations.

Creating a Regular Grid

The simplest method of distribution analysis is to consider a regular grid of cells, much like that used by SQL Server's own sp_help_spatial_geometry_histogram function. The following code listing demonstrates a SQLCLR function that will create a grid of geometry cells covering the full extent of a provided geometry Polygon. However, unlike the single resolution parameter of SQL Server's inbuilt histogram, this procedure will allow you to specify resolutions for the x- and y-dimensions of each cell independently, by dividing the grid into separately specified number of rows and columns. This allows you to create a grid of tall thin cells, or wide short cells, for example. Here's the code:

```
[Microsoft.SqlServer.Server.SqlProcedure]
public static void CreateGeometryGrid (SqlGeometry geom, int columns, int rows)
{

  // Create a rectangular envelope around the supplied geometry
  SqlGeometry envelope = geom.STEnvelope();

  // Get the corner points of the envelope
```

```
double minX = (double)envelope.STPointN(1).STX;
double minY = (double)envelope.STPointN(1).STY;
double maxX = (double)envelope.STPointN(3).STX;
double maxY = (double)envelope.STPointN(3).STY;

// Work out the height and width of the full grid
double gridwidth = maxX - minX;
double gridheight = maxY - minY;

// Calculate the width and height of each individual cell
double cellwidth = gridwidth / columns;
double cellheight = gridheight / rows;

// Create a new List<> to hold each cell in the grid
List<SqlGeometry> Cells = new List<SqlGeometry>();

// Loop through rows/columns to create each cell in the grid
int x = 0, y = 0;
while (y < rows)
{
  while (x < columns)
  {
    // Create the polygon grid cell
    SqlGeometryBuilder gb = new SqlGeometryBuilder();
    gb.SetSrid((int)geom.STSrid);
    gb.BeginGeometry(OpenGisGeometryType.Polygon);
    gb.BeginFigure(minX + (x * cellwidth), minY + (y * cellheight));
    gb.AddLine(minX + ((x + 1) * cellwidth), minY + (y * cellheight));
    gb.AddLine(minX + ((x + 1) * cellwidth), minY + ((y + 1) * cellheight));
    gb.AddLine(minX + (x * cellwidth), minY + ((y + 1) * cellheight));
    gb.AddLine(minX + (x * cellwidth), minY + (y * cellheight));
    gb.EndFigure();
    gb.EndGeometry();

    // Add this grid cell to the list
    Cells.Add(gb.ConstructedGeometry);

    // Move onto the next column
    x++;
  }

  // Move onto the next row
  y++;

  // Reset to the first column
  x = 0;
}

// Define the metadata of the output table
SqlDataRecord record = new SqlDataRecord(
  new SqlMetaData("CellID", SqlDbType.Int),
  new SqlMetaData("Cell", SqlDbType.Udt, typeof(SqlGeometry))
  );
```

```
// Send the metadata
SqlContext.Pipe.SendResultsStart(record);

// Loop through the completed grid cells
for (int c = 0; c < Cells.Count; c++)
{
  // Populate the record with this cell's information
  record.SetValues(c, Cells[c]);

  // Send the record back to the client
  SqlContext.Pipe.SendResultsRow(record);
}

SqlContext.Pipe.SendResultsEnd();
}
```

The geom parameter is used to determine the extent of the grid that will be created. If supplied as a rectangular, axis-aligned polygon, geom will define the exact extents of the grid. However, geom can be any shaped geometry, in which case the grid will be created based on the extent of the envelope around geom. The SRID of the supplied geom parameter must match the SRID of the geometries in the column of data that it will be used to analyze.

Having compiled the function, you can register it in SQL Server as follows:

```
CREATE PROCEDURE dbo.CreateGeometryGrid(@geom geometry, @columns int, @rows int)
AS EXTERNAL NAME Ch13_Clustering.[ProSQLSpatial.StoredProcedures].CreateGeometryGrid;
```

You can now use the CreateGeometryGrid procedure to populate a table with a grid of cells. This table can then be supplied to the usp_geometry_distribution_analysis function, which will determine how many of the features in the base table lie within each of the cells in the provided grid. To test this out, let's start by mirroring the earlier sp_help_spatial_geometry_histogram example, in which we analyzed the points in the HistogramPoints table by creating a grid covering the extent from (0,0) to (10,10), divided into a resolution of 10 in both dimensions. We can recreate this using the following code listing:

```
-- Create a 10x10 grid
DECLARE @Grid CellPattern;
DECLARE @BoundingBox geometry = 'POLYGON((0 0, 10 0, 10 10, 0 10, 0 0))';
INSERT INTO @Grid
EXEC dbo.CreateGeometryGrid
  @geom      = @BoundingBox,
  @columns   = 10,
  @rows      = 10;

-- Plug the grid into the distribution analysis procedure
EXEC usp_geometry_distribution_analysis
@tablename  = 'HistogramPoints',
@columnname = 'Location',
@grid       = @Grid;
```

With the exception of the CellId value and the ordering of the records, the result of executing this code is exactly the same as achieved earlier using the sp_help_spatial_geometry_histogram procedure, and is illustrated in Figure 13-7.

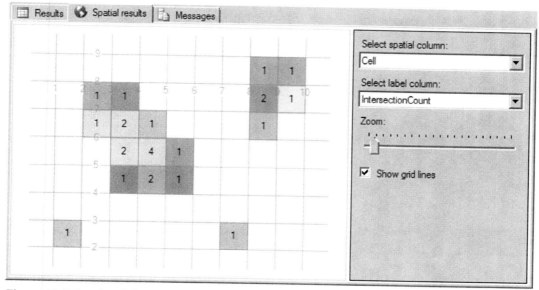

Figure 13-7. *Results of the usp_geometry_distribution_analysis procedure when applied to a regular grid of cells.*

"Why did we go to so much effort to recreate exactly the same result as could be achieved using an inbuilt method?" you may well ask. The answer is that our function can now be customized; suppose that, instead of using a 10 x 10 grid of cells, you wanted instead to analyze the distribution of the data in the HistogramPoints table in a set of horizontal bands. To do so, you could create a grid by calling the CreateGeometryGrid procedure with the @columns parameter set to 1, and @rows set to 5, say. Plugging the resulting table of cells into usp_geometry_distribution_analysis would then give the result illustrated in Figure 13-8. (Note that, although the bounding box is divided into five horizontal bands, no points in the HistogramPoints table intersect the lowest band, from (0,0) to (10,2), so this is not displayed in the results.) Here's the code listing:

```
-- Create a 1x5 grid
DECLARE @Grid CellPattern;
DECLARE @BoundingBox geometry = 'POLYGON((0 0, 10 0, 10 10, 0 10, 0 0))';
INSERT INTO @Grid
EXEC dbo.CreateGeometryGrid
  @geom      = @BoundingBox,
  @columns   = 1,
  @rows      = 5;

-- Plug the grid into the distribution analysis procedure
EXEC usp_geometry_distribution_analysis
@tablename  = 'HistogramPoints',
@columnname = 'Location',
@grid       = @Grid;
```

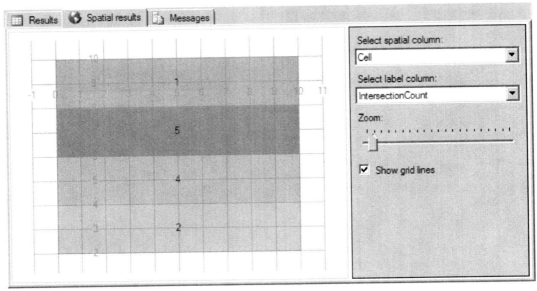

Figure 13-8. Analyzing the distribution of points into a set of horizontal bands.

To create even more customized analyses, you don't have to be limited by the regular pattern of cells as returned by the CreateGeometryGrid function. Instead, you can create other sorts of pattern, as we'll explore in the next section.

Creating a Bullseye Grid

Aside from the regular arranged grid pattern of cells as created by CreateGeometryGrid there are other common patterns used to analyze the distribution of features in a dataset. Since we designed the usp_geometry_distribution_analysis procedure to accept a table of any arrangement of cells as a parameter, we can try passing it more exciting types of grid. One alternative possible cell arrangement is a dartboard or "bullseye" pattern.

A bullseye pattern is formed from a series of concentric circles that expand outwards from a designated center. The parameters required to create such a pattern are the central point, the total number of rings to be created, and the radius by which each subsequent ring extends. The following code listing demonstrates a SQLCLR procedure that can be used to create a set number of circular geometry CurvePolygons expanding around a point.

```
[Microsoft.SqlServer.Server.SqlProcedure]
public static void CreateGeometryDartboard(SqlGeometry centre, int radius, int numrings)
{
  // Create a List<> to hold the cells
  List<SqlGeometry> Cells = new List<SqlGeometry>();

  // Insert the rings into the list
  for (int x = 0; x < numrings; x++)
  {
    // Calculate the "outer" extent of this ring
    SqlGeometry Ring = centre.BufferWithCurves(radius*(x+1));
```

```
    // Calculate the "inner" extent of this ring
    SqlGeometry Hole = centre.BufferWithCurves(radius * x);

    // Subtract the inner hole from the polygon
    Ring = Ring.STDifference(Hole);

    // Add this ring onto the list
    Cells.Add(Ring);
}

// Define the metadata of the output table
SqlDataRecord record = new SqlDataRecord(
    new SqlMetaData("CellID", SqlDbType.Int),
    new SqlMetaData("Cell", SqlDbType.Udt, typeof(SqlGeometry))
    );

// Send the metadata
SqlContext.Pipe.SendResultsStart(record);

// Loop through the cells
for (int c = 0; c < Cells.Count; c++)
{
    // Populate the record with this cells's information
    record.SetValues(c, Cells[c]);

    // Send the record back to the client
    SqlContext.Pipe.SendResultsRow(record);
}

    SqlContext.Pipe.SendResultsEnd();
}
```

You can register the function to create the dartboard of cells as follows:

```
CREATE PROCEDURE dbo.CreateGeometryDartboard(@centre geometry, @radius float, @numrings int)
AS EXTERNAL NAME Ch13_Clustering.[ProSQLSpatial.StoredProcedures].CreateGeometryDartboard;
```

As an example of when you might want to use a bullseye grid, consider the example of the Fukushima Daiichi nuclear power plant in Japan, which was severely damaged by an earthquake and subsequent tsunami in March 2011. The Japanese authorities enforced a 20 km evacuation zone immediately surrounding the plant, and encouraged those living within 20 km–30 km of the plant also to evacuate. The International Atomic Energy Agency tested levels of radiation at the village of Iitate, some 40 km from the site of the plant, which they advised still reached levels exceeding those required for evacuation. The U.S. military enforced a rigorous exclusion zone, preventing any personnel from going within 80 km of the damaged plant.

In order to categorize the levels of risk of features located at different distances from the nuclear plant, you can use the CreateGeometryDartboard procedure to create a dartboard of cells centered on the location of the reactor, with eight expanding circular rings each 10 km apart, as follows:

```
DECLARE @Fukushima geometry = geometry::Point(502912, 4141796, 32754);

EXEC CreateGeometryDartboard
  @centre   = @Fukushima,
  @radius   = 10,
  @numrings = 8;
```

The result created by executing this code listing is illustrated in Figure 13-9.

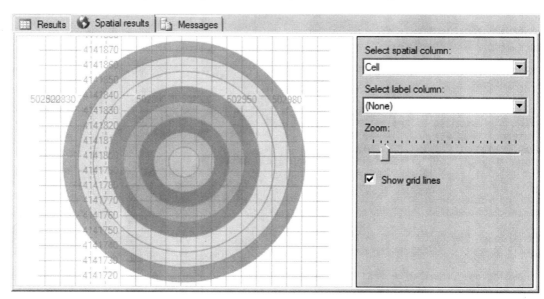

Figure 13-9. A dartboard cell pattern

The resulting pattern of cells could be plugged into the `usp_geometry_distribution_analysis` procedure in order to identify those settlements that lay within high risk zones, based on their proximity to the power plant, for example.

Defining a Custom Pattern of Cells

Both the regular grid and dartboard examples demonstrated so far create a programmatically defined set of cells based on a set of input parameters: for the grid, this is the bounding box, and the number of rows and columns; for the dartboard, the parameters are the center point and number of rings. However, sometimes, you might want to define custom irregular areas against which to analyze distribution of a set of features. One example of such a custom analysis is a *drivetime polygon* analysis. A drivetime polygon is the area containing all those places that can be reached within a certain time from a given point. Due to the irregular nature of the road network, the effect of speed limits on different roads, and other factors, these polygons are often far from regular in shape.

SQL Server does not contain any inbuilt methods to create drivetime polygons (although you certainly could create your own custom method to do so if you had the road data available). However, you can create drivetime polygons using other tools, such as Microsoft MapPoint, which can then be imported into SQL Server. The following C# code listing demonstrates how you can automate Microsoft MapPoint (via its COM interface) to create a geography Polygon of all those points within one hour's drive of an address at 85 Albert Embankment, London:

```
MapPoint.ApplicationClass app = new MapPoint.ApplicationClass();
MapPoint.Map map = app.ActiveMap;

object index = 1;
MapPoint.Location location =
```

```
(MapPoint.Location)map.FindResults("85 Albert Embankment, London").get_Item(ref index);

// Use Mappoint to create a 60 minute drivetime zone around a location
MapPoint.Shape shape = map.Shapes.AddDrivetimeZone(
                        location,
                        60 * MapPoint.GeoTimeConstants.geoOneMinute);

// Create a new geography builder
SqlGeographyBuilder gb = new SqlGeographyBuilder();

// Microsoft Mappoint uses WGS84 coordinates
gb.SetSrid(4326);

// Start creating a polygon
gb.BeginGeography(OpenGisGeographyType.Polygon);

// Loop through the vertices for this polygon
bool firstpoint = true;
object[] vertices = shape.Vertices as object[];
foreach (object vertex in vertices)
{
  MapPoint.Location loc = vertex as MapPoint.Location;

  // First point of polygon must be added with BeginFigure()
  if(firstpoint) {
    gb.BeginFigure(loc.Longitude, loc.Latitude);
    firstpoint = false;
  }
  // Subsequent points are added using AddLine()
  else {
    gb.AddLine(loc.Longitude, loc.Latitude);
  }
}

// Close the polygon by inserting the first point as the last point
MapPoint.Location endloc = vertices[0] as MapPoint.Location;
gb.AddLine(endloc.Longitude, endloc.Latitude);

gb.EndFigure();
gb.EndGeography();

return gb.ConstructedGeography;
```

The address "85 Albert Embankment, London," used in this example, is the headquarters of the British Secret Intelligence Service (MI6). So, let's suppose that the British spy James Bond, codename 007, is evaluating different properties he's interested in buying, and one of the factors he wants to consider is how long it will take him to commute into the office each day. By executing the preceding code listing with different parameter values for the AddDrivetimeZone function, he could create a set of geography Polygons representing the area within 30-minutes' drive, 60-minutes' drive, 90-minutes' drive, and so on of the MI6 building. If he were to do this, he'd get the results as shown in Figure 13-10.

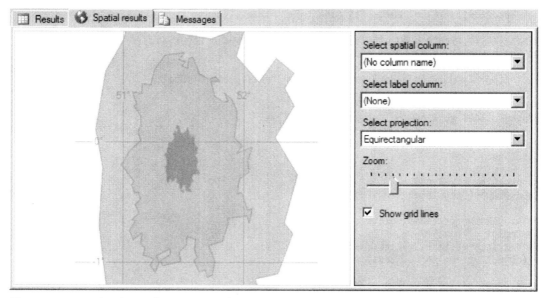

Figure 13-10. Drivetime polygon zones of 30 minutes, 60 minutes, and 90 minutes around the MI6 office in London.

By supplying a table containing the drivetime polygon zones as cells to the `usp_geometry_distribution_analysis` procedure, James Bond could identify the number of properties falling within each area, for example, which would narrow down his search for the perfect London home.

k-Means Clustering

So far in this chapter, we've considered methods that analyze the distribution of values in a column of spatial data by comparing them to a set of "cells," either in a regular pattern such as a grid or dartboard, or defined by a user. In all these methods, the location, size, and pattern of cells are determined independently of, and with no respect to, the distribution of the data itself. It is therefore perfectly possible to imagine a situation in which every data item lies within the same grid cell, or perhaps within its own unique cell, neither of which are particularly useful outcomes when trying to create a descriptive summary of the distribution of the data.

An alternative method of analyzing a large set of data is to cluster items into groups. One well-known algorithm for clustering is called *k-means clustering*. Under this method, a set number (*k*) of initially empty clusters are created. Rather than defining the specific location and bounds within which the clusters lie, the clusters are created at arbitrary locations, and every point is assigned to the cluster point to which it lies closest. The location of the cluster center point is recalculated as points are added to the cluster. In fact, the center of each cluster is defined as the mean average location of all the points in that cluster. (Since there are k clusters, this leads to the name, "k-means.") Therefore the location of clusters will gravitate towards the locations of the points in the set, and there will generally be more clusters in densely populated areas of data and fewer in more sparse areas. This makes k-means a very useful method for analyzing unevenly distributed datasets.

The process for allocating points to clusters using k-means clustering is as follows:

1. Define a chosen number (k) of randomly distributed clusters.

2. Loop through each point in the dataset and allocate it to its nearest cluster.

3. Once all points have been allocated, calculate the centroid of the points allocated to each cluster and set this to be the new center for that cluster.

4. Repeat Steps 2 and 3 until convergence is reached: that is, when, after all the points have been considered, no cluster has been recalculated.

To implement this approach in practice, I'll once again turn to a SQLCLR procedure. Before getting onto the clustering algorithm itself, let's define a few classes that will be required. Rather than store each point in a cluster as a full-blown SqlGeometry instance, we only need a simple structure to record the x- and y-coordinates of each point, as follows:

```
public class kPoint
{
  public double x, y;
  public kPoint(double x, double y)
  {
    this.x = x;
    this.y = y;
  }
  public kPoint()
  {
    this.x = double.NaN;
    this.y = double.NaN;
  }
}
```

Operating on each point as a pair of double coordinates in this simple, lightweight kPoint class will make the procedure more efficient than representing each point as an unnecessarily complex SqlGeometry instance.

We also need a class structure to represent each cluster. A cluster is defined by the location of its centroid and a List<> of the points it contains. It also requires methods to add and remove points from the cluster, and to recalculate the centroid location after the set of points has changed. Here's the full class definition:

```
public class kCluster
{
  public kPoint Centroid;
  public List<kPoint> Points;

  public kCluster()
  {
    this.Centroid = new kPoint();
    this.Points = new List<kPoint>();
  }
  public List<kPoint> GetPoints()
  {
    return this.Points;
  }
  public kPoint GetCentroid()
  {
    return this.Centroid;
  }
  public void SetCentroid(kPoint p)
  {
```

```
        this.Centroid = p;
    }
    public void AddPoint(kPoint p)
    {
        this.Points.Add(p);
        this.RecalculateCentroid();
    }
    public void RemovePoint(kPoint p)
    {
        this.Points.Remove(p);
        this.RecalculateCentroid();
    }
    public int NumPoints()
    {
        return this.Points.Count;
    }
    public kPoint PointN(int n)
    {
        return this.Points[n];
    }
    public void RecalculateCentroid()
    {
        double n = (double)this.NumPoints();
        if (n > 0)
        {
            double avgx = (from p in this.Points select p.x).Sum() / n;
            double avgy = (from p in this.Points select p.y).Sum() / n;
            this.Centroid = new kPoint(avgx, avgy);
        }
    }
}
```

With those class definitions in place, we can get on with the logic of the clustering function itself. Rather than supplying a table and a column name, as with the previous distribution analysis function, the k-means clustering procedure will operate on a supplied MultiPoint geometry instance representing the collection of points to be clustered, together with an int parameter, k, representing the number of clusters into which they should be separated. The procedure returns a table containing a unique ID for each cluster, a geometry Point representing its center, and a geometry MultiPoint column containing each of the points contained within that cluster. Here's the code for the procedure:

```
[Microsoft.SqlServer.Server.SqlProcedure]
public static void GeometrykMeans(SqlGeometry MultiPoint, int k)
{
    // Check that we aren't creating more clusters than points
    if (MultiPoint.STNumPoints() < k)
    {
        throw new Exception("Number of clusters cannot be greater than number of points");
    }

    /**
     * 1.) Initialisation Step
     */

    // Create k empty clusters
```

```
List<kCluster> Clusters = new List<kCluster>();
for (int c = 0; c < k; c++)
{
  // Each cluster starts as an empty collection
  Clusters.Add(new kCluster());
}

// Assign each point to an arbitrary initial cluster
int C = 0;
for (int n = 1; n <= MultiPoint.STNumPoints(); n++)
{
  kPoint p = new kPoint(
    (double)MultiPoint.STPointN(n).STX,
    (double)MultiPoint.STPointN(n).STY
  );
  Clusters[C].AddPoint(p);
  C++;
  if (C >= Clusters.Count) { C = 0; }
}

// Print some debug information
SqlContext.Pipe.Send(
  "There are " + Clusters.Count + " clusters, containing a total of " +
  MultiPoint.STNumPoints() + " points.");


/**
 * 2.) Assignment Step
 * Loop through every point and assign them to their closest cluster
 */

// Keep track of when to break the loop
bool convergancereached = false;

while (!convergancereached)
{
  // On each iteration, assume points won't move clusters
  convergancereached = true;

  // Loop through every cluster
  for (int c = 0; c < k; c++)
  {
    // Loop through every point in this cluster
    for (int pointIndex = 0; pointIndex < Clusters[c].NumPoints(); pointIndex++)
    {
      // Retrieve the next point
      kPoint Point = Clusters[c].PointN(pointIndex);

      // Determine the closest cluster for this point
      int nearestCluster = GetNearestCluster(Point, Clusters);

      // If this is not the cluster in which the point currently lies...
      if (nearestCluster != c)
      {
```

```
                // Add the point to its nearest cluster
                Clusters[nearestCluster].AddPoint(Point);

                // And remove it from its previous cluster
                Clusters[c].RemovePoint(Point);

                // A point has changed clusters, so we need to continue iterating
                convergancereached = false;
            }
          }
        }

      /**
       * 3.) Update Step
       * Compute the new centres of each cluster
       */
      for (int c = 0; c < Clusters.Count; c++)
      {
        Clusters[c].RecalculateCentroid();
      }
    }

    /**
     * OUTPUT
     */
    // Set the SRID of the output to match the SRID of the supplied MultiPoint
    int srid = (int)MultiPoint.STSrid;

    // Define the metadata
    SqlMetaData[] columns = new SqlMetaData[3];
    columns[0] = new SqlMetaData("ClusterID", SqlDbType.Int);
    columns[1] = new SqlMetaData("Centroid", SqlDbType.Udt, typeof(SqlGeometry));
    columns[2] = new SqlMetaData("Points", SqlDbType.Udt, typeof(SqlGeometry));

    // Create a record to represent an individual row in the output
    SqlDataRecord record = new SqlDataRecord(columns);

    SqlContext.Pipe.SendResultsStart(record);

    for (int c = 0; c < Clusters.Count; c++)
    {
      // Set the ID for this cluster
      record.SetValue(0, c);

      // Set the Centroid for this cluster
      SqlGeometry Centroid = SqlGeometry.Point(
        Clusters[c].GetCentroid().x,
        Clusters[c].GetCentroid().y,
        srid);
      record.SetValue(1, Centroid);

      // Create a MultiPoint containing each point in this cluster
      SqlGeometry Points = SqlGeometry.STGeomFromText(
        new SqlChars("GEOMETRYCOLLECTION EMPTY"), srid);
```

```
    foreach (kPoint p in Clusters[c].GetPoints())
    {
      Points = Points.STUnion(SqlGeometry.Point(p.x, p.y, srid));
    }
    record.SetValue(2, Points);

    // Add this row to the output
    SqlContext.Pipe.SendResultsRow(record);
  }
  SqlContext.Pipe.SendResultsEnd();
}

/**
 * Get the index of the closest cluster to a given point
 */
public static int GetNearestCluster(kPoint p, List<kCluster> Clusters)
{
  double minDistance = double.MaxValue;
  int nearestClusterIndex = -1;

  for (int x = 0; x < Clusters.Count; x++)
  {
    // Calculate the distance to the current cluster
    double distance = Math.Sqrt(Math.Pow(p.x - Clusters[x].Centroid.x, 2.0) +
                                Math.Pow(p.y - Clusters[x].Centroid.y, 2.0));

    // If this Cluster is closer than the previous closest
    if (distance < minDistance)
    {
      // Set this cluster as the closest
      nearestClusterIndex = x;
      minDistance = distance;
    }
  }
  return nearestClusterIndex;
}
```

■ **Tip** You can download this code listing (together with all the other examples used in the book) in the accompanying code samples available from the Apress website, http://www.apress.com

You can register the GeometrykMeans function in SQL Server as follows:

```
CREATE PROCEDURE dbo.GeometrykMeans(
  @multipoint geometry,
  @k int)
AS EXTERNAL NAME Ch13_Clustering.[ProSQLSpatial.StoredProcedures].GeometrykMeans;
```

To test out the function, in the code sample that accompanies this book, you'll find a script that creates a table containing details of all antisocial behavior incidents reported to the Norfolk Police Constabulary during the month of June 2011. The table structure and first few rows of data look like this:

```
CREATE TABLE CrimeReports (
  CrimeId int identity(1,1),
  Location varchar(50),
  CrimeType varchar(50),
  Point geometry
);

INSERT INTO CrimeReports(Location, CrimeType, Point) VALUES
('On or near Abbey Close',
  'Anti-social behaviour',
  geometry::Point(621589,314916,27700)),
('On or near Abbey Road',
  'Anti-social behaviour',
  geometry::Point(579778,322936,27700)),
('On or near Abbeygate',
  'Anti-social behaviour',
  geometry::Point(586696,283429,27700));
```

In order to cluster this data into discrete clusters using the GeometrykMeans procedure, we must first create a MultiPoint geometry by aggregating each of the individual point instances in the CrimeReports table. This can be done easily using the geometry UnionAggregate() method. Then, execute the GeometrykMeans procedure to cluster the aggregated MultiPoint geometry into 10 clusters, as follows:

```
DECLARE @ASB geometry;
SELECT @ASB = geometry::UnionAggregate(Point) FROM CrimeReports;
EXEC GeometrykMeans
@multipoint = @ASB,
@k = 10;
```

The result set contains one row for each of the 10 clusters created, as follows:

ClusterId	Centroid	Points
0	0x346C000…	0x346C000…
1	0x346C000…	0x346C000…
2	0x346C000…	0x346C000…
3	0x346C000…	0x346C000…
4	0x346C000…	0x346C000…
5	0x346C000…	0x346C000…
6	0x346C000…	0x346C000…
7	0x346C000…	0x346C000…
8	0x346C000…	0x346C000…
9	0x346C000…	0x346C000…

Unfortunately, since both the centroid at the center of each cluster and the individual items contained within each cluster are represented as Point geometries, there isn't a whole lot to see when you switch to the spatial results tab. To gain a slightly better understanding of the results, rather than returning the results from the GeometrykMeans procedure directly, we can insert them into an intermediate table variable, and from there select the convex hull around the points of each cluster together with a buffer around the points in each cluster, which will make them distinguishable. This is demonstrated in the following code listing:

```
-- Create a MultiPoint containing all the points to be clustered
DECLARE @ASB geometry;
```

```
SELECT @ASB = geometry::UnionAggregate(Point) FROM CrimeReports;

-- Cluster the points and insert the results into a table variable
DECLARE @kMeans table (
  ClusterID int,
  Centroid geometry,
  Points geometry
  );
INSERT INTO @kMeans
EXEC GeometrykMeans
@multipoint = @ASB,
@k = 10;

-- Select the convex hull of the points in each cluster, and buffer the points themselves
SELECT
  CAST(ClusterID AS varchar(32)) AS Label,
  Points.STConvexHull()
FROM @kMeans
UNION ALL
SELECT
  ' ',
  Points.STBuffer(200)
  FROM @kMeans;
```

The result is illustrated in Figure 13-11. For those readers not familiar with the geography of Norfolk, I can tell you that the k-means algorithm in this case has created clusters around each of the main towns and cities in the region—Norwich (Cluster 5), Great Yarmouth (Cluster 0), King's Lynn (8), and Thetford (Cluster 1)—suggesting that these are discrete areas in which occurrences of antisocial behavior have occurred. Further clusters capture the distribution of antisocial behavior offenses in the more remote parts of the county.

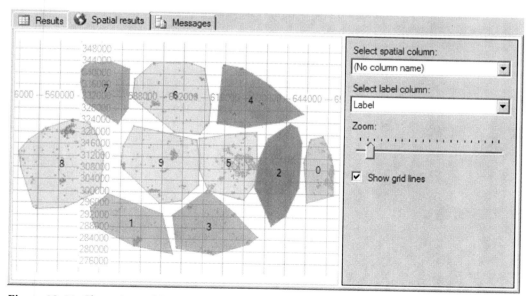

Figure 13-11. Clustering achieved as a result of the k-means algorithm.

351

It is worth noting that, although k-means clustering is an effective method to identify discrete geographic collections of items from a set of data, there are still subjective elements and possible weaknesses with the approach. The most obvious of these is in the selection of an appropriate k value for the number of clusters. Using the wrong value for k could lead to clusters being created that don't naturally correspond to the spread of the data, or failing to identify clusters that should be recognized as separate. You should always exercise care when interpreting results to ensure that you do not try to infer trends in the data that don't really exist.

Summary

In this chapter you learned about clustering and distribution analysis, ways to analyze and summarize the geographic spread of a set of spatial data.

- SQL Server provides two system stored procedures, sp_help_spatial_geography_histogram and sp_help_spatial_geometry_histogram, which can be used to determine the number of items from a column of spatial data that intersect certain cells in a regular grid.

- While SQL Server's histogram functions are helpful in providing a basic overview, they offer limited customization options. They are most helpful for recreating the grids used by geometry and geography indexes in order to aid in performance-tuning.

- I showed you how to create your own distribution analysis procedure that could accept any kind of patterned cell input—a regular grid, dartboard pattern, or custom polygonal areas—and return the number of items that intersected each cell.

- Finally, you considered k-means clustering, which is a method to assign every point in a dataset to one of a number of discrete clusters. The location of each cluster is dynamically determined with respect to the distribution of the points, which makes this a good method to group together unevenly distributed data.

CHAPTER 14

Route Finding

Route finding is the process of finding the optimum path through a network from one chosen location to another. The most familiar examples of route finding are the journey planning features found on in-car satellite navigation systems and travel websites. In such cases, the *network* in question is normally a public road network, and the *optimum path* is the route from A to B that takes the least amount of time, or covers the least distance.

However, route finding algorithms also have practical uses in many other areas; for example, they can be used to plan the most efficient layout of components on a printed circuitboard (where the optimum route may be defined as the circuit that generates least resistance), or in designing the most effective user interface on a website (where the optimum route may be measured by the navigation between two pages that requires the least number of clicks).

In this chapter, we'll take a look at some of the different methods that can be used to determine and evaluate routes in SQL Server, and the ways in which spatial data can be modeled in a network to support such an application.

Graph Theory

Before getting into the practical details of how to code a route finding algorithm in SQL Server, it is worth spending a bit of time considering how to model the network through which that algorithm is expected to navigate.

The way in which data is typically modeled in a route finding system requires graphs. Note that the word "graph" used in this sense does not refer to the line graph or bar chart that you might use to present data in a report but, rather, to a mathematical model used in the discipline of graph theory. A graph, in this context, is defined as a set of nodes connected by edges.

The edges in a graph can either be *directed* (i.e., one-way) or **undirected**, meaning that they can be traversed in both directions. Graphs can also have *cycles*, sets of edges that, when traversed in order, take you back to the node where you started. A graph without cycles is called an *acyclic* graph. Figure 14-1 shows some examples of simple graphs.

Figure 14-1. Undirected, directed, undirected cyclic, and directed acyclic graphs

Graphs of nodes and edges can be used to model lots of different systems: the steps used in a manufacturing process, the path taken by packets of data across a computer network, or the relationship between people in an organizational hierarchy. In the context of spatial data, the most familiar example of a graph is a street map, in which each street is an edge, and the intersections between streets are nodes. One-way streets are directed edges, and if you take a walk around the block you've illustrated a cycle. Therefore, the set of streets used in a route-finding algorithm can be modeled as a cyclic directed graph. Graphs can equally be used to model any other transportation network; a railway network can be modeled as a graph in which train stations are nodes and the lines of track between stations are edges. Similarly, the stops on a bus route, or the airports at which you change on a connecting flight can easily be thought of as nodes connected by edges.

Having conceptually defined a graph that models the nodes and edges in a network, the role of the route-finding algorithm is then to determine the edges that must be traversed to get from a given start node to a destination node. Additional constraints can be placed on the algorithm, so that the route may not be allowed to cross certain edges (consider, for example, a driving route that avoids a particular section of road that is currently closed for maintenance).

If more than one possible path exists between nodes then an optimum route can be determined. The simplest optimum path is the one that minimizes the total distance taken, that is, the total length of all the edges crossed. However, there are many other factors that you might wish to take into account when deciding which route is "optimal." Consider the example of a route across a network of roads: if you wanted to get to the destination in a simple efficient manner, you might prefer to select the route that maximized the part of the journey spent traveling along motorways, rather than narrow, winding country lanes. If you were planning a cycle ride between the same two locations, however, you might do the opposite, favoring the route that took the scenic country route instead. Rather than considering only the length of each edge, there are many other factors that you can use to apply a "cost" to each edge in a road network, including the type of road surface, the degree of uphill or downhill incline, or the speed limit for that section of road. Having assigned a relative cost for each of these factors, the optimum path is then defined as the one of least total cost.

Modeling a Street Network

Having briefly considered the theory behind graph models, let's now crack on with a practical example of how to structure this kind of data in SQL Server. For this example, the network I'm going to model consists of a set of roads close to my house in the city of Norwich, Norfolk. Figure 14-2 illustrates the area in question, as shown on the Bing Maps website (http://www.bing.com/maps).

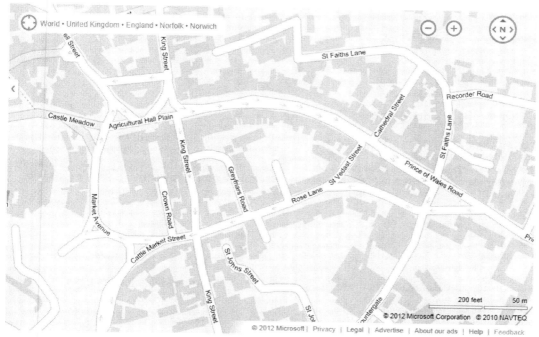

Figure 14-2. Section of the street network in Norwich.

You have probably already realized that the SQL Server spatial datatypes are ideally suited to modeling the individual elements of a network: each node can be represented by a Point geometry, and an edge between two nodes corresponds to a LineString whose start and end points are the two nodes that it connects. But how should we structure database tables to store an entire network?

There are several possible approaches, but perhaps the simplest is to use a column of the geometry or geography datatype to model all the nodes and edges of a graph in a single table. Each row in the table represents an edge in the network, with the shape of that edge represented by a geometry or geography LineString. The start and end points of each LineString implicitly represent the nodes connected by that edge. Several LineStrings starting at the same point represent multiple edges connected to the same node.

Since this model provides a simple compact way of storing the network data in a single table, this is the first approach that we will consider in this chapter.

Defining the Street Names

Although SQL Server is quite comfortable dealing with a map defined in terms of abstract "nodes" and "edges," as humans we generally navigate around using names of streets. To make the output of our routing algorithm more human-readable, we'll create a table to store the names of the streets that are involved in our network model. The following code listing creates a Streets table containing two columns, which record the name of each street and an associated StreetId.

```
CREATE TABLE Streets (
  StreetID int,
  StreetName varchar(50)
  );
```

To begin with, we'll just add three streets to this table:

```
INSERT INTO Streets VALUES
  (1, 'Agricultural Hall Plain'),
  (2, 'Prince of Wales Road'),
  (3, 'Rose Lane');
```

Defining Street Segments (Edges)

Each street will be comprised of one or more segments that represent the edges of the graph that can be traversed. Each segment will be given a unique ID, SegmentID, and will belong to one (and only one) street, the ID of which will be recorded in the StreetID column. We'll use the geometry datatype to store a LineString representing the shape of each segment, which we'll simply call Segment. Here's the table schema that we'll use to record the street segments:

```
CREATE TABLE StreetSegments (
  SegmentID int,
  StreetID int,
  Segment geometry
  );
```

The following code listing inserts the segments relating to each street in the Streets table:

```
INSERT INTO StreetSegments VALUES
  (1, 1, geometry::STLineFromText('LINESTRING(1.297851 52.6292,1.298398 52.629259,1.298548
52.629279,1.299058 52.629328)', 4326)),
  (2, 2, geometry::STLineFromText('LINESTRING(1.299058 52.629328,1.29997 52.629457,1.300898
52.629452,1.301799 52.62928,1.302212 52.62913)', 4326)),
  (3, 2, geometry::STLineFromText('LINESTRING(1.302212 52.62913,1.302432 52.629098,1.302598
52.629028,1.303532 52.628712)', 4326)),
  (4, 2, geometry::STLineFromText('LINESTRING(1.303532 52.628712,1.304401 52.6284)', 4326)),
  (5, 2, geometry::STLineFromText('LINESTRING(1.304401 52.6284, 1.306117 52.627821)', 4326)),
  (6, 3, geometry::STLineFromText('LINESTRING(1.304401 52.6284,1.303327 52.628379)', 4326)),
  (7, 3, geometry::STLineFromText('LINESTRING(1.303327 52.628379,1.302351 52.628599, 1.301638
52.62861)', 4326)),
  (8, 3, geometry::STLineFromText('LINESTRING(1.301638 52.62861,1.299428 52.628089)', 4326));
```

Viewing the Network

At this point, we can examine the network created so far by running the following code listing in SQL Server Management Studio. I've used STBuffer() to buffer each street segment by a small amount to make it easier to see on the Spatial Results tab, and concatenated the ID of each segment and the name of the street to which it belongs:

```
SELECT
  CAST(ss.SegmentID AS varchar(32)) + ' (' + s.StreetName + ')',
  ss.Segment.STBuffer(0.00001)
FROM
  StreetSegments ss
  JOIN Streets s ON ss.StreetID = s.StreetID;
```

Switching to the Spatial results tab illustrates the road network shown in Figure 14-3.

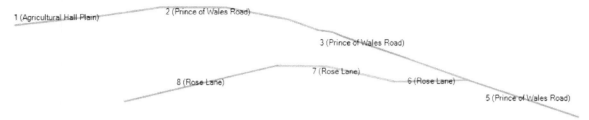

Figure 14-3. *Viewing the street network in SQL Server Management Studio*

Note that, as in the case of Rose Lane and Prince of Wales Road, a single street may consist of several consecutive edges. The end points of each edge denote intersections at which additional streets will be added in the full network.

Brute-Force Routing in T-SQL

Now that we've got our sample data in place, let's have a first shot at creating a path-finding algorithm. For the purposes of demonstration, let's assume that we want to navigate from Agricultural Hall Plain (at the top left of the map) to the end of Rose Lane (at the bottom left).

To start with, we'll declare two geometry Point variables representing the nodes at the start and end points of our route, as follows.

```
DECLARE
  @Start geometry = geometry::STPointFromText('POINT (1.297851 52.6292)', 4326),
  @End geometry = geometry::STPointFromText('POINT (1.29887 52.62802)', 4326);
```

In order to navigate through the network we need to repeatedly look through the edges in the street segments table, experimentally traversing across each edge that connects to our current location to build up a route until we find the destination node. There are a variety of techniques that we could use to write this sort of query: in T-SQL, we could create temporary tables, cursors, or use logic operators to control the flow of the query. We could also use a SQLCLR procedure (more on that later). However, for this first example, we'll use a recursive query based on a Common Table Expression (CTE). A recursive query references itself, repeatedly executing the same query to return subsets of data until the complete result set is returned.

Let's build the query up bit by bit: first, the *anchor* part of the CTE will SELECT all those street segments (i.e., the edges of our graph) that start at the chosen start point, as follows:

```
SELECT
    @Start AS [From],
    Segment.STEndPoint() AS [To],
    Segment
  FROM dbo.StreetSegments
  WHERE
    Segment.STStartPoint().STEquals(@Start) = 1;
```

The *recursive* part of the CTE will select all those subsequent edges that begin where the last edge stopped, using the condition ss.Segment.STStartPoint().STEquals(p.[To]) = 1. The recursive member is shown in the following listing:

```
SELECT
    p.[To] AS [From],
    ss.Segment.STEndPoint() AS [To],
```

```
    ss.Segment
  FROM Paths p
    JOIN dbo.StreetSegments ss ON ss.Segment.STStartPoint().STEquals(p.[To]) = 1
  WHERE p.[To].STEquals(@End) = 0 -- Stop recursion when we reach the end point
)
```

Finally, once recursion has ended, we select the complete route as follows:

```
SELECT
  [From].STAsText() AS theStart,
  [To].STAsText() AS theEnd,
  Segment AS Route
FROM Paths
```

When we put these elements together, we get the full code listing shown following:

```
DECLARE
  @Start geometry = geometry::STPointFromText('POINT (1.297851 52.6292)', 4326),
  @End geometry = geometry::STPointFromText('POINT (1.29887 52.62802)', 4326);

WITH Paths
AS
(
-- Anchor member
SELECT
    @Start AS [From],
    Segment.STEndPoint() AS [To],
    Segment
  FROM dbo.StreetSegments
  WHERE
    Segment.STStartPoint().STEquals(@Start) = 1

-- Recursive member
  UNION ALL
  SELECT
    p.[To] AS [From],
    ss.Segment.STEndPoint() AS [To],
    ss.Segment
  FROM Paths p
    JOIN dbo.StreetSegments ss ON ss.Segment.STStartPoint().STEquals(p.[To]) = 1
  WHERE p.[To].STEquals(@End) = 0 -- Stop recursion when we reach the end point
)
SELECT
  [From].STAsText() AS theStart,
  [To].STAsText() AS theEnd,
  Segment AS Route
FROM Paths;
```

When run against the simple network we've created so far, the output of this query is as follows:

```
theStart                       theEnd                          Route
POINT (1.297851 52.6292)       POINT (1.299058 52.629328)      0xE61000000…
POINT (1.299058 52.629328)     POINT (1.302212 52.62913)       0xE61000000…
POINT (1.302212 52.62913)      POINT (1.303532 52.628712)      0xE61000000104…
POINT (1.303532 52.628712)     POINT (1.304401 52.6284)        0xE61000000…
POINT (1.304401 52.6284)       POINT (1.306117 52.627821)      0xE61000000…
```

POINT (1.304401 52.6284)	POINT (1.303327 52.628379)	0xE61000000...
POINT (1.303327 52.628379)	POINT (1.301638 52.62861)	0xE610000001...
POINT (1.301638 52.62861)	POINT (1.299428 52.628089)	0xE610000001...

Each row in the results represents an edge that must be traveled in the route between the start and end point. The columns show the start and end point of each segment, and the route following that segment. Switching to the spatial results tab does indeed show that the query has returned the set of edges from start to end point.

However, there are several problems with this approach: Firstly, the ordering of the output of a CTE—just like any other query—is not guaranteed without an ORDER BY clause. In this case, the order of results happens to coincide with the order of the segments that must be traversed, but this is only a very small dataset and the computer on which I ran the query has only a single processor. On a bigger dataset, and/or on a server with multiple processors, the result might have been ordered differently.

The second problem may not yet be obvious, since there is currently only one possible path between the start and end points. Let's see what happens when we extend the network slightly by adding some more streets:

```
INSERT INTO Streets VALUES
  (4, 'Cattle Market Street'),
  (5, 'King Street'),
  (6, 'St Vedast Street'),
  (7, 'St Faiths Lane'),
  (8, 'Market Avenue');
```

And now we'll define the associated street segments:

```
INSERT INTO StreetSegments VALUES
  (9, 4, geometry::STLineFromText('LINESTRING(1.29887 52.62802, 1.298209 52.62802, 1.29792
52.628089, 1.297749 52.62818, 1.297679 52.628282, 1.297668 52.628647, 1.297701 52.628899,
1.297851 52.6292, 1.297969 52.62936,1.297947 52.629479)', 4326)),
  (10, 5, geometry::STLineFromText('LINESTRING(1.299058 52.629328, 1.299229 52.628878, 1.29939
52.628481, 1.299428 52.628089)', 4326)),
  (11, 5, geometry::STLineFromText('LINESTRING(1.299428 52.628089, 1.299862 52.627011,1.3002
52.62656)', 4326)),
  (12, 6, geometry::STLineFromText('LINESTRING(1.302212 52.62913, 1.301638 52.62861)', 4326)),
  (13, 7, geometry::STLineFromText('LINESTRING(1.299728 52.629999,1.301102 52.630342,1.301128
52.62994,1.302968 52.63003,1.30366 52.629676,1.303752 52.629311,1.303532 52.628712)', 4326)),
  (14, 7, geometry::STLineFromText('LINESTRING(1.303532 52.628712, 1.303327 52.628379)',
4326)),
  (15, 8, geometry::STLineFromText('LINESTRING(1.299428 52.628089,1.29887 52.62802)', 4326)),
  (16, 8, geometry::STLineFromText('LINESTRING(1.29887 52.62802, 1.298312 52.627778, 1.298118
52.627617, 1.29791 52.627118, 1.297588 52.62685)', 4326));
```

The network now looks like that shown in Figure 14-4.

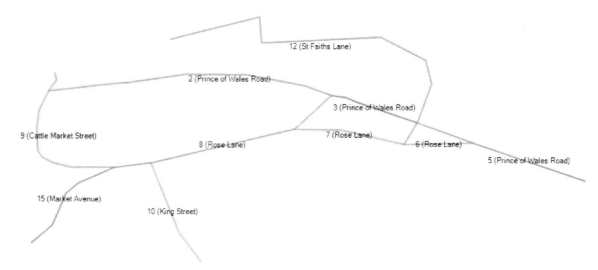

Figure 14-4. *The expanded street network.*

Now try to rerun the previous routing CTE query and you will end up with the results shown in Figure 14-5:

	theStart	theEnd	Route
1	POINT (1.297851 52.6292)	POINT (1.299058 52.629328)	0xE610000001040400000005A4B0169FFC3F43F545227A08950...
2	POINT (1.299058 52.629328)	POINT (1.302212 52.62913)	0xE610000001040500000000F6B6990AF1C8F43F823AE5D18D5...
3	POINT (1.299058 52.629328)	POINT (1.299428 52.628089)	0xE610000001040400000000F6B6990AF1C8F43F823AE5D18D5...
4	POINT (1.299428 52.628089)	POINT (1.3002 52.62656)	0xE610000001040300000000651BB80375CAF43F1AFD68386550...
5	POINT (1.299428 52.628089)	POINT (1.29887 52.62802)	0xE61000000114651BB80375CAF43F1AFD683865504A409C1...
6	POINT (1.302212 52.62913)	POINT (1.303532 52.628712)	0xE610000001040400000000C570740DCD5F43F5C77F3548750...
7	POINT (1.302212 52.62913)	POINT (1.301638 52.62861)	0xE610000001140C570740DCD5F43F5C77F35487504A408EB...
8	POINT (1.301638 52.62861)	POINT (1.299428 52.628089)	0xE61000000114 8EB1135E82D3F43F23F8DF4A76504A40651...
9	POINT (1.299428 52.628089)	POINT (1.3002 52.62656)	0xE610000001040300000000651BB80375CAF43F1AFD68386550...
10	POINT (1.299428 52.628089)	POINT (1.29887 52.62802)	0xE61000000114651BB80375CAF43F1AFD683865504A409C1...
11	POINT (1.303532 52.628712)	POINT (1.304401 52.6284)	0xE61000000114ADA1D45E44DBF43F274D83A279504A4046...
12	POINT (1.303532 52.628712)	POINT (1.303327 52.628379)	0xE61000000114ADA1D45E44DBF43F274D83A279504A4092...
13	POINT (1.303327 52.628379)	POINT (1.301638 52.62861)	0xE610000001040300000092E68F696DDAF43F213F1BB96E5...
14	POINT (1.301638 52.62861)	POINT (1.299428 52.628089)	0xE610000001148EB1135E82D3F43F23F8DF4A76504A40651...
15	POINT (1.299428 52.628089)	POINT (1.3002 52.62656)	0xE610000001040300000000651BB80375CAF43F1AFD68386550...
16	POINT (1.299428 52.628089)	POINT (1.29887 52.62802)	0xE61000000114651BB80375CAF43F1AFD683865504A409C1...
17	POINT (1.304401 52.6284)	POINT (1.306117 52.627821)	0xE61000000114446EA3D95D3DEF43F386744696F504A407EF...
18	POINT (1.304401 52.6284)	POINT (1.303327 52.628379)	0xE61000000114446EA3D95D3DEF43F386744696F504A4092E...
19	POINT (1.303327 52.628379)	POINT (1.301638 52.62861)	0xE610000001040300000092E68F696DDAF43F213F1BB96E5...
20	POINT (1.301638 52.62861)	POINT (1.299428 52.628089)	0xE610000001148EB1135E82D3F43F23F8DF4A76504A40651...
21	POINT (1.299428 52.628089)	POINT (1.3002 52.62656)	0xE610000001040300000000651BB80375CAF43F1AFD68386550...
22	POINT (1.299428 52.628089)	POINT (1.29887 52.62802)	0xE61000000114651BB80375CAF43F1AFD683865504A409C1...

Figure 14-5. *Results of routing through a road network with multiple possible solutions*

There are now multiple possible routes through the network from the start to the end point. The query correctly identifies each possible solution, but the problem is that the edges involved in each route are muddled up in the resultset; it's impossible to separate out which edge belongs to which route.

Tracing The Route

To solve the problem of not being able to separate out which edge belongs to which route, we need to make the CTE "remember" the route that it has already followed on each iteration. To do this, as we traverse across each edge through the graph, we will build up a LineString representing the total route traveled so far from the start point.

Sadly, none of the inbuilt geometry methods can be used to programmatically build up a LineString from an ordered set of points. Fortunately, the SqlGeometryBuilder can help us; the following code listing demonstrates a User-Defined Function, Extend, that will construct a LineString geometry from the ordered points of two supplied geometries.

```
public static SqlGeometry Extend(
  SqlGeometry @geom1,
  SqlGeometry @geom2,
  SqlInt32 @Offset)
  {

    SqlGeometryBuilder gb = new SqlGeometryBuilder();
    gb.SetSrid((int)(@geom1.STSrid));
    gb.BeginGeometry(OpenGisGeometryType.LineString);
    gb.BeginFigure(
      (double)@geom1.STStartPoint().STX,
      (double)@geom1.STStartPoint().STY);
    for (int x = 2; x <= (int)@geom1.STNumPoints(); x++) {
      gb.AddLine((double)@geom1.STPointN(x).STX, (double)@geom1.STPointN(x).STY);
    }
    for (int x = 1 + (int)@Offset; x <= (int)@geom2.STNumPoints(); x++) {
      gb.AddLine((double)@geom2.STPointN(x).STX, (double)@geom2.STPointN(x).STY);
    }
    gb.EndFigure();
    gb.EndGeometry();
    return gb.ConstructedGeometry;
  }
```

The @Offset parameter allows for a set number of points to be omitted from the second geometry. In this example, each subsequent edge in the route begins at exactly the same point that the last edge ended. By setting an @Offset of 1, we can exclude the first point of the second geometry to prevent duplication of that point in the resulting LineString.

Build and import an assembly containing the Extend function into SQL Server, and register the function as follows:

```
CREATE FUNCTION dbo.Extend(@geom1 geometry, @geom2 geometry, @offset int)
RETURNS geometry
AS EXTERNAL NAME
ProSpatialCh14.[ProSpatial.Ch14.UserDefinedFunctions].Extend;
```

Using the Extend function, we can now identify the separate routes through the network by joining together each segment as it is traversed. Because there is now more than one possible route through the network, we'll use the ROW_NUMBER function to assign a unique number to each route, and use STLength() to order the routes from shortest to longest distance. This is demonstrated in the following code listing:

```
DECLARE
  @Start geometry = geometry::STPointFromText('POINT (1.297851 52.6292)', 4326),
  @End geometry = geometry::STPointFromText('POINT (1.29887 52.62802)', 4326);
WITH Paths
AS
(
SELECT
    @Start AS [From],
    Segment.STEndPoint() AS [To],
    Segment,
    Segment AS RunningSegment
  FROM dbo.StreetSegments
  WHERE
    Segment.STStartPoint().STEquals(@Start) = 1
  UNION ALL
  SELECT
    p.[To] AS [From],
    ss.Segment.STEndPoint() AS [To],
    ss.Segment,
    dbo.Extend(p.RunningSegment, ss.Segment, 1)
  FROM Paths p
    JOIN dbo.StreetSegments ss ON ss.Segment.STStartPoint().STEquals(p.[To]) = 1
  WHERE p.[To].STEquals(@End) = 0 -- Stop recursion when we reach the end point
)
SELECT
  ROW_NUMBER() OVER(ORDER BY RunningSegment.STLength()) AS 'Route Num',
  RunningSegment.STLength() AS Length,
  RunningSegment.STAsText() AS RouteWKT,
  RunningSegment.STBuffer(RunningSegment.STLength()/100) AS Route
FROM Paths
WHERE [To].STEquals(@End) = 1;
```

Rather than return a set of individual edges, each row in the results now represents a distinct complete route across the network from the chosen start point to the end point, with the optimum route (i.e., in this case, the route of minimum length) listed first, as follows:

Route Num	Length	RouteWKT	Route
1	0.008026955	LINESTRING(1.297851 52.6292, …	0xE6100000010…
2	0.010745532	LINESTRING(1.297851 52.6292, …	0xE6100000010…
3	0.012352007	LINESTRING(1.297851 52.6292, …	0xE6100000010…

Avoiding Cycles

Unfortunately, there is still a major problem with this approach. Consider what would happen if we were to add a new edge to the graph as follows:

```
INSERT INTO StreetSegments VALUES
(16, 5, geometry::STLineFromText('LINESTRING(1.299428 52.628089, 1.29939 52.628481, 1.299229
52.628878, 1.299058 52.629328)', 4326));
```

This edge creates a cycle, an endless loop in the graph, as shown in Figure 14-6.

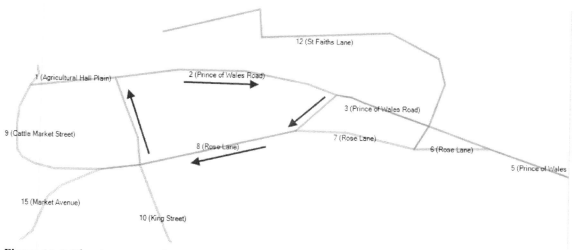

Figure 14-6. *The street network contains a cycle*

Executing the previous route finding query against a cyclic graph will result in an error, because the recursive CTE will attempt to retrace the same edge segments over and over. To prevent this problem, when considering which edges can be traversed from a given node we need to exclude any edge that has already been crossed during this route. This condition can be incorporated into the query by using the STContains() method in the recursive member to check that the RunningSegment does not contain the current Segment edge. This condition is highlighted in bold in the following code listing:

```
DECLARE
  @Start geometry = geometry::STPointFromText('POINT (1.297851 52.6292)', 4326),
  @End geometry = geometry::STPointFromText('POINT (1.29887 52.62802)', 4326);
WITH Paths
AS
(
SELECT
    @Start AS [From],
    Segment.STEndPoint() AS [To],
    Segment,
    Segment AS RunningSegment
  FROM dbo.StreetSegments
  WHERE
    Segment.STStartPoint().STEquals(@Start) = 1
UNION ALL
SELECT
    p.[To] AS [From],
    ss.Segment.STEndPoint() AS [To],
    ss.Segment,
    dbo.Extend(p.RunningSegment, ss.Segment, 1)
  FROM Paths p
    JOIN dbo.StreetSegments ss ON ss.Segment.STStartPoint().STEquals(p.[To]) = 1
  WHERE p.[To].STEquals(@End) = 0 -- Stop recursion when we reach the end point
  AND p.RunningSegment.STContains(ss.Segment) = 0 -- Make sure we haven't already included
this path in the route
```

```
)
SELECT
  ROW_NUMBER() OVER(ORDER BY RunningSegment.STLength()) AS 'Route Number',
  RunningSegment.STLength() AS Length,
  RunningSegment.STAsText() AS RouteWKT,
  RunningSegment.STBuffer(RunningSegment.STLength()/100) AS Route
FROM Paths
WHERE [To].STEquals(@End) = 1;
```

Allowing for Direction

Currently, we are modeling our road network as a directed graph. This means that the LineStrings in every row of the StreetSegments table are considered to have a one-way direction of travel. The algorithm will traverse a LineString from the start point to the end point, but not reverse the journey from the end point back to the start point.

In terms of a road network, our model defines every road as a one-way street, allowing traffic only in the direction in which the LineString has been defined. While this might make sense for some sorts of transport network, generally speaking, most roads can be traveled in either direction. So how do we account for this?

One approach would be to modify the query so that it checked for edges that either start or end at the current node. In either case, we would then define the "To" node as the point that lay at the opposite end of the LineString. For example, the anchor member of the CTE could be modified as follows:

```
SELECT
  @Start AS [From],
  CASE
    WHEN Segment.STStartPoint().STEquals(@Start) = 1 THEN Segment.STEndPoint()
    ELSE Segment.STStartPoint()
  END AS [To],
  Segment,
  Segment AS RunningSegment
FROM dbo.StreetSegments
WHERE
  Segment.STStartPoint().STEquals(@Start) = 1
  OR
  Segment.STEndPoint().STEquals(@Start) = 1
```

A similar change would also have to be made to the recursive member. However, the effect of these changes would be then to treat the entire graph as undirected, which might not be desirable. In doing so, we would lose the ability to define one-way streets, or define junctions at which you could only turn right (or left), for example.

Another alternative would be to maintain the directed nature of the graph but insert additional edges into the table as necessary to represent valid routes. Every two-way road, for example, would then be represented by a pair of edges, one for each direction of travel. This model would support one-way roads (which would only have one edge) and also, because each LineString now represents a carriageway of a road rather than the road itself, would allow for the modeling of dual carriageways where the two carriageways of travel were physically separated. This model provides the most flexibility, but has a disadvantage in that (assuming most roads are indeed two-way) it would require nearly double the amount of rows to be added to the StreetSegments table. A compromise might be instead to insert an additional flag column into the edges table denoting whether an edge was directed or not, which would be taken into account at the query stage. This would make the query slightly more intensive, but would save storage space.

A*: A More Efficient Routing Algorithm?

After a few iterations, we have created a reasonable attempt at a route finding procedure in T-SQL; it avoids cycles and returns every possible route through a network between two specified points, ranked in ascending order of distance. However, the approach taken relies on dumb, brute force; it evaluates every possible combination of paths through the network in order to find the valid routes, and then assesses the best performing one. It makes no attempt to find the route in an efficient or logical manner (by traveling in the direction of the destination, for example), but rather expands outwards in all directions, considering all valid nodes until the destination is reached. This approach is almost certainly not scalable in a production application, as the number of possibilities would grow exponentially with the number of nodes and edges added to the network. What's more, a recursive CTE is probably not the most appropriate construct if we start to add more logic to the procedure or operate on a significant volume of data. Although it is possible to create a CTE that recurses infinitely (by setting the MAXRECURSION query hint with a value of 0) doing so creates the risk of a never-ending, unresponsive query.

In an attempt to improve the performance and robustness of our route finding function, we'll now implement a different algorithm, known as the A* (pronounced "A star") algorithm. Unlike the previous brute force approach, which is guaranteed to find the optimal route (eventually), the A* algorithm attempts to balance the cost (in terms of the effort required to traverse the route) of the result returned against the cost (in terms of the amount of processing required) to calculate that route. Rather than generate and evaluate all possible routes in order to find the optimum solution, A* attempts, at every intersection, to follow those edges that are more likely to lead to the destination. As soon as the first route that leads to the destination is found, the algorithm stops and returns that route. This means that A* may not always return the optimum route, but it should return a "good-enough" route in a faster time than using the previous brute-force method.

Because we need to involve logic and relatively complex conditions to control the flow of the A* algorithm, we'll not use T-SQL but instead create a SQLCLR stored procedure. Over the next few sections I'll discuss different aspects of the implementation of the A* algorithm in isolation, before showing you the complete code sample necessary to create the procedure.

Heuristics

In order to determine the route that leads to the destination most efficiently A* requires some additional properties about each node in the network. Specifically, A* uses an *heuristic*, a value assigned to each node used to determine whether it is likely to lie on the optimum route to the destination.

The additional properties of each node used in the A* algorithm are generally denoted by the identifiers *h*, *g*, and *f*, as follows:

> **h** is an estimate of the remaining cost from this node to the goal (the true cost cannot be known until after the route is found). There are many ways of calculating this estimate but it is important that, whatever method is used, the value of h must not exceed the true cost to the goal (in other words, it must always underestimate or, at best, be exactly equal to the true cost). Since we know where the destination node is (but not how to get there), one possible heuristic is to calculate the straight line distance from any node directly to the destination node. Since, in our model, distance = cost, we can be certain that this estimate will be less than or equal to the true cost of the route from this node to the destination, since there can be no route of less cost to get to the goal than a straight line. In SQL Server, we can calculate this heuristic easily using the STDistance() method.

> **g** is the distance already traveled from the start node to the current node, as measured along the edges traveled through the graph. Where there is more

than one route found from the start point to a given node, the g value of that node is the length of the shortest route found so far.

f is the sum of g + h. It represents the best estimate of the total length of the route from the start point to the goal that passes through this node.

Figure 14-7 illustrates a network consisting of 7 nodes: a start and end point, and five other nodes labeled A–E. Suppose that the A* algorithm has begun to identify possible paths through the network from the start point to the end point. Solid lines represent the (known) length of edges between nodes that have been calculated so far, while dotted lines represent the shortest straight line estimate from each node to the destination.

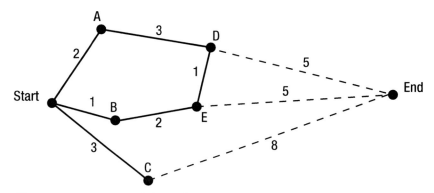

Figure 14-7. *A* traversal through a network*

As shown in Figure 14-7, there are three nodes that could potentially lie on the optimum path from the start to the end point, with the following properties:

- Node D has an estimated remaining distance to the end point (h) of 5, and a distance traveled thus far (g) of 4 (1 + 2 + 1). Therefore, its f score is 9.

- Node E has h of 5 and g of 3 (1 + 2). Therefore, f is 8.

- Node C has h of 3 and g of 8. Therefore f is 11.

At this point in time, Node E has the lowest f score, so it is the node most likely to lead to an optimum route to the goal. Therefore, those edges that lead from E will be considered in the next iteration through the algorithm.

The nodes used in an A* algorithm can be modeled with f, g, and h scores using a simple class as shown in the following code snippet:

```
private class AStarNode : IComparable
{
  public int NodeID;
  public int ParentID;
  public double f; // the total estimated cost of reaching the goal through this node
  public double g; // the cost of the route so far from the starting point to this node
  public double h; // the estimated remaining cost from this point to the destination route

  // Constructor
  public AStarNode(int NodeID, int ParentID, double g, double h)
  {
```

```
    this.NodeID = NodeID;
    this.ParentID = ParentID;
    this.f = g + h;
    this.g = g;
    this.h = h;
  }

  // Implement the iComparable interface to sort nodes by ascending f score
  int IComparable.CompareTo(object obj)
  {
    AStarNode other = (AStarNode)obj;
    if (this.f < other.f)
      return -1;
    else if (this.f > other.f)
      return 1;
    else
      return 0;
  }
}
```

Restructuring the Data

Whereas the primary structures in the brute-force approach were the edges in the graph that were defined in the StreetSegments table, the A* algorithm is instead primarily focused on considering the nodes of the network. In order to allow the A* algorithm to work in an efficient manner, we therefore need to make a few changes to the underlying structure used to store our network model.

Rather than use a single StreetSegments table to define the edges of the graph and only implicitly define the nodes to which each edge connects using the STStartPoint() and STEndPoint() methods, we will create a new table that explicitly defines the nodes, as follows:

```
CREATE TABLE Nodes (
  NodeID int NOT NULL,
  geog4326 geography NULL
);
```

The Edges table will contain details of all the edges that connect pairs of nodes. Rather than joining from the Edges table to the Nodes table on the geog4326 column, which would require a relatively expensive spatial function, we'll instead reference the nodes at the start and end of each edge by their unique integer IDs, which will make traversal through the network significantly more efficient.

```
CREATE TABLE Edges (
  EdgeID int NOT NULL,
  Name varchar(50),
  FromNodeID int NOT NULL,
  ToNodeID int NOT NULL,
  geog4326 geography NOT NULL
);
```

You can find a script to populate these tables in the code download that accompanies this book. The script builds a network containing approximately 1,000 nodes and 2,000 edges representing the streets of the city of Norwich, constructed from data retrieved from Open Street Map (http://www.osm.org). You can examine the street network used in this example by executing the following:

```
SELECT geog4326
FROM Edges
UNION ALL
SELECT geog4326.STBuffer(10)
FROM Nodes;
```

The result is shown in Figure 14-8.

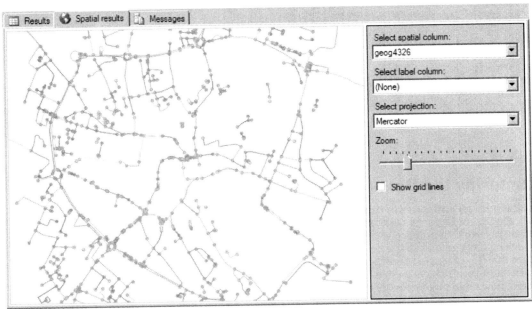

Figure 14-8. Nodes and Edges forming the Norwich road network

Before getting on to the A* algorithm itself, we'll create a couple of supporting stored procedures. The first procedure will be used to identify all those nodes that are connected to a given node. The GetNodesAccessibleFromNode procedure will return the ID of any accessible nodes, the length of the edge that must be crossed to reach that node, and its geographic location. These facts will be used to calculate the g and h scores for that node, respectively:

```
CREATE PROCEDURE GetNodesAccessibleFromNode
  @NodeID int
AS
BEGIN
  SET NOCOUNT ON;

  SELECT
    ToNodeID,
    geog4326.STLength(),
    geog4326.STEndPoint()
  FROM
    Edges
  WHERE
    FromNodeID = @NodeID;
END;
```

The second procedure will return (if one exists) the LineString edge that connects a given pair of nodes:

```
CREATE PROCEDURE GetEdgeBetweenNodes
  @NodeID1 int,
  @NodeID2 int
AS
BEGIN
  SET NOCOUNT ON;

SELECT
  geog4326
FROM
  Edges
WHERE
  FromNodeID = @NodeID1
  AND ToNodeID = @NodeID2;
END;
```

The GetEdgeBetweenNodes procedure will be used to build up the route from the start node to the goal.

Traversing Across the Network

The A* algorithm makes use of two lists to keep track of the nodes in the network: the *open list* and the *closed list*.

The open list holds the set of nodes that have been discovered so far, but have yet to be assessed. When the A* algorithm begins, the only node on the open list is the start node (since, at that point in time, that is the only node that is known).

The closed list holds the set of nodes that have been discovered, visited, and fully expanded; that is, all of the possible successors to that node have been identified already and added to the open list, and there is no more information to discover about this node.

For simplicity, I'm going to implement the Open List as a List collection containing instances of the AStarNode class decribed earlier:

```
List<AStarNode> OpenList = new List<AStarNode>();
```

For the closed list, I'll instead use a Dictionary, in which the AStarNode elements are keyed by ID. This will facilitate quicker scanning through the collection to find if a given Node has already been visited.

```
Dictionary<int, AStarNode> ClosedList = new Dictionary<int, AStarNode>();
```

■ **Note** The structures I'm using for this code example are chosen for their ease of use and understandability rather than for performance reasons. If you wanted to implement the A* algorithm in a production application, you'd probably prefer to implement the open list as a priority queue or similar structure.

A* is an iterative algorithm. On every iteration, the node on the open list with the lowest f score is chosen as the next node to be visited. Based on the information known at the time, this is the node with the best chance of leading to the shortest route to the goal. The node is first checked to see whether it is the goal node; if so, we have found a route through the network! If not, we instead look for all the potential "successor" nodes from the current node: if we follow the edges connected to this node, to what other nodes do they lead us? For this, we'll use the GetNodesAccessibleFromNode stored procedure created earlier. This is demonstrated in the following code snippet:

```
// While there are open nodes to assess
while (OpenList.Count > 0)
{

  // Sort the list of open nodes by ascending f score
  OpenList.Sort(delegate(AStarNode p1, AStarNode p2)
  { return p1.f.CompareTo(p2.f); });

  // Consider the node at the top of the list (i.e. node with lowest f score)
  AStarNode NodeCurrent = OpenList[0];

  // Is this node the goal node?
  if (NodeCurrent.NodeID == GoalID)
  {
    //  GOAL FOUND!
    break;
  }

  // Goal not found yet. Identify all possible successors to this node
  List<AStarNode> Successors = new List<AStarNode>();

  conn.Open();

  using (SqlCommand cmdSelectSuccessors = new SqlCommand("GetNodesAccessibleFromNode",
                                                         conn))
  {
    // Identify all nodes accessible from the current node
    cmdSelectSuccessors.CommandType = CommandType.StoredProcedure;
    SqlParameter CurrentNodeOSODRparam = new SqlParameter("@NodeID", SqlDbType.Int);
    CurrentNodeOSODRparam.Value = NodeCurrent.NodeID;
    cmdSelectSuccessors.Parameters.Add(CurrentNodeOSODRparam);

    using (SqlDataReader dr = cmdSelectSuccessors.ExecuteReader())
    {
      while (dr.Read())
      {
        // Create a node for this potential successor
        AStarNode SuccessorNode = new AStarNode(
          dr.GetInt32(0), // NodeID
          NodeCurrent.NodeID, // Successor node is a child of the current node
          NodeCurrent.g + dr.GetDouble(1), // Distance from current node to successor
          (double)(((SqlGeography)dr.GetValue(2)).STDistance(endGeom))
        );

        // Add the end of the list of successors
        Successors.Add(SuccessorNode);
```

```
            }
        }
    }
    conn.Close();
```

Having identified the list of possible successors, we then need to categorize them. Each potential successor node can be classified according to one of three possibilities:

- The node is already on the closed list. That is to say, it has already been visited and all its successors have been identified. In this case, we do not need to consider this node any further.

- The node already lies on the open list, which signifies that we have already identified at least one alternative possible route to reach that node, but the node itself has not been examined yet. In this case, we compare the g score of reaching that node from the current route to the g score on the open list. If this is a more efficient route to the node (i.e., lower g score) then the value on the open list is updated.

- The node is not currently on the open or closed lists, and is a "new" node previously unknown to the algorithm. In this case, the node is added to the open list.

This logic is demonstrated in the following code snippet:

```
foreach (AStarNode NodeSuccessor in Successors)
{
  // Keep track of whether we have already found this node
  bool found = false;

  // If this node is already on the closed list, it doesn't need to be examined further
  if (ClosedList.ContainsKey(NodeSuccessor.NodeID))
  {
    found = true;
  }

  // If we didn't find the node on the closed list, look for it on the open list
  if (!found)
  for (int j = 0; j < OpenList.Count; j++)
  {
    if (OpenList[j].NodeID == NodeSuccessor.NodeID)
    {
      found = true;
      // If this is a cheaper way to get there
      if (OpenList[j].h > NodeSuccessor.h)
      {
        // Update the route on the open list
        OpenList[j] = NodeSuccessor;
      }
      break;
    }
  }

  // If not on either list, add to the open list
  if (!found)
  {
    OpenList.Add(NodeSuccessor);
```

```
    }
}
```

Once all the successor nodes of a given node have been examined and categorized, the current node itself can be moved onto the closed list.

```
OpenList.Remove(NodeCurrent);
ClosedList.Add(NodeCurrent.NodeID, NodeCurrent);
```

The preceding steps are repeated until either the goal node is found, or until there are no more nodes left on the open list to consider, in which case we can conclude that there is no route through the network from the start node to the goal node. If the goal node is found, then the optimum route path is built up by recursing back through the parent nodes of each goal on the route, calling the GetEdgeBetweenNodes procedure to retrieve the LineString edges of each segment along the route.

```
if (NodeCurrent.NodeID == GoalID)
{

  // Reconstruct the route that led here
  // Keep a list of the edges traversed to get to the goal
  List<SqlGeography> route = new List<SqlGeography>();
  int parentID = NodeCurrent.ParentID;

  // Keep looking back through nodes until we get to the start node (parent -1)
  while (parentID != -1)
  {
    conn.Open();

    using (SqlCommand cmdSelectEdge = new SqlCommand("GetEdgeBetweenNodes", conn))
    {
      // Retrieve the edge from this node to its parent
      cmdSelectEdge.CommandType = CommandType.StoredProcedure;
      SqlParameter fromOSODRparam = new SqlParameter("@NodeID1", SqlDbType.Int);
      SqlParameter toOSODRparam = new SqlParameter("@NodeID2", SqlDbType.Int);
      fromOSODRparam.Value = NodeCurrent.ParentID;
      toOSODRparam.Value = NodeCurrent.NodeID;
      cmdSelectEdge.Parameters.Add(fromOSODRparam);
      cmdSelectEdge.Parameters.Add(toOSODRparam);

      object edge = cmdSelectEdge.ExecuteScalar();
      SqlGeography edgeGeom;
      if (edge != null)
      {
        edgeGeom = (SqlGeography)(edge);
        route.Add(edgeGeom);
      }
    }

    conn.Close();

    // Step backwards to the previous node in the route
    NodeCurrent = ClosedList[parentID];
    parentID = NodeCurrent.ParentID;
  }
```

```
  // Send the results back to the client
  SqlMetaData ResultMetaData = new SqlMetaData(
    "Route", SqlDbType.Udt, typeof(SqlGeography)
  );
  SqlDataRecord Record = new SqlDataRecord(ResultMetaData);
  SqlContext.Pipe.SendResultsStart(Record);
  // Loop through route segments in reverse order
  for (int k = route.Count - 1; k >= 0; k--)
  {
    Record.SetValue(0, route[k]);
    SqlContext.Pipe.SendResultsRow(Record);
  }
  SqlContext.Pipe.SendResultsEnd();

  return;
}
```

Putting It All Together

The following code listing combines the snippets given previously to create the complete code required for a SQLCLR procedure that implements that A* algorithm to traverse the network of roads in the Edges and Nodes tables.

```
[Microsoft.SqlServer.Server.SqlProcedure]
public static void GeographyAStar(SqlInt32 StartID, SqlInt32 GoalID)
{

  /**
   * INITIALISATION
   */
  // The "Open List" contains the nodes that have yet to be assessed
  List<AStarNode> OpenList = new List<AStarNode>();

  // The "Closed List" contains the nodes that have already been assessed
  // Implemented as a Dictionary<> to enable quick lookup of nodes
  Dictionary<int, AStarNode> ClosedList = new Dictionary<int, AStarNode>();

  using (SqlConnection conn = new SqlConnection("context connection=true;"))
  {
    conn.Open();

    // Retrieve the location of the StartID
    using (SqlCommand cmdGetStartNode = new SqlCommand("SELECT geog4326 FROM Nodes WHERE
                                                        NodeID = @id", conn))
    {
      SqlParameter param = new SqlParameter("@id", SqlDbType.Int);
      param.Value = StartID;
      cmdGetStartNode.Parameters.Add(param);
      object startNode = cmdGetStartNode.ExecuteScalar();
      if (startNode != null)
      {
        startGeom = (SqlGeography)(startNode);
      }
```

```
    else
    {
      throw new Exception("Couldn't find start node with ID " + StartID.ToString());
    }
}

// Retrieve the location of the GoalID;
using (SqlCommand cmdGetEndNode = new SqlCommand("SELECT geog4326 FROM Nodes WHERE
                                                  NodeID = @id", conn))
{
  SqlParameter endparam = new SqlParameter("@id", SqlDbType.Int);
  endparam.Value = GoalID;
  cmdGetEndNode.Parameters.Add(endparam);
  object endNode = cmdGetEndNode.ExecuteScalar();
  if (endNode != null)
  {
    endGeom = (SqlGeography)(endNode);
  }
  else
  {
    throw new Exception("Couldn't find end node with ID " + GoalID.ToString());
  }
}

conn.Close();

// To start with, the only point we know about is the start node
AStarNode StartNode = new AStarNode(
  (int)StartID, // ID of this node
  -1, // Start node has no parent
  0, // g - the distance travelled so far to get to this node
  (double)startGeom.STDistance(endGeom) // h - estimated remaining distance to the goal
);

// Add the start node to the open list
OpenList.Add(StartNode);

/**
 * TRAVERSAL THROUGH THE NETWORK
 */

// So long as there are open nodes to assess
while (OpenList.Count > 0)
{

  // Sort the list of open nodes by ascending f score
  OpenList.Sort(delegate(AStarNode p1, AStarNode p2)
  { return p1.f.CompareTo(p2.f); });

  // Consider the open node with lowest f score
  AStarNode NodeCurrent = OpenList[0];

  /**
   * GOAL FOUND
```

```
*/
if (NodeCurrent.NodeID == GoalID)
{

  // Reconstruct the route to get here
  List<SqlGeography> route = new List<SqlGeography>();
  int parentID = NodeCurrent.ParentID;

  // Keep looking back through nodes until we get to the start (parent -1)
  while (parentID != -1)
  {
    conn.Open();

    using (SqlCommand cmdSelectEdge = new SqlCommand("GetEdgeBetweenNodes", conn))
    {
        // Retrieve the edge from this node to its parent
        cmdSelectEdge.CommandType = CommandType.StoredProcedure;
        SqlParameter fromOSODRparam = new SqlParameter("@NodeID1", SqlDbType.Int);
        SqlParameter toOSODRparam = new SqlParameter("@NodeID2", SqlDbType.Int);
        fromOSODRparam.Value = NodeCurrent.ParentID;
        toOSODRparam.Value = NodeCurrent.NodeID;
        cmdSelectEdge.Parameters.Add(fromOSODRparam);
        cmdSelectEdge.Parameters.Add(toOSODRparam);

        object edge = cmdSelectEdge.ExecuteScalar();
        SqlGeography edgeGeom;
        if (edge != null)
        {
          edgeGeom = (SqlGeography)(edge);
          route.Add(edgeGeom);
        }
    }

    conn.Close();

    NodeCurrent = ClosedList[parentID];
    parentID = NodeCurrent.ParentID;
  }

  // Send the results back to the client
  SqlMetaData ResultMetaData = new SqlMetaData(
    "Route", SqlDbType.Udt, typeof(SqlGeography)
  );
  SqlDataRecord Record = new SqlDataRecord(ResultMetaData);
  SqlContext.Pipe.SendResultsStart(Record);

  // Loop through route segments in reverse order
  for (int k = route.Count - 1; k >= 0; k--)
  {
    Record.SetValue(0, route[k]);
    SqlContext.Pipe.SendResultsRow(Record);
  }
  SqlContext.Pipe.SendResultsEnd();
```

```
      return;
    } // End if (NodeCurrent.NodeID == GoalID)

    /**
     * GOAL NOT YET FOUND - IDENTIFY ALL NODES ACCESSIBLE FROM CURRENT NODE
     */
    List<AStarNode> Successors = new List<AStarNode>();

    conn.Open();
    using (SqlCommand cmdSelectSuccessors = new SqlCommand("GetNodesAccessibleFromNode",
                                                           conn))
    {
      // Identify all nodes accessible from the current node
      cmdSelectSuccessors.CommandType = CommandType.StoredProcedure;
      SqlParameter CurrentNodeOSODRparam = new SqlParameter("@NodeID", SqlDbType.Int);
      CurrentNodeOSODRparam.Value = NodeCurrent.NodeID;
      cmdSelectSuccessors.Parameters.Add(CurrentNodeOSODRparam);

      using (SqlDataReader dr = cmdSelectSuccessors.ExecuteReader())
      {
        while (dr.Read())
        {
          // Create a node for this potential successor
          AStarNode SuccessorNode = new AStarNode(
            dr.GetInt32(0), // NodeID
            NodeCurrent.NodeID, // Successor node is a child of the current node
            NodeCurrent.g + dr.GetDouble(1), // Distance from current node to successor
            (double)(((SqlGeography)dr.GetValue(2)).STDistance(endGeom))
          );

          // Add the end of the list of successors
          Successors.Add(SuccessorNode);
        }
      }
    }

    conn.Close();

    /**
     * Examine list of possible nodes to go next
     */
    foreach (AStarNode NodeSuccessor in Successors)
    {
      // Keep track of whether we have already found this node
      bool found = false;

      // If this node is already on the closed list, don't examine further
      if (ClosedList.ContainsKey(NodeSuccessor.NodeID))
      {
        found = true;
      }

      // If we didn't find the node on the closed list, look for it on the open list
      if (!found)
```

```
      for (int j = 0; j < OpenList.Count; j++)
      {
        if (OpenList[j].NodeID == NodeSuccessor.NodeID)
        {
          found = true;

          // If this is a cheaper way to get there
          if (OpenList[j].h > NodeSuccessor.h)
          {
            // Update the route on the open list
            OpenList[j] = NodeSuccessor;
          }
          break;
        }
      }

    // If not on either list, add to the open list
    if (!found)
    {
      OpenList.Add(NodeSuccessor);
    }
  }

  // Once all successors have been examined, we've finished with the current node
  // so move it to the closed list
  OpenList.Remove(NodeCurrent);
  ClosedList.Add(NodeCurrent.NodeID, NodeCurrent);

  } // end while (OpenList.Count > 0)

  SqlContext.Pipe.Send("No route could be found!");
  return;
  }
}
```

■ **Tip** Rather than typing this out, remember that this code listing (and all the code samples in this book) are available in the code download that accompanies this book available from the Apress website at http://www.apress.com

---

Testing It Out

Build an assembly containing the previous procedure and import it into SQL Server. Then register the procedure as follows:

```
CREATE PROCEDURE dbo.GeographyAStar(@StartID int, @GoalID int)
AS EXTERNAL NAME ProSpatialCh14.[ProSpatial.Ch14.StoredProcedures].GeographyAStar;
```

You can then try plotting routes between any two nodes by supplying their node IDs as the @StartId and @GoalId parameters to the GeographyAStar procedure, as follows:

```
EXEC dbo.GeographyAStar
  @StartId = 10,
  @GoalId = 900;
```

The nodes in the network are numbered consecutively from 1 to 995, so try it out with any combination you like (although bear in mind that there are not always valid routes between every pair of nodes). Figure 14-9 illustrates the route between nodes 10 and 900 plotted together with the road segments in the Edges table, as produced by the following code listing:

```
DECLARE @AStarRoute table (geog4326 geography);
INSERT INTO @AStarRoute
EXEC dbo.GeographyAStar
@StartId = 10,
@GoalId = 900;
SELECT geog4326.STBuffer(10) FROM @AStarRoute
UNION ALL SELECT
geog4326 FROM Edges;
```

Figure 14-9. *The A* route calculated between two nodes in the Norwich road network*

Optimizing the Code and Further Enhancements

The algorithm created in this section is a lot more scalable than the earlier T-SQL approach, but can still be improved further. In order to maximize the clarity of the code logic, I've kept to simple structures such as List and Dictionary, and searched for nodes by iterating through the lists in a foreach loop. While this keeps the example relatively simple to understand, it does not result in optimal performance. Every time a new node is chosen, the open list must be re-sorted to find the node with the lowest f score, and this is not very efficient operation.

A more efficient approach might be to keep the lists sorted as nodes are added. This would make inserting new nodes slightly slower, but would make searching and updating the lists faster. In fact, we don't even need to sort every element on the open list; the only operation we need to do is to retrieve the next best node to investigate from the list, that is, the one with the current lowest f score. The best structure for this would be a *priority queue*. Priority queues differ from other collections in that, rather than retrieving items based on the order in which they were added (as in a stack, or a queue), or by retrieving the value associated with a corresponding key (as in a dictionary), they retrieve the next smallest element in the collection. However, .NET has no native implementation of a priority queue and so this would require additional code to implement.

There are still many further enhancements that could be made to this example. For example, driving directions could be added at each node to explain the action that needs to be taken by a person following the route; for example, "Turn left onto Queen's Road" (The Name column of the Edges table can be used to help provide this). Also, you can try experimenting with different heuristic values, assigning a weighting factor to adjust the cost of each edge based on road surface, for example. These are just examples left to you, the reader, to implement.

The Traveling Salesman Problem

Up to this point, we've been considering how best to calculate a route from one node to another chosen node in a network. However, this is not the only kind of routing problem that applies to spatial data. One classic mathematical puzzle based on graph theory is called the Traveling Salesman Problem (TSP). The essence of the TSP puzzle is, given a list of locations and the known distances between each, find the shortest route that visits each location exactly once and returns back to the start.

The algorithms discussed up to now have all been concerned with getting from A to B, but the objective in TSP is slightly different: we generally don't care where we end up or how we get there, so long as we visit the specified set of nodes (or, frequently, all the nodes in the network) in the most efficient way. Although commonly studied as a purely academic, theoretical problem, TSP has many practical applications. The most obvious example is in the field of logistics, for example, planning the route for a delivery driver who must deliver parcels to a list of known addresses and return to the depot, while driving the shortest total distance. TSP can also be applied to find solutions to optimization problems in many other fields, including the biosciences, engineering, and manufacturing industries.

▓ **Note** A similar problem to TSP is the Chinese Postman Problem (CPP). Whereas the objective of TSP is to find the optimum path that visits every *node* in a network, the objective in CPP is to find the optimum path that traverses each *edge* at least once. Like the Traveling Salesman, the Chinese Postman is a simply stated problem, but one for which there is no easy solution. It too has many potential practical applications. As its name suggests, delivering letters or perhaps ploughing snow from roads are obvious uses, but it can also be applied in many other fields.

The most direct way of solving the TSP problem would be to evaluate all possible permutations of routes between the locations and evaluating which took the least distance. As with the brute-force approach to route finding discussed at the start of this chapter, as more locations are considered, the number of possible routes increases exponentially. Taking this approach to find the optimum solution for even a modest amount of cities therefore quickly becomes impractical. The number of possible routes between 10 cities, for example, is $10! = 3,628,800$. For 20 cities, there are $20! = 2,432,902,008,176,640,000$ possible routes! Exact solutions to a TSP scenario using this method are therefore almost always impractical, but there is a range of approximations available. One approach is, from an arbitrary starting point, to always visit the next closest city that has yet to be visited. This "nearest neighbor" approach will probably yield a suboptimal solution, but it is simple and relatively fast to calculate, and it generally avoids making unnecessarily long journeys between locations. We can do this in an SQLCLR function, as follows:

```
[Microsoft.SqlServer.Server.SqlFunction]
public static SqlGeometry GeometryTSP(SqlGeometry PlacesToVisit)
{
  // Convert the supplied MultiPoint instance into a List<> of SqlGeometry points
  List<SqlGeometry> RemainingCities = new List<SqlGeometry>();

  // Loop and add each point to the list
  for (int i = 1; i <= PlacesToVisit.STNumGeometries(); i++)
  {
    RemainingCities.Add(PlacesToVisit.STGeometryN(i));
  }

  // Start the tour from the first city
  SqlGeometry CurrentCity = RemainingCities[0];

  // Begin the geometry
  SqlGeometryBuilder Builder = new SqlGeometryBuilder();
  Builder.SetSrid((int)PlacesToVisit.STSrid);
  Builder.BeginGeometry(OpenGisGeometryType.LineString);

  // Begin the LineString with the first point
  Builder.BeginFigure((double)CurrentCity.STX, (double)CurrentCity.STY);

  // We don't need to visit this city again
  RemainingCities.Remove(CurrentCity);

  // While there are still unvisited cities
  while (RemainingCities.Count > 0)
  {
    RemainingCities.Sort(delegate(SqlGeometry p1, SqlGeometry p2)
    { return p1.STDistance(CurrentCity).CompareTo(p2.STDistance(CurrentCity)); });

    // Move to the closest destination
    CurrentCity = RemainingCities[0];

    // Add this city to the tour route
    Builder.AddLine((double)CurrentCity.STX, (double)CurrentCity.STY);

    // Update the list of remaining cities
    RemainingCities.Remove(CurrentCity);
  }

  // End the geometry
  Builder.EndFigure();
  Builder.EndGeometry();

  // Return the constructed geometry
  return Builder.ConstructedGeometry;
}
```

■ **Note** This method is far from the optimal solution for the TSP. Better methods exist, involving a wide range of genetic algorithms. However, this method is simple to understand, and it demonstrates how we can use methods of the SqlGeometry type to solve interesting problems.

Now suppose that you had a list of locations to visit, defined as a MultiPoint instance as follows:

```
DECLARE @PlacesToVisit geometry;
SET @PlacesToVisit = geometry::STGeomFromText('MULTIPOINT(0 0, 40 30, 25 10, 5 5, 0 1, 1 0,
  2 2, 5 4, 4 10, 12 32, 13 13, 56 60, 45 23, 20 56, 60 40, 34 35)', 0);
```

You can find the route between these destinations using the nearest neighbor approach as follows:

```
DECLARE @TSProute geometry;
SET @TSProute = dbo.GeometryTSP(@PlacesToVisit);

SELECT
  @TSProute,
  @TSProute.STLength();
```

The resulting LineString, 180.6 units long, is depicted in Figure 14-10.

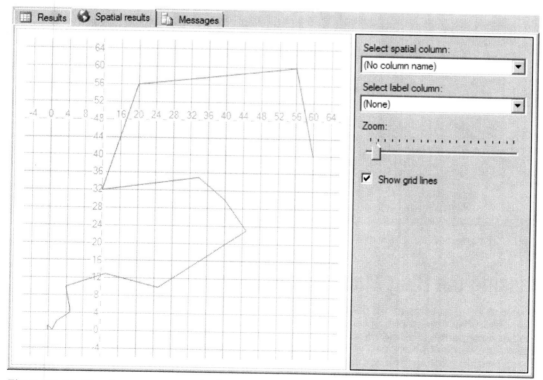

Figure 14-10. The shortest tour as calculated by the nearest-neighbor method.

We can compare this to the route that the salesman would have traveled if he had simply visited each point in the order in which they were originally listed in the MultiPoint, as follows:

```
DECLARE @route geometry;
SET @route = geometry::STGeomFromText('LINESTRING(0 0, 40 30, 25 10, 5 5, 0 1, 1 0,
  2 2, 5 4, 4 10, 12 32, 13 13, 56 60, 45 23, 20 56, 60 40, 34 35)', 0);

SELECT
  @route,
  @route.STLength();
```

This time, the route is longer (371.1 units) and a lot more chaotic, as shown in Figure 14-11.

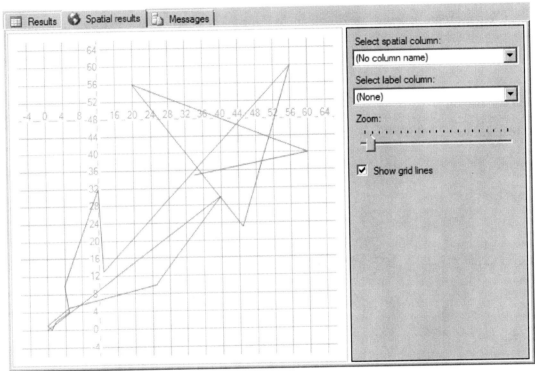

Figure 14-11. The original tour route obtained from visiting each location in the order supplied.

Harnessing the Bing Maps Routing Service

I hope you've enjoyed learning about different approaches to route finding, and finding out some of the complexity involved in implementing such systems. However, you may also be feeling slightly bewildered or disappointed: considering that navigation systems are so commonplace in modern cars, websites, and even on mobile phones, you might have been hoping that I'd provide you with a complete, ready-to-run routing solution. You can certainly build upon and extend the templates I've given in this chapter, but creating a reliable, fully featured routing algorithm is surprisingly complex, especially when you consider elements such as turn restrictions and one-way highways.

All is not lost, however. Remember that, in Chapter 6, I showed you how to create a SQLCLR function that used the Bing Maps REST service to geocode an address? Bing Maps also provides a Routes API that calculates a route between any two locations. The path of the route is returned as an array of latitude and longitude coordinates that can be used to build up a geography LineString representing the journey.

So, rather than try to reinvent the wheel, create a new SQLCLR class library that calls the Bing Maps Routes API as shown in the following code listing:

```csharp
using System;
using System.Data;
using System.Data.SqlClient;
using System.Data.SqlTypes;
using Microsoft.SqlServer.Server;
using System.Net;
using System.IO;
using Microsoft.SqlServer.Types;
using System.Xml;

namespace ProSQLSpatial.Ch14
{
  public partial class UserDefinedFunctions
  {
    [Microsoft.SqlServer.Server.SqlFunction]
    public static SqlGeography Route(SqlGeography Start, SqlGeography End,
                                     SqlString Mode)
    {

      // Check the input parameters
      if (!(Start.STGeometryType() == "POINT" && Start.STSrid == 4326)) {
        throw new Exception("Route start must be a single point defined using SRID 4326");
      }
      if (!(End.STGeometryType() == "POINT" && End.STSrid == 4326)) {
        throw new Exception("Route end must be a single point defined using SRID 4326");
      }
      // Routes API can calculate both walking and driving routes
      string travelMode = ((string)Mode).ToUpper();
      if (travelMode != "DRIVING" && travelMode != "WALKING")
      {
        throw new Exception("Mode of travel must be WALKING or DRIVING");
      }

      // Response returned from the service
      string feedData = string.Empty;

      try
      {

        // Set up the template for the Bing Maps routing request
        // See http://msdn.microsoft.com/en-us/library/ff701717.aspx
        String key = "ENTERYOURBINGMAPSKEY";
        String urltemplate =
"http://dev.virtualearth.net/REST/V1/Routes/{0}?wp.0={1}&wp.1={2}&rpo=Points&optmz=distance&output=xml&key={3}";
        String Startcoords = String.Concat(Start.Lat, ",", Start.Long);
        String Endcoords = String.Concat(End.Lat, ",", End.Long);
```

```
        String url = String.Format(urltemplate, travelMode, Startcoords, Endcoords, key);

        // Call the service
        HttpWebRequest request = null;
        HttpWebResponse response = null;
        Stream stream = null;
        StreamReader streamReader = null;

        request = (HttpWebRequest)WebRequest.Create(url);
        request.Method = "GET";
        request.ContentLength = 0;
        response = (HttpWebResponse)request.GetResponse();

        // Read the (XML) results
        stream = response.GetResponseStream();
        streamReader = new StreamReader(stream);
        feedData = streamReader.ReadToEnd();

        // Clean up
        response.Close();
        stream.Dispose();
        streamReader.Dispose();
    }

    catch (Exception ex)
    {
        // Oops - something went wrong
        SqlContext.Pipe.Send(ex.Message.ToString());
    }

    // Process the XML response
    XmlDocument doc = new XmlDocument();
    doc.LoadXml(feedData);

    // Define the default XML namespace
    XmlNamespaceManager nsmgr = new XmlNamespaceManager(doc.NameTable);
    nsmgr.AddNamespace("ab", "http://schemas.microsoft.com/search/local/ws/rest/v1");

    // Isolate the routepath from the results
    XmlNode routePath = doc.GetElementsByTagName("RoutePath")[0];
    XmlNode line = routePath["Line"];

    // Create a set of all <Location>s in the response
    XmlNodeList Points = line.SelectNodes("ab:Point", nsmgr);

    // Build up a geography LineString connecting the <Location>s
    SqlGeographyBuilder gb = new SqlGeographyBuilder();
    gb.SetSrid(4326);
    gb.BeginGeography(OpenGisGeographyType.LineString);
    gb.BeginFigure(double.Parse(Points[0]["Latitude"].InnerText),
                   double.Parse(Points[0]["Longitude"].InnerText));
    for(int i=1; i<Points.Count; i++)
    {
        gb.AddLine(double.Parse(Points[i]["Latitude"].InnerText),
```

```
                    double.Parse(Points[i]["Longitude"].InnerText));
            }
        gb.EndFigure();
        gb.EndGeography();

        // Return the constructed LineString  to SQL Server
        return gb.ConstructedGeography;
    }
  };
}
```

The code logic is very similar to that used by the geocoding function used in Chapter 6: an HTTPWebRequest is made containing a number of parameters in the URL. These specify the coordinates of the start and end points of the desired route, and whether the method of travel should be "walking" or "driving." You must also supply a valid Bing Maps key when making the request. When the response is returned, the individual points that make up the route are used to construct a SqlGeography LineString, which is returned to SQL Server.

Import the assembly containing this code into SQL Server, remembering to grant it EXTERNAL ACCESS permission. Then register a T-SQL function to call the routing service as follows:

```
CREATE FUNCTION dbo.Route(@Start geography, @End geography, @Mode nvarchar(255))
RETURNS geography
EXTERNAL NAME ProSpatialCh14.[ProSpatial.Ch14.UserDefinedFunctions].Route;
```

To demonstrate the function, you can calculate a driving route between Boston and Miami:

```
DECLARE @NewYork geography = 'POINT(-71.1 42.35)';
DECLARE @Miami geography = 'POINT(-80.2 25.8)';

DECLARE @Route geography;
SET @Route = dbo.Route(@NewYork, @Miami, 'DRIVING');

SELECT @Route, @Route.STLength();
```

The calculated route, 2,360 km in length, is shown in Figure 14-12.

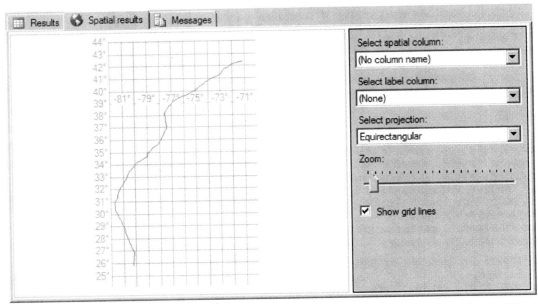

Figure 14-12. The driving route from Boston to Miami calculated from the Bing Maps Route API

Summary

In this chapter, you learned various methods to use SQL Server's spatial datatypes to model and traverse through a network

- Networks are generally modeled as graphs, in which nodes are connected by edges.
- Edges may be directed or undirected, and each edge has a cost associated with crossing it. The cost of an edge may depend on many factors; in the example of a road network this might include the type of road surface, the speed limit, the typical amount of traffic, or the degree of incline.
- A route finding algorithm attempts to find the optimum route from one specified node in the network to another by crossing those edges that have the least resulting total cost.
- You saw two practical implementations of route finding algorithms in SQL Server, one using a brute-force approach in T-SQL, and another implementing the A* algorithm in SQLCLR.
- The Traveling Salesman Problem and Chinese Postman Problem are further examples of mathematical problems from the discipline of graph theory that can be modeled and solved using SQL Server's spatial datatypes.
- The Bing Maps Routes API can calculate walking and driving routes between locations that are used to create corresponding geography LineStrings in SQL Server.

CHAPTER 15

Triangulation and Tesselation

In this chapter I'd like to discuss *triangulation* and *tessellation*, two related topics taken from the computational geometry branch of mathematics, which can be used to provide interesting useful insights about a set of spatial data. Discussion of these topics necessarily involves some mathematical theory, and may initially seem slightly abstract. However, once you've got your head around them you'll see that tessellation and triangulation have plenty of practical spatial applications, and I'll show you just a few of these.

The Importance of Triangles

Triangles are the most basic, and arguably the most useful, type of polygon. Because of their simplicity and the conciseness and efficiency with which they can be defined and used in calculations, triangles are often used as the primitive building block from which more complex geometric structures are created. For example, the three-dimensional models used in computer graphics and animation, such as that illustrated in Figure 15-1, are typically formed from sets of triangular faces.

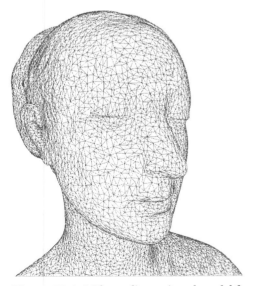

Figure 15-1. A Three-dimensional model formed from a mesh of triangular faces

Three-dimensional models of spatial data are also sometimes based on triangular data structures. For example, a triangulated irregular network (TIN), as illustrated in Figure 15-2, is a method of modeling terrain. A TIN is formed by recording the spot height of different point locations across an area of ground. The network is *irregular* in that the heights do not have to be sampled at regular intervals (although they can be). The network is triangulated by defining a set of triangular faces that connect the points, which creates a faceted surface representing the approximate lie of the land across the area sampled.

TINs, like the geometry types implemented by the geometry and geography datatypes, are an example of vector spatial data; the location of each point in the network is stored as an (x, y, z) coordinate tuple, and the triangular faces are defined by interpolation between the three vertices at the corners of each triangle.

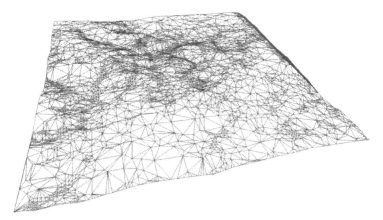

Figure 15-2. A Triangulated irregular network model of a section of terrain

Triangulation

The process required to create the models illustrated in Figures 15-1 and 15-2 involves determining the set of triangular faces that form a continuous mesh connecting a series of points. There may be several different ways to create a triangulated surface from a given set of points, as demonstrated in Figure 15-3.

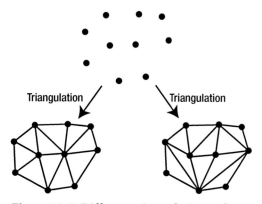

Figure 15-3. Different triangulations of a set of points

Although there are many possible triangulations, when people refer to "triangulating" a set of points, they most commonly mean one specific triangulation, the *Delaunay triangulation*. The Delaunay triangulation has several important properties that make it distinct from other triangulations, as described in the next section.

The Delaunay Triangulation

The Delaunay triangulation, named after Russian mathematician Boris Delaunay, is the particular triangulation of a set of points in which no point lies in the circumcircle of any created triangle (a condition sometimes alternatively expressed as "the circumcircle of every triangle must be empty"). If you're not familiar with geometrical terms, that might be a little hard to grasp, so let's break it down.

Every triangle (and every other regular convex polygon) has a *circumcircle*, the unique circle that passes through all of the vertices at the corners of that shape. The point at the center of a circumcircle is called the *circumcenter*. Similar to the centroid calculated by the STCentroid() method, the circumcenter is one way of thinking about the "center" of a shape (indeed, in the case of an equilateral triangle, the centroid and circumcenter are the same). Also as with a centroid, the circumcenter of a triangle may lie either inside or outside the area of the triangle itself.

Figure 15-4 illustrates a triangle, together with its circumcircle and circumcenter.

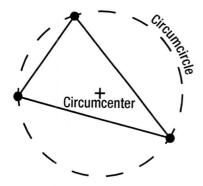

Figure 15-4. The circumcenter of a triangle is the circle that passes through all three vertices

The unique property of a Delaunay triangulation is that it is the triangulation in which the circumcircle of every triangle is empty; that is, the points that define the vertices of one triangle cannot lie within the circumcircle that encloses any other triangle.

Delaunay triangulations have some interesting and useful properties:

- They are deterministic and unique. For any given set of points, there is exactly one possible Delaunay triangulation.

- The Delaunay triangulation tends to create a mesh of relatively evenly-proportioned triangles, which are more aesthetically pleasing than long thin triangles created by some other triangulations.

- The Delaunay triangulation has relationships to other mathematical structures, including alpha shapes and the Voronoi tessellation discussed later in this chapter.

Calculating the Delaunay Triangulation

There are several approaches that can be used to calculate the Delaunay triangulation of a set of points. The general technique that I'm about to follow is an example of an *incremental* triangulation method. This is a commonly used and relatively straightforward method to understand. For readers interested in considering other, possibly more high-performance approaches, I recommend searching the Internet for alternative methods including *Divide and Conquer*, or *Sweepline* techniques.

Using the incremental approach, each point in the dataset is added one at a time into an existing mesh of triangles. If the point being added lies within the circumcircle of any existing triangles, those triangles are removed from the mesh and replaced with smaller empty triangles formed by connecting each of the vertices of the old triangle to the new point. This method ensures that, after the final point has been added, the resulting triangular mesh consists only of triangles whose circumcircles are empty.

One difficulty arising from the incremental approach to triangulation is the question of how to add the very first point from the dataset because, at the start of the triangulation, there is no existing mesh into which to add the point. The general solution to this problem is first to create an artificial "supertriangle" that encompasses the entire dataset, and acts as an initial mesh into which the first points can be triangulated. Once the triangulation is complete, the supertriangle can be removed again, leaving only those triangles defined between points contained in the original dataset.

The steps involved in creating a Delaunay triangulation can be described as follows:

1. Create a "supertriangle" that encompasses all the points to be triangulated (you can think of this supertriangle as similar to a bounding box, but triangular).

2. Select a point to be added to the triangulation, and test whether it lies inside the circumcircle of any of the existing triangles in the mesh. When adding the first point to the mesh this is guaranteed to occur, because the supertriangle covers all the points.

3. For each triangle whose circumcircle contains the added point, remove that triangle, and instead replace it with three new smaller triangles from each of the corners of the original triangle to the added point.

4. Repeat Steps 2 and 3 until all points have been added into the mesh, and no point lies inside the circumcircle of a triangle.

5. Finally, remove any "exterior" triangles from the triangulation, those that connect points that lie on the outside edge of the triangular mesh to the supertriangle.

These steps are illustrated with a dataset containing four points in Figure 15-5.

1. Define points to be triangulated

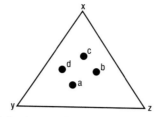

2. Create supertriangle xyz encompassing points

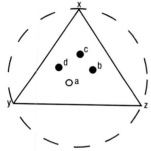

3. Point a lies within circumcircle of triangle xyz

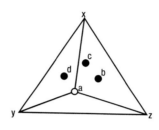

4. Remove triangle xyz
   Insert new triangles ayz, xaz, and xya

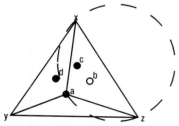

5. Point b lies within circumcircle of triangle zax

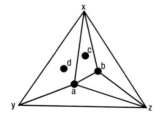

6. Remove triangle zax
   Insert new triangles zab, zbx, and bax

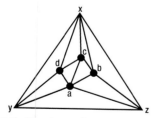

7. Continue to examine each point, creating
   new triangles as appropriate

8. Remove any triangle that shares supertriangle
   vertices x, y, or z

Figure 15-5. Steps involved in an incremental approach to Delaunay triangulation.

An SQLCLR Triangulation Procedure

You've seen the theory behind the incremental method of Delaunay triangulation; now it's time to put that theory into practice with spatial data in SQL Server. In this section, we'll create a CLR stored procedure that triangulates the points in a geometry MultiPoint and returns a table of Polygons representing the triangles created between those points. So, fire up Visual Studio and create a new C# class library project, and let's go!

Data Structures

I said previously that the input to the procedure would be a MultiPoint geometry, and the output would be a set of Polygons. In fact, we could operate on SqlGeometry instances right through the triangulation process; for example, creating new SqlGeometry Polygons as each triangle is added to the mesh, and determining whether the circumcircle of a triangle is empty using familiar methods such as STIntersects() or STDisjoint(). However, carrying around complete SqlGeometry instances like this is quite unnecessary when we only really need a very small subset of that functionality. Creating and manipulating arrays of fully formed SqlGeometry instances would make our code pretty inefficient when we start to work with a large volume of data. So, instead, we'll define some simple lightweight structures to represent a point and a triangle.

The structure used to represent a point needs only two double properties to hold a pair of coordinate values. We'll also implement the IComparable CompareTo method, which will allow us to sort a collection of points by ascending x-coordinate value (we'll use this to make an optimization to the code later), as follows:

```
private struct SimplePoint : IComparable
{
  public double x, y;

  // Constructor
  public SimplePoint(double x, double y)
  {
    this.x = x;
    this.y = y;
  }
  // Implement IComparable CompareTo method to enable sorting
  int IComparable.CompareTo(object obj)
  {
    SimplePoint other = (SimplePoint)obj;
    if (this.x > other.x) { return 1; }
    else if (this.x < other.x) { return -1; }
    else { return 0; }
  }
}
```

The set of points used in the triangulation will be stored in a List collection. That means that each triangle need not explicitly define the coordinates of the vertices from which it is formed, but rather it can simply reference the index value of those vertices from the collection of points. Defining a triangle from three int index values is significantly more efficient than defining a triangular SqlGeometry polygon. We'll also store the circumcenter and radius of the circumcircle along with each triangle rather than calculating them on the fly.

```
private struct SimpleTriangle
{
```

```
  // Index entries to each vertex
  public int a, b, c;

  // Circumcenter and radius of the circumcircle
  public SimplePoint circumcentre;
  public double radius;

  // Constructor
  public SimpleTriangle(int a, int b, int c, SimplePoint circumcentre, double radius)
  {
    this.a = a;
    this.b = b;
    this.c = c;
    this.circumcentre = circumcentre;
    this.radius = radius;
  }
}
```

As stated previously, the advantage of using these stripped-down structures for points and triangles is that it will make our algorithm more efficient. The disadvantage, however, is that we won't be able to use any of the built-in SqlGeometry methods to help us during the triangulation process. So we'll have to create our own functions to perform the necessary calculations instead. Fortunately, these calculations are relatively simple; the following code listing demonstrates a function that calculates the circumradius and circumcenter of a triangle from its three vertices:

```
private static void CalculateCircumcircle(
  SimplePoint p1, SimplePoint p2, SimplePoint p3, // Inputs
  out SimplePoint circumCentre, out double radius // Outputs
)
{
  // Calculate the length of each side of the triangle
  double a = Distance(p2, p3); // side a is opposite point 1
  double b = Distance(p1, p3); // side b is opposite point 2
  double c = Distance(p1, p2); // side c is opposite point 3

  // Calculate the radius of the circumcircle
  double area = Math.Abs((double)(p1.x * (p2.y - p3.y) + p2.x * (p3.y - p1.y) + p3.x
             * (p1.y - p2.y)) / 2);
  radius = a * b * c / (4 * area);

  // Define area coordinates to calculate the circumcentre
  double pp1 = Math.Pow(a, 2) * (Math.Pow(b, 2) + Math.Pow(c, 2) - Math.Pow(a, 2));
  double pp2 = Math.Pow(b, 2) * (Math.Pow(c, 2) + Math.Pow(a, 2) - Math.Pow(b, 2));
  double pp3 = Math.Pow(c, 2) * (Math.Pow(a, 2) + Math.Pow(b, 2) - Math.Pow(c, 2));

  // Normalise
  double t1 = pp1 / (pp1 + pp2 + pp3);
  double t2 = pp2 / (pp1 + pp2 + pp3);
  double t3 = pp3 / (pp1 + pp2 + pp3);

  // Convert to Cartesian
  double x = t1 * p1.x + t2 * p2.x + t3 * p3.x;
  double y = t1 * p1.y + t2 * p2.y + t3 * p3.y;
```

```
  // Define the circumcenter
  circumCentre = new SimplePoint(x, y);
}
```

The next function calculates the distance between two simple points. Rather than replicating the full capability of the STDistance() method, which can compute the distance between complex polygonal or curved geometries, we only need to work out the distance between two points on a flat plane. Therefore, we can apply some straightforward knowledge of high school Pythagorus:

```
private static double Distance(SimplePoint p1, SimplePoint p2)
{
  double result = 0;
  result = Math.Sqrt(Math.Pow((p2.x - p1.x), 2) + Math.Pow((p2.y - p1.y), 2));
  return result;
}
```

The Distance() function will be used to determine whether a point lies within the circumcircle of a triangle, by calculating the distance between the point and the circumcenter of the triangle, and comparing this to the circumradius of that triangle. If the distance from the circumcenter to the point is greater than the circumradius, that point is not contained within the circumcircle of the triangle.

With these structures and functions in place, we can begin to code the main body of the triangulation algorithm.

Setting Up the Points

We'll perform the triangulation using a CLR stored procedure with the following signature:

```
[Microsoft.SqlServer.Server.SqlProcedure]
public static void GeometryTriangulate(SqlGeometry MultiPoint)
```

The procedure will have a single supplied parameter, MultiPoint, which is a SqlGeometry instance containing the points to be triangulated. You could of course adjust the procedure so that the input was read in from individual geometry Point values contained in a specified column of a table; in fact, for practical use in a production environment, this would probably be a better approach. However, for simplicity and ease of demonstration, I'll stick with passing all the points to be triangulated in a single MultiPoint parameter. Note that the CLR stored procedure has no return value; the results will be sent back to SQL Server via the SqlContext pipe instead.

The first step is to initialize and populate a List of simple points from each of the elements in the supplied MultiPoint. We won't simply add every point in the MultiPoint into the network though; while a MultiPoint geometry can contain several Point elements at the same coordinate location, the Delaunay triangulation will fail if the network contains any duplicate points (since this would lead to a triangle being created with an infinitely small edge between those two points). To prevent the chance of this happening, we'll loop through each point in the MultiPoint and only add unique points to the list:

```
List<SimplePoint> Vertices = new List<SimplePoint>();
// Loop through supplied points
for (int i = 1; i <= MultiPoint.STNumPoints(); i++)
{
  // Create a new simple point corresponding to this element of the MultiPoint
  SimplePoint Point = new SimplePoint(
    (double)MultiPoint.STPointN(i).STX,
    (double)MultiPoint.STPointN(i).STY
  );

  // Check whether this point already exists
```

```
if (!Vertices.Contains(Point))
{
  Vertices.Add(Point);
}
}
```

Once the unique points have all been added, we'll sort the list. The `SimplePoint` structure implemented the `IComparable CompareTo` method, so sorting the list using the default comparer will arrange the points in ascending x-coordinate order. Note that it's not strictly necessary to sort the points; the incremental triangulation method will work whatever order the points are added in to the mesh. However, if we sort the list first we can make an efficiency enhancement to the algorithm, as follows.

Remember that, when a point is added, we must identify the circumcircles of all those triangles in the mesh in which the point lies. If points are always added in ascending x order, new triangles will be created in a broad "sweep" from left to right across the surface of the mesh. Therefore, once any triangle lies entirely to the left of the point currently being added (i.e., the x-coordinate of every vertex of the triangle is less than the x-coordinate of the point being added), we know that its circumcircle cannot possibly contain that point, or any future points yet to be added. As such, any triangles that lie to the left of the point being added can be considered "complete" and do not need to be tested again throughout the triangulation process. Making use of this fact will enable our code to be significantly more efficient, and simply requires us to sort the vertex list first:

```
Vertices.Sort();
```

Creating the Supertriangle

We need to ensure that the *supertriangle*—the artificial triangle used to begin the mesh into which points can be added—is large enough to cover the complete extent of the area to be triangulated. To do so, we'll first use the `STEnvelope()` method to create the bounding box around the supplied MultiPoint instance.

```
SqlGeometry Envelope = MultiPoint.STEnvelope();
```

Having created the bounding box around the points, we then need to determine its maximum dimension, that is, whichever of its height or width is greatest. This can be done by working out the difference in coordinate values from the corners of the box and then comparing them as follows:

```
// Width
double dx = (double)(Envelope.STPointN(2).STX - Envelope.STPointN(1).STX);
// Height
double dy = (double)(Envelope.STPointN(4).STY - Envelope.STPointN(1).STY);
// Maximum dimension
double dmax = (dx > dy) ? dx : dy;
```

▦ **Note** The preceding code listing relies on two useful properties of the result returned by the `STEnvelope()` method, which are that the first point, `STPointN(1)`, is always at the bottom left-hand corner of the box, and the remaining points are always listed in counterclockwise order. Knowing these two facts allows you to work out the height and width of the bounding box by simple subtraction of the relevant coordinate values.

Having determined the maximum extent of the bounding box around the points, we also need to calculate the x-and y-coordinates of its centerpoint, which can be done easily using the STCentroid() method:

```
SqlGeometry centroid = Envelope.STCentroid();
double avgx = (double)centroid.STX;
double avgy = (double)centroid.STY;
```

Now, we can define the three vertices, a, b, and c, of the supertriangle of sufficient size to encompass all the points, as follows:

```
SimplePoint a = new SimplePoint(avgx - 2 * dmax, avgy - dmax);
SimplePoint b = new SimplePoint(avgx + 2 * dmax, avgy - dmax);
SimplePoint c = new SimplePoint(avgx, avgy + 2 * dmax);
```

We'll add the vertices of the supertriangle onto the list of vertices, and also add the supertriangle onto a new list of triangles that have been created so far. Finally, we'll set up an empty list to keep track of any triangles that have been completed (those that lie completely to the left of the point being added) that will form the final results of the triangulation algorithm. These steps are shown in the following code listing:

```
// Add the supertriangle vertices to the end of the vertex array
Vertices.Add(a);
Vertices.Add(b);
Vertices.Add(c);

// Create the supertriangle from the calculated vertices a, b, and c. Since these are the
// last points to be added to the vertices array, their corresponding index values will be
// numPoints, numPoints+1, and numPoints+2, respectively
double radius;
SimplePoint circumcentre;
CalculateCircumcircle(a, b, c, out circumcentre, out radius);
SimpleTriangle SuperTriangle = new SimpleTriangle(numPoints, numPoints + 1, numPoints + 2,
 circumcentre, radius);

// Add the supertriangle to the list of triangles
List<SimpleTriangle> Triangles = new List<SimpleTriangle>();
Triangles.Add(SuperTriangle);

// Create an empty list to hold completed triangles
List<SimpleTriangle> CompletedTriangles = new List<SimpleTriangle>();
```

Adding Points to the Triangulated Mesh

We can now begin the incremental process of adding points to the mesh. We'll set up a loop that iterates through each point that is to be triangulated. We'll then use another nested loop to consider each triangle in relation to the point being added. If the circumcircle of a triangle contains this point, the triangle is removed and each of its edges is recorded on a temporary list referred to as the "edge buffer". Alternatively, if the triangle lies completely to the left of the point being added, it is also removed, but this time added to the list of completed triangles.

Once every triangle has been considered, the edge buffer is filtered to remove any edges that have been included twice, and then new triangles are created from each edge in the buffer to the newly added point. This process is then repeated for every point in the dataset. Here's the code:

```
// Loop through each point
for (int i = 0; i < numPoints; i++)
{
  // Initialise the edge buffer
  List<int[]> Edges = new List<int[]>();

  // Loop through each triangle
  for (int j = Triangles.Count - 1; j >= 0; j--)
  {
    // If the point lies within the circumcircle of this triangle
    if (Distance(Triangles[j].circumcentre, Vertices[i]) < Triangles[j].radius)
    {
      // Add the triangle edges to the edge buffer
      Edges.Add(new int[] { Triangles[j].a, Triangles[j].b });
      Edges.Add(new int[] { Triangles[j].b, Triangles[j].c });
      Edges.Add(new int[] { Triangles[j].c, Triangles[j].a });

      // Remove this triangle from the list
      Triangles.RemoveAt(j);
    }

    // If this triangle is complete
    else if (Vertices[i].x > Triangles[j].circumcentre.x + Triangles[j].radius)
    {
      // Move the triangle to the list of completed triangles
      CompletedTriangles.Add(Triangles[j]);
      Triangles.RemoveAt(j);
    }
  }

  // Remove duplicate edges
  for (int j = Edges.Count - 1; j > 0; j--)
  {
    for (int k = j - 1; k >= 0; k--)
    {
      // Compare if these edges match in either direction
      if (Edges[j][0].Equals(Edges[k][1]) && Edges[j][1].Equals(Edges[k][0]))
      {
        // Remove both duplicates
        Edges.RemoveAt(j);
        Edges.RemoveAt(k);

        // We've removed an item from lower down the list than where j is now, so update j
        j--;
        break;
      }
    }
  }

  // Create new triangles from each edge to the current point
  for (int j = 0; j < Edges.Count; j++)
  {
    CalculateCircumcircle(Vertices[Edges[j][0]], Vertices[Edges[j][1]], Vertices[i],
        out circumcentre, out radius);
```

```
    SimpleTriangle T = new SimpleTriangle(Edges[j][0], Edges[j][1], i,
      circumcentre, radius);
        Triangles.Add(T);
  }
}
```

Once all points have been considered we know that no further triangles will be created so, following the end of this loop, we can move any remaining triangles onto the completed list.

```
CompletedTriangles.AddRange(Triangles);
```

Outputting the Results

Once the triangulation is complete, the CompletedTriangles list contains one entry for each triangle that we'll use to populate a resultset in SQL Server. However, each triangle is currently only defined by the int indexes of each of its vertices. To output a column of the geometry datatype, we'll need a function that takes these three vertex references and creates a corresponding triangular SqlGeometry Polygon. This is easily done with a SqlGeometryBuilder:

```
// Construct a triangle from 3 vertices
private static SqlGeometry TriangleFromPoints(SimplePoint p1, SimplePoint p2,
  SimplePoint p3, int srid)
{
  SqlGeometryBuilder TriangleBuilder = new SqlGeometryBuilder();
  TriangleBuilder.SetSrid(srid);
  TriangleBuilder.BeginGeometry(OpenGisGeometryType.Polygon);
  TriangleBuilder.BeginFigure(p1.x, p1.y);
  TriangleBuilder.AddLine(p2.x, p2.y);
  TriangleBuilder.AddLine(p3.x, p3.y);
  TriangleBuilder.AddLine(p1.x, p1.y);
  TriangleBuilder.EndFigure();
  TriangleBuilder.EndGeometry();
  return TriangleBuilder.ConstructedGeometry;
}
```

We'll use the TriangleFromPoints function to output one Polygon for each triangle on the completed triangles list, and send these back to SQL Server via the SqlContext pipe, as follows:

```
// Define the metadata of the results table - a single geometry column
SqlMetaData metadata = new SqlMetaData("Triangle", SqlDbType.Udt, typeof(SqlGeometry));

// Create a record based on this metadata
SqlDataRecord record = new SqlDataRecord(metadata);

// Start to send the results back to the client
SqlContext.Pipe.SendResultsStart(record);
foreach (SimpleTriangle Tri in CompletedTriangles)
{
  // Check that this is a triangle formed only from vertices in the original MultiPoint
  // i.e. not from the vertices of the supertriangle.
  if (Tri.a < numPoints && Tri.b < numPoints && Tri.c < numPoints)
  {
    SqlGeometry triangle = TriangleFromPoints(
      Vertices[Tri.a], Vertices[Tri.b], Vertices[Tri.c], srid
```

```
    );
    record.SetValue(0, triangle);
    SqlContext.Pipe.SendResultsRow(record);
  }
}
SqlContext.Pipe.SendResultsEnd();
```

Registering and Testing the Function

Once you've created a function based on the preceding code listing (or, better still, just download the code from the APress website), register the assembly and function in SQL Server as follows:

```
CREATE ASSEMBLY ProSpatialCh15
FROM 'C:\ProSpatial\Ch15_Triangulation\bin\Debug\ProSpatialCh15.dll'
WITH PERMISSION_SET = SAFE;
GO

CREATE PROCEDURE dbo.GeometryTriangulate(@MultiPoint geometry)
AS EXTERNAL NAME ProSpatialCh15.[ProSpatial.Ch15].GeometryTriangulate;
GO
```

You can then try testing the triangulation. To demonstrate, first create a MultiPoint geometry instance containing a random distribution of 800 points.

```
DECLARE @MultiPoint geometry = 'MULTIPOINT EMPTY';
DECLARE @i int = 0;
WHILE @i < 800 BEGIN
  SET @MultiPoint = @MultiPoint.STUnion(
    geometry::Point(RAND()*100, RAND()*100, 0)
  );
  SET @i = @i + 1;
END;
```

Then create the Delaunay triangulation of this data, and display it alongside the set of points from which it was created by executing the following:

```
SELECT @MultiPoint;
EXEC dbo.GeometryTriangulate @MultiPoint;
```

The results, as shown in the SSMS Spatial Results tab, are illustrated in Figure 15-6.

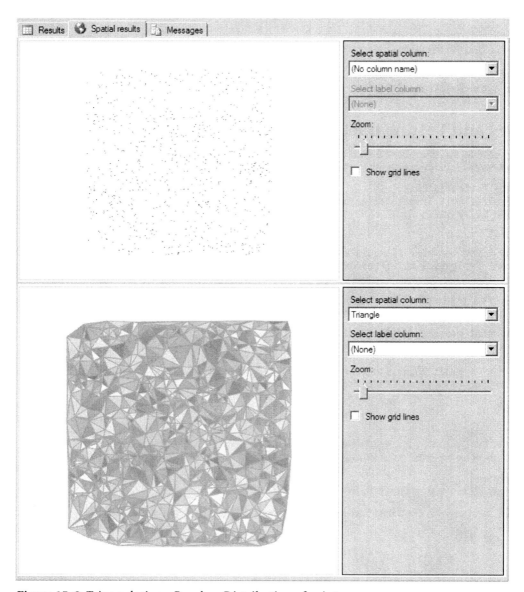

Figure 15-6. *Triangulating a Random Distribution of points*

You may think that seemed like an awful lot of effort to have gone to just to create a pretty mosaic picture from a set of points and, if that were all you could do with the Delaunay triangulation, I would agree with you. Fortunately, however, there are several practical applications that are based on a Delaunay triangulation. In the following sections, I'll show three such practical examples:

- Creating a 3D model representing a terrain surface

- Forming alpha shapes that define the concave hull of a geometry

- Deriving a Voronoi tessellation that materializes the pattern of nearest neighbors around every point

All of these examples reuse the same triangulation code base just created, with only slight additional modifications.

Creating 3D Surface Models

Generally speaking, SQL Server doesn't deal with three-dimensional spatial data. Sure, you can define geometry and geography instances in which the individual points contain z or m coordinate values, but you don't get any obvious benefit from doing so; it won't make a difference to any calculations performed within SQL Server itself. In fact, the results of many of SQL Server's functions will strip off any z or m coordinate values that had been defined in the original instance. However, so long as you avoid using any inbuilt methods, you can still use SQL Server to store and retrieve values for display or analysis in an application that does work with 3D data, and you can define your own functions to operate in 3D space.

In this section, I'll show you how to adapt the Delaunay triangulation code to create a three-dimensional mesh of triangles, similar to that shown in the TIN illustrated in Figure 15-2 near the beginning of this chapter. Then, I'll show you how to display such a model in a Windows Presentation Foundation (WPF) application.

Adapting the Triangulation Code into 3D

To create a 3D triangulated mesh, we need only make a few changes to our existing triangulation code. Namely, we need to modify our simple point structure to possess a z-coordinate value. The necessary changes are highlighted in the following code listing:

```
private struct SimplePoint3d : IComparable
{
  public double x, y, z;
  public SimplePoint3d(double x, double y, double z)
  {
    this.x = x;
    this.y = y;
    this.z = z;
  }
  // Implement IComparable CompareTo method to enable sorting
  int IComparable.CompareTo(object obj)
  {
    SimplePoint3d other = (SimplePoint3d)obj;
    if (this.x > other.x) { return 1; }
    else if (this.x < other.x) { return -1; }
    else { return 0; }
  }
}
```

When adding the points into the list of Vertices at the start of the procedure, we'll check to see if the input point has a z-coordinate value by using the SqlGeometry HasZ property. If the point does have a z-coordinate, we'll retrieve its value via the Z property. If not, we'll assume a default z-coordinate value of 0:

```
for (int i = 1; i <= MultiPoint.STNumPoints(); i++)
{
```

```
SqlGeometry p = MultiPoint.STPointN(i);
SimplePoint3d Point = new SimplePoint3d(
  (double)p.STX, (double)p.STY, p.HasZ ? (double)p.Z : 0
);
// MultiPoints can contain the same point twice, but this messes up Delaunay
if (!Vertices.Contains(Point))
{
  Vertices.Add(Point);
}
}
```

And finally, when we reconstruct each triangle into a geometry Polygon after triangulation is complete, we need to incorporate the Z-coordinate values of each vertex. Note that the BeginFigure() and AddLine() methods of the SqlGeometryBuilder class do not have an overload that accepts only x-, y-, and z-coordinates; to pass in a z-coordinate value you must also supply an m-coordinate value, but I'll leave this as null for this example (if your dataset had m values, you could choose to retain them throughout the triangulation):

```
private static SqlGeometry Triangle3dFromPoints(
  SimplePoint3d p1, SimplePoint3d p2, SimplePoint3d p3, int srid)
{
  SqlGeometryBuilder TriangleBuilder = new SqlGeometryBuilder();
  TriangleBuilder.SetSrid(srid);
  TriangleBuilder.BeginGeometry(OpenGisGeometryType.Polygon);
  TriangleBuilder.BeginFigure(p1.x, p1.y, p1.z, null);
  TriangleBuilder.AddLine(p2.x, p2.y, p2.z, null);
  TriangleBuilder.AddLine(p3.x, p3.y, p3.z, null);
  TriangleBuilder.AddLine(p1.x, p1.y, p1.z, null);
  TriangleBuilder.EndFigure();
  TriangleBuilder.EndGeometry();
  return TriangleBuilder.ConstructedGeometry;
}
```

Those are all the changes required. Note that you don't need to make any changes to the core triangulation process itself; this will still take place in two dimensions. The Z-coordinates of each vertex are simply retained throughout the triangulation process, and required only at the end of the process when the angled triangular faces are created.

Once you've made the code changes described above, recompile the assembly and import it into SQL Server once more (In the code example that accompanies this book, I've created a separate version of the function called GeometryTriangulate3d).

A Practical Example: Creating a 3D Surface from LIDAR Data

To demonstrate the GeometryTriangulate3d procedure, we need some point data from which we can create a triangulated surface model. In the code sample accompanying this book you'll find a MultiPoint instance representing a small sample of LIDAR data. LIDAR technology is similar to familiar RADAR technology, except that it is utilizes pulses of laser or other light rather than radiowaves. A light pulse is emitted from a LIDAR device, and the pattern of diffraction and time taken to receive the reflected beam of light can be used to determine not only how far away a surface is, but also from what sort of material it is made. For example, a light aircraft fitted with a LIDAR device can survey an area of land to determine not only the height of the terrain over which it is flying, but also the canopy height of any trees, and even the type of those trees (since deciduous trees with greater leaf area will produce a different reflection pattern from a coniferous tree).

The supplied MultiPoint instance, @WolfPoint, contains the readings of a set of LIDAR observations taken at Wolf Point, which lies near Mount Saint Helen's in the Pacific Northwest region of the United States. Each point represents a location on the ground, in which the *x*- and *y*-coordinate values are measured using the UTM Zone 10N spatial reference system and the *z*-coordinate is measured relative to the North American vertical Datum of 1988.

■ **Note** The data used in this example was adapted from a set of data published by the United States Geological Survey, hosted at the Washington State Geospatial Data Archive at

http://wagda.lib.washington.edu/data/type/elevation/lidar/st_helens/

The set of LIDAR readings is illustrated, as shown in the SSMS Spatial Results tab, in Figure 15-7:

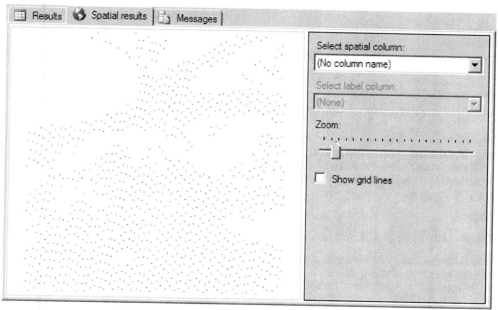

Figure 15-7. A set of LIDAR observations taken at Wolf Point

Although you can't tell from looking at Figure 15-7, it's important to realize that each of the individual points in the @WolfPoint MultiPoint instance has an associated *Z*-coordinate value. So, we can create a 3D surface by triangulating those points as before, but positioning the vertices of each triangle in three-dimensional space rather than on a flat plane.

To test out the GeometryTriangulate3D procedure with the LIDAR data, execute the following code listing:

```
EXEC dbo.GeometryTriangulate3d @WolfPoint;
```

At first glance, the result, shown in Figure 15-8, doesn't seem that different from the result of the GeometryTriangulate method demonstrated earlier.

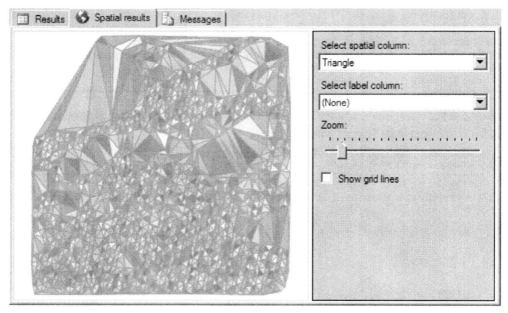

Figure 15-8. *The 3D surface created by the GeometryTriangulate3d method*

The SSMS Spatial Results tab only displays in two dimensions, so you can't tell that the triangular faces contained in the triangulation illustrated in Figure 15-8 do not lie on a flat plane. To really appreciate the difference between the flat triangulation produced by `GeometryTriangulate` and the 3D triangulation produced by `GeometryTriangulate3d`, we're going to need a different visualization tool. And that's where WPF steps in.

Visualizing a 3D Mesh in WPF

The `System.Windows.Media.Media3D` namespace of the .NET framework contains a number of classes for working with 3D objects. One of these classes is the `MeshGeometry3D`, which is described as a "triangle primitive for building a 3-D shape" (http://msdn.microsoft.com/en-us/library/ms604610.aspx), which sounds perfect for creating a WPF application to visualize our triangulated surface mesh.

Before looking at creating the `MeshGeometry3D` class itself, it's worth making a quick observation about the coordinate system used to define 3D space in WPF. Up to now, we've mostly been concerned with two-dimensional planar coordinate sysyems, in which the x-axis extends positively to the right and the y-axis extends positively upwards. In the 3D coordinate space used by members of the `Media3D` namespace, the x-axis extends positively to the right, the y-axis extends upwards, and the z-axis extends positively from from the screen towards the viewer. This is illustrated in Figure 15-9.

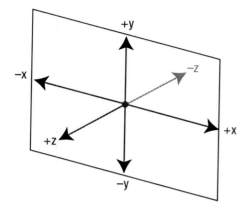

Figure 15-9. WPF 3D coordinate space

In order to take the triangulated mesh illustrated in Figure 15-8 and convert it to a three-dimensional surface model, we must rotate the coordinate reference frame so that the *y*-coordinate axis extends forwards away from the viewer (along the negative *z*-axis), and the *z*-axis maps to the positive *y*-axis. The *x*-axis remains the same in both systems.

The following code listing demonstrates an extract of the code required to create a WPF application that connects to SQL Server, retrieves the triangles in the mesh created by the GeometryTriangulate3d procedure, and uses these to populate a MeshGeometry3D.

```
// Create a new MeshGeometry3D instance
MeshGeometry3D mesh = new MeshGeometry3D();

using (SqlConnection conn = new SqlConnection("server=localhost;Trusted_Connection=yes;
                                              database=ProSpatial")
)
{
  // Define the stored procedure to create the 3D triangulated mesh
  SqlCommand comm = new SqlCommand();
  comm.CommandText = "GeometryTriangulate3d";
  comm.CommandType = CommandType.StoredProcedure;
  comm.Connection = conn;

  // Pass in the MultiPoint to be triangulated
  SqlGeometry WolfPoint = SqlGeometry.STMPointFromText(new SqlChars("MULTIPOINT ((532101.12
5121560.53 432.31), (532100.44 5121557.35 432.62), (532100.22 5121547.64 434.28) …

…(532197.97 5121503.1 447.2), (532198.64 5121506.22 446.86), (532199.36 5121509.24
445.27))"), 26910);
  SqlParameter Points = new SqlParameter("@MultiPoint", WolfPoint);
  Points.UdtTypeName = "geometry";
  comm.Parameters.Add(Points);

  try
  {
    // Open the connection
    conn.Open();
    // Execute the procedure
```

```
SqlDataReader dataReader = comm.ExecuteReader();
// Loop through the results
while (dataReader.Read())
{
  // First column in the results contains geometry triangles
  SqlGeometry tri = SqlGeometry.Deserialize(dataReader.GetSqlBytes(0));

  // Loop through each vertex of this triangle
  for (int n = 1; n <= 3; n++)
  {
    // Retrieve the coordinate values of this vertex
    SqlGeometry point = tri.STPointN(n);
    double X = (double)point.STX;
    double Y = (double)point.STY;
    double Z = point.HasZ ? (double)point.Z : 0;

    // Add this point into the 3D mesh - note X/Y/Z are transposed to X/Z/-Y
    mesh.Positions.Add(new Point3D(X, Z, -Y));
  }
}
}
}
```

The complete source code required to create, render, and rotate around a 3D model formed from this mesh is included in the source code that accompanies this book. A screenshot from this application is illustrated in Figure 15-10.

Figure 15-10. A triangulated 3D surface from LIDAR data of Wolf Point viewed in WPF

Rather than being limited to a plain, slate grey appearance as shown in 15-10, you can also assign texture maps to the WPF 3D model. For example, Figure 15-11 illustrates another 3D terrain model created by triangulating a dataset of points in an area near Mount Snowdon in Wales. The point elevation data in this case was gathered not by LIDAR, but by the NASA Shuttle Radar Topography Mission. After having created the triangular mesh from the set of point readings, I've then applied a texture map that overlays satellite photography of the region on the model.

Figure 15-11. A triangulated 3D mesh with texture map applied

SQL Server's support for 3D spatial data is limited and, if you're dealing with large amounts of 3D information, I would recommend that you use an alternative format that is designed to deal with such data. However, I hope that this example has shown that it is possible to store, retrieve, and perform custom calculations involving 3D data with SQL Server, and how triangulation can help in achieveing that goal.

Creating Alpha Shapes (Concave Hulls)

In Chapter 10, I introduced the STConvexHull() method, which generates a Polygon formed from the convex hull around a set of points. A question that I sometimes get asked is, "How can you create a *concave* hull around a set of points instead?"

This question is harder to answer than at first it may seem. The problem is that, unlike the convex hull, there is no single concave hull around a set of points. Our human brains are very good at looking at a distributed set of points and interpreting the general pattern in which they lie, but doing so involves a degree of subjectivity. Defining this shape precisely or writing a computer algorithm to produce this result is surprisingly complex. However, there is one relatively straightforward approach to creating concave hulls that makes use of the Delaunay triangulation, as follows:

- First, create the Delaunay triangulation of all the points in the shape.
- Select a subset of the triangulation that includes only those triangles whose circumradius is less than a set value.
- Create the union of those filtered triangles.

The resulting union will be formed from all those areas that were triangulated by relatively small triangles (i.e., where the points in the original dataset were close together), and exclude areas of space triangulated by larger triangles, which imply a gap in the data. This approach therefore works quite well to generate a convex hull representing the broad "shape" in which a densely packed set of points is distributed. The single supplied parameter value used to filter the triangles is called *alpha*, and the shapes created by this process are generally known as *alpha shapes*.

Adapting the Triangulation Code to Create Alpha Shapes

To create alpha shapes in SQLCLR, we can reuse almost all the same code as for the original 2D triangulation. The only difference comes right at the end of the procedure where, instead of outputting all of the triangles in the CompletedTriangles list individually, we return the union of those triangles whose circumradius is less than the desired alpha value. The modified code is as follows:

```
SqlGeometry result = new SqlGeometry();
result.STSrid = srid;
foreach (SimpleTriangle Tri in CompletedTriangles)
{
  // Only include triangles whose radius is less than supplied alpha
  if (Tri.radius < alpha)
  {
    SqlGeometry triangle = TriangleFromPoints(
      Vertices[Tri.a], Vertices[Tri.b], Vertices[Tri.c], srid
    );
    // Create union of all matching triangles
    result = result.STUnion(triangle);
  }
}
```

A Practical Example: Calculating the Outline of Massachusetts

To demonstrate alpha shapes in action, we'll reuse the MA_Firestations table from Chapter 12. Recall that this table records Point geometries for all the firestations in Massachusetts. Selecting the records from this table as in the following code listing produces the results shown in Figure 15-12.

```
SELECT Location FROM MA_Firestations;
```

***Figure 15-12.** A set of points representing the locations of firestations in the state of Massachussetts*

Assuming that firestations are spread out across the entire state (though not necessarily consistently spaced), let's see how we can use alpha shapes to try to create a Polygon representing the shape of Massachusetts from this dataset alone. The only factor that will influence the shape of the resulting Polygon is the choice of the single parameter value, alpha. In the following sections, I'll show you the effects of varying this value.

Small Alpha Values

Choosing a small alpha value will create a concave hull formed from only those triangles that connect the most densely distributed points. As alpha approaches 0, the hull created from the union of those triangles degenerates more and more, and the alpha shape created tends towards an empty geometry.

For example, Figure 15-13 demonstrates the hull created from this dataset using an alpha value of 5,000. The code to create this image is as follows:

```
-- First, create a MultiPoint instance containing all the firestations
DECLARE @Firestations geometry;
SELECT @Firestations = geometry::UnionAggregate(Location) FROM MA_Firestations;

-- Create the alpha shape and show it together with the firestations
SELECT dbo.GeometryAlphaShape(@Firestations, 5000)
UNION ALL
SELECT @Firestations.STBuffer(1000);
```

Notice the interior cavities created towards the middle and to the west of the state, where there is generally a greater distance between neighboring firestations. The greater dispersion of points in these areas leads to triangles with circumcircles of radius greater than the supplied alpha value of 5000, so they become excluded from the resulting shape.

Figure 15-13. An alpha shape created from the firestations in Massachusetts using an alpha value of 5,000

Large Alpha Values

As alpha increases, the resulting shape is created from the union of more and more of the triangles from the Delaunay triangulation, making it form a less close fit around the "true" shape of the data it is trying to describe. As alpha approaches infinity, the alpha shape created is formed from the union of all the triangles in the Delaunay triangulation, which increasingly resembles the *convex* hull of the set of points.

Figure 15-14 illustrates the alpha shape created around the firestations of Massachussetts using an alpha value of 30,000, as created using the following code listing:

```
DECLARE @Firestations geometry;
SELECT @Firestations = geometry::UnionAggregate(Location) FROM MA_Firestations;

SELECT dbo.GeometryAlphaShape(@Firestations, 30000)
UNION ALL
SELECT @Firestations.STBuffer(1000);
```

Notice how, rather than hug the coastline around Boston (towards the east of the state, where the points are most concentrated), the alpha shape now incorporates too large an area, including regions of sea in Massachusetts Bay and Nantucket Sound.

Figure 15-14. An alpha shape created from the firestations in Massachusetts using an alpha value of 30,000

Getting the Alpha Value "Just Right"

The alpha value used to create the image in Figure 15-13 was too small, and the alpha value used in Figure 15-14 was too large. But, rather like in the story of "Goldilocks and the Three Bears," somewhere between the two should be a value of alpha that is "just right," one that is small enough to create a hull that hugs the outside boundary of the state closely, while not being so small as to introduce any interior cavities. The exact value to use will vary from dataset to dataset, but in this case I find an alpha value of 11,000 creates a relatively aesthetically pleasing result, as shown in Figure 15-15. The code to create this image is as follows:

```
DECLARE @Firestations geometry;
SELECT @Firestations = geometry::UnionAggregate(Location) FROM MA_Firestations;

SELECT dbo.GeometryAlphaShape(@Firestations, 11000)
UNION ALL
SELECT @Firestations.STBuffer(1000);
```

Figure 15-15. An alpha shape created from the firestations in Massachussetts using an alpha value of 11,000

The result is still not perfect; the islands of Nantucket and Martha's Vineyard at the bottom right of the map have dissolved, as has a section in the middle of the Cape Cod peninsula, However, it successfully captures the general shape of the state more accurately than a simple convex hull.

■ **Note** The photo-sharing website Flickr uses alpha shapes to create outline shapes of different regions of the world. Geotagged photos uploaded to the site are associated with one or more Where On Earth (WOE) identifiers, which are descriptive identifiers of where a photo was taken. By creating alpha shapes around the locations of all those photos identified with a given WOE ID (all photos taken in "London," for example), Flickr has built up a crowd-sourced set of geographic boundaries, quite separate from any political or administrative definition of those locations. It's a fascinating idea, and you can download the resulting dataset in shapefile format from http://www.flickr.com/services/shapefiles/2.0/

Voronoi Tessellations

A Voronoi tessellation (also called a Voronoi diagram), like the Delaunay triangulation, creates a single mesh of connected polygons based on a set of points in a dataset. The key differences between the Voronoi tessellation and the Delaunay triangulation are that:

- In a Delaunay triangulation, the mesh is formed from a set of connected triangular faces. A Voronoi tessellation is also formed from a set of nonoverlapping polygons, but they do not have to be triangles; they can be any n-sided convex polygon.

- In a Delaunay triangulation the triangles are drawn between points, so that each point in the dataset defines a vertex at which triangles meet. However, in a Voronoi tessellation each polygon in the mesh is formed around the points in the dataset. Each Voronoi polygon contains one (and only one) point in the dataset.

The Delaunay triangulation and Voronoi tessellation of a given set of points are directly related: each point at which Delaunay triangles meet corresponds to the center of a Voronoi polygon, and each point at which Voronoi polygons meet is the circumcenter of a Delaunay triangle. In mathematical terms, the Delaunay triangulation and Voronoi tessellation are referred to as *dual structures,* knowledge of either one provides all the information required to create the other.

The relationship between the Delaunay triangulation and Voronoi tessellation of a set of points is illustrated in Figure 15-16.

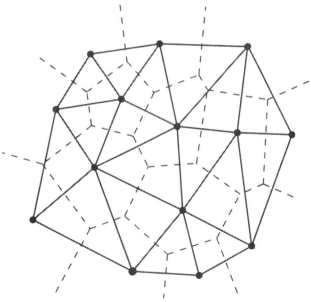

Figure 15-16. Delaunay triangulation (solid lines) and Voronoi tessellation (dashed lines) of a set of points

As with Delaunay triangulations, Voronoi tessellations have applications in three-dimensional computer graphics. They also have uses in spatial analysis, because the Voronoi cell around any site P contains all those points that lie closer to P than to any other site included in the tesselation. You can think of Voronoi diagrams as being a materialized form of the nearest neighbor query. You can easily find the nearest neighbor site of any point in a dataset by simply looking at the Voronoi cell in which it is contained. The shape and size of the polygons in a Voronoi tessellation provide a good visual analysis of the distribution of underlying points.

Adapting the Triangulation Code to Create a Voronoi Tesselation

Just as alpha shapes can be easily derived from the Delaunay triangulation, so too can Voronoi tessellations be created with only minor modifications to the generic triangulation algorithm created at the beginning of this chapter.

Firstly, unlike a Delaunay triangulation, a Voronoi tessellation has no defined boundary and, theoretically, the cells that lie on the exterior of a Voronoi tesselation extend outwards on an infinite plane. SQL Server won't allow us to define a polygon that extends to infinity so, instead, we'll define the exterior Voronoi cells as extending up to the edges of the supertriangle created for the Delaunay triangulation. In order to do this, we need to ensure that we do not remove the supertriangle from the set of triangles after triangulation is complete.

The second change is that once the triangular mesh has been completed, instead of returning each triangle, we will create new convex Polygons by connecting the circumcenters of the triangles around each point. The Polygon created from the circumcenters of all the Delaunay triangles that share a vertex defines the Voronoi cell around that point.

Listed below is the revised output function from the GeometryTriangulate code:

```
foreach (SqlGeometry V in Vertex)
{
  // Initialise a new geometry to hold the Voronoi polygon
  SqlGeometry vp = SqlGeometry.STGeomFromText(new SqlChars("POINT EMPTY"), srid);

  // Look through each triangle
  foreach (SqlGeometry Tri in Triangle)
  {
    // If the triangle intersects this point
    if (Tri.STIntersects(V))
    {
      // Add the circumcentre of this triangle to the list
      vp = vp.STUnion(VCircumcentre(Tri));
    }
  }
  // Create Voronoi polygon from convex hull of the circumcentres of intersecting triangles
  vp = vp.STConvexHull();

  record.SetValues(V, vp);
  SqlContext.Pipe.SendResultsRow(record);
}
```

Having made the necessary changes, import the assembly and register a new GeometryVoronoi function as follows:

```
CREATE PROCEDURE dbo.GeometryVoronoi(@Points geometry)
AS EXTERNAL NAME ProSpatialCh15.[ProSpatial.Ch15.StoredProcedures].GeometryVoronoi;
GO
```

413

A Practical Example: Outbreaks of Cholera in Victorian London

Dr. John Snow was a physician and statistician who lived in Victorian England. He is widely recognized as being the founder of the modern science of epidemiology, and his methods of statistical analysis and pioneering use of maps still influence geographic analysis today in the fields of medicine and beyond.

In August 1854, a severe outbreak of cholera occurred in the Soho district of Central London. At the time, cholera was largely believed to be an airborne disease spread by *miasma* (pollution, or "bad air"). However, Dr. Snow believed instead that the disease was carried through infected water. To prove his theory, he plotted the location of all of the reported cholera deaths on a map, together with the location of all of the water pumps in the area from which people would have drawn their drinking water. His spot map, reproduced in Figure 15-17, was one of the first uses of plotting data on a map in such a fashion.

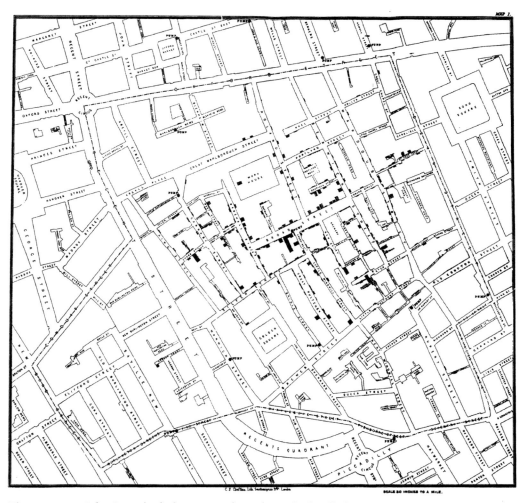

Figure 15-17. John Snow's cholera map of London. Black tally lines indicate the number of reported cholera deaths at each location.

What John Snow discovered was that the vast majority of cholera deaths were centered around the location of a single water pump on Broad Street, or, at those locations for which the pump was closest by travel time, even if not by distance. Assuming that people always obtained their water from the closest water pump, this helped to confirm Dr Snow's theory of how cholera spread. He also explained some of the outlying deaths, as some of those victims had chosen to obtain their water from the Broad Street pump rather than their closest pump (as it was believed that the water of the Broad Street pump tasted better). After Dr. Snow petitioned the council to remove the handle from the Broad Street pump, preventing any water being drawn from it, the death rate dramatically dropped. And the rest, they say, is history.

You can simulate some of Dr. Snow's analysis using Voronoi tessellations in SQL Server. Firstly, we can create a MultiPoint geometry defining the locations of all the water pumps in the Soho area. The coordinate system we'll use will be SRID 27700 (The Ordnance Survey National Grid of Great Britain), as in the following code listing:

```
DECLARE @Pumps geometry;
SET @Pumps = geometry::STMPointFromText('MULTIPOINT ((529180 181359), (529523 181356),
  (529441 181333), (529184 181195), (529194 181079), (529393 181021), (529747 180923),
  (529613 180895), (529451 180825), (529295 180794), (529204 180667), (529589 180666))',
  27700);
```

Now, we can use the GeometryVoronoi tessellation function to define the areas of all those points that lie closest to each pump. However, we won't return the Voronoi cells directly. What we'll do instead is to insert the cells into a temporary table first, as follows:

```
CREATE TABLE #PumpAreas (
  PumpID int IDENTITY(1,1),
  PumpArea geometry
);
INSERT INTO #PumpAreas(PumpArea)
EXEC GeometryVoronoi @Pumps;
```

Why bother with the temporary table? Recall that the exterior cells of a Voronoi tessellation theoretically extend to infinity. In our GeometryVoronoi function, they actually extend to the edges of the Delaunay supertriangle, but this still isn't good, since it suggests that the cells extend beyond the geographic boundaries of the source dataset. To ensure that the analysis remains valid, we'll clip the Voronoi cells to the edges of the dataset from which they were created (since, beyond that, we do not know where the location of any further pumps lie that may alter the nature of the tessellation). We can do this by updating the PumpAreas temporary table, and using the STIntersection() method to clip each Voronoi cell to contain only those areas that lie within the boundaries of the map:

```
DECLARE @MapExtent geometry;
SET @MapExtent = geometry::STPolyFromText('POLYGON ((528895 180562, 529804 180562,
529804 181408, 528895 181408, 528895 180562))', 27700);

UPDATE #PumpAreas
SET PumpArea = PumpArea.STIntersection(@MapExtent);
```

At this point, you can visualize the location of each pump, together with the Voronoi cell around it, by executing the following code listing:

```
DECLARE @Pumps geometry;
SET @Pumps = geometry::STMPointFromText('MULTIPOINT ((529180 181359), (529523 181356), (529441
181333), (529184 181195), (529194 181079), (529393 181021), (529747 180923), (529613 180895),
(529451 180825), (529295 180794), (529204 180667), (529589 180666))', 27700);
```

415

```
SELECT @Pumps.STBuffer(10)
UNION ALL
SELECT PumpArea FROM #PumpAreas;
```

The results are illustrated in Figure 15-18.

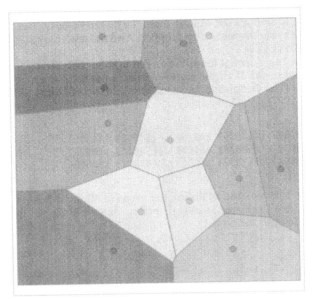

Figure 15-18. *Locations of waterpumps and the Voronoi cells sited around them*

The Voronoi cells illustrated in Figure 15-18 are Polygons that represent the materialized view of the "nearest neighbors" to each pump. (Note that this is a simplified approach compared to Snow's analysis, since the Polygons represent nearest neighbors calculated by simple linear distance and don't account for the travel distance to each pump along the streets of Victorian London, for example.)

To continue the analysis, we now need to consider the number of deaths occurring in locations within each cell.

We'll define the location of each property at which a death occurred, like the pumps, as a Point geom.etry using SRID 27700, and record the number of deaths at that property in an int column, as follows:

```
CREATE TABLE Cholera_deaths(
  ID int IDENTITY(1,1) NOT NULL,
  NumDeaths int,
  geom27700 geometry
);
```

Execute the code listing accompanying this chapter to populate this table with data. Having done so, you can then quickly visualize the distribution of cholera deaths in the regions closest to each pump as shown in the following code listing, the results of which are illustrated in Figure 15-19:

```
SELECT PumpArea
FROM #PumpAreas
UNION ALL SELECT
geom27700.STBuffer(2*SQRT(NumDeaths)) FROM Cholera_Deaths;
```

■ **Note** Rather than buffering each location in direct proportion to the number of deaths, I've buffered each location in proportion to the square root of the number of deaths. This has the effect of creating circles in the Spatial Results tab whose area varies relative to the data value they represent (rather than circles whose *radius* is proportional to the value in question). When creating maps that represent data using proportionally sized shapes this is generally considered a good practice, because users typically perceive and compare elements based on their relative area (as in a histogram) rather than based on a linear dimension such as radius.

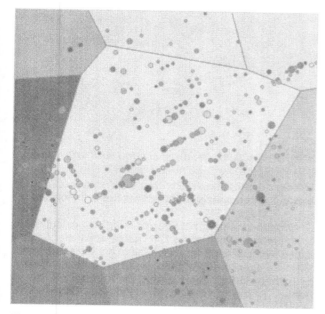

***Figure 15-19.** Plotting proportionally sized circles representing the number of cholera deaths at each property overlaid on the Voronoi cells formed around each pump*

It is obvious from a visual examination of Figure 15-19 that the majority of deaths occurred at locations contained within the Voronoi cell around the central water pump on Broad Street. To quantify this finding, we can execute one last code listing, as follows:

```
SELECT
    PumpArea,
    (SELECT
      SUM(NumDeaths)
      FROM Cholera_Deaths WHERE
      geom27700.STWithin(PumpArea) = 1
    ) AS NumDeaths
FROM #PumpAreas;
```

Switching to the Spatial Results tab and selecting NumDeaths as the label column gives the result shown in Figure 15-20.

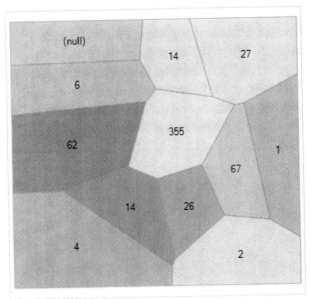

Figure 15-20. The number of cholera deaths occurring within the Voronoi cell around each water pump.

Three hundred fifty-five of the 578 recorded cholera deaths occurred within the Voronoi cell surrounding the Broad Street pump, with hardly any deaths occurring in those Voronoi cells formed around pumps towards the edge of the map.

Voronoi tessellations can be used as an efficient method to perform nearest-neighbor calculations. In this example, we could have calculated the nearest pump for each of the 578 victims separately, using one of the nearest-neighbor query patterns described in Chapter 12 (and we'd have got the same result if we had done so). However, having created the Voronoi tessellation of those points, it is much more efficient to determine the nearest neighbor of any point by simply determining the Voronoi cell in which it lies.

Summary

In this chapter, you learned about triangulation and tessellation.

- The process of triangulation creates a continuous mesh of nonoverlapping polygons formed from a set of points.

- There are many possible triangulations of a set of points, but the most common (and useful) triangulation is the Delaunay triangulation, which is the unique triangulated surface formed from a set of points in which the circumcircle of every triangle is empty.

- Delaunay triangulations have many uses, and I showed you three different practical applications:

    - Creating surface models of 3D terrain

    - Creating alpha shapes that can approximate the concave hull of a shape

    - Deriving a Voronoi tessellation to identify nearest neighbors

CHAPTER 16

Visualization and User Interface

Spatial data, by its very nature, lends itself to graphical display; we do not think of a country, a place, or a route as a set of numeric coordinates, but as a physical object in the world with a location and shape. Text-based formats such as well-known text (WKT) are all very well as a method of exchanging spatial data, but they're simply not viable options for presenting or analyzing that information (and well-known binary is even worse!). Instead, we generally want to portray spatial data in a way that lets us visually examine the shape and location of each element, as well as consider the proximity and relationships between different elements in space. In other words, we expect spatial data to be graphically represented on a map of some sort.

There are many different ways of displaying spatial features with their associated properties on a map; for example, cartographic symbols representing cities can be proportionally sized to represent the population of each city, while polygons representing countries can be colored to represent their relative wealth or another economic or demographic measure. Generally, such thematic maps plot only a single attribute value associated with each feature (i.e., they are univariate). It is also possible to represent multiple attributes on a map by using, say, different sizes, colors, and marker symbols to encode three different dimensions of data. However, this can quickly become confusing, so be careful not to overload your map with too much information.

Computer-based visualizations are not limited only to presenting a static, top-down map view, as used in a traditional cartographic projection, "geobrowsers" such as Google Earth (http://earth.google.com) provide rich graphical interfaces that allow users to explore spatial data in a completely immersive, natural way, enabling multiple layers of information to be placed individually or combined on a virtual globe that can be navigated in three-dimensional space. That data can even be animated to explore changes in spatio-temporal data over time.

In this chapter, we'll examine some of the different options available for visualizing spatial data, and a little about interface design allowing users to interact with that data. Note that the tools provided with SQL Server itself are fairly limited in this respect, so I'll be making use of some well-known third-party applications—Google Earth and Microsoft Bing Maps—to provide ready-made presentation layers for spatial data from SQL Server.

The SSMS Spatial Results Tab

Before looking at more complex visualization solutions, let's start by considering the tools provided "out-of-the-box" with SQL Server itself, such as within SQL Server Management Studio. Normally, the results of any T-SQL statements executed in SQL Server Management Studio are displayed in the Results tab, represented in tabular format. However, after executing a SELECT statement that returns one or more columns of geometry or geography data, you'll also have the option to switch to the Spatial Results tab, which displays the query results in a graphical fashion.

For example, try executing the following code listing, which creates a five-sided geography Polygon containing an interior ring, representing the U.S. Department of Defense Pentagon building:

```
SELECT
  'The Pentagon' AS Label,
  geography::STPolyFromText(
    'POLYGON(
      ( -77.053224 38.87086, -77.054683 38.87304, -77.057880 38.87280,
        -77.058492 38.87022, -77.055563 38.86907, -77.053224 38.87086 ),
      ( -77.055820 38.87029, -77.056936 38.87074, -77.056732 38.87171,
        -77.055477 38.87185, -77.054919 38.87098, -77.055820 38.87029 )
    )',
    4326
  ) AS Geometry;
```

In the results pane at the bottom of the screen, you will see the standard tabular results showing the name of the feature, and SQL Server's binary representation of the geometry. However, notice the choice of three tabs available at the top of the results pane: Results, Spatial Results, and Messages, as illustrated in Figure 16-1.

	Label	Geometry
1	The Pentagon	0xE610000001040C00000081B22957786F434030D7A20568...

Figure 16-1. The Spatial Results tab.

To view the results of the query displayed in a graphical fashion, simply click on the Spatial Results tab. You will see the results illustrated in Figure 16-2.

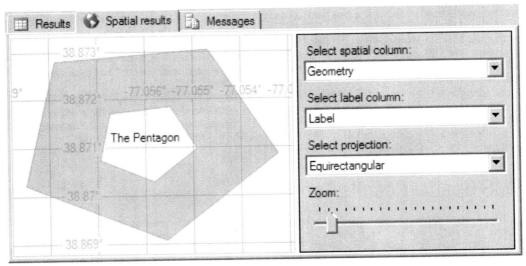

Figure 16-2. Viewing the results of a query on the Spatial Results tab

This is probably pretty familiar to you; I've already illustrated the Spatial Results tab several times in this book to demonstrate the results of various code listings. And this is exactly the purpose of the Spatial Results tab: to provide a quick "sense-check" of the results of any spatial queries. In the following sections, I'll give you a couple of tips to make the Spatial Results tab more useful:

Add a Buffer to Points

When displaying Point geometries, (which, by definition, are infinitely small), you'll find that they are quite hard to see on the Spatial Results tab, plotted as only a single pixel. To make Point data easier to visualize on the Spatial Results tab you can use STBuffer(), BufferWithCurves(), or BufferWithTolerance() to add a buffer of fixed radius around each Point, creating small circular Polygon geometries centered on each Point instead.

You only need to apply this buffer to Points, so use a CASE statement to check the dimension of each geometry in a resultset; if the value returned by STDimension() is 0 then you're dealing with a Point or MultiPoint geometry and a buffer should be applied, otherwise let the geometry pass through as it is. Here's an example code listing:

```
DECLARE @MixedGeometries TABLE (
  geom geometry
);
INSERT INTO @MixedGeometries VALUES
  ('POINT(2 1)'),
  ('POINT(3 4)'),
  ('LINESTRING(1 1, 5 3)'),
  ('LINESTRING(1 4, 2 0)');

-- It's very hard to see the results of this query on the Spatial Results tab
SELECT * FROM @MixedGeometries;

-- Adding a buffer around zero-dimensional geometries creates small circular Polygons
SELECT
  CASE geom.STDimension()
    WHEN 0 THEN geom.STBuffer(0.1)
    ELSE geom
  END AS geom
FROM @MixedGeometries;
```

Note that this is only a "hack" solution to make Point data easier to see in the Spatial Results tab, which may help in performing a quick sense-check of the data. I certainly wouldn't recommend that you change your Point data into Polygons as a general rule for this reason alone!

Create a Base Layer Against Which to Display Your Data

A spatial query will generally return a subset of data containing one or more particular features of interest, but you may well find that those features only really make sense when considered in a wider context. For example, plotting the results of a query to find the current locations of a set of delivery vehicles doesn't help much unless you also consider the road network and locations between which they are traveling. For this purpose, I keep a set of tables representing various simplified "base layers"— country outlines, rivers and roads, major towns, and the like—which I can select and include together with the results of any query to add background context while still in SQL Server Management Studio.

To add context to the Spatial Results tab, use a UNION ALL query to append the geometries from the appropriate base layer to the results of your query. You may also need to add dummy values so that the columns of data in the two result sets are aligned.

▓ **Tip** The sources listed at the beginning of Chapter 5 are good places to look for layers of base data.

For example, suppose that you have a table of all those settlements in Australia with a population greater than 15,000 (a dataset that can be downloaded from http://www.geonames.org). Selected in isolation, the data in this table would be displayed in the Spatial Results tab as shown in Figure 16-3:

```
SELECT Name, geog4326 FROM Australian_Settlements;
```

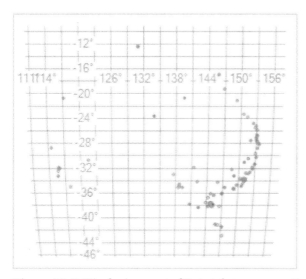

Figure 16-3. *Displaying a set of Point data representing settlements in Australia*

To add useful context to this display, you might want to add a UNION ALL statement to append a Polygon geometry to the result set representing the country of Australia. In the following code listing, I select the appropriate country outline from a Country_Outlines table, which I maintain for exactly this sort of situation:

```
SELECT Name, geog4326
FROM Australian_Settlements

UNION ALL

SELECT Name, geog4326
FROM Country_Outlines
WHERE Name='Australia';
```

The Spatial Results tab would then display the point dataset against a backdrop as shown in Figure 16-4.

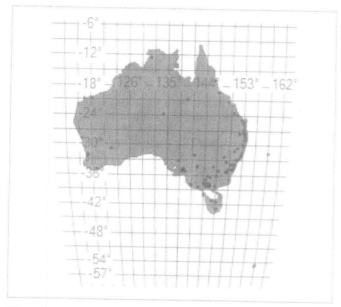

Figure 16-4. Displaying a set of Point data against a background layer representing Australia.

Customize the Display

There are a handful of customization options in the right-hand pane of the Spatial Results tab, as follows:

Select spatial column: Determines which column of geography/geometry from the resultset should be plotted in the display. The Spatial Results tab can only plot data from one column at a time; it is not possible to overlay data from multiple columns. If you execute a SELECT query that returns more than one column of geometry/geography data then you must choose which column should be displayed.

Select label column: Each feature on the map may be labeled according to the value of another column included in the result set, such as an integer id, or varchar description. Labels for LineString features will be placed on the path of the LineString, while labels for Polygons will appear within the Polygon. It is worth noting that SQL Server employs a label placement algorithm that tries to avoid cluttering up the Spatial Results display with too much text, but one side effect of this algorithm is that only some features in a set of results may be labeled. Point features will never be labeled, although it is still possible to view the attributes of a Point by hovering your mouse cursor over the feature on the Spatial Results tab.

Select projection: (geography only) The geography datatype stores angular coordinates from a geographic coordinate system. However, in order to display them on any flat display, including the Spatial Results tab, they must be projected in some way (note that the data itself remains unprojected; it is projected only for the purposes of display). The Spatial Results tab offers four common projection methods: Equirectangular, Mercator, Robinson, and Bonne. If you are plotting results from the geometry datatype, this option is not available. geometry coordinates will always be displayed in the same two-dimensional coordinate system in which they are already defined.

Zoom: This slider allows you to zoom in and out of the rendered map.

Show grid lines: Highlighting this check box allows you to plot the graticule of latitude and longitude (or *x* and *y*) values over the map window.

The options described here are the only customizations available; you can't, for example, choose to color features differently depending on the value of a certain attribute, or change other aspects of their visual appearance. There's also a limit on the total number of elements that can be displayed on the Spatial Results tab, which is capped at 5,000. If your geometries are particularly complex, you may find that you are not able to display this many.

Finally, even if you do end up creating a beautiful display of your data in the Spatial Results tab (such as my attempt to recreate the Mona Lisa as a geometry MultiPolygon, shown in Figure 16-5), there's no way to export the image or embed it in any other application.

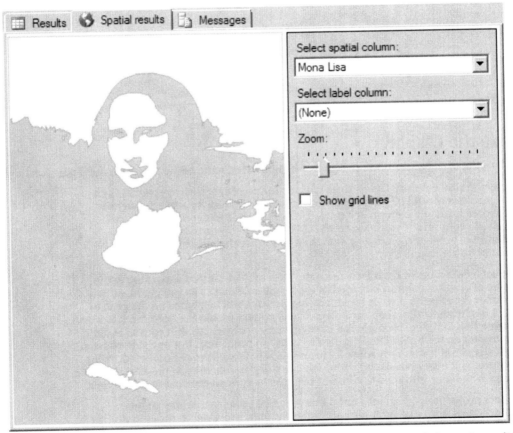

Figure 16-5. Visualizations in the Spatial Results tab, however great their artistic merit, can't be exported

For these reasons, the Spatial Results tab is clearly not a useful tool in terms of presenting or sharing the output of spatial queries with end users. For this, we will have to look to other tools.

Thematic Mapping with Google Earth

Google Earth, the popular "virtual globe" application, is widely acknowledged as contributing to the massive growth in consumer interest and awareness of spatial applications in recent years. The combination of satellite imagery, aerial photography, and other data sources overlaid on a 3D geographic model of the entire globe, together with a responsive and intuitive interface was revolutionary when first released in 2005, and still holds a significant consumer "wow" factor to this day.

The first time I used Google Earth, my immediate first thought (like that, I imagine, of many others) was to see what my house looked like "from space," followed by zooming to various landmarks around the globe (the Eiffel Tower, Sydney Opera House, the Taj Mahal). However, far from being merely a pretty "spinny globe" of amazing imagery, Google Earth also holds significant potential as a graphical user interface in which end-users can explore spatial data from many sources.

To demonstrate this, we'll use Google Earth to display a dataset that shows the ecological footprint of different countries around the world. Broadly speaking, an ecological footprint is a measure of how sustainable a given way of life is, in terms of the amount of resources it demands, and the capacity of the earth to absorb the waste ir produces. An ecological footprint of 1.0 or less indicates that the Earth can sustain a particular way of life. A footprint of 2.0 suggests that it requires the natural capacity of two Earths if the whole of humanity lived according to that lifestyle.

The end result that we're aiming to achieve in this example is shown in Figure 16-6, in which different countries are colored on Google Earth according to their ecological footprint. Clicking on a country brings up an information balloon with additional information.

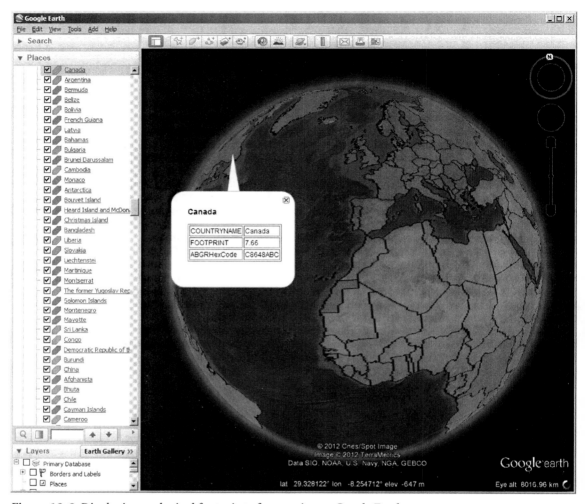

Figure 16-6. Displaying ecological footprint of countries on Google Earth

■ **Note** To follow this example you'll need the Google Earth application, which can be downloaded from
http://earth.google.com

Getting the Data

The source dataset for this example can be found in the code download accompanying this book. It contains three columns: the name of a country, a geography Polygon representing the country outline, and a numeric value representing its ecological footprint as published by the Global Footprint Network in 2010. The structure of the EcoFootprint table is as follows:

```
CREATE TABLE EcoFootprint (
  COUNTRYNAME varchar(255) NULL,
  SHAPE geography NULL,
  FOOTPRINT decimal(18, 2) NULL
);
```

A typical row of data inserted into this table is as follows:

```
INSERT INTO EcoFootprint (COUNTRYNAME, SHAPE, FOOTPRINT)
VALUES (
  'Albania',
  0xE610000001040F0000008E0B0742B2824440A80E80B8AB6F3340FAD5E3BED52C444078812040867A3340FE1…
  1.86
);
```

In order to use this data as the basis for a thematic map in Google Earth, we must first determine the color in which each country should be shown based on its relative footprint, and then export the data in a suitable format. These steps are described in the following sections.

Creating a Color Range

We'll display the data on a *chloropleth* map in Google Earth, in which the footprint of each country is represented by the color in which it is shaded. We therefore need to determine an appropriate color palette based on the range of values in the ecological fooprint column. In keeping with normal user expectation, countries with higher (worse) ecological footprints will be colored red, while countries with lower (better) footprints will be colored green, with a linear gradient being applied to the range of values in between.

The following code listing adds a new column to the EcoFootprint table and populates it with hexadecimal color codes representing the color with which each country will be shaded. The hex color code is stored as a char(8) value, in which the first two characters represent an opacity (alpha) value, and subsequent character pairs represent the blue, green, and red components of each color. This matches the ABGR format used by Google Earth, although note that it differs from the more common ARGB ordering with which you may be familiar. As the value of a country's footprint increases, the red component of the corresponding color increases up to a maximum of 255, while the green component reduces towards 0:

```
ALTER TABLE EcoFootPrint
ADD  ABGRHexCode char(8);
GO

-- Determine the maximum footprint value from the dataset
DECLARE @MaxFootPrint decimal(18,2) = (SELECT MAX(FootPrint) FROM EcoFootprint);

-- Calculate the color code for each country based on their %age of the maximum value
UPDATE EcoFootPrint
SET ABGRHexCode =
COALESCE(
  CONVERT(varchar(max),
    CAST(200 AS BINARY(1)) -- Alpha
    + CAST(100 AS BINARY(1)) -- Blue
    + CAST(CAST(200 - (FootPrint / @MaxFootPrint * 128) AS INT) AS BINARY(1)) -- Green
    + CAST(CAST(127 + (FootPrint / @MaxFootPrint * 128) AS INT) AS BINARY(1)) -- Red
  , 2),
  'ff808080' -- Grey if no data available
);
```

You can, of course, adjust this code listing to apply a different color gradient to the data as you see fit.

Exporting to KML

Google Earth can't query the data in the EcoFootPrint table directly. Instead, the native file format used by Google Earth is Keyhole Markup Language (KML). We'll export the data from the EcoFootPrint table (including the hex color code associated with each country Polygon) to KML using OGR2OGR, as we did previously in Chapter 5.

Here's the code listing:

```
ogr2ogr
  -f "KML"
  "C:\spatial\ecofootprint.kml"
  "MSSQL:server=localhost;database=prospatial;trusted_connection=yes;"
  -sql "SELECT COUNTRYNAME, FOOTPRINT, SHAPE.STAsBinary(), ABGRHexCode FROM EcoFootprint"
  -overwrite
  -nln "EcoFootprint"
  -dsco NameField="COUNTRYNAME"
```

For more information on the general syntax used in this code listing, please refer back to Chapter 5. In this example, the code listing connects to the specified SQL Server instance running on localhost and executes the query listed specified with the -sql flag to select the contents of the EcoFootprint table. The results are converted to KML format as specified by the -f flag, and saved as c:\spatial\ecofootprint.kml, overwriting any previous existing versions of that file. There is one additional option I've included, -dsco NameField="COUNTRYNAME", which is a dataset creation option specific to the KML format; this option specifies that the COUNTRYNAME column from the dataset should be used to populate the name of each placemark in the KML file, which will cause Google Earth to automatically label each country with the correct name.

Styling the KML File

After exporting the data from SQL Server to KML, load up the resulting file, c:\spatial\ecofootprint.kml (or whatever destination you specified in the previous step), in Visual Studio to examine its contents. The following extract shows the start of the file, including the first Placemark feature representing the country of Algeria:

```
<?xml version="1.0" encoding="utf-8" ?>
<kml xmlns="http://www.opengis.net/kml/2.2">
<Document><Folder><name>EcoFootprint</name>
<Schema name="EcoFootprint" id="EcoFootprint">
  <SimpleField name="Name" type="string"></SimpleField>
  <SimpleField name="Description" type="string"></SimpleField>
  <SimpleField name="COUNTRYNAME" type="string"></SimpleField>
  <SimpleField name="FOOTPRINT" type="float"></SimpleField>
  <SimpleField name="ABGRHexCode" type="string"></SimpleField>
</Schema>
<Placemark>
  <name>Algeria</name>
  <Style>
    <LineStyle><color>ff0000ff</color></LineStyle>
    <PolyStyle><fill>0</fill></PolyStyle>
  </Style>
  <ExtendedData>
```

```
<SchemaData schemaUrl="#EcoFootprint">
  <SimpleData name="COUNTRYNAME">Algeria</SimpleData>
  <SimpleData name="FOOTPRINT">1.79</SimpleData>
  <SimpleData name="ABGRHexCode">C864B98D</SimpleData>
</SchemaData>
</ExtendedData>
<Polygon>
  <outerBoundaryIs>
    <LinearRing>
      <coordinates>
        2.96361,36.802216 0.95,36.450272 -2.209445,35.085831 -1.74722,34.747215
        -1.668056,33.26111 -1.01028,32.508331 -1.180556,32.11055 -2.853889,32.088333
        -3.818334,31.69555 -3.626667,30.97055 -4.920556,30.508053 -5.53833,29.902496
        -7.12389,29.636944 -8.66722,28.709442 -8.66667,27.666664 -8.66679,27.29046
        -6.662778,26.129166 -4.80611,25.000275 1.169662,21.102543 1.1675,20.741108
        1.79583,20.308331 3.233055,19.820274 3.331944,18.976387 4.245277,19.146664
        5.812499,19.44611 7.450807,20.852863 11.986475,23.522305 11.558887,24.3025
        10.25222,24.60583 9.398333,26.153332 9.871666,26.514164 9.948332,27.824444
        9.766388,29.427776 9.30389,30.122498 9.537113,30.23439 9.055277,32.099998
        8.34861,32.533333 7.492499000000123,33.887497 8.251665,34.64444 8.183611,36.524162
        8.62203,36.941368 6.398333,37.086388 5.328055,36.640274 4.785832,36.894722
        2.96361,36.802216
      </coordinates>
    </LinearRing>
  </outerBoundaryIs>
</Polygon>
</Placemark>
...
```

You'll see in this code listing the familiar <Polygon> structure describing the coordinates of the geometry representing Algeria. However, what I'd like to draw your attention to are the other elements of the KML file, particularly the <Schema> element at the top of the file, and the <ExtendedData> element attached to the Placemark.

The <Schema> element is a structured type that defines the fields of custom data associated with each element in this KML file. You can think of this element as being roughly equivalent to the .dbf file that defines the nonspatial attributes of each element in an ESRI shapefile. In this KML document, the <Schema> element has been assigned a name and id of "EcoFootprint" matching the name of the file itself. Within the <Schema> element there is a set of <SimpleElement> entities. These correspond to the columns of data returned from the SQL query, and each has both a name and associated type.

Within the <Placemark> element representing Algeria, you'll see an instance of the <SchemaData> element that references the EcoFootprint Schema, which contains the appropriate COUNTRYNAME, FOOTPRINT and ABGRHexCode values for Algeria.

▧ **Tip** For more information about the structure and elements contained with a KML file and how they are interpreted within Google Earth, consult the Google Earth KML reference guide at

https://developers.google.com/kml/documentation/

The KML file generated by OGR2OGR contains all of the fields of information required to create our thematic map, but it requires a little manipulation first. Currently, the color with which we want each country polygon to be filled is specified in the `ABGRHexCode` element, which is part of the extended data for each Placemark. The XML hierarchy to locate this element in the document is as follows:

```
<Document>
  <Folder>
    <Placemark>
      <ExtendedData>
        <SchemaData>
          <SimpleData name="ABGRHexCode">C864B98D</SimpleData>
```

However, Google Earth expects to find styling information in the `PolyStyle` color element located in the `<Style>` element of a Placemark, as shown here:

```
<Document>
  <Folder>
    <Placemark>
      <Style>
        <PolyStyle>
          <color>C864B98D</color>
```

To correct the structure of the KML document, we'll create an XSL transformation that copies the appropriate `ABGRHexCode` value for each Placemark into a `PolyStyle` color element instead. To do so, create a new XSLT file in Visual Studio and enter the code shown in the following listing:

```
<?xml version="1.0"?>

<xsl:stylesheet
  xmlns:xsl="http://www.w3.org/1999/XSL/Transform"
  xmlns:kml="http://www.opengis.net/kml/2.2"
  version="2.2">

  <xsl:output method="xml" indent="yes" omit-xml-declaration="no" encoding="utf-8"/>

  <!-- By default, allow all elements and attributes to pass through unchanged -->
  <xsl:template match="*">
    <xsl:copy>
      <xsl:copy-of select="@*" />
      <xsl:apply-templates  />
    </xsl:copy>
  </xsl:template>

  <!-- Remove any existing styles -->
  <xsl:template match="kml:Style" />

  <!-- For each Placemark element in the KML file -->
  <xsl:template match="kml:Placemark">
    <xsl:copy>
      <xsl:copy-of select="@*" />

      <!-- Add <Style> element based on the value of the associated ABGRHexCode -->
      <Style>
        <PolyStyle>
          <color>
```

```
      <xsl:value-of
         select="kml:ExtendedData/kml:SchemaData/kml:SimpleData[@name='ABGRHexCode']"/>
      </color>
    </PolyStyle>
  </Style>
  <xsl:apply-templates />
  </xsl:copy>
  </xsl:template>
</xsl:stylesheet>
```

Having input the XML transformation, go to the Visual Studio XML menu and select Start XSLT (with or without debugging). On the Choose Input XML Document dialog box that appears, select the `c:\spatial\ecofootprint.kml` file exported from OGR2OGR (you may have to change the file filter to show all files *.* in order to see the KML file).

Visual Studio will apply the XSL transformation to the source KML file to create a new file with the correct styling elements. Save this file and load it in Google Earth to see the output previously illustrated in Figure 16-6.

Taking It Further

In this example, I've demonstrated one way to take data from an SQL Server table and display it in Google Earth. However, there are many ways in which you could improve and extend this idea.

Firstly, rather than manually export a static KML file using OGR2OGR, you could serve the KML file dynamically on-demand via a web service. (KML is, after all, just a dialect of XML, so it is relatively easy to write a .NET handler that will connect to the database and generate the associated XML.) Rather than loading a local static file, this dynamic KML file could be accessed via a network link, meaning users would always see the latest refreshed and updated view of the data in the SQL Server table.

Remember also that Google Earth can not only display shaded polygon areas: it supports polylines equivalent to SQL Server's LineString geometry, and markers that can be used to portray Points using customizable icons. You can even overlay images and text to add additional context to your map, and create some interactivity by launching information windows when certain elements are clicked, and so on.

Furthermore, the example shown here currently makes little use of the fact that Google Earth presents a (pseudo) 3D view of data. Rather than simply coloring each feature on the map, we could create a 3D prism map that extrudes each feature upwards based on its ecological footprint. Prism maps are conceptually a cross between a column chart and a map, in which the height of each feature represents a corresponding attribute value. Figure 16-7 illustrates an alternative view of the ecological footprint data used in this example, in which both the height and color of each country vary according to its footprint.

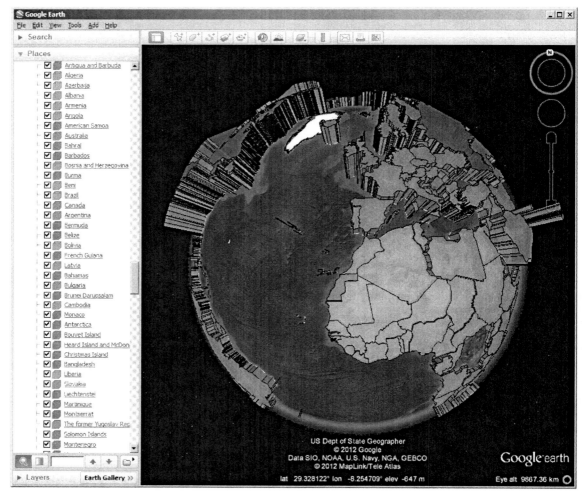

Figure 16-7. A 3D prism map using Google Earth.

Limitations

While Google Earth certainly presents an impressive immersive display medium for users to explore spatial data (particularly datasets that span the whole globe), the level of data interaction it offers is relatively limited. In this example, a single complete KML file containing the ecological footprint of all countries was presented on the map, and no refinement or querying of that data occurs once it is loaded within the Google Earth interface. You can introduce some degree of user interaction with data in Google Earth (displaying pop-up windows with further information when the user clicks on a feature, for example), but the scope of interaction is pretty limited.

Furthermore, it is hard to create a fully fledged, customized application interface based on Google Earth, since you will always be confined to operating within the sandboxed environment of the Google Earth application itself and the functionality it exposes. To overcome this limitation, we can instead create a simple application that harnesses a web-mapping API such as Google Maps or Bing Maps, and this is exactly what I'll demonstrate in the next section.

Creating a Web Map Interface with Bing Maps

Interactive "slippy" map displays such as Google Maps and Bing Maps can be used as a central, two-way user application interface, operating both as a canvas to capture input from users and also to display output to them. In this case, the map becomes not only a presentation layer, but also the main application interface to spatial data held in the database. To demonstrate this approach, we'll create a web application that displays a map of the United States using the Bing Maps AJAX API. When the user clicks any point on the map, the application will trigger a stored procedure that selects information from an SQL Server table about all airports that lie within a certain distance of the chosen location, displays them on the map, and provides a popup information window containing additional information about each. This type of application is similar to that used to provide "store locator" functionality found on many websites, but can easily be adapted to many other situations.

Because we'll be coding this example using standard web conventions such as HTML and Javascript, together with a little .NET server-side scripting, you can extend this example to create a complete customized spatial application incorporating any other web components you desire.

▓ **Note** To follow this example, you'll need to insert a valid Bing Maps key in any code listing where indicated by ENTERYOURBINGMAPSKEY. Instructions on how to obtain a Bing Maps key are described at the beginning of chapter 6. (If you already signed up for a key, you can use the same key here as you did for the geocoding service)

Create the SQL Server Table and Stored Procedure

To begin, execute the SQL script accompanying this chapter to create and populate the table containing details of U.S. airports. The structure of the US_Airports table is as follows:

```
CREATE TABLE US_Airports(
  Code char(4) NULL,
  Name varchar(255) NULL,
  City varchar(255) NULL,
  County varchar(255) NULL,
  State char(2) NULL,
  Location geography NULL,
  Elevation int NULL
);
```

And a typical row inserted into the table looks like this:

```
INSERT INTO US_Airports VALUES (
  '00A ',
  'STONE MOUNTAIN-BRITT MEMORIAL',
  'STONE MOUNTAIN',
  'DE KALB',
  'GA',
  0xE6100000010CC87A6AF5D5E74040D61C2098A30755C0,
  986
);
```

Next, we will create a stored procedure to select all those airports from this table that lie within a given distance of a provided location. This procedure will be called from the web application, which will provide the parameters of where the user clicked on the map (as latitude and longitude coordinates), together with an adjustable radius defining the maximum distance around the point that should be searched. The location of each airport is defined as a geography Point using SRID 4326 so, to be consistent with this, the radius parameter will also be provided in meters.

We'll use the STDistance() method to determine the distance from each airport to the chosen point. Here's the code to create the stored procedure:

```
CREATE PROCEDURE [dbo].[uspAirportLocator]
  @latitude float,
  @longitude float,
  @radius float
AS
BEGIN

  -- Create a geography point from the supplied lat/long
  DECLARE @Point geography;
  SET @Point = geography::Point(@latitude, @longitude, 4326);

  -- Select all airports less than specified distance from this point
  SELECT
    NAME,
    CITY,
    COUNTY,
    STATE,
    Location.Lat AS Latitude,
    Location.Long AS Longitude
  FROM
    US_Airports
  WHERE
    Location.STDistance(@Point) < @radius;
END;
```

That's all that needs to be done in the database back-end, so now we'll turn our attention to creating the client-facing web application.

Creating the Web Application

Launch Visual Studio and select File ➤ New ➤ Project. In the New Project Dialog window that appears, expand the set of installed C# Web templates and highlight the Empty ASP.NET Web Application template. Name the project and choose a location, as shown in Figure 16-8.

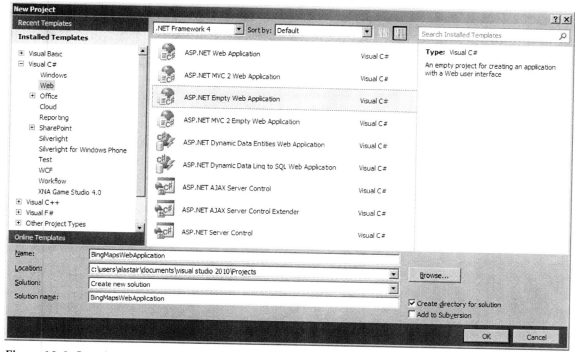

Figure 16-8. Creating an ASP.NET Empty Web Application

Defining the HTML/Javascript

The web application will consist of two elements. The first is the HTML file that defines the structure and elements contained in the user map interface. This file will also contain the Javascript that will add interactivity to the map.

From the Visual Studio menu bar, select Project ➤ Add New Item, and choose to add an HTML Page in the dialog box as shown in Figure 16-9.

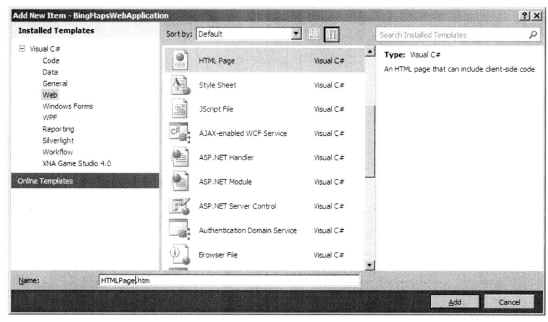

Figure 16-9. Adding a new HTML page to the web application

When the HTML Page has been added it will contain a default template. Replace this with the HTML necessary to define a webpage containing a Bing Maps control, as follows:

```
<!DOCTYPE html PUBLIC "-//W3C//DTD XHTML 1.0 Transitional//EN"
"http://www.w3.org/TR/xhtml1/DTD/xhtml1-transitional.dtd">
<html xmlns="http://www.w3.org/1999/xhtml">
<head>
  <title>Bing Maps Interface</title>
  <script type="text/javascript"
          src="http://ecn.dev.virtualearth.net/mapcontrol/mapcontrol.ashx?v=7.0"></script>
  <script type="text/javascript"
          src="http://ajax.aspnetcdn.com/ajax/jQuery/jquery-1.6.4.min.js"></script>
  <script type="text/javascript">

    // Declare the radius of the search area (in metres)
    radius = 50000;

    // When the browser has finished loading the document
    $(document).ready(function () {

      // Create a new map
      map = new Microsoft.Maps.Map(document.getElementById("mapDiv"),
                        { credentials: "ENTERYOURBINGMAPSKEYHERE",
                          center: new Microsoft.Maps.Location(38, -122),
                          mapTypeId: Microsoft.Maps.MapTypeId.birdseye,
                          zoom: 8
                        });
```

```
  // Listen to mouse clicks on the map
  Microsoft.Maps.Events.addHandler(map, 'click', function (e) {

    // If user clicks on a pushpin
    if (e.targetType == "pushpin") {

      // Create an infobox with information about the selected airport
      var infobox = new Microsoft.Maps.Infobox(
        e.target.getLocation(),
        { title: e.target.Title, description: e.target.Description }
      );

      // Display the infobox on the map
      map.entities.push(infobox);
    }

    // If the user clicks anywhere else on the map
    else {

      // Clear the map
      map.entities.clear();

      // Get the lat/long coordinates of where the mouse clicked
      var point = new Microsoft.Maps.Point(e.getX(), e.getY());
      var loc = map.tryPixelToLocation(point);

      // Draw a circle around this point
      DrawCircleAroundPoint(loc, radius);

      // Find all airports within range of this point
      GetAirportsWithinSearchArea(loc, radius);
    }
  });
});

// Draws a circle of given radius around a location
function DrawCircleAroundPoint(loc, radius) {

  // Convert angular coordinates to radians
  var lat = loc.latitude * Math.PI / 180;
  var lon = loc.longitude * Math.PI / 180;
  var d = radius / 6371000; // angular radius of search area

  // Determine an array of locations lying in a circle around the chosen point
  var locs = [];
  for (var x = 0; x <= 360; x++) {
    var latRadians = Math.asin(Math.sin(lat) * Math.cos(d) + Math.cos(lat) * Math.sin(d)
                        * Math.cos(x * Math.PI / 180));
    var lngRadians = lon + Math.atan2(Math.sin(x * Math.PI / 180) * Math.sin(d)
                    * Math.cos(lat), Math.cos(d) - Math.sin(lat) * Math.sin(latRadians));
    locs.push(new Microsoft.Maps.Location(latRadians / Math.PI * 180,
                                lngRadians / Math.PI * 180));
  }
}
```

```
    // Create a polygon from this array of locations
    var searchArea = new Microsoft.Maps.Polygon(locs, {
      strokeColor: new Microsoft.Maps.Color(150, 255, 0, 0),
      fillColor: new Microsoft.Maps.Color(150, 255, 155, 20)
    });

    // Put the polygon on the map
    map.entities.push(searchArea);
  }

  // Retrieves airports lying within a given radius of supplied location
  // and plots them on the map
  function GetAirportsWithinSearchArea(loc, radius) {
    $.getJSON(
            "Handler.ashx",
            { lat: loc.latitude, long: loc.longitude, radius: radius },
            function (data) {
              for (var i = 0; i < data.length; i++) {
                var loc = new Microsoft.Maps.Location(data[i].Lat, data[i].Long);
                var pushpin = new Microsoft.Maps.Pushpin(loc);
                pushpin.Title = data[i].Name;
                pushpin.Description = data[i].City + ', ' + data[i].State;
                map.entities.push(pushpin);
              }
            });
  }
</script>
<style type="text/css">
  #mapDiv
  {
    width: 800px;
    height: 600px;
    position: relative;
  }
</style>
</head>
<body>
  <div id="mapDiv"></div>
</body>
</html>
```

The preceding code listing defines the HTML document that will be served to the client's web browser. It includes references to the Bing Maps API, defines the overall structure of the page, and contains methods to handle client-side interactivity with the map. It is not my intention to describe this code in any great detail here; readers interested in finding out more about the Bing Maps API should consult the MSDN documentation at http://msdn.microsoft.com/en-us/library/gg427610.aspx.

The primary line of code responsible for adding user interaction to the application is as follows:

```
Microsoft.Maps.Events.addHandler(map, 'click', function (e) { … }
```

This line adds an event handler that listens and responds to mouse clicks on the map. Mouse clicks are handled in one of two ways: if the user clicks anywhere on the background of the map then a circle is first drawn around the chosen point (by the DrawCircleAroundPoint() function) and then the GetAirportsWithinSearchArea() function is called to plot any airports lying within the area selected. Alternatively, if the user clicks on an airport that is already plotted on the map, then an information box is displayed containing additional information about that airport. This logic is contained in the following lines:

```
// If user clicks on an airport pushpin
if (e.targetType == "pushpin") {

  // Create an infobox with information about the selected airport
  var infobox = new Microsoft.Maps.Infobox(
    e.target.getLocation(),
    { title: e.target.Title, description: e.target.Description }
  );

  // Display the infobox on the map
  map.entities.push(infobox);
}

// If the user clicks anywhere else on the map
else {

  // Clear the map
  map.entities.clear();

  // Get the lat/long coordinates of where the mouse clicked
  var point = new Microsoft.Maps.Point(e.getX(), e.getY());
  var loc = map.tryPixelToLocation(point);

  // Draw a circle around this point
  DrawCircleAroundPoint(loc, radius);

  // Find all airports within range of this point
  GetAirportsWithinSearchArea(loc, radius);
}
```

Notice that, on the last line of this event handler, the action to locate and plot airports within the requested search area is handled by a call to another method - GetAirportsWithinSearchArea(). This function is defined as follows:

```
function GetAirportsWithinSearchArea(loc, radius) {
    $.getJSON(
            "Handler.ashx",
            { lat: loc.latitude, long: loc.longitude, radius: radius },

            function (data) {

                // Loop through the response
                for (var i = 0; i < data.length; i++) {

                    // Create a pushpin at each location
                    var loc = new Microsoft.Maps.Location(data[i].Lat, data[i].Long);
                    var pushpin = new Microsoft.Maps.Pushpin(loc);

                    // Add title and description attributes
                    pushpin.Title = data[i].Name;
                    pushpin.Description = data[i].City + ', ' + data[i].State;
```

```
                        // Add the pushpin to the map
                        map.entities.push(pushpin);
                }
        });
}
```

The `GetAirportsWithinSearchArea()` function is responsible for displaying the relevant airports on the map in reponse to a mouse click by the user. However, a Javascript function running in a client browser cannot directly retrieve such information from SQL Server. Instead, it makes an HTTP GET request to the specified URL, `Handler.ashx`, providing the relevant `lat`, `long`, and `radius` parameters. The function then loops through the JSON-encoded response, creating a Pushpin element at each coordinate pair in the results and assigning them a title and description attribute, before adding them to the map. A simplified illustration of the architecture involved is illustrated in Figure 16-10.

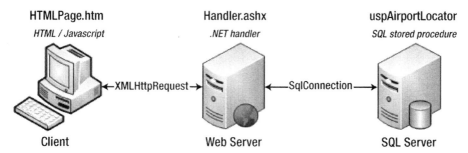

Figure 16-10. *Architecture of a client-side web mapping application interfacing with SQL Server*

We've already created the HTML page and the stored procedure; the final element required for this application is to create the intermediate handler, `Handler.ashx`, which will pass requests from the HTML Page to SQL Server, execute the relevant stored procedure, and return the results. This is discussed in the next section.

Retrieving JSON Data from SQL Server to the Webpage

The intermediate handler could be written in one of several server-side scripting languages; for this example we'll create a generic .NET handler written in C#.

The handler will return results to the web client in Javascript Object Notation format. To do this, we'll make use of the .NET `JSONSerializer` class.

1. To add a new generic handler to the project, select Project ➤ Add New File ➤ Generic Handler.

2. To include the JSONSerializer class, choose Project ➤ Add Reference and, from the .NET tab, highlight `System.Web.Extensions.dll`. Then click ok to add the reference.

The handler will retrieve the three parameters passed from the GET request (lat, long, and radius), and send these to the SQL Server stored procedure. The results of the procedure are read and serialized as JSON, which is then sent back to the webpage to be added to the map. Here's the code listing required for the handler:

```
using System;
using System.Collections.Generic;
using System.Linq;
```

```
using System.Web;
using Microsoft.SqlServer.Types;
using System.Data.SqlClient;
using System.Data.Sql;
using System.Data;
using System.Data.Common;
using System.Web.Script.Serialization;

namespace ProSpatial.Ch16
{
  /// <summary>
  /// Summary description for Handler
  /// </summary>
  public class Handler : IHttpHandler
  {

    public void ProcessRequest(HttpContext context)
    {

      // Define connection to SQL server
      using (SqlConnection conn = new SqlConnection(@"server=localhost;" +
                    "Trusted_Connection=yes;" + "database=ProSpatial"))
      {
        // Open the connection
        conn.Open();

        // Define the stored procedure to execute
        SqlCommand cmd = new SqlCommand("dbo.uspAirportLocator", conn);
        cmd.CommandType = CommandType.StoredProcedure;

        // Send the coordinates of the clicked point
        cmd.Parameters.Add("@Latitude", SqlDbType.Float);
        cmd.Parameters["@Latitude"].Value = context.Request.Params["lat"];
        cmd.Parameters.Add("@Longitude", SqlDbType.Float);
        cmd.Parameters["@Longitude"].Value = context.Request.Params["long"];
        cmd.Parameters.Add("@Radius", SqlDbType.Float);
        cmd.Parameters["@Radius"].Value = context.Request.Params["radius"];

        // Create a reader for the result set
        SqlDataReader rdr = cmd.ExecuteReader();
        var dataQuery = from d in rdr.Cast<DbDataRecord>()
                        select new
                        {
                          Name = (String)d["Name"],
                          City = (String)d["City"],
                          State = (String)d["State"],
                          Lat = (Double)d["Latitude"],
                          Long = (Double)d["Longitude"]
                        };

        // Serialise as JSON
        var data = dataQuery.ToArray();
        JavaScriptSerializer serializer = new JavaScriptSerializer();
        String jsonData = serializer.Serialize(data);
```

441

```
        // Send results back to the webpage
        context.Response.ContentType = "text/plain";
        context.Response.Write(jsonData);
      }
    }

    public bool IsReusable
    {
      get
      {
        return false;
      }
    }
  }
}
```

Remember to change the connection string in the preceding listing as necessary. With the stored procedure, handler, and HTML page in place, we can test out the application. Right-click on the HTML page from the Visual Studio project explorer pane and select View In Browser (or hit Ctrl+Shift+W). You should initially be presented with a map centered on the west coast of America near San Francisco, as shown in Figure 16-11.

Figure 16-11. A Bing Map centered on the west coast of America

Clicking on the map will cause the Javascript event handler to fire, which makes an XmlHttpRequest to the .NET handler. The handler connects to SQL Server, executes the uspAirportLocator stored procedure and returns the results as a JSON string which is deserialized, and pushpins are added to the map at each location.

Clicking on a pushpin creates a popup infobox that displays the title and description attributes of the clicked airport, as shown in Figure 16-12.

Figure 16-12. Clicking on a pushpin displays an information box containing details of the selected airport.

Taking It Further

With the basic structure now in place, it is easy to think of a number of ways in which this application could be modified or extended. For example:

- Users could manually specify the radius of the search area around the clicked point, which could be passed as an additional parameter to the stored procedure.

- Pushpin markers representing each airport could use different icons to represent how many runways they had, the amount of passengers that use that airport, or whether parking was available.

- You could plot many more types of features on the map. The U.S. National Transportation Atlas database from which the data in this example was sourced also contains details of railway tracks, hazardous material routes, ferry terminals, and many other elements that could be added to the map.

- Combine this application with the geocoding function demonstrated in Chapter 6 so that, instead of clicking on a point, the user types in an address as the center point of the search.

- Rather than have a simple site-centered search about a point, let the user trace a line or draw an abstract shape on the map and use the geography STIntersects() method in the stored procedure to determine those airports that lay within the chosen area.

Unlike Google Earth, which is primarily designed as a self-contained desktop application, the Bing Maps AJAX control has a complete application programming interface, documented at http://msdn.microsoft.com/en-us/library/gg427611.aspx, allowing you to customize almost any part of the appearance or behavior of the map, so try experimenting!

Summary

In this chapter, you looked at issues relating to the visual presentation of spatial information from SQL Server, and the creation of user interfaces that allow users to explore and analyze that data.

- SQL Server provides only limited in-built visualization options, in the form of the Management Studio Spatial Results tab.

- To create more engaging and immersive spatial application interfaces, you can use tools such as Bing Maps and Google Earth.

- Google Earth is a desktop application that can display information from SQL Server exported to KML format. It provides a rich graphical interface and allows for some interaction with the data.

- Bing Maps is an AJAX web map control that runs in a client-side browser. It can display information from SQL Server that is accessed via an intermediate server-side handler. Since it is a based on standard web technologies such as HTML/Javascript, it is easy to integrate and customize the Bing Maps control as part of a larger, more complex application.

There is one further visualization option to consider: if you work in an environment that makes use of SQL Server Reporting Services, you can use the new SSRS map component to embed maps in your reports. This will be discussed in the next chapter.

CHAPTER 17

Reporting Services

In the last chapter, I demonstrated some of the ways in which you can visualize spatial information from SQL Server using applications such as Google Earth and Bing Maps. These tools are great for presenting a graphical interface to a dataset represented primarily by simple placement of cartographic features—via markers, lines, or shaded areas on a map—and are suitable in situations when you want the map to be the primary focus of user attention.

However, in practice, location information is rarely treated in isolation, nor is it necessarily the most important element in business databases; more often, it is just one aspect of information, a single dimension that needs to be presented and interpreted in context with other elements of data. When viewing reports, users don't always want to see a full-screen map, but more commonly want to visualize spatial information in a report or dashboard alongside other business data in the form of tables, charts, or graphs that present other facets of related information.

In this chapter we'll examine the SQL Server Reporting Services (SSRS) map component, which can display spatial information as part of a report alongside other data visualization components, presenting a full picture of your spatially enabled datasets.

▨ **Note** SQL Server Reporting Services is Microsoft's business intelligence online reporting environment, containing a rich featureset. In this chapter. I'll demonstrate the process involved in creating a report that displays spatial data from SQL Server, but there are many features that I won't cover including, for example, report parameters, actions, and subreports. For a more thorough treatment of SSRS, I encourage you to read one of the many excellent books dedicated to the subject.

Creating a Simple Report Map

For the example in this chapter, we'll create a report concerning a housing development near to the M6 motorway just north of Birmingham, England. The development contains 300 properties, each represented by a Polygon geometry, shown in the SSMS Spatial Results tab as in Figure 17-1.

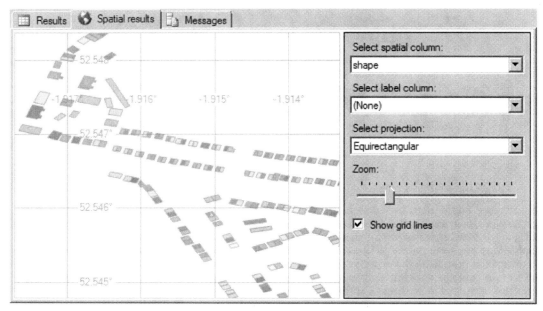

Figure 17-1. A Dataset containing details of 300 properties.

To create the properties table containing this data, and the associated property_prices table used later on, execute the SQL script that accompanies this chapter.

Creating the Report Project

Before getting into the details of adding a map to an SSRS report, we need to begin by creating a basic report project. To do so, follow these steps:

1. Load up SQL Server Data Tools (the Visual Studio environment for creating SQL Server BI applications, known in previous versions of SQL Server as "Business Intelligence Development Studio").

2. From the File menu, click to create a new project. When the New Project dialog window appears, highlight the Report Server Project template from the set of Business Intelligence templates. (If the Report Server Project template is not available, open the SQL Server Installation Center to ensure that the Reporting Services component is installed on your system).

3. Enter a name and location for the project and click OK, as shown in Figure 17-2.

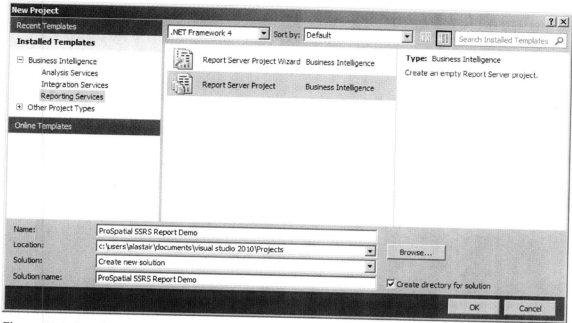

Figure 17-2. Creating a new SSRS Report Server Project

Defining the SQL Connection

The connection(s) through which data is retrieved to populate an SSRS report can be defined and embedded within the report itself. However, I tend to prefer using shared data connections, which are instead managed by the report server and can be reused by a number of different reports. You'll find that using shared connections makes it much easier to manage reports that use data that might be migrated or replicated between different environments, since you only need to update the single shared connection and all reports that use that connection will automatically point to the new data location.

To create a new shared data connection in the report project:

1. In the Solution Explorer pane, right-click on Shared Data Sources and select Add New Data Source.

2. By default, the Microsoft SQL Server connection type will already be highlighted. Click on the button to edit the connection string and, in the connection properties dialog that appears, enter the details of your SQL Server database including any necessary authentication information.

3. Click OK to exit out of the dialog. You should see the new data source appear in the Shared Data Sources folder of the Solution Explorer pane.

Creating a New Report

Having created a new report project and configured a shared data connection, we'll now add a new report to the project.

1. From the Project menu, select Add New Item.

2. In the Add New Item dialog that appears, highlight the Report template, enter a name for the report, and then click Add.

The new report will be added to the project, and you'll see it displayed under the Reports folder of the Solution Explorer pane. The main window display will change to show the design surface of the (currently empty) report as illustrated in Figure 17-3.

Figure 17-3. An empty report template.

▦ **Note** In the Add New Item dialog window, be sure to select the Report item rather than Report Wizard. Using the wizard will force you to step through several screens that aren't relevant to this example.

Adding a Map to the Report

SSRS offers a toolbox containing several different types of report item, which can be combined to provide different ways of visualizing data in a report. In addition to the standard tabular and matrix (or cross-table) items, there are also customizable chart types, gauges, and graphic indicators, similar to those found in Microsoft Excel. The map control, introduced in SQL Server 2008 R2, is a relatively recent addition to the SSRS toolbox, specifically designed for displaying spatial data in reports.

■ **Note** The SSRS map component was originally developed by Dundas Data Visualisation Inc. (http://www.dundas.com), who released it as a third-party plugin called "Dundas Map." The codebase for the Dundas Map component was subsequently acquired by Microsoft, who used it to create the built-in map component now provided in SQL Server 2012.

To explore the SSRS map features, let's now add a map to the empty report. Open up the toolbox and highlight the map report item illustrated in Figure 17-4. Then click anywhere on the design surface to place the map into the report.

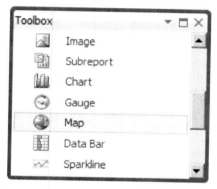

Figure 17-4. Selecting the map component from the report toolbox

When you add a new map to a report, the New Map Layer dialog window will appear. This dialog contains a number of screens that guide you through the process of adding the first layer of data to the map, which are described in the following sections (note that additional layers can be added to the map later following a similar process).

Specify a Data Source

The first page of the new map layer dialog prompts you to select a source for the data, as shown in Figure 17-5.

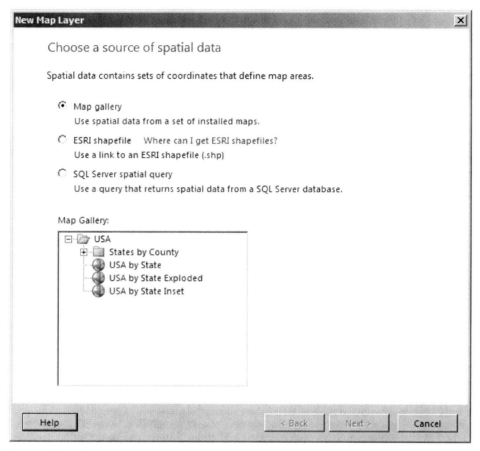

Figure 17-5. Selecting the spatial data source for a map layer

The data displayed in each SSRS map layer can be based on one of three sources:

Map Gallery allows you to create a layer based on one of the inbuilt SSRS map data sets. There are only a small number of items in the map gallery distributed with SQL Server, which cover the states of the United States and the counties within each state (based on TIGER/Line data provided by the U.S. Census Bureau). However, it is possible to add more maps to the gallery, and there is a codeplex project at http://mapgallery.codeplex.com that provides a range of boundaries for other countries and regions across the world. After having downloaded additional map files from the codeplex website, you should copy the .rdl files to the Program Files\Microsoft Visual Studio 10.0\Common7\IDE\PrivateAssemblies\MapGallery folder to make those maps appear in the list of installed map gallery templates.

ESRI shapefile uses a shapefile to provide the data displayed on the map. If you already have spatial data defined in shapefile format you might find this a convenient option to display the data directly from a file, rather than importing the data into SQL Server and then retrieving it from the database again via a query. It is possible to combine the spatial information about a set of features from a shapefile with additional attribute information about those features from a SQL Server analytic dataset, as will be described later. Bear in mind that, if using a shapefile as a datasource, the shapefile containing the map data will need to be in a location that is accessible from the SSRS report server using the credentials under which the Reporting Services account executes.

SQL Server spatial query creates a map that displays geography or geometry data returned by a SELECT query against a SQL Server database.

For this example, we'll be plotting geography data from SQL Server, so

1. Highlight the SQL Server spatial query option and click Next.

2. On the next page of the dialog you'll be asked to choose a dataset for the map. We haven't yet created a dataset in this report, so highlight the option to Add a new dataset with SQL Server spatial data and click Next.

3. When prompted, click to add a New Data Source Connection and, in the Data Source Properties dialog, select the shared data source reference you created earlier, as shown in Figure 17-6.

4. Click OK to add the data source connection, and then click Next to proceed to the next dialog screen.

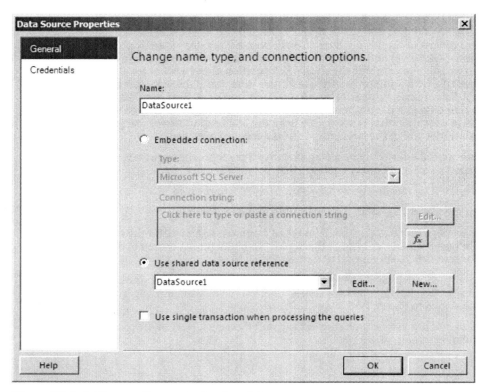

Figure 17-6. Adding a reference to the shared data source

Design the Query

You should now be presented with the query design window, as shown in Figure 17-7. You can use the graphical designer in the top half of the window to select those tables and fields to include in the dataset. However, if, like me, you prefer to write your queries by hand, you can instead just type the required SQL code straight into the bottom half of the window. You can also specify the name of a stored procedure to be used as the datasource for the map but, for this example, we'll just use an ad hoc SELECT statement.

Enter the following query to return the unique id and shape of each property in the properties table:

```
SELECT
  Propid,
  Shape
FROM
  Properties;
```

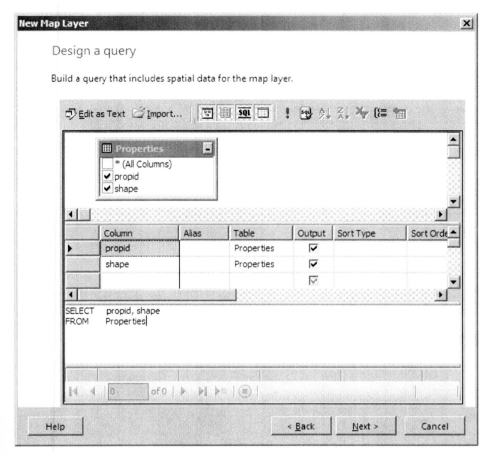

Figure 17-7. The query design window.

After entering the query that will be used to retrieve data for the map layer, click Next to continue through the dialog. The next screen, shown in Figure 17-8, allows you to select the spatial field from the dataset that will be used to populate the map. In this case, our query only returned one suitable candidate field, shape, so that has been automatically chosen as the field containing the spatial data on which the map will be based.

Note that each layer in an SSRS map can contain only geometries of a certain dimension. Since the shape field contains Polygon geometries, the type of this map layer has been set to Polygon accordingly, and a preview of the data is shown in the middle of the dialog box.

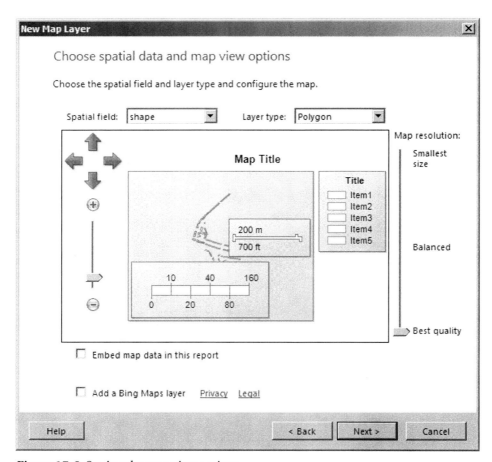

Figure 17-8. Setting the map view options.

Underneath the map preview, there is a checkbox enabling you to embed map data in the report. Generally speaking, every time an SSRS report is run, all of the queries required to populate that report are executed and the report is refreshed with data. Unusually, however, it is possible to embed any spatial data that is displayed on a map layer in the report definition itself, making that data always available within the report without needing to be retrieved at runtime. This option may be useful in cases where you have relatively static boundary data (e.g., county outlines) that are unlikely to change between report runs, making it unnecessary to retrieve each time from a server query. Embedding such data in the report removes load on the database server, and ensures that it is always available at runtime, making the report more self-contained and potentially increasing its portability. However, it also significantly increases the report size, which typically also increases the processing time required to perform any actions on that report.

There are also some other options that you can set on this screen: the vertical slider to the right of the map preview determines the map resolution, and there is a checkbox at the bottom of the screen allowing you to add a Bing Maps layer. For now, just leave these options as default; we'll examine them in more detail later. Continue to click Next to finish the wizard and insert the map into the report.

▧ **Note** Every SSRS map contains one or more layers of data, overlaid one on top of another. When you first add a map to an SSRS report, the New Map Layer wizard is used to specify the datasource and options for the first layer of data. The wizard follows the same process as described here for each additional layer that you add to the map.

Previewing the Report

Once you've finished specifying the options for the map layer, you should see the newly inserted map placed on the design surface of the report. Now, click on the Preview tab at the top of the screen to render the report. You should see the map as shown in Figure 17-9.

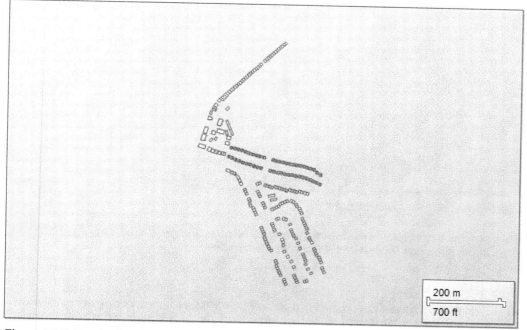

Figure 17-9. Previewing the report

Customizing the Map Viewport

So far, we've created a SSRS report that executes a query, retrieves the results, and plots them on a map layer. However, the result shown in Figure 17-9 is a bit, well, boring. Let's now look at some of the ways that you can customize the appearance of the map.

First, click on the Design tab to return to the report design surface. Then, right-click on the shaded area of the map (the viewport) and click to select Viewport Properties from the context menu. This will bring up a dialog box with a number of settings, as shown in Figure 17-10.

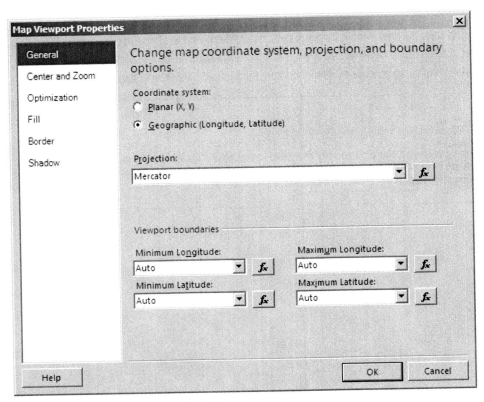

Figure 17-10. Customizing the Map Viewport

There are several tabs available containing groups of settings that affect different aspects of the map viewport. In the following sections we'll examine each in turn.

General Options

The General tab contains a number of options that control mapwide settings affecting the coordinate system, projection, and geographic extent of the map view. Since, in this example, we are plotting a set of data that has been retrieved from a column of the geography datatype, we must (as always) choose an appropriate projection to display that data on a map. The SSRS map component provides all of the same projections as those available within the SSMS spatial results tab, together with a handful of additional common projections. The list of supported projections is as follows:

- Equirectangular
- Mercator
- Robinson
- Fahey
- Eckert1
- Eckert3

- Hammer Aitoff
- Wagner3
- Bonne

The most appropriate projection to use will depend on the extent and location of the data in question. For this example, we'll use the familiar Mercator projection.

■ **Tip** For more information about the properties or method of calculation of any map projections, I recommend you check out the excellent Wolfram Mathworld site at

http://mathworld.wolfram.com/topics/MapProjections.html

By default, the extent of the projection will be set automatically to include the full extent of the data displayed on the map. However, you can also set explicit boundaries on the extents of the map view by specifying a minimum and maximum latitude and longitude. For now, just leave them set to the default auto setting.

Center and Zoom

On this tab you can choose a point on which the map should be initially centered, and the amount by which it is zoomed in. There are four methods of specifying these properties:

Set a view center and zoom level. When using this option, the map center must be given as a percentage in which the default value, 50%, centers the map at the midpoint between the minimum and maximum values in the horizontal and vertical dimensions. The zoom level must also be specified as a percentage, in which the default value of 100% indicates no magnification. Supplying explicit values for the centerpoint and zoom level can be useful when visualizing an unevenly distributed dataset where, instead of displaying the full extent of the dataset, you might want to center and zoom in on a particular area of data.

Center the map to show a map layer. Maps may be composed of several layers, each displaying a different set of data. Use this option to center and zoom the map so that it displays the full extent of data in a particular named layer to which you want to draw the user's attention. Features in the other layers that are contained within this view will also be shown, but any features in those layers lying outside the view will be obscured.

Center the map to show an embedded map element. If the data displayed on the map is bound to a set of analytical data, you can use this option to specify a particular data element on which the map is centered. For example, center the map on the property that has a [PropId] value equal to 123.

Center the map to show all map-bound elements. Use this option to center the map on all elements in the layer that are bound to a set of analytical data.

Optimization

On this pane you can optimize the data used in the map by removing unnecessary detail (using a process similar to that used by the Reduce() method). Higher quality maps take longer to render and, if the spatial data behind the map is embedded into the report, lead to larger report sizes. Lower resolution maps are quicker to render, although they are less accurate. Note that the optimization level is a property applied to the whole map and cannot be set separately for individual layers.

You can set the resolution of the map either by dragging the slider to a position representing the desired tradeoff between quality and performance or, alternatively, you can specify an explicit map resolution. Setting an explicit value lets you decide the minimum resolution that should be distinctly defined on the map; increasing the resolution causes features on the map to become more simplified. For an illustration of the effect of changing the optimization of a map of Italy, refer to Figure 17-11.

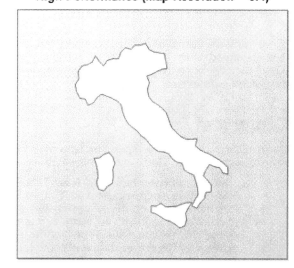

High Quality (Map Resolution = 0)   High Performance (Map Resolution = 0.4)

Figure 17-11. Comparing optimization levels

Fill, Border, and Shadow

These options allow you to change aspects of the viewport appearance to alter the fill (i.e., the background color of the map), border (the edge of the map), and any shadow effect applied to the map frame. These options are common to most Reporting Services elements.

Note that, since we are currently editing properties of the map viewport, these settings affect only the appearance of the viewport itself, that part of the control that contains the map data. If you want to change the fill, border, or shadow of the map *container* (which encompasses not only the viewport, but also elements such as the title, legend, distance scale bar, etc.) then you should right-click somewhere on the map other than the viewport, and select to edit map properties instead.

I've changed the viewport fill to solid white and added a 2 pt dotted gray border. I've also added a title to the map, set the zoom level to 200%, and centered at 60% along the *y*-axis. The result is shown in Figure 17-12.

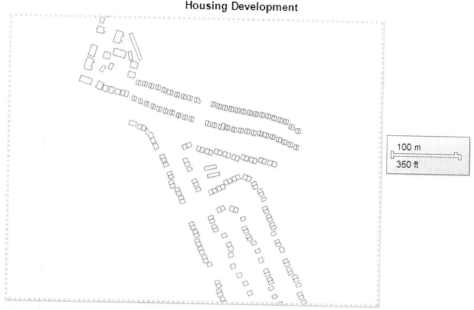

Figure 17-12. The customized map viewport

Adding an Analytic Dataset

Sometimes, plotting the geometric shape and position of items in a dataset is, in itself, the primary objective of a map. This is true, for example, of maps used solely for navigation or planning purposes. However, in a business context, it is more common to require maps that interpret and analyze some additional quality of the data: displaying the number of sales that have occurred in each sales territory, the distribution of customers that have responded to a particular sales campaign, or the routes traveled by certain types of logistic vehicles, for example. To create such thematic maps, it is necessary to link the spatial dataset used to plot the shape of elements on the map with an analytic dataset, which is used to provide additional information about those elements.

Let's add a new dataset to the report that contains an additional field of information, the price of each property on the map.

1. From the Report Data pane (normally displayed to the left of the report design surface), right-click on the Datasets folder and select Add Dataset.

2. Choose to use a new dataset embedded in the report. We'll use analytical data from the same SQL Server database as the spatial data already added to the report, so select the existing shared data source from the dropdown box.

3. In the query box, enter the simple query shown below to retrieve the price of each property, and click ok.

```
SELECT propid, price FROM property_prices;
```

These steps are illustrated in Figure 17-13. For clarity, I've named this dataset *Analytic_DataSet*, and renamed the first dataset added to the report (previously DataSet1) to *Spatial_DataSet*.

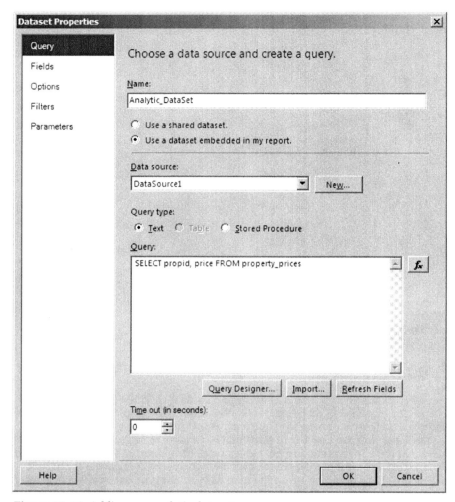

***Figure 17-13.** Adding an analytic dataset*

We now need to join the analytic and spatial datasets together, to relate the price of each property to the corresponding Polygon on the map. To do so:

1. First, click anywhere in the map viewport to display the Map Layers pane.

2. From the Map Layers pane, right-click on the PolygonLayer to bring up the context menu, and select the Layer Data option. The Map Polygon Layer Properties dialog will appear.

3. Click on the Analytical data tab on the left-hand side to be presented with the analytical dataset options.

4. Select the new Analytic_DataSet just created from the dropdown of datasets, and match the spatial dataset to the analytic dataset using the propid field, as shown in Figure 17-14.

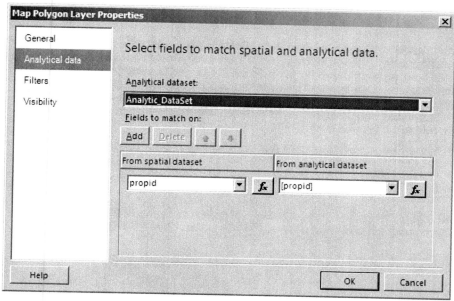

Figure 17-14. Matching an analytic dataset to a spatial dataset

---

■ **Caution** At the time of writing, a bug exists that can cause the selected spatial field to be corrupted after matching the layer to an analytical dataset. After matching the analytical dataset, return to the General tab and ensure that the spatial field is still set to use the shape field from the Spatial_DataSet dataset.

It is worth noting that, in this particular example, it is not strictly necessary to add a separate analytic dataset: since the analytic information is being sourced through exactly the same data connection as the spatial dataset, we could have simply modified the existing data to incorporate both the shape spatial column and the price attribute column in one dataset, as in the following query:

```
SELECT
  s.shape,
  a.price
FROM Properties s
INNER JOIN Property_Prices a ON s.propid = a.propid;
```

If we were to take this approach, there would have been no need to link the two datasets together; the price of each property would automatically be available as a field associated with the appropriate Polygon on the map. However, the ability to link separate spatial and analytical datasets can be useful in other circumstances: remember that a spatial dataset does not have to be sourced from a SQL Server query, but can contain features extracted directly from an ESRI shapefile, or from the in-built SSRS map gallery. In such cases, you might still want to assign attribute data from a SQL Server query to those spatial features. So long as there is a common field between the two datasets—a unique identifier or name that can be used to match the elements together—you can use spatial and analytical datasets from separate sources and combine them in the report itself.

Applying a Styling Rule

Having linked the spatial dataset with associated analytical data, we can now style the map features based on one or more attributes by applying styling rules. Different styling rules can be applied to different sorts of data; the housing plots shown on our map are contained in a Polygon layer, so we'll create a styling rule that determines an appropriate color for each Polygon based on the price of the property. For layers containing line data, a styling rule can be applied to vary the width and color of each line, and a layer of Point data may be styled to use different colors, sizes, and types of marker.

To add a color style rule to the layer,

1. First, highlight the viewport of the map so that the Map Layers pane becomes visible.

2. From the Map Layers pane, right-click on the PolygonLayer (currently, the only layer on the map) and select Polygon Color Rule.

3. The Map Color Rules Properties dialog window will appear as shown in Figure 17-15, which contains options listed under three tabs as described following.

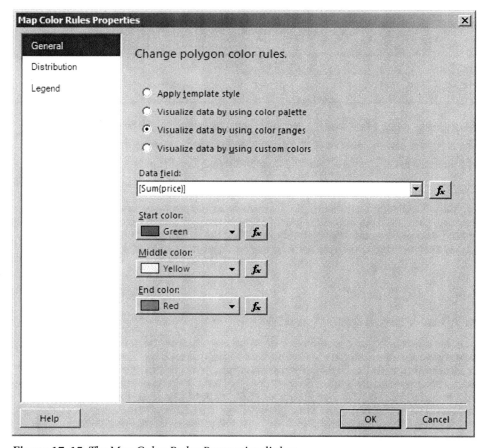

Figure 17-15. The Map Color Rules Properties dialog

General Settings

In this section you can choose the method by which a color is assigned to each item on the map, using one of four methods:

Apply template style. This is the default option, which adds no additional color rules on top of those already defined by the map template.

Visualize data by using color palette. Select this option to let Reporting Services automatically assign colors to each element from a predetermined color palette. The palettes available are Light, Bright Pastel, Semi Transparent, and Random.

Visualize data by using color ranges. This option allows you to create a color palette from a gradient that varies smoothly between two colors. You can also specify an optional midcolor through which the gradient passes. (If you do not want to specify a midcolor, set it to "No Color".) Use this option in order to color elements according to a variable that can be placed in a continuous scale; a common example is to assign a "red, amber, green" color depending on whether a certain property of the feature is poor, acceptable, or good.

Visualize data by using custom colors. Use this option to explicitly set the palette of colors that will be used to assign colors to different features on the map. Colors may be added to the palette by name ("Black" or "Cyan," for example), or by RGB color code. You may also adjust the transparency assigned to each color in the palette. Use this option when you need to assign specific colors manually to features based on an attribute; for example, to color ski runs based on their difficulty as green (easy), blue (intermediate), or black (advanced).

▓ **Note** When visualizing data using custom colors, looking at the color of a feature on the map in isolation will not give any indication as to the range of data values it represents. If you are using custom colors, it is very important also to display a legend so that users can interpret the values associated with each color.

Having chosen any of the visualize data options, you must then also choose the analytical data field that will be used to assign colors from the palette. For the example at hand, we'll color each property on the map according to its price, with the cheapest properties colored green, midpriced properties colored yellow, and the most expensive properties colored red. To do so, choose to Visualize data by using a color range, using [Sum(price)] as the data field. Set the start color to Green, the Middle color to Yellow, and the End color to Red.

Distribution Options

Having specified the color palette that will be used, you must then also determine how the data will be divided into subranges that will be assigned distinct colors from that palette. First, you must decide into how many subranges, or categories, the data should be grouped. For example, if you specify a color palette that ranges from red to yellow, and divide the data into only two subranges, every element will be colored either red or yellow depending on whether they lie in the lower half of the distribution or the upper half. If, however, you create three subranges based on the same palette, elements on the map will be colored red or yellow if they lie at either extreme, or orange if they lie in the middle. Adding further subranges creates more groups of data, which will be colored somewhere on the gradient between red and yellow.

Creating more subranges leads to more distinct categories of features on the map, which is suitable when you want to highlight the differences between elements that span a wide range of values. However, creating too many groups can lead to the styling differences between them becoming too subtle and indistinct, making it hard to tell exactly what subrange a particular element lies in (e.g., it is difficult to discern the different between a Polygon that is orangey-red and one that is reddish-orange!). In practice, for normally distributed data I generally recommend that you create somewhere between three and seven subranges.

Having set the total number of categories, the next step is to assign elements into one of the subranges. There are four methods of doing so:

> **Optimal** is the default option and suitable for most scenarios. It attempts to automatically determine the appropriate boundaries in order to create a balanced distribution of elements between subranges.

> **Equal Interval** assigns elements into subranges by dividing the extent of the dataset into equally-spaced boundaries, although the number of elements contained in each group may vary significantly.

> **Equal Distribution** creates subranges that each contain an equal number of elements, although the range covered by each group may vary significantly.

> **Custom** allows you to specify manually the boundary of each subrange.

To understand the different between the equal interval and equal distribution method, consider a dataset of six items (A–F) that are to be colored according to a datafield that contains values as shown in Table 17-1.

Table 17-1. Sample distribution of a dataset

Item	Value
A	0
B	1
C	2
D	3
E	5
F	8

Now suppose that you wanted to color the items in this dataset based on a styling rule that assigned them one of three subranges, colored red, amber, or green, based on the value of the datafield shown.

> Using the equal interval method, the subranges would each span an equal-sized range of values. Thus the first subrange would contain those elements with values between 0–2, the second subrange from 3–5, and the final subrange from 6–8. Under this rule, items A, B, and C would be colored red, items D and E would be colored amber, and only item F would be colored green.

> Under the equal distribution method, the boundaries of the three subranges would be set so that each contained an equal number of items. Thus, items A and B would be colored red, items C and D would be amber, and items E and F would be green.

The difference between the two methods becomes more noticeable as the underlying data becomes more unevenly distributed. The equal interval method typically emphasizes extreme outlying values in the dataset, which can skew the appearance of the results. The equal distribution method ensures a greater range of contrast across the spread of the data, but can create unbalanced groups that contain very variable ranges of data. The appropriate method depends on the data in question and the way in which you intend to analyze it.

Note also that you can create a restriction so that the rule is applied only to a certain subrange of the data, by providing values for the Range Start and Range End. If either value is not specified, the rule is assumed to apply to the full extent of data.

For this example, create six subranges using the optimal distribution method.

Legend

SSRS will automatically create a legend that displays a key and label for each of the category subranges displayed on the map. The settings on this tab allow you to customize the way in which the label text is displayed, by specifying a pattern containing keywords and custom formats.

For this example, we'd like each legend entry to display the corresponding range of property prices assigned to that color. To display the upper and lower bound of a range, you can use the keywords #FROMVALUE and #TOVALUE, respectively. To format these values as monetary figures rounded to the nearest integer, we'll specify that they should use the currency format C0. To do so, enter the legend text as follows:

```
#FROMVALUE{C0} - #TOVALUE{C0}
```

Click Ok to exit the dialog, and then click to preview the report again. The cumulative result of making the changes described in this section is illustrated in Figure 17-16.

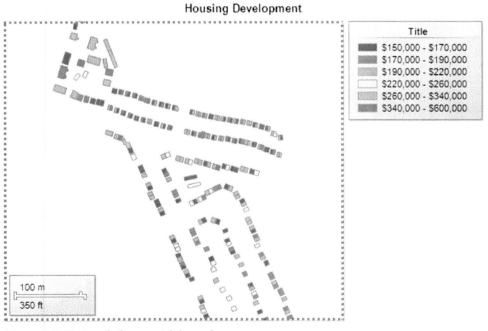

Figure 17-16. *A styled map with legend*

Adding a Bing Maps Tile Layer

One of the pretty smart features of the SSRS map control is that it provides integration with the Microsoft Bing Maps service, allowing you to add a background tile layer automatically to your SSRS map using the same aerial or road imagery that you can see on http://www.bing.com/maps.

There are some limitations to this feature: the Bing Maps background layers are already projected and prerendered onto image tiles, which means that they can be displayed only on SSRS maps that are consistent with the spatial reference system used by the Bing Maps service. Specifically:

- Data on the map must be defined using geographic coordinates based on the WGS84 coordinate system.

- The map viewport must be projected using the Mercator projection.

- The geographic extent of data cannot lie at extreme latitudes close to the Poles (i.e., latitude cannot exceed approximately +85.05 degrees or be less than –85.05).

- As the image tiles must be retrieved from an external source, the Bing Maps tile layer can only be used when the SSRS service has access to Microsoft's tile servers at dev.virtualearth.net. If SSRS is hosted on a server with no Internet access, or if access to that external server is blocked, the tile layer cannot be used.

Seeing as our example map meets all these criteria (and assuming that your SSRS service has access to the Bing Maps tile server), we can add a Bing Maps tile layer, as follows:

1. From the report design surface, click on the map viewport to display the Map Layers pane.

2. Click on the Add Layer button from the top of the Map Layers pane (second icon from the left) and choose Tile Layer from the dropdown.

3. The new tile layer will be added to the Map Layers pane, and displayed in the map preview in the report design surface. By default, the tile layer displays the Bing Maps road style. If you would prefer to display aerial imagery, right-click on TileLayer1 in the Map Layers pane and select Tile Properties. In the Map Tile Layer Properties dialog that appears you can choose either Aerial or Hybrid (Aerial with labels) instead.

Figure 17-17 illustrates the result of adding a road tile layer behind the Polygon layer of properties. You can see that adding the tile layer places an immediate context to the data that can add real benefit to your reports.

Housing Development

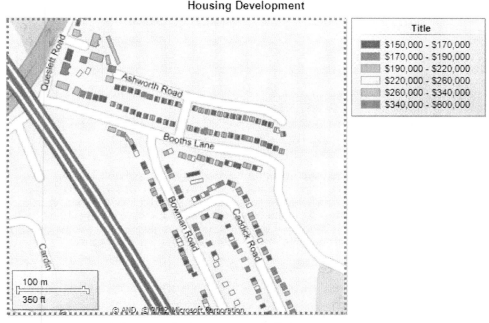

Figure 17-17. A styled map with Bing Maps road tile layer

▓ **Note** Displaying a Bing Maps layer in your SSRS report requires you to agree to the Bing Maps terms of use, which are available by right-clicking on the tile layer in the Map Layers pane and clicking Bing Maps Legal.

Assigning Actions to Map Elements

Although certainly not as immersive as the experience provided by Google Earth, it is still possible to add a degree of user interaction to SSRS maps by assigning actions to elements on the map. An action is triggered when the user clicks on a particular report element, which can redirect them to a new report or URL, for example.

To demonstrate how an action can be used, let's suppose that we wanted to allow users to click on any Polygon on the map. Doing so would direct them to a new detailed report that provided further information about the specific property on which they clicked. To do so, we first need to add a new report to the project that will provide information about an individual property, which we can do using the new report wizard:

1. From the Solution Explorer pane, right-click on the Reports folder and click on Add New Report.

2. The Report Wizard welcome screen will appear. Click Next to proceed.

3. When prompted to select a data source for the new report, choose to select the existing DataSource1 shared data source. Then click next.

4. On the Query Design page, enter the following query which will retrieve the price and area of the property associated with a given propid parameter:

```
SELECT
  p.propid
  price,
  shape.STArea() AS area
FROM properties p
JOIN property_prices pp ON p.propid = pp.propid
WHERE p.propid = @propid;
```

5. Continue to click Next to select the default options for all remaining pages of the dialog.

Once the wizard is complete, you can test out the report by clicking on the preview tab. The dataset in this report is dependent on the @propid parameter so, unlike our first report containing the map, SSRS will prompt you to enter a parameter value before rendering the report. Enter a valid propid value (any number between 1–300) in the text box at the top of the screen and then click on View Report. You will see a very simple table of information about the chosen property, as shown in Figure 17-18. (Note that I've made some simple formatting changes and added a title to the report).

Figure 17-18. *The detailed individual property report*

The next step is to create an action that passes the appropriate propid parameter value and displays this report when the user clicks on any property on the map. So, switch back to the initial map report and follow these steps:

1. With the map viewport highlighted, right-click on the PolygonLayer from the Map Layers pane and select Polygon Properties from the context menu.

2. In the Map Polygon Properties dialog that appears, click to select the Action tab.

3. Select the Go to report action, and specify Report2 as the name of the report to which the action should point (or whatever name you chose for the detailed property report). Although possible to link to any report hosted on the SSRS report server, the dropdown on this screen only lists reports contained in the same project as the current report.

4. In the parameters section, add a new parameter named propid, with a value set to [propid], as illustrated in Figure 17-19. Then click OK.

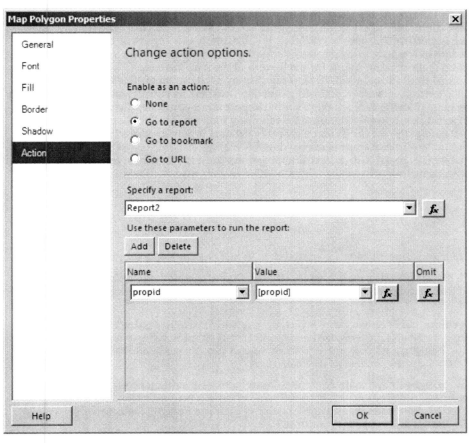

Figure 17-19. Assigning an action to a map layer

The effect of this action will be that whenever a user clicks on any element in the PolygonLayer of the map, the propid of that element will be passed as a parameter to Report2, which will be executed to show further information about the selected property. Click on the Preview tab to try out the new functionality!

■ **Tip** To navigate back to the parent report from the individual property report, click the small blue back arrow in the report toolbar.

Limitations of the SSRS Map Control

The SSRS Map component is a powerful tool that complements and adds to the range of visualization options available in an SSRS report. However, it is not without its limits. The most obvious limitation of the map control is that it can only be used from within an SSRS report. It is not possible to embed the control within a stand-alone WPF application, say, which means that you can only use it in environments where Reporting Services is available. If you already use Reporting Services, it's great to be able simply to drop in a map into your existing reports, but if you don't, it's a lot of upheaval to move an entire reporting environment just for the benefit of the map control.

In terms of technical limitations, an SSRS Map can display a maximum of 20,000 individual elements (or 1,000,000 points). However, you will generally find that, as you add more data to the map, performance suffers long before you reach those limits. Report users generally do not want to wait minutes for a report to render, however detailed the resulting map will be. You should always judiciously filter your data at the server so that only relevant data is retrieved, and make use of the map optimization option to eliminate unnecessary detail.

Also note that, while it is possible to assign simple actions to elements on the map, more advanced user interaction such as panning around the map, smooth zooming, and the like are generally not possible.

Summary

In this chapter, you learned about displaying spatial data in SQL Server Reporting Services reports.

- The SSRS map control is a dedicated tool for displaying spatial data that has been retrieved from a query of the geography or geometry datatype, or from an ESRI shapefile.

- A map is composed of one or more layers, each of which contains either Point, LineString, or Polygon features. In the example in this chapter, a single layer containing Polygon data was added to the map, but you can easily add more layers by repeating the same process as described here.

- Spatial data can be linked to an analytical dataset to create a thematic map, in which features are styled according to the value of certain properties. Styling rules can be used to change the fill and border color of Line and Polygon features, or to assign different markers to Point features.

- You can add a Bing Maps background tile layer to add additional context to data shown on the map.

- The map control exposes many properties common to all SSRS components, enabling you to assign styles and actions to elements on the map and integrate it into a report alongside other more common elements such as tables and graphs.

- The map control can only be used within an SSRS report. To add a map into a custom reporting application you will have to look for other components (such as embedding the Bing Maps AJAX control discussed in the last chapter).

While this chapter has provided an introduction to the core functionality of the SSRS map control, there are several additional features and options not discussed here. For a complete reference guide, you can consult Microsoft Books Online at http://technet.microsoft.com/en-us/library/ee240845%28SQL.110%29.aspx.

CHAPTER 18

Indexing

Effective indexing is fundamental to making database applications find the results you want quickly and efficiently. You're probably already familiar with SQL Server's clustered and nonclustered indexes, which index one or more columns of data, such as columns of int, char, or datetime data. However, SQL Server also includes a type of index specifically designed for indexing spatial data, called (unsurprisingly) a *spatial index*.

A spatial index can be created only on a column of the geography or geometry datatype, and columns of these datatypes can only be added to a spatial index; you cannot include a geography column in a normal nonclustered index, for example.

In this chapter I'll explain how spatial indexes work, and how to make best use of them to improve the efficiency of your spatial queries.

The Need for a Spatial Index

Spatial operations can be complex, and performing them requires a significant amount of processing power. This is particularly true when using methods that compare the relationships between two geometries, such as those discussed in Chapter 12. Consider the process involved in manually determining whether two geometries intersect, as calculated by the STIntersects() method: you'd generally have to evaluate and test the relationship between each coordinate contained in the point set of both geometries. If used to compare two complex geometries, this could involve performing thousands of individual calculations to obtain the desired result. Therefore, a smart design would be to try to find a way to reduce the number of times that expensive methods such as STIntersects(), STDistance(), and STContains() are called.

As a theoretical example, suppose that you had a table containing information about vineyards of the world, in which the location and shape of each vineyard is stored as a geography Polygon. Now suppose that you wanted to identify those vineyards that were located in the Champagne region of France. To do so, you could write a query using the STWithin() method something like as follows (assuming that the variable @Champagne is a Polygon representing the Champagne region):

```
SELECT Name
FROM Vineyards
WHERE Vineyard.STWithin(@Champagne) = 1;
```

To execute this query, SQL Server would have to test every row of data in the Vineyards table, using the computationally expensive STWithin() method to compare the Polygon geometry representing every vineyard against the Polygon representing the Champagne region. You and I know that some vineyards, such as Jacob's Creek in the Barossa Valley of Australia and those in the Napa Valley of California, *clearly* don't lie within the Champagne region of France, since they don't even lie within the country of France itself. However, SQL Server can't apply common sense like this, so (without the presence of an index) it must use STWithin() to evaluate the intersection of every geometry to see if it should be included in the results. This is a lot of effort, and will be a slow laborious query to execute.

To make this query perform more efficiently, we need some way of initially narrowing down the dataset, so that we call the STWithin() method only on those rows that we know are approximately located within the correct area, "in the right ballpark," so to speak. Regular clustered or nonclustered indexes don't help us here, because they can't identify records from the table based on the sort of topological relationships defined between geometries. We need a new dedicated type of index, and this is where the spatial index comes in.

How Does a Spatial Index Work?

Spatial indexes are quite unlike other sorts of SQL Server index. In this section, I'll explain a little more about the theory behind how a spatial index is constructed and how it can be used to make spatial queries more efficient.

The Primary and Secondary Filter

Rather than following the simplistic, brute-force approach of testing every geometry from the source dataset to see whether it meets the conditions for a given query, SQL Server executes spatial queries using a two-stage approach that involves two filters, as follows:

- **Primary filter**: This is a fast approximate method to select a set of potential candidate results for the query. The set of candidates returned by the primary filter is a superset of the actual result set; that is, while it is guaranteed to include all of the records that should be present in the results, it may (and generally does) also include additional "false positive" results.

- **Secondary filter**: This is an accurate, but computationally expensive (and therefore slow to perform) filter that takes the candidate results generated by the primary filter and refines them, removing false positives. The output of the secondary filter is the true result set required by the query in question.

The purpose of a spatial index is that it can be used to provide the primary filter for a spatial query, quickly identifying an approximate set of candidate results. In doing so, it reduces the number of matching records that must be tested by the slower, more accurate secondary filter. The secondary filter, which returns the precise result required by the query, executes the requested spatial method (STIntersects(), say) only on the subset of records identified by the primary filter.

In the example given previously of determining Champagne vineyards, the primary filter would use a spatial index to generate a subset of records from the vineyards table that *could* lie within the Champagne region (eliminating those that clearly didn't). The secondary filter would then use the STWithin() method on this set of potential candidates to determine those records that truly did lie within the Champagne region.

When a spatial index does not exist, no primary filtering of the dataset can occur, so the slower secondary filter must be applied to every row in the source dataset, which can be very costly.

The Grid Structure of a Spatial Index

How, then, do we design an index in such a way that it can perform an efficient primary filter of the results of a spatial query? The entries in a spatial index (as with any type of index) must be sorted in some logical order, so that we can quickly identify and access the set of candidate results that might meet the criteria for a particular spatial query. First, let's consider how values from other datatypes can be ordered in an index:

- Values stored using the int, money, decimal, or float datatype can be sorted in numerical order.

- Values stored using the char or varchar datatype (or their nchar or nvarchar Unicode equivalents) can be sorted in a collating sequence (usually alphabetical) order.

- Values stored using the datetime datatype can be sorted in chronological order.

However, none of these methods are suitable for an index of values of the geometry and geography datatypes, which define the position of objects in space. Instead, the solution used by SQL Server (in common with several other spatial databases) is to define a grid that covers the area of space in which the geometries to be indexed lie, so that every feature intersects one or more cells in the grid. The grid cells are logically arranged and ordered, and the spatial index entry for each feature stores a reference to the grid cells which that geometry intersects.

To explain this concept in more detail, let's consider an example using the simple geometry illustrated in Figure 18-1. For this example, we'll assume that this is the only geometry included in the index although, in practice, an index will normally be created on a table that contains many rows of data.

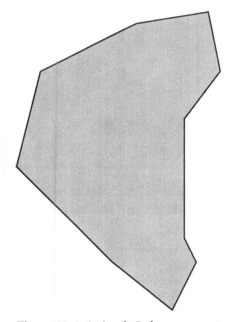

Figure 18-1. A simple Polygon geometry

Now suppose that a regular 4 × 4 grid of cells is laid on top of this geometry. The cells of the grid are numbered sequentially from left to right and top to bottom, starting with cell 1 in the top-left corner and increasing to cell 16 in the bottom-right corner. This is illustrated in Figure 18-2.

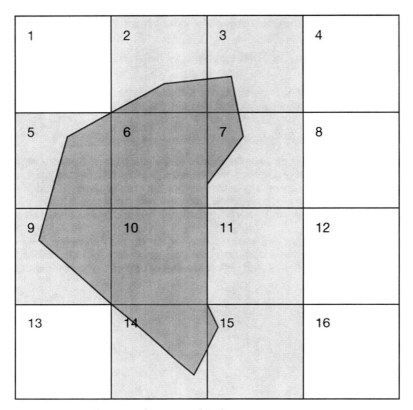

Figure 18-2. A low-resolution grid index

■ **Note** The actual grid cell numbering system used by SQL Server is more complicated than that described here, instead being based on the Hilbert curve model. However, for the purposes of illustration, I will use simple incremental numbering.

The spatial index is formed by describing the relationships between a geometry and the cells in the grid. For example, the geometry illustrated in Figure 18-2 covers cells 6 and 10, partially covers cells 2, 3, 5, 7, 9, 14, and 15, and touches cell 11. The simple relationships to those 10 grid cells, taken together, allow us to deduce enough information to perform a primary filter of this geometry in certain queries without ever needing to consider the detailed shape on a point-by-point basis.

For example, suppose that we were to compare this geometry (let's call it Geometry A), to four other geometries, B–E, as shown in Figure 18-3.

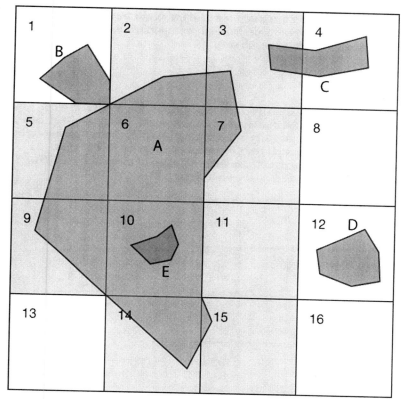

Figure 18-3. Using the grid to determine relationships between geometries

With knowledge only of the grid cells that each geometry intersects, we can make several conclusions about the relationship between these geometries:

- Geometry B touches grid cell 6, which is fully covered by Geometry A. Therefore, Geometry A and Geometry B must themselves intersect.

- Geometry C lies partially in cell 3, which is also partially occupied by Geometry A. Therefore, Geometry A and Geometry C may intersect, but this cannot be determined based on the grid alone.

- Geometry D lies entirely in grid cell 12, which is not intersected at all by Geometry A. Therefore Geometry D cannot intersect Geometry A.

- Geometry E lies entirely in grid cell 10, which is completely covered by Geometry A. Therefore not only do the two geometries intersect, but Geometry E must be entirely contained within Geometry A.

Using this grid as a primary filter to answer the question "Which geometries intersect Geometry A?" we can therefore instantly determine that Geometry B and Geometry E must be included in the results, and that Geometry D should definitely *not* be included in the results. It is only Geometry C that needs to be tested by the more accurate secondary filter to determine whether it truly intersects Geometry A or not.

Even based on this simple example, I hope you can see how the grid index can be used to identify possible candidates for certain sorts of spatial query (and, perhaps more importantly, to discard records that do not meet the criteria for inclusion in the result set).

Refining the Grid

While functional, the index obtained using the method described previously is not very precise; in other words, the grid cells provide only a "loose fit" around the true shape of the geometry. This means that there is a relatively high chance of obtaining results that lie partially in the same grid cell as another geometry, in which case it cannot be determined whether the geometries truly intersect based on the index alone.

In order to make the index more precise, we could increase the resolution of the grid, by dividing the space into 64 cells arranged in an 8 × 8 grid instead, as shown in Figure 18-4.

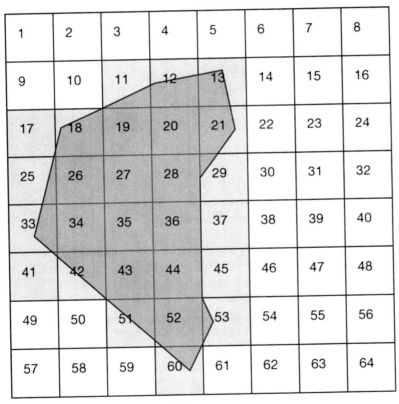

Figure 18-4. A medium-resolution grid index

By increasing the resolution of the grid to contain a total of 64 cells, we obtain a closer fit around the shape of the geometry. Since the index is more precise, this means that a primary filter based on this index will be more selective and return fewer candidate geometries that have to be evaluated by the secondary filter.

However, this introduces a new problem: to be able to describe the geometry, the index must now contain the following grid cells: 11–13, 17–21, 25–29, 33–37, 42–45, 51–53, and 60. The index entry now contains 26 cell values for this geometry, nearly three times as many as in the original index. The increase in precision therefore comes at the expense of a larger index, which has an associated performance cost.

We can extend this approach even further by declaring a high-resolution grid index: a 16 × 16 grid containing a total of 256 cells, as shown in Figure 18-5.

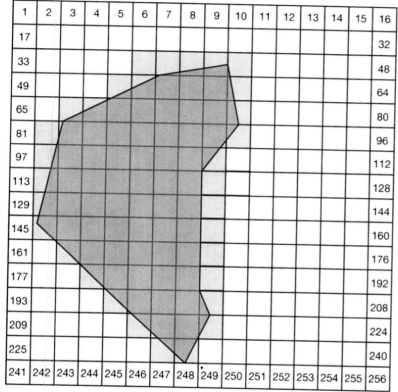

Figure 18-5. A high-resolution grid index

The area described by the cells occupied in Figure 18-5 gives the closest approximation of the true area occupied by the shape, which will optimize the accuracy of the results of the primary filter, but it also leads to the most complex index entry. The larger an index grows, the more unwieldy and slow it becomes, to the point where using an index can actually degrade the performance of a query rather than improve it.

In order to be an efficient primary filter, an index needs to be accurate, but it also needs to be small. So, what is the best compromise between these approaches? The solution used by SQL Server is not to use a single grid as in these examples, but rather to define a multilevel grid. The multilevel grid consists of four levels of grid, nested within one another. For example, the first, level 1 grid might divide the space into 16 cells. The next, level 2, grid then subdivides each of these level 1 cells into a further 16 cells. The third grid subdivides each of those level 2 cells into 16 subcells, and so on until level 4. This creates a multilevel grid as illustrated in Figure 18-6.

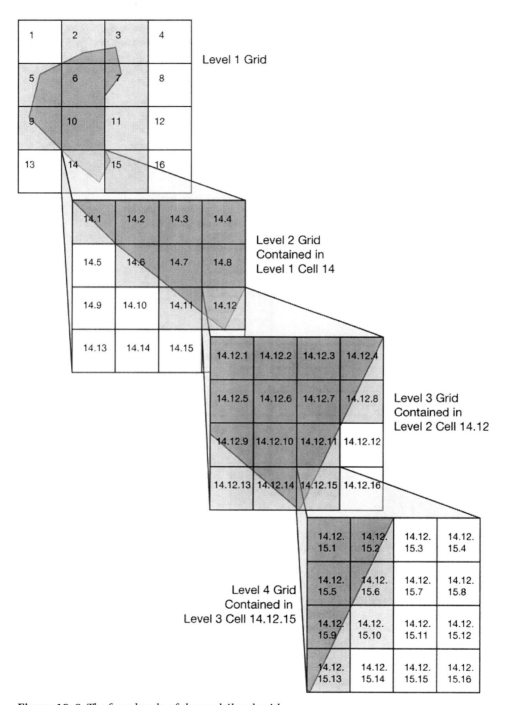

Figure 18-6. The four levels of the multilevel grid.

The numbering convention illustrated in Figure 18-6 expresses the cell reference as you drill down into each subsequent level of the grid, in the format Level1.Level2.Level3.Level4. For example, the cell 3.9.12.1 refers to the first level 4 cell that is located within cell 3 of the level 1 grid, in cell 9 of that level 2 grid, and within cell 12 of that level 3 grid.

The number of cells contained at each grid level may be set independently to one of three predetermined resolutions:

- LOW resolution grids correspond to a 4 × 4 grid, containing a total of 16 cells.

- MEDIUM resolution grids correspond to an 8 × 8 grid, containing a total of 64 cells.

- HIGH resolution grids correspond to a 16 × 16 grid, containing a total of 256 cells.

The default resolution for each grid level is MEDIUM. This means that SQL Server's default spatial index containing four grids, each at MEDIUM resolution, contains 64^4 (approximately 16.7 million) level 4 cells. Increasing the grid resolution to HIGH at all four grid levels results in the maximum of 256^4 cells, which equals approximately 4.3 billion possible level 4 cells!

The Auto Grid

In addition to the manually defined four-level grid defined previously, SQL Server 2012 also introduces an alternative, "auto grid" setting. The auto grid uses eight levels of nested grid rather than the conventional four. The resolution of the auto grid is fixed at HIGH (16 × 16) for the first grid level, and LOW (4 × 4) resolution at all subsequent levels.

The increased number of nested levels means that the auto grid can provide a more accurate filter when used to index objects of varying sizes. The tradeoff is that you lose the ability to define the explicit resolution that should be used at each level of the grid, which can be a powerful tool in performance-tuning. In other respects, the auto grid and the four-level grid operate in exactly the same way, and the techniques discussed in this chapter apply equally to both types.

Optimization Rules in a Multilevel Grid Index

When using a multilevel grid, you might wonder how we go about creating the index entries representing spatial features covered by that grid. In a simple single grid index, such as that discussed at the beginning of this chapter, each geometry's index entry is constructed from a list of all the individual grid cells covered, partially covered, or touched by the geometry. We could do the same for a multilevel grid, storing every cell at every level 1 of the grid that intersects the geometry, then every level 2 cell, every level 3 cell, and so on. However, to do so would be inefficient, and fail to take advantage of some of the beneficial properties of a multilevel grid. The spatial index entry formed from a multilevel grid may contain cells from different grid levels, but it does not need to contain *every* cell intersected by that geometry at every grid level.

To determine those cells that should be included in a spatial index, SQL Server applies three rules:

- The covering rule

- The deepest-cell rule

- The cells-per-object rule

The purpose of these rules is to ensure that each index entry includes only the necessary cells to maximize the accuracy of the index, while minimizing the total amount of information required to do so. Let's look at how each rule operates, in turn.

Covering Rule

The covering rule states that if a cell at any grid level is completely covered by a geometry, the index entry for that geometry should not contain any cells that further divide the covered cell into lower grid levels. For example, if a level 1 cell is completely covered by a geometry, we know that every level 2 cell contained within that level 1 cell must, by implication, also be completely covered (as must every subsequent level 3 and level 4 cell). Therefore, performing this subdivision and storing every lower-level subcell would occupy a lot of space in the index while providing no new information. In these cases, only the completely covered cell needs to be stored in the index. Figure 18-7 illustrates how the covering rule can be applied to an example geometry.

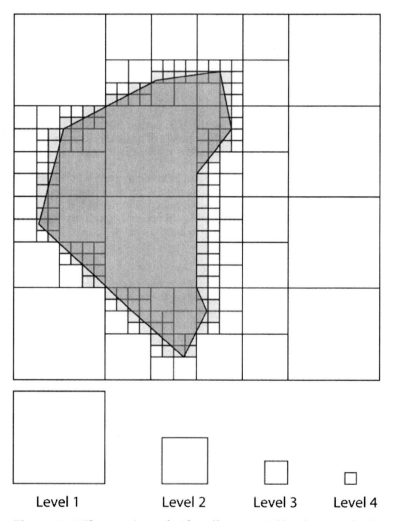

Level 1   Level 2   Level 3   Level 4

Figure 18-7. The covering rule. If a cell at any grid level is completely covered by the geometry, it is not further subdivided into lower grid levels. For illustrative purposes, the level 1 grid resolution in this example is 4 × 4 cells, and levels 2, 3, and 4 are all 2 × 2 cells.

Deepest-Cell Rule

The deepest-cell rules states that when a partially covered cell is subdivided, only the cell or cells that lie at the deepest nested grid at which intersection occurs need to be added to the index, not the cells at any higher grid levels in which those cells are contained. Since every level 4 cell lies within one (and only one) level 3 cell, and that level 3 cell lies within one (and only one) level 2 cell, and so on, once you know that a level 4 cell (the deepest level) intersects the geometry, you know by implication that the cells at each higher grid level in which that level 4 cell lies must also partially intersect the geometry.

To use an example based on the numbering system illustrated in Figure 18-6, if the level 4 cell 10.2.31.5 intersects the geometry, then the cells 10.2.31 (level 3), 10.2 (level 2), and 10 (level 1) must also intersect that geometry, since they contain the stated level 4 cell. As such, only the deepest cell, 10.2.31.5, needs to be added to the index describing that feature.

Note that the deepest cell does not always lie in level 4; according to the covering rule, if a cell at any level is completely covered by the geometry it is not subdivided further. Therefore, the deepest cell in such cases lies at the first grid level in which the cell is completely covered.

Cells-Per-Object Rule

Even after applying the deepest-cell rule and the covering rule, the index entry necessary to describe a complex geometry might still require many distinct grid cells. While this maximizes the precision with which the index describes the extent of a geometry, it can lead to poor performance of the index.

The cells-per-object rule mitigates the risk of a spatial index becoming too large, by allowing you to place an explicit limit on the number of cells that will be stored for each object. In situations where subdividing a cell would lead to this limit being exceeded, the cell will not be subdivided, and the cell at the current grid level will be included in the index instead (overruling the behavior dictated by the deepest-cell rule). The value of the CELLS_PER_OBJECT parameter on which the cells-per-object rule is based must be specified at the time a spatial index is created, and may be set to any value between 1 and 8,192. The default value is 16 cells per object.

■ **Note** The only circumstance in which SQL Server will break the cells-per-object rule is if the number of level 1 grid cells required to cover a large object exceeds the specified CELLS_PER_OBJECT value. In this case, SQL Server will include as many level 1 grid cells as are necessary to ensure that the object is fully covered.

Creating a Spatial Index in T-SQL

Now that I've shown you the mechanics behind how spatial indexes work, let's look at the syntax of how to create a spatial index in T-SQL. To start with, let's create a simple table onto which the index can be applied, containing two columns, as follows:

```
CREATE TABLE Points (
  id char(1) NOT NULL,
  shape geometry
);
```

Even though this table contains a column of the geometry datatype, we can't add a spatial index to it quite yet. A spatial index identifies which grid cells belong to each geometry by relating the cells to the primary keys of indexed objects. The index itself essentially takes the form of a set of (grid_cell_id, primary_key) pairs. Therefore, you can only add a spatial index to a table that has a primary key.

To add a clustered primary key index on the id column of the Points table, execute the following code listing:

```
ALTER TABLE Points
ADD CONSTRAINT idxCluster PRIMARY KEY CLUSTERED (id ASC);
GO
```

■ **Caution** You can only create spatial indexes on columns of a table that has a clustered primary key.

With the primary key in place, we can now go about creating the index. The syntax to do so is shown in the following code listing:

```
CREATE SPATIAL INDEX sidxPoints ON Points(shape)
USING GEOMETRY_GRID WITH (
BOUNDING_BOX = (0, 0, 4096, 4096),
GRIDS = (
  LEVEL_1 = MEDIUM,
  LEVEL_2 = MEDIUM,
  LEVEL_3 = MEDIUM,
  LEVEL_4 = MEDIUM),
CELLS_PER_OBJECT = 16);
```

Let's break this listing down line by line:

The first line follows the regular T-SQL syntax for creating any kind of index, stating the name of the index and the table and column on which the index will be applied. It is possible to have multiple spatial indexes on the same column, although each individual spatial index can be placed on only a single column of data.

The geometry and geography datatypes each have their own distinct grid type; as the shape column on which I'm creating this index is of the geometry datatype, I've specified USING GEOMETRY_GRID so that the manual geometry grid should be used in this case. I could alternatively have specified GEOMETRY_AUTO_GRID to create the eight-level nested auto grid. If creating an index on a column of geography data, you can use either the corresponding GEOGRAPHY_GRID or GEOGRAPHY_AUTO_GRID instead.

The BOUNDING_BOX parameter states the total extent of the area to be covered by the index, in the order xmin, ymin, xmax, ymax. Even though the geometry datatype allows for geometries to be placed on a theoretically infinite flat plane, the grid that divides that space used by a spatial index can only be applied within the limits of a finite space. You must therefore always specify the extent of the BOUNDING_BOX for any spatial index applied to a geometry column. The coordinate values of the bounding box may be any floating-point values so long as xmax is greater than xmin, and ymax is greater than ymin; in this example, I'm creating a square grid ranging from (0,0) to (4096,4096).

The GRIDS parameter sets the resolution of cells contained at each of the four levels of the grid. They can be set independently but, for this example, I'm using a MEDIUM resolution at all four levels. Note that this parameter is not required (nor valid) if using the GEOMETRY_AUTO_GRID option.

The CELLS_PER_OBJECT limit determines the maximum number of cells that will be added to the index to describe each individual geometry. I've used 16 here, which is the default.

▧ **Note** The parameters just described relate to properties that are specific to spatial indexes. You can also set a number of options that are generic to all index types in SQL Server, such as DATA_COMPRESSION, PAD_INDEX, and SORT_IN_TEMPDB. For a full list of available index options, consult

http://msdn.microsoft.com/en-us/library/bb934196.aspx.

The values used in this example were chosen carefully. In what way? Well, remember that the MEDIUM grid resolution corresponds to an 8 × 8 grid. Therefore, as the index covers the extent from (0,0) to (4096,4096), each level 1 grid cell will be 512 units high by 512 units wide. Each level 2 cell will then be 64 × 64 units, each level 3 grid cell will be 8 × 8 units, and each level 4 cell in the grid will be 1 × 1 unit. These values were chosen to simplify the analysis in the following sections, since each level 4 grid cell will be a simple unit square.

Analysing How the Index Is Used

To understand how SQL Server uses a spatial index to fulfill a spatial query, let's now insert some sample data into the Points table just created. We'll insert four points, identified by the letters A–D. Since these are just abstract points I'll insert them into the geometry Shape column using SRID 0.

```
INSERT INTO Points VALUES
('A', geometry::Point(0.5, 2.5, 0)),
('B', geometry::Point(2.5, 1.5, 0)),
('C', geometry::Point(3.25, 0.75, 0)),
('D', geometry::Point(3.75, 2.75, 0));
```

Figure 18-8 illustrates the points contained in the Points table, together with the individual Level 4 grid cells in which each point lies.

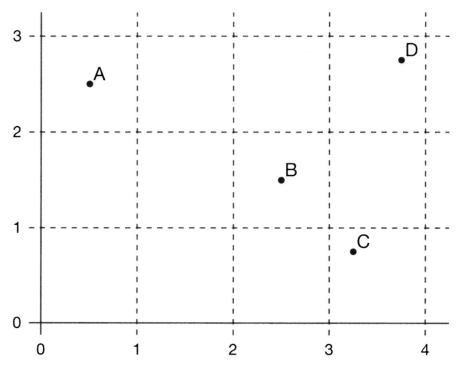

Figure 18-8. *A set of points lying in distinct level 4 grid cells.*

To see how the index is used to fulfill a typical query, let's consider a very common query pattern to identify those records from the Points table that intersect a given Polygon. The Polygon we'll use in this example will be a square Polygon, 2 units high × 2 units wide, as shown in Figure 18-9 (You might want to take good note of this diagram, as I'll be referring to the elements several times in the upcoming sections).

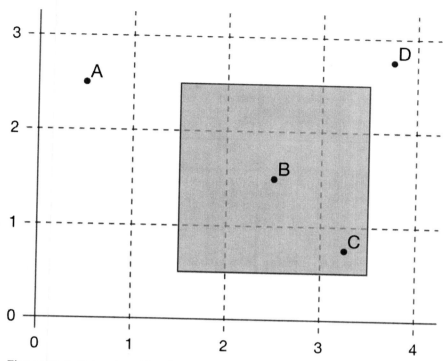

Figure 18-9. *Using the grid to determine those points that intersect a square Polygon*

The query to identify those points lying within the Polygon is as follows (note that the query includes an explicit index hint to make sure that the execution plan uses the spatial index just defined; this will be explained shortly!):

```
DECLARE @Polygon geometry='POLYGON((1.5 0.5, 3.5 0.5, 3.5 2.5, 1.5 2.5, 1.5 0.5))';

SELECT id
FROM Points WITH(INDEX(sidxPoints))
WHERE shape.STIntersects(@Polygon) = 1;
```

To analyze how SQL Server makes use of the sidxPoints index to fulfill this query, we can make use of one of a set of spatial helper stored procedures: because we're using a geometry index in this example, the appropriate stored procedure is sp_help_spatial_geometry_index (the equivalent sp_help_spatial_geography_index can be used to describe geography indexes).

The sp_help_spatial_geometry_index returns a table containing a range of useful information about how a particular geometry index can be used in spatial queries in relation to a provided query sample. Spatial indexes are used to provide a primary filter of results by comparing them to another geometry, and the query sample is simply the other geometry against which the geometries in the index are to be compared (say, by the STEquals() or STIntersects() method).

The following code listing demonstrates how to call the sp_help_spatial_geometry_index method to analyze the sidxPoints index in relation to a query sample based on the square Polygon illustrated in Figure 18-9.

```
EXEC sp_help_spatial_geometry_index
@tabname = Points,
```

```
@indexname = sidxPoints,
@verboseoutput=0,
@query_sample='POLYGON((1.5 0.5, 3.5 0.5, 3.5 2.5, 1.5 2.5, 1.5 0.5))';
```

■ **Tip** To get even more information about the spatial index, you can call `sp_help_spatial_geometry_index`
with `@verboseoutput=1`.

The stored procedure will output a table containing several properties describing the way in
which the `sidxPoints` index can be used by a spatial query involving the specified query sample. These
properties are discussed in the following sections.

Tesselation Information

The first statistics reported by `sp_help_spatial_geometry_index` give tessellation information about the
index, that is, information about the grid cells in which geometries in the index lie. In this case, the
`sidxPoints` index contains four Points, each of which lies in its own distinct level 4 grid cell. This is
reported in the following lines:

```
Total_Number_Of_Intersecting_ObjectCells_In_Level4_In_Index        4
Total_Number_Of_ObjectCells_In_Level4_In_Index                     4
```

An important concept to grasp is that, in order to use the grid as a primary filter, the query sample
(i.e., the other geometry against which we are making a comparison) must also be tessellated to the
same grid as the geometries in the index itself. The query sample in this case is the square Polygon,
which, as can be seen in Figure 18-9, completely covers one grid cell, and partially intersects a further
eight cells. This is reported in the following lines:

```
Total_Number_Of_Interior_ObjectCells_In_Level4_For_QuerySample         1
Total_Number_Of_Intersecting_ObjectCells_In_Level4_For_QuerySample     8
Total_Number_Of_ObjectCells_In_Level4_For_QuerySample                  9
```

■ **Note** In order to be used as a primary filter, both the geometries in the column on which a spatial index is
created and the other geometry to which they are being compared must be tesselated to the same grid.

Primary Filter Selectivity

The next set of properties returned by `sp_help_spatial_geometry_index` gives statistics relating to the
use of the index as a primary filter of records compared to the query sample. In this example, based on
the index alone, we can be certain that Point A does not intersect the query sample (because it lies
solely in a cell not intersected by the Polygon geometry). As there are four records altogether in the
index, the primary filter excludes 25% of the rows, as reported by:

```
Percentage_Of_Rows_NotSelected_By_Primary_Filter       25
```

The remaining three rows, Points B, C, and D, are selected by the primary filter:

```
Number_Of_Rows_Selected_By_Primary_Filter                    3
```

Internal Filtering

At this point, you may think that all three rows selected by the primary filter must be passed to the secondary filter. However, we can make that process more efficient. Consider Point B, which lies within a grid cell completely covered by the square Polygon geometry. Therefore, it is possible to preselect this row into the query result set based on the primary filter alone, without needing to call the secondary filter for confirmation. This preselection of rows based on the primary filter is known as "internal filtering," as reported by:

```
Number_Of_Rows_Selected_By_Internal_Filter           1
```

This measure is also reported as a percentage, with the number of rows selected by internal filtering given as a percentage of the number of rows selected by the primary filter. In this case, of Points B, C, and D, only Point B was selected by internal filtering:

```
Percentage_Of_Primary_Filter_Rows_Selected_By_Internal_Filter    33.3333333333333
```

Needless to say, it's desirable for this measure to be as high as possible, because every row selected by the internal filter is one less row that has to be processed by the secondary filter.

Secondary Filtering and Output

Using the primary filter based on the grid index, SQL Server has been able definitely to include Point B through internal filtering, and definitely exclude Point A. That leaves two points that need to be passed to the secondary filter, Points C and D, as reported by:

```
Number_Of_Times_Secondary_Filter_Is_Called     2
```

The secondary filter is precise, and accurately determines that Point C lies within the Polygon while Point D lies outside it. Therefore, the total number of points that intersect the provided query sample is 2, and this is the number of rows output by the query:

```
Number_Of_Rows_Output     2
```

Efficiency Measures

The final two properties reported by the sp_help_spatial_geometry_index procedure are also arguably the most important, since they relate to the efficiency with which the index can be used to answer queries of this data based on the supplied query sample.

The first efficiency measure is calculated as the number of rows selected by the primary filter as a percentage of those included in the final output. This is a useful measure in that it represents the accuracy of the "first guess" based on the primary filter alone. The more false positives that are included in the primary filter, the lower this percentage becomes. In this example, the primary filter selected 3 rows: B, C, and D. Of these, rows B and C were correct, so the primary filter efficiency is 2/3 = 66.66%.

```
Primary_Filter_Efficiency    66.6666666666667
```

The second efficiency measure is calculated as the number of rows preselected by the internal filter as a percentage of those in the final output. In this case, there were two rows in the final output

(Points B and C), of which Point B was preselected by the internal filter. So, the internal filter efficiency is $1/2 = 50\%$:

```
Internal_Filter_Efficiency    50
```

These two measures are very useful when evaluating the relative efficiency of different index settings. Generally speaking, when tuning a spatial index for optimum performance, you should always seek to maximize both the internal filter efficiency and the primary filter efficiency.

Creating a geography Index

So far in this chapter, I have demonstrated only examples of geometry indexes, in which a grid system is overlaid onto a flat, two-dimensional plane. You may then be wondering how SQL Server applies a grid index onto the three-dimensional, curved surface used by the geography datatype? The answer is, quite simply, that it doesn't.

As with the geometry datatype, geography indexes are based on a multilevel grid system. However, rather than being applied directly onto a round model of the earth, SQL Server first implicitly projects all geography data onto a flat plane prior to indexing.

The particular projection used by SQL Server to facilitate indexing is as follows:

- Two quadrilateral pyramids are placed over the poles of the earth. The bases of the two pyramids touch at the equator, so that they fully cover the northern hemisphere and southern hemisphere, respectively.

- Geometries lying in each hemisphere are projected onto the sides of the appropriate pyramid.

- The pyramids are vertically flattened and joined together to form a single projected image.

This process is illustrated in Figure 18-10.

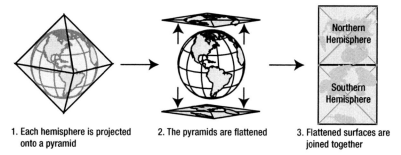

1. Each hemisphere is projected onto a pyramid   2. The pyramids are flattened   3. Flattened surfaces are joined together

Figure 18-10. Projecting the geography globe onto a flat plane for indexing

Once the two hemispheres have been projected and combined into a single image, a grid can be applied just as with the geometry datatype. This process of projection occurs automatically and transparently whenever you create a spatial index on a column of geography data. As a result, you can apply the same basic set of rules for a multilevel grid system for either the geometry or geography datatype, and SQL Server will handle the "behind-the-scenes" conversions for you.

There are just a few differences to be aware of when working with geography indexes, as follows:

Firstly, indexes created on columns of the geography datatype must specify the appropriate tessellation grid, using GEOGRAPHY_GRID or GEOGRAPHY_AUTO_GRID as required.

Secondly, unlike with the geometry datatype, there is no need to specify a BOUNDING_BOX parameter. All geography index grids are assumed to cover the entire globe and you cannot specify an explicit bounding box. Other settings regarding grid resolution and cells per object apply to geography indexes exactly as they do to geometry indexes.

The following code listing demonstrates an example of the syntax required to create an index on the geography column of a table:

```
CREATE SPATIAL INDEX idxGeography ON Table ( geogColumn )
USING  GEOGRAPHY_GRID
WITH (
  GRIDS = (
    LEVEL_1 = MEDIUM,
    LEVEL_2 = MEDIUM,
    LEVEL_3 = MEDIUM,
    LEVEL_4 = MEDIUM),
  CELLS_PER_OBJECT = 16
);
```

▓ **Note** "Behind-the-scenes," SQL Server uses projection to apply a grid index to geography data, but the column of data on which the index is based remains as unprojected geographic coordinates.

Designing Queries to Use a Spatial Index

Generally speaking, queries that make use of a spatial index as a primary filter perform better than those that do not. However, not all spatial queries can use an index. In this section, we'll consider a number of factors to bear in mind when designing queries so that they can make use of an index.

Supported Methods

A grid index describes the approximate topological relationship between geometries. Therefore, it can be used only to fulfill queries that, in themselves, are concerned with testing the toplogical relationship between two geometries.

Specifically, SQL Server supports the use of a spatial index as a primary filter only for queries that use one of the following methods:

- Filter()
- STContains()
- STDistance()
- STEquals()
- STIntersects()
- STOverlaps()
- STTouches()
- STWithin()

SQL Server cannot use a spatial index to fulfill other types of query condition: for example, to identify geometries of a certain length using STLength(), or geometries of a certain type using STGeometryType(). To support such queries, you can instead create a persisted computed column based on the result of the method in question and create a regular clustered or nonclustered index on the computed column.

For example, consider the following code listing, which creates a table containing a geometry column and then creates a spatial index based on that column:

```
CREATE TABLE IndexTest (
  id int NOT NULL,
  geom geometry,
  CONSTRAINT pk_IndexTest PRIMARY KEY CLUSTERED (id ASC)
);

CREATE SPATIAL INDEX sidx_IndexTest ON IndexTest(geom)
WITH ( BOUNDING_BOX = (0, 0, 10, 10) );
```

The spatial index created in this example, sidx_IndexTest, can be used in an execution plan to fulfill the following query:

```
SELECT * FROM IndexTest
WHERE geom.STIntersects('POINT(3 2)') = 1;
```

However, it cannot be used in the following query:

```
SELECT * FROM IndexTest
WHERE geom.STLength() > 100;
```

To create an index that can be used in conjunction with the second query, we can add a persisted computed column to the table that stores the length of each geometry, and then create a nonclustered index on this column as shown in the following code listing:

```
ALTER TABLE IndexTest ADD geom_length AS geom.STLength() PERSISTED;
CREATE INDEX idx_geom_length ON IndexTest(geom_length);
```

Correct Syntax and Query Form

When designing a query that makes use of one of the supported methods listed previously, there are several additional conditions that must be met to ensure that a spatial index can be employed.

Firstly, the spatial method must appear within a condition contained in the WHERE clause of the query (i.e., it cannot be used in the SELECT, HAVING, or GROUP BY clause). The method itself must be applied on a column of data on which a spatial index has been created.

Secondly, the query condition must be expressed using the general syntax of GeomA.Method(GeomB) = 1, in which the method is evaluated on the left hand of the expression. Even though generally considered normal coding practice, this requirement can still present a bit of a gotcha; even though they are logically identical, the following code listing can make use of a spatial index on the geom column:

```
SELECT * FROM IndexTest WHERE geom.STEquals('POINT(3 2)') = 1;
```

whereas this query cannot:

```
SELECT * FROM IndexTest WHERE 1 = geom.STEquals('POINT(3 2)');
```

Indeed, trying to force the use of a spatial index by adding an index hint to the second query will result in an error.

One minor exception to the general syntax described previously is when using the STDistance() method in a query condition. In this case, a spatial index can be used to filter those results lying within a certain distance of another geometry using either of the following two query patterns:

```
SELECT * FROM IndexTest WHERE geom.STDistance('POINT(3 2)') < 25;
SELECT * FROM IndexTest WHERE geom.STDistance('POINT(3 2)') <= 25;
```

Checking if a Spatial Index Is Being Used

When it comes to executing a query, frequently there is more than one approach that SQL Server can use to locate and return the necessary results from the database. SQL Server's query optimizer generates a number of alternative query plans, together with an estimated cost of each plan. The actual execution plan chosen to fulfill the query is the one that has the lowest estimated cost, that is, the most efficient query.

In general, this process happens automatically and is not something you need to worry about. For example, if an index exists on a table, and the query optimizer estimates that using that index would lead to the most efficient query, the index will automatically be used. Spatial indexes make spatial queries more efficient, so, having created a spatial index and designed a query that meets the conditions for that index to be used, you don't need to do anything else, right? Unfortunately, this isn't quite true. In fact, there are two false assumptions in the previous sentence; let's look at each one in turn.

Firstly, using a spatial index does not always lead to a spatial query being more efficient. Setting inappropriate values for the GRIDS, CELLS_PER_OBJECT, and BOUNDING_BOX parameters can actually lead to a spatial index that is more cumbersome to use than methods executed directly against the table on which the index is based. In this case, the query optimizer might (correctly) choose not to use a query execution plan that employs the spatial index, since it has a high associated cost.

Secondly, remember that the query optimizer chooses between various execution plans based on their lowest *estimated* cost and, sometimes, these estimates aren't accurate. While this problem occurs with any type of query plan, it is particularly difficult to assign cost estimates to spatial queries correctly. As a result, the optimizer sometimes decides not to choose a query plan that uses the spatial index because it has failed to estimate the associated cost accurately in comparison to the other plans. As previously, this leads to the spatial index not being used, however, in this case, the query optimizer has made an incorrect decision, and the query execution plan chosen is not optimal.

To demonstrate a query execution plan that makes use of a spatial index, enable the SSMS option to display the execution plan (Tools ➤ Include Actual Execution Plan, or Ctrl + M). Then execute a spatial query that makes use of a spatial index, such as that shown below:

```
SELECT * FROM IndexTest WITH(INDEX(sidx_IndexTest))
WHERE geom.STIntersects('POINT(3 2)') = 1;
```

After the query has finished executing, switch to the Execution Plan tab, which should appear as shown in Figure 18-11.

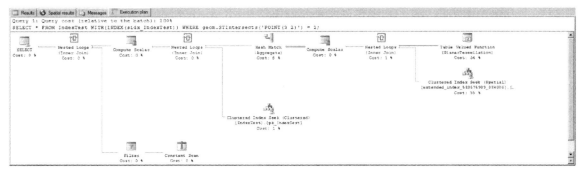

Figure 18-11. A query execution plan containing a spatial index seek

This plan may look quite complicated for what seems like a relatively straightforward query, but don't let that worry you. The thing to notice is the item illustrated in Figure 18-12, which is a Clustered Index Seek (Spatial).

Clustered Index Seek (Spatial)
[extended_index_533576939_384000].[…
          Cost: 55 %

Figure 18-12. The Clustered Index Seek (Spatial) icon

The presence of a Clustered Index Seek (Spatial) element shows that, instead of performing a scan, this execution plan performs a seek into the spatial index, using it to perform a primary filter of those geometries from the IndexTest table that intersect the requested Point at POINT(3 2).

If you're familiar with the symbology used in SQL Server's execution plans, you might notice the little yellow exclamation mark displayed at the bottom right of the Index Seek icon in Figure 18-12, which indicates a warning in relation to this element. Hovering your mouse cursor over the Index Seek icon will present further information, indicating that the warning in this case is because there are no statistics available for the column.

This is nothing to worry about; in contrast to "traditional" index types, spatial indices in SQL Server are stored in internal tables that maintain their own statistics. Unfortunately, the "Missing Column Statistics" event does not correctly recognize this and so generates a false warning, which you can safely ignore.

■ **Tip** To find out whether the query optimizer has chosen a plan that uses a spatial index, select Query ➤ Include Actual Execution Plan in SQL Server Management Studio before you execute the query. If the execution plan contains a step called Clustered Index Seek (Spatial), then you know that the index was used as part of the query execution.

Adding an Index Hint

To make sure that a spatial index is used to execute a particular query, you can use an index hint as used in the previous code sample. Adding an index hint to a query forces the query optimizer to choose an execution plan that makes use of that particular index (or indexes). You can specify an index hint by using the WITH(INDEX(indexName)) clause in your query following the name of the table on which the index is placed, as highlighted in the following example:

```
SELECT * FROM IndexTest WITH(INDEX(sidx_IndexTest))
WHERE geom.STIntersects('POINT(3 2)') = 1;
```

If possible, SQL Server will then generate an execution plan for this query that uses the sidx_IndexTest index as a primary filter to determine those geometries from the IndexTest table that intersect the Point at POINT(3 2).

▦ **Caution** Although using a spatial index can improve the performance of a spatial query, forcing the use of an inappropriate index can degrade query performance just as much.

Optimizing an Index

The key properties of a primary filter are that it must not only be fast, but also minimize the number of false positive results returned. The degree by which a spatial index succeeds in meeting these two aims is largely determined by the values chosen for the grid resolution, the bounding box, and the cells per object parameters.

It is very hard to give foolproof guidance on the appropriate values to use for each of these parameters, because they depend very much on the exact distribution of the particular dataset in question. However, in this section I'll give you some general ideas to bear in mind when determining the settings for a spatial index.

When tuning spatial index settings, in addition to general performance-testing measures, remember to use the sp_help_spatial_geometry_index and sp_help_spatial_geography_index procedures described previously to compare and analyze the relative efficiency achieved from your changes.

▦ **Tip** You can create multiple spatial indexes on the same column using different settings for each index. You may find this particularly useful to index unevenly distributed data.

Grid Resolution

Choosing the correct grid resolution—the number of cells contained at each level of the grid—is a matter of balancing the degree of precision offered by the index (the "tightness of fit" around features) with the number of grid cells required to obtain that precision. When attempting to achieve the optimum grid resolution, you should consider the following factors:

If you set the resolution of the grid cells too low (i.e., the index contains a small number of relatively large grid cells), then the primary filter will return more false positives, features that intersect the grid cell that don't actually intersect the geometry in question. These false positives will lead to more work having to be done by the secondary filter, leading to query degradation.

If you set the resolution of the grid cells too high (i.e., the index contains a large number of grid cells, but each one is individually small), then the resulting index will contain more grid cell entries for each geometry, which means that it will take longer to query the index, degrading query performance. There is also the risk that the total number of cells required to describe the geometry fully will exceed the cells per object limit.

How, then, should you go about determining the optimum grid resolution for a particular dataset? Unfortunately, there are no definitive rules to follow, and the "correct" answer largely depends on the particular dataset in question. One approach to determine the appropriate grid size is as follows:

1. Create and populate a table with no spatial index at all. Run a set of typical queries against the data contained in this table and record how long they take to execute. You will use these results as a benchmark against which to measure any improvements gained from the addition of an index.

2. Create an appropriate geometry or geography index, initially using the LOW resolution at all levels of the grid. This creates the most generalized index.

3. Rerun the same set of queries that you originally used to set your benchmark, and assess the difference in performance. (Remember that you may have to use an index hint to ensure that the new index is used by the query optimizer.)

4. Drop the existing index, and re-create a new index, increasing the resolution of each level from LOW to MEDIUM.

5. Rerun the benchmark tests and record the results.

6. Repeat Steps 4 and 5, increasing the resolution of each grid one level at a time, for as long as you continue to receive performance benefits. If increasing the grid resolution makes your query perform more slowly then stop and re-create the index that gave the best performance setting (or use no index at all).

This approach can be used to help give you an initial indication of the appropriate grid resolution required for a spatial index, but it is a very crude method. An alternative approach is to rely on the GEOGRAPHY_AUTO_GRID or GEOMETRY_AUTO_GRID settings, which removes the need to state the resolution of each grid level explicitly in favor of the automatically predetermined eight-level grid. Using SQL Server's auto grid will produce good performance in most situations and removes the need to decide on individual grid settings, although it will not necessarily result in optimal performance and cannot be adjusted.

In practice, the optimum grid resolution settings cannot be determined in isolation as they depend on the values chosen for the bounding box and cells-per-object parameters discussed in the following sections. Bear in mind also that if the data contained in the table changes, the optimum index design might also change.

Bounding Box

The bounding box of a spatial index applied to a geometry column determines the extent of space over which the grid is overlaid. Your first instinct might be to specify a bounding box that covers the full exten of all the data contained in the table to which the index is applied, but this is not always the best choice.

The area contained within the bounding box will be decomposed into a fixed number of cells, as specified by the parameters supplied for the resolution at each level of the grid. Specifying a smaller bounding box but keeping the number of cells in the grid the same will lead to each grid cell being smaller. Therefore, the grid cells can achieve a more precise fit around any features.

Suppose you have a dataset that contains a densely populated central area together with a few extreme outlying features. Specifying a grid that covers the full extent of data means that each grid cell would be relatively large, since the grid must extend to cover the far-outlying features. By specifying a bounding box that tightly fits around only the dense area of data, the index can more accurately depict the majority of data contained in this area, with only the few outlying features excluded from the index. Just because these features aren't contained in the index doesn't mean that they won't be contained in any results when you come to query the table, just that they won't be obtained from a primary filter of the index.

Alternatively, if you want to include the full extent of your data in your index, you may also want to include a buffer that enlarges the bounding box slightly to provide capacity for future growth.

For geography indexes, the bounding box parameter cannot be set, as all geography indexes explicitly cover the entire globe.

▧ **Tip** You can set the extent of the bounding box based on the maximum and minimum coordinate values of the geometry data contained in your table, but narrowing the bounds of the index may result in better performance because it allows the index grid to be more granular.

Cells per Object

The CELLS_PER_OBJECT parameter allows you to explicitly state the maximum number of grid cells that will be stored to describe each feature in the spatial index. The optimum number of cells per object is a value that balances the precision of each entry against the size of the index. This optimum value is intricately linked to the resolution of the cells used at each level, since a higher-resolution grid will contain smaller cells, which might mean that more cells are required to cover the object fully at a given level of the grid. The following are a few factors to keep in mind when you're attempting to set the ideal number of allowed cells per object:

> If you set the CELLS_PER_OBJECT limit too low, then each index entry might not be allowed to contain the total number of cells required to describe a geometry based on the deepest-cell rule and the covering rule. In such cases, the grid cells will not be fully subdivided and the index entry will not be as accurate as it could be.

> If you set the CELLS_PER_OBJECT limit too high, then each index entry will be allowed to grow to contain a large number of cells. This may lead to a more accurate index, but a slower one, thereby negating the purpose of using a spatial index, which is to speed up the results of spatial queries.

As with the other index parameters described previously, determining the optimum setting involves a degree of manual trial and error, based on a particular dataset. If you are not sure what value to set, use the default CELLS_PER_OBJECT value of 16, which works reasonably well in the majority of situations.

Performance Comparison

Spatial indexes are most effective when used by queries that are highly selective; that is, the window within which intersecting geometries are chosen is relatively small compared to the overall extent of the dataset. As the percentage of rows selected from the underlying table increases, the cost of performing lookups against the spatial index begins to outweigh the cost of performing a full table scan, to the point that using a spatial index actually degrades a query performance rather than improves it.

Figure 18-13 illustrates a graph plotting the time taken to execute a simple SELECT query against a randomly distributed set of points in a RandomPoints table, based on the following general syntax:

```
DECLARE @Window geometry
SET @Window = geometry::STPolyFromText('POLYGON((0 0, 1 0, 1 1, 0 1, 0 0))', 4326)

SELECT *
FROM RandomPoints
WHERE geom.STIntersects(@Window) = 1;
```

The query was executed repeatedly against a base table while increasing the number of rows, and specifying increasing lengths for the sides of the square Polygon @Window. For each size of window, the query execution time was recorded.

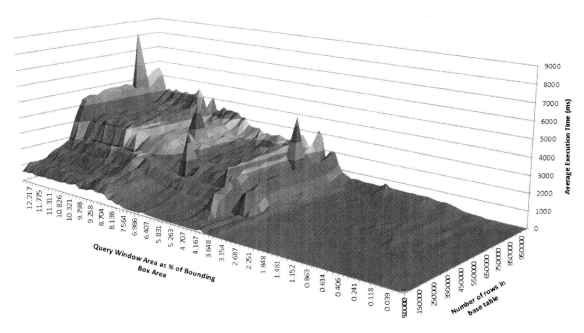

Figure 18-13. *A graph comparing the time taken to execute a query for increasing size of query window*

As can be clearly seen in Figure 18-13, the spatial index in this example proves most beneficial when the size of a query window is small relative to the overall extent of the data contained in the index. When the area of the query window is less than 3% of the total area covered by the index, execution time increases only very slightly, even when the base table contains 1,000,000 rows. As the size of the query window increases and the total number of rows returned by the query increases, the primary filter becomes less efficient, leading to dramatically longer execution times.

Note that this comparison is based on results obtained from a single artificial dataset. The relative benefits of using a spatial index in a particular application depend on a number of factors, and may vary from those illustrated here. To create a more thorough investigation, you would also need to repeat this set of tests using different combinations of grid resolution and cells per object.

Summary

In this chapter you learned about spatial indexes, and how you can use them to improve the performance of queries against spatial data. Specifically, you learned the following:

- A spatial index acts as a primary filter for the results of certain spatial operations.

- The primary filter provides a fast approximate set of candidate geometries that is guaranteed to include the results of a query, but may include additional "false positive" results.

- The secondary filter is used to refine the results of the primary filter into the true result set. Secondary filters are slower but more accurate than primary filters.

- To create an index of spatial features, SQL Server allocates features to cells within a multilevel grid.

- SQL Server applies the covering rule, the deepest-cell rule, and the cells-per-object rule in an attempt to maximize the precision of an index entry while minimizing the number of grid cells required to do so.

- You may create spatial indexes that apply to either the geography or geometry datatype by using either T-SQL or SQL Server Management Studio.

- Sometimes, it is necessary to force the query optimizer to use a spatial index, by specifying a query hint.

There are a number of factors that affect the performance of a spatial index, and each one must be balanced to obtain the optimum trade-off between speed and accuracy.

Appendix

This appendix contains various tables of reference information that you might find helpful when working with spatial data in SQL Server, as follows:

- Methods available for the geometry and geography datatypes
- Exception codes and descriptions
- `IsValidDetailed()` response codes and descriptions
- Common SRIDs

Method List

This section contains a summary of all the methods and properties provided by the geometry and geography datatypes.

Static Methods

The following tables list static methods that can be used to instantiate items of geometry or geography data.

Well-Known Text

Method	Description	geometry	geography
STPointFromText()	Creates a Point from supplied WKT	•	•
STLineFromText()	Creates a LineString from supplied WKT	•	•
STPolyFromText()	Creates a Polygon from supplied WKT	•	•
STMPointFromText()	Creates a MultiPoint from supplied WKT	•	•
STMLineFromText()	Creates a MultiLineString from supplied WKT	•	•

Method	Description	geometry	geography
STMPolyFromText()	Creates a MultiPolygon from supplied WKT	•	•
STGeomCollFromText()	Creates a GeometryCollection from supplied WKT	•	•
STGeomFromText()	Creates any kind of supported geometry from supplied WKT	•	•
Parse()	Creates any kind of supported geometry from supplied WKT	•	•

Well-Known Binary

Method	Description	geometry	geography
STPointFromWKB()	Creates a Point from supplied WKB	•	•
STLineFromWKB()	Creates a LineString from supplied WKB	•	•
STPolyFromWKB()	Creates a Polygon from supplied WKB	•	•
STMPointFromWKB()	Creates a MultiPoint from supplied WKB	•	•
STMLineFromWKB()	Creates a MultiLineString from supplied WKB	•	•
STMPolyFromWKB()	Creates a MultiPolygon from supplied WKB	•	•
STGeomCollFromWKB()	Creates a GeometryCollection from supplied WKB	•	•
STGeomFromWKB()	Creates any supported geometry from supplied WKB	•	•

Geography Markup Language

Method	Description	geometry	geography
GeomFromGML()	Creates any supported geometry from supplied GML	•	•

Other Static Methods

Method	Description	geometry	geography
Point()	Creates a Point from supplied coordinate values	•	•

Representation Formats

Method	Description	geometry	geography
STAsText()	Returns the Well-Known Text representation of a geometry	•	•
ASTextZM()	Returns the Well-Known Text representation of a geometry including Z and M values	•	•
ToString()	Returns the Well-Known Text representation of a geometry including Z and M values	•	•
STAsBinary()	Returns the Well-Known Binary representation of a geometry	•	•
AsBinaryZM()	Returns the Well-Known Binary representation of a geometry including Z and M values	•	•
AsGML()	Returns the Geographic Markup Language representation of a geometry	•	•

Aggregate Methods

Method	Description	geometry	geography
CollectionAggregate()	Creates a collection containing geometries from a column of spatial data	•	•
ConvexHullAggregate()	Creates a convex hull around the geometries in a column of spatial data	•	•
EnvelopeAggregate()	Creates the envelope around the geometries in a column of spatial data	•	•
UnionAggregate()	Creates the union of geometries in a column of spatial data	•	•

Describing Properties of a geometry

Method	Description	geometry	geography
STSrid	Sets or retrieves the SRID in which an instance is defined	•	•
STGeometryType()	Returns the name of the type of a geometry (e.g., "Point")	•	•
InstanceOf()	Tests whether an instance is of a particular geometry type	•	•
STDimension()	Returns the number of dimensions occupied by a geometry	•	•
STIsSimple()	Tests whether a geometry is simple	•	
STIsClosed()	Tests whether a geometry is closed	•	
STIsRing()	Tests whether a geometry is a ring (a simple, closed LineString)	•	
STNumPoints()	Returns the number of points in a geometry	•	•
STIsEmpty()	Tests whether a geometry is empty (contains no points)	•	•
STIsValid()	Tests whether a geometry is valid	•	•
IsValidDetailed()	Tests if, and describes why, a geometry is invalid	•	•
HasM	Tests if an instance has M coordinate values	•	•
HasZ	Tests if an instance has Z coordinates values	•	•

Calculating Metrics

Method	Description	geometry	geography
STLength()	Measures the length of a geometry	•	•
STArea()	Measures the area contained within a geometry	•	•

Returning Coordinate Values

Method	Description	geometry	geography
STX	Returns the X coordinate of a Point	•	
STY	Returns the Y coordinate of a Point	•	
Lat	Returns the latitude coordinate of a Point		•
Long	Returns the longitude coordinate of a Point		•
M	Returns the M coordinate of a Point	•	•
Z	Returns the Z coordinate of a Point	•	•

Isolating Points from a geometry

Method	Description	geometry	geography
STPointN()	Returns the nth point of a geometry	•	•
STStartPoint()	Returns the first point of a geometry	•	•
STEndPoint()	Returns the last point of a geometry	•	•
STCentroid()	Returns the centroid of a geometry	•	
EnvelopeCenter()	Returns the center of the envelope around a geometry		•
STPointOnSurface()	Returns an arbitrary point from the interior of a geometry	•	

Isolating Curve/Line Segments from a Geometry

Method	Description	geometry	geography
STNumCurves()	Returns the number of segments in a LineString, CircularString, CompoundCurve, or MultiLineString	•	•
STCurveN()	Returns the nth curve segment from a geometry	•	•

Dealing with Polygon Rings

Method	Description	geometry	geography
STExteriorRing()	Returns the exterior ring of a Polygon	•	
STNumInteriorRing()	Counts the number of interior rings in a Polygon	•	
STInteriorRingN()	Returns the specified interior ring of a Polygon	•	
NumRings()	Counts the total number of rings in a Polygon		•
RingN()	Returns the specified ring from a Polygon		•

Describing the Extent of a geometry

Method	Description	geometry	geography
STBoundary()	Returns the boundary of a geometry	•	
STEnvelope()	Returns the bounding box of a geometry	•	
EnvelopeAngle()	Determines the angle between the center of a geography instance and its most outlying point		•

Working with Geometry Collections

Method	Description	geometry	geography
STNumGeometries()	Returns the number of geometries in a geometry collection	•	•
STGeometryN()	Returns the nth geometry from a collection	•	•

Modifying a geometry

Method	Description	geometry	geography
TBuffer()	Applies a buffer around a geometry	•	•
BufferWithTolerance()	Applies a buffer with a given tolerance	•	•
BufferWithCurves()	Applies a buffer that uses curved geometries	•	•
MakeValid()	Makes a geometry valid according to OGC specifications	•	•
Reduce()	Simplifies a geometry	•	•
ReorientObject()	Reorients the rings of a Polygon, inverting its interior and exterior		•
TConvexHull()	Creates the convex hull around a geometry	•	•
TCurveToLine()	Converts a curved geometry to the equivalent linear geometry type	•	•
CurveToLineWithTolerance()	Converts a curved geometry to the equivalent linear geometry type, approximating curved sections to within a specified tolerance	•	•
TUnion()	Combines two geometries	•	•
TIntersection()	Returns the intersection created between two geometries	•	•
TDifference()	Returns the difference between one geometry and another	•	•
TSymDifference()	Returns the symmetrical difference between two geometries	•	•

Testing Relationships Between geometries

Method	Description	geometry	geography
STEquals()	Tests if two geometries contain exactly the same set of points	•	•
STDistance()	Calculates the shortest distance between two geometries	•	•
ShortestLineTo()	Determines the shortest straight line connecting two geometries	•	•
STIntersects()	Tests for any degree of intersection between two geometries	•	•
Filter()	Performs a primary filter (based on a spatial index) to test whether two geometries intersect	•	•
STDisjoint()	Tests whether two geometries are disjoint	•	•
STTouches()	Tests whether two geometries touch	•	
STOverlaps()	Tests whether two geometries overlap	•	•
STCrosses()	Tests whether one geometry crosses another	•	
STWithin()	Tests whether one geometry is contained within another	•	•
STContains()	Tests whether one geometry contains another	•	•
STRelate()	Tests whether two instances exhibit the relationship specified using the DE-9IM model	•	

Exception Codes and Messages

The following table lists the codes and corresponding description for exceptions that can occur while working with geometry or geography datatypes (or their SqlGeometry and SqlGeography equivalents).

Code	Description
24100	The spatial reference identifier (SRID) is not valid. SRIDs must be between 0 and 999999.
24101	The distance parameter ({0}) for ({1}) is not valid. Distances cannot be infinite or not a number (NaN).
24102	The point index n ({0}) passed to STPointN is less than 1. This number must be greater than or equal to 1 and less than or equal to the number of points returned by STNumPoints.
24103	The geometry index n ({0}) passed to STGeometryN is less than 1. The number must be greater than or equal to 1 and should be less than or equal to the number of instances returned by STNumGeometries.
24104	The ring index n ({0}) passed to STInteriorRingN is less than 1. The number must be greater than or equal to 1 and should be less than or equal to the number of rings returned by STNumInteriorRing.
24105	The geometryType argument in InstanceOf ('{0}') is not valid. This argument must contain one of the following types: Geometry, Point, LineString, Curve, Polygon, Surface, MultiPoint, MultiLineString, MultiPolygon, MultiCurve, MultiSurface, GeometryCollection, CircularString, CompoundCurve, CurvePolygon, or FullGlobe (geography Data Type only).
24108	The tolerance ({0}) passed to BufferWithTolerance is not valid. Tolerances must be positive numbers.
24109	The intersectionPatternMatrix argument to STRelate is not valid. This argument must contain exactly nine characters, but the string provided has {0} characters.
24110	Character {0} ({1}) of the intersectionPatternMatrix argument to STRelate is not valid. This argument must only contain the characters 0, 1, 2, T, F, and *.
24111	The well-known text (WKT) input is not valid.
24112	The well-known text (WKT) input is empty. To input an empty instance, specify an empty instance of one of the following types: Point, LineString, Polygon, MultiPoint, MultiLineString, MultiPolygon, CircularString, CompoundCurve, CurvePolygon, or GeometryCollection.
24114	The label {0} in the input well-known text (WKT) is not valid. Valid labels are POINT, LINESTRING, POLYGON, MULTIPOINT, MULTILINESTRING, MULTIPOLYGON, GEOMETRYCOLLECTION, CIRCULARSTRING, COMPOUNDCURVE, CURVEPOLYGON, and FULLGLOBE (geography Data Type only).

Code	Description
24115	The well-known binary (WKB) input is not valid.
24117	The LineString input is not valid because it does not have enough points. A LineString must have at least two points.
24118	The Polygon input is not valid because the exterior ring does not have enough points. Each ring of a polygon must contain at least four points.
24119	The Polygon input is not valid because the start and end points of the exterior ring are not the same. Each ring of a polygon must have the same start and end points.
24120	The Polygon input is not valid because the interior ring number {0} does not have enough points. Each ring of a polygon must contain at least four points.
24121	The Polygon input is not valid because the start and end points of the interior ring number {0} are not the same. Each ring of a polygon must have the same start and end points.
24125	The tolerance ({0}) passed to Reduce is not valid. Tolerances must be positive numbers.
24126	Point coordinates cannot be infinite or not a number (NaN).
24128	The Geography Markup Language (GML) input must have a single top-level tag.
24129	The given XML instance is not valid because the top-level tag is {0}. The top-level element of the input Geographic Markup Language (GML) must contain a Point, LineString, Polygon, MultiPoint, MultiGeometry, MultiCurve, MultiSurface, Arc, ArcString, CompositeCurve, PolygonPatch, or FullGlobe (geography Data Type only) object.
24130	The given XML instance contains attributes. Attributes in Geography Markup Language (GML) input are not permitted.
24131	The given pos element provides {0} coordinates. A pos element must contain exactly two coordinates.
24132	The posList element provided has {0} coordinates. The number of coordinates in a posList element must be an even number.
24133	The linearRing input is not valid because there are not enough points in the input. A linearRing must have at least four points, but this linearRing input only has {0}. l24304: Nesting overflow. The call to {0} would result in {1} levels of nesting. Only {2} levels are allowed.
24134	Sequential parts of a compound curve must have one common end point. Add a common end point. All coordinates, including optional Z and M, must be equal.
24141	A number is expected at position {0} of the input. The input has {1}.

Code	Description
4142	Expected "{0}" at position {1}. The input has "{2}".
4143	The posList element provided is empty.
4144	This operation cannot be completed because the instance is not valid. Use MakeValid to convert the instance to a valid instance. Note that MakeValid may cause the points of a geometry instance to shift slightly.
4149	FullGlobe cannot have internal elements and must be the only object in the instance. Remove any other objects in the same geography instance.
4150	FullGlobe instances cannot be objects in the GeometryCollection. GeometryCollections can contain the following instances: Points, MultiPoints, LineStrings, MultiLineStrings, Polygons, MultiPolygons, CircularStrings, CompoundCurves, CurvePolygons, and GeometryCollections.
4151	The curve index n ({0}) passed to STCurveN is less than 1. This number must be greater than or equal to 1 and less than or equal to the number of curves returned by STNumCurves.
4152	The tolerance ({0}) passed to CurveToLineWithTolerance is not valid. Tolerances must be positive numbers.
4200	The specified input does not represent a valid geography instance. Use MakeValid to convert the instance to a valid instance. Note that MakeValid may cause the points of a spatial instance to shift slightly.
4201	Latitude values must be between −90 and 90 degrees.
4202	Longitude values must be between −15069 and 15069 degrees.
4204	The spatial reference identifier (SRID) is not valid. The specified SRID must match one of the supported SRIDs displayed in the sys.spatial_reference_systems catalog view.
4205	The specified input does not represent a valid geography instance because it exceeds a single hemisphere. Each geography instance must fit inside a single hemisphere. A common reason for this error is that a polygon has the wrong ring orientation. To create a larger than hemisphere geography instance, upgrade the version of SQL Server and change the database compatibility level to at least 110.
4206	The specified input cannot be accepted because it contains an edge with antipodal points. For information about using spatial methods with FullGlobe objects, see Types of Spatial Data in SQL Server Books Online.
4207	The specified buffer distance exceeds the full globe. Decrease the buffer distance.
4209	Unexpected end of input. Check that the input data is complete and has not been truncated.

Code	Description
24210	{0} type with an unexpected version of {1} received; only versions up to {2} are accepted.
24211	The specified operation cannot run under the current compatibility level. A common reason for this issue is that the object contains circular arcs. Change the database compatibility level to 110 or higher, or use STCurveToLine.
24212	The CircularString input is not valid because it does not have enough points. A CircularString must have at least three points.
24213	The CompoundCurve input is not valid because it does not have enough points. A CompoundCurve must have at least two points.
24214	Circular arc segments with Z values must have equal Z value for all three points.
24215	Bounding box input is not valid. The value of parameter '{0}' must be greater than the value of parameter '{1}'.
24216	The arc must contain exactly three points.
24300	Expected a call to {0}, but {1} was called.
24301	Expected a call to {0} or {1}, but {2} was called.
24302	No more calls expected, but {0} was called.
24303	The OpenGis{0}Type provided, {1}, is not valid.
24305	The Polygon input is not valid because the ring number {0} does not have enough points. Each ring of a polygon must contain at least four points.
24306	The Polygon input is not valid because the start and end points of the ring number {0} are not the same. Each ring of a polygon must have the same start and end points.
24307	Different SRIDs encountered.
24308	Objects with compatibility level 110 cannot be populated using IGeometrySink. Use IGeometrySink110 instead.
24309	Objects with compatibility level 110 cannot be populated using IGeographySink. Use IGeographySink110 instead.

IsValidDetailed() Response Codes

The following table lists the possible codes and descriptions returned by the IsValidDetailed() method when used to test the validity of a geometry.

Code	Description
24400	Valid
24401	Not valid, reason unknown.
24402	Not valid because point ({0}) is an isolated point, which is not valid in this type of object.
24403	Not valid because some pair of polygon edges overlaps.
24404	Not valid because polygon ring ({0}) intersects itself or some other ring.
24405	Not valid because some polygon ring intersects itself or some other ring.
24406	Not valid because curve ({0}) degenerates to a point.
24407	Not valid because polygon ring ({0}) collapses to a line at point ({1}).
24408	Not valid because polygon ring ({0}) is not closed.
24409	Not valid because some portion of polygon ring ({0}) lies in the interior of a polygon.
24410	Not valid because ring ({0}) is the first ring in a polygon of which it is not the exterior ring.
24411	Not valid because ring ({0}) lies outside the exterior ring ({1}) of its polygon.
24412	Not valid because the interior of a polygon with rings ({0}) and ({1}) is not connected.
24413	Not valid because of two overlapping edges in curve ({0}).
24414	Not valid because an edge of curve ({0}) overlaps an edge of curve ({1}).
24415	Not valid because some polygon has an invalid ring structure.
24416	Not valid because in curve ({0}) the edge that starts at point ({1}) is either a line or a degenerate arc with antipodal endpoints.

Common Spatial Reference Identifiers

This section contains SRIDs for some common spatial reference systems. To look up details of any reference systems not listed here you can consult http://www.epsg-registry.org or http://www.spatialreference.org.

Geographic Coordinate Systems

SRID	Description
4326	Global - WGS84
4230	European – ED50
4267	North America – NAD27
4269	North America – NAD83

National Grids

SRID	Description
27700	OSGB 1936 British National Grid
29900	TM65 / Irish National Grid
20790	Lisbon (Lisbon)/Portuguese National Grid
2100	GGRS87 / Greek Grid
20499	Ain el Abd / Bahrain Grid
2391	KKJ / Finland zone 1
2392	KKJ / Finland zone 2
2393	KKJ / Finland Uniform Coordinate System
2394	KKJ / Finland zone 4
28600	Qatar / Qatar National Grid

UTM North Zones (Meter Units)

SRID	Description		SRID	Description
32601	WGS 84 / UTM zone 1N		32631	WGS 84 / UTM zone 31N
32602	WGS 84 / UTM zone 2N		32632	WGS 84 / UTM zone 32N
32603	WGS 84 / UTM zone 3N		32633	WGS 84 / UTM zone 33N
32604	WGS 84 / UTM zone 4N		32634	WGS 84 / UTM zone 34N
32605	WGS 84 / UTM zone 5N		32635	WGS 84 / UTM zone 35N
32606	WGS 84 / UTM zone 6N		32636	WGS 84 / UTM zone 36N
32607	WGS 84 / UTM zone 7N		32637	WGS 84 / UTM zone 37N
32608	WGS 84 / UTM zone 8N		32638	WGS 84 / UTM zone 38N
32609	WGS 84 / UTM zone 9N		32639	WGS 84 / UTM zone 39N
32610	WGS 84 / UTM zone 10N		32640	WGS 84 / UTM zone 40N
32611	WGS 84 / UTM zone 11N		32641	WGS 84 / UTM zone 41N
32612	WGS 84 / UTM zone 12N		32642	WGS 84 / UTM zone 42N
32613	WGS 84 / UTM zone 13N		32643	WGS 84 / UTM zone 43N
32614	WGS 84 / UTM zone 14N		32644	WGS 84 / UTM zone 44N
32615	WGS 84 / UTM zone 15N		32645	WGS 84 / UTM zone 45N
32616	WGS 84 / UTM zone 16N		32646	WGS 84 / UTM zone 46N
32617	WGS 84 / UTM zone 17N		32647	WGS 84 / UTM zone 47N
32618	WGS 84 / UTM zone 18N		32648	WGS 84 / UTM zone 48N
32619	WGS 84 / UTM zone 19N		32649	WGS 84 / UTM zone 49N
32620	WGS 84 / UTM zone 20N		32650	WGS 84 / UTM zone 50N
32621	WGS 84 / UTM zone 21N		32651	WGS 84 / UTM zone 51N

SRID	Description		SRID	Description
32622	WGS 84 / UTM zone 22N		32652	WGS 84 / UTM zone 52N
32623	WGS 84 / UTM zone 23N		32653	WGS 84 / UTM zone 53N
32624	WGS 84 / UTM zone 24N		32654	WGS 84 / UTM zone 54N
32625	WGS 84 / UTM zone 25N		32655	WGS 84 / UTM zone 55N
32626	WGS 84 / UTM zone 26N		32656	WGS 84 / UTM zone 56N
32627	WGS 84 / UTM zone 27N		32657	WGS 84 / UTM zone 57N
32628	WGS 84 / UTM zone 28N		32658	WGS 84 / UTM zone 58N
32629	WGS 84 / UTM zone 29N		32659	WGS 84 / UTM zone 59N
32630	WGS 84 / UTM zone 30N		32660	WGS 84 / UTM zone 60N

UTM South Zones (Meter Units)

SRID	Description		SRID	Description
32701	WGS 84 / UTM zone 1S		32731	WGS 84 / UTM zone 31S
32702	WGS 84 / UTM zone 2S		32732	WGS 84 / UTM zone 32S
32703	WGS 84 / UTM zone 3S		32733	WGS 84 / UTM zone 33S
32704	WGS 84 / UTM zone 4S		32734	WGS 84 / UTM zone 34S
32705	WGS 84 / UTM zone 5S		32735	WGS 84 / UTM zone 35S
32706	WGS 84 / UTM zone 6S		32736	WGS 84 / UTM zone 36S
32707	WGS 84 / UTM zone 7S		32737	WGS 84 / UTM zone 37S
32708	WGS 84 / UTM zone 8S		32738	WGS 84 / UTM zone 38S
32709	WGS 84 / UTM zone 9S		32739	WGS 84 / UTM zone 39S
32710	WGS 84 / UTM zone 10S		32740	WGS 84 / UTM zone 40S

SRID	Description		SRID	Description
32711	WGS 84 / UTM zone 11S		32741	WGS 84 / UTM zone 41S
32712	WGS 84 / UTM zone 12S		32742	WGS 84 / UTM zone 42S
32713	WGS 84 / UTM zone 13S		32743	WGS 84 / UTM zone 43S
32714	WGS 84 / UTM zone 14S		32744	WGS 84 / UTM zone 44S
32715	WGS 84 / UTM zone 15S		32745	WGS 84 / UTM zone 45S
32716	WGS 84 / UTM zone 16S		32746	WGS 84 / UTM zone 46S
32717	WGS 84 / UTM zone 17S		32747	WGS 84 / UTM zone 47S
32718	WGS 84 / UTM zone 18S		32748	WGS 84 / UTM zone 48S
32719	WGS 84 / UTM zone 19S		32749	WGS 84 / UTM zone 49S
32720	WGS 84 / UTM zone 20S		32750	WGS 84 / UTM zone 50S
32721	WGS 84 / UTM zone 21S		32751	WGS 84 / UTM zone 51S
32722	WGS 84 / UTM zone 22S		32752	WGS 84 / UTM zone 52S
32723	WGS 84 / UTM zone 23S		32753	WGS 84 / UTM zone 53S
32724	WGS 84 / UTM zone 24S		32754	WGS 84 / UTM zone 54S
32725	WGS 84 / UTM zone 25S		32755	WGS 84 / UTM zone 55S
32726	WGS 84 / UTM zone 26S		32756	WGS 84 / UTM zone 56S
32727	WGS 84 / UTM zone 27S		32757	WGS 84 / UTM zone 57S
32728	WGS 84 / UTM zone 28S		32758	WGS 84 / UTM zone 58S
32729	WGS 84 / UTM zone 29S		32759	WGS 84 / UTM zone 59S
32730	WGS 84 / UTM zone 30S		32760	WGS 84 / UTM zone 60S

U.S. State Plane Projections (Meter Units)

SRID	Description		SRID	Description
26929	NAD83 / Alabama East		26991	NAD83 / Minnesota North
26930	NAD83 / Alabama West		26992	NAD83 / Minnesota Central
26932	NAD83 / Alaska zone 2		26993	NAD83 / Minnesota South
26933	NAD83 / Alaska zone 3		26994	NAD83 / Mississippi East
26934	NAD83 / Alaska zone 4		26995	NAD83 / Mississippi West
26935	NAD83 / Alaska zone 5		26996	NAD83 / Missouri East
26936	NAD83 / Alaska zone 6		26997	NAD83 / Missouri Central
26937	NAD83 / Alaska zone 7		26998	NAD83 / Missouri West
26938	NAD83 / Alaska zone 8		32100	NAD83 / Montana
26939	NAD83 / Alaska zone 9		32104	NAD83 / Nebraska
26940	NAD83 / Alaska zone 10		32107	NAD83 / Nevada East
26941	NAD83 / California zone 1		32108	NAD83 / Nevada Central
26942	NAD83 / California zone 2		32109	NAD83 / Nevada West
26943	NAD83 / California zone 3		32110	NAD83 / New Hampshire
26944	NAD83 / California zone 4		32111	NAD83 / New Jersey
26945	NAD83 / California zone 5		32112	NAD83 / New Mexico East
26946	NAD83 / California zone 6		32113	NAD83 / New Mexico Central
26948	NAD83 / Arizona East		32114	NAD83 / New Mexico West
26949	NAD83 / Arizona Central		32115	NAD83 / New York East
26950	NAD83 / Arizona West		32116	NAD83 / New York Central
26951	NAD83 / Arkansas North		32117	NAD83 / New York West

SRID	Description		SRID	Description
6952	NAD83 / Arkansas South		32118	NAD83 / New York Long Island
6953	NAD83 / Colorado North		32119	NAD83 / North Carolina
6954	NAD83 / Colorado Central		32120	NAD83 / North Dakota North
6955	NAD83 / Colorado South		32121	NAD83 / North Dakota South
6956	NAD83 / Connecticut		32122	NAD83 / Ohio North
6957	NAD83 / Delaware		32123	NAD83 / Ohio South
6958	NAD83 / Florida East		32124	NAD83 / Oklahoma North
6959	NAD83 / Florida West		32125	NAD83 / Oklahoma South
6960	NAD83 / Florida North		32126	NAD83 / Oregon North
6961	NAD83 / Hawaii zone 1		32127	NAD83 / Oregon South
6962	NAD83 / Hawaii zone 2		32128	NAD83 / Pennsylvania North
6963	NAD83 / Hawaii zone 3		32129	NAD83 / Pennsylvania South
6964	NAD83 / Hawaii zone 4		32130	NAD83 / Rhode Island
6965	NAD83 / Hawaii zone 5		32133	NAD83 / South Carolina
6966	NAD83 / Georgia East		32134	NAD83 / South Dakota North
6967	NAD83 / Georgia West		32135	NAD83 / South Dakota South
6968	NAD83 / Idaho East		32136	NAD83 / Tennessee
6969	NAD83 / Idaho Central		32137	NAD83 / Texas North
6970	NAD83 / Idaho West		32138	NAD83 / Texas North Central
6971	NAD83 / Illinois East		32139	NAD83 / Texas Central
6972	NAD83 / Illinois West		32140	NAD83 / Texas South Central
6973	NAD83 / Indiana East		32141	NAD83 / Texas South

SRID	Description		SRID	Description
26974	NAD83 / Indiana West		32142	NAD83 / Utah North
26975	NAD83 / Iowa North		32143	NAD83 / Utah Central
26976	NAD83 / Iowa South		32144	NAD83 / Utah South
26977	NAD83 / Kansas North		32145	NAD83 / Vermont
26978	NAD83 / Kansas South		32146	NAD83 / Virginia North
26979	NAD83 / Kentucky North		32147	NAD83 / Virginia South
26980	NAD83 / Kentucky South		32148	NAD83 / Washington North
26981	NAD83 / Louisiana North		32149	NAD83 / Washington South
26982	NAD83 / Louisiana South		32150	NAD83 / West Virginia North
26983	NAD83 / Maine East		32151	NAD83 / West Virginia South
26984	NAD83 / Maine West		32152	NAD83 / Wisconsin North
26985	NAD83 / Maryland		32153	NAD83 / Wisconsin Central
26986	NAD83 / Massachusetts Mainland		32154	NAD83 / Wisconsin South
26987	NAD83 / Massachusetts Island		32155	NAD83 / Wyoming East
26988	NAD83 / Michigan North		32156	NAD83 / Wyoming East Central
26989	NAD83 / Michigan Central		32157	NAD83 / Wyoming West Central
26990	NAD83 / Michigan South		32158	NAD83 / Wyoming West
			32161	NAD83 / Puerto Rico and Virgin Islands

Index

CPSIA information can be obtained at www.ICGtesting.com
Printed in the USA
LVOW030719170512

282117LV00005B/1/P

9 781430 2349